Baptist Autographs in the

John Rylands University Library

of Manchester, 1741–1845

MERCER
UNIVERSITY PRESS

Endowed by
TOM WATSON BROWN
and
THE WATSON-BROWN FOUNDATION, INC.

Baptist Autographs in the John Rylands University Library of Manchester, 1741–1845

transcribed and edited by

Timothy Whelan

Mercer University Press
Macon, GA
July 2009

Isbn 9780881461442 / H780

Baptist Autographs in the John Rylands
University Library of Manchester, 1741–1845
Copyright ©2009
Mercer University Press, Macon, Georgia 31207
All rights reserved
Printed in the United States of America
First edition July 2009

The paper used in this publication meets the minimum requirements
of American National Standard for Information Sciences—
Permanence of Paper for Printed Library Materials,
ANSI Z39.48-1984.

Mercer University Press is a member of Green Press initiative
(greenpressinitiative.org), a nonprofit organization working
to help publishers and printers increase their use of recycled paper
and decrease their use of fiber derived from endangered forests.
This book is printed on recycled paper.

Library of Congress Cataloging-in-Publication Data

Baptist autographs in the John Rylands University Library of
Manchester, 1741-1845 / transcribed and edited by Timothy
Whelan. -- 1st ed.
    p.   cm.
 Includes bibliographical references and index.
ISBN-13: 978-0-88146-144-2 (hardcover : alk. paper)
ISBN-10: 0-88146-144-X (hardcover : alk. paper)
    1. Baptists--England--Correspondence. 2. Baptists--England--
History--18th century--Sources. 3. Baptists--England--History--19th
century--Sources. I. Whelan, Timothy D. II. John Rylands University
Library of Manchester. III. John Rylands University Library of
Manchester.
BX6493.B38 2009
286'.14209033--dc22
                                    2009021725

To my father,
Rev. Eugene Whelan,
Independent Baptist minister,
and my mother,
Betty June Whelan,
his helpmate in the ministry

Contents

Part Two: 1780–1799   43

Part Three: 1800–1809 103

Part Six: 1841–1845   221

Part Seven: Undated Letters   327

Acknowledgments

The discovery of these Baptist letters within the autograph albums of the Thomas Raffles Collection and the Methodist Archives at the John Rylands Library of Manchester came about largely by accident. I was looking for a letter by Joseph Cottle of Bristol, but when I received the large album that included his letter, I decided to look through the entire album just for fun. What I discovered were several letters written to John Sutcliff, Baptist minister at Olney. I was quite familiar with Sutcliff at that time, so out of curiosity I began to call up other volumes, including three titled "Nonconformist Divines," and in these volumes were more letters to Sutcliff, and letters of numerous other Baptist ministers scattered throughout the leaves. By the time I had finished going through some thirty volumes of the pertinent collections in the library, I had found more than 330 Baptist letters written between 1741 and 1900, of which only a handful had ever been noted before.

I wish to thank the John Rylands University Library of Manchester for granting me permission to print this marvelous collection of Baptist letters that have lain so long in obscurity. I could not have accomplished this task without the gracious assistance and expertise of the librarians and staff at the John Rylands Library, Deansgate, Manchester, who during the past seven years have copied hundreds of pages for me and lugged out volume after volume from the Raffles Collection and numerous other collections in the library. My thanks especially to John Hodgson, Keeper of Manuscripts and Archives; Alistair Cooper, Jackie Hardcastle and Jean Bostock (now retired) from Reader Services; Dr Peter Nockles, Assistant Librarian responsible for the Methodist Archives; Anne Young, Senior Bibliographical Assistant; Carol Burrows and Anne Clarkson in Reprographic Services; Dr Peter McNiven, former Head of Special Collections (now retired); and Dr Stella Butler, formerly Head of Special Collections and now Deputy University Librarian; and to the porters, who were always so friendly and helpful to me during my many visits. My thanks as well to the staff of Mercer University Press, especially Marc Jolley, Director, and Edmon Rowell, Jr., Senior Editor, for their acceptance of this project and their help and expertise in preparing the manuscript for publication.

Besides these individuals from the John Rylands Library, I am indebted as well to the following individuals and libraries that have graciously shared their time and resources with me: Sue Mills, Librarian (now retired), Jennifer Thorp (former archivist), and Julian Lock, current archivist, and the outstanding collections of the Angus Library, Regent's Park College, Oxford;

Dr. John Briggs, Director, Centre for Baptist History and Heritage, Regent's Park College, who has shared so much of his time and expertise with me during the past six years as I have worked on this project—the final result owes more to him than I can adequately state; Dr. David Wykes, Director, and the staff of Dr. Williams's Library, Gordon Square, London, to whom I will be forever indebted on this and so many other projects; Dr. Roger Hayden, whose knowledge of Bristol Baptists is encyclopedic and who graciously read through a draft of the biographical index and offered invaluable corrections and suggestions; the librarians and staff at Bristol Baptist College, who have been more than generous in their time and attention to my numerous requests for materials; the staff and librarians of the Pitts Theology Library and Special Collections, Candler School of Theology, Emory University, Atlanta, Georgia; the staff and librarians of the Special Collections, Jack Tarver Library, Mercer University, Macon, Georgia, and the Monroe F. Swilley, Jr., Library, Mercer University, Atlanta, Georgia; the Bodleian Library, Oxford University, Oxford; the Central Library, Bristol, and the Bristol Record Office; the Northamptonshire Record Office, Northampton; the Cambridge Central Library and the Cambridgeshire Record Office, Cambridge; the British Library, London; the Newspaper Library, Colindale, London; the Guildhall Library, London; the Family History Library, London; the Senate House Library, University of London; Metropolitan Baptist Tabernacle, London; the Tate Library, Manchester Harris College, Oxford; the Central Library, Manchester; Special Collections, Perkins Library, Duke University, Durham, North Carolina; the Spencer Research Library, University of Kansas, Lawrence, Kansas; Cooper Library, University of South Carolina, Columbia; the William E. Partee Center for Baptist Historical Studies, Curry Library, William Jewell College, Liberty, Missouri. I would also like to thank Cynthia Frost and the staff of the Interlibrary Loan Office, Henderson Library, Georgia Southern University, for their patience with my numerous requests for materials. I also wish to thank the following libraries and individuals for permission to quote from their collections: the University Librarian and Director, John Rylands University Library of Manchester; Bristol Baptist College, Bristol; Angus Library, Regent's Park College, Oxford; the Spencer Research Library, University of Kansas, Lawrence, Kansas. My thanks as well to my college English teacher and mentor, Dr. Robert Miller, whose suggestions greatly improved the Introduction. I also wish to thank my lovely wife, Yixing, for her patience and her invaluable assistance in creating the Index.

Note on the Text

In transcribing the following letters, I have tried to adhere as closely as possible to the original manuscripts. Archaic and unusual spellings, variations in spellings of the same word or name, and typical eighteenth-century capitalization of nouns have not been changed. In most cases variant spellings are followed by [*sic*]. Superscripts have been retained, as well as apostrophes for deleted letters and the use of "y" for "th." At times, salutations and closing lines in these letters can be problematic due to the abbreviations used by the writers. In many cases, "D^r S^r" is used, which means "Dear Sir." Other abbreviations to note are "y^e" (the), y^m (them), y^n (then), and y^r (your), the latter often attached at the end of a letter to other abbreviations, such as "F^r" (Friend), "B^r" (Brother), or "S^{vt}" "Servt" (Servant); also, many words are shortened at the end, such as "congreg^n" (congregation). These words will usually be accessible to the reader due to the context of the sentence. Dashes, which in eighteenth- and early nineteenth-century manuscripts often served for periods, have been retained as well. In cases where words have been left out (but were clearly intended given the context of the letter), I have added these words within brackets. Where the text is unreadable, either due to damage received from the folding of the letters or by the removal of the wafer used to seal the letter, I have inserted the word "illegible" within brackets. In the following 267 letters, I have identified over 850 individuals in the footnotes. Those names that appear in **bold print** are also included in the biographical index at the end of the book in case the reader wishes a more complete history of a particular person.

Introduction

In 1989, Clive D. Field, speaking about Nonconformist materials in the John Rylands Library, noted that "apart from a volume containing 88 portraits and letters of Baptist ministers of the eighteenth and nineteenth centuries (English MS 861) and a modest collection of periodicals and other printed works, the Library was poorly endowed with Baptist materials before the receipt on 'permanent loan' in 1980 of the historical collection of the Northern Baptist College. This consists of 4,683 printed items and 79 manuscripts from the former Manchester Baptist College (founded in 1866) and, at one and two removes respectively, from Rawdon (1804) and the Midland General Baptist (1797) Colleges."[1] Field listed the total number of Baptist manuscripts and archival materials held by the Rylands after the acquisition of the Northern Baptist College collection at 300, representing "the sum of (a) items in identifiable denominational collections, whether written by members of that denomination or not, based so far as possible on a detailed shelf-to-shelf count and (b) nonconformist items held outside identifiable denominational collections, including transcript and microform materials, estimated on the basis of subject catalogues and impressionistic surveys."[2]

The use of such criteria may explain why Field cited only Eng. MS. 861 as comprising the bulk of the Library's Baptist manuscripts prior to the acquisition of the Northern Baptist College materials. Within this volume are 69 autographs of Baptist ministers from 1746 to 1907, collected by Thomas Raffles, Congregational minister in Liverpool, and his son, Thomas Stamford Raffles. Among these autographs are letters from C. F. Aked, John Aldis, C. W. Birrell, William Brock, Hugh Stowell Brown, J. P. Chown, John Clifford, T. S. Crisp, James Culross, F. W. Gotch, Samuel Green, I. N. Haycroft, John Howard Hinton, E. H. Jackson, William Landels, F. B. Meyer, Arthur Mursell, Baptist Noel, C. H. Spurgeon, F. C. Spurr, Edward Steane, D. J. Hiley,

---

[1]Clive Field, "Sources for the Study of Protestant Nonconformity in the John Rylands University Library of Manchester," *Bulletin of the John Rylands University Library of Manchester* 71 (1989): 106. For a more detailed summation of the Northern Baptist Collection, see Ian Sellars, "The Northern Baptist College Historical Collection," *Baptist Quarterly* 32 (1987-88): 52. For a comprehensive look at the current state of Nonconformist collections, see Clive Field, "Preserving Zion: the Anatomy of Protestant Nonconformist Archives in Great Britain and Ireland," *Archives* 33 (2008): 14-51.

[2]See Field's table, "Principal Nonconformist Holdings in the John Rylands University Library of Manchester," in "Sources," 138.

J. C. Rook, J. H. Shakespeare, W. J. Henderson, and many others, including two women, Mary Brock (wife of William Brock of Bloomsbury Baptist Church, London) and Mrs. C. H. Spurgeon. These 69 letters form only a portion, however, of the Baptist letters in the Rylands Library. Within the Library's collections are another 268 letters scattered throughout the volumes of the Thomas Raffles Collection (156 letters), the Raffles Handlist (9 letters), and the Methodist Archives (103 letters), bringing the total number of Baptist letters to 337, composed between 1741 and 1907. This book contains transcriptions and annotations of 267 of these letters, written between 1741 and 1845 by some of the period's most prominent Baptist ministers, missionaries, and laypersons.

Thomas Raffles, Minister and Antiquarian

Thomas Raffles (1788-1863)—noted preacher, educator, and antiquarian—labored for more than fifty years (1812-1863) as pastor of Great George Street Chapel in Liverpool. During that time he actively supported pastoral education, assisting in the founding of Blackburn Independent Academy in 1816. The institution moved to Manchester in 1843 and became Lancashire Independent College; Raffles served as chairman of the college from 1842 to 1863. After his death, his massive collection of autograph letters, portraits, and personal manuscripts was deposited at the college. In 1896 this collection was purchased by Enriqueta Augustina Rylands, the wealthy widow of the Manchester industrialist, John Rylands, one of the first collections to find a home in the manuscript division of the John Rylands Library of Manchester. The library, a magnificent structure built in honor of her husband, was nine years in the making. When it opened on 6 October 1899, the building was described in the *Baptist Magazine* as "an addition of rare value to the architectural wealth of Manchester."[3] Mr. Rylands had affiliated at various times with both Baptists and Congregationalists, so it was fitting that Raffles's autograph collection should find a home in the Rylands Library. The Raffles Collection (Eng. MS. 343-87) includes original letters of some 230 poets, 390 artists, over 540 members of the English nobility, 133 English nonconformist divines (composed between 1658 and 1821), 135 missionaries and 2,260 authors (chiefly English), as well as eight boxes of letters and papers written or signed by

---

[3]Principal Fairburn, who gave the inaugural address that day, boasted that the architect "had adorned Manchester and enriched England with one of the most distinguished and the most perfect architectural achievements of this century." See James Stuart, "The John Rylands Library," *Baptist Magazine* 91 (1899): 509-515. Quotations from pp. 511, 513.

various notables, English and foreign.[4] Another part of the Raffles's collection consists of 64 small volumes of letters and portraits of ministers, missionaries, and evangelists of the second half of the nineteenth century.[5] Some years later, Lancashire College deposited a second collection of Raffles's letters and manuscripts at the Rylands Library, comprising five volumes of autograph letters from more than 400 ministers, mostly nonconformist divines, compiled by his son, Thomas Stamford Raffles. Now known as the Raffles Handlist, this collection also includes twenty-eight unbound volumes of sermons by Raffles as well as his three-volume manuscript, "Collections for a History of the Nonconformist Churches of Lancashire," composed between 1819 and 1821.[6]

Raffles's passion for collecting autograph letters was well known during his lifetime. He solicited ministers and literary figures not only for their own letters but also for any letters written to them from prominent individuals that Raffles wished to add to his collection. For instance, in the collection is a letter dated 29 May 1823 Raffles received from Joseph Cottle of Bristol, friend and early publisher of the Romantic poets Coleridge, Wordsworth, and Southey, in which Cottle writes, "I have not yet been successful in my endeavour to obtain an Autograph of our poor unfortunate Chatterton. I have still one clue which may conduct to the desired result, but should any impediment arise in that quarter, why I will then, even filch a bit from my own continuous MS; so much is it my wish to comply with your request."[7] Francis Wrangham, a clergyman and autograph collector himself, in a letter dated 15 October 1836, expresses his "gratitude for y[r] [Raffles's] attention upon several of the autographs indeed—Wardlaw, Hutchinson, Jeffrey, etc. I place a particular value to these names. I might truly add your own."[8] John Ryland, Jr., on 22 February 1821, offers Raffles autographs of two prominent evangelical clergymen, John Newton and Thomas Scott, as well as prominent Baptists Andrew Fuller, Robert Hall, Samuel Pearce, John Foster, and William Carey.[9]

---

[4]"Notes and News," *Bulletin of the John Rylands University Library of Manchester* 59 (1976): 5.

[5]Lizzie Boxall, "Portraits and autographs collected by the Rev. Thomas Raffles, John Rylands Library, Manchester" (Manchester: John Rylands University Library of Manchester, 1991).

[6]See "Notes and News," 6.

[7]Eng. MS. 351, f. 49.

[8]Eng. MS. 355, f. 227.

[9]Eng. MS. 383, f. 1773. The Baptist autographs Ryland sent to Raffles now comprise a part of this book. Autograph letters were not only traded among collectors but may have been "pilfered," along with rare books, from various library collections. C. S. Crisp, Principal of Bristol Baptist College, writing to Charles Godwin on 30 April 1847, thanks him for his gift to the college library but also admits that the library has "not been without some proof that the kind of pilferring to which you

Raffles, Joseph Angus, and the BMS

Raffles owned the largest private collection of Baptist letters from the late eighteenth and early nineteenth centuries ever assembled, largely through his acquisition of a major portion of the correspondence of John Sutcliff (1752-1814), Baptist minister at Olney (1775-1814) and a member of the Baptist Missionary Society [BMS] Committee between 1792 and 1814. A letter from Raffles to Joseph Angus (7 June 1844) substantiates this claim.[10] The letter had been placed loosely between the leaves of a volume from the BMS Archives (now housed at the Angus Library, Regent's Park College, Oxford) titled "Original Letters: A. Fuller to J. Sutcliff, 1790-1814," a collection of letters that passed between Andrew Fuller (1754-1815), Baptist minister at Kettering and one of the founders of the BMS and its first secretary, and Sutcliff. The letter reveals that this volume, now viewed as one of the most important in the early history of the BMS, was originally a part of the Thomas Raffles Collection before it became a part of the BMS Archives.[11]

In early June 1844, Angus (1816-1902), Secretary of the BMS (1841-49) and President of Regent's Park College, London, 1849-93, discovered that Raffles possessed these valuable autographs. Angus immediately wrote to him, requesting that he donate the volume to the BMS after his death:

> Baptist Mission House,
> Moorgate Street, London
> 7th June 1844

> My dear Sir
> I am not sure that my present application is not open to the charge of something like an impertinent intrusion. If

---

refer is practis'd, tho' happily we have scarcely suffer'd at all." See Eng. MS. 861, f. 17.

[10]Sue Mills, former librarian of the Angus Library, brought the letter to my attention.

[11]Sutcliff and Fuller, along with the overwhelming majority of the Baptist ministers whose letters were collected by Raffles, were Particular Baptists, agreeing with the paedobaptist Independent (Congregationalist) Raffles in theology (Calvinism) but differing in baptism. On the other hand, General Baptists were Arminian in theology, and by the late eighteenth century many General Baptist ministers (though not always their congregations) had adopted Arian and Socinian positions. Raffles the Calvinist obviously did not hold the General Baptists in the same regard as he did his Particular Baptist friends, and his autographs bears this out. Only three letters by General Baptist ministers found their way into the Raffles Collection: one by Dan Taylor, founder of the New Connection and a friend to many Particular Baptist and Independent ministers; and two by Joshua Toulmin, prominent General Baptist minister at Taunton and Birmingham.

so, I hope you will excuse it and let the motive of the appli-
cant be regarded as a palliation of the offence.

A friend of mine told me the other day that he understood you had a large collection of the letters of Fuller, Carey, Sutcliffe and others relating principally to our Mission.

It is on all accounts desirable that there s^d be as complete a collection as possible of such documents: and as we
have the larger proportion of this early correspondence & I
am doing what I can to make it complete, will you forgive
me in suggesting that ultimately your volume w^d find its
most appropriate & certainly a most honoured resting
place among the archives of our Mission.

I trust that many many years will elapse before your
volumes change hands, but when they change, if that one
volume c^d be intrusted to us, as none w^d be more likely to
prize it, so none w^d be more grateful for the gift.

Very sincerely & esp^y Y^{rs}

Joseph Angus

Rev Dr Raffles

Written on the first page of the above letter, next to the picture and logo
of the Mission House in Moorgate, is this response by Raffles, dated 3
October 1844:

My wish & desire is, that the request contained in this
note should be complied with, & this volume, after my decease, presented to the Baptist Missionary Society.

Tho Raffles

Oct. 3. 1844.

This volume of BMS letters addressed to Sutcliff was not the only one
that Raffles possessed. He also owned one titled "Original Letters of the
Revd. Dr. Fawcett, Revd. Andrew Fuller, Mr. J. W. Morris, and Revd. Dr.
Ryland, 1773-1813" that now stands alongside the previous volume at the
Angus Library. In both volumes, the letters are addressed solely to Sutcliff.
Whether Angus was aware in his June letter that the BMS correspondence
owned by Raffles consisted of *two* valuable volumes of Sutcliff's letters is
unclear, but within a few months he had learned of this fact and wrote to
Raffles about the matter, recorded in the following entry in the BMS Com-
mittee Minutes for 10 October 1844:

Read a letter from the Rev: Dr Raffles, of Liverpool, (in reply to one from the Secretary) stating that he had left in-

structions with his eldest son to give to the Society after his decease two volumes of MS. letters by the Rev. A. Fuller & others:—Resolved, that the cordial & respectful thanks of the Committee be presented to D[r] Raffles for this intended donation.[12]

In case there was any doubt as to his wishes concerning the second volume, Raffles left this inscription inside the front cover:

It is my desire that, after my decease, this Volume may be presented to the Baptist Missionary Society, whose House of Business is now in Moorgate St. London.
Tho Raffles.
Liverpool.
Nov. 12. 1847.[13]

Both volumes bear the seal of Thomas Raffles and are identical in their physical properties to the remaining volumes of the Raffles Collection at the Rylands Library.

In 1857 Raffles and Angus entered negotiations once again about some autograph manuscripts. It is unlikely that Angus provided Raffles with any Sutcliff letters at this time, given the fact that Raffles already owned the majority of the extant Sutcliff letters.[14] Instead, Raffles probably obtained from Angus autographs of other Baptist figures, enough to warrant Raffles sending Angus a collection of autographs of literary figures, autographs Angus eagerly desired to exhibit in his new library at Holford House, Regent's Park, London.[15] Some of the Baptist letters currently residing in the

---

[12]BMS Committee Minutes, Volume J (30 May 1844—29 July 1847), ff. 49-50, Angus Library, Regent's Park College, Oxford.

[13]Frederic Trestrail, secretary of the BMS, 1849-1869, should have had first hand knowledge of the letters, since they arrived sometime after Raffles's death in 1863, during Trestrail's tenure as secretary. His memory, however, was fading when he wrote the following to a correspondent in Liverpool in 1880: "Dr Raffles had a strong passion for autographs & had a large collection some of w[h], I think, his son gave to our Mission Library & he seems to have infected you with his passion" (Raffles Handlist, fasc. 42, f. 17).

[14]Isaac Mann (1785-1831), Baptist minister at Shipley, Yorkshire, and at Maze Pond, Southwark, owned 18 Sutcliff letters. These letters, and the remainder of Mann's important collection, are now held by the National Library of Wales. For a complete summary of the Mann Collection, see "Calendar of Letters, 1742-1831, Collected by Isaac Mann," *Baptist Quarterly* 6 (1932-33): 39-43, 83-85, 173-86, 218-26, 277-83, 318-22, 373-79; and 7 (1933-34): 39-46, 89-91, 138-39, 175-85, 235-38.

[15]In the library at Holford House, these autographs had been placed in glass frames and hung on the walls of the library. When Regent's Park College moved from London to Oxford in the late 1920s, these autographs (67 in all, now kept in a

Raffles Collection may have come from that autograph exchange in 1857, for, as Angus mentions in his June 1844 letter to Raffles, he was already building the BMS collection of letters and may have had some letters he felt he could offer in an exchange.[16]

Thus, two volumes of letters addressed to Sutcliff by Fuller, Ryland, Fawcett, and Morris made their way to Moorgate Street after Raffles's death in 1863. A substantial body of Sutcliff letters pertaining to the BMS, however, remained in the Raffles Collection. These autographs, along with the Baptist letters Raffles acquired from Angus and other individuals, would eventually find their way to Manchester and the John Rylands Library. Now, after more than a century, a full accounting can be made of all the Baptist letters originally collected by Thomas Raffles and his son.

The Sutcliff and BMS Letters

The 75 letters addressed to John Sutcliff (composed between 1773 and 1814, the residue of the massive Sutcliff correspondence originally owned by Raffles) comprise the most striking feature of the Baptist correspondence within the Raffles Collection.[17] Raffles also retained in his collection two autographs of Sutcliff: one to John Ryland, Jr. (1753-1825), Baptist minister at Northampton and Bristol and one of the founders of the BMS, written sometime in late 1794 or early 1795; and one to Samuel Bagster

---

box in the Angus library) were placed in storage and forgotten until their discovery in 1999. Among these autographs, many of which undoubtedly came from Raffles and his massive collections, are letters from Byron, Coleridge, Southey, John Foster, George Dyer, Washington Irving, Letitia Landon, Lydia Sigourney, and James Montgomery. For more on Raffles and his exchange with Angus, see Timothy Whelan, "Joseph Angus and the Use of Autograph Letters in the Library at Holford House, Regent's Park College, London," *Baptist Quarterly* 40 (2004): 455-76; idem, "Coleridge, the *Morning Post*, and a Female 'Illustrissimae': An Unpublished Autograph, February 1800," *European Romantic Review* 17 (2006): 21-38.

[16]Trestrail appears to have continued Angus's tradition of viewing BMS letters as personal possessions. His Liverpool correspondent (see above, n12), after securing an autograph of William Knibb, was told by Trestrail that if he had not been successful, "I would have got one from the Mission House."

[17]A smaller set of 18 Sutcliff letters was owned by Isaac Mann (1785-1831), Baptist minister at Shipley, Yorkshire, and at Maze Pond, Southwark. Mann's collection of Baptist letters is now held by the National Library of Wales and forms an excellent companion to the Baptist letters at the Rylands library. For a complete summary of the Mann Collection, see "Calendar of Letters, 1742-1831, Collected by Isaac Mann," *Baptist Quarterly* 6 (1932-33): 39-43, 83-85, 173-86, 218-26, 277-83, 318-22, 373-79; and 7 (1933-34): 39-46, 89-91, 138-39, 175-85, 235-38; Timothy Whelan, "A Calendar of Baptist Autographs in the John Rylands University Library of Manchester, 1741-1907," *Baptist Quarterly* 42 (2008): 577-612.

(1772-1851), Baptist bookseller in London, dated 19 March 1813.[18] Many of the letters addressed to Sutcliff are from some of the greatest Baptist ministers in English history, including eleven from John Ryland, Jr., four from Andrew Fuller, two from John Rippon (1751-1836), John Gill's successor at Carter Lane in Southwark and editor of the influential *Baptist Annual Register* (1790-1802), and one from the incomparable Robert Hall (1764-1831), successor to Robert Robinson at St. Andrew's Street in Cambridge and later to John Ryland at Bristol.[19] These letters reveal a striking closeness between these men at a pivotal time in their denomination's history, sharing concerns about their local ministries as well as the larger work of the Baptist Missionary Society and evangelical Christianity, both Nonconformist and Anglican, in England and America. Other correspondents of Sutcliff include nearly every leading Baptist figure of his day, such as John Fawcett, Hugh and Caleb Evans, William Hartley, James Turner, James Ashworth, Joseph Jenkins, Thomas Langdon, John Rippon, William Steadman, Samuel Kilpin, Joseph Hughes, F. A. Cox, J. W. Morris, Christopher Anderson, William Newman, Joseph Ivimey, Joseph Kinghorn, Robert Hall, and William Richards. The Sutcliff letters provide a remarkable commentary upon the Olney minister's pervasive presence in matters of Baptist concern, especially the work of the BMS, during a span of more than four decades.[20]

Many of the Sutcliff letters kept by Raffles involve the latter's correspondence with various BMS missionaries, an activity Sutcliff maintained

---

[18]See Eng. MS. 384, f. 1949; Eng. MS. 371, f. 116. The Sutcliff correspondence in the Rylands Library is surpassed only by the Sutcliff Papers and BMS Home Office Papers in the Angus Library. Within the Angus collections are approximately 340 letters addressed to Sutcliff by various individuals. Both collections are similar in one important aspect: neither possesses any significant body of letters written by Sutcliff himself. In fact, I have found only one letter by Sutcliff in the BMS papers to go with the two letters by him in the Raffles Collection (there are also two letters by Sutcliff in the Isaac Mann Collection, and two letters by Sutcliff in the Walter Wilson Collection, Bodleian Library, Oxford). It may be that Sutcliff requested of his heirs that his own letters be burned, which would explain their scarcity. If so, the loss has been a grievous one to the history of English Baptists and the BMS. For the best account of Sutcliff's life and career, see Michael A. G. Haykin, *One Heart and One Soul: John Sutcliff of Olney, his Friends and his Times* (Darlington: Evangelical Press, 1994).

[19]Within the collection of Baptist letters at the Rylands Library are eighteen letters to or from Ryland (composed between 1774 and 1823), ten letters by Fuller (between 1790 and 1814), six letters to or from Rippon (between 1791 and 1802), and seven letters by Hall (between 1811 and 1827).

[20]Another aspect of the Baptist letters in this collection is the pervasive influence of Bristol Baptist Academy. As a result of the work of Hugh and Caleb Evans, and especially John Ryland after his arrival in Bristol in December 1793, the Academy played a preeminent role in fomenting the spirit of evangelism and missionary enterprise among Baptist men and women throughout England, Scotland, and Wales during the first three decades of the BMS.

faithfully between 1792 and 1814. Raffles also owned a number of other letters involving BMS personnel, both in England and abroad. In his collection are fifteen letters from various members of the Carey family. Eight are by William Carey (1761-1834), including three addressed to John Shepherd, director of the Botanical Gardens in Liverpool, and one to Nathaniel Wallich, renowned botanist in Calcutta, all of which detail Carey's horticultural activities at Serampore, including extensive lists of his plants. Five are by Carey's nephew, Eustace; one by his father, Edmund; and one by his sister, Mary. Over all, the Raffles Collection contains thirty-two letters to and from BMS missionaries in India and Jamaica. Among these correspondents are William Ward (four letters), Joshua Marshman, William Knibb, John Lawson, Joshua Rowe, and John Chamberlain.

The Raffles Collection also includes letters by Particular Baptist laymen, General Baptist ministers, and letters by prominent Independent ministers and non-Baptists to their Baptist friends. Among these correspondents are Joseph Cottle, Bristol bookseller and member at the Baptist meeting in the Pithay and at Broadmead; Benjamin Flower, Cambridge printer and member at St. Andrew's Street; Dan Taylor, founder of the New Connection of General Baptists; Joshua Toulmin, General Baptist (Unitarian) minister at Taunton; Independent ministers James Burgess, Benjamin Brook, William Bull, Samuel Greatheed, and Matthew Wilks; the American Baptist minister and scholar, William Rogers, of Philadelphia; the revered Anglican Evangelical divine, John Newton; and James Boswell, biographer of Samuel Johnson.

Other letters are of interest as well: George Whitefield, the great evangelist, pleads for funds for his orphanage in Georgia; John Ryland, Jr., secretly tells a young John Sutcliff to come to Olney, where John Newton "is the freest of a party Spirit of any one in Olney," even though "his wife is more of a Bigot"; James Ashworth, Baptist minister at Gildersome, informs Sutcliff that William Hartley's situation in Halifax has been made worse "on acc^t of our Brother's amours"; John Rippon, after the Priestley Riots of 1791, expresses his loyalty to dissenters by suggesting to Sutcliff that "it is feared in Town that ye High Church employed the mob at Birmingham. Don't government prefer papists to the dissenters?" A frustrated William Carey complains to his sister about not being allowed "to write about experience, or any of the common topics of Religion; nor to say any thing about the Doctrines of the Gospel" because his correspondents only want to hear about "News, and continual accounts of marvellous things are expected from me. I have however no news to send, and as every thing here is the same, no Marvels"; William Ward notes in the journal he kept on his initial voyage to India in 1799 a confrontation with a French ship in which cannon balls "whizze[d] over [his] head" and flew "over the shrouds," testing his faith in the face of capture and the possibility of spending time in "a French prison"; Mary Carey writes to Sutcliff about the death of her brother-in-law, Charles Short, in India, anguishing over the fact that William Carey did not reach Short in time "to see him die" and "longing that someone present with keen and inquisitive feelings [would have] urged Mr Carey to have ventured tho at midnight," for had she been there she "would have mounted an eastern Elephant and set off in the deepest shades for Hindostan"; John Foster, the Baptist essayist, after praising Carey's brilliant mind, speaks ill of Carey's recently deceased third wife, who "was no friend to the Marsh-man family—one therefore the less regrets her removal." The list could go on and on, but these examples demonstrate the rich material found within this remarkable body of letters.[21]

Baptist Letters in the Methodist Archives

Besides the Baptist autographs within the Raffles Collection, more Baptist materials have also been found in the holdings of the Methodist Archives, a massive collection that came to the John Rylands Library in 1977.[22] Scattered among the Archives are letters from such Baptist figures as Anne Dutton, Andrew Fuller, John Gill, John Ryland, Jr., Robert Hall, John Rippon, Samuel Pearce, William Steadman, and Joseph Stennett, including a letter from Benjamin Flower to the radical Methodist leader, Alexander Kilham. Of even more significance, however, is Box 39 of the Achives, a remarkable collection of 88 autograph letters originally belonging to the Home Office of the Baptist Missionary Society when it was located in Fenchurch Street, London (this collection comprises the majority of the letters in Part Six). All but four of these letters were composed between March 1842 and March 1843, during the Jubilee Celebration of the BMS. Seventy of these letters are addressed to Joseph Angus, BMS secretary at that time, providing a rare look into the day-to-day activities of Angus and his associates during an important year in the history of the BMS. Whether Angus or one of his successors removed these letters is unclear; it is also unclear how these letters found their way into the Methodist Archives, but given how little of the BMS correspondence for that period has survived, the letters within Box 39 form an invaluable addition to the history of the Society.[23]

---

[21]The largest collection of letters to or from BMS missionaries, including the majority of those missionaries cited in this collection, belongs to the BMS Archives, now housed at the Angus Library, Regent's Park College, Oxford. The bulk of this material is available on microfilm. Another good source of BMS letters is the Reeves Collection, also at the Angus Library.

[22]"Notes and News," *Bulletin of the John Rylands University Library of Manchester* 60 (1978): 269.

[23]The BMS Home Office Papers, H/11 and H/12 (Angus Library, Regent's Park College, Oxford), covering the years of Angus's tenure as secretary of the BMS, contain only a handful of letters addressed to the Mission House between the years

Among the letters addressed to Angus are eleven by John Clarke, BMS missionary to Jamaica, and two by his traveling companion, the Jamaican doctor, G. K. Prince. These letters were written between 20 September 1842 and 21 March 1843, when the two men toured England attempting to raise support among Baptist congregations for the new BMS mission at Fernando Po on the coast of West Africa and the Cameroons. Much of Clarke's correspondence concerns his desire in 1843 that the BMS purchase a steam-powered schooner to transport missionaries to West Africa and the West Indies, as well as assist the mission work along the coast and inland rivers of West Africa. Five other letters in this collection discuss the purchase of a schooner, including one from Edward Cowper, noted professor of engineering at King's College, University of London, about the possibility of a boat equipped with an "Archimedes Screw." The campaign led by Clarke would culminate in 1844 with the BMS's purchase of the *Dove*. Within Box 39 are also letters from such Baptist leaders as C. E. Birt, Christopher Anderson, William Colgate, J. M. Cramp, Richard Pengilly, James Peggs, Charles Kirtland, J. G. Pike, and Frederick Trestrail; five letters from BMS missionaries other than Clarke and Prince, as well as letters from individuals who applied to become missionaries, such as Edgar Anthony Low, Thomas Parkinson, Joseph Clare, Thomas Thompson, and Owen Johnson Birt. The collection includes several letters from Baptist laymen, such as manufacturer Samuel Giles of Manchester, printer Josiah Fletcher of Norwich, engineer Richard Johnson of Liverpool; soap manufacturer William Colgate of New York; and two London laymen, George Bayley (ship inspector for Lloyd's Register of London) and Joseph Fletcher (owner of a prominent London shipping business). Within the collection are also letters from some prominent Baptist laywomen, including Elizabeth Ivimey (third wife of Joseph Ivimey), Sophia Parsons (BMS missionary to India), and Rachel S. Voigt (daughter of Joshua and Hannah Marshman). These letters from the Methodist Archives, all relating to the activities of the BMS, coupled with the letters from the Raffles Collection, make the John Rylands Library an important centre for the study of English Baptist missions, 1792-1845.

Biographical and Historical Annotations

Within the footnotes of this book are identifications of more than 850 individuals, including 480 Baptist ministers, missionaries, and laypersons, of which nearly 300 can be found in the Biographical Glossary at the end of

---

1841 and 1843. A bound letter book contains carbon copies of 280 letters to and from Angus, beginning on 3 July 1848 and ending on 3 October 1849, but very little correspondence exists from Angus's earlier years at the Mission House. According to the Committee Minute books, between 3000-4000 letters a year arrived at the Mission House during the 1840s, most of which are now lost.

the volume. The remaining individuals are primarily ministers of other denominations, political figures, merchants, and writers, of which approximately 90 can be found in the Glossary. The biographical information on Baptists ministers and laypersons provided in this book will be of considerable value to students and scholars of Baptist history.

Only a few of the Baptist letters in the John Rylands Library have appeared in the published memoirs of the various individuals who either wrote or received the letters. Michael Haykin, Baptist historian, in *One Heart and One Soul,* cites fifteen letters written to John Sutcliff from Eng. MS. 369-71.[24] Photocopies of twelve letters by John Ryland, Jr., Caleb Evans, Hugh Evans, and John Fawcett, all from the Raffles Collection, can be found at the Bristol Baptist College Library.[25] A version of John Newton's letter to Arthur Clegg (Eng. MS. 347, f. 240) was published in the *Congregational Magazine* in 1825. A portion of a letter from Andrew Fuller to John Ryland, Jr., dated 7 January 1791, is included in John Ryland's *Life of Andrew Fuller,* which may be the "specimen" of Fuller that Ryland refers to in his letter to Thomas Raffles, 22 February 1821.[26]

W. Wright Roberts, surveying the manuscript holdings of the Rylands Library in 1941, briefly commented on the Raffles Collection, noting that, given the sheer quantity of the collection, it "cannot be adequately surveyed in small space. Covering the first sixty years of so of the nineteenth century and containing autograph letters from many prominent Englishmen and Englishwomen of those times, it is a vast quarry for students of biography, church history, theology and politics, no less than for the student of literature."[27] Field is correct in his assessment of the nonconformist materials at the Rylands Library, noting that "many gaps remain to be filled, of course, and much cataloguing and listing has still to be done, but the claims of the John Rylands University Library to be regarded as a national and international centre of excellence in this area cannot possibly be denied."[28] The

---

[24]Haykin quotes from letters by John Geard (Eng. MS. 370, f. 51); John Fawcett (Eng. MS. 369, f. 46); John Ryland, Jr. (Eng. MS. 371, f. 107); Hugh Evans (Eng. MS. 369, f. 44); Caleb Evans (Eng. MS. 369, f. 43); Joseph Jenkins (Eng. MS. 370, f. 69); Thomas Steevens (Eng. MS. 371, f. 115); Thomas Langdon (Eng. MS. 370, f. 75); Andrew Fuller (Eng. MS. 369, f. 50); Samuel Greatheed (Eng. MS. 370, f. 54); Christopher Anderson (Eng. MS. 369, f. 4); and Rev. William Bull (Eng. MS. 369, f. 19), all transcribed in this volume.

[25]These letters can be found in Eng. MS. 369, f. 43 a-b; 369, f. 44; 369, f. 46 a; and 371, f. 107 a-g.

[26]For Fuller to Ryland, see Eng. MS. 861, f. 21; for Ryland to Raffles, see Eng. MS. 383, f. 1773; see also John Ryland, *The Work of Faith, the Labour of Love, and the Patience of Hope, illustrated; in the Life and Death of the Rev. Andrew Fuller* (London: Button and Son, 1818), 225.

[27]W. Wright Roberts, "English Autograph Letters in the John Rylands Library," *Bulletin of the John Rylands Library* 25 (1941): 129.

[28]Field, "Sources," 139.

discovery and publication of the following body of Baptist letters is an attempt to fill one of those "gaps" and mine a portion of the vast "quarry" of manuscript material held by the John Rylands Library. Without question, the Library stands as one of the more significant depositories of Baptist archival materials in the United Kingdom.

Part One

1741–1779

1. George Whitefield,[1] London, to Joseph Stennett,[2] London, 1 June 1741.[3]

    Believing you are ready to every good word & work I am embol-den'd to write this. My arrears upon the Orphan-house account at present are very large. In order to discharge them & prevent publick Collections for the future I am now getting annual Subscriptions to be-gin at Midsummer. Will you be pleasd to become a Subscriber, & use your interest among your Friends? In so doing I believe you will please our Common Lord; & much oblige your very weak but affect: Brother & Ser[vt] in X[t]

GW

---

[1]George Whitefield (1714-1770), the dynamic Calvinistic Methodist evangelist, originally followed the Wesley brothers to Savannah, Georgia, in 1738 as a missio-nary for the Church of England. The Bethesda Home (the "Orphan house" mentioned in this letter), the first orphanage in America, was established by a grant of 500 acres from the Colony of Georgia in 1739. The idea for the home originated with Charles Wesley and Georgia governer James Oglethorpe, but it was mainly through the efforts of Whitefield that the orphanage became a reality in March 1740. Savan-nah resident James Habersham (c. 1712-1775) became the orphanage's first schoolmaster. Whitefield would cross the Atlantic thirteen times during his thirty-two years of ministry, primarily to raise funds for the orphanage. Just before his death, Whitefield willed the orphanage to the Countess of Huntingdon, his wealthy patron in England. She spent considerable funds to repair the buildings in 1773 and planned to build a Calvinistic Methodist college on the grounds patterned after her college at Trevecca, Wales, but the American War of Independence postponed her plans. The college finally opened in 1788, but after the death of the Countess in 1791, the property and control of the orphanage was assumed by the state of Georgia. The orphanage fell into a state of neglect and decay during the next ten years. Eventually the orphanage was taken over by the Union Society of Savannah and continues to this day on its original site. See George Whitefield in Savannah to James Habersham in Charleston, 18 January 1747, John Rylands University Library of Manchester [hereafter JRULM], Eng. MS. 347, f. 185; Edward J. Cashin, *Beloved Bethesda: A History of George Whitefield's Home for Boys, 1740-2000* (Macon GA: Mercer Press, 2001) 106ff; *Savannah* (Savannah GA: Review Print Co., 1937) 172.

[2]**Joseph Stennett** (1692-1758), Baptist minister at Exeter and Little Wild Street, London (1737-1758).

[3]MAM. PLP. 113.1.5, JRULM.

PS
God has been with me in the Country & continues to be with me in London in an Extraordinary manner—help me to adore Free Grace.—

2. Micaiah Towgood,[4] Exeter, to Joseph Stennett, London, 3 December 1743.[5]

Rev.[d] Sir
     The unhappy Sufferers whose Case this printed Letter represents, being Objects truely worthy Comiseration; we beg leave, at their desire, to recomend [sic] them to your Compassion; & to request your good Offices in recomending them to such as may be disposed to contribute to their Relief.[6]

[Signed]   Jo: Walrond
             John Lavington
             James Green
             Jos. Hallett.
             Ed[rd] Jones
             Mic. Towgood

---

[4]**Micaiah Towgood** (1700-1792), Arian minister at George's Meeting (Presbyterian), Exeter, 1749-1782, and tutor at the Exeter Academy.
[5]Eng. MS. 344, f. 73, JRULM.
[6]The accompanying letter representing the "unhappy Sufferers" is missing. Most likely they were aging Particular Baptist ministers (though the monies may not have not been necessarily restricted to Baptists) experiencing pecuniary distress and had applied to Stennett and the Particular Baptist Fund in London for assistance. All the ministers who signed the above letter, however, were Presbyterians, both Arians and Calvinists. John Walrond, first ministered at Ottery St. Mary, then at the Bow Meeting (Presbyterian) in Exeter from 1729 until his death in 1755. At Bow, he joined his friend, John Lavington (1690?-1759), who had been a minister there since 1715. Lavington, a friend and correspondent of the Baptist poet and hymn writer Anne Steele (1717-1778) of Broughton, would remain at Bow until his death in 1759. It was primarily Lavington, along with Walrond (then at Ottery) and some other dissenting ministers in Exeter and Devon, who led the orthodox ministers in their attack against **James Peirce** and Joseph Hallett II, forcing the latter two out of their positions at the James Meeting in 1719 because of their Unitarian beliefs (see letter 22). Joseph Hallett III (1691/2-1744), son of Joseph Hallett II (d. 1722), was trained in his father's academy in Exeter and ordained in 1715. When his father lost his position at the James Meeting, the younger Hallett went with his father as his assistant at the new Mint Meeting, later serving as minister there from 1722 until his death in April 1744, about five months after the date of the above letter. James Green was a minister at the James Meeting in Exeter from 1724 to 1749. Jones I have not identified. See Jerom Murch, *A History of the Presbyterian and General Baptist Churches in the West of England* (London: Hunter, 1835) 386-404, 412.

3. Two MS. pages from the diary of John Collett Ryland,[7] Warwick, Sept. 5-9, 1746.[8]

Business for the Month September:

1. Holy Scriptures.— (viz.) Bible. Com. Pla Book.
   Concordance—M.[r] Henry on Pray.[r9] & Clark. Promises[10]
2. M[r] Henry Exposit.[n] on Genesis Ch. VIII.[11]
3. M[r] Gill on Matthew—Chap. VII &c[12]
4. M[r] Charnock on God's Holiness. Goodness. Dominon. Patience & Providence—[13]
5. Boylean Lectures. 1.st Vol. Folio.[14]
6. Proceed in y[e] New Adversaria—& fill up more of y[e] Old one[15]
7. Compose New Sermons if possible every Week and revise y[e] Old ones—
8. Go to Evesh. Bourt.—& Abing:[16]
9. Compose—a Brief Memorial of Encyclopaed:—for a Friend.—
10. Read the Husbandman's Calling—by M.[r] Steele[17]

---

[7]**Ryland, John Collett** (1723-1792), Baptist minister at Warwick (1746-1759), College Lane, Northampton (1759-1785), and well-known educator at Northampton and Enfield (1785-1792).

[8]Eng. MS. 861, f. 48, JRULM. Another portion of Ryland's diary, April 1744-September 1745, can be found at the Angus Library, Regent's Park College, Oxford, shelfmark 6.e.27; a portion of which was printed in "A Student's Programme in 1744," *Baptist Quarterly* 2 (1924-1925): 249-52. For more on Ryland's diary, see H. Wheeler Robinson, "A Baptist Student—John Collett Ryland," *Baptist Quarterly* 3 (1926-1927): 25-33.

[9]*A Method for Prayer, with Scripture-Expressions Proper to be used under each Head* (1710) by Matthew Henry (1662-1714).

[10]*A Collection of the Promises of Scripture under their Proper Heads* (1720) by Samuel Clarke (1684-1750).

[11]Probably *An Exposition on the Old and New Testament* (1737-38) by Matthew Henry.

[12]*An Exposition of the New Testament.* (1746-1748) by John Gill (1697-1771).

[13]Probably a reference to *The Works of the Late Learned Divine Stephen Charnock, B.D., Being Several Discourses upon the Existence and Attributes of God* (1699).

[14]A series of lectures founded by Robert Boyle (1627-1691) in 1692 to provide a platform for sermons on the evidences of God. Richard Bentley (1662-1742) delivered the first two lectures in the series: *The Folly and Unreasonableness of Atheism Demonstrated from the Advantage and Pleasure of a Religious Life*; and *Matter and Motion Cannot Think, or, A Confutation of Atheism from the Faculties of the Soul.*

[15]Possibly a version of *Thomae Gatakeri Londinatis, Adversaria Miscellanea* (1659) by Thomas Gataker (1574-1654).

[16]Evesham, Bourton, and Abingdon.

11. pursue Heads of Meditation every Lords Day for the whole Week.—
12. proceed in Improv[t] Mind—in Logic—and in Lat. Gr. & Heb.—& Divinity—wth M[r] H.[18]
—On y[e] Head of Meditation—every Week—State y[e] Doctrine clearly & largely—Answer all Objections—Solve all Questions & Doubts on—Resolve all Cases of Conscience—Explain—& enforce y[e] Practice of all y[e] Duties—& describe the part of Christian Experience belonging to it—Make all Sorts of Uses or Improvements.

Friday Septem.[r] 5. 1746—
1. Finish.[d] an Extract of Satan's Devices[19]
2. Scheme of Rhetoric from M.[r] Holmes[20]
3. Ames's Cases of Conscience.—translated part.[21]

Saturday Sep.[r] 6—1746—
Spent chiefly with M.[r] Benj[n] Stennett.—[22]
—in y[e] Evening Rec'd my Books from Lond[n]—

Lord's Day sep.[r] 7. 1746—
Mr. Stennett preached for me—Rom. 5: 3"—We glory in tribulations.—
In the afternoon John. 12. 21. Sir we wou'd see Jesus

Monday Sep.[r] 8—
1. Began M.[r] Weston's Stenography—Or Short Hand.—8[vo] pr. Vol[23]

---

[17]*The Husbandman's Calling, Shewing the Excellencies, Temptations, Graces, Duties &c of the Christian Husbandman: Being the Substance of XII Sermons Preached to a Country Congregation* (1670) by Richard Steele (1629-1692).

[18]James Hervey (1714-1758), evangelical, Calvinistic Anglican divine from Northampton, who was a popular cleric at Weston Favell and Collingtree, 1752-1758. He was a friend and correspondent of Ryland. A number of letters between the two (composed c. 1752-1758) appeared in Ryland's *The Character of the Rev. James Hervey* (London: W. Justins, for R. Thompson and H. D. Symonds, 1790).

[19]*Precious Remedies Against Satan's Devices* (1669) by Thomas Brooks (1608-1680).

[20]*The Art of Rhetoric Made Easy, or, The Elements of Oratory Briefly Stated, and Fitted for the Practice of the Studious Youth of Great Britain and Ireland* (1739) by John Holmes (1703-1759).

[21]*Conscience with the Power and Cases Thereof, Divided into Five bookes* (1639) by William Ames (1576-1633).

[22]Benjamin Stennett was a Seventh-day Baptist minister in Ingham, Norfolk, 1736-48. He was the youngest son of Joseph Stennett the elder (d. 1713). See Bryan Ball, *Seventh Day Men: Sabbatarians & Sabbatarianism 1600-1800* (Oxford: Clarendon Press, 1994) 260.

2. Spent wth M.[r] St. & in reading D.[r] Mathers Manuduct:[24]

Tuesday Sep.[9]—
    1. Serm: xxxv—Imitation of Christ in his Example and Life—1 Jn 2:
    6— M.[r] Hubbard[25]
    2. Began A Defence of Natural and Revealed Religion—3 Vol.[s] Fol:
    —M.[r] Boyle's Lectures from 1692 to 1732.
    —Vol. 1.—Serm. 1.—D[r] Bentley On the Folly of Atheism.—Ps.
        14:1—
        Serm. II. A Confutation of Atheism from the Faculties of
        the Human Soul.—[26]
Wrote Letters to Bristol & Transcribed Hints on Cycloped.—

4. Anne Dutton,[27] Great Gransden, to George Whitefield [accompanied by a note to Mrs. Whitefield], 20 June 1752.[28]

Great Gransden   June 20, 1752

Reverend & very Dear Sir,
    Your most kind Letter, & valuable present, with that of your dear Consort's, which to me is most acceptable, I received with humble Joy in God, & gave Thanks to Him, from whom all Blessings flow, & pray'd for y[e] choicest Favours to descend upon you both, as a rich Reward of your abundant Goodness to unworthy me.—I knew not how to take it, that you should be ashamed of y[e] smallness of y[r] Present, which surpris'd me with its Greatness, & melted me into Tears of Joy; yea, struck my Heart with an holy Fear, lest I should not render unto God y[e] Glory of this his great Goodness; cast upon worthless me, thro' you his worthy

---

[23]*Stenography Completed, or, The Art of Short-hand Brought to Perfection; Being the Most Easy, Exact, Lineal, Speedy, and Legible Method Extant* (1727) by James Weston.

[24]*Manuductio ad Ministerium: Directions for a Candidate of the Ministry* (Boston, 1726) by Cotton Mather (1663-1728). J. C. Ryland would later issue his own edition of Mather's work, titled *Dr. Cotton Mather's Student and Preacher: Or, Directions for a Candidate of the Ministry* (1781).

[25]Possibly a reference to a sermon by John Hubbard (1691/92-1743) titled *Christ's Loveliness and Glory, in his Personal and Relative Characters, and Gracious Offers to Sinners: Consider'd in Twelve Sermons Preach'd at Mr. Coward's Lecture* (1729).

[26]*A Defence of Natural and Revealed Religion; Being a Collection of the Sermons Preached at the Lecture Founded by the Hon. Robert Boyle (From the year 1692 to the year 1732)* (3 vols., 1739), edited by Sampson Letsome.

[27]**Anne Dutton** (1692-1765), a prolific writer, was a friend and frequent correspondent of Whitefield.

[28]MAM. PLP. 36.51, JRULM.

Servants. No Part of your kind Favours to me seem'd small, but great Love, struck my Eyes, & broke my Heart in all. Please to accept yᵉ utmost Acknowledgements, that a Heart warmed with deepest Sentiments of Gratitude is capable of giving. Surely I am your Debtor: God grant me Grace, to seek your present Joy & eternal Glory, as an Hundredfold Reward of this your Labour of Love, shewn towards yᵉ Lord's name, & yᵉ least & last of those that belong to Him! I do indeed accept your Token of Love, as from Love unfeigned: And as it is for Jesus Christ's Sake; it gives me double Joy; and your Reward from Him, shall be ineffable & eternal.

But why do you ask me, Sir, "What I want *further*? Hav't you lov'd me enough already? Wou'd you yet do more for me? Wou'd you be glad to help me? Yea, think it your Privilege, your great Privilege, to minister to my necessities? This is wondrous Love! The God of Love reward you, not only according to what you have done, but also according to what you would do for Him, & for poor me as related to him! Your Love to Christ herein, comforts my Heart greatly, tho' yᵉ worm you wou'd favour, is most unworthy. Our Lord will write, *Loved*. And you will find all that you would have done for Him & His; recorded in the Book of his Remembrance, for a full Reward, at his glorious appearing, & Kingdom.—And as I find, that when you have done your utmost, to proclaim yᵉ Redeemer's Gospel, & to win yᵉ Lamb's Redeemed to yᵉ Lord-Redeemer, you still lament yᵗ you can do no more with an "Oh how little do I do for God!" And mournfully add, "I am ashamed from my inmost Soul of my unfruitfulness:" Behold herein, how Jesus loves You! Is it not enough for Christ to give you an Heart to do so much for him, as he enables you to do; but has he given you such a Largeness of Heart, that your Desires after a more abundant Service, & a more exceeding Fruitfulness, to his more abundant glory in & by You, are as it were insatiable? Oh what Love is this, in yᵉ Lord of Love, to draw out your Soul thus to love him! And what an abundant Reward, think you, will yᵉ Prince of Grace bestow upon yʳ Soul in future Glory, which in yᵉ present State, he draws out to love him thus ardently! Rejoyce & be exceeding glad, & even leap for Joy, for great is your Reward in Heaven! And, Go on, Happy Soul, to love & serve yᵉ Lord your infinite Lover; till increasing Love & Duty, shall rise to their meridian Brightness, & be crown'd with eternal Glory!—But I am to answer your Query: And at present, Dear Sir, I want no more, either for Food or Raiment, nor have a Prospect of so doing for this year, if the Lord spares my Life. I have All and abound, having received yᵉ things which you sent: which I doubt not being given to Jesus Christ & for his Sake, are by him presented as an Doer of a Sweet Smell, or Sacrifice acceptable & well-pleasing unto his & your God & Father.—I am a Partaker of your Bliss, in yᵉ joyful Days you see at London: The Lord continue & increase them! And may his Kingdom come with Power & great Glory, till yᵉ whole Earth universally, & all opposite Power fall before it speedily! Amen. Even so, come Lord Jesus, come quickly!—I remember you before yᵉ Lord, & as he enables me, shall endeavour to hold up your Hands in his work. I commit you to his Love & Care. Great Grace be with You! I subscribe, with great Affection & under great Obligation,

Reverend Sir,

Your most humble Serv.ᵗ in yᵉ Lord,

Anne Dutton.

To Mrs. Whitefield,[29]

Dear Madam,

Your generous & agreeable Present, I accept with all humble Thanks: And yᵉ undeserved Love of yᵉ Giver in the Gift, brings a sensible Endearment with it. May yᵉ Lord refresh & comfort you with yᵉ Joys of his infinite Favour & clothe you sensibly in yᵉ view of Faith, with yᵉ Garments of Salvation, with yᵉ Robe of Righteousness; that as yᵉ Lamb's [paper torn] made ready, you may with Him inherit yᵉ Throne of Glory: while his own all-gracious Hand, according to his all-faithful Word, bestows on you yᵉ promis'd Crown of Righteousness, to your ineffable & eternal Bliss!—I am very Affectionately,

Dear Madam,

Your most thankful & obliged hble Serv.ᵗ,

Anne Dutton

5. John Tommas[30] of Pithay church, Bristol, to his parents at Skipton, 27 November 1757.[31]

Bristol Novᵇʳ 27 1757

Dear Parents

Am sorry that my long Silence who.ᵈ give any trouble however shall endeavour to make it up by writing more frequently. I have to tell you we are all well and have been ever since I writ to you before. The continuance of your health gives real pleasure to us may God help you to

---

[29]George Whitefield married Elizabeth Burnell James (d. 1768), a widow ten years his senior, in 1741. They had one child, John, who died in 1744.

[30]**John Tommas** (1723/1724-1800), Baptist minister at Gildersome (1745-1753) and at the Pithay in Bristol (1753-1800).

[31]Eng. MS. 371, f. 122, JRULM. Also included in this folio section are some writings by Tommas in Hebrew, sent to **Alvery Jackson** (1700-1763) at Barnoldswick (Jackson is mentioned in this letter).

Improve it. The affairs of our Church is near the same my work is great but there is sufficient strength in him that head in all things to the Church. Old Mr. Beddom[32] left this world about a month ago we are as far from meeting with one to help me as ever but hope God will keep us in the way of duty.[33] You by this time want some help I have on the other side desired M.ʳ Jackson to let you have one Round ten shilling till I come which I hope will be in the begining [sic] of the Summer. My Wife joines me in love & duty and our grown son &c

Jo.ⁿ Tommas

6. John Newton,[34] [Liverpool], to Rev. Mr. Caleb Warhurst[35] at Arthur Clegg's,[36] Manchester, undated [but written in late September 1762].[37]

Dear Brother

Thoˢ Rothwell called at my house yesterday but I was from home— I have long been endebted a visit to Bolton—& likewise desirous of the sight of Mʳ Warhurst (since I cannot get a letter from him)—I now propose to spend this next Sabbath at Bolton if the Lord please, & to call on you at Manchester on Monday—unless I should (which I question) find

---

[32]**John Beddome** (1674-1757), Baptist minister at the Pithay in Bristol, 1725-1757.

[33]Tommas's desire for an assistant would be met shortly after the date of this letter, when **James Newton** (1733-1790), a member at Maze Pond in Southwark, arrived in early 1758. See "Sketch of the Life of the Late Rev. John Tommas, Pastor of the Baptist Church in the Pithay, Bristol," *Baptist Annual Register*, 4 vols. (London: Dilly, Button, Thomas [and others], 1790-1802) 3:313-319; also letter 8.

[34]**John Newton** (1725-1807), later popular vicar at Olney and St. Mary Woolnoth, London, and author of "Amazing Grace." Newton was making frequent visits to Manchester at this time as he was considering becoming a dissenting minister. John Byrom recorded in his diary (20 April 1762) that Newton had "come to Manchester upon account of the opening of the new meeting (house) [Cannon Street] at the upper end of this Croft to-morow, and to see some ministers and friends," among whom, as this letter suggests, were Warhurst and Clegg. See William Urwick, *Historical Sketches of Nonconformity in the County Palatine of Chester* (London: S. Fletcher, 1864) 293.

[35]**Caleb Warhurst** (d. 1765), an Independent, ministered to the Baptist congregation (a mixed congregation of paedobaptists and anti-paedobaptists) at Coldhouse Lane, Manchester, 1756-1762, at which time the paedobaptists withdrew with Warhurst to form an Independent congregation in Cannon Street, Manchester.

[36]**Arthur Clegg,** member at Coldhouse Lane, Manchester, till 1765, and most likely later (with his relation Edmund) at Shudehill till about 1781.

[37]Eng. MS. 347, f. 240, JRULM. The postmark appears to bear a Liverpool stamp; internal evidence suggests that Newton was in Liverpool when he wrote the letter. A version of this letter was published in the *Congregational Magazine* 8 (1825): 132.

it convenient to stretch forward into Yorkshire, in which case I shall not be with you till the end of the week.

But as M[r] Burgess[38] informed me in his last that M[r] Waldegraves[39] Ordination is to be sometime in this month, I wish this to beg, that if it should be fixed for next week, you would inform me by tomorrow or Thursdays post, that when I am at Bolton I may turn my horses head to Tockholes at once—& perhaps M[r] Burgess' notice might come on Saturday when I am not in Liverpool to receive it.

I should be glad of an opportunity to see M[r] Scott[40] either at Tockholes or at his own house to let him know that I am disposed to accept a call with in his connection, & under the sanction of his judgment & recommendation, if any favourable opportunity should offer, & he thinks proper to encourage me. I begin to be weary of standing all the day idle & there seems not the least probability of beginning any thing at Liverpool. The Lord has made me willing nay desirous to set about it. I would prefer it to any thing else. I have made all the overtures towards it that the situation of things will bear—but it will not do there is not a person (one woman excepted) who is willing to concur in the necessary preliminaries.

If I should not have opportunity of meeting wth M[r] Scott, I take the liberty to desire you to acquaint him with my case. And to tell him that so far as I know my own heart, I have quite done with the established Church so called—not out of anger or despair, but from a conviction that the Lord has been wise & good in disappointing my views in that quarter   And I believe if the admission I once so earnestly sought was now freely offered, I could hardly if at all accept it.

If I come to Manchester on Monday I hope to stay two days—but I am deeply engaged to lodge with M[r] Philips—as they were so kind as to abide with us, I make the first advances towards an acquaintance.

I hope your soul prospers—that the Lord comforts refreshes & strengthens you in your inner man & your outward labours. I hope the house which you have built to his name, is plied with his glory—Happy they that know the grace of our Lord Jesus Christ—but happy above all others are those who receive appointment & power to proclaim this

---

[38]**James Burgess** (d. 1804), Independent minister for many years in Lancashire (see letter 256).

[39]**Thomas Waldegrave** (1732-1812), Independent minister at Tockholes (1756-1771) and Bury St. Edmunds (1771-1801). Newton's desire to attend Waldegrave's ordination service is not surprising, for, according to Thomas Raffles, Waldegrave "was almost deified in Tockholes and Manchester." See Robert Halley, *Lancashire: Its Puritanism and Nonconformity* (Manchester: Tubbs and Brook, 1872) 510.

[40]**James Scott** (1710-1783), Independent minister who operated an academy for training ministers at Heckmondwike, 1754-1783.

grace to poor sinners, & who find the Lord confirming their word with signs following—To be thus engaged—among a few faithful lively pecple, to dispose all my faculties studies & time to this service, is the one thing that I continually desire after the Lord, & which I think I could without hesitation prefer to the honours & possessions of a Lord or a prince.

I believe you pray for me Dear Sir continue so to do—entreat the Lord to empty me of self, to fill me with grace—to make me humble obedient watchful & spiritual in all things—to nourish me daily with the bread & water of life to favour me with these transferring manifestations of his love, which the world knows nothing of, & then let him do with me as seemeth good in his sight. And to this purpose my poor petitions shall not be wanting for you My love to M^r & Mrs Clegg & all their family   May the love of God our Saviour be with you & with y^r affecti^e

J Newton

7. *John Gill,*[41] *Camberwell, London, to John Collett Ryland, Northampton, 20 March 1771.*[42]

Dear Sir

I received some little time ago a few lines from your son by means of Mr Warne,[43] acquainting me that you had sent me an hare, which I have received & give you thanks for it; it proved a good one & I eat a tolerable good dinner of it— Your son also intimates your desire of being favoured with a loaning of Mr Messey's M.S. Translation of John Bunyan[44]—that I delivered to Mr Keith[45] two years ago, & quickly after Mr Messeys Son & I suppose his executor called upon him for it— Addingtons Book of Baptism[46] I have not seen nor do I chose to see it; I have done with all controversies & especially about Baptism; I have exhausted that subject all I can & I think I have wrote enough to convince any man of the Truth whose mind is open to conviction what you propose viz. reprinting all I have wrote about it in my Body of Practical Di-

---

[41]**John Gill** (1697-1771), High Calvinist Baptist minister at Horsleydown (later Carter Lane), Southwark, 1719-1771.

[42]MAM PLP 44.47.1, JRULM. O the back page of the MS. **John Ryland, Jr.,** has written, "Dr Gill respecting Addington on B[aptism]. March 20th 1771."

[43]**Joshua Warne**, deacon at Carter Lane, Southwark.

[44]I have been unable to identify this individual and the provenance of this MS.

[45]**George Keith** (d. 1782), Gill's son-in-law, member at Carter Lane, and a prominent London dissenting printer and bookseller.

[46]**Stephen Addington** (1729-1796), at that time Independent minister at Market Harborough and author of *The Christian Minister's Reasons for Baptizing Infants* (1771).

vinity will answer no end at all for that party who always cry up every new thing as unanswerable, never think any thing answered tho' it has been done over & over again unless a formal answer is given to it, which if you think it necessary it should be done by one of you ministers in Northamptonshire or Leicestershire & there are [enough] of you capable of it as your self Mʳ Woodman[47] &c. & I imag[ine] it will give you but little trouble it having nothing new unless it be scandal & that stands for nothing—they have now nothing to throw out but their old assumptions their old thread bare arguments, which are quite wore out, so that you will have nothing to do but to return our arguments upon 'em! I think Mʳ John Browne of Kettering[48] is yᵉ properest person to undertake yᵉ work, he has wrote against this same man heretofore & a very good thing which I suppose sticks in this mans stomach & is yᵉ occasion of his writing this & thereat he entitles his pamphlet the ministers reasons for baptizing infants &c. he may entitle his by way of contrast yᵉ ministers reasons for not baptizing infants & for acknowledging the ordinance not by sprinkling or pouring water but by Immersion only of which he is very capable of giving & who also may be supplied with arguments & answers to objections if necessary from my last Treatise & others which he has by him for as they give us nothing but their old reasons & arguments we must return ours, in our own defence; but if you chuse another person of your body of ministers, he will find no great difficulty in encountering those doughty advocates for infant sprinkling, a cause which no man of Taste chuses to engage in. I indeed then beg leave! enough wrote on both sides yᵉ question to satisfy any man who is desirous of knowing on what side truth lies, at least, so as to determine for himself.

I desire the two of you to acquaint Mʳ Davey[49] of your Town, that whereas I now live a little way out of yᵉ city by reason of my age & growing infirmities I very rarely attend any of the meetings of the Fund,[50] & therefore I desire that he will send up his next letter to yᵉ

---

[47]**Isaac Woodman** (1715-1777), Baptist minister at Sutton in the Elms.

[48]**John Brown** (d. 1800), Baptist minister at two congregations in Kettering, 1751-1786. Gill is referring to Brown's *A Sermon Preached at a Public Administration of Baptism Interspersed and Enlarged with Testimonies from Learned and Judicious Writers, who Espoused Infant-Sprinkling* (1764), which was sold by George Keith.

[49]**Henry Davis (Davy)** (1700-1780), Strict Baptist minister in Northampton.

[50]The Particular Baptist Fund was formally organized in June 1717 in London, with Thomas Hollis (1659-1731) serving as the first trustee and treasurer (he left £500 to the Fund in his will). The Fund initially used Pinners' Hall in London as its headquarters. Its objective was primarily educational—to develop and maintain an effective ministry within the Particular Baptist denomination, or, as the original 1717 letter reads, "for the support and maintenance of honourable Ministers, and providing for a succession of such." From the beginning the country churches often distrusted the London churches, and in 1717 a separate fund in Bristol was estab-

Fund to some other person either to D[r] Lewelyn in Southampton Street Bloomsbury,[51] or to one of y[e] Treasurers of y[e] Fund, or to M[r] James Smith,[52] watchmaker in Bunhill row near Morefield, auditor of 'em or to M[r] John Robinson, stationer in Shad Thames Southwark Secretary of y[e] Fund[53] or to any minister he has any acquaintance or correspondence with & I should be glad if you could convey by any means y[e] same intelligence to M[r] Cole of Long Bugby,[54] in doing which you greatly oblige

your affectionate Friend & Bro. in X

John Gill

Camberwell March 20th 1771.

8. John Fawcett,[55] Wainsgate, near Hebden Bridge, Yorkshire, to John Sutcliff,[56] care of Hugh Evans,[57] Bristol Academy, 29 May 1773.[58]

My dear dear Brother,

You desire in yours to Brother Tommas to know when our association is to be, & express a desire to be at it. Please then to observe that it is fixed for the 16 & 17 of June.[59] If possible I could wish to have your company at that time, & to hear you preach. What I am going to relate will doubtless give you a good deal of concern.

---

lished. The minister and one messenger could be sent by a church, primarily in London and its surrounding areas, to the meetings of the Fund for each £50 contribution made by that church to the Fund. Other individuals, not affiliated with these churches, could also serve as messengers to the Fund based upon their own private contributions. John Gill's congregation in Southwark was one of the six London churches instrumental in the formation of the Fund, and Gill, while still at Kettering, received one of the first educational grants from the Fund in 1718. Gill would play a major role in the affairs of the Fund for the next 50 years. See Theo. F. Valentine, *Concern for the Ministry: The Story of the Particular Baptist Fund 1717-1967* (Teddington: Particular Baptist Fund, 1967) 1-12.

[51]**Thomas Llewelyn** (1720?-1793), Welsh Baptist historian and educator in London.

[52]**James Smith**, deacon at Little Wild Street, Lincoln's-Inn Fields, London.

[53]**John Robinson**, Baptist bookseller in Southwark and member at Carter Lane.

[54]William Cole (1718-1794), Baptist minister at Longbuckby, 1768-1794.

[55]**John Fawcett** (1740-1817), Baptist minister at Wainsgate, Hebden Bridge, near Halifax, Yorkshire, 1777-1817.

[56]**John Sutcliff** (1752-1814), Baptist minister at Olney, 1775-1814.

[57]**Hugh Evans** (1712-1781), minister at Broadmead, Bristol, and Principal of Bristol Baptist Academy, 1758-1781.

[58]Eng. MS. 369, f. 46a, JRULM.

[59]A reference to the annual meeting of the Lancashire and Yorkshire Baptist Association (founded in 1720).

Your friend & mine above named is sick, & unable to answer your letter.[60] His disorder is—what he has much dreaded—*the small pox.* I have just been with him. He is very full, but they are not of the worst sort. He is often very serene & well composed in his mind. His hope is steadfast in Christ. He has just been saying— "Since the small pox came into the neighbourhood, I have endeavourd to live in a habitual prepa-redness for death." I could be glad—exceeding glad to see him safely recover. O the dear ties of exalted friendship by which he has been bound to my heart! I would gladly hope he will get thro', but he has ap-peared for some time like a person ripening for glory.—We shall be able to inform you in a post or two how his disorder is likely to turn.

Pray order to be with us at the association if possible.

Grace be with thy spirit. Amen

J. Fawcett

Wainsgate   May 29 1773.

My best respects to Mess.rs Evans's[61] &c
In haste—

9. John Geard,[62] Chacewater, to John Sutcliff, Strathtay, Scotland, to be left at John Fawcett's, Hebden Bridge, Yorkshire, 5 July 1773.[63]

Chacewater   July y.e 5.th 1773

---

[60]I have been unable to identify this "Brother Tommas." He was most likely a member of Fawcett's congregation.

[61]A reference to Hugh Evans and his son, **Caleb** (1737-1791), the latter serving as assistant pastor for many years under his father before becoming pastor at Broadmead and Principal of the Academy, 1781-1791.

[62]**John Geard** (1749-1838), later Baptist minister at Hitchin, Herts., 1774-1831. As this letter reveals, efforts by Geard and others (primarily Benjamin Francis) in itinerant preaching in Cornwall and the West Country in 1773, commissioned by the newly-formed Bristol Education Society (1770), preceded by many years the formation of the London Baptist Society for the Encouragement and Support of Itinerant and Village Preaching in 1797. Another letter by Geard to Sutcliff and Thomas Purdy, dated 9 August 1773, can be found in the BMS Archives, Angus Library, Regent's Park College, Oxford. See Roger Hayden, *Continuity and Change: Evangelical Calvinism Among Eighteenth-Century Baptist Ministers Trained at Bristol Academy, 1690-1791* (Chipping Norton UK: Roger Hayden and Baptist Historical Society, 2006) 129-130; Deryck W. Lovegrove, "Particular Baptist Itinerant Preach-ers during the late 18.th and early 19.th Centuries," *Baptist Quarterly* 28 (1979-1980): 127-131.

[63]Eng. MS. 370, f. 51, JRULM.

Dear friend

I am now sat down in order to communicate some intelligence to my friend in Yorkshire. I did not come into Cornwall so soon as I intended when I left Bristol on the account of the complaint in my breast. Yesterday sennight was the first Lords day I spent in Cornwall. I am not sorry that I deferred my journey for a week. I apprehend that it would not have been the most surprizing news to you that ever was heard, if I should have informed you that by preaching and journeying I had knocked myself up but I have no such intelligence to communicate. The week before the last, I rode about 170 miles and preached 8 times. Last week I rode 40 miles and preached 7 times. This week I have rode 6 miles or thereabout and preached 3 times, and have appointed for twice more already, viz this evening & tomorrow evening. Blessed be God for a good constitution, and for a desire, I hope in a measure at least to improve it for his honor and glory and the good of precious souls. I feel no bad effects at present of journeying or preaching. I have had no very bad opportunities in preaching since I came into Cornwall. The Lord be praised if I have solid reason to think I have enjoyed any thing of his spiritual presence, and may his divine blessing accompany what I have attempted. I should be better able to give you an account of particular matters had I staid longer before I had written. The number of people at Falmouth have not been as yet large since I came. At Chacewater last night the company was quite numerous considering that the meeting house is not very large, and that it has no gallery. The house was upon the whole pretty well stuffed, and some for ought I know out of doors. I expect young Preceptor[64] by next Lord's day. I intend to ride part of the road towards Plymouth to meet him, but I expect a letter from him informing me at what particular place to come. Brother pray for me that the Lord may cause his grace to abound towards me. O what a good master you and I profess to serve! What pleasures are comparable to the pleasures of religion! To be employed as the ambassadors of Christ, to be honored so as to carry the messages of God to men, what can be likened to this! And what art thou O Sutcliff, and what am I, or what are our fathers houses that we should be advanced hitherto, if in reality we are the ambassadors of Christ. May the Lord if he has counted us faithful and put us into the ministry, make us eminently useful & may we have a disposition & ability to abound in the work of the Lord. May we never preach an unfelt gospel but continually feel the power and influence of the truths we deliver unto others upon our own hearts. May Gods strength be made perfect in our weakness. Send me an ans.ʳ as soon as possible that I may receive it before I leave

---

[64]Preceptor [Praeceptor] served, mostly as a supply minister or assistant, in several Baptist congregations in the southwest of England in the 1770s. Whether he was a classmate of Geard's at Bristol is unknown.

Cornwall. Let me know how it is with you as to your health. The Lord bless and be with you and cause his face to shine upon you! May he establish your bodily health if it be agreeable to his will. May you grow and flourish in the best things. May you be an instrument of doing much good! Give my respects to relations & friends tho' to me unknown, as well as to y.ʳ pastor. I now subscribe myself your affectionate friend

John Geard

P.S. Direct for me to be left at M.ʳ Richard Muttons[65] in Falmouth Cornwall. The complaint in my breast is pretty nearly if not quite gone. The greek testament &c are left at Montacute.

10. *William Hartley,*[66] *Halifax, to John Sutcliff, Dr. Evans's house, No. 2 Stokes Croft, Bristol, 16 November 1773.*[67]

Halifax Nov 16—73

Dear B.ʳ

This is the second time I take up my pen to write to my dear friend, since I either see him, or heard from him. My last scrawl after a considerable delay came to hand again; since which time I have been very poorly as to my health. My disorder, of which I had been better for some time, returned again with renewed vigour. But I hope, I shall get the better of it soon; if not, the will of the L.ᵈ be done. "Good when he

---

[65]Richard Mutton [Motton] was a pawnbroker in Falmouth. He was baptized by Philip Gibbs, the Baptist minister at Plymouth, on 25 June 1769, and became a member of the Baptist meeting at Chacewater, which was organized in September 1769. The Baptist church at Falmouth was formed shortly thereafter, and the two congregations met as one until June 1772, when the Falmouth congregation was granted a dismissal to form its own congregation, much to the disappointment of the Chacewater congregation. Richard and Mary Mutton signed as members of the new Falmouth church. Neither meeting was able to support a minister for some time, and both were supplied for several years by students from Bristol, including a young John Rippon in July of 1771. The two congregations were reunited briefly again in 1776; they would share ministers at other times as well during the remainder of the eighteenth century. See *The Universal British Directory,* 5 vols. (London: Printed for the Patentees [Peter Barfoot and John Wilkes], and sold by Champanye and Whitrow, Jewry Street, Aldgate, 1791-1798) 3:99; Leonard Alfred Fereday, *The Story of the Falmouth Baptists, with Some Account of Cornish Baptist Beginnings* (London: Carey Kingsgate Press, 1950) 42-50.

[66]**William Hartley** (1740-1822), between 1771 and 1822, ministered to Baptist churches at Halifax, Bingley, Lockwood, Newcastle, and Stockton-on-Tees.

[67]Eng. MS. 370, f.59a, JRULM. On the back page Sutcliff has written, "Rec.ᵈ Nov.ʳ 28. 73. Ans.ᵈ Dec.ʳ 22. 73."

gives, supremely good. Nor less when he denies; Ev'n crosses from his sovereign hand, are blessings in disguise." Jehovah leads his people thro' the fire & the water unto a wealthy place   Our afflictions are weighed in the balances, of yᵉ [Contrary?]; and will work together for our best intrest [sic]—And tho', in themselves they are not joyous, yet the effects thereof under the teaching of divine grace are useful & salutary. David could say, before I was afflicted, I went astray, but now have I kept thy word   One of the antient fathers, being for a considerable time afflicted with a violent head-ach, prayed earnestly to God for the removal of it. *God heard him*, but withal thought meet to exercise him, with the *powerful workings* of lascivious lust. The old Father after strugling [sic] for a season with his new affliction, prayed to God for the removal of it and the return of his old companion. Thus you see, he judged it wiser to be exercised with a pained head than with unclean desires. Yet after all it must be acknowledged that health in itself considered is one of the greatest blessings in life. Nay may I not say the greatest. For, not all the variegated beauties of summer can charm, nor all the musick of the woods in that intervening season can delight us, when health is departed. Food is the object of lothing [sic], friends are dull companions, & our favourite studies are painful labours when destitute of health. May you, & I, improve every d[e]gree of it we are, or may be the subjects of, to yᵉ praise and glory of God—

Your uncle W.ᵐ S—f[68] informed me that you was quite clear of your complaint; on which account I rejoice with you, may the Lord establish and continue it.

I heard a few days ago that the Baptist church at Shrewsbury had given you a call—& that you had accepted of it, may the Lord make yᵉ step happy & prosperous. I rejoice in hope of your settlement—near your native country. May yᵉ God of Israel smile upon it I hope when you are settled there, that a circulation of letters will be more easy, & that we can mix our joys & sorrows more feelingly, as our work then will be similar.   .

You wished in your last that the suspended affair between S— M— & me, was agreeably decided. I have the pleasure to inform you that it is (I hope) honorably concluded. I gave her a letter at the appointed period instead of going over, in which I informed her of the State of my mind relative to it— of the difficulties lying in the way—and of what our friends said concerning it. In answer to which she told me yᵗ she had been much affected with it, and was willing upon the above consid-

---

[68]William Sutcliff, John's uncle, was a member of John Fawcett's congregation at Wainsgate; he was a close friend of the Rev. James Turner of Birmingham. See Michael A. G. Haykin, *One Heart and One Soul: John Sutcliff of Olney, His Friends and his Times* (Darlington: Evangelical Press, 1994) 58, 66, 87, 93, and 118.

erations (*at present*) to drop it. So that now I am on that [paper torn] entirely at liberty. Nor have I any engagements [of] the like nature any where else. Have never been [illegible word] since you left Yorkshire. The affair concerning MP. have laid honestly before a judicious friend, who declared he is amazed that any person (who has any knowledge of those concerns) should say that I ever proposed to that wo—n in what I had said—

My child has had yᵉ smallpox since she came to Halifax, in which she was sorely afflicted; but is well again.

The relation between M.ʳ Dracup[69] and his flock, at Bingley is dissolved. He is where he was; & the church is supplied from Wainsgate. M.ʳ George Hains[70] from M.ʳ Francis's church,[71] is, I hear come to Shipley. George Townsend[72] I hear is inclined to Hawkshead-hill. I am informed that John Hindle[73] is under the eye of the church—at Bingley. I heard Peter[74] is entered upon his studies at Wainsgate.

Dear B.ʳ if you would be so obliging as to inquire secretly & judiciously [sic] into the circumstances of yᵉ widdow [sic] Lady you mentioned; I shall lay it before M.ʳ Haldene if you are kind enough in your next to give me some knowledge of it. Write soon and seal it up safe, as the last came to hand open. Ever, ever yours,

Wm Hartley

11. Thomas Harmer,[75] Wattisfield, near Bury St. Edmunds, Suffolk, to Josiah Thompson,[76] London, 7 March 1774.[77]

To the Revᵈ Mʳ Thompson, London.

Revᵈ & Dʳ Sʳ

With this I return your M.S.[78] and am very much obligᵈ to you for the Pleasure & Instruction it has afforded me. I have as you desired ven-

---

[69]**John Dracup** (1723-1795), former Independent turned Baptist minister in Lancashire and Yorkshire, 1772-1795.

[70]**George Haines** (d. 1780), Baptist minister at Shipley, 1771-1780.

[71]**Benjamin Francis** (1734-1799), Baptist minister at Horsley, 1759-1799.

[72]**George Townsend** (1744-1783), Baptist minister at Accrington, 1775-1783.

[73]**John Hindle**, Baptist minister at Bingley before removing to Pellon Lane, Halifax, 1779-1789.

[74]Unidentified.

[75]**Thomas Harmer** (1714-1788), Independent minister at Wattisfield, 1734-1788.

[76]**Josiah Thompson** (1724-1806), Baptist minister at Unicorn Yard, Southwark (1746-1761), and Nonconformist historian.

[77]Eng. MS. 370, f. 57, JRULM.

tured to make two or three alterations or additions, in the Counties of Norfolk & Suffolk, & in them only have I taken that Liberty.

I showed the Book to a young Minister of this County who was here last week, & who took much pleasure in finding out his Fellow Pupils in their several stations. He, or rather a Relation of his, complained a little that the Names of the Ministers that concurred in the late Application to Parliament[79] are not placed in *Alphabetical* Order, which rendered his Search less easy.

This young Minister was also a little hurt at finding M[r] Belsham's[80] Name among the Students at Daventry. He says he is now a Sub-Tutor in that Academy, & was so at the time when these enquiries are supposed to have been made, 1772, 1773. He was, I think he said, first Classical Tutor, & since Mathematical.

There are very considerable differences, in the Names of divers places, I find, from the vulgar Orthography: whether this is owing to the Neglect of those that gave you the Lists, or the Refinements of Criticism, I will not pretend to decide. It would be improper, in a peculiar manner, for me to take any notice of these matters, since the Orthography of the Village in which I myself live is so much unsettled, having found it written six or seven different ways in books & inscriptions. I will not therefore point out any thing of this sort, excepting one which may serve as a specimen of what I mean. In Middlesex I find there are two Congregations said to be at Branford, which, I suppose, is the town I have hitherto allways seen written Brentford. As these papers are with great Propriety, designed to answer the purposes of a kind of Record, perhaps you will think this circumstance not alltogether unworthy of Attention.

There are some other things which appear to me rather in the light of oversights, with which however your Correspondents are the people that are chargeable. Thus I find in Worcestershire, among the Ministers that concurred in the Application to Parliament John or Noah Jones[81] &

---

[78]Thompson's chief work, "The State of the Dissenting Interest in the several Counties of England and Wales ... The First Part, c. 1774," was never published (the manuscript is now at Dr. Williams's Library, London). In this work, Thompson acquired information on over 600 dissenting congregations in England and Wales at the time of the application to parliament in 1772 for the relief of dissenting ministers. As the above letter reveals, Harmer had just reviewed Thompson's MS., most likely in preparation for Harmer's own work on the history of dissenters in Norfolk and Suffolk.

[79]In 1772 a group of dissenting ministers applied to parliament for a repeal of the Test and Corporation Acts; their efforts, however, were not successful.

[80]**Thomas Belsham** (1750-1829), former Independent turned Unitarian minister in London, 1794-1829.

[81]**Noah Jones** (1725-1785), Welsh Baptist minister at Walsall, Staffordshire, 1762-1784.

Risden Darracott.[82] Mr Darracott's name is struck out. If that was proper I should imagine Mr Jones's also should have been expunged, since they seem both to stand on the same footing, being both mentioned in Staffordshire, as related to Walsall.

I hope you will receive this safe, & that the M.S. will receive no hurt in it's Return to you. I expect to send it by a Youth belonging to this Assembly this afternoon; but if I should be disappointed as to that I will send it by another method the end of this week, lest you should be disappointed as to the sending it the time you proposed into Shropshire.

My Son desires his Compliments, & with great Thanks for this Favour, I am

Revd & Dr Sr

Yr affectionate Brother

& faithfull humble Servt

Thomas Harmer

Watisfield, (near Bury St Edmds)
Suffolk, March. 7. 1774.

12. *James Turner,*[83] *Birmingham, to John Sutcliff, Salop [Shrewsbury], 25 August 1774.*[84]

My very dear friend

How will you be surpriz'd, when I tell you, that I have seen your Unkle William[85] since you did, & consequently knew more than half of what is contain'd in your letter before I saw it.

The truth of all is as follows—Mr Holden[86] & his Lady (married at Xmas last) came here on yesterday 30 July, on their way to Lancashire. His mother & two of his brothers being dead since he was there, he was sent for to settle matters &c They were very desirous of my going with them, & as it happened I had an opportunity (a supply dropping in) tho' I had left off all thoughts of visiting that Country this summer.

---

[82]**Richard Darracott** (1751–1795), Independent minister in Somerset, 1773–1793. His name may have been marked out because he was no longer in Staffordshire by 1772.

[83]**James Turner** (1726–1780), Baptist minister at Birmingham, 1755–1780.

[84]Eng. MS. 371, f. 125b, JRULM.

[85]William Sutcliff (see letter 10).

[86]Holden was at this time pastor of the Baptist church at Lockerly, near Romsey, Hampshire. In 1775 he became a subscriber to the Bristol Education Society. See *An Account of the Bristol Education Society Anno 1770* (Bristol: M. Ward, 1776) 24.

Accordingly on the Wednesday morning following we set out, they in a one horse Chaise, which they keep, & I on horse back. A delightful journey we had indeed. The weather, the roads & agreeable conversation, made it truly pleasant: and thro' mercy our coming up was as delightful. I wrote a line to your Unkle but did not expect to see him, & was surpriz'd to hear he was come on the Lord's day morning. I had but very little time with him, some part of which was spent in conversing about you. He gave me an account of y^r ramble to Wrexham, Liverpool &c—well, if you can travel 130 miles & preach 9 or 10 times in 8 or 9 days I just give you the preference. But I know there are few such do-little's as I am.

I am glad to hear of the success at Liverpool Mr Medly[87] seems to be the very man for them. But is it man, without the blessing of God?

I am sorry your auditory is so small. I am in hopes that case will be alter'd ere long. To be sure you came at a critical season. Well, the Lord's ways are in the deep, & his footsteps none can trace. Go on, & fear neither death nor devils.

Religion seems to be gaining ground in our Country. At Bacup they are going to enlarge their House[88]; and at Rochdale they talk of building a new one.[89] At the latter place they have an Auditory of near 200. I saw your Unkle Clayton,[90] Mr Bamford is not likely to continue long at Accrington.[91] Things get worse & worse. Tottlebank, I apprehend, is the place he is likely to go to. There is not a very good understanding between him & a gentleman above mention'd, but I don't like fishing in troubled waters. "Jealous is cruel as the grave." Ministers should be healers of breaches & restorers of paths to dwell in.[92]

---

[87]**Samuel Medley** (1738-1799), Baptist minister at Byrom Street, Liverpool, 1772-1799.

[88]**John Hirst** (1736-1815) was the Baptist minister at Bacup, 1772-1815. A new chapel was opened in 1777. See Frederick Overend, *History of the Ebenezer Baptist Church, Bacup* (London: Kingsgate Press, 1912) 165.

[89]John Dracup (see letter 10) ministered at Rochdale, 1772-1783.

[90]Unidentified.

[91]**Charles Bamford** (1727-1804), Baptist minister in Yorkshire, 1755-1804.

[92]The church at Tottlebank was formed in 1669, making it the oldest nonconformist church in Lancashire. David Crosley (1669-1764) spent eight years there as minister between 1696 and 1704, before removing to Currier's Hall in London. At the time of the above letter, the church had been unsettled for some time. After Joshua Kettilby's resignation in 1770, probationers came and went and the church seemed in no hurry to name a successor, disagreeing over monies derived from church property. The church resided on a large farm it had purchased at the close of the seventeenth century and from which it received annual rents. Other monetary bequests had been left to the church as well. Some other nearby communities that had formed with the Tottlebank church many years earlier believed they were entitled to some share of the proceeds of the church's investments. An entry in the

Sometimes the very contrary is the case.

I cannot now say any thing to yᵣ question about *unbelief*; Mᵣ & Mᵣˢ Holden are here & I have very little time to write—& besides, I am such a queer creature, that 'tis but now & then that I am in an agreeable humour for writing.

I am surpriz'd to hear that Mᵣ Pyne[93] has had an invitation to Warwick; Tho I have a *notion* I heard something of it before. I hear nothing what's come of Mᵣ Shaw.[94] What a *day*! what a *world*! what a *Church*, do we live in! no; I dare say Pyne would not go for an 100 a year. Well, all will be right by & by.

I dare say Mᵣ Hall[95] would not come to Salop on the errand you mention, on any account.

Tottlebank Church Book, dated 12 April 1769, reads: "Be it remembered that it is agreed for the time being by us whose names are hereunto subscribed that the people in communion with the church of Tottlebank residing in Broughton Dunnerdale and Ulpha hath a right to one half of the one hundred and Twenty Pounds being part of the stock belonging to Tottlebank Pursueant to which it is agreed that the Rev Mᵣ Kettilby is to officiate at Broughton one whole Lord's day every Month agreed to by us whose names are here under written this 12ᵗʰ day of April 1769." Later, when the estate deed for the farm was renewed, the church book notes that it had been "Purchased by Monies which the Church had as a Common Stock . . . and no Member or Members could have any Personal, particular or Party claim but must remain as Common to the whole while a Church in Communion and that each Individual has an equal right to the one common whole thereof and no more." A Mr. Hutton briefly followed Kettilby, but he settled instead at Little Broughton in Cumberland. The church book notes for 1775: "After the remove of M.ᵣ Hutton we were again supplied providentially (as a Probationer towards taking the Pastoral Charge of this Church) by M.ᵣ Bamford from Acronton [Accrington] who staid about three years, but on Trial had, in that space of time was judged not likely for the Increase and comfort of the Body; therefore he also removed." A Mr. Harper came for a few months in 1779, but he left for Warrington and later became an Antinomian. Apparently, William Hartley was also considered by Tottlebank (he may have been related to the Hartley's who were members there), but he chose to go elsewhere (see letter 23). Eventually, Thomas Harbottle came from Hawkshead Hill in 1780, but he did not officially become pastor until 1783. Harbottle remained at Tottlebank until his death in 1824. See Tottlebank Church Book (MS., Angus Library, Regent's Park College, Oxford) ff. 74-78; Foster Sunderland, *A Brief History of Tottlebank Baptist Church, Greenodd, Ulverston: The Oldest Baptist Church in Lancashire* ([Tottlebank]: n.p. 1965?) 14-15; Margaret F. Thomas, *A History of the Tottlebank Baptist Church 1669-1999* (n.p.: [1999]).

[93]**John Pyne**, Baptist minister in Shrewsbury, 1762-1773.

[94]William Shaw (d. 1803) pastored the Baptist congregation at Collingham, Nottinghamshire, 1777-1803. Sutcliff became acquainted with Shaw in 1773. See Haykin, *One Heart*, 304.

[95]**Robert Hall, Sr.** (1728-1791), Baptist minister at Arnesby, 1753-1791.

Yesterday the New Chapel[96] here was consecreated (as 'tis call'd.) A dry ceremony indeed. Mr Holden & I had Tickets and got in & saw the whole proceeding.

Respects to self, Mrs Harley, M^r & Mrs Phillips[97] & all friends. Mrs Egerley's sister,[98] is, I believe, very well, and I doubt not, a very godly (more of this) good Girl.—The Lord be with you Amen

Birming. 25 Augt 74
A long letter will always be acceptable &c

13. John Ryland, Jr.,[99] Northampton, to John Sutcliff at Mr. Harley's, Shrewsbury, 12 November 1774.[100]

Rev^d & dear Bro^r

Yesterday I received your last letter—I think I had not answered the former—however I will not be long now and I hope soon to see you—I observe this moment upon receiving your last that it shou'd seem it was sent to Mr Ryland, however as it was given to me and I have begun to write I go on to answer it—it was I that sent to Mrs Andrews[101]—as to Olney people there are *many* of each Denomination that are *excellent* people—thro' the tatling of outward Court worshipers and the stiffness of inward Court worshipers there is too much prejudice between godly folks of each sort—there is nothing but Gospel in the Town—yet too little Love—I believe Mr. Newton[102] (who is Omicron) is the freest of a party Spirit of any one in Olney nor do I know any man more so in the world—his wife is more of a Bigot and so are *many of each* Denomination—the stiffness of the Baptists has hurt

---

[96]The dedication service for the new chapel at the New Meeting (Presbyterian) in Birmingham, where **Joseph Priestley** would pastor, 1780-1791.

[97]Thomas Phillips (d. 1815) was a deacon in the Baptist congregation at High Street in Shrewsbury and author of a history of Shrewsbury. A number of his letters to Sutcliff can be found in the Sutcliff Papers, Angus Library, Regent's Park College, Oxford. For more on Phillips, see Haykin, *One Heart,* 65-66.

[98]A Mr. Edgerley, cheesefactor, and a Mr. Edgerley, Jr., grocer, appear in the *Universal British Directory,* but without addresses. Mr. Harley was a watchmaker and goldsmith (iv.418). See *Universal British Directory*, 4:418.

[99]**John Ryland, Jr.** (1753-1825), Baptist minister at Northampton (1785-1793) and Bristol (1793-1825) and one of the leading Baptists of his day.

[100]Eng. MS. 371, f. 107a, JRULM.

[101]Mrs. **Mary Andrews** of Olney, in whose house Sutcliff lived until his marriage in 1795.

[102]John Newton, then vicar at Olney. "Omicron" is a reference to the *nom de plume* used by Newton in his popular publication, *Omicron* (1774), a series of letters on religious topics.

them, but yet they are well attended 300 or 400 people, in afternoon and night I suppose, are able to maintain a minister comfortably, and if a man of a gospel spirit should go there and determine to believe No Tales and labor by gentle degrees to undermine a party spirit and try to outdo Mr N. in Candor & Love for all that love Christ I believe he would have a *good* prospect—and would find that the Interest wou'd gain more than it lost by the Gospel in the Church—this is a plain faithful acc.ᵗ as far as I can judge who know a good deal of Olney people both Church people and Dissenters—I think you had better by all means to come and try and doubt not but you'll call at Northampton and then we can consult further—My Parents & Mr. Burley[103] send Respects— Excuse haste May the Lord direct you—

I am

Yours in our dear Lord,

John Ryland jun.ʳ

I need not mention that I write freely and shou'd not desire others to know who gave you such and such information.

14. *John Ryland, Jr., Northampton, to John Sutcliff, Birmingham, 26 January 1775.*[104]

Revᵈ and honor'd Bro.ʳ

---

[103]**George Birley**, General Baptist minister and educator at Northampton and St. Ives, 1768-c.1818. He tutored for several years at J.C. Ryland's academy in Northampton.

[104]Eng. MS. 371, f. 107b, JRULM. Sutcliff must have left Birmingham before he received this letter, for he has written on the back that the letter was not received until 1 March and answered that day. Sutcliff would begin his ministry at Olney about the time of this letter. The above letter was written on the back of a handbill titled "Useful Questions for Self-Examination," apparently inspired by Psalms iv. 4. Questions include: "Have I been much in holy Ejaculations?" "Have I not inordinately minded earthly things?" "Have I been temperate and self-denying in the use of creatures?" "Have I been diligent and watchful?" "Have I been led to Gospel Duties by Gospel Motives? Have I ask'd every Blessing in the Name of CHRIST, and attempted every Duty in the strength of the SPIRIT." The author is unknown [possibly Ryland or Sutcliff]; however, the author affixed this interesting note at the bottom of the printed list of 15 questions: "Paste this within the cover of your Bible, or pin it against the back of your bed: for God's sake, read it over every night or morning; and, as in his sight, answer yes or no to every Question, with a low voice—if you are a true Christian, and reap no benefit by this practice at one month's end, you may light your pipe with it." Just beneath this Ryland has written, "Price 4ᵈ pʳ doz. or 2ˢ pʳ hundred."

Indeed I began to be uneasy in not hearing from you, therefore rec.[d] your kind Letter with much pleasure—am sorry to hear of M[r] Turners[105] Illness which I had but a very slight Intimation of before—I trust God will own you at Birmingham for much good—there's people enough there for you and M[r] Ryland[106] and M[r] Pomfield[107] all of you to find Work plenty among them I think.—

Poor Hervey[108] is silenc'd by the Bishop and tempted much to sad conformity to get into favor—he is naturally of a weak capacity surrounded with Enemys—dares not see a godly person—all things considered he deserves much pity tho' I can n't say he deserves no censure—

I am glad you have been to see friend Guy[109]—God is with him I am persuaded.

My Mama and Mr. Birley send their kind Resp. to you—

She joins me also in saluting all friends—Perhaps I may see you ere very long—do preach up Generosity & Liberality mainly ere I come for we want help much as to our Enlargement of our place of Worship—

I hope by this time you have preach'd away your Cough. M[r] Ryland[110] is in London—I have [been] preaching six times a week except sometimes our Deacon helps once in the Sabbath—I wish we cou'd see & hear you ag.[n] Peace be with you—Pray for a poor carnal stupid Wretch but

Yours affectionately in our dear Lord,
John Ryland jun.

Respects in particular to M[r] Turner M[r] Mosley M[r] Hill—M[r] Rubins M[r] Berry M[r] Hayes M[r] Pomfield if you know them and sh[d] see them soon—[111]

---

[105]James Turner (see letter 12).

[106]**John Riland** (1736?-1822), Anglican evangelical minister at St. Mary's, Birmingham.

[107]Probably the Rev. John Punfield of Exeter Row. See *Universal British Directory* 2:207.

[108]**Thomas Hervey** (1741-1806), Anglican evangelical clergyman near Kendal.

[109]**William Guy** (1739-1783), Baptist minister at Shepshed (Sheepshead), Leicestershire, 1774-1783.

[110]John Collett Ryland.

[111]Robert Mosely, sword cutler in Suffolk Street, Birmingham, and deacon at Cannon Street; a number of Hills are listed in the *Universal British Directory*; David Berry, a pocket-book lock and clasp maker in New Meeting Street, or Thomas Berry, a bone mould-turner in Loveday Street; Joseph Hayes, pawnbroker in Lower Temple Street. See *Universal British Directory*, 2:228, 223, 211, and 222.

15. Hugh Evans, Bristol, to John Sutcliff, Birmingham, 28 February 1775.[112]

Bristol Feb[y] 28th 1775

Dear Sir

As usefulness is the great end of life with respect to our selves and others: As I now hear that one M[r] Jones (who is one of Lady Hunting-ton[s] young men)[113] has left Falmouth, where he has been some time and there are many in those parts like Sheep with[t] a Shepherd, and others thirsting for the word, as you are not engaged, I have been thinking, it would give you an opportunity of seeing more of the world, and I hope of doing much good, if you were to pay them a Visit for 2, 3 or 4 months and see what the event might be. Your expenses will be paid, as we have an Order for some allowance for it from the education Socie-ty.[114]—If you are willing to take such a tour, let me have a line as soon as may be, that I may write to them on that head. If you are applied to from any other place you prefer, I don't wish to prevent what may be for your advantage.

There is a wide door opened in Cornwall, if we could but enter in while it is open. If you go, I imagine it will be best to purchase a strong

---

[112]Eng. MS. 369, f. 44, JRULM.

[113]Probably the same Mr. Jones who was at one time an assistant to Andrew Kinsman at the Plymouth Tabernacle, a congregation organized by Whitefield in the 1740s and finally established by Kinsman c. 1750. In 1763 Kinsman established a similar tabernacle in Dock, and was finally set apart to the pastoral office at Broad-mead in Bristol on 4 August 1763, with Hugh Evans taking part in the service. Kinsman's obituary in the *Evangelical Magazine* (1793) notes that his most distin-guished assistants in the early 1770s were Dunn and Padden at Plymouth, and Jones and Lake at Dock, "each of whom continued for some time in the exercise of his talents, with success, until invited to the pastoral office at other places." See *Evangel-ical Magazine* 1 (1793): 55.

[114]The Bristol Education Society (see letter 9) was formed in 1770 by the citi-zens of Bristol and the Baptist congregation at Broadmead, solely for the purpose of raising funds for the maintaining of a learned ministry through the means of Bristol Academy. It held its annual meeting every August, and began publishing the ser-mons preached at the meeting in 1773. A similar organization, the London Baptist Education Society, formed by Dr. Llewelyn, had existed since 1752. The leading officers for the collection of monies for the Bristol Society in 1776 were Frederick Bull, Esq., Leadenhall Street, London; John Reynolds, Artillery Court, London; Isaac Woodman, Thorpe, Leicestershire; J. C. Ryland, Northampton; Robert Robinson, Cambridge; John Bull, Esq., Treasurer; and Thomas Mullett, Secretary, the latter two from Bristol. See *Account of the Bristol Education Society*, 12; Norman S. Moon, *Education for Ministry: Bristol Baptist College, 1679-1979* (Bristol: Bristol Baptist College, 1979) 115.

hardy horse, as you will have it to carry you round the country there as well as to go down and return. We have nothing new here but that my son[115] is in a measure recovered of a nervous fever, wch had greatly reduced him. He has not preacht the 3 last Lord's Days, but hopes to do it next L'ds day. He & family are at Hanham for the air. We got our Members of parliament established & yesterday Mr Cruger[116] was introduced by a vast Number of foot Horse & carriages into our city and conducted thro' a triumphal arch at the bottom of Corn Street erected on the Occasion, to his house in Park Street. Mr Burke[117] declined coming down on Acc^t of business in the House of Commons &c—we all join in kind respects to you & Mr Turner in wch my family join. I am

Your's affec^ly

H Evans

16. John Fawcett, Wainsgate, near Hebden Bridge, Yorkshire, to John Sutcliff, Brick-kilne Lane, Birmingham, 10 April 1775.[118]

Wainsgate April 10. 1775

Dear Brother

I thank you sincerely for your very welcome letter which reach[ed] my hands a few days ago. I find you are yet involved in uncertainties. It is a true saying, Ου εχομεν ωδε μενουϛιν [sic] πολιν[119] I hope you will not conclude that I am void of sympathy with or concern for you. It is far from being the case. I apprehend, that considering your youth, your

---

[115]**Caleb Evans** (1737-1791), Baptist minister at Broadmead, Bristol, and Principal of the Academy.

[116]Henry Cruger (1739-1827) was originally from New York but emigrated to England prior to the American Revolution. He settled in Bristol, where he became a prosperous merchant. He was twice elected to parliament, first in 1774 and again in 1784. He served as Mayor of Bristol in 1781. He returned to New York in the late 1780s and was elected to the state senate while still a member of the British parliament. He died there in 1827. See Lewis Namier and John Brooke, *The House of Commons 1754-1790*, 3 vols. (Oxford: Oxford University Press, 1964) 2:280-282.

[117]Edmund Burke (1729-1797) was one of the greatest statesmen of his day. His opposition to the American War gained him the admiration of dissenters and reform-minded citizens throughout England and America, but after his harsh judgment of the French Revolution, recorded in his most famous work, *Reflections on the Revolution in France* (1790), Burke became the universal enemy of the radical reformers. Burke served in parliament as a representative for Bristol from 1774 to 1780.

[118]ENG. MS. 369/f.46b, JRULM. On the back page Sutcliff has written, "Rec.^d April 24. 75 Ans.^d 2 June—."

[119]Taken from Hebrews 13:14—"here have we no continuing city."

trials have been singular. Yet hitherto the Lord has helped you, and I trust you will find in the End that all has been ordered for the best.

I am obliged to you for your Subscription towards my little Book, tho' I know not when it will see the Light.[120] If you can be of any Service in promoting the Sale of the Sick Man's Employ,[121] I shall take it as a Favour, as the Copy is mine.

I know not whether Mr H.[122] will stay at Shipley or no. Mr Crabtree[123] &c have refused to assist in his ordination, and as such, he is not ordained. I cannot inform you of their reasons.—An unhappy difference about some unimportant matters is the cause of Brother Hindle's leaving Bingley. They are likely to be quite destitute.

Brother Townsend has a call to Akringdon,[124] & inclines to accept it, tho' he is much perplexed about giving up the poor people in Bolland.[125] I suppose you have heard that Brother Greenwood[126] is married to Miss Jackson. I think he goes on well at Rochdale. They are engaged in Building a meeting-house which will be a weighty Affair to them.

I am very much straitened for time, having so many concerns on my hand. I have been endeavouring to get an assistant to take off part of my School-Work, but cannot yet succeed. I am generally very happy in the pulpit, and in my preparations for it. The means of grace are well attended here. Last Wednesday preached from Gen. 17.1. I am the Almighty God, walk before me &c I scarcely ever had a better season. May you & I, my dear Brother, be helped to walk before the All-sufficient God, in dependence on him and devotedness to him. Pray give my best respects to Mr Turner.

I am Dear Brother

Most cordially yours

J. Fawcett

---

[120]Most likely a reference to Fawcett's *An Epitome of Christian Doctrine, Experience and Practice. In Prose and Verse. For the Instruction of Youth*, which he advertised at the end of the second edition of his *Advice to Youth; or, the Advantages of Early Piety*, a work that appeared sometime around 1778. The *Epitome* never appeared in print.

[121]Fawcett's *The Sick Man's Employ* first appeared in 1774; it was reprinted in 1809 and 1837.

[122]**George Haines** (see letter 10).

[123]**William Crabtree** (1720-1811), Baptist minister at Bradford for more than fifty years.

[124]Accrington.

[125]For Hindle and Townsend, see letter 10.

[126]**Abraham Greenwood** (1749-1827), Baptist minister at Rochdale (1775-1780), Dudley (1780-1786), and Oakham (1787-1796).

17. Caleb Evans,[127] Abingdon, to John Sutcliff, Birmingham, 30 June 1775.[128]

Abingdon June 30. 1775

My Dr Friend,

By the desire of our friends at Olney, I write to you earnestly to request that you would as soon as possible set out to pay them a visit and supply there for a few Lord's Days, that you may be the better able to judge whether it may be the will of providence that you sh^d become their stated Minis^r, sh^d y^r Minis^y be approved of by them. In this request Mr Beddome[129] Mr Dunscombe of Coate,[130] & myself, who have all been at Olney, unite with the people, & unless your engagem^t where you are sh^d be very urgent indeed, we shall take it unkind if you do not comply with this request, as it cann^t possibly do you any injury to pay the people a visit, and then to act as providence may direct, which is all that is desir'd of you.—The interest at Olney is considerable, a good house, a large congregation, and were there an acceptable Minis^r, a prospect of it's becoming much larger, an agreeable neighborh^d with respect to other churches & Minis^s, & many circumstances of a very encourag^g nature. With respect to the people, *some* of them are pretty high in their sentenc^s, & are perhaps too fond of a doctrinal Ministry, but in the gener^l, a spir^l experimental evangelic^l Minis^r w^d be highly acceptable, & I verily believe ye people would unite cordially in such a man. Mr Sackett[131] that was lately with them appears to have been useful to many, & his going away was against the will of many y^t attended, but the majority by far of the Church Memb^s could not approve of his being settled amongst them. They tho't him too rambling, superfic^l and methodistical. The independ^t Min^r is laid aside & not likely to be able to preach any more,[132] and sh^d ye independ^s be provided with a lively min^r whilst the Bapt^s are destit^e, it is fear'd the Inter^{t133} w^d suffer greatly—but on the

---

[127]See letter 15.

[128]ENG. MS. 369/f.43a, JRULM.

[129]**Benjamin Beddome** (1717-1795), Baptist minister at Bourton-on-the-Water, 1743-1795.

[130]**Thomas Dunscombe** (1748-1811), Baptist minister at Coate, 1773-1797.

[131]Apparently Sackett supplied briefly at Olney between William Walker's departure in 1773 and Sutcliff's arrival in 1775.

[132]John Drake pastored the Independent meeting in Olney from 1735 until his death on 10 August 1775, only a month and a half after Evans's letter to Sutcliff. Cowper greatly admired him and occasionally attended his services. John Whitford, a friend of John Newton, succeeded Drake. See *History of the Congregational Church, at Olney* (Olney: Cowper Memorial Congregational Church, 1929) 6-7.

[133]Interest.

other hand, sh^d the Bapt^s be provided first they s^d have the advantage. Upon the whole, we all think it highly probable y^r ministry will be acceptable to all the people, & sh^d it be so, that you might be remarkably useful in this situation. But at present all we desire is, as they are & will be destit^e till you come or send an answ^r to them, that you would *immed^y* pay them a visit & stay with them as long as you can, and then look up to God for further direction. Y^r present duty, as things appear to us, seems clear & evident, & it will give us great pain if you refuse to comply with our joint request.—Please to send a line to Mrs Andrews, inform^g her when you intend being at Olney, & how you think to go. We apprehend you might come in the Coach to Stony Stratford, & Olney friends would send a horse to meet you there if you inform them when they may expect you. Indeed two of them would have come to Birming^h for you, but that we tho't ye affair might as well be conducted by letter. We all join in Xtian repects to you & Mr Turner, who is, as we are glad to hear, better. May the Lord confirm his health and extend his usefulness! I am, my Dr Friend,

Your affect^e friend & bro^r in Christ
C Evans

P.S. I am going to Bro'ten,[134] hope to be at Bris^l in a fortn^t, when I sh^ll be glad to hear from you. Please to write to Mrs Andrews with^t delay—Mr Bedd^me lately preach'd from—and do you now pract^s —the words—The King's Busn^s requireth haste.

18. *James Ashworth,*[135] *Gildersome, Yorkshire, to John Sutcliff, Olney [via Northampton], 9 October 1775.*[136]

Very dear Brother

Your kind letter of the 23rd Sept^t came safe to hand. I readily grant your excuse, for your long silence, when I see the reasonable reason. I own I expected hearing from you before I did, but never once doubted your reception of mine, but thought you had took the hint which I gave you, viz. that my letters wou'd not be worth postage. Shou'd this have been the reason, it wou'd not have grieved me, because I wrote what I thought.

---

[134]Evans was close friends with the family of William Steele in Broughton, especially the two women poets in the family, Anne Steele (1717-78)("Theodosia") and Mary Steele, her niece (1753-1813).

[135]**James Ashworth** (d. 1802), Baptist minister at Gildersome, 1770-1797.

[136]Eng. MS. 369, f. 8, JRULM. On the back page Sutcliff has written, "Rec.^d Octr 13. 75. Ans.^d Decr 27. 75."

I am still pleased to hear of the success of the ever blessed gospel; and more especially others you told me, chiefly amongst the BAPTISTS. Writing baptists in large hand, is to let you know how greatly I love the cause, and trust I shou'd abide by it was it as much upon the decline, as I believe it upon the advance. No cause in reference to its goodness, can be known by the numbers that espouse it, but by its corresponding with the scriptures of truth. In this view, I apprehend, ours has greatly the preference.

We have had no additions to our Ch^h since I last wrote you, except one man from Pudcy,[137] which has join'd us. We have had a considerable increase of hearers this summer, of strangers y^t I do not know, that seem to settle. We have no spare room in our meeting house, especially in the latter part of the day. I hope the Lord has some kind end in view by bringing them under the word. I have been well helped, lately in my work; do generally preach with good liberty; you know that then the work is pleasant.

We are still at peace among ourselves, except one woman member, who has been very disorderly in her walk; one of Pauls busy bodies in other mens matters. I believe we shall be obliged to cut her off, in order to preserve the body from being hurt. It is altogether heavy work to me; any thing of this nature; but it is necessary to be done, and must be done, or Churches cannot be kept from disorder & corruption.

My health sometime back has but been poor, have found an inward weakness, and faintness attending me, which ended in the jaundice, to a great degree. I believe this bodily disorder was one cause of my work being so burdensom. It cost me many a wrestling hour at the throne of grace, for the quickening influences of God's holy spirit. It has given me a fresh proof of the influence ye body has upon the soul, as well as the soul upon the body; the union is so close, near & nice. I have been down at Scarborough, the middle of last month, for the benefit of the waters, both drinking and bathing, and have found surprising advantage, under a divine providence from them. I have got to my own feeling, a quite new inside, and my natural spirits are become a great deal more brisk & lively than before. Help me, dear B^r to be thankful!

There is a small interest of baptists at Scarbro', much upon the revival. They have had eleven members added to them last year. I doubt not this acc^t will be pleasing to you. The minister's name is Hague,[138] a sober, serious & judicious man. He has but had small advantages for improvement, but I am informed, he has grown abundantly in ministerial qualifications. I heard him preach once, he was upon redemption, was much pleased with his performances. He seems to reign in the af-

---

[137]Pudsey.
[138]**William Hague** (1736-1831), Baptist minister at Scarborough, 1771-1819.

fections of his audience, and is of good report in the Town. They have at present only an upper room which they have took to meet in, but are now intending to build.[139] One Mr Flight of London[140] has engaged to secure them a hundred pounds towards defraying the expence. I was there nine days & preach'd three times to them. The last time, the place was so crowded that all cou'd not get in but obliged to return.

I make no doubt you have heard they have had some uneasiness in the Ch^h at Halifax on acc^t of our Brother's amours; it had like to have ended in a seperation [sic], but I believe things are now comfortably settled.[141] I believe, dear B^r Hartley has been to blame in equivocating. Let this learn us to be quite plain, explicit & upright in every thing we do, for plain truth will stand its ground. I think our B^r is not very happy in the choice he seems to make of a companion for life. Whenever, my dear B^r, you shall think of taking such a step be prudent in it, and much in prayer to the Lord for direction. Much of the happiness of life depends upon a suitable companion, in a marriage relation. Ever remember, that a prudent wife is from the Lord. From him, therefore, seek her.

You ask me the reason of Mr. Whitford's[142] leaving Kipping, I do not [know], any further than hearing that the people there are never long satisfied with any man as their minister. I believe they are a restless uneasy Ch^h. I have never had much acquaintance with Mr. Whitford, and never heard him preach but once, and that was before he came to settle in Yorkshire, perhaps it is 16 years since. If I remember right I was well pleased with his discourse, according to the judgement I then had. However, I believe he is not in great repute as a preacher, even amongst his independant [sic] Brethren. I believe, according to what I have heard, he is a man of a hasty spirit, soon moved. I suppose the reports that have been spread, of his being fond of women, cannot be proved. I have now told you all that I know materially concerning him. Accept my fraternal respects to you in w^h my wife joins, from, Sir, y^r affectionate Brother in Xt

Ja^s Ashworth

---

[139]A meetinghouse was erected at Quay Street in 1776, not long after the date of the above letter, and enlarged three times during Hague's ministry. See C. E. Shipley, ed., *The Baptists of Yorkshire: Being the Centenary Memorial Volume of the Yorkshire Baptist Association* (London and Bradford: n.p., 1912) 204-205.

[140]**Thomas Flight** (d. 1800), a wealthy China merchant and leading member at Maze Pond, Southwark.

[141]See letter 10 for Hartley's difficulties with a woman in the Halifax church.

[142]**John Whitford**, former Independent turned Baptist minister, serving at Bicester, Oxfordshire, in the 1780s.

19. Caleb Evans, Bristol, to John Sutcliff, Olney, 23 October 1775.[143]

My D[r] Friend,

Enclos'd you have a pamphlet lately published by me in ans[r] to one wrote by M[r] Wesley.[144] I did not put my name to it, but a large edition is printing in Lon[n], to which my name will be prefix'd, at the importunity of sev[l] of my friends; tho' contrary to my own judgm[t]. Please to present one, with my Chris[n] respects, to M[r] Newton, tho' I am persuaded he is not of my mind, & will probably blame me for meddling with politicks. Nor sh[d] I have done it, had it not been for the shameful inconsistency of M[r] Wesley, & y[e] assiduity made use of in y[e] spread of his pamphlet. We do not al[ys] see alike, but I can truly say I wrote that pamphlet from con-scient[s] motives and in y[e] fear of God.—When y[e] Soc[y] Serm[n][145] is printed, how shall I send you a few of y[m]? The printer is at present so hurried y[t] he cannot take it in hand.—And now, in y[e] lang[e] of one of old, I am ready to say—Is it peace? Oh w[t] a pity it is that *Brethren* sh[d] fall out by the way! When will the breaches at Olney be made up—when will that meek & quiet spirit, which so eminently adorns your pious hostess, un-iversally spread am[g] the people & leaven y[e] whole lump! We are com-manded to pray for y[e] peace of Jerusalem—when will our prayers be ans[d] with respect to that part of our Jerusalem where you are at present situated? I long to rec[e] good tidings.

M[rs] Evans & my D[r] children are well, but we have had 2 of our fami-ly dangerously ill, & have a Serv[t] now lying, we fear, at y[e] point of death in the small pox. Sis. Mullett[146] has lost her two dau[s] in it, as she once

---

[143]Eng. MS. 369, f. 43b, JRULM.

[144]In 1775 Evans engaged in a controversy with John Wesley over their diver-gent views of the war with the American colonies. Wesley had just published *A Calm Address to our American Colonies*, in which he took a very pro-British stance against the revolutionaries; Evans responded with *A Letter to the Rev. Mr. John Wesley, Occasioned by his Calm Address to the American Colonies*, defending the colonists for upholding values of freedom and toleration long held dear by Englishmen.

[145]*Kingdom of God. A Sermon Preached before the Bristol Education Society, August 16, 1775* (Bristol, 1775), by Caleb Evans

[146]Mary Evans Mullett (1743?-1800) was the daughter of Hugh and Sarah Evans (his first wife) and sister to Caleb Evans. She was baptized and admitted as a mem-ber of the Baptist congregation at Broadmead on 9 August 1765. She spent her last years in London, worshiping at Devonshire Square under Timothy Thomas, who had married her half-sister, Sarah. Sarah died in London in October 1800 and was buried in Bunhill Fields. Mary's husband, **Thomas Mullett** (1745-1814) was a prosperous paper-maker and stationer in Bristol before removing to London, where he began operating as an American agent in partnership with his wife's nephew and his son-in-law, Joseph Jeffries Evans (1768-1812). See "Alphabetical List of Members in 1802," Broadmead Church, Bristol (Bristol Record Office, Bd/R/1/4d) f.31; *Baptist Annual Register*, 3:269; 324-327.

before lost her 2 sons in y[e] sore throat, so that she is now childless. These are sore trials, but to y[se] y[t] love God shall work for good. "The bud may have a bitter taste, But sweet will be the flower."

A young Lady, Sis[r] of M[r] Lewis, died lately at my father's in [words marked out] Consumption—How loudly & how pathetically do these providences speak to us?[147]

I shall be glad to hear from you when agreeable, & espec[y] to hear good tidings of y[r] own Soul & of the souls of th[s] to whom you minister. I am mindful of you, forget not to pray for me, who am

with sincere affect[n]

Yours.

C Evans

Bris[l] Oct[r] 23. 1775

20. Dan Taylor,[148] London, to John Fawcett, Brearley Hall, Yorkshire, 21 February 1777.[149]

Belovd & esteemed Friend and Bro[r],

Two days ago I received a letter from M.[r] Beatson[150] desiring to send the pamphlets which I have of his to M.[r] Edwards's Halifax.[151] I desire to know what number you have sold, and what you have of those I sent you, order that I may write to him, as he requires from me a speedy answer to his letter.

---

[147]David Lewis joined the Baptist congregation at Broadmead in 1764 but was excluded sometime before 1802. The Broadmead Subscription Book notes that David Lewis paid £2.2 for his pew on 14 April 1775. An entry for 6 January 1778 lists his occupation as a barber. Lewis was still paying his pew subscriptions in 1788. In 1770 Lewis also became a subscriber to the Bristol Education Society, paying £1.1 in dues. See "Alphabetical List," f. 29; Broadmead Subscription Book, no. 3, 1772-1813 (Bristol Record Office, Bd/A2/2); *Account of the Bristol Education Society,* 12.

[148]**Dan Taylor** (1738-1816), General Baptist minister at Birchcliffe and Halifax (1763-1785) before removing to London and the General Baptist church at Church Lane, White Chapel (1785-1812). He was instrumental in the founding of the General Baptist New Connection in 1770.

[149]Eng. MS. 371, f. 118, JRULM.

[150]**John Beatson** (1743-1798), Baptist minister at Hull, 1771-1794. The two pamphlets mentioned by Taylor are Beatson's *The Divine Character of Christ Confirmed and Vindicated in a Series of Dialogues* (Leeds, 1773-1774) and *The Divine Satisfaction of Christ Demonstrated in a Series of Discourses* (Leeds, 1774).

[151]William Edwards was a bookseller in Halifax. See *Universal British Directory,* 3:322.

As my pen is [in] my hand, also, I beg you would take it in good part, if I venture to ask you a Question respecting myself, and desire a direct and immediate answer. It is said by some in this neighbourhood, that a certain serious and judicious minister has declared that I behave in a cruel manner to my people. I have desired to know who the minister is; but can't obtain the information. As the report spreads, and may both injure my character as an individual, and my usefulness as a minister, especially considering the authority with which it is stamp'd, as coming from a minister both serious and judicious, I think, I ought to know from whence it arose if I can. Had it been merely the Clamor of the multitude I sh^d not have thought it worth while to regard it. I beg leave therefore in Christian love to ask, if these or the like words have been spoken by you? & if so, to what part of my behaviour they refer? I know your caution & prudence too well, my Bro^r, to imagine you would say any such thing, unless such a representation of me was laid before you as made my conduct appear to you in this disagreeable light. If you be the person from whom the report is propagated, I shall acknowledge it as a very great favor if you will permit me to lay before you the circumstances of that conduct to which your words refer. But if the report came not from you, I trust you will excuse the freedom I now take. As the affair is tender, & of considerable importance, I beg you would write immediately, and this will oblige thirst.

Your sincerely affectionate Bro.^r
Dan Taylor

Feb. 21. 1777.

21. Joseph Jenkins,[152] Wrexham, to John Sutcliff, Olney (by favor of Mr. Sample), 19 March 1777.[153]

Wrexham March 19 1777

Dear Sir,

Surprized as I was at receiving a letter from you, I was not the less pleased on that account: I was almost ready to think that, removed as you are to such a distance, you had forgot me; and tho' when I was nearer you than Wrexham, I thought of you and should have been glad to call on you, I was so circumstanced as not to be able. By being nearer

---

[152]**Joseph Jenkins** (1743-1819), ministerial tutor in London before becoming the Baptist minister at Wrexham (1773-1793) and Blandford Street, London (1793-1798) and Walworth (1798-1819).

[153]Eng. MS. 370, f. 69, JRULM. On the back page Sutcliff has written, "Rec.^d March 28. 1777. Ans.^d June 26——."

you I mean, that we were called up to Dunstable in the month of January by the death of Mrs Jenkins's brother. I desire to rejoice in the appearances of usefulness you have, at the same time that I am very sorry to hear of the ill state of your health. Indeed I can sympathize with you in this respect from experience; my own health has been of late but in a very precarious state; I have been confined last week and this week, only that I made shift to go out on Lord's day. My disorder is in my Breast and Back, and they say is Rheumatic & Nervous &c. Writing hurts me, and so does speaking in public; but I must *go forward*, and thro' mercy I have hitherto found that as my day is so &c I wish I could say that there is any revival in Wrexham; but, tho' as many people attend as usual, I can perceive but little concern about the best things; I say but *little*, for I dare not say there is *none*. God is pleased to try his ministers in this respect as well as others. It will be well for you to look for it as what may happen amongst you. It is our duty to wait on the Lord & keep his ways if we could but do it with patience.— Providence has been very kind to me in other respects; in connecting me with one that fears God, and possesses Religion; we have also a Son, (a fine Boy) of the name of John, called so after my Grandfather John Jenkins an eminent Baptist minister in South Wales.[154] Mrs Jenkins is a member of Mr Gill's Church at St Albans.—[155] I have seen the sequel to Mr Lindsey's Apology[156]; but he takes no notice of me, so I do not think myself under any obligation to answer him; indeed I lost so much money by my last reply, that I chuse to leave the field open to other advocates; and I have less time for it now, than I had formerly, as I have several young Gentlemen under my care, who engross a great deal of my time: I don't know whether I sent you the *Christian's strength* a Sermon that I published; and the Orthodox Dissenting Minister's Reasons for applying again to Parliament.[157]— I shall always be glad to hear from you, and pray that God may be with you & go on to do you good. Remember us; at the Throne of Grace particularly. I am Dr Sir, Your affectionate Fr^d and brother in Christ

J Jenkins

---

[154]**John Jenkins** (1656?-1733), Welsh Baptist minister at Rhydwilym, 1689-1733.

[155]**John Gill** (d. 1809), nephew of the legendary John Gill of London and Baptist minister at St. Alban's, 1758-1809.

[156]**Theophilus Lindsey** (1723-1808), influential Unitarian minister at Essex Street in London, 1778-1793. The text mentioned here is Lindsey's *An Apology on Resigning the Vicarage of Catterick, Yorkshire* (1774); the sequel appeared in 1776.

[157]Jenkins is referring to three of his publications: *Reflections on the Apology of the Rev. Theophilus Lindsey, M.A., late Vicar of Catterick in Yorkshire* (1774), *The Orthodox Dissenting Minister's Reasons for Applying Again to Parliament* (1772), and *The Christian's Strength: A Sermon Preached at Wrexham, in Denbighshire* (1775).

P.S. Have you seen Medley's answer to Decorcy?[158] You may see in it some traces of your friend Jenkins; I wrote in conjunction.

22. *Joshua Toulmin,*[159] *Taunton, to Joseph Fownes,*[160] *Shrewsbury, 7 July 1778.*[161]

Rev[d] & Dear Sir

I am afraid to see the date of your last favour; but many impediments, which you chiefly conceive attendant on my situation, & will candidly make an indulgent allowance for, have arisen to produce an undesigned neglect in acknowledging it.

I am perfectly satisfied with M[r] Eddowes[162] conduct in the disposal of the six copies of Socinus & the remittance he has made to M[r] Browne: He had acted, I apprehend, quite agreeably to the method of Trade.

M[r] Taylor's[163] Question leads me to think that my assertion p. 280 of the life of Socinus, that "many societies of Protestant Dissenters have

---

[158]In 1776 the Rev. Richard De Courcy (1743-1803), Vicar of St. Alkmonds, Shrewsbury, published *A Letter to a Baptist Minister: Containing Some Strictures on his Late Conduct in the Baptization of Certain Adults at SY— ; With a Particular Vindication of the Right of Infant Baptism* (Shrewsbury, 1776). The following year Samuel Medley published a response to De Courcy, titled *Intemperate Zeal Reproved, and Christian Baptism Defended, in a Letter to the Rev. Richard De Courcy.* Jenkins would later publish *A Calm Reply to the First Part of Mr. De Courcy's Rejoinder: As far as it Relates to the Scriptural Mode of Baptism: in a Letter to a Friend* (Wrexham, 1778). De Courcy had previously engaged in a brief pamphlet war with Thomas Phillips, deacon at the Baptist meeting at High Street, Shrewsbury (see letter 12). In 1776 Phillips published (with the assistance of John Sandys, his pastor) *An Address to the Baptist-Church, Meeting in High-Street, Shrewsbury,* which then occasioned two responses by De Courcy: *A Word to Parmenas: Occasioned by his "Address to the Baptist-Church, Meeting in High-Street, Shrewsbury"* (dated 5 March 1776) and *A Reply to Parmenas,* a much longer response, dated 28 March 1776. Later, Benjamin Francis would engage in the pamphlet war with De Courcy with his anonymous *The Salopian Zealot* (1778), a satiric poem attacking the Shrewsbury vicar.
[159]**Joshua Toulmin** (1740-1815), General Baptist (Unitarian) minister at Taunton (1774-1814) and Birmingham (1814-1815).
[160]**Joseph Fownes** (1715-1789), Presbyterian (Unitarian) minister at High Street, Shrewsbury, both as copastor and pastor, 1748-1789.
[161]Eng. MS. 371, f. 123, JRULM.
[162]J. Eddowes was a printer and stationer in Shrewsbury; by 1790 he was in business with his son, W. Eddowes. Although Eddowes printed several works by De Courcy, he primarily printed works by dissenting ministers, such as Joseph Fownes, Benjamin Fawcett, Joseph Jenkins, John Fletcher, Edward Williams, Job Orton, Robert Gentleman, and others. See *Universal British Directory,* 4:418.
[163]William Tayleur, Esq., of Shrewsbury (1712-1796), was a member of Fownes's congregation at Shrewsbury and a prominent Unitarian layman.

become communities of *professed* Unitarians," was not expressed with sufficient accuracy & precision. Your answer to that Gentleman's Enquiry seems to supersede any I can attach to it. Except the Mint Society at Exeter formed under Mr Peirce,[164] scarcely any have made the Unitarian Principle the avowed ground of the manner of conducting their worship[165]—yet many have not disdained the denomination of Unitarians, & on account of the known sentiments of the generality of their members have been stigmatized for their disbelief of the Trinitarian scheme: such are the Society I served at Colyton in Devonshire before the alteration of my sentiments on the subject of Baptism & the Baptist Church I now serve.

However your view of the matter, Sir, is on the whole, I think, more just & accurate than what my expressions intimate.

Soon after the rec^t of your former letter, I took the liberty with it on writing to Dr Priestley,[166] to give him your sentiments on his late publication concerning Necessity: for which he returns his thanks; adding, "I have seen Mr Fownes formerly & heard him preach with much pleasure. If you write to him give my respects to him."

The Title, Nabob of Archot,[167] was given to me thro' the hands of a friend, by the agent of this East Indian Prince residing then in London. The Nabob understand English.

It will, I am sure, give you pleasure to hear, that our worthy Friend Mr Ward's[168] health is greatly improved: I am charged with his respects to you.

My best wishes for your long & increasing usefulness & felicity, I beg, may be acceptable. With great esteem & affectionate regard, I am

Dear Sir,

Your obliged hble Ser^t &
sincere Fr^d & Bro^r
Joshua Toulmin

Taunton. July. 7. 1778.

---

[164]**James Peirce** (1673-1726), Presbyterian minister at Cambridge (1701-1706), Newbury (1706-1713), and Exeter (1713-1726).

[165]Toulmin is referring to the use of a revised liturgy being used at the Mint Meeting, introduced by David Williams, minister from 1761 to 1770, and continued by John Hogg (1772-1789).

[166]**Joseph Priestley** (1733-1804), noted scientist, philosopher, and Unitarian minister at the New Meeting, Birmingham, 1780-1791. Toulmin is referring here to Priestley's *The Doctrine of Philosophical Necessity Illustrated* (1777).

[167]Probably a reference to *An Impartial View of the Origin and Progress of the Present Disputes in the East-India Company Relative to Mahomed-Ally-Khan, Nabob of Arcot, and Tulja-gee, Raja of Tanjore to which are Annexed, Observations on Mahomed-Ally-Khan's Letter to the Court of Directors* (1777).

[168]John Ward (1712-1797) was the minister of the New Meeting (Presbyterian) in Taunton from 1759 to 1793. See Murch, *History*, 224-225.

23. William Hartley, Chester, to John Sutcliff, Olney, 14 September 1779.[169]

Dear Brother

Your's of the 24 of April I duly received, for which testimony of your disintrested [sic] regard—I sincerely thank you. You wonder, I doubt not, why I have not writ sooner. The reason of my delay has been this, I have all along hoped to have some particular account to give you of the designs of providence respecting my fixation; but this I have not yet, been able to do. The congregation here gathers strength in point of number: and considerable attention, and solemnity, rest upon it. More young people incline to meet with us, than could have been expected for the time; and some, appear much affected under the word. It is a thousand pities that such a promising prospect should be blasted; & yet, I fear, this will be the case. My Spouse and Children come over in June on a visit, for sometime, at the earnest request of Friends here. They pressed me to engage to make trial of them for a year; but I only consented to stay with them for an uncertain time. Upon this bottom they promised to solicit the people at large to enter into a subscription in order to support the cause of Christ in Common hall Lane; but some discouraging circumstances have prevented the attempt. M.r Dix, fearing a Baptist Intrest [sic] would be established signified to M.r Mellor his design to withdraw his subscription, except mixt communion would be allowed. M.r Crane, a Johnsonian,[170] did not appear willing to be bound to advance any particular or specified sum. But what is still more painful, M.r Roberts, a steady, generous Baptist, a member with D.r Stennett, and a Grocer & Ironmonger in this City has found it very hard work to keep open his shop for sometime past: and it would have been shut before now, had not M.r Mellor advanced considerable sums of money for him. This affliction has taken off the wheels of their religious Chariots, so that they have moved heavily indeed. Their principles of action have really stagnated. And if those who are leading men in any religious assembly are thunderstruck by any trial so as to fall into the deeps of despondency, what can their minister do?[171] Was not this the

---

[169]Eng. MS. 370, f. 59b, JRULM. On the back page Sutcliff has written, "Rec.d Sep.r 19.79. Ansd. D.o."

[170]**John Johnson** (1706-1791), High Calvinist Baptist minister in Liverpool, 1740-91.

[171]These individuals were all attendants in the fledgling Baptist interest at Common-Hall Lane in Chester in the late 1770s. No one by the name of "Dix" appears in the *Universal British Directory*, but a "Mr. Dixon" of Queen's Street does appear, and that may be the individual Hartley has mentioned. John Mellor was a plumber and shot-maker in Common-Hall Lane in 1794; he had purchased the building that was being used by the church, a building formerly occupied by the

case here, I should hope something considerable might be done for the King of Sion; but as it is, my expectations are almost dead. Have had two Letters lately from the Church at Bingley, in which the people press me in the most affectionate manner to return into Yorkshire, and settle with them. M.ʳ Medley of Liverpool is come over to visit a Convict under sentence of death in the City's Prison: and would have me, if I leave Chester, to make a trial of a people at Tottlebank in Lancashire. Understand that there are considerable Legacies left to that place; so that it would exceed Bingley in a temporal view; but this I hope, is far from being the chief object with me. There have been hurtful counteractions at Tottlebank. Whether they are quelled, or no, I cannot say. The Church gave me an invitation last summer to go over for sometime upon trial; but my hands were too full to comply with it.[172]

You ask me a few questions about persons, and Churches: I shall answer them as well as I can. M.ʳ Hughes[173] has been laid up, and entirely incapacitated for preaching above a year and an half. Brassey-Green is entirely destitute: Fear M.ʳ Hughes will never Preach there again. Some of that little congregation are running into strange notions, under the influence of Clegg of Manchester.[174] Chetham [of] Stockport,[175] and Smith of Tarporley, who, once preached at Brassy-Green,

---

Independent congregation. Thomas Crane was a cork-cutter in Barrell-well. His daughter would marry the Scotch Baptist layman and writer, **William Jones**. Mr. Roberts was apparently dead by 1791, but a Mrs. Roberts was listed as a grocer and tea-dealer in Nicholas Street. At the time of this letter, there had been no permanent pastor for the Chester meeting. Samuel Medley of Liverpool and Joseph Jenkins, then at Wrexham, occasionally preached at Chester, as did John Sandys when he was Shrewsbury. Apparently, Hartley was being considered on trial in 1779. A work was not established at this time, but in 1782 several members from Joseph Jenkins's church at Wrexham were dismissed "for the purpose of joining with others to form a Particular Baptist Church in Common Hall Lane, Chester." Some of these individuals, such as Thomas Crane, would eventually form, under the leadership of **Archibald McLean** and William Jones, a Scotch Baptist congregation in 1786 (see letter 49). The first minister appears to be a Mr. Ecking, who had been baptized by John Sandys and called out by the Shrewsbury church. He arrived at Chester in April 1783, but he died in early 1785. Alexander McLean came to Chester in October 1786 and spent five weeks, essentially turning the small congregation into a Scotch Baptist meeting. See William Jones, *Autobiography of the Late William Jones, M.A.* (London: J. Snow, 1846) 10-31; Margaret F. Thomas, *Brassey Green & Tarporley: A Baptist History* (n.p.: 1984) 9; *Universal British Directory*, 2:709, 718, 714, 720.

172For the Tottlebank church, see letter 12, n. 88.

173**John Hughes** (d. 1783), Baptist minister at Brassy Green, 1775-1783.

174Arthur Clegg of Manchester (see letter 6).

175Probably Isaac Cheetham, pastor of the Particular Baptist Chapel at Millington, Cheshire, from 1766 until his death in 1800. He was succeeded by John Cheetham [his son?], who remained until his death in 1819. According to Urwick, Stock-

and now preaches in private houses to them.[176] M.r Walley of Taten-hall Lanes is averse from their Schemes.[177] Have paid him many visits. Gave your respects to him, as desired, and now return his to you.

Hear that M.r Sandys's congregation[178] does not increase; and M.r Phillips told me lately that there was no prospect of it. M.rs Philips, I found, when I was [at] Salop last Spring, is, by no means, happy in her Pastor. M.r Gentleman[179] is removed to Caermathen. He is the Master of ye Academy there. His successor at Shrewsbury (M.r Lewis if I mistake not his name) gives great satisfaction to the people.—[180] [illegible name][181] more friendly with M.r Armitage[182] than he is with me; tho' I have reasons to say, that he is as free as can be expected. Believe his congregation is pretty large. Some of his people are remarkably bitter against the Baptists. M.r G——s[183] spoke of leaving W——m on account of the smalness [sic] of his income: tho' he is not on the best terms with some of his congregation, which is small. He is finishing the publication of [paper torn] Vol.s of Sermons on Historical subjects [I] suppose you

---

port had no regular Baptist meeting at this time. See Urwick, *Historical Sketches,* 350, 450.

[176]According to M. F. Thomas, "The only known Smith to feature in connection with Brassey Green is Mr. John Smith of Wirswell, to whose home Miss Anne Walley was sent after her father's death, and where she was brought up. John Smith's wife, Mary, nee Richardson, was a sister-in-law of Mr. Samuel Walley of Brassey Green, Anne's great uncle. John Smith himself was too young to have had any influence with Cornelius Gregory, but census returns show that he was born in Beeston, so it is quite likely that the two families were in contact. No documentary evidence has been found to show that any member of the Smith family preached at Brassey Green, but this does not preclude the possibility." If Hartley can be trusted, it would appear from this letter that Smith did indeed preach at Brassey Green. Another possibility is a William Smith who ministered in the 1790s at Hag Gate in Lancashire. See Thomas, *Brassy Green,* 15; *Baptist Annual Register,* 1:7; 2:7; 3:21.

[177]Numerous Walleys were involved in the Baptist churches at Brassy Green, Tattenhall, and Wrexham. John Walley (1689-1776) was instrumental in founding the work at Tattenhall, having his house licensed as the first meeting place for the congregation. He nephew at that time was the landlord for the Brassy Green church property. See Thomas, *Brassy Green,* 15.

[178]**John Sandys** (d. 1803), Baptist minister at Shrewsbury (1777-1781), Watford (1786-1791), Harlow (1791-1795), and Hammersmith (1795-1801).

[179]**Robert Gentleman** (1746-1795), Independent minister at Shrewsbury (1767-1779) and later at Kidderminster (1784-1795).

[180]The name Hartley was searching for was **Samuel Lucas** (1748-1799), Independent minister at Shrewsbury, 1779-1799.

[181]The letters appear to be "Aon"; the reference, however, is to a name clearly known to Hartley and Sutcliff.

[182]**William Armitage** (1738-1794), Independent minister at Common-Hall Lane, Chester, 1772-1794.

[183]Possibly "Y——s."

have heard of them.[184] Have received [a let]ter from Dan Taylor to day, in which he desired to take a Licence out of the Bishops Court [illegible word] for a Room he has taken lately in the Market place Burnley. What an indefatigable little great man is he! May his zeal provoke the particular Baptists around him to greater activity![185] Am stealing this opportunity to scribble this scrawl, from M.ʳ Medley, who has consented to Preach tonight in Common hall Lane. He has contracted a particular hoarseness by preaching too often when in London. He is advised to abstain from preaching for a while, which he designs to comply with. And now Dear Brother you will permit me to exercise freedom with you and confidence in you, as a bosom friend. My Spouse is still inclined, if the Lord s.ᵈ point out the way, to remove into your parts, for reasons before given, and at a settlement where I could enjoy now and then a personal interview with you would be very acceptable to me for many reasons, shall take it as a very great favor if [you] will inform me whether any thing suitable has come to your knowledge lately   If nothing of this nature exists in the line of your acquaintances please to give me your advice respecting Bingley and Tottlebank. Should have given the Church at Bingley a final answer before now. I know not how I can defer it another week. Yet in order to have your advice shall attempt it. Do Good Brother, let me have a line by return of Post without fail. And let no man ever know of the freedom I take with you, let me abuse it to my hurt. You are a tried friend; therefore shall rest in your faithfulness. May the Lord cause his face to shine evermore upon you. Spouse joins in tenders to you; tho' I ought to exceed her, seeing I am

Your Old, tho' unworthy Brother
And Friend
W.ᵐ Hartley

N.B. Do not mention M.ʳˢ Roberts case particularly, lest she s.ᵈ be hurt, and I blamed—Pardon haste

P.S. Please to direct for me at Mellor's Northgate Street, Chester/ [illegible word]

---

[184]I have not been able to identify this minister or his publication.

[185]According to Whitley, Burnley was about five miles to the west of two hamlets, Worsthorne and Haggate, where Dan Taylor (see letter 20) had already begun village preaching. Taylor found the place "wretched," with "no religion, in or near it." In September 1779 he hired a house in the market place and procured a license from the Bishop of Chester and opened a General Baptist chapel; shortly thereafter Richard Foulds took over as the church's first minister, remaining there until 1789. See W. T. Whitley, *The Baptists of North-West England* (London: Kingsgate, 1913) 158.

24. James Turner, Birmingham, to John Sutcliff, Olney, 10 October 1779.[186]

Mr Harris not going so soon as I expected, enables me to add a line more Mr Butterworth,[187] it seems, has been down in Lancashire to open the New Chapel at Crawshawbooth (Taylor's)[188] somebody (I have not learnt who) assisted him. He set off on the Monday, reach'd there on Wednesday & the place was open'd on Thursday. He prd there the Sabbath following to a vast concourse of people & return'd the following week. These kind of revolutions are seldom attended with prudence in their cause, or wth success in their effects. How things may issue in the present instance, time only can determine. It is the part of candor however, to wish well, & of charity [paper torn] well. If the end aim'd at be good, tho' the means to attain it may [be] liable to some censure, one can [paper torn] desirous of success. I hear nothing what comes of [G]reaves and his Chapel at Rattanstall.[189] Whether it stays a monument of human folly, or of divine mercy. So many Meetings, in so little compass, must, I shd think, greatly injure one another; &, instead of forwarding must hinder the success of religion.

I shall not add any thing further, but my wishes that if you should Convert an ho—se into [illegible word] it may be well. And may the Lord of hosts be with you bless you & do you good—so pray & so leaves off

your affte Friend &c
Js Turner

---

[186]Eng. MS. 371, f. 125a, JRULM. On the back page Sutcliff has written, "Rec. Oct. 10. 79. Ansd — 13."

[187]Probably **John Butterworth** (1727-1803), minister of the Particular Baptist church at Cow Lane, Coventry, 1753-1803. He was originally from Rossendale in Lancashire.

[188]**Henry Taylor** (d. 1789) left Crawshawbooth, Lancashire, to minister to the Baptist church at Cannon Street, Birmingham, 1782-1789.

[189]I have not been able to find any record of this chapel at Rawtonstall, Yorkshire.

Part Two

1780–1799

25. Samuel Medley, Liverpool, to James Dinwiddie,[1] Manchester ("P[r] favor of M[r] Spear Jun[r]"), 9 August 1782.[2]

Liverpool 9th Aug[st]—1782

Dear Sir—Or (plainly if you please) *Dear Cousin*

There's an Address for You!—Such a One as I never wrote you before—such a One as you never received from one before—And pray who can tell what this same *Cousinship* may one Day produce, especially if *You* should become One of his Maj.[ty] Principal *Secretarys of State*— And I should become *Arch Bishop* of *Canterbury*—And be assured of this—that if ever we are to become such—we are nearer to it than ever we were—Well, but—*Dear Cousin*—again You see I am as pleased with

---

[1]Dinwiddie, Medley's cousin by marriage, was an Independent layman in Manchester associated with the firm of Dinwiddie, Kennedy, and Dinwiddie, Merchants and Cotton-Manufacturers, 4 Red-Cross Street. In the Thomas Raffles Collection is an undated letter from Thomas Barnes, minister at Cross Street Presbyterian Chapel in Manchester, to Dinwiddie, then living in King-Street, in which Barnes responds to a request by Dinwiddie for assistance concerning some business of the "Institution," the forerunner of the Independent College in Manchester which later became Lancashire Independent College. Barnes declined, arguing that

> it would not add much to the credit of this Establishment with many persons to whom you will make application, if a Dissenting Minister were one of the petitioners—This consideration has influenced me upon many occasions besides the present. My feelings would have led my to step forward, & to take an active share in some public business; but prudence dictated caution & reserve.—
>
> Your situation in life, your general character, & I am happy now to add, your Office among us, qualify you to take a lead in this important affair with peculiar advantage.—

Dinwiddie subscribed 1£1s. to the Sunday School Society in London in 1789. He may be the same individual to whom William Steadman writes on 27 February 1835, asking his influence in procuring admission to the congregational school at Lewisham for a young relative of Steadman's wife (see letter 151). See *Universal British Directory*, 3:806; Eng. MS. 369, f. 11, JRULM; *Plan of a Society Established in London, Anno Domini 1785, for the Support and Encouragement of Sunday-Schools in Different Counties of England* (London: Sunday School Society, 1789) 24.

[2]Eng. MS. 370, f. 84a, JRULM.

this new Relation as a Boy with a new son—Well but once more—*Dear Cousin*—Your very acceptable favor of the 5th Curr^t I duely rec.^{d}—thank You for Your early Intelligence of what had taken place the forenoon of that Day—You know my poor heart was much in it—and very anxiously concerned for Your mutual Comfort and Happiness—And be asured [sic] I am not less so—*No.* now the sacred relation has commenced—Be asured Both of You of my Best Love—And (if it be worth any thing)—my hearty Blessing upon You Both—for Body and Soul—for Time and Eternity. I almost long to hear how you were received on Monday afternoon at Ships-[car?]—And how you have been helped to manage matters since—do drop me a Line informing me when You are returned to Manchester—with that Dear Dear Creature with You—I trust if I am spared to see You both Happy—both for Time and Eternity—I shall Love You and rejoice in You both more than ever—I pray You may live and walk with God and with one another as Heirs together of the Grace of Life—as helpers of Each others Faith and forwarders of each others Joy—that Your Prayers nor Your Peace may never be hindered or interrupted.—But that You may go on Your way with One Heart and with One Soul, rejoicing in Christ Jesus—And in a truly Sanctified and Subordinate Sense—rejoicing in *Each other*—God help you both to keep near to him—Remember—Creature Comforts are but Time Comforts—Consequently—Cannot last forever.

If I knew when Mrs Medley returned to Manchester in her way home—And if at that time You and Mrs Dinwiddie were at home—I would come and meet her at Manch^r—And at the same time should have an Opportunity of paying my respects to You both—In *Propria Personae*—perhaps You may be able to Inform me in a Line respecting this Matter.

All my Children here at home join me in presenting their Love to M^r and Mrs Dinwiddie and wish them much happiness in their new relation—

I called as desired upon Mr Poole,[3] but could not find him within Mrs Poole I was informed was but poorly in her Chamber and it was not Convenient to see her as he was Expected to Call at Mr Hope's[4] in Pool Lane they promised me to inform him as desired.

---

[3]Given Dinwiddie's occupation as a cotton merchant, this may be Charles Poole, collector of the Dock duties, whose offices were located in the Old Church Yard, Liverpool. See *Universal British Directory*, 4:716.

[4]**William Hope**, linen and woolen draper, at 14 Pool Lane, Liverpool. His son, William Hope, Jr., and their relation **Samuel Hope**, were all members of Medley's congregation at Byrom Street. For more on the Hopes, see letters 122 and 125; See *Universal British Directory*, 4:703.

For the present I take my leave, hoping amidst all the Hurry which may take place in consequence of Your marriage you will not forget or neglect to favor me with a Line from You—

And once more for the present *Adieu* The God of Heaven forever Bless You Both and make You Blessings and Comforts to Eaach other So wishes and prays—*Dear Cousin*—(for the last time in this Letter)
Yours most affectionately
in the whole of my Relation to You
Sam Medley

26. John Collett Ryland, Northampton, to Mr. Charrier,[5] Teacher of the French Language at the Royal Academy, Portsmouth, 4 December 1782.[6]

Dear Mr. Charrier

In Portsmouth Town on the Point you will find a worthy Man and a Christian M[r] Pearsan attorney at Law[7] ask him to introduce you to some good People.

M[r] Thomas Whitewood Glazier to his Majesty.[8] he will introduce you to M[r] Wichell,[9] to the Rev[r] M[r] Tuppen[10] and Rev[d] M[r] Cox with other kind Christians

---

[5]Jacques Samuel Charrier, French Master at the Academy at Portsea, Hants. See *Universal British Directory*, 4:202.

[6]Eng. MS. 371, f. 106, JRULM. In October 1782, two months before the date of this letter, John Collett Ryland had been in Portsmouth to assist in the formation of a second Baptist church, located in White's Row. Those forming this new church had previously been members of Joseph Horsey's congregation on Portsmouth Common, Meeting-house Alley. Henry Dawson, who had been recommended by Ryland, became the initial pastor of the new congregation, but he was replaced in 1785 by **Peter Edwards**. Dawson would also minister briefly at Tuthill Stairs in Newcastle-upon-Tyne. See "Calendar of Letters," *Baptist Quarterly* 6 (1932-33): 180; P. Ridoutt, *The Early Baptist History of Portsmouth* (Landport: G. Chamberlain, 1888) 60-61; *History of Bewick Street Baptist Church: A Lecture Delivered by John Bradburn, before the Bewick Street Mutual Improvement Society, on January 18th, 1883* (Newcastle-on-Tyne: J. Bell, 1883) 5.

[7]Possibly Charles Piers or William Piercy, both of whom were attorneys in nearby Portsea. See *Universal British Directory*, 4:203.

[8]Thomas Whitewood, stationer. He was probably the son of either Thomas Whitewood (d. 1767)—one of the trustees when the Baptist Church at Meeting-house Alley, Portsea, was purchased in 1755, and who later served as minister to the Baptist church in Reading (1749-66)—or Daniel Whitewood (Thomas's brother), who served as a deacon and assistant minister at Meeting-house Alley from 1732 until shortly before his death in 1765. See *Universal British Directory*, 4:206; Ridoutt,

As I believe you love Christ they will be glad of your Company and to M^r and Mrs Howard[11] at the Ladies Boarding School [Lake?]. Mrs Whitewood will also introduce you. The Lord Jesus bless you for ever and ever I am

Your cordial Friend
John Ryland

December 4. 1782

27. Thomas Steevens,[12] Colchester, to John Sutcliff, Olney, 10 November 1785.[13]

Colchester Nov 10th 1785

Dear Brother
    It would give me great pleasure to be instrumental of good to you in Body or mind. I am therefore willing that my last should produce a friendly smile or even a laugh; as I learn from the faculty that laughing is an exercise promotive of health.
    But you mistook me in one thing—Mr Perkins[14] had given me the shadow of an hope, that you would visit Colchester. I aimed to give substance to this shadow & referred the consideration of your queries 'till your self should explain them.—However I have reviewed them & am apprehensive that our views would very nearly coincide. They are now

---

Early Baptist History, 32-44; Arthur S. Langley, "Baptist Ministers in England about 1750 A.D," *Transactions of the Baptist Historical Society* 6 (1918-19): 143.

⁹Thomas Whichell, Drawing Master, Academy at Portsea. See *Universal British Directory*, 4:203.

¹⁰**Thomas Tuppen** (1742-90), follower of Whitefield who preached in chapels in Portsea and Bath, 1768-90.

¹¹He may be the same Mr. Howard who attended the Baptist meeting in Plymouth Dock and who, in 1800-1801, contributed 10s.6d to the Baptist Missionary Society (hereafter BMS). See *Periodical Accounts Relative to the Baptist Missionary Society*, 6 vols. (Clipston: J. W. Morris; London: Burdett and Morris, 1800-1817) 2:210.

¹²**Thomas Steevens** (1745-1802), Baptist minister at Colchester, 1773-1802.

¹³Eng. MS. 371, f. 115, JRULM. On the back page Sutcliff has written, "Rec.^d Mr Steevens Novr 30. 1785. Ans^d sometime."

¹⁴No Perkins appear in the *Universal British Directory* for Colchester, but a James Purkiss, a wheelwright and a freeman, does appear. See *Universal British Directory*, 2:524.

in London: Mʳ Thomas of Devonshire Square[15] wishing to weigh them, & avail himself of you or me in an attempt to bring his Father to see with Mʳ Fuller.[16]

You wish to know my thoughts of that gentlemens publication—I will be perfectly free, however much I may prove myself precipitate & even ignorant in what I wrote before.—I admire the Spirit of the author—it appears plain I think that his alone wish is to propagate Truth—I admire the perspicuity of his manner which conveys at once his meaning to the mind—Nor can I find anything to say against, but much to say for the Sentiment. I was rather averse to it before, either because I did not understand it, or because it was wrongly stated by others—the last I think was the chief reason; for I now recollect, that for seven years past & more I have been coming over to his mind tho' I did not know, that I had any Partners—thinking upon that text with a view to the pulpit "ye will not come to me that you may have Life" led me into a quite (for me) new train of Thought upon mans Inability & I found & said it lies in his will.

The wiseacres in your Parts will do as they please I suppose, but it pleases me, that some very sensible Independents here about have the Book & esteem it—But my baptist Brethren will not receive it & some of them already deem me an Arminian for only attempting to explain to them the meaning of the phrases moral & natural Inability[17]—I have had some warm, I dont mean angry, disputes upon the Subject—but alas it is a Task indeed to "tell Persons a Story & find them Ears," or which is much the same—state a Truth & give them understanding— Indeed there is one very great unhappiness attendant upon the Statement of this case—Mʳ Fuller is obliged to use the word natural inability. We have been accustomed to say man is a Sinner by Nature—is by Nature averse to God & therefore knows not how to drop the common Idea when we mean to express something very different by the same word, hence many exclaim "no need then for divine Influence"; but I sincerely wish they would read the Book once & again before they reply.

---

[15]**Timothy Thomas** (1753-1827), Baptist minister at Devonshire Square, London, 1781-1827. His father was Joshua Thomas, Baptist minister at Leominster, 1753-97.

[16]**Andrew Fuller** (1754-1815), Baptist minister at Kettering (1782-1815) and first secretary of the BMS.

[17]A reference to High Calvinist Baptists who, influenced by the writings of John Gill and John Brine, were keen to oppose what appeared to be Arminian elements in Fuller's theology. See E. F. Clipsham, "Andrew Fuller and Fullerism: A Study in Evangelical Calvinism," *Baptist Quarterly* 20 (1963-64): 99-114; 146-54; 214-25; 268-76.

Mr Fullers Idea of Faith will not, I conceive, easily gain ground with those who have been accustomed to view Faith as being somehow or other, a belief of personal Interest in Jesus Christ & this must occasion the rejection of his whole System. But had I known his mind upon this article before I should have been a Believer e'er I had seen his performance; for I think his definition of Faith entirely incontrovertable, tho I suppose he finds a need to enlarge his Definition sometimes, in order to show, that none but those whose Faith actuates the whole Soul are real Believers in the Son of God.

It appears to me that M^r F— deserves the thanks of all the Lovers of simple Truth & I am not without hope, that some who cannot fully adopt his view will yet so far profit by it as to address their fellow Sinners more in the Style of Scripture. I know two or three already who mean to make this use of his work.—But what think you Bro^r? a neighboring minister seriously very seriously proposed to me the following Queries a few months since—"But if it is the Duty of Sinners to believe in Jesus Christ, is it my Duty to exhort them to it? This is what I want to know!" By this I think you will be informed that we have wiseacres with us too.

Your views & mine agree with respect to Scripture language in the main, but I still think, that there are in use many Terms which some hold sacred, that give very unscriptural Ideas—I remember to have heard a Reverend divine in London spend a whole hour to prove the propriety of the Term offer & so foolish was I as to think Mr Fuller meant to plead the same cause. I ask his pardon for condemning him unheard.

Many thanks to you for the circular Letter I deem it very valuable— lent it to my Friends at a Prayer meeting which was unusually well attended, but I fear I have lent it till it is lost—I have read a Sermon by the same author: alltogether lead me to form the best opinion of the man & to hail the church happy that has such a Pastor—the association favored that has such a member.[18]

Thro mercy we have Peace—I mean we are not at war professedly, but some of my People charge me with "wishing them to be more holy than God requires"! I sometimes say where will these things end? —we have some prosperity in the addition of members, but I want to see much more.

May you be held as a Star in the redeemers right hand & be happily instrumental in leading many Souls to him. Such is the wish of

Your affectionate Friend

Thos Steevens

---

[18]Most likely a reference to *The Nature, Evidences and Advantages of Humility*, the 1784 circular letter for the Northamptonshire Association, written by John Ryland, Jr.

28. *Caleb Evans, Bristol, to [Samuel] Jackson,*[19] *London, 14 December 1785.*[20]

Dear Sir,

I have only time to say that M[r] Madgwicke[21] hopes to be in town on Friday, & will endeav[r] to comply with y[r] request of preach[g] at Unicorn Yard while he remains in town. But return he must, & will, after a few weeks absence, as I have no authority at all to discharge him from his present obligations till the vacation, nor has he any desire to be releas'd from them. Four or five months, at the most, cann[t] be very material; but material or not, my young friend will not be at liberty sooner. I write thus fully on this point, to preclude any further application relative to it. With the sincerest good wishes for yourself & the whole church, I remain

In haste,

Y[rs] sincerely &c

C Evans

29. *Thomas Langdon,*[22] *Leeds, to John Sutcliff, Olney, 17 June 1790.*[23]

Leeds. June 17. 1790.

My dear Friend,

A M.[r] Smithers is going to send a parcel to M.[r] Palmer of your town, I cannot help embracing the opportunity of sending you a line, just to tell you that I am still alive.

I was very much grieved yesterday on hearing that you had been in Yorkshire without giving me the pleasure of seeing you at Leeds. Had you known how happy I should have been to have enjoy'd an interview with you, I am perswaded you would either have come this way, or given me an opportunity of meeting you at some other place. However, I will hope that when you come into this country again, you will not forget your old friend Langdon.

A M.[r] Temple has established a connexion at Olney, I hope soon to have an opportunity of sending you a *Letter*: at present I have only time to tell you, that (thro mercy) I go on pretty comfortably here; that I intend to spend the next Month in Ireland, and to preach under the direc-

---

[19]**Samuel Jackson**, a deacon in the Baptist meeting at Unicorn Yard, Southwark.

[20]Eng. MS. 861, f. 19, JRULM.

[21]**William Madgwick[e]**, at that time a student at Bristol Academy.

[22]**Thomas Langdon** (1755-1824), Baptist minister at Leeds, 1781-1824.

[23]Eng. MS. 370, f. 75, JRULM. On the back page Sutcliff has written, "Ans.[d] March 31. 1791."

tion of the *Evangelical Society*, lately established there; that I shall be happy to receive a line from M.ʳ Sutcliffe; and that I am

Your affectionate Friend and Brother
Tho.ˢ Langdon

P.S. Mess.ʳˢ Smithers and Temple are persons for whom I have a very great regard, and I was happy when I found M.ʳ Palmer had given them an Order. They are I believe very *honest worthy* Gentlemen. M.ʳ S. is one of our Congregation.

Pray forgive my hasty scrawl

30. Andrew Fuller, Kettering, to John Sutcliff, Olney, 10 August 1790.[24]

Kettering Aug. 10. 90

D.ʳ Bro.ʳ

Thank you for your kind enquiry after my health I have been getting better for weeks, and am now I think as well as usual—M.ʳ Wallis[25] is better we hope—M.ʳˢ Baker & M.ʳˢ Gotch[26] went to Bath last week—He has written since their arrival & says they each say they *know* he is better—His Physician proposed then, (Friday, 6ᵗʰ Ins.ᵗ) for him to [stay at] Bath a week longer, & then drink the waters a few days more—and then he said he should dismiss him, hoping that his complaints would gradually go off—Possibly he may be at Birm.ᵐ at the Ordination[27] on his return but I cannot tell—have sent him word of it I have an invita-

---

[24]Eng. MS. 369, f. 50b, JRULM. Fuller and Sutcliff were frequent correspondents for more than thirty years. Over 150 letters by Fuller to Sutcliff can be found in the BMS Archives at the Angus Library, Regent's Park College, Oxford. See Ernest A. Payne, "Andrew Fuller as Letter Writer," *Baptist Quarterly* 15 (1953-54): 290.

[25]**Beebe Wallis** (1735-92), a deacon in the Kettering church. He would die on 2 April 1792, just a few months before his home would give birth to the BMS.

[26]Mrs. Baker and Mrs. Gotch were members of Fuller's congregation in Kettering. John Gotch, Mrs. Gotch's husband, was best known for promising a young but determined William Carey 10 shillings a week so that he could quit his shoe-making business and devote his time to his studies and pastoral duties at Moulton. See E. A. Payne and A. R. Allan, *Clipston Baptist Church* (Northampton: n.p., 1932) 8-9.

[27]Fuller did attend the ordination of Samuel Pearce at Cannon Street in Birmingham in August 1790; Caleb Evans delivered the charge in the morning service and Fuller laid hands on Pearce. John Ryland, Jr., delivered the ordination sermon, along with Robert Hall, Sr. Fuller preached in the evening service. Most likely Sutcliff attended as well.

tion—Shall be for trying to get there if I can—Shall be at Arnsby the following Sabath [sic]—I hope to see you at Birm.^m

Mr Bland of Soham[28] is about being married to Miss Adam, daughter of the late independent minister there[29]—She is an industrious, intelligent girl, and in a pretty business—keeps a shop of Grocery Drapery &c We are all as usual—Write in love to Self M^r [?]

Y^rs Affec.^y   A Fuller

P.S. Am going thro' the Psalms on L.^ds day forenoon   last L.^ds day expounded the 14.th in Course—preached afternoon f.^m 2 Pet. 1. 12. *We not only need to be established in the truths of the gospel, but to be constantly reminded*

31. John Ryland, Jr., Northampton, to John Sutcliff, Olney, 10 December 1790.[30]

Dec. 10. 1790

Dear Bro Sutcliff

I've only time to say I am just return'd yesterday—Settled wth Lepard[31] as follows—

Rev^d Jn Sutcliff with John Pelly Lepard

1789

O^r Aug 1	By 50	Edwards Attempt[32]	
D Duct Oct. 2	By 25	Sent Mr Ash[33]	I did not see
	25		him since I

---

[28]**Francis Bland** was pastor of the Baptist meeting at Soham (1788-1802), where Fuller began his ministry. Bland was originally a member of the Soham church and studied at Bristol Academy from January 1787 until July 1788. See *Baptist Annual Register*, 1:4.

[29]Miss Adam was the daughter of **William Adam** (1710-82), Independent minister at Soham.

[30]Eng. MS. 371, f. 107c, JRULM.

[31]**John Pelly Lepard** (d. 1796) worked with his father, **William Lepard**, as London stationers, rag merchants and paper makers.

[32]Jonathan Edwards's *Humble Attempt to Promote Explicit Agreement and Visible Union of God's People in Extraordinary Prayer for the Revival of Religion and the Advancement of Christ's Kingdom on Earth, Pursuant to Scripture-Promises and Prophecies Concerning the Last Time* (Boston, 1747). The work was reprinted (Northampton: T. Dicey, 1789) primarily through the efforts of Sutcliff.

[33]William Ash, bookseller at 15 Tower Hill, London; he was most likely a Baptist. See *Universal British Directory*, 1/2:472.

called on Ash,
perhaps this
is a mistake
for Button[34]

<u>1790</u>
Nov. 17 Returns　　　　<u>16</u>
to pay for　　　　　　9　@ 7ᵈ　————　5..3

Deduct Car.g' Porterage　　　————　<u>1..4</u>
　　due to Mʳ Sutcliff　　　　　　3..11　This he pᵈ me

XII Copies of Edw. out of the above 16 I left with Vernor[35]　IX I re-turn—and send with them 2 Edw. on Ch. Fellowship[36]　II at 3ˢ .4ᵈ the two, & one Robinsons secᵈ Vol[37] at 3ˢ

If you like to keep all, you will owe me 2..5

Thro' Mercy we had a good Journey & met wᵗʰ much friendship—Mʳ Newton sent Carey[38] a Guinea—said it did not suit him before, but he cᵈ afford it now for his Baptist Bro.ʳ—Mʳˢ N. was living when I left Town —You must excuse haste—I'll get Mʳ Rippon to enquire of Lepard about the above. He will settle yʳˢ with Palmer of Bucklands other Execʳ when he settles for himself & for me—Our Respects to Mʳˢ A.

　　　　　　　　Yʳˢ cordially
　　　　　　　　　J. R. j.

Send any or all back if you don't want them

On the back cover is the following note to Sutcliff:

If Mʳ Palmer[39] goes to Holland can you not engage him to make some Enquiries into the State of Religⁿ

---

[34]**William Button** (1754-1821), pastor of the Baptist congregation at Dean Street, Southwark, 1775-1815, and a bookseller, first at Newington Causeway and later in Paternoster Row.

[35]**Thomas Vernor** (d. 1793), London bookseller in Birchin Lane and Baptist layman

[36]Most likely a reference to Jonathan Edwards's *An Humble Inquiry into the Rules of the Word of God, Concerning the Qualifications Requisite to a Complete Standing and Full Communion in the Visible Christian Church* (Boston, 1749), which was republished in Edinburgh in 1790.

[37]Probably a reference to Robert Robinson's translation of Jean Claude's *An Essay on the Composition of a Sermon*, 2 vols. (editions in 1788 and 1789).

[38]**William Carey** (1761-1834), Baptist minister at Moulton and Leicester before serving in India and Serampore as the first BMS missionary, 1793-1834. The guinea came from Ryland's friend, John Newton (see letter 6).

[39]Possibly **John Palmer** (1768-1823), Baptist minister at Shrewsbury.

32. Portion of a letter by Andrew Fuller, Kettering, to John Ryland, Jr., Northampton, 7 January 1791.[40]

. . . As to my Everton Journey, I wrote something as it was then fresh upon my mind better than I can now—I greatly admired that divine savour that all along mingled with his[41] facetiousness, and sufficiently chastised it—His conversation tended to produce a frequent, but guiltless smile, a smile accompanied with a tear of pleasure—His love to Xt appears to be intense. I requested him to give us a few of the outlines of his life & ministry. These were interesting, but too long to write—they will enrich an evenings conversation if I should some time come to Northampton—When he had gone thro' I asked him to pray for us—he was so faint, he said he could not yet—he requested me to pray—I prayed, & concluded as usual by asking all in Xs name—He, without getting off his knees took up the prayer where I had left it, in some such manner as this "O Lord God! This prayer has been offered up in the name of Jesus, accept it I beseech thee . . . & so on, for five or six minutes in a most solemn & savory manner. We then took leave with solemn prayer for blessings on each other as if we had been acquainted for 40 years, & were never to see each other again in this world—The visit left a strong & lasting impression on my heart of the beauty of holiness, of holiness almost matured. . . .

---

[40]Eng. MS. 871, f. 21, JRULM. This letter is included (with numerous punctuation changes, word alterations, additions and deletions, as well as the important substitution of "Mr Berridge" for "his" in the second sentence) in Ryland's *Life of Andrew Fuller*. One of the chapters in the *Life* was titled, "Extracts from Mr. Fuller's correspondence, chiefly with the author of these memoirs, for two-and-thirty years..." The above letter may be the "specimen" of Fuller's handwriting that Ryland refers to in his letter to Thomas Raffles of 22 February 1821 (see letter 135). Sutcliff accompanied Fuller on his visit with Berridge, an account of which can be found in Morris. See John Ryland, *The Work of Faith, the Labour of Love, and the Patience of Hope, Illustrated; in the Life and Death of the Rev. Andrew Fuller* (London: Button and Son, 1818) 225, 212; J. W. Morris, *Memoirs of the Life and Writings of the Rev. Andrew Fuller*, 2nd ed. (London: Wightman and Cramp, 1826) 47.

[41]John Berridge (1716-93), evangelical Methodist vicar at Everton (1758-93), was a confidant of the Wesleys, Whitefield, and Newton. He was widely noted for his piety and religious convictions, even among dissenters, as this letter demonstrates. He was instrumental, through his village preaching, in establishing numerous chapels throughout the vicinity of Everton.

33. John Rippon,[42] Southwark, London, to John Sutcliff, Olney, 20 July 1791.[43]

Southwark. July 20. 91.

My dear Bro.[r]

    I heartily thank you for y[e] line last night contain[g] corrections—the womans name is *Richard*. I can't answer your question, ab[t] Market S[t] Herts. *Elden* in Norfolk, I suppose, is an abridgement of *Great Ellingham*.

    I intend to have what I am sure will be absolutely necessary; as we have so much to do with names & dates, 3 or 4 pages, in y[e] manner of y[e] Gent[s] Magazine, of Addenda & Corrigenda, to be placed at the *end* of y[e] volumes—these will have y[e] appearance of notes —to be placed before y[e] *Index* which must be unavoidably in Vol. 1st very large because of y[e] names of persons & places.[44] As you have begun I request you to continue your communications. I shall advertise on y[e] blue cover for annual accounts of all the ordinations in y[e] denominations—y[e] time of them, circumstances, persons engaged, just their texts &c &c this *universally* regarded, would of itself, be an inconsiderable step towards a future history of the English Baptists when we are dead & gone. Give me an acc[t] of all you can for 1789 & 90.

    The 2[d] part of y[e] Register I hope will be out in ab[t] a fortnight.

    My particular reason for writ[g] now is that you may *directly* send me the *whole* acc[t], dates &c &c w[c] you have rec[d] from M[r] Botsford.[45] Do let me have it, by Sat. sennight, don't abridge it.

    I have Lelands Chronicle[46] 8 pages 1789 & 45 pages 1790 with the address of y[e] Committee in Aug[t] 89 to Presid[t] Washington & his answer.[47] I am much pleased with it. Two or three words excepted, I think it is a good composition—and as it shows y[e] state of civil & relig[s] liberty among them, I had thought of introducing it into y[e] 2[d] part of the Register. As I suppose you have it I request you to look at it again, and say whether you think it w[d] be improper to give it to the public with us. I

---

    [42]**John Rippon** (1751-1836), Baptist minister at Carter Lane and New Park Street, Southwark, 1772-1836.

    [43]Eng. MS. 371, f. 101, JRULM. On the back page is written in Sutcliff's hand, "Rec.[d] July 22. Ans.[d] D.[o] 24. 1791."

    [44]The Index comprised seventeen pages in vol. 1.

    [45]**Edmund Botsford** (1745-1819), Baptist minister in Georgia and South Carolina.

    [46]**John Leland** (1754-1841), American Baptist evangelist and writer.

    [47]See "The Address of the Committee of the United Baptist Churches in Virginia," assembled in Richmond on 8 August 1789, as well as George Washington's response. See *Baptist Annual Register*, 1:168-71.

shall give ye 33 lines of Leland, leav^g out y^e *jumping* part, and ye enthu-siasm.

Have you Georgia Association Letters of 1789 or 1790, or the "United Baptist Association" (formerly called the Kentuky [sic] Associa-tion) of 1790. I have the Danbury of 90 & the Charleston of 90[48]—some considerable packets sh^d have arrived this spring from America w^c I have not rec^d—perhaps they will come just as my register is out—too late. Have you seen Revd Jed. Morses American Geog:^{y}+[49] *you* will have an intellectual feast in it. He preaches close to Boston, is named in the Register for 81. I have written to him to send some over, as I have ap-plied & can get none in England, tho' I have seen it.

I wish soon to have in ye Register an acc^t of y^e *monthly meeting for prayer,* to which your piece refers—what sh^d I add to your preface—or would two or three pages newly drawn up by you, be better. On ye ground of Your piece I have opened a meeting somewhat like it *quarter-ly.* We have had but one, consisting of ab^t 300 people—& in a word, I believe we have not had a better meeting since I have been pastor—it will be forever remembered by our people.[50]

Do excuse this scrawl—we are printing 5000 Selec^s 4th ed: and a new Selection of Tunes will be given to ye engraver in a few days & out we suppose in little more than 2 months.

Ever affec^y Yrs
J. Rippon.

It is feared in Town that ye High Church employed the mob at Bir-mingham.[51] Don't government prefer papists to the dissenters?

What books & pamphlets of the denominations (not Baptists) do you wish me to mention in ye Register? in this 2^d part—if you name any give me the full title.

I have not yet rec^d any *full* acc^t of ye Commencement at Rhode Isl-and in 1790.[52]

---

[48]Minutes of Association meetings, letters from pastors, and circular letters from American Baptist associations were regularly printed in the issues of the *Baptist Annual Register*, including the ones from 1790 mentioned above, representing Georgia, Kentucky, Connecticut, and South Carolina. See *Baptist Annual Register*, 1:98-117.

[49]**Jedediah Morse** (1761-1826), minister of the Congregational Church in Char-lestown, Massachusetts.

[50]Most likely this is a reference to Sutcliff's republication of Jonathan Edwards's *Humble Attempt.* See advertisement in *Baptist Annual Register*, 1:126.

[51]A reference to the Priestley Riots in Birmingham in July 1791, in which Priest-ley's home, including his scientific equipment and important manuscripts, as well as the homes of several other dissenters (mostly Unitarians) and some dissenting meeting-houses were destroyed or damaged during three days of rioting.

+It includes an acc^t of all ye denominations in *all* ye States, at least ye 13 States.[53]

34. John Ryland, Jr., Northampton, to John Sutcliff, Olney, undated, but received on 26 January 1792.[54]

Dear Bro^r

I have been wishing to write to you & have been hindered—I have not been nearer London than Luton[55] since I saw you at Northampton—My child was dangerously ill but thro mercy is recovered—I hear Mr Grunden[56] refus'd to visit Hunts followers here[57]—I sent 25 to each

---

[52]The account of the 1790 Commencement at the Baptist College, Providence, Rhode Island (now Brown University), appeared in the *Baptist Annual Register*, 1:177-79.

[53]Rippon's note.

[54]Eng. MS. 371, f. 107d, JRULM.

[55]Ryland preached at Luton on Wednesday, 4 January 1792. See "Text Book John Ryland, D. D. 1766-1825" (MS., Northamptonshire Record Office, MS. CSB) non-paginated.

[56]**Richard Grunden** (Grindon) (d.1814), Baptist minister at Sharnbrook.

[57]**William Huntington** (1745-1813) was a controversial High Calvinist preacher in London. By the date of this letter, there was no love lost between John Ryland and Huntington. In 1791 Huntington, as a part of his ongoing pamphlet war with Maria de Fleury, launched a scurrilous attack on John Collett Ryland (then a schoolmaster at Enfield) in *The Broken Cistern, and the Springing Well: or, The Difference Between Head Notions, and Heart Religion; Vain Jangling, and Sound Doctrine. Addressed to the Rev. John Ryland, Senior, at Enfield* (London: G. Terry [and others], 1791). Later that year, in October 1791, the younger Ryland and his congregation at College Lane excommunicated John Adams, a member of the church, as a result of his propagation of Huntington's teachings. In a breach of church etiquette, Huntington published Ryland's private letter of excommunication to Adams in *Excommunication, and the Duty of All Men to Believe, Weighed in the Balance. In a Letter to Mr. Ryland, Junior. Occasioned by a Letter of Excommunication, Sent to Mr. Adams, Mine Host, at Northampton* (London: G. Terry [and others], 1791). Ryland never forgot this incident. In the library at Bristol Baptist College is an annotated copy of a pamphlet titled *The Voice of Years, Concerning the Late Mr. Huntington* (London: A. Maxwell, 1814), by a Rev. Lincoln. Nearly twenty-five years after his contest with Huntington (who was known for his vicious personal attacks on other dissenting ministers), Ryland writes in a marginal note, "After all, can any one testify that upon *any* occasion Mr H. ever discover'd Humility or Self Abasem.^t? Did he ever shew any other Love to God, but what arose from a previous confid.^ce that he was a favorite of heaven? . . . I never saw into M^r H's [heart], and do not pretend to be his Judge, but if, like Paul, he 'delighted in the Law of God after the inner man,' he had a strange way of shewing it" (p. 21).

London bookseller[58]—know not *how* I had best send to Sheffield—I gave pres[ts] to Hervey,[59] Forsaith,[60] Evans,[61] Okely,[62] Edw[d] Scott, Newton, *Rippon, Booth,*[63] *Thomas,*[64] Pearce, M[r] Sprig sen.[r] [65] D[r] Williams,[66] D[r] Edw.[67] D[r] Stillman—[68]

You must fight your Antinom[s] by fasting and prayer. God is doing great things in Guilsboro, & a Revival seems beginning at Clipston by this means, they have begun at Leicester—and we had a good Meeting last Wed. f[m] 8 till 2. Bro[r] Edm[d69] and his people are all alive indeed— You do owe me for Stratford serm[s]—Bro[r] Fuller I believe pretty well— Hunts folks have had one Hoxton or Hodgson or some [paper torn] name down—He explained the 4 Judgments threaten'd to the [paper torn] Famine Sword Pestilence Evil Beasts—" Now I'll show you a Mystery—The *Sword* means the *Law*—Evil Beasts false Teachers &c." They

---

[58]It is not clear what publication Ryland is referring to in this instance. Most likely it is the Northamptonshire Association sermons preached by Sutcliff and Fuller at the 1791 meeting at Clipston, published as *Jealousy for the Lord of Hosts, and the Pernicious Influence of Delay in Religious Concerns. Two Discourses Delivered at the Meeting of Ministers at Clipstone, April 27, 1791* (1791). The thirteen "sermons" sent to Leicester, mentioned later in this letter, are most likely copies of these same Clipston sermons (see letter 37).

[59]**Thomas Hervey** (1741-1806), Anglican evangelical clergyman.

[60]**Robert Forsaith** (1749-97), at that time an Independent minister in Northampton.

[61]**John Evans**, Baptist minister in Foxton, Northamptonshire.

[62]**Francis Okely** (1719-1794), Moravian minister.

[63]**Abraham Booth** (1734-1806), Baptist minister at Little Prescot Street, Goodman's Fields, London.

[64]Most likely Timothy Thomas of Devonshire Square or his father, Joshua Thomas of Leominster (see letter 27). Ryland, on 4 and 6 December 1791, preached for Rippon at Carter Lane. While he was in London, he probably distributed copies of the sermons to Rippon, Booth, and Thomas (who was also a bookseller). See "Text Book John Ryland."

[65]Most likely this is either William Sprigg, a subscriber in 1800-1801 to the BMS, or James Sprigg, who also subscribed in 1804-1805; both men, possibly father and son or brothers, were from Birmingham and may have been members at Cannon Street. See *Periodical Accounts,* 2:207; 3:127.

[66]**Edward Williams** (1750-1813), at that time minister at Carrs Lane Independent church, Birmingham.

[67]**Dr. Jonathan Edwards** (1745-1801), son of the famous leader of the American Great Awakening.

[68]**Samuel Stillman** (1737-1807), minister of the First Baptist Church in Boston, 1765-1805.

[69]**John Edmonds,** Baptist minister at Guilsborough, 1781-c.1811. Three days after Sutcliff received the above letter, Ryland would preach three times for Edmonds on Sunday, 29 January 1792. See "Text Book John Ryland."

have met 2 Sabbaths by themselves for prayer & Reading—None yet have joined them that we account a loss to us—

I sent 13 Serm^s to Leicester—Sh^d have exchanged wth Faukner[70] last Lords Day or next but both times put off—Shall not go now I suppose—probably may change with Bro^r [Eden?] next L. day & night—Excuse great haste—We write in Love to you All—I owe you for the Charity School Girl Acc^t 5/6—Did—yes I did shew you Jones's Good News from Wales[71]—Can you do poor [Motick?] one good yet—I want you to have another Letter from Botsford.[72] I am

Y^{rs} cordially

John Ryland Jun.

On the back page Sutcliff has added:

Rec^d with this
1 Edw^s on Redemp.[73]   3^{s}6^d
2 Flemming versified at   6^{s}1^d

35. John Ryland, Jr., Northampton, to John Sutcliff, Olney, 7 March 1792.[74]

My dear Bro^r

I wrote the Letter about Thursday last & sent it to W. Law's,[75] but M^r B^n did not come—I order'd a man to call on Saturday Ev. and see if it

---

[70]Most likely Ryland is referring to Robert Faulkner, who was pastor of the Baptist meeting at Thorn at that time. By 1794, Faulkner had gone elsewhere. See *Baptist Annual Register*, 1:3.

[71]**David Jones** (1741-1792), Baptist minister at Pontypool in Wales. The Welsh Bible mentioned by Ryland was published by Jones and Peter Williams as *Y Bibl Sanctaidd: Sef Yr Hen Destament a'r Newydd . . .* (1790). Jones spent considerable time and effort promoting the book through travels and correspondence, which is probably how Ryland received a copy of the book. Those efforts destroyed his health and he died on 24 January 1792, oddly enough the same day Ryland composed his letter to Sutcliff. See *Dictionary of Welsh Biography*.

[72]See previous letter.

[73]Jonathan Edwards's *History of Redemption* (Philadelphia, 1773; London, 1788).

[74]Eng. MS. 371, f. 107e, JRULM.

[75]A William Law joined the congregation at College Lane on 9 April 1773 and died July 1809. A note added to his membership entry says that Law was "called out to preach," but whether he actually pastored is unknown. See College Lane Church Book, Northampton, 1781-1801 (MS., Northamptonshire Record Office, CSBC 48) f. 185.

was gone, & if not send it by the Newsman—I think you w^d have had it on Lord's Day.

Bro^r D^{t76} wanted you or Bro.^{r} Fuller to be here on our Lord's Supper Day—Bro.^{r} N.^{n} is near to Milton & can preach there at another time—Mr Evans told me you were governed by the Moon in your L. Sup.^{r}—I therefore concluded that the 8.th w.^{d} be your L. Supper Day, and another wished B. Fuller to be *here* on the 8.th & you on the 1st—As I supposed the 1st was Bro.^{r} F. & H.^{77} L Sup^r Day—I thought this Arrangm.^{t} w.^{d} suit all best—and told B. F.^{78} so—but have not had his Ans.^{r}—I find he is gone to Arnsby & Leicest.^{r} Will let you know as soon as I hear f.^{m} him—

In all probability your coming Ap. 1st will be the best Day for you to come. I have sent word to B. Heighton^{79} of your not coming next L. day am glad to hear your good News—May God revive his Cause more & more—If anything comes f^m America you shall be very welcome to it—I have nothing yet—Pray for us!

N.B. Your petition must be sign'd *not merely by* the Chairman—the Committee w.^{d} be glad of a Copy of the Petition & the N^o of Names

The House rec.^{vs} no petitions without more Names than the Chairman^{80}— I am

Y^{rs} most cordially

J Ryland

36. *William Carey, Leicester, to John Sutcliff, [Olney], 11 May 1792.*^{81}

My dear Bro.^{r}

---

^{76}**Joseph Dent** of Milton, **Ryland's** brother-in-law.

^{77}Fuller and William Heighton (see below).

^{78}Ryland's abbreviation of "Brother Fuller."

^{79}**William Heighton** (1752-1827), Baptist minister at Roade.

^{80}Ryland is probably referring to a petition by Sutcliff and his congregation at Olney, or possibly the churches of the Northamptonshire Association, regarding the upcoming debate in parliament over abolition of the slave trade. Numerous petitions poured into members of parliament from across England in 1791 and 1792. Despite the overwhelming evidence accumulated by the abolitionists against the slave trade, William Wilberforce's motion was defeated on 19 April 1791 by a vote of 163 to 88. Wilberforce had to settle for a partial victory for the abolitionists in early April 1792, when the House voted for a *gradual* abolition of the slave trade, eventually setting 1 January 1796 as the date of final abolition. The House of Lords, however, immediately implemented delay tactics, and by the end of 1793 it had become clear to most abolitionists that the movement had lost momentum and the slave trade would most likely not end in 1796.

^{81}Eng. MS. 374, f. 361a, JRULM.

I have sent you 25 Copies of my *Enquiry*. Accept one yourself—and sell as many as you can—I hope to see you as you go to the Association.[82] We are well except my youngest Child which for this Fortnight has been at the point of Death with a peripneumary she is now some thing better—we have had Baptizing three Months successively—and have one proposed for the next—Wm Hind[83] was among the last—he gave an acc.^t of his experience much beyond my expectation—I send a letter from him with this—which you will take care of

Yours Affectionately

W. Carey

Leicest.^r May 11. 1792.

NB my resp.^ts to all friends shall be glad if you will present one to my Brother Smith[84] when you see him with my love—and tell him of our Health &c

37. John Ryland, Jr., Northampton, to John Sutcliff, Olney, July 1792.[85]

Dear Bro^r

Somebody, I forget who, s^d you [were] just thro Kettering last Week. I was in hope you w^d have come this Way & shou'd have been glad to see you. I hope you are however got home safely & in health. I shall be glad to hear from you—

Bro^r Carey had pretty good Success in London but has left about 35£ not gather'd—I think you & Mrs A.[86] advanced 10£ or Guineas he cou'd not tell which—I suppose also your people will be willing he sh^d sometime collect at Olney—When will that be?—Will you be satisfied with half what you & Mrs A. lent & wait for the rest till he collects at your Town—He left the Money with me—Five of our friends had advanced 5 Guineas—these I have reduced to 2£ each which is less than

---

[82]The Northamptonshire Baptist Association meeting was held from 29-31 May 1792 at Nottingham. Ryland wrote the circular letter, titled *Godly Zeal Described and Recommended*, and Carey preached his famous sermon on missions that led to the formation that October of the Baptist Missionary Society. Shortly before the May meeting, Carey had published his famous discourse, *An Enquiry into the Obligations of Christians to Use Means for the Conversion of the Heathens* (1792).

[83]A John Hind, possibly William's father, was a dyer living in West Bridge. See *Universal British Directory*, 3:597.

[84]This could be Thomas Smith, butcher; or Michael or Charles Smith, lace manufacturers in Olney. See *Universal British Directory*, 4:89.

[85]Eng. MS. 383, f. 1773a, JRULM.

[86]Mrs. Andrews, in whose home Sutcliff lived (see letter 13).

their Share of the Money collected   But—two of their Neighbours, who are but cool in their Love to the Cause need to be paid the whole of their 5£ or Guineas—and the Carpenter wants as much as can be spared him, so that if you can let half lie you will do them a Kindness, and may get the remainder soon

Let me hear from you speedily & I will send what you require—Or shall I pay the printers Bill for the Clipstone Sermons[87] with it, which was 5£ 10 and 4s 6d for 250 Title pages—Indeed half will not be enough for that—You cannot come over just at present—I wish I cou'd see you much—Have recd last Week a new & urgent Applicn from Bristol—Carey says all the London Minrs are for it, but One who is always contrary to the Majority & wonders I shd have the least hesitation on the Subject. We unite in Respects to yourself & to Mrs Andrews &c. I am
Dear Bror
Yours Affectionately
John Ryland Junior

38. *James Boswell, London, to John Fawcett, Brearley Hall, Halifax, Yorkshire, 12 October 1792.*[88]

Sir,

I am very much flattered by your letter which though in a high strain of compliment, appears to me to be sincere, and therefore gratifies both my vanity and my benevolence; for, believe me, Sir, the hope of giving instruction and entertainment is a great motive to my literary labours.

I should have thanked you for your letter, and complied with your request sooner; but to make amends for the delay, I enclose you a small piece of the handwriting of my illustrious friend.[89] I am Sir

---

[87] See letter 34.

[88] Eng. MS. 343, f. 43, JRULM.

[89] Fawcett's "request" of Boswell (1740-1795), the Scottish-born biographer of Johnson, is unknown, but what he received from Boswell is most likely the letter from Dr. Samuel Johnson to John Ryland of London, January 1756 (Eng. MS.343, f. 44, JRULM, published in *The Letters of Samuel Johnson*, ed. Bruce Redford, 5 vols. (Oxford, 1992-1994), 1:127-128). This Samuel Johnson letter may be the same letter Boswell gave to Fawcett, as noted in the above letter. In August 1814, Thomas Raffles visited Fawcett at Ewood Hall, receiving from Fawcett several autographs, including an MS. of Oliver Heywood. Thomas Raffles, Jr., noted that his father "ever preserved it amongst his most cherished treasures" Raffles may have received the Boswell and Johnson letters from Fawcett at this time as well. See Thomas Stamford Raffles, *Memoirs of the Life and Ministry of the Rev. Thomas Raffles, D.D., LL.D.* (London: Jackson, 1864) 124-125.

your much obliged
humble servant
James Boswell

39. Samuel Medley, London, to John Smallshaw,[90] Sparling Street, Liverpool, 22 December 1792.[91]

London 22[d] Dec.[r] 1792

My dear Brother and Sister Smallshaw
        In writing to many of my dear and much-loved friends in Liverpool as now absent from them—you both, as a peculiar part of that number must not be forgotten of or neglected by me   I trust I can say You are not in any sense so far as in my power   I daily think of you in my poor way   I daily pray for you—that the gracious Blessing Promise and Consolation of our God and Heavenly Father in Christ Jesus may be ever with You—that his Heavenly and Everlasting Arms may be underneath You and that the Banner of his Love may be ever over You—that You may thro Grace cleave to the Lord with purpose of heart—and so be enabled to look upward and to press forward and rejoice in hope of the Glory of God—And that tho You are now getting into years and so drawing towards the Evening of Life Yet You may find his Grace to be sufficient for You and his Strength to be made perfect in Your weakness—and that You may daily and universally come up from this wilderness looking to and living upon the Lord Jesus Christ as your Beloved and as Your friend—and this I trust thro Grace You know Him to be—and therefore You cannot nor will You part with him or give up or let go Your claim of or hold upon him   O my dear friends Christ and his Grace and Love are precious Realities—And will stand us instead when flesh and Heart fail us as they will do   O what an unspeakable mercy it is to be brought to some Experimental Knowledge of—Faith in—and Love to Him as an Able—Willing—Kind—Wise—Only—Faithful—Free Faithful Unchanging and Everlasting Savior And all this he is to his dear Children and People—well might the apostle Paul say of him what I trust You can and do say of him also—viz that he is—*All and in all*—It has pleased the Father that in Him should all fullness dwell—And O it is Your great mercy and mine also my dear friends to believe out of and from his Blessed fullness and grace for grace and that we may do so we

---

[90]John Smallshaw was a Liverpool ship-builder and member of Medley's congregation at Byrom Street. In 1804-1805 he subscribed £2.2 to the BMS as part of a special collection for Carey and his Serampore work in translating the Bible into the Eastern languages. His daughter, Elizabeth, married Medley's son, Samuel, in 1818. See *Universal British Directory*, 3:721; *Periodical Accounts*, 3:149.
        [91]Raffles Handlist, unlisted fascicle no. 367, JRULM.

are Warranted Invited and Encouraged to Come Humbly and yet Boldly to his Throne of Grace that we may obtain mercy and find Grace to help us in everytime of Need—may we be made truly thankful for—and make both diligent and constant use both of the Word and of the Throne of Grace also—O may we love and delight in and find Blessing daily flowing to us from the Word of God and Prayer for I am well persuaded and assured that if thro Grace our Souls are truly alive to God we do not we cannot live without them—The Bible—and Prayer—are Heaven's appointed means for the maintaining and strengthening the spiritual life and comfort of the Real Christian as I trust your souls find by happy Experience   I hope and pray this hasty Line may meet you both and all the dear children mercifully well—Accept my best Love to yourselves and present the same to them also—Tell Dear Hannah that I purpose if possible I can get time to drop her a line before I leave London—But my Engagements are very many in publick and I [am] almost always in a hurry while I am here in London—I have been very much indisposed since I have been here with a most violent cold thro the Goodness of God I have been of late considerably better tho not quite rid of it yet—my publick Labors here are many O that the Lord may Commend his gracious Blessing on my poor attempts for his Glory—I hope the good Lord feeds Your Souls with his Blessed word at home tho I am not with You—May You indeed be fed with it and truly grow thereby—till we reach to the Better Brighter world above and so are ever with the Lord   I hope to see you again soon if the Lord please by the first Sabbath in January I think of and pray for me that I may be returned to you in safety & peace and that we may rejoice in Christ Jesus and be mutual Comfort and Blessings to one another   My Son[92] his Wife and M[rs] Arthur join in kind respects to You all—Grace be ever with You   so prays

Yours most affectionately
Sam Medley

40. MS. copy of a letter from C[hristian]. I[gnatius]. LaTrobe,[93] [London], to John Rippon, Southwark, 26 June 1793.[94]

---

[92]**Samuel Medley, Jr.**, (1769-1857), painter and leading Baptist layman in London.

[93]This letter is a response by La Trobe to a request from the leaders of the BMS concerning the Moravians' ideas about proper qualifications for a missionary. C. I. La Trobe (1758-1836) spent most of his adult life promoting the cause of Moravian missions, first as secretary to the Society for the Furtherance of the Gospel in 1787, then as editor of the Society's *Periodical Accounts*. The *Baptist Annual Register* included not only "An Account of the Particular Baptist Society for Propagating the Gospel among the Heathen; including a Narrative of its Rise and Plan; with a short

London, June 26, 1793.

Dear Mʳ Rippon,

Mʳ Dixon has by your desire transmitted to me Nº 6 of Your instruc-
tive Work, *The Baptist Annual Register*, for which I sincerely thank you,
and have given Mʳ Dixon the 9ᵗʰ Nº of the little Accounts concerning our
Endeavors to propagate the Gospel among the Heathen which he promised to send or deliver to you. I have just received them from the Press,
for I am sorry to say that my printer has unaccountably delayed these
publications, to put forward a work of his own. Otherwise they would
have appeared a month ago.

I have this morning perused the accᵗ of the rise of the *Particular
Baptist Society for propagating the Gospel among the heathen*, & trust
that our Lord will lay his blessing upon your Endeavors, and by your
means also extend his glorious Kingdom on Earth. You have made honourable mention of us—but no praise is due our poor labors. What
could we poor insignificant people have done, had not our blessed Savior himself done the work, and to shew his power, made use of the
weakest & most insufficient instruments? I think the rise, progress and
success of the Brethren's missions are the greatest Proofs on Earth of
the Truth of our Lord, *my strength is made perfect in weakness*.

In Your account, the following articles are proposed for Examination & discussion in a diligent & impartial manner (Nº 5 p. 378.) 1.
What qualifications are especially requisite in missionaries? 2. What
advice should be given to the Missionaries, or what regulations adopted
concerning them &c. I did not find any answers to, or further Discussion
of these subjects in Your 6ᵗʰ Nº p. 485. except that You have met with 2
Brethren willing to go among the East indian heathen. To the first question we Moravian Brethren should answer simply thus— The Love of
God shed abroad in our hearts by the Holy Ghost. A heart cleansed in
the blood of Christ, and from Love & gratitude to Him who hath purchased him with his own blood, truly & wholly devoted to his Service;
assured, that in *life & death* thee is the Lords & will abide with Him for-

---

Address earnestly recommending this benevolent Design" but also an extract from
the papers of Samuel Watson, a Moravian missionary to the West Indies, as well as a
printed copy of the La Trobe letter. This MS. copy of La Trobe's letter, with corrections by Rippon, was also sent to John Ryland, who made numerous corrections and
alterations in his own hand on the letter. The printed version in the *Baptist Annual
Register* incorporates nearly all of Ryland's and Rippon's corrections and alterations
exactly as they appear on this MS. When compared with the original letter, we get
rare glimpse into the editing techniques of Rippon (and in many respects late
eighteenth-century editors in general) when printing manuscript letters. See *Baptist
Annual Register*, 1:371-378, 1:531-533.
⁹⁴Eng. MS. 861, f. 88, JRULM.

ever; void of self-love, self-seeking, self-complacency & the whole poisonous system of *Self*; conscious of numberless wants & infirmities, but by experience acquainted with the saving power of Jesus, & the sanctifying merits of His precious atonement; filled with Love to their fellowman, as being bought with an inestimable price, and consequently precious in the Sight of our Savior, however depraved & corrupted, & however despicable in the sight of men; shunning no danger, no trial, no persecution when engaged in the Cause of the Savior, & always hoping, believing; unweariedly following the poor straying sheep; & even without present prospects, relying upon that gracious promise, *that the Word of the Lord shall not return unto Him void, but accomplish that,* in due time, *& whereunto he has sent it.* Those of our Missionaries, whose labors the Lord has blessed have had these qualifications. Learning, & what the world calls, accomplishments, we have not experienced to be of much use. A true Christian has always those accomplishments he wants; he is kind, courteous, gentle, peaceable & full of good will. Let the world produce any better principles of Conduct. He must put up with shame, because he has not the truth in him. 2. What advice &c should be given to yᵉ Missionaries

When the Brethren went first among the heathen, they thought that they must first enter upon an explanation of the greatness, justice, omnipresence &c of God of the heinousness of Sin &c. but they soon found that *"to know nothing among them save Jesus & him crucified"* was the right way; the Word of the Cross, proved the power of God unto Salvation, and every other good thing followed. The minds of the converts were by degrees open to all other religious subjects. Therefore our advice is, that they preach the *crucified Jesus*; that they in externals look more for real conversion of heart in the few committed unto their care, than for numbers: that they carefully & kindly keep to the discipline of the Church, excluding transgressors, yet not forsaking them, but endeavoring by Gods grace to lead them gently into the right track; that they are continually watchful to prevent hurt to the Souls, to become acquainted with every individual, & baptize none but those in whom a Change of heart is visible. That is to Externals, they be satisfied with whatever Providence may appoint; & frugally manage their housekeeping. The Lord be praised, who has hitherto given us such ? subjects for our Missions. May he also give them to your dear people, and hear your prayers in behalf of all men. In those ideas contained in the preamble p. 372, is contained everything needful for a missionarys Consideration &c a complete answer seems to me to be given to these questions. Did our Savʳ do so much for us—how much then ought we to be devoted to Him!

I have been much too prolix & must beg yʳ pardon for interfering in your Concerns; Nor was my opinion asked & I am sure you have persons in your society much more able to say something to the purpose, on these subjects, but I have simply written what just struck my mind in perusing your book. We differ in a few things, but we are I trust one in Jesus, and do what we do in His name. You are at liberty to insert what you please concerning us & our Missions into your work, if you think it can give any pleasure to your good people. I remain with sincere Esteem

Dear Sir

Your affec[te] friend & humble Serv[t]

C. Ig. LaTrobe

41. Matthew Wilks,[95] London, to John Sutcliff, Olney, 6 November 1793.[96]

My old friend

We are both embarked in the same work of doing good, in the execution of which experience testifies that we also frequently get good. For he that watereth shall be watered again.

I hear you are now a favourer of E. Mag.[97] by recommending its sale, for which you are entitled to thanks. Though you are not an editor, I do not see why you should not be a contributor, and furnish us with a few short productions of y[r] leisure hours.

A good friend informs me, that you can favour me with some pretty biographical pieces, with some entertaining anecdotes, and Experiences of living and dying Saints. As productions of this nature are very interesting to the generality of our readers, you dont know how much I should be obliged by such favours.

As our plan is liberal, I do not see why we should not make it a common course, I hope y[r] modesty will not enslave y[r] mind so far as to prevent y[r] assistance. Many mites make a large sum.

---

[95]**Matthew Wilks** (1746-1829) was an Independent minister at the Moorfields and at the Tottenham Court Road Chapel, London.

[96]Eng. MS. 371, f. 129, JRULM. On the back page is written in Sutcliff's hand, "Rec.[d] Nov.[r] 7. 1793. Ans.[d] (inclosing M[rs] Jarvis Case) Dec.[r] 2. 93."

[97]The *Evangelical Magazine* began in 1793, the work of several London Evangelical (Anglican and Nonconformist) ministers and laymen. Sutcliff, Fuller, and others would write a number of articles for the magazine during their careers. Among the stated contributors and trustees listed on the initial title page in 1793 were John Eyre of Homerton, George Burder of Coventry, Andrew Fuller of Kettering, Samuel Greatheed of Newport Pagnell, John Ryland of Bristol, and Matthew Wilks of London.

Should you have a known object to [paper torn] probably some of our London Editors may have no application, and if you will send it to me as directed in ye Mag. I will do what I can for the object.

I hope the dear Lord is with you in y^r great work of winning Souls. In this may you abound yet more, and more, till y^r work terminates in everlasting rest. Awaiting y^r favourable answer I remain in the best of bonds. Dr Sir   y^rs

M Wilks

London Nov. 6. 1793.

42. William Steadman,[98] *Northampton, to John Sutcliff, Olney, 4 January 1794.*[99]

My dear Brother,

I am sorry I happened to be out of Town when the Parcell came; so did not open it till to day, else sho.^d have written sooner—Mr Dent[100] delivered the inclosed Letter to Mr Fitzhugh.[101] Hope the Delay was not of any bad Consequence.

Am much obliged to my good Brother for his kind presents—the Books & pamphlets, and also for his kind Enquiries. In Answer to which I would inform him, that I found my way without much difficulty, and got to N—[102] between 3 and 4 oclock. Was a good deal fatigued, and nearly as much in want of a *Dinner* as I was of a Breakfast the preceeding Thursday when I reach^d Olney. But a Chair & a good Fire to sit by relieved me from the former, and a Piece of a roast Sparrib removed the latter.—

Made Enquiry after the Registers.[103] Mr Chapman[104] undertook to send the number you wished. Hope he has accomplished his Promise.

---

[98]**William Steadman** (1764-1837), Baptist minister at Broughton (1789-1798), Devonport (1798-1805), and Bradford, Yorkshire (1805-1837). Steadman was supplying at College Lane in Northampton immediately after Ryland's removal to Broadmead in Bristol.

[99]ENG. MS. 371/f. 116a, JRULM. On the back page is written in Sutcliff's hand, "Rec. Jan. 5. 1794. Rev. William Steadman." This letter is not in Thomas Steadman's *Memoir of the Rev. William Steadman, D.D.: Pastor of the First Baptist Church, Bradford, Yorkshire, and President of the Northern Baptist Education Society* (London: Thomas Ward, 1838).

[100]Ryland's brother-in-law, Joseph Dent (see letter 35).

[101]Charles Fitzhugh was the proprietor of the London stage wagons in Northampton. He joined the College Lane church on 2 June 1774, but was excluded in 1805. See College Lane Church Book, f. 13; *Universal British Directory*, 4:88.

[102]Northampton.

[103]Presumably a reference to Rippon's *Baptist Annual Register.*

I rejoice to hear of Mrs Andrews' happy deliverance; and congratulate her and her Yokefellow on the Increase of their Family, and from my very Heart wish them much Joy of the Daughter born—

Thank you my dear Brother, for your wishes respecting my safe return Home, and my Comfort and Usefulness there. The former will I trust be accomplished next week and the latter be accomplishing thro' Life.—And in Return can only wish you much of the divine presence, all needed Guidance, and constant Success in your attempts to promote the Redeemer's Glory.

Beg you will present my Christian Love to Mrs Andrews and repeat my Thanks for her great kindnesses.—And to all Friends—

I remain

Dear Brother

most affectionately yours

W Steadman

Northampton
Jan: 4.th 1794

43. *Andrew Fuller, Kettering, to John Rippon, Southwark, London, 6 August 1794.*[105]

Kett^g 6 Aug. 94

Dear Bro.^r

On 29.th July for the first time I rec^d a Letter from each of our Brethren in India they are all well and as happy as can be expected—They met with great civility from the Captain, who is an Englishman tho' Commander of a Danish Ship—He has promised to make Interest for

---

[104]Probably John Chapman, who joined the congregation at College Lane on 10 November 1780; he was excluded at one point, but later restored. He died in 1830. See College Lane Church Book, f. 15.

[105]MAM. PLP. 42.47.3, JRULM. The letter from Carey that Fuller has just received resides now in the Isaac Mann collection at the National Library of Wales; it is dated 17 October 1793, with additions on 14 and 25 November, and 16 December. A note on this letter in Fuller's hand reads: "Mr. Carey's 1st letter dated Oct. and Nov. 93. Arrived beginning of Aug. 94."—which was actually, as the above letter reveals, 29 July 1794. Carey's letter was reprinted in the *The Periodical Accounts, Relative to the Baptist Missionary Society*, a monthly periodical that commenced about two years after the founding of the BMS, publishing letters from the mission fields and keeping supporters at home aware of the mission's activities and progress. Fuller met with the Committee at Guilsborough on 4 August 1794, replying to Carey and Thomas on behalf of the Committee in a letter written that day and published by Rippon in the *Baptist Annual Register*, 2:174-175. See also *Periodical Accounts*, 1:61-70.

them with the Danish Governor, who resides but about 16 miles from Calcutta, where they now are and which is a matter of great importance *if the English Company should frown upon their undertaking.*[106]

After escaping one most imminent danger in which they were on the point of giving up all for lost, they arrived in the Bay of Bengal and were safely landed Nov[r] 7. 1793 not five months after their departure— During the Voyage they had translated the Book of Genesis into Bengallie—Carey is got very forward in that language, and Thomas[107] in the Sancrit, which is the learned language of Indostan in w[h] are written all their sacred writings—The voyage or its dangers does not appear in the least to have damped their spirits, but rather to have produced a contrary effect—Thus writes M[r] *Thomas* while they were tossing about in the Bay of Bengal—almost in sight of the place of destination "We have been burthened with many sorrows but at present I rejoice—I rejoice because God is with us, the throne of grace is open and the precious word of God is unsealed to us—I rejoice to be so near my family, and so near a flock of black sheep—I rejoice to run and roll away the storm from the wells mouth that they may drink!"

On their arrival they met with *Ram Ram Bashoo*[108] who to their great grief they found had been again bowing down to Idols! They still however think well of him—Carey gives the following account of his temptations and fall as expressed by himself— "Forsaken by European Christians, and discarded by the Hindoos, very ill of a flux, nothing to support me or my family—all said M[r] Thomas would never return—I knew that Roman Catholics worshiped Idols—I thought I had seen but a small part of the Bible—*Perhaps* the worship of images might be commanded in some parts of it which I had not seen—I hesitated—and complied, but it was for a piece of bread—and I still love Xnity much the best." Carey speaks after wards of his having engaged him to teach him the language and as being "much pleased with his conversation."

---

[106]At the bottom of the page Fuller writes, "I learn by other Letters he has made application, & succeeded. You must not publish this however," for that would "offend the Company." He advises Rippon that they must be silent about Carey's "application to the Danish governor."

[107]**John Thomas** (1757-1801) joined Carey as a BMS missionary to India in 1793.

[108]Ram Ram Bashoo (Bashu, Basu) was supposedly converted by John Thomas during the latter's first visit to India, but when Thomas returned with Carey in 1793, Bashoo, a Hindoo, was once again worshiping idols. Carey nevertheless liked him and used him as an interpreter, but eventually Bashoo, like several of the other early guides and interpreters used by Carey and Thomas, did not remain a Christian. See F. A. Cox, *History of the Baptist Missionary Society, from 1792 to 1842*, 2 vols. (London: T. Ward, and G. and J. Dyer, 1842) 1:93-96.

Parbotee,[109] they found stood well, and he and Mohun Chund[110] were coming from a distant part of the country to see them and unite with them. Only three days passed after their arrival ere they began to work—Their first entrance on it is thus described by Carey— "On the 10th of Novr Mr Thomas and I began our labours—We came in a Pansowah (a boat) from the ship, and at slack water we lay to at a Bozar (or market) where Mr T preaches to the people—They left their merchandise immediately and listened for three hours with great attention— One of them prepared us a dinner which we ate—A plantain loaf was our dish, and plates, and instead of knives and forks we used our fingers—when we left them they desired us to come again!" In his concluding paragraph dated Decr 16th he says, "We have frequent opportunities of addressing the Hindoos, and their attention is astonishing— Last Lords day we went and Mr Thomas preached to near 200 of them at La Gange, a village near us they listened with great seriousness; and several followed us to make further enquiries about what is the way to heaven? and how they should do to walk therein? Every place presents a pleasing prospect to us of success, and we are of one mind, & of one soul!— Pray for us we daily remember you, & the prosperity of the Society lies very near our hearts."

"I hope, adds he, the Society will go on and increase—and that the multitudes of heathens in ye world may hear the glorious words of truth—Africa is but a little way fm England—Madagascar but a little farther—South America and all the numerous and large Islands in the Indian & Chinese Seas I hope will not be passed over—A large field opens on every side, and millions of perishing heathens tormented in this life by means of Idolatry Superstition and Ignorance and subject to eternal misery in the next, are pleading! Yes all their miseries plead as soon as they are known with every heart that loves God, and with all the churches of the living God! O that many labourers may be thrust into the vineyard of our L. J. C.[111] and that ye gentiles may come to the knowledge of the truth as it is in him!" By this if you knew not before you may know the man & his communication.

Both Thomas & Carey speak highly of each other—at their outset when they were Sea-sick T speaks of Car[ey] "leaning over the sides of the Ship to relieve his stomach, and expressing what Joy he felt in contemplating the goodness of God!" C. on the other hand speaks of T as, "A

---

[109]Parbotee, like Mohun Chund, was a Brahmin and a devoted Hindoo; he was converted under Thomas and became a great help to Carey and the others in their translation work. See Cox, *History*, 1:93-96.

[110]Mohun Chund was a Brahmin who supposedly had been converted to Christianity by Thomas, but he returned to his former religion, which was a bitter loss to the early work in India. See Cox, *History*, 1:93-96.

[111]Lord Jesus Christ.

holy-man—that the more he knows him the better he loves him, tho, adds he, his faithfulness is apt to degenerate into personality—It is thus I account for his former differences with M^r C—I speak not this of myself for we live in the greatest love."

Their expences are more than they expected—Carey has to pay a Mumshee, or interpreter, for teaching him the language—-and Thomas a Pandit for teaching him the Sancrit—These are absolutely necessary for translating the scriptures, on which their hearts are set—they request a Polyglot Bible which will cost 8 or 10 guineas to be sent them— and some other books—and when they have translated enough into manuscript to think of printing, we must either have it printed in London or send them types which will cost 3 or 400£—but if God be with them & prosper them we shall not want for money—I have collected this spring in London and the Country near 300£—

While they were tossed about in the Bay of Bengal Carey writes thus "Many private seasons I have enjoyed (on board) of great pleasure and have a growing satisfaction in having undertaken this work and a growing desire for its success, tho I feel so much barrenness and so little of that lively continual sense of divine things upon my mind that I almost despair of ever being of any more, but in general I feel a pleasure in the thought that Christ has promised to be with his Ministers to the end of the world and that as our day is so shall Our strength be have often felt much pleasure in recollecting the times of Publick worship in the Churches in England and reflecting that now perhaps Hundreds if not Thousands are praying for me   you will also easily believe that my friends have not been forgotten by me on those occasions your 10 oclock in the Morning will be 4 in the afternoon there being 6 hours difference of time between you and us Mr Thomas has laboured indefatigably in translating the Book of Genesis which he has now accomplished   in short we are now expecting to join Ramboshee and Parbotee in a few days

Dear Bro^r —We have had a Committee meet^g last Monday when it was Resolved amongst other things to print an Account of the Origin and Progress of the Society[112]—and w^h will contain extracts of the letters lately Rec^d as are proper to be made publick—This will be printed with all convenient Expedition—and f^m this you may take what you please for y^r Register—You will have no objection I presume to our printing in this acc^t the Narrative of Mr Thomas w^h appeared in y^r Register—Y^r affec^e

A. Fuller

My Respects to Mrs R. &c

---

[112]The beginning of the *Periodical Accounts* of the Baptist Missionary Society, which were published serially between 1794 and 1817.

44. Andrew Fuller, Kettering, to John Sutcliff, Olney, 30 August 1794.[113]

Kett.ᵍ 30 Aug. 94

My dʳ broʳ I have been much concerned to hear of your indisposition and very much wished ere now to have come over; but cᵈ not possibly accomplish it—Am going into Camb—shire next Monday—wish you could give me a line when there, informᵍ me how you do & how Mʳˢ A. is—and whether I might have any dependance on an exchange with you on the Sabbath after the Ministers Meeting, wʰ is on Sep. 30. at Kettᵍ and Oct. 1ˢᵗ at Walgrave.

Direct to me at Mʳ Robert Fuller's Isleham near Newmarket Cambridgeshire.[114] My Respects as due.

I am affecʸ yʳˢ
A. Fuller

P.S. The writing so much on the Missions business has made me ill for 2 or 3 weeks but am rather better.

45. John Gill, St. Albans, to John Sutcliff, Olney (By favor of Mʳ Harris), 29 December 1794.[115]

Dear Brother,

I chearfully embrace an Opportunity of Sending you a few Lines by Mʳ Harris of Tilsworth, in which are enclosed 2ˢ for the Letters which came safe to Hand.

We are exhorted to rejoice with them that do rejoice, and weep with them that weep. I have sometimes communicated to you some unpleasant things, But now I trust I can tell you of some of the pleasant things of Zion, the King of glory hath heard our mourning Voice, and hath come in, and comforted our wast places, and caused some little revivings in our Bondage. Early in the Spring the last Day in Feb.ʸ we had the ordinance of Baptism Administered to one Person, it was a remarkable Good Season, and I think will be long remembered by some who were much affected. Surely the Lord was Among us, and I began much to hope for Some Happy Consequences to Appear, but Huge were some intervening Clouds, and any hope was stricken a little, especially when

[113]Eng. MS. 369, f.50c, JRULM.

[114]Possibly Fuller's eldest son, but most likely this is Fuller's cousin, also named Robert. See Donald M. Lewis, ed., *The Blackwell Dictionary of Evangelical Biography: 1730-1860*, 2 vols. (Oxford: Blackwell, 1995) 1:415; Fuller to Sutcliff, 21 November 1808, MSS. BMS, vol. 4, Angus Library, Regent's Park College, Oxford.

[115]Eng. MS. 370, f. 53, JRULM. On back page in Sutcliff's hand we find, "Rec.ᵈ Jan. 5. 1795. *Good news.* Ans.ᵈ July 9. 95."

the Separation came on, however, I was unwilling to put off my Helmet, tho' the Divil told me I might as well do so, but I was enabled to wait and found I trust the presence of God with me in my work and some appearance of the Spirit that moved upon the face of the deep at the Creation, moving upon the Hearts of Some, and Stirring to Unity Love and Zeal.

We set apart a Time in the month of Oc.ᵗʳ for prayer, and I think the Spirit of Grace and Supplication was given. I preached from Isaiah 7 Ch. 7 Vers. we met again in the Evening for prayer and I spoke from Nahum ch. 7. We had a Good Season, surely the Lord hath Shewed us some tokens for Good. Since then we have been more comfortable than heretofore, and our prayer meetings have been attended with Double the Number, and some are coming forth to embrace the ordinances of Jesus Christ and unite in fellowship with us.

Last Thursday I baptized five Persons 4 Women, 1 Man, It was a Solemn and a Rejoicing Season, many were present, the Spectators behaved well, with Serious attention some were in tears, the Subjects were comfortable, and it was a good time to me, tho, a Day or two before the Divil lay hard at me, to put it off on Accᵗ of the Weather, and he raised such a Storm in my mind, as almost frightned me, but I was enabled to resist his Temptation, and found the Grace of Christ sufficient for me, preachᵈ in the Evening from Isaiah 19. latter part 20.

Yesterday morn from Acts 8. 39. afternoon from Psal. 27. 1. a funeral Serm for Mʳˢ Packman who hath walked honourably in fellowship 35 years, She had a Good hope thro Grace, which lasted to the end, and had an easy Dismission from this world of Sin and Trouble to the World of everlasting rest and peace.

In the Evening Lecture I spoke from 1 Thes. 1.5.

Our Lectures have hitherto been well attended—

We have Some expectation of Some others coming who are standing at the door ready to enter in. When the Lord worketh none can hinder that which is impossible with us is possible with him and easy to perform

I have been some times much affected with the Goodness of God when I think how he Supports and Supplys me and Carries thro, the Services which he calls one to, and that he is now appearing to save this little part of Zion,—where he hath fixed my Station for many Years past how long my Time may be is not for me to know at present. May the Lord keep me in a humble waiting Posture doing his will with courage and Faithfulness and Crown my poor Endeavors with Success.

I cannot help mentioning a Circumstance or two which hath Sometimes melted me into tears.

Mʳ Gillie who some years back resided here lately sent me a very affectionate Letter expressing his Good will to me and the Interest and in order to encourage us beged [sic] his Name might be put Down as a Subscriber for two Guineas a year.[116] Some friend and minister at a Distance have expressed their concern for me on Acc[t] of the change which hath taken place.

It is pleasing to have the Good will of our fellow Creatures, but that is changeable, but to have the Good will of him that dwelt in the Bush is far more and of the Greatest importance, that is unchangeable, his Counsels shall stand and he will do all his pleasure.

If M[rs] Andrews is living pray give any kind Love to her, tell her M[rs] Packman hath got the Start of her is gone to heaven but a little before remember me to M[r] Andrews and all friends, excuse inaccuracies I have not time to Correct being about to Visit some Friends wishing you much of the presence of the God of all Grace. Fare well Affectionately
John Gill

S[t] Albans
Dec.[r] 29. 1794.

46. John Sutcliff, Olney, to an unnamed correspondent [John Ryland, Bristol], undated [late 1794 or early 1795, but shortly before the death of Mrs. Andrews on 9 March 1795].[117]

Dear Brother!
I must defer writing to M[r] Tommas[118] to another time. Sincerely wish you, M[rs] R. and any who travel with you, a good journey.—Am much fatigued with the exertions of yesterday. Hope I shall be better, when the weather becomes a little cooler.—M[rs] Andrews continues very ill.

M[r] Newton[119] has had a hurt at Bedford, but I do not know particulars. One report says, it was thro' a fall he had, as he descended the Pulpit stairs. Do not learn that the effects are alarming.

I remember Brother Fuller once mentioned to me, a Sermon of your's on Gal. iv. and perhaps 1/2 a score of the last verses. How many you read as your text, I cannot tell; but your design was to elucidate the whole passage. Could you not with little trouble, work up your leading

[116]Presumably he wished to subscribe to the BMS.
[117]Eng. MS. 384, f. 1949, JRULM.
[118]John Tommas, minister at the Baptist meeting in the Pithay, Bristol (see letter 5).
[119]John Newton (see letter 6).

ideas into a short Essay, and insert it in the Evangelical Magazine?[120] I wish you to give the question a thought.

With usual love,
Your's very cordially,
John Sutcliff

Olney, Monday Morning

47. *William Bull,*[121] *Newport Pagnell, to John Sutcliff, Olney, 13 March 1795.*[122]

Newp.ᵗ 13—Mar. 95

Dear Sir

I truely feel for you on the present painful occasion, & thank you for your two notes, & for many others. I pray the Lord to be your support & strength so also that of our two cousins, who I doubt not, feel much on this occasion—I was from home on Monday & Tuesday & was waiting to hear again from you.

I am much surpriz'd at the Burial being at midnight, & suspect you must have made some mistake—indeed I much fear that it will be extremely dangerous to us both to be out at that late hour—I wish you had pointed out a mode for us to come, we must have a post chaise, but whether we should speak for it to stay all night, to wait for us, or send it home, & order another to come for us on Monday morn'g I am doubtful.

We have both of us colds & coughs, poor Thomas also has a cold & a hoarseness & a good deal of the fever with it—I wish we could have come & returned in a day, but if it was our late dear friends dying request that we should be sent for, I will try all that is possible to attend, & will speak for the chaise to leave home at half past four,

I think we must set off at four, & get there about half past five, if any thing wants explaining give me a line by the postman

---

[120]Ryland's essay, "Thoughts upon the Allegorical Application of the History of Sarah and Hagar" (taken from Galatians 4:21-31), appeared in the *Evangelical Magazine* 3 (1795): 64-69. The copy in the Bristol Baptist College library has been annotated by Ryland.

[121]**William Bull** (1738-1814), Independent minister and teacher at Newport Pagnell.

[122]Eng. MS. 369, f. 19a, JRULM. The occasion of this letter is the funeral service for Mrs. Mary Andrews, in whose home Sutcliff had lived since his arrival in Olney in 1774. She died on 9 March 1795. Her sister, Hannah (d. 1814), was married to William Bull. Haykin notes that Mrs. Andrews had requested Sutcliff not to preach a funeral sermon on her behalf; the midnight timing of the funeral, however, was not uncommon at that time. See Haykin, *One Heart*, 115, 240-241.

I am with love to cousins
Dear Sir
your affectionate Bro^r & serv^t
W. Bull

48. Samuel Greatheed,[123] Newport Pagnell, to John Sutcliff, Olney, 14 March 1795.[124]

Newport Pagnel
14 March 1795

Dear Sir,

I thank you for the trouble you have taken to get me the Books, and am glad to have them on the whole, altho' several of them are imperfect, which Friend Button[125] ought to have mentioned in his Catalogue.

The loss of a cordial Friend and pious Housemate, of so long standing, must doubtless be felt by you. I heartily pray that you may find it sanctified, and your future situation rendered comfortable and profitable by the Guidance and Blessing of Him who is alone the same yesterday, today, and forever.

The request of our late worthy Friend, about the funeral Sermon, was, I am confident, from a good motive; yet I think it a pity the occasion should not be improved for the benefit of the living; and I suppose you will endeavour to do this, as much as you can without infringing upon her injunction. Her death will certainly be mentioned in the Magazine[126]; and you are best qualified to give a proper account of it. Any hint that may tend to vindicate our deceased Friend from the common charge of parsimony, will, I think, be seasonable. If you favor me with the Account, I will take the care of its insertion. If done in a day or two it may yet come into the next number.

When your spirits are sufficiently reestablished I shall hope you will oblige me with some further help in the Review. I have much need of it. I have requested for dismission from my Charge in this matter on account of the irregularity & deficiency of assistance; but the reply is, that, if I dont persevere, neither will Mr Eyre[127] in the final Editorship; which I fear would be very detrimental to the Cause. If I dont hear from

---

[123]**Samuel Greatheed** (d. 1823), Independent minister at Woburn, Bedfordshire.

[124]Eng. MS. 370, f. 54a, JRULM.

[125]William Button (see letter 31).

[126]*Evangelical Magazine*.

[127]**John Eyre** (1754-1803), Anglican clergyman at Homerton and one of the first editors of the *Evangelical Magazine*.

you on the Subject I shall conclude you are offended at the alterations I made in your last favour.

"Whatsoever thy Hand finds to do" &c never struck me more forcibly than of late. Death does not limit his attacks to the aged and infirm. At Woburn, young Dover, who used to be at M[r] John Butfield's,[128] has lately gone off very suddenly. You have doubtless heard of M[r] Humphrey's[129] decease, at Daventry, in the midst of usefulness & comfort, after very few days illness.

The sudden & severe changes of weather, affect most people here, and myself with a slight sore throat. M[rs] G. desires you to accept her cordial respects & best wishes. I am,

Dear Sir,

Yours affectionately in Xt.

Sam.[l] Greatheed

P.S. I inclose 1 1/2 Guinea, and when you find a convenient Opportunity you may send me another of Carey's Enquiries, & make up the Charges, but for this there is no hurry.

49. Archibald McLean,[130] Edinburgh, to John Brown,[131] Wigan, 10 June 1795.[132]

---

[128]Unidentified. He may have been a relation of William Butfield (d. 1776), who served for many years as the Baptist minister at Thorn, Bedfordshire, where he was succeeded by Robert Faulkner (see letter 34). Butfield was a boyhood friend of Edmund Botsford (see letter 33). See Charles D. Mallary, *Memoirs of Elder Edmund Botsford* (Charleston: W. Riley, 1832) 15-17.

[129]Possibly the Rev. Samuel Humphreys, Anglican minister at Daventry. See *Universal British Directory*, 2:772,

[130]**Archibald McLean** (1733-1812), a leader among the Scotch Baptists.

[131]A number of Browns figure in the early Baptist history of Wigan. This particular Mr. Brown was involved with a group of believers who had been meeting with an Independent congregation in Wigan but had recently (as this letter suggests) to the influence of McLean, developed Baptist convictions. In 1796 this group would begin meeting in a room in Brick Kiln Lane and, with the encouragement of John Hirst of Bacup (see letter 12) and James Hargreaves of Bolton, organized into a Baptist church later that year. They would not have a pastor until 1803 (William Wrathall of Skipton), at which time a chapel was built in Lord Street. Later the church moved to Scarisbrick Street, where it remains to this day. McLean's correspondent in this letter may be the same John Brown in Wigan who was listed as a bookseller in Mill Gate in Holden's 1811 *Directory*. See *Holden's Triennial Directory* (2 vols. London: W. Holden, 1811); Ian Sellers, "Other Times, Other Ministries: John Fawcett and Alexander McLaren," *Baptist Quarterly* 32 (1987-1988): 9.

[132]Eng. MS. 370, f. 79, JRULM.

Dear B.ʳ

I just now received yours, and have sent you 2 Copies of the Im-
portᵉ of Baptism.¹³³ I have published nothing of late

M.ʳ Jones¹³⁴ wrote me lately from Liverpool, and informed me of
some addition to the church at Chester; but said nothing of the sickness
which has been among them. I hope they are all now recovered; and I
am also glad to hear that you are so far recovered. We have lately been
deprived of three of our members by death. One of them was killed by
the fall of a wall, while he was assisting in extinguishing a fire which
happened last week. He has left a wife and two children. He was a most
amiable christian, and is regretted by every body that knew him. These
instances of our mortality ought to have a suitable effect upon us, that
we may so number our days as to apply our hearts unto wisdom. The
rest of us are much in our ordinary way, tho' never all well at once. I
have enjoyed a pretty good state of health since I saw you last. I hope
you and the rest at Wigan are well, and continuing in unity and love. Mʳ
Jones writes me that he could wish to have you all settled at Liverpool,
if providence should favour it in other respects. This would surely contribute to your comfort & edification.

Give my love to the brethren with you, and believe that I am Dear
Bʳ

Yours with sincere affection
Arch.ᵈ McLean

Edin.ʳ June 10ᵗʰ 1795

50. William Bull, Newport Pagnell, to John Sutcliff, Olney, 13 February 1796.¹³⁵

Sat. even'g Feb.ʸ 13—96

My dear Sir

I sent for Mʳ Couch this morn'g & conversed with him near an hour
on the nature of settlements & learn there two things,

1) if there is any *real estate* there must of necessity be a Trustee otherwise the estate will go to the heirs at law of the husband,

---

¹³³McLean's *A Defence of Believer-Baptism, in Opposition to Infant Sprinkling: In
a Letter to a Friend. Being an Answer to a Pamphlet, entitled, Remarks on Scripture
Texts Relating to Infant Baptism* (Liverpool: W. Jones, n.p.).

¹³⁴**William Jones** (1762-1846), McLean's Liverpool publisher and a prominent
Scotch Baptist layman, writer, and periodical editor.

¹³⁵Eng. MS. 369, f.19b, JRULM.

2) the particulars of the personal estate must be named & the several securities of the estate in the deed,

3) *there may be an article in the deed, whereby the parties* while both are yet living, may revoke the first deed of settlement & make a new one if circumstances should render it desireable

4) that said Trustee shall have no power to act while the parties are both living, I have desired Couch to wait on you on Monday morn'g, therefore keep in the way

My own opinion is, that the parties ought to take each others solemn promise, (or else not come together) about the *personal* estate, & as to the *real*, to have a Trustee & a settlement—with a reserved power to revoke the first deed of settlement, & make a new one, at any time hereafter, if the parties should be both agreed so to act—this will guard against every inconveniency arising from the death of the Trustee or any change in his temper—circumstances—or situation,

I am Sir
your faithfull & affectionate
Bro.ʳ & Serv.ᵗ
W. Bull

51. William Rogers,[136] *Philadelphia, to unnamed correspondent [Thomas Williams*[137]*], London, 27 February 1796.*[138]

Phil.ᵃ Feb.ʸ 27. 1796

My dear Sir,

On the 22.ᵈ ult: I wrote to the Rev. M.ʳ Button, by the Sally, Cap.ᵗ Weaks, in which I enclosed N.º 1. of a bill of exchange for £32 Sterl.ᵍ— £20 of which I requested him, on receiving, to pay into the hand of M.ʳ John Gill[139]—and the remaining £12 to keep untill further orders—I hope the whole has gotten safe to London. I now forward N.º 2 of the same tenor to date, which be so obliging as to deliver yourself to Mʳ Button.—

In my letter to him I mentioned the unwearied pains I took in order to find out the Box, which your agreeable favor of Oct.ʳ 26. 95. authorized me to expect from him—I have enquired & searched a number of

[136]**William Rogers** (1751-1824), pastor of the First Baptist church in Philadelphia (1772-1775) and Professor of Oratory and English literature at the College of Philadelphia (and later the University of Pennsylvania), 1789-1811.

[137]**Thomas Williams** (1755-1839), London Calvinistic preacher (Independent), writer, and bookseller.

[138]Eng. MS. 371, f. 105, JRULM.

[139]Baptist minister at St. Albans (see letter 45).

times since the Sally sailed—*but in vain*!—A Disappointment indeed!—
as I very much want to see the Historic Defence,[140] with the pamphlets
you mention—the Box certainly could never have been sent, or I must
have come by this time to some knowledge of it—I greatly hope now,
when it does arrive, that I shall find the Vol.ˢ put into blue boards, as
this will save me very considerable trouble—I would just inform you
here that your esteemed favor came to hand Janʸ 14, nearly 3 months
after date—When the Historic defence arrives I will in your name

---

[140]Thomas Williams, *An Historic Defence of Experimental Religion; in which the Doctrine of Divine Influences is Supported by the Authority of Scripture, and the Experience of the Wisest and Best Men in all Ages and Countries*, 2 vols. (London: T. Heptinstall and William Button, 1795). See also William Rogers of Philadelphia to William Button, 24 Paternoster Row, London ("fav.d by Cap.t Tillinghast of the Ship Amiable"), 3 July 1799:

Dear S.ʳ
    The 24.ᵗʰ ult.º I wrote to our common friend M.ʳ Williams, begging him to call on you & enquire into the cause of Bunyan's pilgrim &c not being sent me—from 6 to 8 Ships have lately arrived in our Port directly from London, & not a line even, from you or any others of my Correspondence—what can be the matter?
    This goes by Cap.ᵗ Tillinghast of the Ship Amiable, a Gentleman with whom I am particularly acquainted & who on his return will take charge of any thing for me—I wrote to you by him Dec.ʳ 7.ᵗʰ last—to which letter I beg leave to refer you—in that letter I solicited certain information &c—
    Can you, or will you solicit D.ʳ Rippon to send me his 2.ᵈ <u>vol.</u> of the Bapt. Reg.ʳ to correspond with my 1.ˢᵗ, which is 1/2 bound with a red leather back. The 15.ᵗʰ n.º has my portrait—the D.ʳ says a *correct* one—so say not, those who know me—M.ʳˢ Rogers & some of my female friends feel somewhat mortifyed—but it is all *vanity*!—My family *now* are thro' mercy tolerably well, M.ʳˢ Rogers unites in Christian love to Self, M.ʳˢ Button, M.ʳ Williams &c—
Affectionately your's,
W.ᵐ Rogers

(MS. Montagu d. 15, f. 252 (r. and v.), Bodleian Library, Oxford)

present a Copy to the respectable library of Phil.ᵃ[141]—& another to that of R. Island College.[142]

I shall use my endeavors to prevent a republication of it in this City—but this I am fearful will be a difficult task as "Self Interest here, as in Europe, is the governing passion still"—the 2.ᵈ part of Paine's Age of Reason[143] has not, to my knowledge, yet arrived in America—It need not be worse than the 1ˢᵗ p.ᵗ—If it be, it must be devilish indeed!—Dont fail in sending me the 2.ᵈ part of the age of infidelity.

You may have a small view of my thoughts respecting the Missionary Society by perusing a short preface to the enclosed Acc.ᵗ of the Same, extracted from the Baptist Reg.ʳ—M.ʳ Ustick[144] thought a few words addressed to the American Reader necessary, & I undertook to give them.

I feel myself highly flattered in what you intimate relative to your 2.ᵈ Vol.—but why profess yourself under such a weight of obligation to me!—I cannot divine what I have done to merit such a compliment—as it is paid, accept my thanks therefore, but be assured, it might have been dedicated to a thousand other persons whose influence in spreading so valuable a publication ought principally to have been considered.—

In general it is a very dead time among our churches in the middle States of America, & for ought I know to the contrary, in the Eastern & Southern States likewise—Oh for the outpourings of Jehovah's Spirits—

---

[141]The Library Company of Philadelphia, the oldest lending library in America, was founded by Benjamin Franklin and several other leading citizens of Philadelphia in 1731. The library was located on Fifth Street, between Chesnut and Walnut Streets, adjacent to the State House Square, and opposite the Philosophical Society. By 1793 the library had become the model for the soon to be instituted Library of Congress. Among its members in the 1780s and '90s were ten signers of the Declaration of Independence, including Robert Morris, Benjamin Rush, and Thomas McKean. The library owned some 15,000 volumes in 1794, of which only about 5000 were available to the general public.

[142]Rhode Island College, now Brown University, was founded by William Staughton, a former student at Bristol Academy, in 1764. A copy of Williams's *Historic Defence* is still owned by the library of Brown University (shelfmark CE W67) and bears the following inscription: "In testimony of persevering regard, this excellent defence of experimental religion, consisting of 2 vols., is presented for the library of Brown University, State of R. Island. By Wm. Rogers. Univʸ of Pennsa. Octʳ 16. 1805." I am indebted to Dr. Bruce Graver of Providence College for this inscription.

[143]Thomas Paine (1737-1809), radical political writer, was most famous for the publication of *Rights of Man*, in two parts (1791, 1792). The work referred to here is his *Age of Reason*, of which Part 1 appeared in 1794 and Part 2 in 1795.

[144]**Thomas Ustick** (1753-1803), senior pastor at Philadelphia's First Baptist Church, 1782-1803.

The time to favor Zion, if I understand the Scriptures, certainly draweth nigh—let us pray for this auspicious event—how happy will our world then be compared with what it now is!

What increasing esteem I subscribe myself, very dear Sir, your's most affectionately,

Wm Rogers

P.S. Please to present my Christian love to M.ʳ Button & show him this hasty scrawl. Do you know the Rev. Morgan J. Rhees[145]—he was married last Monday Evening to a young Lady of our Society, of pleasing prospects as to fortune.—The portrait of the Presid.ᵗ of the U. S.[146] is called an exact likeness.

52. Samuel Pearce, Birmingham, to Samuel Etheridge,[147] Bullion Office, Bank of England, London, 20 April 1796.[148]

Dear Sir

By a Letter from Broʳ Fuller to Mʳ King, (Treasurer to the Mission Socʸ)[149] which Mʳˢ K. put into my hands yesterday, I find, that you have kindly advanced £70 on the Society's behalf, & which Mʳ Fuller desires may be remitted to you without delay. This wᵈ most certainly have been done by this days post, had Mʳ King been at home' but as he is out on a Journey, I hope it will not prove inconvenient to you to wait 3 or 4 days longer—He is fully expected to return by next Saturday at farthest, & *then* you may depend on a remittance. I thought it necessary to say thus much, lest you shᵈ suspect that your kind advance had not been acknowledged wʰ the speed it undoubtedly demands.

I hope you & Mʳˢ E. are preserved in the sweetest enjoyment of evangelical hopes & pleasures. The affliction of your good Lady makes this peculiarly desirable, for when flesh & heart fail, it is *GOD* alone who can strengthen the heart, and support the sinking spirits of our feeble nature.

Most affectionately so I embrace this opportunity of acknowledging the pious satisfaction I enjoyed in your Society when last in Town—My

[145]**Morgan Rhees [Rhys]** (1760-1804), Welsh Baptist who emigrated to Pennsylvania in 1794.

[146]George Washington.

[147]**Samuel Etheridge**, deacon at the Baptist meeting at Little Prescot Street, Goodman's Fields, London.

[148]MAM PLP 81.63.1, JRULM.

[149]**Thomas King** (1755-1831), deacon at Cannon Street in Birmingham and treasurer of the BMS.

agreeable interviews w^h you on earth have enlarged my prospects of celestial pleasures, where our communion shall neither be damped by affliction, nor interrupted by local removals.

Dear bro^r Savage[150] is gone to glory before us; "but thro the grace of our Lord Jesus Xt we hope to be saved even as he." I was much affected w^h the news of his death, not only on my own acc^t, & the acc^t of the Society he so much befriended, but on your acc^t also. In our path thro life, tho we meet w^h so many travellers, & we hope w^h many who are going to Zion w^h their faces thitherward; yet, it is not often that we meet w^h men, whose openness of mind, steadiness of attachment, & spirituality of temper, invite our friendship w^h such force & sweetness as our departed Friends—What a mercy, my dear Sir, that we have *one friend who never leaves us nor forsakes us*! To *him*, I trust, we commend each other in our warmest devotions, that guided by his counsel we may at length meet in Glory.

Dear bro^r Swain[151] is also removed—my heart bleeds w^h his flock, his family, & his friends. There are not many such men of God in Israel. I knew him intimately, & felt an unusual oneness of Soul w^h him—but we must submit—The Lord is righteous in all his ways. Ever yours in the indissoluble bonds of grace

S. Pearce

Birmingham Ap^l 20th –96

53. Benjamin Flower,[152] Cambridge, to Alexander Kilham,[153] Sheffield, 23 October 1797.[154]

Cambridge   Oct. 23. 1797.

Dear Sir

In reply to your Favour I transmit you on the other side a copy of the letter you mention, and I fear I must give it to the public together with the resolutions referred to, and which are not other than those figured by Dr Coke[155] and Mr Bradburn[156] Leeds Aug 1797. but which

---

[150]**James Savage**, the BMS's India House counselor.

[151]**Joseph Swain** (1761-1796), minister at the Baptist meeting at Walworth.

[152]**Benjamin Flower** (1755-1829), radical editor of the *Cambridge* Intelligencer, 1793 to 1803.

[153]**Alexander Kilham** (1762-1798), founder of the Methodist New Connection in 1797.

[154]Methodist Archives, Alexander Kilham Correspondence, JRULM.

[155]**Thomas Coke** (1747-1814), John Wesley's assistant and leader among the Methodists in England and America.

really have nothing to do with the famous resolution about "Sedition and the Established Church," and I wish entirely to avoid any dissention respecting the interior management of religious societies which those resolutions more particularly refer to.

I have already brought on myself some ill will and the charges of partiality, and making myself a party man in the controversy now carrying on amongst the Methodists. To get rid of the charge of Partiality I must publish the note of the Lover of Truth, to let the public see I was justified in my remarks. As to the other charges I regard them not. In this age of extreme degeneracy, (I fear of all sects that have yet a name) I earnestly wish there could be found a party of honest enquirers after Truth, who have no other views in their enquiry, that they may be made thereby wiser and better, more intimately acquainted with their own characters, as they appear in the sight of God, and more ardently concerned for the welfare of all mankind. Such a party I hope I am willing to declare myself in favour of let it be called by any name, which either a great or a little man may please, as the whim or caprice or just judgment of mankind may direct. Names are nothing, but the Reality is all in all.

I sent a paper with my Remarks on the letter of the "Lover of Truth," directed to Mr Bradburn, I want to get at his *conscience*. As to Dr Coke, and all the ministers of the Church of England, to a man, I have charged them so repeatedly and in such plain home language of Prevarication and Prying, that I have nothing more to say to them. I know not whether you have seen what I have said on these subjects in my Remarks on the French Constitution, and in the "Necessity of a Reformation in Church and State," a £6/8vo both Editions published in '92; and "National Sins considered in Letters to the Revd T. Robinson of Leicester &c" a 2/6 pamphlet published 96.[157] If you will inform me how I can send you these or if I can leave them for you in London I shall request your acceptance of them. I will likewise thank you to inform me where the Methodist Monitor[158] is printed in London.

---

[156]**Samuel Bradburn** (1751-1816), one of the leading Methodist itinerant ministers of his day.

[157]The two works mentioned here from Benjamin Flower's pen are (1) *The French Constitution: With Remarks on Some of its Principal Articles: in which their Importance in a Political, Moral and Religious Point of View is Illustrated: and the Necessity of a Reformation in Church and State in Great Britain, Enforced* (1792); and (2) *National Sins Considered, in Two Letters to the Rev. Thomas Robinson on his Serious Exhortation to the Inhabitants of Great Britain with Reference to the Past . . . to which are added a Letter from Rev. Robert Hall, to the Rev. Charles Simeon, and the Reflections on War, by the late Rev. W. Law* (Cambridge, 1796). Robinson was the vicar of St. Mary's, Leicester.

[158]The *Methodist Monitor*, a periodical published by Kilham.

With respect to the second Letter in the *Courier*,[159] I have my doubts whether it would be proper to publish it. It only confirms what was in the former Letter, and refers to Letters & resolutions which were I not to insert, would have the appearance of partiality. I think I had better now leave the adresse[e] party to attack what I have already said or to answer the first letter. If they do not think the triumph on the side of the Rights of Conscience, and of the Rights of Man, is *complete*, so far as relates to the Controversy in my paper. I can not help remarking, that if Priestcraft had not deeply insituated itself, or rather did it not form a part of the essence of the souls of some people, they could not bear the strong language I used respecting Dr Coke or the insinuation respecting Mr Bradburn without a reply. You mention in your letter that the above party "are now obliged to fly to the secular arm to defend their plan." Does this allude to the resolution at Leeds, or to any particulars of their Conduct? If the latter I must wish to be informed of it, as anything of the kind, I would be sure to inform the public of thro' the medium of my paper, which notwithstanding the new duty, has still an extensive circulation amongst I believe all sects and parties from the High Churchman, to the lowest Unitarian. Dr Priestley has a set sent him to America by every conveyance.

I have only to add, that it is my sincere wish, that the *principles* on which your new societies profess to act, may be preserved *inviolate*, for I am persuaded that it is only in proportion as they are so, that pure vital christianity as taught by the precepts and example of our common Lord & Master can possibly flourish or spread

Y^rs Respectfully
B Flower

On the back is a copy of the letter to Flower by "A Lover of Truth":[160]

---

[159]A London newspaper.

[160]In his editorial in the *Intelligencer* on 14 October 1797, Flower noted that he had received the letter from "A Lover of Truth" charging Kilham with propagating "falsehood and miresspresentation" in his article titled "The Methodists," which appeared in the *Intelligencer* on 30 September 1797 under the *nom de plume* "Philanthropus." In his letter, Kilham leveled serious charges at the Methodist leaders, primarily Dr. Coke and Samuel Bradburn, who had expelled him from the Methodist leadership for his "seditious" activities and writings, including what would soon become an issue the leadership could not avoid—the reality that many Methodists had, in fact, already become dissenters. He writes, "Ought not the [Methodist] Conference to define what they mean by 'holding and propagating opinions inimical to the Civil Government and established Religion of the Country.' Are the proceedings of the Methodist Conference, and their measures in the different circuits which they reveal, every way agreeable to the established Religion of this Nation? Are they not as much Dissenters as any sect in the Kingdom? If they refute 'connection and fellowship' to all who are inimical to the National Church, must they not dismiss a

Sir,

    Lately reading in your instructive and useful paper of the 29th of Sept. an address to the people called Methodists; I was much concerned at the falshood [sic] and misrepresentation with which that address is replete. The author either wants information or integrity, or both. As the following address will fully evince⁺ the readiness of the Conference to meet the wishes of the people in every thing consistent with the preservation of the beautiful Structure of Methodism; and as you are no less the patron of Truth and Justice than of Religious liberty; I doubt not but you will have the goodness to insert the address as soon as possible.

A Lover of Truth

+Address to the Methodist Societies
dated—Leeds Aug. 7. '97, signed by Dr C. & M^r B— [161]

P.S. Altho' I am obliged to insist on postage from the common herd of writers, or I should be ruined both in time & money, but I never expect it from a private correspondent whose letters I at all think worth reading. Your Letters will be always welcome, & I shall expect to pay the postage of them in future *myself.*

54. Samuel Kilpin,[162] Bedford, to John Sutcliff, Olney, 27 January 1798.[163]

---

great part of their body? And if they expel all who will not reverence the establishment, must they not expel a great number of the traveling preachers? If dissenting from the Church of England 'disturb the public weal,' and be a 'nursery of Sedition,' are not they among the first in the Nation who ought to be expelled from holding fellowship and connection with the truly pious, of every denomination?" Flower writes in his editorial on 14 October that he will not print the letter from "A Lover of Truth" because the writer has not "proved his charge" against Kilham. To Flower, Kilham was correct in his observations, noting that "since Mr. Wesley's death the societies have been governed by a kind of arbitrary, 'Dutch Aristocracy;' and we find that this Aristocracy, perceiving the eyes of the Methodists to be opening, now profess—"They are willing to make, (to use their own words) 'considerable sacrifices in respect to authority,' and to give up the greatest part of their Executive Government.' That is," Flower contends, "like Executive Governments of another description, *they keep the power from the people as long as they can in their own hands, and when they can hold it no longer, most graciously resign a part, to retain the rest.*" Though Flower tells Kilham in the above letter that, out of fairness to his Methodist readers, he intends to publish in the *Intelligencer* the letter by "A Lover of Truth" and some other documents relating to the controversy, he never did.

    ¹⁶¹Rev. Coke and Bradburn.

Dear Sir

I intend being at Olney God willing on Wednesday next on my Road to Newport and if agreeable will preach in the Even^g   I expect that some of my Cousins from Newport will meet me at Olney & if they do I must return with them to Newport that Night. The People at Ridgmount have given me an Invitation to settle amongst them but I dont see any prospect of being happy I wish to consult with you on the Business.

Father & Mother desire their respects to yourself & Mrs Sutcliff. I am quite well though weary & subscribe myself

Y^r f^d

S Kilpin

Bedford Jany 27. 1798.

---

55. Joshua Toulmin, Taunton, to unnamed correspondent, 29 January 1798.[164]

Dear Sir

Your polite Favour, enclosing a Bank post Bill for Mrs Morris,[165] to the amount of Five Pounds, was delivered *last* Night, after ten oclock.

This circumstance, together with the fatigue of three services, which I always very sensibly feel, will be admitted as an apology for my not acknowledging the receipt of it by this mornings post.

I beg the Trustees for the distribution of the Profits of the Evangelical Magazine to accept my thanks for their kindness to Mrs Morris, & their handsome attention to my Suit on her behalf.

I think myself obliged & honoured by "the Sentiments of personal regard" with which you favour me: and can not but consider this as expressive of your candour & liberality of mind; giving you a claim on my esteem & gratitude. I am

Revd Sir,

Your obed^t h'ble Ser^t:

Joshua Toulmin

Taunton. 29 Jan^y: 1798

---

[162]**Samuel Kilpin** (d.1830), student at Bristol Academy and later minister of the Baptist congregation at Church Street, Exeter.

[163]Eng. MS. 370, f. 72, JRULM.

[164]Eng. MS. 344, f. 70, JRULM.

[165]Probably the wife of Thomas Morris, a printer and bookseller in Taunton. See *Universal British Directory*, 4:588.

56. Joseph Hughes,[166] Northampton, to John Sutcliff, Olney, 26 February 1798.[167]

Dear Sir

    I feel myself obliged by your invitation but shall probably be in Town before you receive this note—-& cannot therefore, at the present season, enjoy the pleasure of an Olney visit—I beg to be respectfully remembered to M[r] Horne[168]—& tho unknown to M[rs] Sutcliffe—-I remain—

yours with esteem
J Hughes

Northampton
Feb: 26—1798

57. Samuel Pearce, Northampton, to William Summers,[169] 98 New Bond Street, London, 12 July 1798.[170]

Northampton July 12.th 98

    Blessed be God that he hath again wrought deliverance for the partner of my very dear Friend & put a new song into All our mouths—Happy sh.[d] I be to witness the grateful devotion of your amiable Family but many things forbid our going by way of the Metropolis to Plym.[h]—I now hope to see you soon & therefore have the less concern to tell you all the Whys & Wherefores of my plan in this letter—You shall know all when w meet

    The Plan Itself is this

Next Lords day—July	15—-I preach here
	16—-Return to Birm.
	18—-Go to Bristol
	19—to Exeter
	20—to Plymouth
Lords Day	22

---

[166]**Joseph Hughes** (1769-1833), Baptist minister at Battersea and one of the founders and secretaries of the Religious Tract Society (1799) and the British and Foreign Bible Society (1804).

[167]Eng. MS. 370, f. 67, JRULM.

[168]**Melville Horne** (1761-1841), Anglican clergyman who played a prominent role in the beginnings of the missionary movement in England in the late eighteenth and early nineteenth centuries.

[169]**William Summers**, close friend and correspondent of Samuel Pearce.

[170]Eng. MS. 371, f. 97, JRULM.

d°		27 Spend at Plymouth or its neighbor-hood
d°	Augst—	3
		5—Return to Exeter
		6 —to Bristol
Lords day		10—Preach at Bristol or its neighbor-hood—perhaps at Uley if you c.^{d} meet me there but I cannot promise till I have seen Dr Ryland
		12—Go to Oxford
		14—Preach at the opening of a meet.^{g} there
		15—Return again to "that *dear hut* our home."

Meet me as soon as you can—if possible at Plymouth for my Father[171] is really anxious to entertain you & enjoy your company—But write me as soon as you have fixed your plan—Perhaps you c.^{d} send by Saturday's post so as to meet me at Birm. Our love to yours & you.—

S. Pearce

58. Samuel Greatheed,[172] Newport Pagnell, to [Thomas] Williams, 2 Foy Place, [Henton], near London, 30 October 1798.[173]

Newport Pagnel, 30 Oct. 1798

Dear Sir,

Accept my warmest thanks for the Care and trouble you have taken in circulating the Addresses to so many associated Bodies of Religious people. May the lord unite all their hearts more to himself and to each other by the means used to promote that great end!

---

[171]William Pearce, a watchmaker in Plymouth. See *Universal British Directory*, 4:269.

[172]Greatheed (see letter 48), along with Samuel Hillyard of Bedford and William Bull of Newport Pagnell, helped found the Bedfordshire Union of Christians in September 1797. In Greatheed's *Address* (most likely the work referred to in the above letter) delivered on 31 October at the Old Meeting, he commented: "Surely it is time that the keen edge of bigotry, which has so long mangled and separated the members of Christ's body, should be taken off for ever. What are the points of difference between real Christians, compared with the greatness of those objects in which we all agree." See H. G. Tibbutt, *Bunyan Meeting Bedford 1650-1950* (Bedford: Trustees of Bunyan Meeting, [1950]) 48-49.

[173]Eng. MS. 370, f. 54b, JRULM.

By a letter from brother Eyre this Morning I find that the Business of preparing the Address for a more extensive Circulation with the Evangelical Magazine devolves also into your hands. Conscious that they are sufficiently full already, I can only say that I feel the greater obligation on the Account for your attention to an Object which I have so much at heart, and shall be very glad to embrace any opportunity of rendering you a similar Service.

My Brethren who have united in this part of the Country are desirous of having the Address in its Octavo Form printed as nearly as possible uniform with the Sermon,[174] and the report of our Proceedings (which is in the same Type with the Sermon), that these, and any other paper we may have occasion to print, may the better bind together in a Volume. I have too little experience in printing to judge precisely how many Octavo pages the Address will fill upon the same letter and paper with the Sermon, but I suppose it cannot exceed twelve.

I am not aware of more than one error which escaped in printing the former Copies. It is in page 4. There ought to be no paragraph between "may present." & "It seems," but a short break, like those in the 16th & 22d lines, between "formed.—It is obvious," and "frustrated.—It appears."

If it will be of use to save room, no spaces need be left between any of the paragraphs.

Should you meet with any difficulty be so kind as to inform me of it by post. Every incidental Expense, with that of postage already incurred, I will either defray, when next in town, or Mr Reyner[175] will, whenever applied to. When the Charge of printing is ascertained, and communicated to me, I will direct Mr Foster our Treasurer[176] to defray it.

The hurry of the Missionary publications obliges me to postpone at present any attempt to bring forward the Cause of Union in the Christian Spectator, but I shall gladly avail myself of your hint the first leisure I can find for the purpose.

It gave me pleasure to learn from my friend Fuller that you have undertaken the good work of replying to Mr Belsham's Review of

---

[174]Greatheed's *General Union Recommended to Real Christians in a Sermon Preached at Bedford, October 31, 1797* (1798) was printed by Thomas Conder, one of London's leading dissenting printers and booksellers. It was reviewed in the *Evangelical Magazine* 6 (1798): 128-129.

[175]**Joseph Reyner** (1754/5-1837), a successful London cotton importer and shipper and supporter of numerous religious societies.

[176]**John Foster** of Biggleswade (1765-1847), a prosperous merchant and prominent Baptist layman.

Wilberforce.[177] I am provoked at the impudence of the Socinians in assuming that Scriptural Criticism is on their side. I have critically attended to the various readings of the New Testament, and more particularly of the Epistles, and know the reverse to be true, except in the single Instance of I John 5: 7, which is unquestionably spurious. I mentioned Mr. Fuller as Authority that I think would appear with advantage in replying to Mr B.s dogmatical assertions. It is that of the great Michaelis and the passage is quoted in the Review of Marsh's Translation of that incomparable Critic's Introduction to the New Testament.[178] Evang.¹ Magazine, March 1794 p. 126, 127. I take this Opportunity of pointing it out to you, in case Mʳ F. should omit doing so.

It will give m pleasure to hear from you on any subject.

Believe me

Very sincerely and affectionately

Yours

Sam.¹ Greatheed

59. William Carey, Mudnabatty, Bengal, to Ann Hobson[179] at Mr. W. Hobson's, Cottesbrooke, Northampton, 27 November 1798.[180]

---

[177]The devout Evangelical William Wilberforce (1759-1833) led the movement in parliament from 1787 to 1807 to abolish the slave trade throughout the British Empire. He was beloved by most dissenters for his position on this issue. Many dissenters, however, divided with Wilberforce over his refusal to repeal the Test and Corporation Acts when it came before parliament in 1787, 1789, and 1790, as well as his support of the war with France. The work referred to in the above letter is Wilberforce's *A Practical View of the Prevailing Religious System of Professed Christians in the Higher and Middle Classes of this Country Contrasted with Real Christianity* (1797). Thomas Belsham, the Unitarian minister at Gravel Pit, Hackney, responded to Wilberforce's book with *A Review of Mr. Wilberforce's Treatise, entitled A Practical View of the Prevailing Religious System of Professed Christians, &c. In Letters to a Lady* (1798). Thomas Williams then responded to Belsham's review with *A Vindication of the Calvinistic Doctrines of Human Depravity, the Atonement, Divine Influences, &c: In a Series of Letters to the Rev. T. Belsham, Occasioned by his "Review of Mr. Wilberforce's Treatise" with an Appendix Addressed to the Author of "Letters on Hereditary Depravity"* (1799).

[178]*Introduction to the New Testament* (Cambridge, 1793) by Johann David Michaelis (1717-1791), translated by Herbert Marsh (1757-1839).

[179]**Ann Carey** (b. 1763), William Carey's sister, married William Hobson, a Cottisbrooke farmer. Both she and her younger sister, **Mary Carey**, were ardent supporters of Carey's work in India.

[180]Raffles Handlist, fasc. 40, f. 8, JRULM. The calendar of the Raffles Handlist denotes this letter as being written to Mary Carey, but it would appear that it was actually written to Ann Hobson—note the reference to "Polly" in the letter, the appellation used by Carey when referring to Mary, not Ann; also note the reference to Mr. Hobson near the end of the letter. For a similar letter by Carey to his sisters

Mudnabatty 27 Nov[r] 1798

My Dear Sister

I just snatch an Hour after the Family are gone to rest and it is almost Midnight, to write you a short Letter, and you must be contented with a short one (for I have so much exceeded all bounds in some which I have written, and which you will see, or the substance of them, that I have no time left, nor any thing to say.)

No one expects me to write about experience, or any of the common topics of Religion; nor to say any thing about the Doctrines of the Gospel, but News, and continual accounts of marvellous things are expected from me. I have however no news to send, and as every thing here is the same, no Marvels.

What then shall I say? That I and my Family are in good Health and spirits.[181] This is true, and you will undoubtedly be glad to hear it. (M[r] & M[rs] Short[182] are returned to England.) Our two eldest sons are very great stout Lads and the other two very fine Boys indeed.[183] You would be much diverted to hear them carry on their discourses, their Play, and every thing in the Bengal Language. These however are little things.

Both M[r] Fountain[184] and myself often Preach; sometimes with considerable pleasure, and often with as great Pain. We have had pleasing hopes blasted, our impatient minds almost ready to fret at our want of Success, and at best we scarcely expect to be any thing more than Pioneers to prepare the Way for those who coming after us may be more useful than we have been. I know success depends entirely upon the blessing of God, and therefore in him I will trust and not be afraid.

The principal thing we see is the translation of the Bible into the Bengal Language.[185] This is now in considerable forwardness, and I expect will be finished in the next year, if God continue Health, and other requisite abilities: nor do I think that we are entirely without Seals to our Ministry, tho it is a difficult thing to say any thing confidently.

---

shortly before he died, see "A 'Carey' Letter of 1831," *Baptist Quarterly* 9 (1938-1939): 239-241.

[181]Carey appears to make a gracious reference here to his wife, Dorothy, whose mental deterioration began shortly after Carey's arrival in Bengal. As George Smith notes in his biography of Carey, "Never did reproach or complaint escape his lips regarding either her or Thomas, whose eccentric impulses and oft-darkened spirit were due to mania." See George Smith, *Life of William Carey* (London: J. M. Dent, 1909) 135.

[182]**Charles Short**, William Carey's brother-in-law (see letter 70).

[183]Carey's sons at this time were Felix (b. 1785), William (b. 1788), **Jabez** (b. 1793), and Jonathan (b. 1796).

[184]**John Fountain** (1766-1800), BMS missionary to India.

[185]Carey's Bengali New Testament appeared in 1801; the Old Testament wasn't completed until 1809.

Polly writes in the old complaining style. If she continues it much longer no one will believe her in earnest, it will appear like a Lesson got by Heart. What shall I say to her. Has she no reason to rejoice, can she look back on all that God has done for her, and not be ashamed of complaining. No doubt but some, or much evil remains, but is all that God has done from the first day till now, to be buried in forgetfulness, or smothered under the remains of Sin—No. Give to God the glory due to his name, and give thanks at the remembrance of his Holiness—I could complain too, but the worst of it is, no body believes a Word I say when I do that, or if they do, or say they do, never condole with or try to comfort me. I have therefore nearly left off complaining to Men, and wish to be more serious in Groaning and Prayers to my God.

I have written to my Father,[186] and intend to write to my Brother tomorrow. I have written more than once to him and he is much on my Heart. I hope he will be enabled to fill up the station in which he is in a Christian like manner.

Brother Hobson must always understand that what I say to you, I say to him; my Letters contain no secrets, but I mean them for your whole Family. Give my Love to the Children, and to Thomas's Children too.[187] Poor Children I often feel an aching Heart for them—

Is Mr Perfect living, give my respects to him. I have sent a Quantity of Seeds to Mr Pearce of Birmingham, and mentioned Mr Perfect as a proper Person to get some of them. I dare say he will send some.

Give my Love to all the Ministers, to Mr James[188] & John Hobson with their Spouses—and to all with whom I was acquainted. Do you ever see any of Moulton Friends, if you see them, or any of them, give my kindest Xtian Love to them, especially Mr Trushes[?], Dore, Mrs [P?], or indeed any other. How does Mr Sherman.[189] I still hope God will recover

---

[186]Edmund Carey of Paulerspury, Northamptonshire, Carey's father, was a handloom weaver and occasional schoolmaster who ardently supported Carey's work in India (see letter 95).

[187]Carey's brother, Thomas (b. 1768), was the father of Eustace Carey, who later served as a BMS missionary in India.

[188]John James joined the Baptist church in Olney on April 1782 and became a deacon on 23 March 1809. He died on 12 October 1814, aged 56. He was buried near Sutcliff on the church cemetery. He was also a subscriber to the BMS in 1800-1801 (£1.1) and 1804-1805, submitting £2.2 to Sutcliff's collection that year. See "List of Persons Dead Among the Congregation of Dissenting Baptists in Olney, Bucks 1775-1835" (MS., Angus Library, Regent's Park College, Oxford) f. 27; Olney Church Book, 1752-1854 (MS., Angus Library, Regent's Park College, Oxford) ff. 43, 101; *Periodical Accounts*, 2:205; 3:139.

[189]**Edward Sharman** ministered at the Moulton church in the 1790s after Carey's removal to Leicester. Apparently, he was out of the ministry by 1798, though he does appear in letter 79.

him out of the snare of the Devil, and this is the effect of real Love to his Soul, which I fear is in an awfully forlorn State

Your affect^e Bro^r

W. Carey

60. Samuel Greatheed, Newport Pagnell, to John Sutcliff, Olney, 6 December 1798.[190]

Dear Brother,

I transmit to you the Minutes of the Conference at [Ampthill] in 1797, by desire of Mr Livius,[191] who will be obliged to you for letting Mr Horne[192] have them as soon as you can, with directions to return them to Bedford by the earliest opportunity after he has read them.

I think you may promise yourself much pleasure from the perusal. To see Good Men of various descriptions and from distant situations confessing and corresponding upon the foundation of their hope & the Source of their Comfort and communicating mutual advice and encouragement suited to their different Circumstances, affords some similitude of the Communion we hope fully to enjoy with them hereafter, when all Error being done away there shall be no hindrance to the completeness of our fellowship with Christ & all his people.

The pleasure which these pious Correspondents express at what they have heard of the Missionary Society in England, and at all foreign Communications on the things of Christ, has led me to try at sketching such an Address from our Union as might afford them some Gratification. When I have got it into a little form I shall be glad to find an Opportunity of obtaining your Sentiments upon it, before proposing it to our next Committee Meeting.

You have probably observed Brother Burder's Advertisement of Village Tracts[193] I have promised him some help, though my incessant

---

[190]Eng. MS. 37, f. 54c, JRULM.

[191]George Livius, Esq., of Bedford. He was a member of Samuel Hillyard's Independent congregation at the Old Meeting and committee member of the Bedfordshire Union of Christians (see letter of Fuller to Hillyard in the biographical appendix under "Hillyard" for more on Livius). Sutcliff preached at the 1797 meeting of the Union. See *Universal British Directory*, 2:320; *Evangelical Magazine* 7 (1799): 216.

[192]Melville Horne (see letter 56).

[193]*Village Sermons; or ... Plain and Short Discourses on the Principal Doctrines of the Gospel; Intended for the Use of Families, Sunday Schools, or Companies Assembled for Religious Instruction in Country Villages* (7 vols, 1798), by George Burder (1752-1832), Independent minister at Coventry, 1783-1803. One advertisement for *Village Sermons* in the *Baptist Annual Register* noted: "These Sermons are intended, pri-

application to the M.ᵞ Socʸˢ Business[194] has prevented me as yet from taking my share. We shall be heartily glad of your Cooperation in the work; which is I think capable of being well adapted to do good.

With this I send you Horne Tooke's Book,[195] which I am sorry that I forgot to do before, and can only plead in Excuse that my thoughts have been so much occupied upon one object as to exclude almost all others. I thank God that I have now got nearly through this business, before my strength was quite exhausted. My head was more afflicted by it than by any thing I have attempted. May the Lord render it useful to his Cause!

I also return some of your books with many thanks. The others I beg leave to retain for the present. I expect, God willing, to be at Mʳ Hillyards[196] next Lords day, and hope for the pleasure of seeing you before I come back.

> Mʳˢ G. joins in Xtian respects to Mʳˢ S. with
> Yours affectionately in the lord
> S. Greatheed

6 Dec.ʳ 98.

P.S. The Duff[197] was in the Downs on Monday waiting for a wind. Matthew Wilks and Mʳ Fenn of Cornhill[198] are gone with the Missionaries in

---

marily, for the use of those pious and zealous persons, who, pitying the deplorable ignorance of their poor neighbours, are accustomed to go into country villages to instruct them: a practice, which, though but lately adopted, bids fair to produce the most substantial and extensive advantages." The sermons are "very *plain* and *short*, yet on the most interesting subjects, and with frequent appeals to the conscience." The advertisement also notes that Sunday school teachers "may, perhaps, think proper to read them to the children." See *Baptist Annual Register*, 3:469.

[194]London Missionary Society (founded in 1795), the Congregational counterpart to the BMS.

[195]**Horne Tooke** (1736-1812), an Anglican priest turned radical politician in the 1770s, founding member of the Constitutional Society in 1780, supporter of the French Revolution, and ardent advocate of political reform in parliament in the 1780s and '90s. The reference to a "book" by Tooke in the above letter is somewhat obscure. It could refer to several publications, including *The Trial of John Horne Tooke for High Treason* (1795) or *Epea Pteroenta; or, The Diversions of Purley* (1798-1805); most likely, however, the reference is to Tooke's *Speeches during the Westminster Election, 1796* (1796).

[196]**Samuel Hillyard** (1770-1839), minister at the Old Meeting at Bedford, 1790-1839, and one of the early leaders of the Bedford Sunday School Union and Bedfordshire Union of Christians.

[197]The *Duff* was purchased by the London Missionary Society to transport missionaries overseas. On this particular mission, the *Duff* sailed from Spithead on 20 December 1798, carrying nearly thirty missionaries destined for the South Sea Islands. The French navy captured the ship as it neared Rio de Janeiro. After several

her. Brookshank[199] is gone to convey the Women & Children by land to Portsmouth from whence they are expected to sail almost immediately. B[r] Haweis[200] writes that ["]nothing can be [more] promising than the commencement of the voyage has been."

61. Samuel Medley, Liverpool, to Mrs. Thomas Wilson,[201] 16 Artillery Place, London, 4 March 1799.[202]

Liverpool 4th March 1799.

My very dear and kind friends M[r] and M[rs] Wilson.

I have no doubt but you must have heard, how sorely in the Course of his Holy and wise providence, it has pleased my gracious God and Heavenly Father in Christ Jesus to visit poor me with very violent and painful Illness since my Return from London. Indeed I have been and am but exceeding low in respect of my Bodily Health and Constitution. All I went thro while in London, sore as it was—was but a kind of a prelude to, or Introduction of, what I have suffered since I came home. Never had my poor Clay Tabernacle such a shake or so many wide and gaping Cracks in it, (if I may so express myself) as it has had and still has.—It would be only tedious and painful to you my dear Friends to enumerate or make a detail of particulars in this Respect—I am still a Closely confined prisoner to my House as not having yet dared, or indeed been able to put my Head out of the doors.—Yet—and I well know it will afford you pleasure to be informed of it—It appears at present, at least in some small degree, as if it was the pleasure of the Lord to bless the use of Means towards my Recovery. I do find in several Respects that some of my Complaints—are beginning to give way and lessen and my Medical friends here, tell me that however it has been a very tedious and painful, yet they have no doubt but it will in the end, prove a profitable Crisis to my Constitution even at this advanced period of my Life— Thus far they—But kind and attentive to me as they are I trust I am

---

months of captivity, the missionaries were allowed to return to England. See *Evangelical Magazine* 6 (1798): 509-510; 7 (1799): 80-81, 124.

[198]**John Fenn**, hosier at 78 Cornhill, London.

[199]**Joseph Brooksbank** (1762-1825), Independent minister at Haberdashers' Hall, London, 1785-1825.

[200]**Thomas Haweis** (1734-1820), Anglican evangelical who served as rector at All Saints, Aldwincle, Northamptonshire.

[201]**Thomas Wilson** (1764-1843), London silk merchant and Independent layman.

[202]Eng. MS. 370, f. 84b, JRULM. A note on the back page reads, "M[r] Medleys last Letter to M[rs] Wilson."

enabled to look above and beyond them as Men—even to the Hills from whence & whence only Cometh my Help—Mourning indeed I have been and am still called to and daily made to Experience—But I trust and desire to be thankful for it I am kept from the power and prevalence of Indulged Murmuring against his Holy wise and Sovereign Hand as now laid upon me—And I hope I desire to Consider and esteem this as among the many wonderful and undeserved Mercies I am yet the partaker of—I hope I do love and often am I led to Reflect upon and Expect to myself those sweet words of the Psalmist where he says— "I know O Lord that thy Judgments are right and that those in faithfulness hast afflicted me."— And those of the Apostle Peter— "Tho now for a season if needs be, ye are in promises thro manifold Trials" —And again those words to the Hebrews— "My Son, despise not those the chastning [sic] of the Lord neither faint when thou art rebuked of him &c &c—and especialy [sic] where it is said in the same Chapter— "But He for our proffit that we might be made partakers of his Holiness"—And those words in the 27th Chapter of Isaiah— "By this therefore shall the Iniquity of Jacob be purged and this is all the fruit to take away his Sin"—And those words in Deuteronomy— "To humble thee and to prove thee and to do thee good in thy latter end"—And many more—And so I think I find and Experience somewhat of the Truth of what I have often said in publick—viz "That truly sanctified afflictions are some of the sweetest and most blessed Expositors of Gods Holy Word—And but for them we should not know the meaning of several parts of and passages in it— "But who teacheth like Him—Of whom it is said by the Prophet— "Who teacheth thee to thy profit, and leadeth thee by the way in which thou shouldest go."—which may well lead this afflicted Christian, without fear of being mistaken to say— "It is all well now and shall be Eternaly [sic] better by and by. Blessed by God for this. I would not have you my dear and much lov'd friends—Suffer from all or any thing I have thus written to You—That I have no conflict with, or painful disturbance in my Soul from a Corrupt Nature, or the sad, sinful and shameful working of an Evil heart of Unbelief. Indeed the truth is I have much of this—in my daily Experience and yet the Lord is good, his Mercy is Everlasting and his Truth Endureth to all Generations—Yea his compassions fail not & therefore it is that I am not Consumed"— O what a Song will it be to sing in a brighter world to all Eternity"—that he has led us forth by the right way, to bring us to a City of Everlasting Habitation" I hope and pray, my dear friends that these few lines may meet You both and your dear Infant Children all mercifully well. And that the gracious blessings of the presence power and peace of the Lord are with you all, enabling you more and more to look to and love, and live, upon him and like Him also; in humble and in holy walking with Him and in so doing to persevere to the End and then to be with him in Glory World without

End Amen   Mrs Medley and my family here join me in presenting our
Xtian Love and best Respects—And I have particularly to Request again
that you will kindly accept my sincere thanks for all the many and repeated Instances of Your very great kindness to me while lately with
you in London   the Lord himself reward You with a Thousand-fold better Blessings in Your own Souls—For the present therefore my Dear
Friends farewell—And now Commanding You both and all Yours most
Cordialy [sic] to the Lord I remain with all due Respect and gratitude
your greatly oblidged [sic] and very affectionate Friend and willing Servant in the Lord Jesus and for his sake

Sam Medley

*62. William Ward,²⁰³ Serampore, Bengal, to unnamed correspondent
[John Rippon in London], 16 December 1799.²⁰⁴*

Serampore, Dec. 16, 1799.

Very dear Brother,

On the 24ᵗʰ of May 1799, we entered the Criterion at London.
On the 12ᵗʰ October we left it in the river near Calcutta, and the next
morning we landed at Serampore. We had a very favourably [sic]
voyage. I was almost the only one who escaped the sea sickness. We
preached to the sailors on deck on a Lord's day morning, & in our room
to ourselves in the evening. The Capt. indeed always joined us, & took
the lead in his turn in family worship. He is a godly elder of a Presbyterian church at Philadelphia, under the pastoral care of the Rev. D^r
Smith.²⁰⁵ We had the pleasure of introducing two of the sailors, appar-

---

²⁰³Portions of the journal of William Ward (1769-1823) are reprinted in S.
Pearce Carey's *William Carey, D.D.* (London: George H. Doran, 1923) 174-175, but
this letter is not mentioned.

²⁰⁴Eng. MS. 387, f. 94, JRULM. This letter was written to a member of the BMS
committee, most likely John Rippon.

²⁰⁵Capt. Benjamin Wickes often used his ships to transport missionaries to India during the early years of the BMS. An elder in the Third Presbyterian Church in
Philadelphia, Wickes was nevertheless a strong supporter of the BMS, informing the
London Committee, upon learning that his passengers for India were BMS missionaries, that "my heart rejoiced," bringing "to my mind a desire which I had felt some
years past . . . that I might have command of a ship that should convey some of these
messengers of peace to the heathen." According to S. Pearce Carey, Wickes was the
son of a Baptist minister. Wickes would later serve as an honorary member of the
first board of the General Missionary Convention of the American Baptists in 1814.
John Blair Smith (1756-1799), after graduating from the College of New Jersey in
1773, served as an educator for many years, including a stint as President of Hamp-
den-Sydney College in Virginia (1779-1789). Smith then served as minister of the

ently under serious concern, unto our Lord's day evening worship in our own room for a few times. We were once under alarm from privateers & once from violent weather. I will copy a short extract or two from my Journal:—

Tuesday, June 11. At 12 oclock Bay of Biscay 300 miles to our left. Several vessels just in sight, supposed to be privateers. The men go thro' their exercise at the guns. The vessels get nearer. The Capt. has his fears, & says he shall expect us to take a Musket. Shall I then aim an instrument of death against my fellow creatures?—Unable to answer this solemn question to the satisfaction of my conscience, what shall I do?— The Lord does not put it to the test: *1/2 past One*. Capt. says the enemy is gone.—-*Four o'clock*. A vessel is still pursuing us, which the Capt. believes to be a Frenchman. I feel some alarm, most for our women & children. Oh! Lord! be thou our defender! The vessel seems to make way upon us. *Quarter past eleven at night*. There is no doubt of the vessel being a French privateer: when we changed our course this afternoon she changed hers. We have since dark changed into our old course again, so that possibly we shall lose her. Two of our Brethren have engaged in prayer, and our minds are pretty comfortable. Thank God there is an hour coming when "The wicked *shall* cease from troubling" &c. "Thou art my portion, O Lord."

Wednesday, June 12. Blessed be God, & blessed be his glorious name forever! We are still in tranquillity on board our vessel, & the enemy has disappeared. The women manifested a deal of courage last night, & slept soundly in spite of the Frenchman.

Thursday, June 13. *One o'clock in the morning*. Our friends have just waked me out of sleep, with the information that two large vessels are just upon us, & that one of them has fired a gun to bring us to. I dress myself in a hurry, & go upon deck. All hands are at their posts, & the matches are lighted. I go to the end of the ship. I can just see the vessel, tho' it is very foggy. A ball whizzes over my head, & makes me tremble. I go down, & go to prayer with our friends. My mind calm: we leave ourselves in the hands of our God, that he may decide, whether we shall go to a French prison or to India. Another ball goes over the shrouds. The Capt. thinks its an English frigate. He has scarcely any doubts, & now,

---

Third Presbyterian Church in Philadelphia (1791-1795) before removing to Schenectady, New York, where he served as President of Union College until his death in August 1799. Captain Wickes would have at one time been under the care of Smith during the latter's pastorate in Philadelphia, but neither Wickes nor Ward would have known of Smith's death due to their being at sea since May of 1799. See Cox, *History*, 1:50, 156; Carey, *William Carey*, 182; *Periodical Accounts*, 1:505; Roger Hayden, "Kettering 1792 and Philadelphia 1814: The Influence of English Baptists upon the Formation of American Baptist Foreign Missions 1790-1814," *Baptist Quarterly* 21 (1965-1966): 11-13; 71-72.

lest the mast should be shot away, he orders to haul to, for the ship gets nearer and nearer. The sails are furled & she is coming along-side. Its a fine sight. The lights thro' the portholes, & that on the surface of the sea around the vessel, make it charming, even amidst the fear of its being an enemy. They demand our name, our destination, &c. and then inform us, theirs is an *English frigate*!!   As soon as the sound of these words caught my ears, I was electrified with joy, & word was immediately carried to our friends below; who, however, were greatly supported. The Lieutenant comes on board, & we are all busy writing letters. After the vessel has left us, we fall down & thank our Saviour, & retire to rest.

Friday, Aug. 9. *Opposite the Cape of Good Hope.* The weather is so pleasant even here, that our sisters have been telling Capt. Wickes, he must have been joking, when he talked of such terrible weather, & that they should never learn to be sailors on a smooth sea. He told them to wait a little, & they should see he was not joking. In the afternoon we had presages of an approaching storm: the wind was boisterous & the sea rough. We held our prayer meeting & retired to rest. The rocking of the vessel almost threw us out of our beds. The night was very dark, & at one time the vessel seemed to be sailing on a sea of fire, the agitation of the waves around the ship causing a friction of the particles of salt in the water, & producing a flood of sparks like those from an electrical machine.

Saturday, Aug. 10. The sea was rough most of the day, but in the evening it became terrible to our sisters. Whilst Brethren Marshman[206] & Brunsdon[207] were sharing just before dusk, the vessel gave such a violent shook, as to throw the former backwards, with an open razor in his hand, & the great stool upon which he sat rolled upon him. I expected his back was broken. He was only very slightly hurt on the arm, & the looking-glass broken. But the whole room was thrown into confusion & uproar; every person & thing almost reeling to & fro like the drunkard. Picture to yourself a scene like this below, & then ascend the deck: the rain pours, the winds roar in the shrouds, & the waves bellow around us, dashing against the vessel, & covering the forecastle with waters.—Now she seems to be climbing a steep hill, now descending into the valley; now reeling to one side, then to the other; the Capt. causing his voice to be heard amidst the storm, & the men running to & fro on the deck of the reeling ship to straiten or take down the sails. You would be delighted to see us at dinner, which is placed on a tray, & the tray tied to the table, & the table fastened to the floor. There the difficulty is to secure our food & our plate, every thing sliding first to one

---

[206]**Joshua Marshman** (1768-1837) of Broadmead in Bristol sailed for India with Ward, Brunsdon, and Grant in 1799.

[207]**Daniel Brunsdon** (1777-1801) and his wife sailed with the Marshmans, William Grant, and William Ward in 1799.

end of the tray & then to the other. Now we hold ourselves, & the plate takes its chance. Sometimes a single sweep of the ship overturns mug glasses, & plates, & blends them all in one common mass. We have been talking of imitating the natives, & eating out of a bucket.

In general we had all pretty good health, except sister Brunsdon, who had much sickness & a miscarriage. On Monday evening we had a prayer-meeting—Tuesday evening a text discussed; Wednesday evening experience meeting; Thursday evening question discussed; Friday evening a prayer-meeting; & Saturday evening a meeting to adjust differences, confess faults, & promote brotherly love. We had the Lord's Supper three times, in which our beloved Capt. joined.[208] We instructed the sailors daily in reading, writing & accounts; & on some impressions apparently were made, but we fear whether any were savingly enlightened. The boys we instructed in Dr Watts Catechism.[209] For a time there was an evident reformation, but at the close of our voyage the blasphemies of some were more terrible than ever, encouraged, I suppose, by two or three profane gentlemen on board. On our arrival at this place we made preparations for going up the country & joining our Brethren, but the Government of the Company prevented us. Our Brethren, therefore, are coming to join us at this place, where the seat of the mission will be placed. This place belongs to the Danes. There is no church. The governor & several gentleman attend preaching at our house. We have preached once in the Governor's hall. We have all the patronage we could expect, & we can go any where to itinerate. Paper, press, types are ready & before this reaches you, no doubt some part of the Bible will be printed in Bengalee. Our Brethren are still sowing in hope, tho' in tears. I know not when I shall be able to join them.— Descriptions of the country must be sent in my next. We have lost by Death our dear Brother Grant.[210] He has left a widow & two children. Tho' well on landing, he died in three weeks after our arrival, of a fever. Brother Carey still looks young. He sends his love to you & family, & begs me to make his acknowledgment for the books. He, however, talks

---

[208]During this voyage, Ward and the other BMS missionaries on board practiced "open communion" with Wickes and other sailors on the *Criterion*, a practice not followed at that time by Carey at Serampore or advocated by Fuller in England. In 1805, Ward's open position would triumph at Serampore, but only until 1811, when closed communion was reinstituted once again. See E. Daniel Potts, "A Note on the Serampore Trio," *Baptist Quarterly* 20 (1963-1964): 115-117.

[209]Isaac Watts (1674-1748), Independent minister, private tutor, and greatest hymnwriter of the eighteenth century, spent most of his adult life in Stoke Newington, near London. His *Catechism* (first published in 1730) was decidedly Calvinistic and was widely used in England and America, going through numerous editions in the eighteenth century.

[210]**William Grant** sailed with Ward, the Marshmans, and the Brunsdons to Serampore in 1799.

of writing. Let me hear from you while either of us live, & send me an account of the Yorkshire churches, & you will increase those many obligations under which you have laid

Your sincerely affection^e son & Servant

Wm Ward

My unfeigned love to Mr Johns & *all* your family, as well as to M^r & Mrs Greaves,[211] & all your church.

---

[211]**William Johns**, a member at Carter Lane in Southwark, would sail for India in 1810 with John Lawson to join Ward and Carey at Serampore. Greaves is unidentified.

Part Three

1800–1809

63. Final portion of a letter from John Ryland, Bristol, to John Sutcliff, Olney, postmarked 25 April 1800.[1]

". . . to find money to pay for all we have already, as there are 3 on the Broadm'd Benefactions, which will not well maintain above two and a half—On these accts. I cannot buy many books this year, either for my-self or the Library.—Morgan[2] is at Oxford.—I hear they like him well—Webb[3] is just return'd from Plymouth Dock where he went to assist Birt in the time of his afflictn. He bears his sore bereavemt well. His Ch. & Bror Steadmans are now distinct—both places well filled—and both Congregats very harmonious[4]—We unite in Love to yourself Mrs Sutcliff and Miss Johnston[5]   I am

Dear Bror
Yours cordially
John Ryland

---

[1]Eng. MS. 861, f. 47, JRULM. Included here are also two portraits of John Ryland, Jr.

[2]Most likely this is **Thomas Morgan** (1776-1857), who would later become the Baptist minister at Cannon Street, Birmingham (1802-1811), and afternoon preach-er, copastor, and eventually pastor at Bond Street, Birmingham (1815-1846). He was probably supplying for James Hinton of New Road, Oxford.

[3]**Joseph Webb** (1779-1814), William Steadman's brother-in-law, while still a student at Bristol Academy, supplied at Cannon Street in Birmingham in February and March 1801. In the fall of 1801 he would assume the pastorate of the Baptist congregation at Tiverton, where he remained until 1804.

[4]**Isaiah Birt** (1758-1837), Baptist minister at Plymouth Dock (1781-1813) and Cannon Street, Birmingham (1813-1827). William Steadman (see letter 42) arrived in Plymouth Dock in 1798 to become the initial pastor of a Baptist congregation in Liberty Fields, founded by former members of Birt's congregation, which was meeting at that time in Morice Square.

[5]Sarah Johnston was the unmarried sister of Jane Johnston Sutcliff (d. September 1814). After Sutcliff's marriage to Jane in 1796, Sarah lived in the Sutcliff's home in Olney. See Haykin, *One Heart*, 249.

64. MS. of Andrew Fuller's record of the receipts from the sale of publications for the benefit of the BMS, December 1791 to 21 May 1800.[6]

Rec.[d] [received] And.[w] Fuller

M[r] C's Acc.[t]		
1792		
May 2[d]	6 Careys pamphlets[7]	

Acc.[t] of Miss: Serm.[s]

Dec. 23. 1791	Rec[d] 100 f.[r] North.ton	
	sent them all to Clipstone—	
Jan. 3. 92	Rec.[d] 100 more—Sent	
	36 to Arnsby giv.[g] M[r] Blundell[8]	
Jan. 10	Rec.[d] of M[r] Blundell—	0..13..0
	—M[r] B. 10 Remained with him.	
	—6 Sold at home—	3..0
	—7 Sent to Rev.[d] Butler[9] —	3..0
Feb 2. 92	Rec.[d] of Collins[10] for 8—	3..4
Jan. 8. 93	Rec.[d] of M[r] Morris[11]	
	for 74—	1..17..0

N. B. 26 at that time in hand
& 8 M.[r] Edmonds[12] has unaccounted for.

_____

2..19..4

[?] sold [in?] India

---

[6]Eng. MS. 369, f.50, JRULM.

[7]Most likely copies of William Carey's *An Enquiry into the Obligations of Christians to Use Means for the Conversion of the Heathens* (1792).

[8]**Thomas Blundel, Sr.** (1752-1824), Baptist minister at Arnsby (1791-1804), Luton (1804-1812), and Keighley (1812-1823).

[9]William Butler ministered to the Baptist meeting at Gretton, Northamptonshire, in the early 1790s. The church was without a pastor in 1794, and Butler does not appear to have preached anywhere at that time or in 1798. See *Baptist Annual Register*, 1:9, 2:9, 3:27.

[10]Probably **Luke Collins** (d. 1805).

[11]**John Webster Morris** (1763-1836), Baptist minister at Clipston (1785-1803) and Dunstable (1803-1810).

[12]Either **John Edmonds** (d. 1823), Baptist minister at Guilsborough, Northamptonshire, 1781-1811, or his brother, Edward Edmonds (c.1750-1823), who ministered at the Baptist meeting at Bond Street, Manchester, 1785-1823. A third possibility, though unlikely, is another brother of the previous two Edmonds, Thomas Edmonds, who ministered at this time at Upton-on-Severn, Worcestershire. See Arthur S. Langley, *Birmingham Baptists Past and Present* (London: Kingsgate Press, 1939) 81-83; Ralph F. 1963) 12.

Sermons at home w[h] are not down— say—	..3..8
161 Disposed of—	3..3..0

May 21. 1800 Paid M[r] Sutcliff	£3..3..0

65. Andrew Fuller, Kettering, to John Sutcliff, Olney ("By fav.[r] of M[r] Clarke"[13]), 15 June 1801.[14]

Monday Morn.[g] June 15. 1801

My d[r] bro.[r]

I sent up the Receipts to Burls[15] on Saturday with a direction to him to distribute the P. A.[16] w[h] I hope are or will be there to day. Yesterday I rec.[d] a Letter f.[m] a M.[r] Brown now in London, who was at Serampore in Dec.[r] Past. By him Carey sent a short note just to introduce him to me, and makes mention of hav.[g] written more largely the day before by the ships. As therefore the Fleet is come in I expect Letters every day. They *may* require an ans.[r] in a few days, to go by our Packet. I will do every thing as quick as possible. if a ride over to Olney latter end of the week be necessary I'll come. Griffin the Bristol student[17] was sent to Plymouth Dock a day before my L.[r] arrived. Bro[r] Ry.[d] will be at North.[n] [18] on *Friday* next—Goes with me to Boston.[19] If a L.[r] sh.[d] come in a day or two, could not we meet on Friday at North.[n] & consult bro.[r] R. then you'd see him before you go.— I am invited to Norwich by Mark Wilks[20] to Collect for Mis.[s][21] Think of being there the first Sab. in July & go thro' London perhaps between that & the Second

Affec.[y] Y.[rs]

A. Fuller

---

[13]Possibly Thomas Clark of Kettering, hairdresser and dealer in hats. See *Universal British Directory*, 3:479.

[14]Eng. MS. 376, f. 716a (originally catalogued as f. 4057), JRULM.

[15]**William Burls** (1763-1837), wealthy London merchant, Baptist layman, and one of the chief financial officers of the BMS for many years.

[16]*Periodical Accounts.*

[17]Unidentified.

[18]John Ryland; Northampton.

[19]Fuller promoted the BMS in Boston that summer, receiving £7.7 from a collection organized by a Mr. Trotman of Boston. See *Periodical Accounts*, 2:208.

[20]**Mark Wilks** (1748-1819), Baptist minister, Norwich, 1788-1819.

[21]Fuller collected £8.6 at Mark Wilks's congregation and £3.12.6 at Joseph Kinghorn's in Norwich that summer. See *Periodical Accounts*, 2:203.

P.S. If I hear nothing f.ᵐ you nor you from me between now & Friday, let us meet that day by dinner at North-[amp]ton

66. *John Chamberlain,²² Bristol, to John Sutcliff, Olney, 24 October 1801.²³*

Bristol. Oct.ʳ 24ᵗʰ 1801.

Dear Father,
 An opportunity of sending a few lines to you occurring, I embrace it. A Member of the Church at Blunham²⁴ being now at Bristol, who I expect will return next week, & will take this to Newport, & send it thence to Olney.
 Since my return hither, I have been ill, & am now weak, tho' much recovered. A cold & a slow fever have brought me low. I fear the cold was occasioned by sitting imprudently at my desk with the window open & without my coat a month since yesterday. After preaching the next Sabbath, I was very hoarse & more wearied than ever before in the good work. The hoarseness was soon gone but the cold has remain'd ever since. This with the fever have forced me to lay every thing aside for several days & render'd me incapable of doing much the past month. But blessed be God, I am much better, yet my breast is in such a state that I dare not sit long at writing. My spirits have been low at times, but I have much reason to be thankful that on the whole they have been no worse. I wish it were more evident that my affliction has been good for me & it gives me sorrow that it is not.
 It affords me great pleasure to find that the Lord is carrying on his work at Olney. O may his arm be more gloriously displayed. Doubtless you will rejoice, that he is also gathering in his elect at Bristol. The work seems going on among the young people at Broadmead. Last Thursday sennight. D.ʳ Ryland baptized 17 persons. Sixteen of whom joined the church. Mʳ Edmond's Son²⁵ who is at our house was one. The day be-

---

 ²²**John Chamberlain** (1777-1821) studied at Bristol Academy (1799-1802) before serving as a BMS missionary to India, 1803-1821. During 1798 he had studied at Sutcliff's academy in Olney.
 ²³Eng. MS. 387, f. 21a, JRULM. On the back page is written in Sutcliff's hand, "Rec. Nov. 7. 1801. Ans. — 23. —." Chamberlain's final note is dated 26 October.
 ²⁴Blunham, a village near Bedford; Martin Mayle was the Baptist minister at that time. See *Baptist Annual Register*, 3:1.
 ²⁵**Thomas Edmonds** (1784-1860), son of John Edmonds, Baptist minister at Guilsborough (see letter 65). The younger Edmonds would later serve as pastor at St. Andrew's Street, Cambridge, 1812-1831.

fore, M.ʳˢ Skinner[26] was baptized. Few knew of it till after wards. She has not joined the Baptist Church, but sits down with Mʳ Skinner in the Independent communion. It is reported that both M.ʳ or Mʳˢ Skinner have left M.ʳ Hey,[27] not approving of his controversy with Mʳ Biddulph.[28] M.ʳ S. is a very pious man, & one of the most generous in this city. May his life long be spared, & his usefulness greatly extended.[29]

M.ʳ Hall of Cambridge is here, M.ʳ Lowell & he having made an exchange.[30] He preaches at Bridge street in the morning & at Broadmead

---

[26]**William Skinner** (d. 1834), Bristol banker and prominent member of the Independent congregation at Broadmead (see letter 80).

[27]John Hey (1734-1815), pastor of the Independent congregation at Castle Green, Bristol, 1789-1804.

[28]**Thomas Tregenna Biddulph** (1763-1838), evangelical vicar at St. James, Bristol.

[29]The entry in the Broadmead Church Book for Thursday 8 October 1801 provides further details about Chamberlain's comments: "At xi o'clock in the morn.ᵍ Broʳ Page began divine Service w.ᵗʰ singing, readᵍ & prayer, the Pastor preached from Luke xii. 50. "I have a B.ᵐ [baptism] wherewith to be B.ᵈ [baptized] and how am I straightened till it be accomplished." After w.ᶜʰ a hymn was sung while the Candidates prepared for B.ᵐ and the Ord.ᶜᵉ was administer'd to the following persons, six Men to join Bmᵈ & one who remains at Tabernacle & ten Women." The names were Mr. Morgan, Short, Shrive, Pring, Thomas Edmonds, another Mr. Morgan (a member of Tabernacle, nephew to Mrs. Fido), and Mr William Merrick, Jr. Ryland comments in the margin, "It was a pleasant & solemn Season   Blessed by God!" He then adds at the bottom of the page: "Mʳˢ Skinner was B.ᵈ more privately yesterday afternoon— She joins the [Independent] Church with her husband." They were received into the church on Sunday 11 October. An entry in the Church Book for the Broadmead Independent Church, 1757-1818, for 11 October 1801 reads: "Mʳ Will.ᵐ Skinner and Mʳˢ Mary Skinner returned to this Church, having for some years withdrawn to the Church in Castle Green." A note in parentheses adds, "on acc.º of the assistant minister being a materialist." A controversy arose over this circumstance, resulting in a controversy between Thomas Biddulph and John Hey. Hey published *The Important Question at Issue: Between the Editors of a Periodical Publication, entitled Zion's Trumpet and a Non-conformist, in a Letter to those Rev. Gentlemen* (Bristol, 1801), to which Biddulph responded in *An Appeal to Public Impartiality, or, The Manner in which the Dispute Concerning "The Important Question at Issue, &c." has been Conducted* (Bristol, 1801). Hey responded with *The Important Question still under Consideration, but Approaching to a Decision: or, An Address to the Rev. Tho. T. Biddulph, Minister of St. James's Bristol; in Reply to a Letter Lately Published in Answer to a Pamphlet entitled, "The Important Question at Issue"* (Bristol, 1801). See Broadmead Church Book, 1779-1817 (MS., Bristol Record Office, Bd/M1/3) f. 221, 222; Broadmead Independent Church, 1757-1818 (MS., Bristol Record Office, Bd/M2/1) f. 49.

[30]**Robert Hall** (1764-1831), at that time the celebrated Baptist minister at St. Andrew's Street, Cambridge, was visiting in Bristol in October 1801, having exchanged pulpits with **Samuel Lowell** (1759-1823), pastor of the Independent congregation at Bridge Street, 1799-1823. Chamberlain noted Hall's visit in his diary

in the evening   D.ʳ Ryland & M.ʳ Page[31] preach for him in the afternoon. I am inform'd that Broadmead is crouded to hear him & that he preaches astonishing sermons, but on account of illness I have not yet heard him. Last Sabbath afternoon D.ʳ R. preached a thanksgiving sermon on the pleasing return of peace & plenty, from Psalms the 147.ᵗʰ the 12.ᵗʰ or 14.ᵗʰ verses. He enlarged much on the manner in which christians should evidence their gratitude. One remark was "That as Merchants will be looking out for new resources of trade so Christians should enlarge their views respecting the propagation of the Gospel & multiply their endeavour to promote it. Now (said he) the destroyer Apollyon is chain'd, let the armies of Immanuel go forth, & spread abroad over the whole Earth." O may we see it realized. I look over the vast regions of France with reviving hopes. Surely God will appear for his own cause & dispel the darkness that covereth the people, & confound the infidelity with which many are infatuated. O verily there is a loud call. "Come over & help us." O may many hear it & obey its voice! When I reflect on these things I long to be employed in the good work with all my might, & can hardly satisfy my self to remain as I am, but a moment's consideration of my self restrains my anxiety, & almost makes me asham'd of my pretensions. O what am I that I should aspire to a work so important or glorious? Let me wait & see what Jehovah hath appointed for me.

I am much obliged to you, Dear Father, for what you said to me & for your advice, when I was at Olney. I cannot speak well of myself, but it often occasions much to me that I am not otherwise. I trust that I am sincere in saying that nothing pierces my heart more than the thought of going to Bengal or to be the occasion of trouble & uneasiness to the dear Brethren there. What you intimated to me concerning my temper, had caused me many painful feelings before, & it has not been a little on my mind since. It has at times almost brought me to relinquish every thought of missionary services & of the ministry also. But I cannot rest here, perhaps it would be better if I could. But I am most composed & satisfied when I leave every thing as it is & wait the approaching conclusion. I am happiest when my expectations are low, or my will rec-

---

that he kept during his years as a student at Bristol. He writes in October 1801, "Have been hearing an excellent sermon to young people at Broadmead, by Mr. Hall of Cambridge. May it be attended with a divine blessing. He was very earnest. May he have seals to his ministry in this place." See William Yates, *Memoirs of Mr. John Chamberlain, Late Missionary in India* (Calcutta: Baptist Mission Press, 1845) 45.

[31]**Henry Page** (1781-1833), assistant pastor at Broadmead and secretary and tutor at Bristol Academy, 1802-1817.

lines on the divine pleasure. O that I had more of this experience! blessed be God for any.[32]

Being ill & poorly so much of the time since my return, & having a library exercise to prepare I can give but little account of my proceedings. M.ʳ Page has put me in another class, in which I read Virgil &c in the Collectanea majora. This is a fortunate circumstance with respect to learning Greek. For this class learn 3 or 4 Greek lessons a week while the other learns but one. I am pleased with Virgil have read his Eclogue's & some of his Georgic's, but expect to make the Greek my chief study for a time, that I may make some proficiency in it. If we had a French Tutor, I would begin the French immediately, but we have not & I cant afford to pay 2 guineas a year for one. In reading, I have attended to little but history. Read Grays Key to the Old Testament[33] & thought it a good performance. Last week read Michaelis's Introductory lectures on the New Testament[34] found much information there tho' I cant believe all he says. Have Perkins[35] 2 vˡ Sermons in hand, but I can attend to divinity but very little & am sorry for it. Expect to read Campbell on the Gospels[36] soon, but an Oration will require my alteration for a time. Some of the Brethren have agreed to study different sciences, have a lecture once a week prepared by one of them. I approve of their plan & wish them much success.[37] Was over at the French prison to day to see

---

[32]Chamberlain's diary entry for 19 October 1801 records his struggles at that time concerning his calling as a missionary: "Through what changes hath the Lord brought me; and what a multitude of tender mercies has he bestowed upon me! What a trial was that with which I was exercised concerning the mission! How great the perplexity of mind I then experienced! and yet I survey it with joy. I now see that it was indeed wisely ordered of the Lord, to shew me what there was in me. It was my longest trial, and I hope it has done me the greatest good. The survey makes me think of what my dear Brunsdon said to me: he sympathized with me like a brother, and told me I should see it was all right in the end." On 29 December he wrote about Carey's famous sermon at Nottingham in May 1792 from Isa. liv. 2, in which he paraphrases Carey as saying "it is the bounden duty of Christians to expect great things from God, and to attempt great things for him." See Yates, *Memoirs of Mr. John Chamberlain,* 50-51, 58.

[33]*A Key to the Old Testament and Apocrypha; or, An Account of their Several Books, Their Contents and Authors, and of the Times in which they were Respectively Written* (1790), by Robert Gray (1762-1834).

[34]*Introduction to the New Testament* (1798), by Johann David Michaelis (1717-1791).

[35]William Perkins (1558-1602), early Puritan divine.

[36]Probably a reference to *The Authenticity of the Gospel-History Justified: and the Truth of the Christian Revelation Demonstrated, from the Laws and Constitution of Human Nature* (Edinburgh, 1759) by Archibald Campbell (1691-1756).

[37]Chamberlain regretted that so much of his time at Bristol was spent in literary studies, not divinity. One entry in his diary reads, "I am exceedingly liable to be carried away by the levity that surrounds me, and to which I am so inclined. I am

them once more before they depart. Their joy is very great in the prospect of returning home. Met with one Man, who has been in Bengal 6 years & can speak Bengallee. He spoke a little at my request & I could but rejoice to hear it.

Thro mercy I am recovering my strength & hope soon to resume all the course of my studies. The prospect is pleasant, may the Lord prosper me & help me to glorify his Name. Please to remember me most affectionately to M.rs Sutcliff to Miss Johnston & to Brother Brown if he be at Olney. Shall esteem it a great favor to receive a line from you at any time. May the blessing of [illegible word] be with you to render you happy, & your labour prosperous.

Most affectionately Yours

J Chamberlain.

Oct.r 26.th 1801

P.S. D.r Ryland desires his Love to you. The family is well.

67. *John Chamberlain, Bristol, to John Sutcliff, Olney, 23 December 1801.*[38]

Bristol Dec.r 23.rd 1801

Dear Father,

D.r Ryland being about to send a parcel to Northampton, I drop a line to send in it, tho at this time I have little to write. I presume that you are already apprized of what has passed between Dr Ryland & me concerning the Mission. This morning he read me some things out of your letter relative to this affair & remarked some things of which I suppose you will hear before this arrives. I perceive that he has already anticipated some things about which I was thinking of writing to you

---

convinced that true religion and levity are quite inconsistent with each other, and are, and ever will be, irreconcilable. Religion, if it has a prevailing influence on the mind, will be an antidote against a volatile and trifling disposition." Concerning Chamberlain's studies at Bristol, William Yates writes: "There have perhaps been few students in divinity, that have endeavoured more sedulously to improve time, to grow in grace, and to avoid the temptations attendant on a retired and collegiate life, than Mr. C. did; and yet we find him frequently lamenting over his failings in these things, particularly over his proneness to a light and trifling spirit: from which we may learn, that they are most sensible of their faults, who strive most against them, and that they are most conscious of their errors, who are most ardent in pressing toward perfection." See Yates, *Memoirs of Mr. John Chamberlain,* 43.

[38]Eng. MS. 387, f. 21b, JRULM. On the back page Sutcliff has written, "Rec. Jan.y 2. 1802."

such as coming up into Northamptonshire to stay a little before the time of departure. From some hints which have been dropped this morning I conjecture that you will soon expect me in your parts, but D.ᴿ Ryland thinks I might stay some time longer. He mention'd what you wrote concerning Persic & will I expect write to you farther about these things. Respecting coming up I should like it, but am at your disposal. Duty & interest I think require me if possible to spend some time among my Friends. I confess that I should like to be two by three months here to apply to the Greek but yet this is of inferior importance. Much better shall I like to have my heart & mind engaged in a nobler employ. If it be judged proper, that I should attend to Persic, if health permit I will do it with vigorous application. Some things occur to me which I now write concerning my connection with H. S³⁹ which I doubt not you have already anticipated. If there be any prospect of our embarking for Bengal soon, would it not be eligible for her to give Mʳ Green⁴⁰ as early notice as possible? that he may the better provide against the event? Would it not be necessary & prudent for her to spend a month at least among her friends if they approve of it? These seem to me necessary precautions. In bringing them forth, I have no thought of protracting the time so far from it that I wish we were now sailing on the spacious main, or were the day of embarkation to morrow, I should rejoice.

I cannot be sufficiently thankful for that composure of mind I enjoy in the prospect of so important an undertaking. Blessed be God I am neither flushed with flattering hopes, nor depressed with discouraging fears. Being firmly persuaded that the cause is Jehovah's my mind is not greatly moved in the prospects of difficulty or danger & being brought about by divine Providence in such a way to present my self for this work, I cannot dispute my call, while at the same time, I tremble at my-self & think nobody so unworthy or unfit, for such a momentous concern. I am fully assured that were it not for a conviction of the reality extent & sufficiency of the divine promises & grace, I should sink under the load & never rise again. But thanks be to God he supports me in the prospect of this work, & will also I hope, if he call me to its execution. My Mind has been in a happy state in general since the prospect of my going on the Mission became more evident. I was more discouraged respecting this affair a little before this event, than at any period since I left Olney. I began to conclude that I had no heart for this affair, & that if I were called upon to give an account of myself relative to this matter

---

³⁹Chamberlain's fiancée, Hannah Smith, was a member of Sutcliff's congregation at Olney. They were married in 1802, but she died shortly after their arrival in India in 1804.

⁴⁰Possibly Thomas Green, for many years pastor of the Baptist church at Middleton Cheney, Northamptonshire. See *Baptist Annual Register*, 3:28.

whether I would go or not, I should not hesitate to decide it negatively. All my hopes, desire, & prospects seemed gone, past all return. I rejoice the trial has proved otherwise. They were only overwhelmed in thick gloom, when the light arose they again appeared, & came into delightful exercise with reanimated vigor. Thus I am happily disappointed in the conclusion I too rashly made & rebuke myself for my precipitancy. It gives me pleasure to see my way begin to appear, but being sensible that it may again be beclouded I am taught to be moderate in my joy. An hour of sunshine may be followed with many stormy days. I feel more of the necessity of inward religion without which all outward pro-fession is but a mere flash. My soul longs for the experience of the con-straining love of Christ in my heart that this may be the main spring to every action. O how important is this for a Missionary especially! This will support the sharpest trials, & stimulate to undertake the most ar-duous enterprizes in the promotion of his blessed cause. O may I have a large portion of this blessed principle to constrain me to the perfor-mance of the divine will in all things.

I am sincerely obliged to you for the letters you lately sent me & for the suitable advice it contained concerning reading & books. My prac-tice for some time past has been agreeable to it. But now it seems that I am about to resign the priviledges [sic] I have so long enjoyed. I am sor-ry that they have been no better improved that my time has been no better spent. The remembrance of Bristol will ever excite gratitude & sorrow in my mind. Should I shortly leave, I hope to do it in resignation to the divine will, & trust that a divine blessing will be added to what-ever knowledge I have attain'd here. Just received a letter from my Dear H. S. which affords me much pleasure respecting the good work before us. Her heart is stedfast trusting in the Lord. Blessed by God. My Chris-tian Love to M.rs Sutcliff & to Miss Johnston. Soliciting an intrest [sic] in your prayers, that I may be directed into the whole will of God

I remain

Affectionately Yrs

J Chamberlain

68. *John Rippon, London, to John Sutcliff, Olney, 12 February 1802.*[41]

Feb 12. 1802

My dear Sir,

---

[41]Eng. MS. 383, f. 1710, JRULM. On the back page Sutcliff has written, "Rec. Feb. 16, 1802. Ans.d May 20. [1802]."

As you expressed yourself, in two diff^t conversations, well pleased with ye design of ye arrangement of Dr Watts[42] I wanted to print your name, tho' you had not seen ye book, one other brother also was in ye same condition—I now request your acceptance of a Copy.

We have some in 24mo —same letter & paper. An edition, longer letter will be out, begin^g of next month   I hope 3/6 £ in calf & bettr paper 4 or 4/6 £—

7 Copies of any sent for 6 Copies. I have sent 2 doz Selec^s to India,[43] this day, by order of Mr Fuller to Mr Burles[44]—you sometime since mentioned 2 doz of Watts for India—but I have not sent them, lest that order might have been altered, as it was given long since; but they shall be sent whenever you receive y^r order.

I have rec^d an *host* of handsome letters concern^g ye arrangement—I wish it may please you.

Y^r affect^t bro^r & sv^t
J Rippon

69. *John Webster Morris, Clipston, to John Sutcliff, Olney, 11 June 1802.*[45]

Dr Bro.

Ever since the receipt of yours, I have been waiting a conveyance for a parcel to Olney, and must send by Coach at last. Will now make it as large as I can.—Have heard more heavy tidings. The amiable Mrs Wragg of Nottingham[46] was setting out last week for the association, in-

---

[42]*An Arrangement of the Psalms, Hymns and Spiritual Songs of the Rev. Isaac Watts . . . Including (what no other volume contains) All his Hymns . . . now Collated with Each of the Doctor's Own Editions: To Which are Subjoined, Indexes, very much Enlarged, both of Scriptures and of Subjects . . .* (1802), printed by William Button.

[43]*A Selection of Hymns; From the Best Authors, Intended to be an Appendix to Dr. Watt's Psalms and Hymns* (1801), sold by John Rippon.

[44]See letter 65.

[45]Eng. MS. 381, f. 1437a, JRULM. On the back page Sutcliff has written, "June, 1802. Acc.^t of Periodical Acc.^t"

[46]Ann Wragg (sometimes spelled "Ragg") joined the Baptist meeting at Friar Lane in Nottingham on 22 February 1789; her husband, Thomas Wragg, joined on 18 December 1796. Mrs. Wragg died on 6 June 1802, aged 37. She had seven children, the last born on 27 December 1800. J. W. Morris included a short summary of Mrs. Wragg's death in *the Biblical Magazine* (1802), noting that, at the time of her decease, she had been visiting some relations, "intending afterwards to be at the Baptist association held at Northampton on June 15: but while passing through the streets of Nottingham she fainted in the carriage, was taken out by her friends, and immediately expired!" See *Lists of Members of the Baptist Church, Friar Lane, Nottingham, 1769-1815* (Nottingham: n.p., 1901) 11, 14; John T. Godfrey and James

tending to spend a day or two at Arnsby, Leicester, and Clipstone in her way. Bro. Blundel went to Leicester to meet her there by appointment, and was informed that she had set out in a carriage, had scarcely left the streets of Notting.^{m}, fainted, was taken out, and expired in the arms of her friends before they could convey her home!—Heard from Mr Fuller today: all well.—I sent the "Circular Letters" for this year; fearing you should forget to *return* it by the association.^{47} —Mr F. says he does not understand the subject of religious melancholy.—Hope to see you on Tuesday.—Mrs M. is very poorly—

Y.^{rs} truly
J. W. Morris.

June 11. 1802.

3	Period. Acc.^{t}	Vol. I—see 6/6—		
12 ~~25~~	D^o —	N.º 9 —	/6—	
6 ~~25~~	D^o —	N.º 8 —	6—	
6	Watts Hymns — — — — —	3/3— —18/—		

Instead of 25   N.º 9, only 12.
D.^{o} N.º 8, only   6.

70. M[ary]. Carey to John Sutcliff, Olney, 4 October [1802] [postmarked from Wobourn].^{48}

Sir,

Altho I cannot suppose you are ignorant of a circumstance which has appeared in the Biblical Magazine^{49} yet so my dear Mrs Short sensibly feels that her vow is upon her and that she wont be freed therefrom till you are thro my kindness informed of that intelligence which she has received.

Ward, *The History of Friar Lane Baptist Church, Nottingham* (Nottingham: H. B. Saxton, 1903) 140, 252; *Biblical Magazine* 2 (1802): 359.

[47]One of the circular letters (presented at the Association meeting a few days after the date of the above letter) was Andrew Fuller's *The Practical Uses of Christian Baptism[,] a Circular Letter from the Ministers and Messengers of the Several Baptist Churches of the Northamptonshire Association, Assembled at Northampton, June 15, 16, 1802, to the Churches in Their Connexion* (1802).

[48]Eng. MS. 387, f. 19, JRULM.

[49]The *Biblical Magazine* was edited and printed by J. W. Morris at Dunstable from January 1801 until December 1803, when it merged with the *Theological Magazine*. The notice about Short's death appeared in the *Biblical Magazine* 2 (1802): 384.

I take this early opportunity of saying that yesterday and not till yesterday we heard the melancholy account of M[r] Shorts death.[50] It was transmitted us by M[r] Morris of Clipstone who received it from M[r] Carey.[51] I lament that M[r] C— was not present with him in his last expiring moment—and could with an empassioned heart exclaim

"Oh not to see him! not to see him die!
"Catch his last glance and close his languid eyes."

I feel it much—yet feared in time it could not well be otherwise—tho' I cannot help longing that someone present with keen and inquisitive feelings had urged M[r] Carey to have ventured tho at midnight—but I have no philosophy on such occasions and therefore perhaps am less qualified to articulate the principles of my wiser friends. I am sensibly fearful of all large animals yet I know not in that case but I would have mounted an eastern Elephant and set off in the deepest shades for Hindostan—but he is now no more! and I fear we shall never know at home the real feelings of his mind at the last—if they can be gathered only by bits and scraps as it were I know it would be [a] matter of great comfort to M[rs] Short. M[r] S- dies informed and I am persuaded he knew the doctrines of the Gospel theoretically. Oh that he may have received the love of the truth—then is he saved!

I cannot well write any more
Believe me with real esteem
Yours
M Carey

M[rs] Short intends writing M[r] Carey by the post [illegible word] —will M[r] Sutcliffe do us the favour to say how the letter may be convey'd? [?] respects [?] M[rs] S yourself, and Miss J—

October the 4th

---

[50]See letter 59.

[51]Carey wrote to Morris from Calcutta on 25 February 1802; the letter arrived sometime in late September and was published in the *Periodical Accounts*. Carey writes that in the first week of March he was informed that Short was near death. "I set out at daybreak on Tuesday morning," Carey writes, "but he had been dead about four hours when I arrived. I paid him every possible attention while he lived, and afterwards saw him decently interred. His health was visibly on the decline ever since his arrival in this country." Mary Carey believed that if her brother had left "at midnight," rather than daybreak, he would have seen Short *before* he died, a moment of great significance within the evangelical English culture of the eighteenth and nineteenth centuries. See *Periodical Accounts*, 2:230.

71. Charles Taylor,[52] Hatton Garden, London, to John Sutcliff, Olney, 21 October 1803.[53]

Sir
     Though I have long been under obligation to your good opinion yet this is the first direct intercourse which has taken place between us, and I avail myself of it, with great pleasure, as an opportunity of paying my personal respect, and acknowledgement.
     M[r] Morris of Dunstable writes me that a wish is expressed by a benevolent friend to find a copy of Calmet to the Missionaries in India pay[g] £5.5. for it—I need not inform you that this is less than the price of Calmet only but being desirous of forwarding the laudable objects of the Mission I send you, at that price, a fine paper copy of Calmet, complete, and a copy of Scripture Illustrated Complete also the whole half bound in calf How this kind of binding may be proper I do not know as the order was for one *in boards*—if it was intended to be pulled to pieces in order to be rebound in any other manner, then certainly, the present binding is waste, and this Copy may be exchanged; but if this binding will answ.[r] the intention it is much at your service
     If there was a thought of sending several *commonpaper* copies I should be happy to make a considerable abatement by way of compliment to the Mission—but these must be distinct from the binding—
                    I am Sir
                         very respectfully
                              W.[m] le Charles Taylor

Oct.[r] 21. 1803.
N[o] 108 Hatton Garden

72. Joshua Rowe,[54] in the Bristol Channel on board a ship, to John Sutcliff, Olney, 3 January 1804.[55]

                              Bristol Channel Jan[y] 3. 1804

     Very dear Sir

---

     [52]**Charles Taylor** (1756-1823), biblical commentator and editor of *Calmet's Great Dictionary of the Holy Bible* (1797).
     [53]Eng. MS. 384, f. 1980, JRULM. On the back page Sutcliff has written, "Rec. Oct. 22, 1803. Ans.— 27."
     [54]**Joshua Rowe** (1781-1822), BMS missionary to India, 1804-1822.
     [55]Eng. MS. 387, f. 108, JRULM. On the back page John Ryland has written, "a scene of sea sickness"; also written in Sutcliff's hand, "Rec. Jan. 17. 1804."

Have but just time to write a few lines, to send on shore by the Pilot, who intends leaving the ship much sooner than we expected, on account of having such a fine breeze to take us down the channel. Suppose you were very anxious to know whether we were at Sea in the late storm. Thro: mercy we did not sail at the time appointed, a vessel that sailed at the time we intended was lost! Our hearts are much revived at the pleasing intelligence rec.[d] from India: and we hope to meet with Dear Capt.[n] Weaks.[56] We left Bristol this morning, after taking leave of D.[r] Ryland, M.[r] Page, M.[r] Sharp,[57] Students, and many other friends, of both sexes, who accompanied us down to Pill.[58] We breakfasted, sang an hymn or two, and D.[r] R—prayed at an Inn near the river: after w.[h] we were accompanied by M.[r] Page and some other friends into the Ship, then stood on the Quarterdeck & sang M.[r] Saffery's 2nd hymn.[59] Have not time nor ability to enlarge—if I had I w.[d] give you an account of the scene w.[h] present[ed] themselves to my view. The Captain has been sick. Find it very difficult to please our sisters. On my left hand is M.[rs] Moore very sick, calling out lustily for a pot: bro: Moore holding her head and calling for a bucket. Complains of being sick himself. Mary Biss vomiting upon her Mother. Bro: Mardon ascending the ladder for fresh air, but obliged to discharge the contents of his stomach before he could get on the deck. M.[rs] Biss very sick: bro: Biss holding her head, and very quamish himself. M.[rs] Mardon sitting down on the floor of the state room casting up her accounts.—Betsy looking pale, and putting on a kind of sham cheerfulness, saying she is not sick—The vessel begins to heave much now, I do not know what kind of a night we shall have. All are now gone to bed, myself excepted. I find myself very quamish,

---

[56]Probably the same Capt. Wickes mentioned in letter 64.

[57]**John Sharp** (1741-1805), Baptist minister at Oakam (1770-1785), Manchester (1785-1797), and the Pithay, Bristol (1797-1805).

[58]According to an entry in the Broadmead Church Book, "On Dec[r] 8.th [1803] A solemn Meeting of Prayer was held at our place for the Designat.[n] of 4 Missionaries about to be sent by the Baptist Society, to New York in their way to Serampore in the East Indies." These were Joshua Rowe, Richard Mardon, John Biss, and William Moore. Saffery and Sutcliff were both in attendance. Sutcliff provided the laying on of hands, with the other ministers joining him. Andrew Fuller also spoke to the missionaries. Ryland concluded in prayer—"It was a day much to be remembered— The Meeting was well filled." Sutcliff preached at Broadmead on 8 December and twelve new members were baptized that day and received on 11 December. See Broadmead Church Book, 1779-1817, ff. 259, 260, 261; "Calendar of Letters," *Baptist Quarterly* 6 (1932-33): 283, 320-21, 376.

[59]**John Saffery** (1763-1825), Baptist minister at Brown Street, Salisbury, 1790-1825.

and wish to lie down, therefore must draw to a close: it is with great difficulty that I have written this.—[60]

Have left some profiles for you, Miss J.—[61] & M.rs Fuller,[62] with D.r Ryland.—M.r Tho.s Ransford[63] gave me the two first vols: of Scott on the Bible[64]   w.d thank you to send me the third, when published.—Hope that "I am among you as one that serveth" will be engraven upon my heart. Have great reason to think that unanimity will subsist among us. If I could, I w.d write you a long letter. Could you realize what I now feel from sickness you w.d freely pardon me; tho' I am obliged to write five letters.

All of us write in love to you M.rs S. Miss J and all enquiring friends—

Your's in our dear Lord
Joshua Rowe

N.B. The Knife w.h bro. Moore wrote to M.r [paper torn] about, proves to be bro: Mardon's, w.h [paper torn] in mistake. It was paid for.—

73. *Andrew Fuller, Kettering, to S[amuel]. J. Button,*[65] *24 Paternoster Row, London, 1 May 1804.*[66]

Ketter.g May 1. [1]804

Dear Sir,

---

[60]Besides Rowe, the other missionaries sent out on this day from Bristol were **William Moore** (1776-1844) and his wife, Eleanore; **John Biss** (d. 1807) and his wife, Hannah, and their daughter, Mary; and **Richard Mardon** (1776-1812) and his wife Rhoda.

[61]Miss Johnston, Sutcliff's sister-in-law.

[62]Miss Ann Coles, daughter of **William Coles** (1735-1809), Baptist minister at Maulden, became Andrew Fuller's second wife on 30 December 1794. His first wife died in 1792.

[63]**Thomas Ransford**—of Ransford and Sons, hat manufacturers, in Wine Street, Bristol—was a prominent member of the Broadmead church. See *Matthew's Bristol Directory for 1794* (Bristol: Matthews, 1794) 68.

[64]Thomas Scott (1747-1821), evangelical Anglican divine in Olney and a popular Bible commentator, was also a correspondent of John Ryland, Jr. The work mentioned here is his *Holy Bible, Containing the Old and New Testaments: with Original Notes and Practical Observations*, 3 vols. (1802–1804).

[65]Samuel Button, son of William Button, Baptist minister at Dean Street, Southwark, was a partner in his father's printing house in London, 1802-1819. Samuel was a subscriber to the BMS in 1804–1805. See *Periodical Accounts*, 3:131.

[66]MAM. PLP. 42.47.2, JRULM.

I am much obliged to Mr Bevan[67] for the labour he has bestowed on the Articles *Behmanists, Mystics, Quietists,* & *Friends*, all w^h I have duly rec.^d The first is gone to press, and I believe with out any alterations. The Second & Third I have not had time to examine. The last which came yesterday I have read to day. It is long, but I w.^d not object to it on that acc.^t: And as I approve of the principle of every denomination being allowed to speak for themselves, I see nothing to object to on any other, except the last note which he is not anxious to have inserted, and the first two pages, respecting their history. These I think have rather too much asperity and reflection for a simple statement. If it were a vindication it might be less objectionable. I also conceive *that part* sh.^d be given by the Editor; and that it w.^d be more to their honour to have it so. As it is, it would be manifest to every discerning reader that it was done by one of themselves, and that rather as an advocate than a simple narrator. That the account of their principles sh.^d be thought to be drawn up by one of themselves is highly proper; and it w.^d add weight & worth to it. In that part therefore I shall intimate as much. I submit the following to Mr B.s remarks instead of those two first pages, w^h if he approve, he need not trouble himself to write: if not, I will thank him for a few lines. All the rest I approve.[68]

Friends or *Quakers*, a religious society wch began to be distinguished about the middle of the 17.th Century. The doctrines peculiar to this society were first promulgated by George Fox in Eng.^d about the year 1647, for wch he as imprisoned at Nott.^m in 1649, and in ye year following at Derby. The appellation of *Quakers* was given them by way of con-

---

[67]**Joseph Gurney Bevan** (1753-1814), a leading Quaker writer.

[68]The work under discussion and to which Fuller contributed, with assistance from Bevan, was a new edition of Hannah Adams's *An Alphabetical Compendium of the Various Sects which have Appeared in the World from the Beginning of the Christian Aera to the Present Day. With an Appendix Containing a Brief Account of the Different Schemes of Religion now Embraced Among Mankind, etc.* (Boston, 1800 and 1801) which first appeared in England in 1805, printed by J. W. Morris of Dunstable for William Button and Son, and for Thomas Williams (another edition appeared in 1814). Added to the 1805 edition was a preface by Fuller entitled "An Essay on Truth" (pp. 5-30). The article on "Behmanists" appeared on pp. 90-93; "Mystics" on pp. 229-232; "Quietists" on pp. 272-273; and "Friends" on pp. 138-158. At the end of the article on "Friends," the following editorial note was added: "In apology for the length of the foregoing article, in which the reader is referred to the authorities cited at the foot of the page, it is proper to say, it was inserted at the request of an intelligent *Friend*, and in consequence of complaints of misrepresentations in other publications. The contrary opinions on several points will be found under the articles Calvinist, Baptist, Episcopalians, &c." (p. 158). Obviously, that "Friend" was Bevan, though no acknowledgment concerning any of the authors of the articles in the book is given. Paragraphs 2-7 appeared in the 1805 edition (pp. 138-139) largely as written by Fuller, with some deletions and additions.

tempt: some say on acc.^t of the tremblings and quakings, under an impression of divine things, whch appeared in their publick assemblies; but they themselves say, it was given them by one of the Justices, who imprisoned Fox on acc.^t of his bidding him, and those about him *tremble* at the word of the Lord. Whatever was the origin of the name, it has remained their usual denomination, but they themselves adopted the appellation of *Friends*.

From their first appearance they suffered much persecution. In New England they were treated with peculiar severity. To what has been alleged ag.^t them they do not justify every thing done by individuals—that the extravagances and blaphemies of *James Nayler*,[69] and his associates were disapproved at the time, and parties disowned; nor was he restored till he had given signs of sincere repentance, and publicly condemned his error—and that many of those who suffered were persons of unimpeachable character. The treatment which they as a body received, they consider, and so we apprehend must every true friend to liberty of conscience, as anti-christian and cruel.

During the persecutions which they met with in New England, they applied to King Charles the Second for relief, who granted a Mandamus, dated September 9. 1661 to put a stop to them. Neither were the good offices of this Prince in their favour confined to the colonies; for in 1671 he released under the great seal 400 of these suffering people, who were imprisoned in Great Britain.

In 1681 the same king granted to Willm Penn the province of Pennsylvania. Penn's treaty with the Indians, and the liberty of Conscience which he granted to all denominations, even those, which had persecuted his own, do honour to his memory.

In the reign of James the IInd, the *Friends*, in common with other English dissenters, were relieved by the suspension of the penal laws. But it was not till the reign of W.^m & Mary that they obtained any thing like a proper legal protection. In 1696 an Act was made which, with a few exceptions, allowed to their affirmation the legal force of an oath, and provided a less oppressive mode of receiving tythes under a certain amount; which provisions in the reign of Geo. the first were made perpetual. For refusing to pay tythes, &c, however, they are still liable to suffer in the exchequer and ecclesiastical court, both in Great Britain and Ireland.

---

[69]James Naylor (1617?-1660) was an English Quaker from Yorkshire who, after his conversion through the preaching of George Fox, suffered considerably for his Quaker beliefs. He was tried and convicted of blasphemy in 1651 by parliament, and after two years of imprisonment was released into the custody of some Friends. His collected *Writings* were published posthumously in 1716.

The doctrines of the Society of Friends have been variously represented: we shall give the reader an account of them as drawn up by one of themselves, and nearly in the words of their principal writers.
Kind respects to your own & fathers family & am affec.ʸ y.ʳˢ
A. Fuller

P.S. Mʳ Bevan & you must have patience—My hands are so full of other matters, & my Journies so many & long, that I shall not be able to get on very fast. I suppose I shall not be able to sit down to it another day till the latter end of July.

74. *Joseph Hughes, Battersea, London, to John Sutcliff, Olney, 19 July 1804.*[70]

Battersea   July 19, 1804

Dear Sir,
I understand Mʳ Carey has opened a magnificent plan relative to the translation of the Scriptures into various languages.[71]
This idea is so coincident with the views of the *Bible Society*, that I cannot but wish for some information relative to it.
Will you favour me with a few lines containing an Extract from *Carey's* Letter, such as I may lay before the Committee. I wish for it by return of post that I may have ready next Monday—
Yours affect.ʸ
J Hughes
Secretary

Be kind enough to direct your letter for me at Mr Button's to be left till called for—

---

[70]Eng. MS. 346, f. 156, JRULM.

[71]Carey's ambitious plan to translate the scriptures into several Eastern languages was the primary reason for Fuller's fundraising trip to Scotland in the summer of 1805. Collections and donations received during that trip totaled £1298.9.10. See *Periodical Accounts*, 3:146-150.

75. James Hinton,[72] Oxford, to John Fawcett, Hebden Bridge, Halifax, 21 September 1804.[73]

Oxford Sep 21. 1804

Dear Sir

I have been duly favoured with both your letters; & I remark with sincere pleasure the ardent & anxious zeal which you manifest, to serve the cause of God & truth—The esteem which your works had excited, your letters have confirmed—

I hope I have not, on my part, incurred the charge of neglect, in the "important business" on which you write. On receiving your first letter, I resolved to take 3 or 4 days for consideration & prayer—I did so—At the end of 3 or 4 days (I believe) I received a letter from my friend and late Tutor M[r] Hall, who entered more largely on the subject & certainly removed some of my objections to the proposal I had received. I now thought it right to lay the matter before a few of my friends whom I am in the habit of consulting, both in Oxford and in the neighborhood & the result I wrote to M[r] Hall in a week after I received his application & begged him to transmit it immediately to the Society. You probably know, ere now, what the result is. I thought the matter too important to decide at once, & where any hesitation rests, on such a business, the answer ought not perhaps, to be more speedy than mine has been.[74]

My Love to my people, & their pleas with me, would not alone prevail, but when disinterested men are clearly & unanimously of opinion that public good (tis *their* expression) demands a continuation of my labours in Oxford, I am obliged, tho with a more cordial wish to serve the interests of your rising Society, to listen to the decisions of one who will I doubt not, provide you with a more able Tutor; for which blessing [paper torn] for every one, personal, domestic, & [paper torn] on your own behalf, accept the wishes & be assured of the prayers of

---

[72]**James Hinton** (1761-1823), Baptist minister at Oxford, 1787-1823.

[73]Eng. MS. 378, f. 953, JRULM. On the address page is written in John Fawcett's hand, "This letter to be returned to J. F."

[74]In this letter Hinton is declining the presidency of the Northern Education Society's new academy at Bradford, which had been first offered to Joseph Kinghorn at Norwich, who had also declined. The position was eventually filled by William Steadman. John Fawcett had written to Robert Hall, enlisting the latter's aid in procuring a president after Kinghorn had rejected the offer; apparently Hall had considered Hinton a viable choice to head the new academy. Fawcett had written Hinton twice about the proposed presidency, to which Hinton finally responded. See Mary Langdon, *A Brief Memoir of the Rev. Thomas Langdon, Baptist Minister, of Leeds* (London: Simpkin and Marshall, 1837) 46-47.

Dear Sir
y^r oblig'd fr^d & Bro^r
Ja^s Hinton

76. *John Ryland, Bristol, to John Sutcliff, Olney, 23 January 1805.*[75]

My dear Bro^r

We have got nearly three thousand pounds subscribed for our Building,[76] particulars I have no time to relate—I send this on a printed paper the better to conceal the inclosed which you will be so good as to acknowledge in a day or two—9.3.9. is for yourself, including 1 Guinea for D. Dossett's[77] pocket money—which will pay you for 1 Q^r at the rate of 32 Guineas p^r Ann. Board & Tuition—the same as is paid here—the remaining 4£. 6.3 you will pay to Bro^r Fuller for the Mission Society, particulars shall be sent as soon as I can—I rec^d 50 Guineas last week thro Mr Biddulph.[78]

On the opposite page are these figures:

Board & Tuition	9. 3. 9
Dan Dossett	48. 6. 3
	57.10.7

---

[75]Eng. MS. 371, f. 107g, JRULM. The letter is postmarked 23 January; on the back page Sutcliff has written: "Rec. Jan. 24. 1805. Ans. — 25. —."

[76]Ryland oversaw the move of the Academy from North Street to Stokes Croft. The new building, including the Museum, cost £12,000 and was not completed until 1811. See Norman S. Moon, *Education for Ministry: Bristol Baptist College, 1679-1979* (Bristol: Bristol Baptist College, 1979) 34.

[77]Daniel Dossett was studying for the ministry under Sutcliff at Olney, although he does not appear in the list of students mentioned in "Sutcliff's Academy at Olney," *Baptist Quarterly* 4 (1928-129): 276-279. Apparently, he was receiving some monetary support from the Bristol Education Society, which would explain the receipt of a guinea from Ryland. Dossett would later pastor the Baptist church at Gold Hill, Bucks., c. 1811-1823. Along with Sutcliff and forty-three other ministers, he attended the initial meetings in London on 24-25 June 1812 that led to the formation of Baptist Union. See Seymour J. Price, "The Early Years of the Baptist Union," *Baptist Quarterly* 4 (1928-1929): 58, 131.

[78]The total received from Biddulph came from Miss P. G. Smith of Bradford, and amounted to £52.10. See *Periodical Accounts*, 3:128.

77. John Ryland, Bristol, to John Sutcliff, Olney, postmarked 1 March 1805.[79]

My dear Brother

I rec[d] by this days post a Letter from M[r] Beeching of Maidstone,[80] M[rs] Clark's Agent,[81] by w[ch] I find the sole Cause of the Draft's being returned, is the failure of the Maidstone Bank. Being ten or eleven days clear from the date of the Draft, before they stopt paym[t], M[r] Beeching concluded it had been presented & accepted by their Bankers in town, previous to the 29th of January, w[ch] was the day they first refused to accept. Bills sent to Lond[n] are always presented for acceptance the day received or the next, or otherwise the Holders make them their own. But when sent so far distant as Bristol the Case no doubt is different, says he.

The Expences on the Bill are not easily to be accounted for. M[r] Skinner the Banker[82] thinks them exhorbitant, and indeed I cannot make out how they are reckoned. The following is a Copy of the Paper confer'd on, to the Note.[83]

A Letter came to our House on Lord's day for M[r] Coles of Bourton[84] from Marshman, dated Sept[r] 1804, in which there is very little News. But a few lines I transcribed, viz.

> The first Edition of the Bengalee N. T. is nearly distributed, & another is begun, in which we have advanced as far as the 2[d] Epistle to the Corinthians. Luke the Acts & the Romans are not however included, as it is our intention to strike off 10,000 Cop[s] extra of the 3 Books, when we print them; this necessarily occasioning a considerable addition of Exp[ce] in Paper, causes a little delay.
>
> Lord's day Sept[r] 2. we Bap[d] 3 Hindoos, one of them a young Brahman, Soroop by name the Son of a considerable Teacher

---

[79]Eng. MS. 383, f. 1773b, JRULM. On the back page Sutcliff has written: "Rec.[d] Mar. 26. 1805."

[80]John Beeching, salesman. See *Universal British Directory*, 3:874.

[81]Mrs. Clarke of Bristol was the descendant of John Clarke (1687-1734), early 18th c. Latin scholar and translator of *Cornelii Nepotis Vitae Excellentium Imperatorum; . . . Or, Cornelius Nepos's Lives of the Excellent Commanders* (1723), the fifteenth edition appearing in London in 1797. Her donation (£2.2, plus another £2.8 from the "profits on Clarke's Lives") to the BMS was received for 1805. See *Periodical Accounts*, 3: 127.

[82]William Skinner of the Broadmead church in Bristol (see letter 67).

[83]Unfortunately, no other paper is included with this letter.

[84]**Thomas Coles** (1779-1840), Baptist minister at Bourton-on-the-Water, 1801 to 1840.

among them. Before his B^m his Father came & with many Tears and entreaties besought his Son to return, but he very steadily refused, saying, "that to return to Hindooism, was to plunge himself into Hell." The other two are young men of the writer Cast.[85] These make the N° 12, which we have B^d this year.—We have however been greatly afflicted wth the walk of some of our Members this year; have been compelled to suspend some, & exclude others: yet we cannot but conclude that there is among them a holy seed wch shall be unto the Lord for an eternal Excellency.

If you have had any Letters from India, I hope you will soon let me know some of the News. When will N^o xiv. be out?[86] Would it be worth while to send Mr Morris this extract from the Letter to Coles? No other Letter is come hither.

I sh^d have expected that Marshman's Journal w^d have come by the same conveyance probably directed for me—I guess'd Bro^r Fuller might have opened it in Lond^n but then I sh^d tho't it w^d have been forwarded by this time.—I think Care sh^d no[w] be taken to abridge their Acc^ts of the Discipline, & there is no Need of letting all the World know every Difficulty of that sort, any farther than just to shew the faithfulness of the Men. We make no other Church Transcriptions public.

I sh^d not have delay'd sending you the money, but Mr Skinner tells me it will not be safe to do it, till I hear again from Maidstone, under present Circumstances, as the Bill was not presented for Accept^ce nor return'd in time.

[no signature]

78. J. W. Morris, Clipston, to John Sutcliff, Olney, 30 March 1805.[87]

Dr Bro.

---

[85]The three men were Ram Kaunt, Hawnye, and Soroop. Soroop was about 20 years of age. His father was a Gosaic, "or great Goroo," and had many followers, according to William Ward's journal as printed in the *Periodical Accounts*. "This man had four or five disciples with him," William Ward writes. "He wore two malas, (or necklaces) one of which had large beads, made of the wood of the sacred Toolsee tree. He has a number of disciples at Serampore." Soroop's baptism was a significant moment in the early history of the Serampore mission. See *Periodical Accounts*, 3:44-45.

[86]A reference to the next number of the *Periodical Accounts*.

[87]Eng. MS. 381, f. 1437, JRULM. On the back page Sutcliff has written: "Rec. Mar. 30, 1805."

I can send you only one copy at present of H. Adams:[88] we have no more boarded, and some of the sheets we want are gone to Button's. I have written to him twice about it, but there is no end of his teasing dilatory conduct.— I enclose only 2 copies of P. A.[89] vol. ii. We have none of N.º X to complete the sets: if you have any to spare, let me have them without delay, or we must reprint that N.º —I enclose you Ward's letter:[90] but do not forget to return it by first opportunity. M.ʳ Fuller has seen it: it came just before he called lately. I do not hear whether any others have come to hand.—You will think to give me directions in time about the box for India, and what articles will be wanted from Dunstable. If possible you had much better make us the box yourself: there is no trusting to Button—We cannot yet complete the Connec. Mag.ᵉ — The TH. M.[91] was sent into the binding room to be done uniformly, and I thought it had been so.— We are now upon M.ʳ Fuller's Exposition on Genesis,[92] which will make near 400 pp.— Also trying at Blundel's sermons: but they are as if they were put together with wooden skewers. We shall proceed very slowly, if indeed we can proceed at all.—[93]

We are all tolerably well. M.ʳˢ M. seems at present to bear this Spring rather better than the last. We are glad to hear that you and yours are in better health, and that poor Mary is returned more comfortable: this is a very pleasing circumstance.—We are to have a Min. Meeting here on *Easter Tuesday*! Brethren Wake,[94] Blundel and Sutcliff are requested to preach: do not disappoint us!— Our united love to all yours.

Yours always

J. W. Morris

Mar. 30. [1]805.

---

[88]Probably *An Abridgement of the History of New-England for the Use of Young Persons* (Boston, 1805) by Hannah Adams (1755-1831). The work was reprinted by Morris in Dunstable in 1806.

[89]*Periodical Accounts.*

[90]William Ward had sent Morris a copy of his journal from 1 January through 30 November 1804, which was printed in the *Periodical Accounts*, 3:29-58. Morris was the printer of the *Accounts* from its inception until sometime in 1810 or 1811.

[91]The *Theological Magazine* began in 1800 and in January 1804 it joined with the *Biblical Magazine*, becoming known as the *Theological and Biblical Magazine*, which ran until 1807.

[92]*Expository Discourses on the Book of Genesis Interspersed with Practical Reflections* (1806) by Andrew Fuller and published by Morris.

[93]*Sermons on Various Subjects* (1806) by Thomas Blundel (see letter 64); also published by Morris.

[94]**Thomas Wake**, at that time Baptist minister at Leighton Buzzard, Bedfordshire.

79. Christopher Anderson,[95] Olney, to John Sutcliff, "care of M.ʳ Mellor, Hebden Bridge, Halifax, Yorkshire," 19 July 1805.[96]

Olney 19ᵗʰ July 1805.

Dear & esteemed Brother

The day after you left home a letter came from Mʳ Fuller which Miss Johnstone thought it best to open, thinking he would mention to you in it the days he required assistance at Kettering—he does so—the 1ˢᵗ & 2ⁿᵈ Lord's days in August. There has not yet any line come from Mʳˢ Fuller. You will excuse me copying the whole of his letter—the principal intelligence is as follows— "Collected at Lincoln 8 Guineas—At Hull & Cottingham (4 miles off) £153.—Scarboro £40. At Alnwick £20. did not call at Newcastle—Mʳ Fyshwick[97] being absent.—" Arrived at Edinʰ Saturday Evening 11 o'clock—had a cold ever since the Association which is much against me. Mʳ Haldane's book[98] will be sent you— perhaps some Sandemanianism[99] in it. "To be sure (says Bro: Fuller to Mʳ R. H.) after all this minute attention to Scripture rules, we shall hear

---

[95]**Christopher Anderson** (1782-1852), Baptist minister at Edinburgh and strong supporter of the BMS.

[96]Eng. MS. 372, f. 44a, JRULM. On the back page is written in Sutcliff's hand: "Rec. July 1805."

[97]**Richard Fishwick, Esq.** (1745-1825), a leading Baptist layman in the north of England during the last quarter of the eighteenth century.

[98]**Robert Haldane** (1764-1842), along with his brother **James**, was a prominent figure in the evangelical revival of Scotland in the late 1790s and early 1800s. At the time of this letter, Haldane was pastor of the Tabernacle Church in Edinburgh, a leading congregation of the New Congregational Churches of Scotland, formed in 1799. Haldane was still a paedobaptist at this time, which explains Fuller's comments. Haldane did not accept baptism by immersion until 1808, at which time his church adopted Baptist polity. See Brian Talbot, *The Search for a Common Identity: The Origins of the Baptist Union of Scotland 1800-1870,* Studies in Baptist History and Thought, vol. 9 (Carlisle UK: Paternoster Press, 2003) 73-114; William W. Lawson, "Robert and James Haldane," *Baptist Quarterly* 7 (1934-1935): 283.

[99]Sandemanians were a sect that originated in Scotland under the leadership of John Glas (1695-1773) and his son-in-law, Robert Sandeman (1718-71). In 1730 Glas, an ordained minister in the Church of Scotland, withdrew from the Scottish church and began an independent sect, known in Scotland as Glassites. Eventually, through the efforts of Sandeman, the sect spread to London and America, where Sandeman died in 1771. As a result, in England and America the sect became known as Sandemanians. Among the group's major tenets was the complete separation of church and state; a belief in a "reasoned faith" (as opposed to emotion, "religious affections," or a personal experience) as the only grounds for a true relationship with God and the attainment of salvation; and the reinstituting of certain New Testament practices, such as the love feast, foot washing, a limited community of goods, and church governance by bishops, elders, and teachers.

in a little time how surprized you are at yourselves in having so long stuck fast by Infant Baptism!"—"I have so many places to preach at during the ensuing week & so large a Circuit, that I have little hope of being with you at the Leeds Meeting"—D[r] S.[100] goes with me hence on Tuesday (letter dated 4th July) morning the 9th by Dunfermline—Kirkaldy—Dundee—Montrose—Aberdeen—on y[e] Lords day in Perth—Stirling—Glasgow &c. &c. &c.[101] He is afraid the Glas[w] Collections will not be so large owing to the News about the French Fleet arriving in the West Indies. But hopes in one place & ano[r] to get his usual Sum—Sent home already £310 Stg. i.e in the faith of the Tab. Collection being £100. had collected already £220—(and I observe by the Newspaper the collection was £126!)   He had called on M[r] McLean & talked over many things very amicably. Informed him that altho he had given up the idea of ask[g] him for 2 years—did not know but that he would do it yet.

I preached on Wednesday Evening after you went, & last Evening—M[r] Wake[102] came on Saturday—left this on Tuesday Afternoon—M[r] Sharman is come—I preach at Stoke L[ds] day Evening—(they applied)—and intend if the L[d] will to be at Kettering the days M[r] Fuller mentions—M[r] Robertson[103] leaves this on Wednesday next for Bristol—I

---

[100]**Dr. Charles Stuart** (1746-1826).

[101]Anderson traveled extensively for several months in 1805, arriving in London in the middle of May to stay for about a month, largely to promote BMS activities, during which time he also visited Bristol. In mid-June he went to Olney to spend time with Sutcliff, attending the Midland Association meeting at Dunstable on his way. His stay with Sutcliff was "as pleasant as it was profitable to him," Hugh Anderson writes. "Literary advantages, indeed, there were not many; but the conversation and remarks of his revered tutor were valuable, the opportunities he had of public address were numerous, while the free criticisms on his written exercises by his fellow-students, who were not more in number than an ordinary family circle, could not fail to keep in check the self-esteem which his growing popularity in the villages and neighbouring towns might create." He kept a journal of his travels the month before this letter was written, preaching in Bedford at Hillyard's church; then at Lavendon; entertaining John Ryland on 2 July in Olney; and preaching in Olney on 7 July. According to his journal, he was in Birmingham on the 19th, but according to this letter, he was actually in Olney. Fuller returned on 14 August from Scotland with nearly £1300. Anderson eventually left Olney for London on 30 October 1805. An account of Fuller's journey through Scotland that summer raising funds for Carey's translation work at Serampore can be found in Morris's *Memoir of Fuller*. The total amount collected by Fuller and others in Scotland and the north of England appeared in the *Periodical Accounts*. See Hugh Anderson, *Letters of Christopher Anderson* (Edinburgh: W. P. Kennedy, 1854) 59-61, 33-36; Morris, *Memoirs*, 129-153; *Periodical Accounts*, 3:146-150.

[102]See letter 78.

[103]Two possibilities exist here. James Robertson (1778-1861), from Inchture, Perthshire, was one of Haldane's first students in 1798. He ministered in a Congregational church briefly at Aberdeen before settling at Stuartfield in 1800. Eventually,

have not received any letters from Scotland since you left us—M[r] Hillyard[104] called just now to see if I could preach L[ds] day Evening—but as I am engaged for Stoke I could not. Your letter dated Saturday did not arrive here till Yesterday Morning! We were anxious to hear from you, how you had got forward—but it relieved Miss J[s] mind &c.—The "two manuscripts" were sent away, before your letter arrived—also the parcel directed to M[r] Wheeler[105]—Miss Johnstone desires her love to you both & all friends—She is well & Mary apparently in her ordinary—If any interesting News come from Scotland I shall let you know—May the Lord be present with you, to render your Sowing pleasant & useful & may grace & peace be multiplied to you and your affectionate Bro: who remains with much esteem yours &c. in

the LORD.

Christ[r] Anderson

80. S[amuel]. Barnard, Jr.,[106] Boston, [Lincolnshire], to John Sutcliff, Olney, 5 February 1806.[107]

---

he immigrated to America, ministering in Vermont (1832-1836) and later in Canada (1836-1861). George Robertson (1778-1854) was a Haldane convert who studied under Greville Ewing at Glasgow before becoming a Scottish congregational minister in the church at Inverkip, near Greenock, from 1800 to 1807. He then ministered at Paisley (1807-15), Orkney (1814-1834), and finally at Thurso, Caithness (1833-1847). See *American Congregational Quarterly* (1862): 214; James Ross, *A History of Congregational Independency in Scotland.* (Glasgow: J. MacLehose, 1900) 218, 252-253, 254; *Congregational Year Book* (1855): 234.

[104]Thomas Hillyard (d. 1828), father of **Samuel Hillyard** of Bedford, was the Independent minister at Olney.

[105]Possibly John Wheeler, who was baptized in the Northampton church in 1798. Originally from Gloucestershire, he was working for a tallow chandler in Northampton when he was drawn to Christ by the singing of a Cowper hymn at College Lane. He was soon called to preach and in 1805 led a group from College Lane into forming a meeting at Bugbrooke, where Ryland and Fuller had often preached. His descendant was H. Wheeler Robinson. See Ernest A. Payne, *College Street Church, Northampton, 1697-1947* (London: Kingsgate Press, 1947) 27.

[106]Two Samuel Barnards, father and son, lived at Boston at this time, and were most likely Baptists, for the elder Barnard was a subscriber to Robert Robinson's *Ecclesiastical Researches* (1792). The writer of this letter and author of the work under discussion, *The Essence, Spirituality, and Glorious Issue of the Religion of Christ Jesus to All God's Chosen: Exhibited in Remarks on the Expression, "Verily, Verily," as used by our Blessed Saviour in many Parts of Scripture* (1806), is Samuel Barnard the younger (b. 1784). The work was published by W. Nicholson of London, not Thomas Williams and William Smith. Samuel Barnard the elder (1752-1810) was a banker and merchant in Boston. The author of the above letter and work should not be confused with another Samuel Barnard (d. 1807), Independent minister for many years at the New Chapel, Dagger-lane, Hull, and later at Hope Street, Hull, and finally

Boston. Feb^r 5, 1806

My dear Sir

    I have just rec^d my Manuscript & your Letter, by the hand of Mr Talbot, & by him I now write these few Lines in Return—& thank you for the few Hints you have given me concerning them. At present I am not at work upon the other Parts of them. A smaller Work has risen out of them, which I am now publishing, having just set my finishing hand to the Work. It will comprise about 300 Pages of common Octavo & nearly 1/2 is printed off. It consists of short Remarks on the Verses in the New Testament which begin with the double Expression Verily, verily. They are in Number about 22, are all contained in John's Gospel, & are the Words of our Saviour, & my design in writing was to discuss what might be the doctrinal Points which our Lord pressed upon his Disciples here below. Williams & Smith have it in Lon^n & I hope it will be out in 3 or 4 months.

    I think with you that the Manuscript I sent you is not in a suitable State for the public Eye, & I think would be more suitable to present taste in some kind of [illegible word].

    Mr Stevens[108] who preaches at St Neots is yet with us & I think it seems probable will soon have an Invitation from the Particular Bap. Church to take the office of Pastor here. He is much liked by People in the Country, more so than by the Town People, tho the former in general can only get to hear him in the Summer.

    I am glad to hear so good an Acc^t of John Smith,[109] to whom please remember me, also to Mr Dobney[110] if still with you.

---

at Howard Street, Sheffield, from 1803 to 1807. His publications appeared between 1786 and 1804. Some papers belonging to the Boston Barnards can be found in the Barnard-Talcot-Hollerith family papers at George Washington University. See *Universal British Directory*, 2:338; Miall, *Congregationalism in Yorkshire*, 293, 355.

    [107]Eng. MS. 372, f. 113, JRULM. On the back page Sutcliff has written: "Rec. Mar. 14. 1806. Ans: — 20. —."

    [108]**John Stevens**, Baptist minister at St. Neots (1799-1805) and later at Meard's Court, Wardour Street, London. In 1794 the *Universal British Directory* noted that Boston, Nottinghamshire, could claim Baptist (both General and Particular), Presbyterian, Methodist, and Quakers meetings, adding that "the number of Dissenters is, of late years, considerably increased." See *Universal British Directory*, 2:336.

    [109]John Smith was originally from Boston, where he would have known Barnard. He was a student of Sutcliff's at Olney and was ordained pastor of the Baptist congregation at Burton-on-Trent, Staffordshire, on 10 May 1809, having been dismissed from the Olney church on 23 February 1809. See *Baptist Magazine* 1 (1809): 341; Olney Church Book, f. 58.

    [110]George Dobney was also one of Sutcliff's students; he ministered at Wallingford in 1814. See P. B. Gravett, *Over Three Hundred Years of God's Grace: A Short*

I remain in best Wishes
Dear Sir Yours truly
S. Barnard, Jun[r]

81. *Francis Augustus Cox,*[111] *Clipston, to John Sutcliff, Olney, 20 February 1806.*[112]

My very dear Sir
  I am extremely sorry after having written you word of my coming Mar. 5 to put it off—but this I hope you will have the goodness to excuse as it is only for *one week*—I have received a letter from Cambridge inviting me to supply there the *first* & *second* Sabbaths in *March.* I intend therefore (God willing) to be with you on *Wednesday* the 12.th of *March* & you may depend upon it that no engagement shall alter this.
      I rem.[n]
                Y.[rs] very affectionately
                        F A Cox
Clipstone
Feb. 20. 1806

82. *Christopher Anderson, London, to John Sutcliff, Olney, 19 June 1806.*[113]

London 19.th June 1806

  Much respected Brother
    I left Bristol with D.[r] Ryland on Tuesday at 12 oclock. He stopped that night to preach at Newburgh, and has arrived in Town this morning. I have been very kindly treated at Bristol indeed. I mentioned the Ed.[n] business[114]—called on Friends there and have received about

---

History of Sutcliff Baptist Church (Olney: n.p., 1987) 27; "Sutcliff's Academy at Olney," *Baptist Quarterly* 4 (1928-1929): 277.

  [111]**Francis Augustus Cox** (1783-1853), after two years at Clipston (1804–1806), spent two years at St. Andrew's Street in Cambridge (this letter denotes the beginning of that connection) as Robert Hall's successor. He would pastor the Baptist church in Mare Street, Hackney, for more than forty years.

  [112]Eng. MS. 375, f. 473a, JRULM. On the back page is written in Sutcliff's hand: "Rec. Feb. 21. 1806."

  [113]Eng. MS. 369, f. 4, JRULM. On the back page is written in Sutcliff's hand: "Rec. June 21, 1806. Ans.— 25.—."

  [114]Most likely this is a reference to Anderson's involvement with the newly formed London Baptist Education Society (1804), which initially provided financial

£150.—I intend preaching at Mr Booths two next L.^{ds} Days, tho' perhaps the D.^{r} will exchange next L.^{ds} day and in that case I may be at Carter Lane in the afternoon. Is there any thing I can do for you while in London—I think of leaving on this day fortnight—in which case I may once more be indulged with the sight of my Olney Friends. I shall at all events spend that Sabbath with you. I suppose I must be at Wellingboro on the Monday Evening & with Bro Fuller on the Tuesday—I have never enjoyed his Company a single day together—and as he leaves Kettering the week following for Birmingham—I must be punctual.

I have not heard yet whether you are to be at Birmingham on the 16 prox.^{o}—But as Bro Fuller—Ryland—Page—Coles[115] &c are to be there I suppose it is probable.

Give my love to Mr Wilson—please to inform him of my being in Town—If his business should lead him to London on Monday week—we could return together on the Thursday or Friday.

Could you oblige me by mentioning to Mr Fuller that I intend being at Kettering after seeing you, and if it is convenient may accompany him (on my way home) to Birmingham—as I intend being there while he is.

Excuse my concluding. M.^{r} & Mrs Burls kind respects. My Love to all Friends—and in prospect of seeing you soon &c   I am   My dear sir
with much esteem
Your bro in ye L.^{d}
Christ.^{r} Anderson

Mrs Burls is rather poorly, and the child who has been so poorly some time, tho still ill is rather I believe recovering—

London 19 June

---

support for a select number of promising ministerial candidates each year. A report of the Society's annual meeting in May 1809, which appeared later that year in the *Baptist Magazine*, proclaimed that the Society's primary goal was to provide Baptist "churches with godly ministers, not wholly uneducated, at a time when education is sought after by reflecting persons of every class. It aims, not to make its pupils acquainted with the learned languages, but to give them such a knowledge of their mother tongue as to raise them above the charge of illiteracy. It seeks to inform their minds in Theological subjects, so far as to enable them to comprehend scriptural truths in their connection and harmony, and to express their ideas with clearness and precision, with sound speech that cannot be condemned." Anderson spoke at the 1809 meeting, which was followed the next year by the founding of Stepney College. See *Baptist Magazine* 1(1809): 342.

[115]**William Coles** (1735-1809), Andrew Fuller's father-in-law and Baptist minister at Maulden, Long Buckby, 1758-1805.

83. J. W. Morris, [Dunstable], to John Sutcliff, Olney, 21 November 1806.[116]

Dear Bro.

    Your American order was sent to Boston in May last, but am greatly afraid that both of them are lost, and also another parcel in Jan.ʸ, as I have heard nothing from Boston since Oct. [1]805. However I have this week sent again, & again copied your order.— D.ʳ Ryland and Fernandez[117] just called, but it was very transient. He was full of wrath about our review of Rippon! It was written by a person in London whom I do not know: but it was sent to me for revision, and I laid at least a discount of 40 p cent upon it, or it would have killed him quite![118]—I wish much to be at Northampton, but the weather and roads are forbidding, and I am still very poorly of a cold caught for my journey to Biggleswade. If I were to come I could not preach without injury to my self; and perhaps might venture out if I were excused from preaching, as indeed I ought to be. I have not been well this fortnight or more. Blundel is better, but is not likely to stir out.— No preaching at Hockliff[119] last sabbath, but I sent one of our friends to read: the place was suffocating—[Tift?] will be there next sabbath, and now I hope there will be no further mistakes.

Yours affec.ᵗ
J W Morris

Nov. 21. [1]806.

---

[116]Eng. MS. 381, f. 1437c, JRULM.

[117]**Ignatius Fernandez (**1757-1830), BMS supporter in India.

[118]The review appeared in the November 1806 issue of the *Theological and Biblical Magazine* (502-508), is which Rippon was severely criticized in an unsigned review of Rippon's *Memoir* of Abraham Booth, which Rippon had delivered at Booth's interment on 9 February 1806. The *Memoir* was published in connection with James Dore's funeral sermon for Booth. Apparently, Booth had left explicit commands that there were to be no memorials of his life and work spoken at his funeral or interment. The anonymous reviewer praised Dore for following those wishes, but brutally lambasted Rippon at length for failing to do so.

[119]There is no record of a Baptist church in Hockliff at this time, but, as this letter suggests, there may have been a small group of Baptists (not organized as a church) meeting in a home. One group of dissenters (possibly the group mentioned by Morris) registered with the Archdeacon's Court on 27 January 1806 to meet in the house of William Read, Hockliff. See Edwin Welch, ed., *Bedfordshire Chapels and Meeting Places: Official Registration, 1672-1901* (Bedford: Bedfordshire Historical Record Society, 1996) 86.

2	Memoirs of Miss Anthony[120]—-	3/6 —	6.0
2	D.º Pearce, common[121] ———	1/6 —	2.6
1	Watts, red Rone ———	4/6 —	4.--
1	Hopkins on Holiness[122]———	2/ —	1.8
			14.2

84. Olinthus Gregory,[123] Royal Military Academy, Woolwich, to an unidentified bookseller in London, 12 January 1807.[124]

Royal Military Academy
Woolwich. Jan 12. 1807.

Gentlemen
    I will thank you to send me as soon as you can conveniently, the following articles, or such of them as you have:

Montucla's History of Mathematics, 4 vols 4ts.[125]
The 3.ᵈ vol. of Prony's Architecture Hydraulique.[126]
The Connaissance des Terms for 1808, (an. 16)[127]

    I will call at Soho and pay for them, the first time I come to that part of the Town.
    Be so good to inform me, if you have lately imported any new Math.ˡ Works—with their title and price. Let the parcel be directed to me to come by the Woolwich Barrack Coach from the White Swan, Charing Cross—

---

[120]*The Life and Character of Miss Susanna Anthony* [1726-1791], *Consisting Chiefly in Extracts from her Writings, with Some Brief Observations on Them* (Worcester, MA, 1796), ed. by Samuel Hopkins (1721-1803) of Rhode Island. In 1803 John Ryland issued his own edition of this work, now titled *Memoirs of Miss Susanna Anthony*, printed at Clipston by Morris and sold in London by William Button, among others.

[121]*Memoirs of . . . the Rev. Samuel Pearce; With Extracts from his Letters*, by Andrew Fuller, was first published by Morris at Clipston in 1800.

[122]*An Inquiry into the Nature of True Holiness* (1773; 1791) by Samuel Hopkins.

[123]**Olinthus Gregory** (1774-1841), mathematics professor at the Royal Military Academy at Woolwich and prominent Baptist layman.

[124]Eng. MS 343, f. 3, JRULM. This folder also includes a portrait of Gregory.

[125]*Histoire des Mathematiques*, 4 vols. (1798-1802) by Jean Etienne Montucla (1725-1799).

[126]*Nouvelle Architecture Hydraulique*, 2 vols. (Paris, 1790-1796) by R. Prony (1755-1839).

[127]Probably *Hydraulique Physique, ou, Connaissance des Phenomenes que Presentent les Fluids* (1809) by Joseph Mollet (1756-1829).

I am,

Gents,

Yours respectfully,

Olinthus Gregory.

85. William Newman,[128] *Bromley, near Bow, [London], to John Sutcliff, Olney, 21 September 1808.*[129]

Bromley near Bow   21ˢᵗ Septʳ 1808

Dear Sir

I am very much obliged by your present of valuable pamphlets. I wish it was in my power to repay you in the same coin. — In persuance of what passed betweeen You and Mʳ Fuller and myself respectᵍ Mʳ Worth,[130] I have taken measures to get an Opportunity of hearing him. I have also put into his hands Mason's "Student & Pastor"[131]—have given him this Question to discuss on paper—'What is the difference between justification & sanctification'—and have desired him to draw out two or three Schemes of sermons. In the midst of this, I have exhorted him to work with his hands, if he could get any employment, that his money might not melt away too fast. I have only to say, 'Go, and he goeth' so he went & bought a Millers frock, and spent one day with a Miller, a friend of mine, in this neighbourhood, but the labour was too hard for him. He has been sore and stiff ever since!

Lords Day Septʳ 11. at 12 oclock, I took him to our Female Sunday School. He discoursed about 20 Minutes to 100 girls. The first impression I received was quite in his favour.

---

[128]**William Newman** (1773-1835), Baptist minister at Old Ford, Bow, 1795-1835, and principal of Stepney College, 1810-1827.

[129]Eng. MS. 381, f. 1485a, JRULM. On the back page Sutcliff has written: "Rec.ᵈ Sep. 23. 1808. Ans. Dᵒ."

[130]Richard Moss Worth, after spending some time with Newman in London, studied with John Sutcliff from 1808 to 1810, apparently receiving some financial support from the London Education Society and the Particular Baptist Fund, as this letter suggests. Newman wrote to Sutcliff on 31 December 1808, inquiring about Worth's progress and hoping for "a favourable report." Worth inherited a baronetcy not long after leaving Olney, and failed to make any mark as a Baptist preacher. For more on Worth, see letter 103; see also "Calendar of Letters," *Baptist Quarterly* 6 (1932-1933): 373; Gravett, *Over Three Hundred Years*, 28.

[131]*The Student and Pastor; or, Directions how to Attain to Eminence and Usefulness in those Respective Characters* (1807) by John Mason (1706-1763). The work was originally published in the mid-1700s.

Friday the 16.th He called in the morn^g to say he shuddered at the thought of going into the Ministry— could not see a clear call—and must give it up. I endeavoured to console him, and engaged him to go with me in the afternoon to our Female Charity School, where he spoke to about 22 Children on Acts. 17. 'The unknown God'   The Children were very attentive—the Mistress thanked him most heartily and begged him to come again. I was very much gratified.

He has shown me 3 MS Discourses which I wish You to see.

Lords Day the 18.th   At 4 oclock, he went with me to our Sunday School and addressed about 100 boys from Gen. 41. 55   Go unto Joseph &c. I heard him with pleasure.

Monday, the 19.th   At three oclock, he went with me to a little female Day-School, kept by one of my friends.—There he had another little Congregation, which he addressed with great familiarity & affection from Matt. 18. 3   'become as little children' &c

His modesty, simplicity & affection have very much endeared him to me. There are some little defects in his elocution which I think may be cured.

It is proper that I have seen Mr Smith, the Pastor of the Church at Ilford.[132] I inquired if he thought these measures would be displeasing to the Church. He replied, 'I believe the Church would *wish* him to be tried by others'

On the whole, *I dare not withhold encouragement*—but I distrust my own judgment. He is certainly a practised speaker among children. How he might appear among other classes of hearers, I cannot tell.

Now I wish to ask You, my dear Sir, whether You will allow him to spend *3 or 4 weeks with You on a visit*, as Mr Fuller suggested—he paying for his board &c—

If Your Judgment sh^d be in his favour, I think we could get him patronage from the Education-Society or from the *Fund*. I shall not tell Mr Worth I have written this Letter till I receive your answer. The occasion is urgent—He can do nothing in secular business till this question is set at rest; therefore You will excuse my sending this by post without delay.

With the most fervent prayers for Your long life and increasing usefulness,

I am Dear Sir

Cordially Your's

Wm Newman

---

[132]**James Smith** (1781-1839), Baptist minister at Ilford, 1808-1834.

P.S. Since I wrote the above Mr Worth has been with me to a Prayer Meeting at Mrs West's Boarding-School in Bow—He spoke from Gen 3. 'Where art thou' to about 25 Young Ladies & 12 or 13 other persons. I thought he displayed more ability than on any former occasion. I need not add, I shall be obliged by Your finding me an answer as soon as convenient—

Thursday morning—

86. Joseph Ivimey,[133] *London, to John Sutcliff, Olney, 14 November 1808.*[134]

London Novr 14. 1808

Dear Sir,

I have nearly prepared the life of Bunyan[135] I am disappointed in the painting you mentioned which is in the possession of M^r [Lanascar?] whose wife is a great-great-grand daughter of Mr B. I am much obliged for your friendly letter. Will you give Lawson[136] leave to go to Bedford to ask a few questions for me and to consult the Church book. I have written to Mr Hilliard[137] to ask permission but have not heard from him. I shall take it a great favour also could you ascertain for me the meaning of the following statement. About five years ago Mr Bull said to the late Mr Knight[138] in a Hackney Coach when none were present that there was something respecting Mr Bunyan very interesting that had never yet appeared on account of some persons who were descended from his persecutors being alive but that it would soon be published. Did you ever hear any thing of this? and if there be any manuscript can I get it for love or money?

---

[133]**Joseph Ivimey** (1773-1834), Baptist minister at Eagle Street, London, 1805-1834.

[134]Eng. MS. 378, f. 1056a, JRULM. On back page Sutcliff has written: "Mr Ivimey Rec.^d Nov. 15. 1808. Ans. — 25. —."

[135]Ivimey's *The Life of Mr. John Bunyan, Minister of the Gospel at Bedford; in which is Exemplified the Power of Evangelical Principles*, appeared in 1809, printed in London for (among others) two Baptist booksellers, William Button and Samuel Bagster.

[136]**John Lawson** (1787-1825), after a period of study with Sutcliff in Olney and training in London as a miniature painter and engraver, served as a BMS missionary to India, 1812-1825.

[137]**Samuel Hillyard**, Independent minister, Bedford.

[138]Most likely **James Knight**, Independent minister at Nightingale Lane, London. See *Evangelical Magazine* 2 (1794): 30.

I am Dear Sir
yrs respectfully.
J. Ivimey

Was it Elstow or Edworth where Mr B. lived? Where was he appre-
hended? at Samsell or [Gansell?] or Eaton or Harrow? What day of the
month was he baptized? Are there any remains of the families of his
persecutors? named Cobb. Twisdom. Huling &c

*87. Benjamin Brook,[139] Tutbury, to John Sutcliff, Olney ("Fav.r by M.r
Fletcher"[140]), 23 December 1808.[141]*

Tutbury Dec 23—1808

Dear Sir
    A short time ago Mr Abraham,[142] your acquaintance, called upon
me with your kind respects, for which I am much obliged to you. In our
conversation I was led to say, that I am compiling a biographical work,
which, if it should ever be published, may perhaps be entitled, The Memorial of the Puritans. Having told me that you were a great Collector
of such old and scarce publications as I appeared to want, I requested
him to mention to you what I am about, and make some inquiries. But
by the favour of B.r Fletcher, I wish to say something more on the same
subject. I am collecting materials for a work of the above description,
and hitherto have been tolerably successful. It is designed to give a full
and circumstantial account of the lives, sufferings, deaths, & printed
works of the Puritans, and will perhaps include all such as died from
the rise of Puritanism in 1556, to the coming out of the Act of Uniformity in 1662, so far as accounts can be collected.
    I wish you, Sir, to say whether you think such a publication is likely
to meet the approbation of the public; and more especially, whether
you think it is likely to be *useful*. If you approve of the object I have in
view, be so good as give me any hints which, you think, may prove useful in the compilation. And as you have been in the habit of collecting
scarce articles, if you have any thing that will be of advantage, and you

---

[139]**Benjamin Brook** (1776-1848), Independent minister at Tutbury, 1801-
1830.
    [140]Mr. Fletcher was the Baptist minister at Burton-on-Trent. He retired c. 1808
and was replaced by John Smith. See *Baptist Magazine* 1 (1809): 341.
    [141]Eng. MS. 373, f. 256a, JRULM.
    [142]Most likely Thomas Abraham, who joined Sutcliff's congregation at Olney in
1794, coming from the church at Carleton. He was eventually returned to the church
at Carleton in August 1818. See Olney Church Book, ff. 42, 71.

feel disposed to favour the undertaking, I shall be very much obliged to you for the use of them. I have given Mr Fletcher a list of Books, to make some inquiry of a Bookseller, part of which I am anxious to obtain. If you have got any of them, or any others that will afford me any assistance, the loan or purchase of them will be esteemed a very great favour. The works which I principally want, are Clark's Lives, 2 Vols; Clark's Mirror; Fuller's Worthies; Fuller's Church Hist; Crosby's Hist. of the Baptists; and Part of a Register. Do you know, Sir, whether Robinson's Hist. of Baptism, gives an account of the lives & sufferings of the Baptists, in the time of Queen Elizabeth, King James I or Charles I? Can you inform me what is the most likely place to obtain such Books as I want? Do you know where is the manuscript so often referred to in Vol. I of Neal's History?[143] Of whom had I best inquire? If possible, I must obtain the use of it. Thus, Sir, I have stated my present persuits [sic] and necessities. I have already collected and transcribed upwards of fifty lives; and some of them are at considerable length, others are somewhat shorter.

I wish the Lord may abundantly bless you in your own soul, and in your public work; and make your last days appear but days. Your kindly answer to this hasty scribble, by B.[r] Fletcher, will very much oblige your

Most Af.[t] Ser[t]

In Christ

B Brook

88. John Ryland, [Bristol], to unnamed correspondent [John Sutcliff, Olney], 22 December 1809.[144]

My dear Bro[r]

---

[143]The books mentioned in this letter are as follows: *The Marrow of Ecclesiastical History: Divided into Two Parts: the First, Containing the Life of Our Blessed Lord & Saviour Jesus Christ; With the Lives of the Ancient Fathers, School-Men, First-Reformers and Sovereign Princes* (1675) and *A Mirror or Looking-Glass both for Saints and Sinners* (1671) by Samuel Clark (1599-1682); *The History of the Worthies of England* (1662) and *The Church-History of Britain from the Birth of Jesus Christ until the Year M.DC.XLVIII* (1655) by Thomas Fuller (1608-1661); *The History of the English Baptists, from the Reformation to the Beginning of the Reign of King George I* (1738-1740) by Thomas Crosby; *The Fourth Part of a Brief Register, Kalender and Survey of the Several Kinds, Forms of Parliamentary Writs* (1664) by William Prynne (1600-1669); *The History of Baptism* (1790) by Robert Robinson (1735-1790); *The History of New-England Containing an Impartial Account of the Civil and Ecclesiastical Affairs of the Country to the Year of our Lord, 1700* (1720) by Daniel Neal (1678-1743).

[144]Eng. MS. 383, f. 1773, JRULM.

You wrote to me sometime since about a young man's coming to Bristol, do you think of sending him? On what foundation? Do you wish the Education Society[145] to adopt him?—If so, w^d he be willing that *they* sh^d send *him* into Cornwall to Mr Rowe[146] of Redruth? I do not know that I c^d get them so to do. But I w^d be willing to give up *my* advantage, if it be one, for the sake of Rowe's having some assistance— and Rowe c^d do as much as most persons for a young man's improvement. Rowe and Webb are much the best Scholars we have had here in my time, who finished their Educat^n at Bristol. Stennett[147] might equal them in some respects, but they have much more natural *Genius* than he—

Or your young man might go to Redruth only for half a year & come to B^l next Augt if he wishes it—

I will describe the Case in Rowe's words.

> "A person of the name of Michell[148] has been with me for 18 months, in conseq^ce of which, regular preaching has been maintained every Lord's day at Redruth, St Die, Chacewater & Pool. He has been supported by subscriptions, Chacewater 15£ Pol 10 £ Opie Smith[149] 10£ & the B^l [Bristol] Fund 5£ together with some trifling extra helps.
>
> In conseq^ce of extreme & culpable inattent^n on Michell's part, Cap^tn Morcom (Captain of a ship, a Deacon of Truro, & occasional preacher)[150] has declined assisting any longer

---

[145]Bristol Education Society (see letter 15).

[146]**William H. Rowe** (1777-1817), itinerating Baptist preacher in Cornwall.

[147]**Joseph Stennett** (d. 1824), Baptist minister at Coate (1798-1810) and Calne (1810-1824).

[148]Possibly James Mitchell, a Scotch Baptist who ministered at Cateaton Street in London c. 1806 before leaving to itinerate in Cornwall under the sanction and support of the Haldanes of Scotland Another possibility is James Mitchell (1781-1834), who served several years with the London Itinerant Society before becoming minister of a new Baptist congregation in Chapel Street, Borough, in 1813. See Walter Wilson, *The History and Antiquities of Dissenting Churches and Meeting Houses, in London, Westminster, and Southwark; Including the Lives of Their Ministers, from the Rise of Nonconformity to the Present Time*, 4 vols. (London: W. Wilson for W. Button, 1808-1814) 2:522; *Evangelical Magazine* 12 (1814): 154; J. A. Jones, ed., *Bunhill Memorials, Sacred Reminiscences of Three Hundred Ministers and Other Persons of Note, who are Buried in Bunhill Fields* (London: J. Paul, 1849) 177.

[149]**Opie Smith**, wealthy brewer in Bath and prominent member of the Particular Baptist congregation at Somerset Street.

[150]Morcom appears in William Steadman's diary during one of his itinerating sojourns in Cornwall in August 1797. Concerning the fledgling Baptist congregation at Chacewater, Steadman writes, "Went afterwards to Chasewater, and preached in the Baptist meeting ... with a good deal of liberty and comfort. The house was very

than Christmas, and the conseq^{ce} of the loss of the 15£ from Chacewater, raised in Capt. Morcom's family, must be Michell's retiring, which will throw me into considerable embarrassm^t. You yourself know St Die. Owing to the unhappy affair of Godwin that Cause is reduced, but there is still a Congregat^n and Subscript^s to the amount of 10 or 12£ p^r Ann. I do not like the Idea of shutting up a house (a very good one I have preached there) the debt on which is not yet paid, but it is the only alternative of my having no Assist^{ce} and will occasion a loss in my income of ten or twelve £ which altogether is but about 60£ p^r Ann.

Either Pool or St Die must be given up. Indeed Redruth is so increased in importance, & my scholastic engagements so many, that I believe both must be resigned—Pool is an important little interest, we have already two members from it, & maintain a very respectable congregation, tho the place of worship is inconveniently situated. I could not in Conscience resign that, in ord^r to preserve the dwindled concern at St Die, where there has been no hopeful promise of conversion from the beginning. Pool is situated at the west of Redruth, where there is no Methodist Congregat^n, but they abound in the neighbourhood; & if we once dip our foot out I am convinced it will be difficult, on acc^t of Method^t Infl^{ce} to procure a place of worship again.

I am decidedly of Captn Morcom's Opinion, relative to Michell's removal. He has been a very unsuitable person. His intellect is not many removes from that of an Ouran Outang, he has been famously discipled in the false Calvinistic School, & after all my efforts to give him better views, I must pronounce him incurably infected wth that moral Miasma. Captn Morcom says he will manage Chacewater himself, & I sh^d have no objection to his trying for a few months to convince him, he will find a great^r difficulty in it than he is aware of. I don't doubt he will get so thoroughly tired & sick in 3 months, that he will give 20£ a year rather than be without assist^{ce}.

I have just stated these particulars, in ord^r to request your advice as quickly as possible. I will retain Michell if possible a week or two, till it be determined if either St Die

---

crowded, and a few stood without. Suppose there was upwards of 400; found it a solemn, pleasing opportunity ... Went afterwards to Wheal Virgin, a mine to which one of the Chasewater people, Captain Morcom, belongs. It is one of the largest mines in the county, having upwards of 700 men employed in it." See Steadman, *Memoir of the Rev. William Steadman*, 167.

must be given up or whether it is possible for you to provide an assist^t for me— I think there is no doubt 50£ c^d be
raised to transport a suitable person, c^d such a one be procured. He should be a prud^t Man, of sound but moderate
notions, & of tolerably decent talent. Could such a person
be procured, I think we w^d have a considerable opportunity of doing good, & may be thus prepared for a more important Station in the Church—I have not written to M^r
Opie Smith, neither do I intend it, I have already written on
the Subject repeatedly, but the good man appears to be
more concerned to get his money in, than for any other
branch of the Cornish Business. I suspect he w^d not like the
idea of St Die being given up on that Acc^t— (I own I sh^d not
like it) If St Die be given up, must I as a trustee keep the
key? I must have instructions on that head, as I have no
doubt but the Harveys will make an immediate effort to
procure possession for the Independ^{ts}."

So far Rowe—I do think it w^d be the easiest method of all, (to accomplish this Object, wch I think very important) to let your young man go
to Redruth for one half year—If you and he consent, I will try to get him
the Bm^d Benefactions[151]; and I hope I can surely accomplish that—
Rowe w^d help him on well in Learning—& get him some pocket money—I w^d very readily send down a Stud^t who is already here; but probably B^r Page w^d oppose it, and I neither like to conquer him, nor to let
him conquer me—It w^d be worth while for the Mission Society, or any
Body that cares for the Cause of Christ to help—Let me hear speedily—
Or if you prefer any other plan, propose it.
                    [Concluding portion of the letter is missing]

---

[151]Besides the Bristol Baptist Fund, established in 1717 "to make provision for
the support of and succession in the Baptist Ministry," some students at the Academy were also beneficiaries of the Terrill Fund, which was begun in the late 1680s
and fully instituted in 1715 by Robert Bodenham (d. 1726) of Broadmead. The
Terrill Fund was based primarily upon properties left to Broadmead from the estate
of Edward Terrill (1634–c.1685), a leading member of the Broadmead church in the
seventeenth century. By the late eighteenth century, the Terrill Fund was earning
about £60 a year, enough to support two ministerial students. Other bequests, such
as that from the estate of Bernard Foskett (1685-1758), enabled these Broadmead
Funds to support several more ministerial students. These two Bristol funds served
as a West Country counterbalance to the Particular Baptist Fund (sometimes called
the "London Fund"), which was also founded in 1717 to assist Baptist ministerial
students. See Roger Hayden, ed., *The Records of a Church of Christ in Bristol, 1640-
1687* (Bristol: Bristol Record Society, 1974) 10-11; Raymond Brown, *The English
Baptists of the Eighteenth Century* (London: Baptist Historical Society, 1986) 49;
Moon, *Education for Ministry*, 104, 106-107.

Part Four

1810–1819

89. John Lawson,[1] London, to John Sutcliff, Olney, 20 January 1810.[2]

London Jany 20. 1810.

My dear Sir

When last I saw you I promised to write soon, and give you information respecting the unpleasant concern we were then talking of. I believe you saw brother Johns[3] after I left you in Cloth Fair,[4] who I suppose informed you of the success of that day. His sister is now with him in the Kent Road, this is all I know, because it would perhaps be improper for me to make inquiry in such a circumstance. I could wish to see her not quite so cheerful after such an affair. I had the pleasure of being in the company of D[r] Ryland a few evenings ago, who honour'd me by requesting a copy of a Poem which I have lately finished called the *Maniac*. I hope to send it to you soon. It has been inspected & approved by Rev.[d] T. Beck,[5] and is now I believe in the hands of M[r] Parkin the editor of the Ecclectic [sic] Review.[6] —It consists of fiction and fact blended together, and is divided into three parts.

---

[1]See letter 87.

[2]Eng. MS. 353, f. 132, JRULM. On the back Sutcliff has written: "Rec.[d] Feb. 6. 1810. Ans.[d] — 12." This letter was placed by Raffles in the volume "Original Letters: Poets," most likely because of the reference to Lawson's *Maniac*.

[3]William Johns (see letter 62).

[4]A street in the Smithfield section of the old City of London, near the Barbican, where the annual Cloth Fair was held.

[5]**Thomas Beck** (1755?-1844), Independent minister at Bury Street, St. Mary Axe, London 1788-1825.

[6]Daniel Parken, a Baptist, along with Samuel Greatheed and Thomas Williams, both Independents, were the initial editors of the first series of the *Eclectic Review* (vols. 1-10, 1805-1813). The *Eclectic Review* would continue until 1868, with later editors including Josiah Conder and J. E. Ryland. *The Maniac* (1810) was reviewed in the *Eclectic* in December 1810, but not favorably. The reviewer suggested that Lawson would do well to study "the best models" and learn to "distinguish simplicity from dulness, or energy from bombast." He did note, however, that Lawson was not "deficient in sensibility, or destitute of imagination" (1137). The long narrative poem about two brothers, written in the form of a dialogue, was marked by a "continual strain of lamentation, scarcely ever diversified by a striking event, a

Sometime ago I received a letter from Northampton, in which my brother informed me that Mr Fuller wish'd to forward the business of his settlement there. He has open'd his mind freely to me & appears to like Mr Berridge very well, & wishes matters to be concluded. —-In about a quarter of a year my 12 months at Mr Colwell's[7] will be expired. I should like to know whether or not I shall then be expected at Olney.— Mr Johns when I was last with him projected a plan which is as follows—he thinks that (as Dr Ryland wishes very much that I should be a good miniature painter) it would be advantageous if I were to live at his house & continue my studies under Mr Medley.[8] He likewise proposes for our mutual improvement, that we should together apply to the Greek & Latin languages. We both submit this to your consideration.

Perhaps you have heard that I consented to preach for Mr Stevens.[9] I was more comfortable a great deal than I expected to be, excepting one part only, where I was obliged intirely to leave out one subdivision. On the 14th of Jany I spent the Sabbath at Crouchend. In the morning I preach'd to sixteen & in the evening to twenty-two.

I feel, & have felt for a long time past, quite in an unsettle'd state, nor do I think I shall be happy or settled till I am doing something in India. I struggle with much corruption & sometimes am bowed down under the weight of my sins, yet it is my desire even if I should be finally disapprov'd by the Master, to work according to my ability in his vineyard.—Present my love to Mrs S. Miss Jo.[10] and all the family.

I am Yours
Most affectionately
John Lawson

vigorous thought, or a brilliant expression, and giving only the form of verse to the substance of prose." Parken appears to have worshiped at Eagle Street under Ivimey. He was also a good friend of Crabb Robinson and appears frequently in the early volumes of Robinson's diary. For an account of Christopher Anderson's meeting with Parken at Eagle Street in July 1806, see Anderson, *Letters of Christopher Anderson*, 58.

[7]The only Colwell listed in the *Universal British Directory* was an Edward Farnell Colwell, ironmonger, at 58 Haymarket Street. In *Holden's Directory* for 1805, besides Edward Colwell in Haymarket, a Charles Colwell, in business with a Mr. Fisher, was operating an Irish linen warehouse at 29 Great Russell Street, Bedford Square. In *Holden's Directory* for 1809, Edward Colwell is listed again, as is a Thomas Colwell, tailor, with locations at 67 John Street, Fitzroy Square, and 24 Upper Titchfield Street, Cavendish Square. See *Universal British Directory*, 1/2:109; *Holden's Triennial Directory* (1805); *Holden's Triennial Directory* (1809), non-paginated.

[8]**Samuel Medley, Jr.** (1769-1857), artist and portrait painter (see letter 39).

[9]**John Stevens**, formerly of St. Neot's, was at that time ministering among the Strict Baptists at Meard's Court, Wardour Street, London. See letter 81.

[10]Johnston.

P.S. M^r & Mrs Johns send *their love.*

90. F. A. Cox, Clipston, to John Sutcliff, Olney, 13 March 1810.[11]

Clipstone, Mar. 13. 1810

My Dear Sir

I am engaged to preach for poor Bro^r Morgan[12] the three first Sabbaths in April. I shall be obliged to you to send a supply to Clipstone the third Sabbath April 15.th and will thank you to send me word.

Our Friends as well as myself will be exceedingly happy to see you at our usual Minister's Meeting in Easter Week—I rem.^{n}

Yours affection.^{y}

F A Cox

All our best regards await yourself & family

91. J. I. Fernandez, London, to John Sutcliff, Olney, 7 May 1810.[13]

London   May 7.th 1810.

Rev.^{d} & dear Sir,

I received your note & favour of M.^{r} [Clarke?]; I intended writing to you before this, but one thing and another prevented me. Saml Brunsden[14] has been very ill with the scarlet fever, but, through mercy is rather better, and appears to be in a convalescent state. Mrs Rolt[15] was very much alarmed at first: her health is but middling;—has fatigued herself, very much, with sitting up at nights. She was under the necessity of removing Saml from Mr Thomas's,[16] for fear the other children

---

[11]Eng. MS. 375, f. 473b, JRULM.

[12]**Thomas Morgan** (1776-1857), Baptist minister at Cannon Street, Birmingham (1802-1811) and Bond Street, Birmingham (1822-1846).

[13]Eng. MS. 387, f. 37, JRULM. On the back page is written in Sutcliff's hand: "Rec.^{d} May 8. 1810."

[14]Most likely the son of **Daniel Brunsdon**, BMS missionary to India, who died in 1801.

[15]Mrs. Rolt was the former wife of Daniel Brunsdon. See note, letter 62.

[16]**Timothy Thomas** (1753-1827), minister at Devonshire Square (1781-1827), also conducted a school in Islington. His cousin, **Thomas Thomas** (1759-1819), Baptist minister at Mill Yard (1789-1799) became one of the first secretaries of the Baptist Union in 1813. See "Dissenters' Schools, 1660-1820," *Transactions of the*

should catch it—she has procured lodgings in the outskirts of Islington. Says she cannot leave London, till Sam.ˡ is quite well. I have not heard her intimate any thing about her returning with Capt.ⁿ Reid—She seems rather at a loss what to do for want of money.

I have stayed hither beyond my time, but I could not, very well, help it. This week are the Missionary meetings. It will be a very, very interesting week, I am told. I, never being present at one before, am inclined, once more, to transgress; a good many of my friends have said, That it would be a very great pity not to embrace such a favourable opportunity as this. What to do I know not. I hope, I may not displease you. Hitherto, I have used the money you gave me—& have had no occasion to apply to M.ʳ B-[17] for any; but I believe, *shall* need a little assistance from that quarter.

M.ʳˢ Rolt did, in my hearing, make some enquiries, respecting Capt.ⁿ Reid; but M.ʳ Burls could not give any satisfactory reply;—whether he has, since, made any enquiries, I cannot say.

I intend calling upon M.ʳ Burls soon, when I shall interrogate him on the subject.—I have once or twice felt very poorly, but thro' tender mercy, am pretty well, at present. I am happy to hear, M.ʳˢ Sutcliff has recovered; I hope yourself & the rest of the family are well.

Please to give my very kind respects to all. Accept the same yourself, from, Rev.ᵈ & dear Sir,

yrs very sincerely & cordially,

J. I. Fernandez

92. Benjamin Brook, Tutbury, to John Sutcliff, Olney ("Favᵈ by Rev. Mr Smith"[18]), 9 June 1810.[19]

Tutbury June 9. 1810.

Rev. sir,

You greatly obliged me by sending Baylie's Dissuasive. I have found great assistance from your various communications; for which, I shall

---

Baptist Historical Society 4 (1914-1915): 227; Ernest A. Payne, *The Baptist Union: A Short History* (London: Carey Kingsgate Press, 1959) 24, 26.

[17]William Burls (see letter 65).

[18]**John Smith**, Sutcliff's former student, was ministering at Burton-on-Trent, Staffordshire, not far from Tutbury. Brook may have known Smith prior to his coming to Burton-on-Trent, for he spoke, along with Fuller, Sutcliff, and others, at Smith's ordination on 20 May 1809. See *Baptist Magazine* 1 (1809): 341; Olney Church Book, ff. 97, 101.

[19]Eng. MS. 373, f. 256b, JRULM. On the back page Sutcliff has written: "Rec. June 13. 1810."

never by sufficiently thankful. Agreeable to your request, I have here sent you a list of the articles, with which you have kindly favoured me:

Fuller's Church Hist. & Hist. of Cambridge.
Part of a Register.
Life of T. Cawton.
Fuller's Worthies.
Backus's Hist of New Eng. Baptists, Vol. I.
Pagit's Arrow against the Brownists.
Ainsworth's Counterpoison.
Prince's Chronological Hist. of New Eng. Vol. I.
Life of T. Wilson.
Baylie's Dissuasive.[20]

B Brook

93. Joseph Kinghorn,[21] Norwich, to John Sutcliff, Olney, 26 March 1811.[22]

---

[20]The books are as follows: *The Church-History of Britain from the Birth of Jesus Christ until the Year M.DC.XLVIII* (1655) and *The History of the University of Cambridge Since the Conquest* (1655) by Thomas Fuller (1608-1661); *The Fourth Part of a Brief Register, Kalender and Survey of the Several Kinds, Forms of Parliamentary Writs* (1664) by William Prynne (1600-1669); *The Life and Death of that Holy and Reverend Man of God, Mr. Thomas Cawton* (1662) by Thomas Cawton, Jr. (1637-1677); *The History of the Worthies of England* (1662) by Thomas Fuller; *A History of New-England, with Particular Reference to the Denomination of Christians called Baptists* (Boston, 1777) by Isaac Backus (1724-1806); *An Arrow Against the Separation of the Brownists* (Amsterdam, 1618) by John Paget (d. 1640); *Counterpoyson, Considerations Touching the Points in Difference Between the Godly Ministers and People of the Church of England, and the Seduced Brethren of the Separation* (1642) by Henry Ainsworth (1571-1622?); *A Chronological History of New-England in the Form of Annals Being a Summary and Exact Account of the Most Material Transactions and Occurrences Relating to this Country, in the Order of Time wherein they Happened, from the Discovery by Capt. Gosnold in 1602, to the Arrival of Governor Belcher, in 1730* (Boston, 1736) by Thomas Prince (1687-1758); *The Life and Death of Mr. Tho. Wilson, Minister of Maidstone, in the County of Kent, M.A.* (1672) by George Swinnock (1627-1673); *The Dissuasive from the Errors of the Time: Vindicated from the Exceptions of Mr. Cotton and Mr. Tombes* (1655) by Robert Baillie (1599-1662). Some of these books had been requested by Brook in letter 87.

[21]**Joseph Kinghorn** (1766-1832), Baptist minister at St. Mary's, Norwich, 1789-1832.

[22]Eng. MS. 379, f. 1152a, JRULM. On the back page Sutcliff has written: "Ans. April. 3. 1811."

Dear Sir

M.ʳ Ryland of Biggleswade²³ has called on me & told me of the situation of M.ʳ Jo.ˢ Patrick of Southhill;²⁴—he stated that he had been unpleasantly circumstanced & considered him as moveable, & asked me if I knew any situation hereabouts where he could keep a school & preach occasionally.

I have long been on the look out for a minister for a small people at Aylsham 11 miles from hence. They are but low, but I think there is a good probability of a school, as Aylsham is a Market Town, and not provided with a good common School. But a good deal depends on the man, what think you of him in point of *seriousness—sentiments—& talents*? I have made, & shall make, no application till I hear concerning him, & your free opinion will much oblige me.

The Interest at Aylsham is a small one about 26 Members, their situation not rich.—They could not do more at present than raise ab.ᵗ £30 An. I should not like to see them fall into the hands of a man who s.ᵈ drive his doctrinal opinions to the extreme sometimes witnessed, nor of one who for fear of that would keep on such general grounds that it would be hard to say what he did believe. It is desirable that a feeble Interest should have some one, who would not sink it into contempt. Your reply with your opinion on any circumstances of his case & character which you may think important, will be esteemed. Has he had any education—does he speak decently correct English?—

I need make no apology to you for this trouble;— as it is for the Church of the Lord,—I know you esteem that a sufficient reason for intruding on your valuable time.

May the Blessing of the Lord attend your labours in his cause,— I remain

Dear Sir

Yours in the Gospel of X.ᵗ

Jo.ˢ Kinghorn

Norwich   March 26. 1811

---

²³**Benjamin Ryland** (d. 1832), Baptist layman formerly of London and Cambridge.

²⁴**Joseph Patrick**, Baptist minister at Southill (1804-1811) and later (after 1812) at Fenny Stratford, Bucks.

94. Edmund Carey, Paulerspury, to John Sutcliff, Olney, 28 March 1811.[25]

Revd Sir

My Daughter inform'd me that Mr Fernandez was soon to set out for the Indies, hope he will favour me with conveying a letter to my Son, we had flattered ourselves with the hopes of seeing Mr Fernandez at our house before he went to the Indies, but now it seems we must not expect that favour; Our kind respects to M^r & Mrs Sutcliff and to Mr Fernandez if at your House,—

Our kind love to our Grandson Eustace[26]

Y^r Humble Servt

Edm^d Carey

95. Robert Hall, Leicester, to John Sutcliff, Olney, 25 May 1811.[27]

May 25. 1811—

My dear Friend,

The last time I had the pleasure of seeing you at Arnsby, you were so kind as to express a wish that I should give you a sermon at Olney. It always gives me unfeigned pleasure to spend a few hours with my highly esteemed friend, and as I shall be returning to Leicester next week I purpose, if it be suitable to spend Thursday evening with you and to give you a short lecture. I find there is a Wellingborough Coach passes through Olney and by that I intend, God willing, to come   My kind respects await Mrs S. I remain dear Broth^r

Your affect^e Broth^r

R. Hall

---

[25]Eng. MS. 387, f. 17, JRULM.

[26]**Eustace Carey** (1791-1855), William Carey's nephew and BMS missionary to India (1814-1824) and later deputation director for the BMS. At the time of this letter, he was studying under Sutcliff at Olney.

[27]Eng. MS. 377, f. 859a, JRULM. On the back page is written in Sutcliff's hand, "Rec'd. May, 26. 1811."

96. George Barclay,[28] Kilwinning, to John Sutcliff, at Mr. Greville Ewing's,[29] Carleton Place, Glasgow, 5 July 1811.[30]

Kilwinning 5th July 1811

Dear Bro: Sutcliff

By a letter from Bro: Anderson of last week I am informed that you intended visiting Ayrshire and would if possible be with us soon upon a Lord's day. I need not say how happy I shall be to see you under my humble roof and in our meeting, and especialy [sic] for the sake of Saviours cause in India. However in order to our making your visit as public as possible it will be necessary that I hear from you on the Sab: previous to your coming, and that you will mention the different places in Ayrshire where you intend to preach and make collections.

May I suggest that you might preach in Saltcoat? Kilwinning Irvine Ayr & Kilmarnock, on your way from Greenach you make [may?] take Saltcoat on friday or saturday, Kilwinning on Sabbath afternoon as we meet there in the forenoon and afernoon of the 2 & 3[d] sabbaths of the month, in the evening of either of those days you can be in Irvine, take Ayr on the Monday or Tuesday following, and Kilmarnock next even[g].

Being from home upon a preaching tour this week I could not write sooner, as I only arrived last night, yet if you have not written to me already, if you write on receiving this, I shall get your letter before lesson on Sab: evening, and can intimate your intentions in regard to Ayrshire in our evening meetings, and can get it sufficiently circulated in other places through the week by an Advertisement in the Ayr newspaper which is published on friday and by other means which I can adopt. Only I beg to suggest in regard to Kilmarnoch that it might be proper for M[r] Wardlaw of Glasgow[31] to write to M[r] Jeffreys the Burgher Minister there, requesting the favour of his place of meeting, and that he would intimate your intentions, you can be accomodated [sic] with the Tabernacle in Ayr, yet if you or friends in Glasgow thought it more adviseable to preach in the Burgher meeting house, it will be necessary to write to M[r] Shaw[32] requesting that accommodation.

---

[28]**George Barclay** (1774-1838), minister to a Baptist congregation at Kilwinning (1804-1838) and strong supporter of the BMS in Scotland.

[29]**Greville Ewing** (1767-1841), Congregationalist minister and educator in Glasgow, 1799-1836.

[30]Eng. MS. 372, f. 109, JRULM.

[31]Ralph Wardlaw was a Congregationalist minister in Glasgow and a supporter of the BMS; he was involved in the collection of BMS subscriptions in Glasgow in 1804-1805. See *Periodical Accounts*, 3:148.

[32]Unidentified.

I shall at any rate expect you here upon a Lord's day and so do my people. I suppose I shall not see nor hear D:ʳ Ryland except I come to Paisley on Monday evening, well if I can I shall, but I cannot at present promise myself that pleasure, my love to him I should have been happy could he have accompanied you to Ayrshire. I shall if the Lord will accompany you to the different places in Ayrshire, and if you judge it needfull or desirable I could be with you in Greenach also.

I beg my comp:ˢ to Mʳ & Mʳˢ Ewing expecting to hear from you by the first post after you receive this I hasten to say that I am

your affectionate

Brother in Jesus

Geo: Barclay

97. *A detailed invoice of goods received by William Carey in Serampore, Bengal [India] by ship from England, entered (in Carey's hand) February 1812.*[33]

Includes four boxes of printing type; also some cloth, millboards, books, magnifying glass, clocks, microscope, books from William Button (over £134), and other items. The total bill came to just over £515! Also received were 3000 copies of various unnamed pamphlets, along with 12 pairs of "cloggs" and one "Sunday Pair pattens—a present." Carey adds this note: "also some few Books a present from D Lister Esqʳ *let there be a Letter of acknowledgement for these* this Friend has sent presents before, he has a great regard for the Mission."[34]

98. *Joshua Marshman, a printed letter to John Ryland, 12 March 1812 [received 9 September 1812].*[35]

Entitled "To the Friends of Christianity and Oriental Literature," the letter was probably printed in Edinburgh, for donations were requested to be received in Edinburgh by Dr. Charles Stuart of George Square, and Christopher Anderson, as well as James Deakin[36] in Glasgow. Marsh-

---

[33]Eng. MS. 387, f. 20a, JRULM. The invoice is in Carey's hand, with notes on some of the items.

[34]David Lister of Hackney, who contributed two guineas to the BMS in 1800-1801 and 1804-1805. See *Periodical Accounts* 2:205; 3:134.

[35]Eng. MS. 387, f. 123a, JRULM. This letter was printed in the *Baptist Magazine* 4 (1812): 444-446.

[36]James Deakin, a Baptist layman in Glasgow, was an active supporter of the BMS in Scotland, working closely with Barclay and Anderson (see letter 133). For correspondence between Andrew Fuller and James Deakin, see "Andrew Fuller and

man's letter informs Ryland of the destruction of the Mission Printing Office by fire on 11 March 1812, with losses estimated at £12,000. Marshman writes, "How it arose we know not. Brother Ward and others think it must have been done by design, and that some Idolater among our servants, turning pale with envy at the sight of the Bible printing in so many languages, contrived this mode of stopping the work. This, however, is mere conjecture. Be strong in the Lord, my dear Brother, he will never forsake the work of his own hands."

99. *Christopher Anderson, Edinburgh, to John Sutcliff, Olney, Wednesday ? 1812.*[37]

Edin.[r] Wednesday

My Beloved Brother

Our Saviour being in *an Agony prayed the more earnestly* oh that we may resemble him on this occasion! Over all this *desolation* let us be assured my dear Brother we shall, er'e long, sing a Hymn of wonder, love, & Praise. It is our duty in the meanwhile to be busy, and need oh need I say can I help you in any way. No you need no assurance as to my [hearts][38] willingness. In a few days I hope to send 200 or 300£ and in the meanwhile I send information which is perhaps *as material*. I have heard from Bro: Ryland & send him the same letter for substance as this & the same book. The same of both to Bro: Burls. If the order is not given for the types in London pause a moment—& consider. Observe the difference of *prices* at the end of the book—the *peculiar beauty* of the article—This Man sends types to *London* now & rivals the first Makers. He will send at *these rates carriage free* to any Port where the types are to [be] shipped. Perhaps you never saw a finer type, and as the Maker is an enterprizing Man—rivalling the first Maker & only begun a few years he is the more likely to be on honour. I requested a reply from D.[r] R. & M.[r] B.[39] but uncertain where I should write, I knew that my dear Brother is engaged in this department of the Mission.—I only heard yesterday—You observe no time has been lost. All here feel the deepest simpathy [sic]—and if we have this called forth on our behalf the Money will be soon ready—Write if it be but two words to London

---

James Deakin, 1803," *Baptist Quarterly* 7 (1934-1935): 326-333; "Letters to James Deakin," *Baptist Quarterly* 7 (1934-1935): 361-373.

[37]Eng. MS. 387, f. 123b, JRULM. This letter is attached to the printed letter by Marshman (see letter 102 as well).

[38]Anderson has drawn a heart followed by "ts."

[39]Ryland and Burls.

to me that I may know how to proceed. Excuse haste but I lose the Posts My kind love to Bro Wilson[40] & all friends—with much Esteem

Christ.ʳ Anderson

Millar might have a part of the order if not the whole, though from the difference of price p.ʳ the whole would be better.[41]

100. Eustace Carey, Bristol, to John Sutcliff, Olney, 19 August 1812.[42]

Bristol August 19.ᵗʰ 1812

Rev.ᵈ & dear Sir.

Must say I much regret my not having seen you during the whole of last vacation; and more so, as I fear it has justly led you to suspect my mindfulness of your passed [sic] favours. My own feelings assure me this is not the case, and knows the difficulties under which I laboured, as to be convinced he will fully forgive me. It would grieve me to forfeit the regard of one, to whose salutary counsels I have been so much obliged, and to whom I hope still to look up with confidence and respect.

It will be necessary, Sir, for me to give you a little account how I disposed of my time, which, will enable you to judge of the reasonableness of my excuse. The D.ʳ[43] was kind enough to give me a fortnight for my journey. Set off from Bristol on the Monday as the Dʳ arrived on the Saturday Reached Leicester late on Tuesday night. Now a previous application had been made by some methodist friends of Willoughby in Notinghamshire [sic] for me to preach for their Sunday-school, to which (as the Leicester friends desired me) I acceded. I stoped [sic] at L— till Saturday and then went to Willoughby. Preached for them on the Sabbath and Monday even. Returned to Leicester on the Tuesday. Was necessitated, I may say, to preach at [Streetend?] (in Leicestershire) on

---

[40]Possibly the **Thomas Wilson** of letter 63. Another possibility is **John Broadley Wilson** (1765-1835) of Clapham.

[41]The individual Anderson is referring to is William Miller, typefounder. After working for Alexander Wilson in his type foundry at Glasgow (1800-1808), Miller established his own foundry in Edinburgh in 1809. Though he was in the early years of his career when Anderson sought his help in supplying new types for the print-shop in Serampore, Miller would soon become one of Scotland's most successful typefounders, serving in that capacity for Scotland to the King of England from 1825 to 1833. His company would eventually produce one of the most famous types of the nineteenth century, the Scotch Roman font.

[42]Eng. MS. 387, f. 18a, JRULM. The letter is postmarked from Maidenhead. On the back page Sutcliff has written: "Rec.ᵈ Aug.ᵗ 25. 1812."

[43]John Ryland, Jr.

the Wednesday. Then comes Thursday, when I was very unwell. Friday thought to have set off to Northampton, but the coach being full, and there being no other that day, was obliged to defer it till Saturday.

Now Tuesday was the day for my going back to Bristol (and this was a persian law which could not be altered) It therefore became impossible to see Olney, a place that will ever be dear to me. Thus Sir, you have heard my tale, and trust, you will admit it as my apology. The academy has received an accession of five; and four of them are men of considerable abilities   One of them is the son of a Mr Simmons[44] a baptist Minister who once lived at Braunson[45] near Daventry. Mr Newman gave a very excellent address from "be ye followers of me as I am of Christ." He 1.st delineated the Apostle's character, then, 2.^{ly}, fixed upon one feature which he enforced, his conduct to his fellow labourers, illustrated in the cases of Timothy & Titus. He then in the 3.^{d} place addressed the students and committee. First he addressed the students as literary characters, secondly, as christians, and, thirdly, as candidates for the ministry. His sermon was very cool, discriminate, and replete with good sentiment. He read it all   It's to be published in the baptist magazine.[46] Last week, Mr Stedman from West[gate] was at Bristol. He had been at Plymouth to ordain one of his students over the church he had formerly been pastor of himself. He gave us some most excellent advice.[47]

We this week heard from Mr Howlet: he is geting [sic] much worse, and has given up all hope of returning to study. While they were at meeting last sabbath evening his fathers premises caught fire, and have sustained considerable injury   Believed he says they were ensured; but not to the full amount. Was very sorry to hear of Mr Marriott's death,[48]

---

[44]**John Simmons**, Baptist minister at Wigan and Braunston, and his son, **John Edmund Simmons**, minister at Stoney Stratford, Bucks, 1823-1830, and at Bluntisham, Hunts.

[45]Braunston.

[46]*Paul's Liberality in his Conduct Towards his Fellow-Labourers: A Sermon Addressed to the Members of the Bristol Education Society, Assembled at Their Annual Meeting in Broadmead, on Wednesday, August 5, 1812* (1812), by William Newman. A review of the sermon appeared in the *Baptist Magazine* 4 (1812): 85-86.

[47]**William Steadman**, formerly at Broughton and Plymouth Dock, was at that time President of the Baptist Academy at Bradford and pastor of the Baptist church there.

[48]A number of Marriotts were members of the Olney church. A John Marriott joined the church in December 1776. His date of death, however, is listed as 15 May 1816; another member, Martha Marriott, died on 1 February 1813. See Olney Church Book, ff. 23, 26, 34.

and especially as it was so premature. Poor Gamby,[49] hope he may be spared, am grieved to learn he is so ill.

Feel increasing pleasure in my studies, and wish much to go to India, if it should prove to be will of Saviour to send me. Hope you and M.ʳˢ Sutcliff: Please to give my kind respects to her, together with Miss Johnstone, hope she is well. Accept of thanks for the kindness you have shown to me. Hope you will remember me kindly to my dear fellow students often think of them with more esteem than I can express, especially Peters who is as dear to me as a brother. Should write them, but [fear?] the time that letter-writing consumes, and the expence they would be at in receiving them. Hope, Sir, you will privilege me (when convenient) with a few lines; as perhaps shall be a little uneasy till I hear from you.

> I remain,
>> d'r Sir, with much deference &c respect,
>> yours &c.
>> Eustace Carey

P.S. I'm thinking the sending of this letter by the post is a freedom I have no right to take, but was anxious to write you, and knew not any other way of geting [sic] it forwarded. Do Sir give my respects to Mʳ Osborn,[50] M.ʳ Wilson,[51] M.ʳ James, and M.ʳˢ Denney. Must not farther obtrude.

101. Andrew Fuller, Kettering, to James Deakin,[52] Glasgow, 29 October 1812.[53]

Dear Sir

Since I wrote you I have learned that the subscriptions towᵈˢ the loss[54] in London amount to £1500; and as from accounts recently received from India it appears that the pecuniary loss will not exceed

---

49**William Gamby** (1790-1813) of Southill, Bedfordshire, one of Sutcliff's students.

50Thomas Osborne was most likely a member of Sutcliff's congregation at Olney. He subscribed £1.8 in 1800-1801 to the BMS, and another £1.1. as part of a collection by Sutcliff for the Baptist Missionary Society in 1804-1805. See *Periodical Accounts*, 2:206, 3:139.

51William Wilson was most likely another member of Sutcliff's congregation. He submitted £1.1 to the BMS in 1801-1801 and in 1804-1805; he also served on the BMS Committee in 1812. See *Periodical Accounts*, 2:207; 3:139; Cox, *History*, 2:221.

52See letters 98 and 132.

53Raffles Handlist, fasc. 37.1.

54The BMS Printing Office fire in Serampore (see letter 98).

£10,000, some of our friends do not scruple to say "It is repaired." From the best estimation I am able to make this is not yet the case; but as I am persuaded it will be so very soon, I do not wish you to push the subject at Glasgow. If any chuse to contribute, we will thank them, and when the loss is repaired, whatever is overplus shall be applied to the translations.

Among the rubbish were found uninjured by the flames, nearly 4000 steel punches, the loss of which could not have been repaired in less (they say) than six years. The metal of w[h] the types were composed also was found melted in large stakes, to the amount of about 3 1/2 Ton w[h] which they have already begun to recast, and on the 25th of April had even begun to print with the recast types in *Orifson & Hindoosthanee!* The work of God they say was never more encouraging.

Affec[e] Y[rs]

A. Fuller

Kett[g] 29 Oct 1812

102. Eustace Carey, Leicester, to John Sutcliff, Olney ("by favour of M[r] Gamby"), 30 October 1812.[55]

Leicester Oct. 30, 1812

My dear M.[r] Sutcliff

As I have long been anxious of writing you, am glad of the opportunity of droping [sic] you a line by M.[r] Gamby.[56]

Perhaps you have heard of my being unwell from D.[r] [Ryland] Left Bristol last week and got to Leicester on Saturday. Have not been able to attend to any work for this six or seven weeks. Am now something better, but as my medicine is chiefly mercurial am obliged to use great care; The friends there are very kind to me and hope to be able to get about again soon. My complaint is principally in my liver, and is attended with the same symptoms as when at your house, a pain in the back and side with a considerable weakness

On our way hither we stayed a day at Birmingham and M.[r] Hall preached at night for the mission, and collected near £50. They have gathered between three and four hundred in all. Thus God is opening the hearts of those who have the silver and the gold, to dedicate it to the service of the sanctuary. I hope the loss will soon be made up, and be

---

[55]Eng. MS. 387, f. 18b, JRULM. On the back page Sutcliff has written: "Rec.[d] Oct. 31. 1812."

[56]See letter 100.

over ruled for the furthering of the blessed work. The missionary society have been making a sweeping effort at Bristol and have got £1000.
They have voted 50 to the Baptists, but this is old news to you.

Mr Hoby[57] of whom Lawson used to speak to you is now at Bristol.
He is truely a sweet man in his disposition and character and is much
devoted to God. I think he will offer himself to the society, as soon as an
opportunity presents itself for going. Miss Fasbrook[58] has a brother
who has been an officer in the [East India] company's service. She says
persons may get out under their protection who have relations in India.
Perhaps I could get out this way, but this you will judge of. As soon as
I'm able, hope to reach Olney. Poor Howlet is no better, believe he's
now with M.r Scot. He is happy in his mind. Please to remember me
kindly to M.rs Sutcliff Miss Johnstone, Mary Pillin,[59] and all in the house.

I remain dear Sir, most dutifully,
Yours
Eustace Carey

103. William Newman, Stepney, to John Sutclif, Olney, 31 October 1812.[60]

Stepney   31 Octr [18]12

My dear Sir

I return the inclosed according to your request the sheet wanting
is—*the first 8 pages of the work itself* not of the Life of Confucius[61]
which I now return. Perhaps you can send it up by some friend that
comes to London.

I rejoice to hear that the loss at Serampore is made up—having
done with loss, let us now think of gain. How easily can the Omnipotent
turn a curse into a blessing!

---

[57]**James Hoby** (1788-1871) ministered to Baptist congregations in London,
Birmingham, and Twickenham during his career and was an active supporter of the
BMS.

[58]Mary Fasbrook of Leicester would marry Eustace Carey on 9 December 1813.

[59]Miss Pillin[g] was a member of Sutcliff's church at Olney. She later married a
John Robinson, also of the Olney Church, who later was minister to the Baptist
church in Gretton, Northamptonshire. See Olney Church Book, ff. 72, 80.

[60]Eng. MS. 381, f. 1485b, JRULM. On the back page Sutcliff has written: "Rec.d
Nov. 7. [18]12. Ans.d [Nov.] 17. [1812]."

[61]Marshman's *Elements of Chinese Grammar, with a Preliminary Dissertation on
the Characters, and the Colloquial Medium of the Chinese, and an Appendix Containing
the Tahyoh of Confucius with a Translation*, printed in two parts at Serampore in
1814.

I have been much perplexed with the case of R. M. Worth—but seem to come to this conclusion—that he is not able to go through the course of studies prescribed—and that it will be more suitable for him to go out and travel as an Itinerant Preacher—or go into secular business and preach in a village as far as opportunity may be afforded. I am truly sorry to part with him but if I make this report to the Committee, he tells me he shall acquiesce in it. May the God of wisdom direct!

I have seen a letter from Mr Ward to Mr Lindeman[62] in which I think he speaks of *eleven* churches at Asia—this is new to me.

At the house of Mr L. I saw the other ev^g three Missionaries from the Society at Rotherham—waiting in London—destined for the East Indies—

By the way, I have heard of several letters from our Missionaries which have arrived since You left London but I have not heard from any quarter, what has been *collected in Calcutta*—

When do you expect the next N^o of P. Accounts? Let me hear from You from

Your's very affect^y

Wm Newman

P.S. I have been long contemplating a small publication on the state of females in Pagan & Mahametan Countries and in the course of this winter, I shall publish it, if I am not prevented by other things[63]—I should like to see Mr Ward's book on the manners of the Hindoos[64]—If you see Mr Fuller shortly or send to him—will you do me the favor to ask him to lend it me for a few weeks. I shall gladly pay the carriage—

On the back page is another note by Newman to Sutcliff:

D^r S^r

I beg your acceptance of a copy of my Bristol Sermon.[65] —shall be glad if You can promote the circulation of it   Yours

W N

Monday 2 Nov^r [18]12

---

[62]William Lindeman, at that time an attorney at Upper Crown Street, Westminster, and significant BMS supporter. See *Holden's Directory* for 1811 (non-paginated).

[63]I have found no record of this publication.

[64]*Account of the Writings, Religion, and Manners, of the Hindoos: Including Translations from Their Principal Works*, 4 vols. (Serampore, 1811) by William Ward.

[65]See letter 100.

104. Eustace Carey, Leicester, to John Sutcliff, Olney, 18 December 1812.[66]

Leicester Dec.ber 18.th, 1812

To My Dear, and much respected Tutor

No doubt you will begin to feel some sort of surprise at not having seen or heard from me since my being at Clipston, and as I've no opportunity of sending but by post, so hope you will excuse me in addressing a line to you. It was my full intention to reach Olney the begining [sic] of the week, but after the exercise of the Lords day I was so excessively weak that I was afraid to undertake the journey and my friends at Cottesbrook dissuaded me from it. If all be well have engaged to preach for them again a fortnight next sabbath, and then will find my d'r M.r Sutcliff's, a place much beloved by me. M.r Hall is going to baptise next sabbath, his back is something better. Wishes me to preach for him at night. Have engaged for him one Wednesday night before but felt considerable inflamation [sic] afterwards. M.r Mack[67] is here from Bristol and is going to Clipston next sabbath he left the D.r[68] well. It's now Christmas, and I [have] not been able to do much since last vacation. I hope shall soon hear something about India, but I endeavour to feel my mind resign'd to the Divine dispose[r] in all things. I have lately had such a sense of my incompetency for the work of the ministry that I've been almost overwhelmed with discouragement, and do think I err'd perhaps in devoting myself to it. But I knew but very little and that little I valued ten times too highly, but if it does but end in making me more humble and in bringing me ultimately nearer to God, shall rejoice.

Hope my dr M.r Sutcliff is better. Please to present my kind regards to M.rs S— and Miss Johnstone, & Mary Pillin. Respects to all my fellow students. M.r & Mrs Gates desire their kind remembrance

I remain, Dear Sir, yours in the most grateful and obedient regards,
Eustace Carey

P.S. Miss Fasbrooks respects to M.r & M.rs Sutcliff.

---

[66]Eng. MS. 387, f. 18c, JRULM. On the back page Sutcliff has written: "M.r Carey. Dec.r 21. 12."

[67]**John Mack** (1797-1845), future BMS missionary to India and professor at Serampore College, 1821-1845.

[68]John Ryland, Jr.

105. John Sutcliff, Olney, to Samuel Bagster,[69] *Paternoster Row, London, 19 March 1813.*[70]

Sutcliff is adding several more books (some of which have a large "X" placed beside them) to a previous order. Though near the end of his life and writing in a very fragile and difficult hand, Sutcliff is still concerned about the quality and appearance of the books he orders; he notes at the bottom of the letter, "Let the Edges of Board be sprinkled with blue." The books he ordered are as follows: *Private Thoughts on Religion, and Other Subjects Connected with It* (York, 1786; Philadelphia, 1803) by Thomas Adam (1701-1784); *A Brief Declaration and Vindication of the Doctrine of the Trinity as also of the Person and Satisfaction of Christ* (London, 1669; Glasgow, 1798) and *Christologia, or, A Declaration of the Glorious Mystery of the Person of Christ* (London, 1679; 1812) by John Owen (1616-1683); *The Christian Monitor for the Last Days, or, A Caution to the Professedly Religious Against the Corruptions of the Latter Times, in Doctrine, Discipline, and Morals* (London, 1799) by John Dyer (1766-1822); *The Pleasantness of a Religious Life Opened and Proved* (London, 1758) by Matthew Henry (1662-1714); and *The Life of the Rev. John Wesley . . . : To Which is Prefixed, Some Account of his Ancestors and Relations: With the Life of the Rev. Charles Wesley*, ed. John Whitehead (1740?-1804) (London, 1793-96; 2nd. ed., Dublin, 1805-1806).

106. William Richards,[71] *[King's] Lynn, to John Sutcliff, Olney ("Favd by Mr Welsh"), 18 May 1813.*[72]

Lynn 18th May 1813.

Dear Sir,

I avail myself of Mr Welsh's[73] regretted departure from Lynn to drop you a line, which I hope will not be unacceptable.

---

[69]**Samuel Bagster** (1772-1851) established his bookselling and printing business in London in 1794.

[70]Eng. MS. 371, f. 116b, JRULM. This letter was placed under Steadman's folio number, apparently by accident, and was not listed under Sutcliff's name in the 1896 handlist.

[71]**William Richards** (1749-1818), Baptist minister at Lynn, 1776-1798.

[72]Eng. MS. 383, f. 1700, JRULM. On the back page Sutcliff has written: "Rec. May 20. 1813. Ans.d [May] 28. [1813]."

[73]**Thomas Welsh** [Welch], Baptist minister at King's Lynn, 1811-1813.

Since I became pretty well acquainted with Mr Welsh I have much wished his settlement here had proved permanent, tho' I all along feared it w^d not turn out so. I knew the people too well to entertain very sanguine hopes that he would be long very comfortable here. I had been myself their minister above twenty years, which is twice as long as any other minister has staid with them, & ten times as long as most of them did stay. Durrant[74] was their minister the longest next to me, but he living out of town, & not taking any thing for his services, & seldom seeing them except on the Lord's Day, got on pretty quietly, but the society & congregation dwindled, till the numbers at last were reduced to little more than a dozen, whereas they were once in my time about fourscore.

I much regret the departure of Mr Welsh. The more I knew him the better I liked him; & I promised myself much pleasure from his acquaintance had he continued here: & in all probability should have attended at no other place. But that is now all over, & it is not likely that the minister the managers here will choose will be much to my liking. A noisy, ranting preacher will suit some of them best, who will draw a crowded audience to fill the pews, that the rents of them may pay the minister's Salary, & so save the pockets of the managers of the place. But we will drop this subject.

I enclose some little papers published here—merely as a token of sincere & undiminished respect, of near 40 years standing.[75] However you may occasionally disagree with certain passages in them, I trust you will meet with nothing that will seriously offend you.—I often wish I had been situated nigher to you, that I might have the pleasure of seeing you now & then—I had many warm friends in different parts of the kingdom; but death hath deprived me of most of them: I have now very few left; & have spent a very cheerless life ever since I buried my dear wife about nine years ago, who was a most affectionate & excellent wife. It would give me no small pleasure to hear from you now & then: but whether you will indulge me with that favour or not, I shall assuredly remain very sincerely & affectionately

your Friend & Servant

W Richards

---

[74]**Timothy Durrant**, minister at King's Lynn, 1800-1808.
[75]Richard's *History of Lynn* (Lynn, 1812).

107. John Ryland, Bristol, to John Sutcliff, Olney, [postmarked 13 August 1813].[76]

My dear Bro[r] Sutcliff

I hear that by some *oversight* M[r] Hall was not p[d] for his Journey to London, and was somewhat disturbed about it, as he had not taken with him money enough to take him back, had he not rec[d] 2 Guineas for preaching at M[r] Dore's.[77] This was a pity, I cannot think how it came to pass, as the Expence of his Journey ought certainly to have been defray'd out of the Collection.

We had an agreeable annual Meeting. Bro[r] Coles gave an excell[t] Address to the Stud[ts]. That thou mayst know how to behave thyself in the house of God w[ch] is his Church.[78]

Bro[r] Roberts[79] has exerted himself wonderfully, he got near 600£ lately in Bristol, for our Building, and expects to get a good deal more — much of it from people of no Religion.

I lately rec[d] a Letter from poor Moses Baker,[80] he wishes we c[d] send a Missionary to Martha Brae or that Neighbourhood, and I wish so too, if we c[d] find a Man on whom we might depend. But I will copy his letter, which is dated

Hamstead   April 16. 1813

Rev[d] & dear Friend

I embrace this opportunity of sending you these few lines, hoping they may meet you and your whole Society, in a perfect state of good health, and prospering in the work of the Lord. I have been

---

[76]Eng. MS. 383, f. 1773d, JRULM. On the back Sutcliff notes that he received the letter on 14 August 1813.

[77]**James Dore** (1763/64-1825), Baptist minister at Maze Pond, Southwark, 1783-1815.

[78]*Advice to Students and Ministers: A Sermon, Preached at Broadmead, Bristol, August 4, 1813, before the Bristol Education Society, and Published at their Request* (Oxford, 1813), by Thomas Coles (1779-1840), Baptist minister at Bourton-on-the-Water (see letter 80).

[79]**Thomas Roberts** (1780-1841) ministered to the Baptist congregation in the Pithay, Bristol, 1807-1841.

[80]This letter is mentioned in the *Periodical Accounts,* with additional information that **John Rowe**, member of the church at Yeovil and a student at Bristol Academy, would be going to Jamaica to assist **Moses Baker** (1755-1822), former slave turned preacher. Rowe would be the first of a remarkable succession of Bristol students who would serve as BMS missionaries in Jamaica, as numerous letters in this collection will demonstrate. See *Periodical Accounts*, 5:289-293; Gordon A. Catherall, "Bristol College and the Jamaican Mission: A Caribbean Contribution," *Baptist Quarterly* 35 (1993-1994): 294-302.

long wishing for an Opportunity and praying to hear from you. I have just now rec^d a message from Mr Stephen Cooke in Kingstown,[81] who rec^d a letter from Lady Gray of Portsmouth[82] in England directing him to deliver to me the sum of 5£ sterling from the honorable Lady Gray for the help and support of my poor, distressed Family. Mr Cooke obliged me to give him three receipts for the same. I have also written to her Ladyship & the whole Society has joined me in prayer love & thanksgiving for the kind offering from her Ladyship to us poor Creatures. There was a Gentleman who was a friend to the Gospel, who saw the State and condition of my poor distressed family, & went over to Portsmouth, & informed the hon^ble Lady who took it immediately into Consideration; which I now beg that your Congregation will take it into Consideration.

On another page Ryland writes, "Moses Baker's Letter continued"

From Decr 20. 1811   I have rec^d liberty to stand up and open the Gospel on the Estate of Mr Samuel Vaughn,[83] called Flamstead. Mr V. applied to the General Assembly for a License for me to preach the Gospel, and it was granted on these terms, that I should enter on no estate except his own, i.e. Flamstead and Crooked Spring. But, as the Lord w^d have it one Gentleman gave his People Liberty to come and hear me. Mr Vaugh'n said Now Mr Baker I will give you liberty to preach on Vaugh'ns field, but now you are not allow'd to preach, nor teach, nor marry, nor B^ze[84] nor suffer any other people to come to your Meetings, except Mr Vernon's and my own. They obliged Mr Vaugh'n to agree wth them, to hold the Licence in his own hands and bring me und^r there [sic] rules. When Mr V. read these regulations to me, I answered, Now, Sir, as you are desirous for the Gospel, let us put God before us in all we think, say or do. Notwithstanding these charges I remembered that this thing was not done in a corner. So contrary to these rules I gave out to all my poor brethren thro' the regions round about us, that I intended if it was the Lord's Will to stand up once more in the Cause of my blessed Lord C. J^s; and gave them to understand that it w^d b. on the first day of Jan^y—I begg'd the favor of Mr V. for a horse & serv^t to send to

---

[81]**Stephen Cooke**, merchant in Kingston and correspondent of John Rippon.

[82]Possibly the wife of Francis, 14th Lord Gray (b.1765), who served as a Peer from 1812-1842. He married Mary Anne Johnston (d. 1858) in 1794. See Bernard Burke, *Peerage and Baronetage*, 104th ed. (London: Burke's Peerage, 1967) 1091-1092.

[83]**Samuel Vaughan, Esq.**, proprietor of the large estate at Flamstead where Moses Baker preached and a friend to the BMS in Jamaica.

[84]Baptize.

Martha Brae for Sister Baker to come home to help me in the Gospel. On the appointed day we went to the Meeting-house, & after
waiting some time, I stood up, and we raised a hymn, the meeting
was crouded wth strange brethren, not belonging to the place. All
that I c^d do was to try according to the scriptures to find out the
state and condition that they now stand in. On the next Lord's Day
they came from every estate where they had heard from me, so that
the Meeting house c^d not hold Mr Vaughns people for the strangers.
The Meeting house is close to the King's road, about a stone's throw
from Mr Vaughns house   Mr V. and some other Gentlemen seeing
this congregat^n he was angry, knowing they were not all his own
and said to me Mr Baker, you must ord^r this people away. I answered him, Sir, I am not to leave the word of God, but if these Gentlemen do not chuse that their serv^{ts} sh^d hear the word of God, let
them send their Bookkeepers to order them away. From that there
was a complaint from every Estate where I had brethren. Most of
the Masters of these Estates are Magistrates. Mr Vaugh'n went
down to Montego Bay, & they told him they were determin'd to put
an end to my preaching, as they found that I was not abiding by the
articles of agreem^t. They told Mr V. that they had entered upon Articles of Agreement and were determined to call their slaves from
every Estate, & to persuade them that whatever Mr Baker had
taught them was of no manner of Consequence, but now, said they,
we will call for the parson of the English Church, and you all shall
have liberty to change from that name by which Mr Baker B^{d85} you;
you may chuse your names after the first Gentlemen and Ladies in
the Country. You are to chuse the White People for your Godfathers
& Godmothers, you shall have time to go to the Protestant Church,
and the time shall be appointed,+ what days he sh^d meet at the dif-
fer^t Estates. They enq^d of some of my Brethren what did Mr Baker
charge for Baptizing you. They answered, Master not a shilling. The
protestant Min^r told them, I shall only charge you a dollar for yourself and a dollar for your Child, this was agreed upon between their
Masters & themselves. Many of my poor breth^n came to me by night
to know what they sh^d do in this matter. I told them as to christening of you, it can do you no harm, therefore tell your Masters that
you will be very happy to please them, but we are poor and some of
us have got child^n and the times are hard. The Min^r began with
them and christen'd on the different Estates. This too tedious to
add here the heavy trials and persecutions I now labor under but I
glory in them, and trust it is the Lord's Will.

---

[85]Baptized.

But I am growing very dark & my sight fails me. A Testam^t with a large print, one of Dr Watts's Hymn books with a large print and a pair of glasses to suit my eyes, (I am near 70) w^d be very serviceable; and then wth the help of the Lord I might be able to finish the course & to keep the faith. The Reason that they are so severe ag^t me in the part where I am, our poor dear Brethren in Kingston are pulling & hauling one another who shall be the greatest among them. Our poor dear Bro^r Swigle[86] is departed this life.

I think I will write so that you may cut off all that concerns Baker, with^t any one's seeing other things that I may mention here—Miss Matthews a member of our little Ch. is just marry'd to the Revd Berry of Warminster,[87] she has a considerable fortune, was a niece of Mrs Chandlers, who had lent our Building 100 [£], which Miss M. gave up, just before her Marriage. Old Mr Ransford, who is very feeble and not likely to continue long has given up his 200£ also—And Mrs Pasco 100.—If you sh^d come to Welsh's Ord^n at Newberry[88] I hope you will come thro to Bristol. We sh^d be very glad to see you. I have not heard anything of Bro^r Fuller since he has been in Scotland. I have been exceedingly languid and weary almost ever since I saw you, I suppose thro some what of a low fever—They requested me to print my Serm^n at Lyme, wch I have done, and will send you a Copy the first Opportunity, "On the Necessity of the Trumpet's giving a certain Sound."[89] We unite in cord^l Love to yourself Mrs Sutcliff and all friends

I am y^{rs} affect^{ly}
John Ryland

Trowt seems a very good man[90]

+so these Episcopalians turn Anabaptists, to get away the Baptist Memb^s of Baker's Ch. *[Ryland's note]*

---

[86]**Thomas N. Swigle** (d. 1811), black Baptist minister in Kingston, Jamaica.

[87]Joseph Berry (d. 1864) was an Independent minister in Warminster. This was apparently his second marriage, for he already had a son, Henry Lea Berry (1807-1884), who would also become an Independent minister, serving as chaplain at Homerton Academy (1826-1831), chaplain and headmaster at Mill Hill School (1831-1834), classical tutor at Homerton (1840-1843), before ministering to Independent churches in Scotland and Hampstead.

[88]Thomas Welsh (see letter 106).

[89]*The Necessity of the Trumpet's Giving a Certain Sound: A Sermon Preached Before the Ministers and Messengers of the Baptist Churches, Belonging to the Western Association at their Annual Meeting held at Lyme on Thursday, June 10th, 1813* (Bristol, 1813) by John Ryland.

[90]**Thomas Trowt** (1784-1816), BMS missionary in Java, 1814-1816.

108. Eustace Carey, Collingham, Nottinghamshire, to John Sutcliff, Olney, 25 September 1813.[91]

Collingham Sept.[ber] 25 1813

My Dear Sir

I have this week receiv'd my watch with a kind note from my be-loved tutor and therefore wish to make the earliest acknowledgement of his kindness

I understand the parcel has been at Leicester this week or two, but as I've been at Nottingham supplying for a month, had not the opportu-nity of receiving it. Thank you kindly for this, and every token of your regards   As to D.[r] Fawcett's Bible[92] I shou'd like it. Some time since, re-ceived M.[r] Cecil's life and remains[93] for wh.[h] also am truly grateful. Thro' great mercy am well and *happy*. Am this way now to preach for M.[r] Jarman's school sabbath-night;[94] But hope to get to Southampton by the meeting, where I may enjoy the happiness of seeing my D.[r] M[r] Sut-cliff. Do remember me affectionately to M.[rs] S— & Miss P[n][95] M.[r] Ni-chols[96] sends his respects to you and yours

I am most gratefully Yours,
Eustace Carey

pay my kind respects to all the students

---

[91]Eng. MS. 387, f. 18d, JRULM. On the back page Sutcliff has written: "Rec.[d] Sep.[r] 30. 1813."

[92]*The Devotional Family Bible Containing the Old and New Testaments: With Notes and Illustrations, Partly Original, and Partly Selected from the Most Approved Expositors, Ancient and Modern, and a Devotional Exercise to Each Chapter* (1811), by John Fawcett (1740-1817).

[93]*Life, Character, and Remains of the Rev. Richard Cecil* (3rd ed., 1812), collected and revised by Josiah Pratt. Cecil was the biographer of John Newton.

[94]**John Jarman** (1774-1830), Baptist minister at Nottingham, 1804-1830. The church at Nottingham founded a Sunday school in 1799; by 1815 more than 300 pupils attended. Jarman was a major advocate of Christian education, as evidenced in his 1816 circular letter for the Northamptonshire Association titled *The Regard which a Christian ought to pay to his Principles in the Education of his Children*. According to an entry on 5 July 1813 in the Friar Lane Church Book, Jarman was experiencing an "indisposition" in his health which required the church to procure the services of other ministers for a time. This may explain Eustace Carey's month-long supply in Nottingham, as mentioned in the above letter. See F. M. W. Harrison, "The Nottinghamshire Baptists and Education," *Baptist Quarterly* 27 (1977-1978): 95; Thornton Elwyn, "Particular Baptists of the Northamptonshire Baptist Associa-tion as Reflected in the Circular Letters 1765-1820," *Baptist Quarterly* 36 (1995-1996): 375-376; John T. Godfrey and James Ward, *The History of Friar Lane Baptist Church, Nottingham* (Nottingham: H. B. Saxton, 1903) 39, 47, 56, 199-203.

[95]Miss Pillin[g] (see letter 102).

[96]**William Nichols**, Baptist minister at Collingham, 1807-1835.

109. James Bicheno,[97] Astor, near Witney, to John Sutcliff, at Mr. Pecks, Linen Draper, Newbury, 23 Oct. 1813.[98]

My d[r] Sir, having parted with you last Tuesday, & having the honour of so little acquaintance with you, it may surprise you to receive a letter from me on the present occasion; but I am sure what follows will suggest to a person of your goodness of disposition a sufficient apology for the liberty I take in thus troubling you, & which I hasten to do because I understood you to intend returning to Newbury on Tuesday next & to go for Buckinghamsh[e] on Wednesday.

When I arrived at home last evening I found a letter on my table, from which, in opening it, I learnt that in the 2nd week of the present month was held at Northampton your autumnal meeting of ministers, where I concluded you were present. At that meeting M[r] Hall spoke favorably of some parts of my writings, & mentioned a remarkable dream which I had relative to the taking of Rome by the French in Feb[y] 1798 when M[r] A. Fuller did not satisfy himself with opposing M[r] Hall's opinion, but insinuated what was disadvantag[s] to my reputation &c. that is, I conclude, that I invented the dream after I had heard of the capture in question, meaning thus to stab my character & rob me of that *good name* which I have, without interruption, now enjoyed for more than 40 years. Till I met M[r] Fuller in Leicestersh[e] in April 1810, I had not seen him more than once or twice, nor been in his company one hour, for 42 years, & never either injured or offended him in my life in any way. Was delighted to see him at Arnsby, but he treated me with illtemper & rudeness.—But to the present business about the dream, concerning which I have never said much, unless in reply to inquirers; but as you may satisfy yourself while at Newbury as to the truth of the facts & justify me among our brethren from the foul insinuations of slander, I shall state the facts, & you may apply to M[r] Tho[s] Hedges of Newbury, to whom & M[r] S. Edkins, who now lives at Warwick. I told the dream 13 days before the news reached Newbury by the Reading Mercury; or you may inquire of M[r] Weeden to whom M[r] Hedges has related the fact, or of M[r] Lloyd to whom M[r] Edkins told it, as well as to 80 more in the town, & who have heard M[rs] Bicheno relate, or bear testimony to the circumstances. Or if you or M[r] Hall, or Cuttriss,[99] or any of your brethren in whose presence I was attempted to be assassinated would write

---

[97]**James Bicheno** (1752-1831), Baptist minister and prophetic writer at Newbury (1780-1807), Coate (1811-1819), and Newbury once again (1820-1824).

[98]Eng. MS. 373, f. 165, JRULM.

[99]William Cuttriss (d. 1829) attended Bristol Academy in 1807. He served as Baptist minister at Arnsby, 1810-1818, and Ridgmount, Bedfordshire, 1818-1829. See *Baptist Magazine* 22 (1830): 30.

or call upon M[r] Edkins at Warwick I should be extremely obliged[100]—
This is the plain story. On the morning of the 10th of Feb[y] 1798—I cannot tell the time to an hour or two—I hear a mans voice, as tho' he
stood at the fire place opposite the beds foot, but with a voice as loud as
a person calling from 20 or 30 yards distance, or more, saying "Babylon
is taken." I started up, while my blood ran chill, & exclaimed, *Rome is
taken! wife! Rome is taken.* She waked & cried, "what is the matter?"
*Why, Rome is taken. I this moment heard a voice that called, "Babylon is
taken."*— "Do hold your nonsense & go to sleep, I don't care about Babylon"—*Yes, but let us remember, it was not Babylon is fallen, but Babylon is taken. It does not fall yet, it is only taken.*— "I sha'n't remember
any thing about it, go to sleep."— In the morning I told it at the breakfast table, & wrote in my pocket book, now before me, against Feb[y] 10th
"Dreamed I heard a voice saying, *Babylon is taken!*" This was Saturday.
On Monday evening met M[r] Edkins at M[r] Hedges', to spend an hour or
two together—as we did usually once a fortnight at each others houses
alternately. There & then I told them of my dream, but no more than
Babylon is taken. M[r] Edkins replied, "Ah! dreams are nothing." & he
went on talking, that no more was said about it. Nor did I mention it
more that I remember, but the Sabbath fortnight—15 days after the
voice, some one told me that it was in the Reading paper that the
French had taken Rome, but it coming so quick after, I could have no
idea that my dream could agree in time with it. On Monday morning I
went to M[r] Lloyds to see the Reading paper, & was surprised that the
capture was so lately & said to him, 'why I lately dreamt &c &c, but I
forget what morning it was. I'll run home & see, for I put it down in my
pocket book.' I went home & was astonished to find it *exact*, for the paper said the French entered it on the morning of the 10th at daylight.[101]

In the afternoon of this Monday, M[r] Edkins called upon me, I called
to his recollect[n] what I had said about my dream on that day fortnight.
He remembered it & expressed surprise. M[rs] B. beg'd him not to mention it for I should only be laughed at. However when the coach came in
he went to the Coffee room to see the papers & there he told the com-

---

[100]According to the *UBD*, these men were Thomas Hedgis [Hedges], corn-
chandler, or William Hedgis, millwright; Samuel Edkins, Esq., and Samuel Lloyd,
Esq.; Timothy Weedon, taylor and habitmaker; or John Weeden, haberdasher. Most
likely these men were members of the Baptist congregation at Newbury, for Edkins
and Hedges were both subscribers to Robert Robinson's *Ecclesiastical Researches* in
1792. See *Universal British Directory*, 4:81, 79, 82.

[101]For more on the importance of this event in Bicheno's prophetic scheme, see
John Oddy, "Bicheno and Tyso on the Prophecies," *Baptist Quarterly* 35 (1993-94):
81-89. Fuller wrote to Sutcliff on 15 November 1813 and said he had written
Bicheno "and set the matter straight," it being all a misunderstanding. See BMS
Archives, Letter vol. IV, Angus Library, Regent's Park College, Oxford.

pany of my dream. It was soon noised about town, & it was in every bodys mouth, "Mr Bicheno had the first intelligence." This is the plain, straightforward story, & you have it in your power to ascertain the truth, or prove me that impious & lying scoundrel which Mr A. Fuller wishes the public to believe me to be. Will thank you to read this to Mr Hall, to Mr Fuller, & to all, if convenient, that heard Mr Fuller's insinuations, & to report what you learn.

My son[102] I conclude is gone to London. Should be glad if our friends could be informed, that I found M.rs Bicheno worse. The servant called me his morning, thinking her dying. I thought so too, & ordered a man & horse to be got to go to Newbury. But she took a little coffee & revived, before the medical man came. He thought her not very near death, but cannot be expected to live long. Extremely weak; swelling increases & scarcely knows me. I wish my son to know this, but don't know how to inform him. Love to M.rs Sutcliff, M.r & Mrs Welch. Pray for us. May every blessing attend you   pray yours

J Bicheno

110. William Newman, Stepney, to John Sutcliff, Olney, 27 November 1813.[103]

Stepney

My dear Sir

I heard lately that you passed through London and should have been happy to see you but I suppose you were in haste to get home.

Mr Singleton, a very valuable man, who has been with me two years, is likely to succeed Smith at Tiverton.[104] If I could have had my will, he would have gone to another place—but the will of the Lord be done!

---

[102]James Ebenezer Bicheno (1785-1851) was for many years secretary of the Linnean Society. Included under MS. 373, f. 165, are two letters by the younger Bicheno: 18 April 1827, addressed to N. A. Vigors, Esq., concerning the Linnean Society; and 14 December 1840, to an unknown correspondent.

[103]Eng. MS. 381, f. 1485c, JRULM. On the back page Sutcliff has written: "Rev. M.r Newman   Rec.d Dec.r 2. 1813."

[104]**Thomas Smith**, previously at Shipston-on-Stour, Worcestershire, pastored the Baptist congregation at Tiverton, 1807-1812. Singleton, then a student at Stepney College, came as a probationary candidate in 1813 and was ordained at Tiverton on 10 August 1814, where he continued as pastor until 1844. During his tenure at Tiverton, some 280 individuals joined the church. See H. B. Case, *The History of the Baptist Church in Tiverton 1607-1907* (London: Baptist Union Publishing Department, 1907) 53-60.

We have *nine* left and there are *nine* others waiting at the gates for admission but for want of funds we cannot at present admit any of them. And this lies heavily on the minds of some of our friends. I hope some exertions will be made this winter to assist us.

I have not yet seen Mr Johns[105] nor the account Mr Fuller has published concerning him.

The last N.º of Period. Acc^ts is very interesting and it is excellently printed. [106] I begin to be looking for a letter from Professor Carey and some elementary books for the Lascars and Chinese. Mr Atley[107] is still very zealous and some good fruits, I trust, will appear. There is a young man who has made considerable proficiency in the Chinese. He has been here several times to see what you sent us from Dr Marshman. Dr Gregory of Woolwich[108] I am told, is much disposed to favor the scheme that relates to the Lascars.

Have the goodness to read the envelope to this and if you see any remarkable omissions, point them out, as I intend to print it again before long.

By the way, I think you were to review my little pamphlet on "Baptism a pre-requisite &c[109] I wish I could have your thoughts on that subject at length, for I cannot help thinking that it is probably the attention of the public will be drawn to that subject before long. I have been told that Bro^r Edmonds[110] of Cambridge intends to publish in defence of Free Communion.

Excuse this hasty scribble with which I assure you that I remain
                    Your's very affect^y
                         Wm Newman
Novr 27. [18]13—

---

[105]**William Johns** (see letters 62 and 89).

[106]The printer at this time was Andrew Fuller's son, J. G. Fuller, still living in Kettering. He would later remove to Bristol.

[107]Possibly the son of a Mr. Atlie of Harlington, Middlesex, who married a member of William Button's congregation at Dean Street, Southwark. Though inclined toward paedobaptism, the senior Atlie and six other individuals from Harlington were baptized by Button in 1798. That same year Atlie and the others formed a Baptist church. In 1804-1805, he was a subscriber to the Baptist Missionary Society. See *Periodical Accounts*, 3:130.

[108]See letter 84.

[109]Newman's *Baptism an Indispensable Prerequisite to Communion at the Lord's Table* first appeared in 1805.

[110]Newman and Thomas Edmonds, then pastor at St. Andrew's Street in Cambridge, were on close terms. Edmonds preached a benefit sermon for Stepney College in 1816 entitled *The Gospel Committed to Faithful Men: A Sermon Delivered in London, on Thursday, June 20, 1816, before the Subscribers and Friends of the Stepney Academical Institution* (Cambridge, 1816). No record exists of Edmonds writing a defense of Free Communion.

111. Eustace Carey, on board the Europe, *to John Sutcliff, Olney, 22 February 1814.*[111]

Ship—Europe   Tuesday 1814.

My D.ʳ M.ʳ Sutcliff

I have only time to say to you that we are on board, are getting under way, & have every prospect of being happy on our voyage. We have two serious men on board with whom we have family worship—we do not stop at Madiera but whenever we can we will drop you a line.

Adieu Adieu. but not forever—
Our love to all.
Most affect.ˡʸ
Yours.
E. Carey

Feb. 22

112. William Steadman, Horton, to Daniel Sutcliff,[112] *Hebden Bridge, 23 September 1814.*[113]

My dear friend

From further consideration, and in compliance with the opinion of my friends to whom I have shewed M.ʳ Wilson's letter, I have determined to go myself to Olney, & see to the packing of the books.[114] But owing to our Double Lecture at Shipley on the 5 of Oct.ʳ and likewise to a meeting of the bible society to be at Bradford the following week, I shall not be able to set out till Monday the 17ᵗʰ of Oct.ʳ Should you have any letters I shall be glad to convey them, or command to execute them—with christian love to M.ʳ Fawcett &c I am,

Yours very sincerely
W Steadman

Horton
Sep.ʳ 23.ʳᵈ 1814

---

[111]Eng. MS. 387, f. 18e, JRULM. On the back page Sutcliff has written: "Rec.ᵈ Feb. 22. 1814. Ans.ᵈ — 24. —."

[112]John Sutcliff's younger brother.

[113]Eng. MS. 384, f. 1909a, JRULM.

[114]After John Sutcliff's death in 1814, his library was given to Horton Academy at Bradford, of which Steadman was principal.

113. Joseph Kinghorn, Norwich, to Messrs. Duncan and Cochrane, 295 Holborn, London, 10 October 1814.[115]

Gent.^m

I rec.^d your parcell, though by some accident it was a slow traveller, & perhaps loitered some days on the road, for I found it did not come [with] our direct Waggons.—It arrived however safe.—

I now owe you Int.^t £5.5.— From what I hear of your mode of doing business with others, I hope you will allow me some Discount— Please to call on Mr Button I have requested him to pay you, leave any general memorandum of the amo.^t that he may send me.—And if Robertson's Heb. Gram.^r[116] be come have it directed for me & put the amo.^t to my Acc.^t & take the money for altogether.—I am

Gent.^m your Hble Ser.^t

Jo.^s Kinghorn

Norwich Oct 10. 1814

114. Andrew Fuller, Kettering, to Daniel Sutcliff, Pickhaven Gate near Hebden Bridge, Halifax, 27 October 1814.[117]

My dear Friend,

I have received y.^rs. I was detained from drawing out the Sermon, and writing The Memoirs[118] partly by my long Journey into the North, partly by another Journey I was obliged to take immediately on my return, to London, where I was kept three weeks, and partly by a severe illness which has laid me by several weeks. It is done however now, and in the press.

As to the sentence which you correct, I hope you will excuse the liberties I have taken with your account; as I have altered the sentences in that and several other instances, and some paragraphs are omitted. I

---

[115]Eng. MS. 379, f. 1152b (originally catalogued as f. 4073), JRULM.

[116]*Grammatica Linguae Hebraeae: Cum Nottis et Variis Quaestionibus Philologicis . . . In Usum Juventutis Academicae* (Edinburgh, 1758), by James Robertson (1714-1795).

[117]Eng. MS. 376, f. 716b, JRULM.

[118]Fuller would preach Sutcliff's funeral sermon in June 1814, which was published, along with the memoir, in October as *The Principles and Prospects of a Servant of Christ: A Sermon Delivered at the Funeral of the Late Rev. J. Sutcliff, A.M. of Olney, on June the 28th, 1814; With a Brief Memoir of the Deceased* (Kettering, 1814). Sutcliff's obituary, as this letter suggests, was probably written by Daniel Sutcliff; it appeared in the *Baptist Magazine* 6 (1814): 332.

suppose the Sermon and Memoir must be sold for 2 Shillings: but in sending your parcel I wish to charge you only what they cost me.

The *sketch* which you have sent, has some good bones, but it is a mere skeleton; and I doubt whether our dear friend would have approved, could he have been consulted, of its appearing in public. If however it does appear in the B. M. I think it should be *after* his *Memoir*, a considerable part, if not the whole of which will probably be copied with the Magazine.

I was lately told of a sermon which your brother preached from Isai. 40. 30, 31. which was peculiarly interesting. If I could get a sketch of it, I should like to insert that after his memoir is out, and perhaps this also: but I am rather doubtful. Posthumous publications are delicate things, and seldom do justice, to say nothing of honour, to the deceased. When I die I think of leaving a prohibition, that nothing found among my papers shall be published after my decease.

In your account you say "mostly enjoyed a settled peace, which sometimes rose to joy," yet you represent him almost immediately after as saying, "as to strong consolation or triumph, I know nothing of it." Now it appears to me that *joy* and *strong consolation* are so nearly the same thing that to affirm the one, and disown the other has the appearance of a contradiction. I have therefore left out what you said of joy. I have also omitted giving the name to his disorder, save that it was a dropsy, lest there should be some mistake on a subject, beside the promise of persons unacquainted with the science of medicine.

Make my kind respects to dear M.ʳ Fawcett Sen.ʳ & Jun.ʳ when you see them

I am y.ʳˢ Sincerely
A. Fuller

Kettering 27.ᵗʰ of Oct. 1814.

115. William Steadman, Little Horton, to Richard Fawcett, Esq., Horton Lane, Bradford,[119] for the Committee of the Woodhouse Grove Seminary, 16 February 1816.[120]

To the Committee of the Woodhouse Grove Seminary[121]

Gentlemen

With respect to the business on which you condescended to employ me, I beg leave to make the following Report.

M.[r] Crowther[122] appears to me well qualified for the situation he fills. With much pleasure I heard him read, in a very masterly style, without any mistake, or scarcely any hesitation, portions of Virgil, Horace, Cicero, the Greek Testament, & Homer, selected by myself on the spot, and of which selections he w[o]uld not therefore have had the least previous intimation. His Latin version of Knox's 72[nd] Essay I have perused with all the care and attention I am capable of and find to be correct both in construction and spelling, and also to be expressed in as classical latin, as the Subject would well admit of, & could reasonably be expected from a person who had not been very much questioned to write on that language. I do not expect to see its equal soon.

The pupils went through their exercises as well as I could reasonably expect, while at the same time their performances left sufficient room for improvement. The first class did well; the inferior classes moderately well. The different capacities of the pupils together with the different spaces of time they may have spent in their application to the latin and Greek, sufficiently account for the deficiencies of any of them, without the imputation of neglect to their tutor.

Were I to suggest any improvement in the plan of education, it should be what I took the liberty of mentioning to M.[r] Crowther, that of introducing some of the lesser classics, such as Eutropius, Nepos, Justin

---

[119]Richard Fawcett, Esq., was a wealthy Methodist layman who would later occupy two country estates—Westbrook-House, in the township of Great Horton, 2 miles from Bradford, and Acacia Cot, in the township and parish of Guiseley, 4 miles from Bradford. See Thomas Langdale, *A Dictionary of Yorkshire: Containing the Names of All the Towns, Villages, Hamlets, Gentlemen's Seats, &c. in the County of York* (Northallerton: J. Langdale, 1822) 433, 211.

[120]MAM. PLP. 100.9.8, JRULM. Apparently Steadman had tested the pupils at the Seminary in Greek and Latin and was reporting on the results of the proceedings to the overseeing committee.

[121]Woodhouse Grove Seminary, near Bradford, was established in 1812 for the purpose of educating the sons of Methodist ministers. The school still exists as a preparatory school for students between the ages of eleven and eighteen.

[122]**Jonathan Crowther** (1794-1856), headmaster at Woodhouse Grove (1814-1816) and at Kingswood (1823-1825).

&c prior to the pupils proceeding to Virgil and Horace; to which I would have added had it then occurred to my recollection, and submitted it to M.ʳ C—s consideration, that the use of literal translations, such as those of Clark[123] and Davidson,[124] would very much facilitate and expedite the learning of the Latin tongue; whilst a little care and attention on the part of the tutor would sufficiently guard the pupils against the abuse of such assistances.

Of M.ʳ Parker, as he declined an examination, I can say but little. His Latin epistle written partly with design to be a specimen of his proficiency in that language, has certainly many blunders in it, in the voice and syntax, whilst in some instances it shews him to have attained to a considerable degree of knowledge of the peculiarities of the Latin tongue. I would willingly have imputed the mistakes to the haste with which his letter must have been composed, and therefore wished him, when I saw him the day following the examination, to write another letter, with more attention, & favour me with a sight of it; but as I have not yet rec.ᵈ any such communication, I can say nothing farther on the subject.[125]

---

[123]Some of the Latin texts by John Clarke (1637-1734) that were widely reprinted throughout the eighteenth century include *Historiae Phillippicae: . . . , or, The History of Justin* (8ᵗʰ ed., 1780), *Introduction to the Making of Latin* (1721), *A New Grammar of the Latin Tongue* (1733), and *A Dissertation upon the Usefulness of Translations of Classick Authors* (1734).

[124]James Davidson (1732-1809) authored *A Short Introduction to Latin Grammar for the Use of the University of Pennsylvania, in Philadelphia* (Philadelphia, 1783), as well as a translation of Ovid (1790).

[125]Thomas Steadman says of his father's classical instruction:

> Free from scholastic pride, he divested learning of it technicalities, and taught its elementary branches with studied simplicity; wishing to see real rather than rapid and superficial progress. . . [His methods of teaching] did not materially differ from those usually followed under similar circumstances; nor would it be reasonable to expect that languages could be taught with elaborate exactness, where the only teacher had to lecture on Theology, History, and Composition, besides fulfilling the onerous duties which devolved on the pastor of a growing congregation and church.

> Many would object, with considerable justice, to the free use of translations; a practice which our tutor, allowed, especially in reading the initiatory authors, both Greek and Roman. In granting this indulgence, he conceded something to the disadvantages under which his pupils had previously laboured, and yet more to the confidence he felt that they would not abuse it. No scholar will require to be informed that the conduct of the disciples did not invariably justify the confidence reposed in them by their master....

See Steadman, *Memoir of the Rev. William Steadman,* 253-254.

I am
Gentleman
Yours very respectfully
W. Steadman

Little Horton
Feb. 16. 1816

116. William Steadman, Bradford, to Thomas Raffles,[126] *Liverpool, 5 September 1816.*[127]

My very dear Sir
    In reply to your enquiry, I am free to say, That as far as I am able to judge an academy supported by your friends in Lancashire appears to me a very desireable object.[128] Were it practicable an academy for young men in our denomination would be very useful on that side the mountains. We have not at present young men enough to supply the demands upon us; and if we had the distance and expence of travelling are very serious inconveniences. I am aware that your denomination is better supplied with Seminaries than ours, having two in the county of York, the smaller of which is nearly as large as ours: how far they may be adequate to the demands of Lancashire, or whether the expences of travelling &c may be surmounted is what I am unable to say. But admitting both, the distance is such as an amount of the consumption of the young mans time to form a formidable objection, and to render an academy on the spot very desireable   I sincerely wish you success in your attempt, and should you succeed in it, I pray God he make the seminary a blessing to the country.
                    I am
                My Dear Sir
            Yours very sincerely
                    W Steadman

Sep.ᵗ 5.ᵗʰ 1816

---

[126]**Thomas Raffles** (1788-1863), Congregational minister at Great George Street in Liverpool, 1812-1863.

[127]Eng. MS. 384, f. 1909b, JRULM.

[128]In 1816, Raffles, with the assistance of George Hadfield, was instrumental in the founding of Blackburn Academy to train Independent ministers in the north of England. In 1843 the school, again with Raffles's help, moved to Manchester and changed its name to Lancashire Independent College.

117. Robert Hall, Leicester, to Thomas Raffles, Liverpool, 12 March 1817.[129]

12 March 1817

Rev. & dear Sir

I feel myself much honoured by the regard of so respectable a Society[130] to officiate at its anniversary. Be assured my readiness to do so is not the least diminished by a difference of opinion on one religious subject, the importance of which has been in my humble apprehension now much overrated. Instead the circumstance to which I allude would rather operate as an inducement than as an impediment. But still there are powerful reasons which compel me to decline an invitation which does me honour. I feel that my powers of voice are by no means adequate to reach the audience which may be expected on such an occasion. Next, I am already engaged the ensuing spring & summer to be absent in different places for as much time (I might say more) as I can with the least propriety be spared from my home engagements. Finally though I have the highest respect for the motives which actuate the members of your most respectable Society, & other similar ones, yet I have always disrelished the air of publicity & attention with which the operations of missionary Societies are usually conducted. For my own denomination, I never yet took a part, nor ever intend in any meeting when speeches were delivered &c. &c. I have been too strongly impressed, whether correctly or not, with the perception that these meetings are repugnant to the simplicity of the gospels, & that they tend too much to assimilate the Kingdom of Christ to the spirit & maxims of the World. I cannot forget our Savior's divine aphorism, the Kingdom of God cometh not with observation, or as Cambell[131] has it, not with parade. I am far from wishing to censure others, but such are my feelings & convictions, to which as an honest man, while they continue to be such, my conduct must be conformed.

Permit me my dear Sir, to thank you very cordially for the present of your travels.[132] I have been reading them only with Mrs Hall with very

---

[129]Eng. MS. 377, f. 859b, JRULM.

[130]Most likely a reference to the London Missionary Society.

[131]**John Campbell** (1766-1840) was one of Scotland's most notable missionaries in the early years of the nineteenth century. In 1812, 1814, and 1818-1821 he toured parts of South Africa on behalf of the London Missionary Society. He published an account of his first journey, *Travels in South Africa, Undertaken at the Request of the Missionary Society* (1815), from which Hall has probably taken the reference mentioned above.

[132]A reference to Raffles's *Letters During a Tour Through France* (1818).

great delight. I admire greatly the judicious selection of objects—the brevity of the style & the force & vivacity of the descriptions. You have planted your reader in the very heart of the scene you are exhibiting whether it be the tumultuous magnificence of Paris, or the solitary & romantic grandeur of the Alps.

I have read nothing on the same subject with equal pleasure. Wishing a perpetual increase in usefulness & happiness, I remain dear Sir

Your affectionate friend & Brother

Robert Hall

118. Robert Hall, Leicester, to the Rev. Mr. Richard, Attercliff, near Sheffield, 31 March 1817.[133]

March 31. 1817

Dear Sir

I am deeply sensible of the Honour the Auxiliary Society for Yorkshire[134] has shown me, on the present occasion, by inviting me to be one of the preachers at their anniversary & was I so situated as to give one sermon, it would afford me pleasure. I consider it not only as a common cause, & rejoice greatly in the brilliant success with which providence has crowned the efforts of your Society, in Africa, the South Sea Islands, &c. &c. May that noble vision send forth its bounty to the rivers, & fill the seas of the Earth with fruit. But the truth is, all the time, I can with the least propriety be absent from Home, & more than I ought is already engaged, & on that account, feel myself under the necessity of most respectfully declining an invitation which I shall always consider as no small honour.

My sense of this you will oblige me by conveying in the most respectful terms to the Society in whose behalf you write.

I remain dear Sir

Yours most sincerely

Robert Hall

---

[133]Eng. MS. 377, f. 859c, JRULM.

[134]Probably another invitation to Hall by an auxiliary of the London Missionary Society.

119. Olinthus Gregory, Royal Military Academy, [Woolwich], to T. J. Pettigrew Esq.,[135] *Bolt Court, Fleet Street, London, 3 October 1817.*[136]

R. M. A. October 3.[d] 1817.

My dear Sir,

You have most probably read before this time, the extraordinary account given in the last N.[o] of Thomson's Annals,[137] by the Rev. T. Glover, of a Miss M'Evay of Liverpool, who is blind, but who can perceive and distinguish the shape and colour of objects, whether distant or near, by passing the extremities of her fingers along the surface of a piece of glass which is so interposed between her and the objects that optical rays fall upon the glass. The circumstances mentioned quite surpass credibility; yet they are well authenticated, and are clearly of such a nature, that the deception, if any, cannot be practised by Miss M'Evay but by those who describe her case. Too many, however, have described it in different newspapers, &c. to leave any room to doubt that there is something truly surprizing in the business.—

Mr. Glover states that some competent person at Liverpool is preparing a fuller account than his. Cannot you, through the medium of Mr. Raffles, get this account for vol 1. of the Transactions? It is not merely a matter of wonderment; but, if Glover's account be throughout correct, may lead to an extension of our knowledge concerning light and colours.—I could almost wish that a deputation from the Society, of persons possessing the requisite degree of optical and physiological knowledge, should go down to Liverpool, and so direct, vary, modify, and extend their enquiries and experiments upon Miss M'Evay, as to educe from her singular (and perhaps fugitive) faculty, all that it may be capa-

[135]A London surgeon and antiquarian, Thomas Joseph Pettigrew (1791-1865) was a founding member of the Philosophical Society of London as well as secretary of the Royal Humane Society from 1813 to 1820, during which time he published *Memoirs of the Life and Writings of John Coakley Lettsom, M.D.* (1817). In the 1830s he began to focus on his antiquarian interests, serving as the first treasurer of the British Archaelogical Society in 1843. Among his publications are *Bibliotheca Sussexiana* (1827), *A History of Egyptian Mummies* (1834), *Medical Portrait Gallery* (London, 1838-1840), *Memoirs of the Life of Vice-Admiral Lord Viscount Nelson* (1849), and *Chronicles of the Tombs* (1857).

[136]Eng. MS. 377, f. 813, JRULM. Gregory spoke before the Philosophical Society of London in June 1817. His *Oration, Delivered at the Anniversary of the Philosophical Society of London, June 12, 1817*, appeared in the *London Pamphleteer* (1818): 529-548.

[137]*Annals of Philosophy, or, Magazine of Chemistry, Mineralogy, Mechanics, Natural History, Agriculture, and the Arts* (1813-1827), by Thomas Thomson (1773-1852), who also had recently published his *History of the Royal Society, from its Institution to the End of the Eighteenth Century* (1812).

ble of furnishing: and I regret that I cannot volunteer to make one of such a party.

Do you know Dr. Bostock,[138] or does Mr. Raffles? The Doctor, I apprehend, could furnish an interesting paper on the subject.— But many means of correct and philosophical information will suggest themselves to your mind.

I certainly feel very solicitous that the Philosophical Society should have the start of the Royal Society or of any other, in presenting to the public a full and accurate account of this extraordinary digital perception, together with such physiological, optical, or other theoretical observations, as will naturally flow from so singular a case: —and this must be my apology for troubling you with a hasty letter upon the subject.

I hope you safely received Dr. [Pomerdston's?] paper.

Have you received good accounts from Mrs Pettigrew since she has been in the Country?

I am my dear Sir,
Ever truly yours,
Olinthus Gregory

120. Autographed note by Joseph Kinghorn, Norwich, to unnamed correspondent, 12 November 1817.[139]

I beg my respectful remembrances to your friends at whose request you wrote your Letter; I thank them for such a mark of their esteem, however unmerited, and I remain
Dear Sir
Yours very sincerely
Jo:ˢ Kinghorn

---

[138]Dr. John Bostock (1773-1846) was born in Liverpool and educated at Edinburgh University, where he received his M.D. in 1798. His thesis was dedicated to William Roscoe of Liverpool. He returned to Liverpool and established his medical practice there. In 1817, however, he moved to London, and shortly thereafter published *Account of the History and Present State of Galvanism* (1818). Earlier he had authored *Observations on Diabetes Insipidus* (Liverpool, 1812), and *On the Nature and Analysis of Animal Fluids* (1813). Shortly after his arrival in London, he gave up medicine and turned to chemistry, physiology, and general science, publishing *An Elementary System of Physiology* (1824). He quickly became a member of the Royal Society and served as president of the Geological Society in 1826.

[139]Eng. MS. 861, f. 31 & 32, JRULM.

121. Joshua Marshman, Serampore [Bengal], to William Hope,[140] *Liverpool, 13 January 1818.*[141]

Serampore
Jan.ʸ 13.ᵗʰ 1818

My dear Sir,

Permit me tho' personally unknown to you, to drop you a few lines to express the satisfaction and esteem excited in our minds by the interest so generously taken by you and your Son and your excellent family, in what we are enabled to do at Serampore to promote the cause of God. Some years ago either you or your Son kindly sent me a copy of Lancaster's System,[142] enriched with some highly sensible observations in m.s. The book unhappily did not reach me till some years after, which prevented my acknowledging your goodness sooner, but I now beg you to accept my sincere thanks, together with a copy of a small work on National Schools,[143] from which you will see that the Lord is blessing us in this way far beyond our expectation; and that if due means be afforded, there is reason to suppose that these schools will prove of the highest value in diffusing abroad the light of Divine revelation

---

[140]**William Hope**, Esq., of Liverpool, served for many years as the director of the Yorkshire and Lancashire Auxiliary Society of the BMS. His son, also mentioned in this letter, was an active supporter as well. In the early part of the nineteenth century William Hope (most likely the father) built the first house in what became Hope Street in Liverpool.

[141]Eng. MS. 387, f. 123c, JRULM. Letter is marked on first page "Rec^d 10 July."

[142]**Joseph Lancaster** (1778-1838), education entrepreneur and founder of the Lancastrian system.

[143]**Joshua Marshman's** *Hints Relative to Native Schools, Together with the Outline of an Institution for Their Extension and Management* (Serampore, 1816, 1817). The education of native children had long been a concern of the Serampore mission, with instruction primarily in the vernacular languages. Carey opened his first school at Mudnabatty in 1794. In 1802 the mission published its *Plan for the Education of the Children of Converted Natives*, patterned at that time after traditional models of English nonconformist education. Marshman was instrumental in founding the Benevolent Institution in Calcutta in 1810, and by 1813 sixteen schools were operating in India under its auspices, all of them patterned now after a Lancastrian model. Between July 1816 and October 1817, as G. E. Smith writes, BMS missionaries opened 103 schools, instructing more than 6,700 students. By the time of the above letter, BMS missionaries in the East were operating 126 schools with a student population of more than 9000. See Cox, *History*, 1:231-33, 315; G. E. Smith, "Patterns of Missionary Education: The Baptist India Mission 1794-1824," *Baptist Quarterly* 20 (1963-1964): 300; M. A. Laird, "The Serampore Missionaries as Educationists 1794-1824," *Baptist Quarterly* 22 (1967-1968): 320-25; Keith Farrer, *William Carey: Missionary and Botanist* (Kew, Victoria, Australia: Carey Baptist Grammar School, 2005) 41-46.

I have taken the liberty of sending you and your Son, who is held in the highest estimation by my son as well as myself; a copy of the Pentateuch in Chinese just completed with our metallic moveable characters, of which lot we expect your kind acceptance.[144] You will perceive that the whole Pentateuch is brought into a volume quite portable; and that the latter part and that only, is printed on *both* sides of the page without any injury to them legibly. Had the whole volume been thus printed, as we now print all we do, the size would have been still more reduced; and the New Testament which contains only a sixth part more of letter press, will when printed on both sides, make a volume little as nothing exceeding that in size.

I have also taken the liberty to send to your kind care by Cap^tn [?] of the [Bounty?] Hall four other copies, which if you will kindly send to Dr Ryland at Bristol, in a way the cheapest and most expeditious, you will very highly oblige me. I have also further troubled you by thus directing to your kind care a large packet of Letters for Dr Ryland, which you will greatly oblige me by sending in the same manner, as speedily as you can. It struck me that this ship may arrive with in four or five days of the Annual Baptist Meeting in London held the 25.th of June, and in this case, as Dr Ryland will be in London, the parcels directed to him there, to the care of Wm Burls Esqr of Lothbury, would reach him more quickly. Pardon, my giving you so much trouble, and believe me with kindest regards to your Son & Mrs Hope

My dear Sir

Most respectfully yours

J Marshman

P.S. Mr Pearce[145] and Mrs Ward want to be kindly remembered to you. Let me hope to be indulged with a line answer—[paper torn] your worthy Son.

†pray is my worthy friend Dr Adam Clarke[146] in Liverpool? If he be kindly present him with the *blank* copy of the Pentateuch with my cordial regards

---

[144]During his years at Serampore, Marshman devoted himself in particular to mastering the Chinese language, the results of which were several significant translations of Chinese works into English and from English into Chinese. Among these were *The Works of Confucius* (Serampore, 1809), *Elements of Chinese Grammar* (1814), and the translation of the Bible into Chinese (mentioned in the above letter) between 1818 and 1824.

[145]**William Hopkins Pearce** (1794-1840), BMS missionary to India, 1817-1840. See also letter 127.

[146]**Adam Clarke** (1760?-1832) was a Wesleyan preacher, Biblical commentator, theologian, linguist, and scholar.

122. Robert Hall, Leicester, to Jabez Bunting,[147] Wesleyan Missionary House, No. 77 Hatton Garden, London, 23 February 1818.[148]

Rev and dear Sir

I feel myself highly honored by the invitation you have transmitted to me to preach one of the sermons at the approaching anniversary of the methodist missionary society. The respect I have long entertained for yourself and the highly esteemed body in whose names you write render me very reluctant to decline any proposal issuing from such a quarter. But permit me to say that reasons of great moment impel me however reluctantly to take that step on the present occasion. I could not visit the Metropolis this summer without materially changing plans and engagements, already formed. Add to this that I am convinced from painful experience of my total inability to render myself audible to such assemblies as are accustomed to convene on such occasions, in consequence of which my engaging would obstruct rather than aid the design of the anniversary. I had the mortification to find that when I officiated on a similar occasion in behalf of the baptist mission, I was not heard by one half of the audience. I must therefore be permitted decidedly to decline the honour intended me, in which I can say with the utmost truth that I am so far from being influenced by a feeling of party-spirit, that on the contrary few things would please me more than a proper opportunity of evincing my cordial esteem of my methodist brethren; to whose exertions in the cause of religion, both foreign and domestic, the Public, are in my humble opinion, indebted to an incalculable degree. That this success may be still more extended, and your invaluable labours among them may be crowned with a blessing commensurate to your largest wishes is, dear Sir the prayer of your obliged friend & brother

R. Hall

Leicester. 23 Feb.ʸ 1818

---

[147]**Jabez Bunting** (1779-1858), Methodist leader who helped form the Methodist Missionary Society in 1813.

[148]MAM. PLP. 48.25.5, JRULM.

123. Thomas Langdon, Leeds, to John Fawcett, Jr., Halifax, 7 August 1818.[149]

My dear Friend,

The inclosed is as nearly as I can recollect what I said at the Missionary meeting.[150] If you think it proper to publish it with your memoirs,[151] it is quite at your service. And if you wish to have it inserted in the Baptist Magazine, I have not the least objection, if you would get it transcribed, and send it to the editors. On the other side you will find the memorandums you requested, respecting the Dr's preaching at Leeds, &c.

I have only time to add that M[rs] Langdon and Mary[152] unite in kind respects to you and M[rs] Fawcett, and to our dear young friends, with

Your affectionate Friend

Tho[s] Langdon

Leeds
Jan[y] 13, 1818.

For the year 1779, a few persons at Leeds, of the Baptist denomination, hired a part of the Old Assembly rooms; and requested the Rev. D[r] Fawcett, and the Rev. John Parker,[153] of Barnoldswick, to preach on the occasion of its being opened for public worship. The D[r] delivered a very ingenious sermon, which was greatly admired, from Neh. 4. 2 "What do these feeble Jews?" This may be considered as the commencement of the Baptist interest in Leeds. And in 1781 he delivered a judicious and solemn discourse, on occasion of opening the present Baptist Chapel in that town, from Gen. 28.17. "How dreadful in this place! This is none other than the house of God, and this is the gate of heaven."

In 1792, after the death of D[r] Caleb Evans, D[r] Fawcett was invited, by the Bristol Education Society, to become the President of the Bristol Academy; and Alderman Harris, and Thomas Ransford Esq[r][154] were delegated by the Society to wait on him with the invitation.

---

[149]Eng. MS. 379, f. 1182, JRULM.

[150]The BMS annual meeting that year was held in London on 25 June (see letter 124).

[151]A reference to *An Account of the Life, Ministry, and Writings of the Late Rev. John Fawcett, D.D.* (London: Baldwin, Cradock, and Joy, 1818) by John Fawcett, Jr.

[152]Langdon's daughter, who would later publish her father's *Memoir* in 1837.

[153]**John Parker** (1725-1793), Baptist minister at Barnoldswick, 1763-1790.

[154]**John Harris, Esq.** (1727?-1801), deacon at Broadmead for more than forty years and mayor of Bristol in 1790; for **Ransford**, see letter 72.

124. William Carey, Serampore [Bengal], to S[amuel]. Hope,[155] Esq., Hope Street, Liverpool, 21 November 1818.[156]

My Dear Sir

Accept my thanks for the present of 5 Doz. of Beer, and two Cheeses, which Bro.^r Pearce informed me you had sent for my acceptance. I received them safe and in good order. I have also to thank you for the present of a very fine Kalaidascope which I have also received safely. This instrument is certainly a wonderful application of the science of Optics, and colours. I saw one for the first time a few days before I received your kind present, which is the property of the Physician of the Place.

I formerly wrote you some account of the exertions, which are making all over India to instruct the rising Generation. Last year a School Book Society was constituted in Calcutta, which promises to be of much advantage. The first hint of this Society arose from the Countess of Loudoun; but it has now assumed a much more substantial form, and greater extent than was at first contemplated.[157]

We have tried with various success for some years past to establish Schools in the villages around us: Many Gentlemen in different parts of the Country have also set up Schools upon our plan; and three or four years ago Government made one experiment of the same kind, and employed Bro.^r May, now deceased, as superintendent of them. We have the last year being [been] exerting ourselves to improve the native Schools in which the parents pay the Masters; and have considerable hopes of success; A good number of these schools for a small encouragement have adopted the plan suggested by us, and their instruction may be extended much further than it could be on the plan of wholly supporting them at our own expence.

One of the most important events which has lately occurred of this kind is the proposed introduction of Schools into all the newly conquered Provinces, now called Rajpoothana.[158] A country nearly as large again as England. This work originated with the Marquis of Hastings,[159]

---

[155]**Samuel Hope** (1760-1837), prominent Baptist Liverpool banker and active supporter of the BMS.

[156]Eng. MS. 387, f. 20b, JRULM. This letter sent by the ship *Princess Charlotte*.

[157]Flora Mure-Campbell (1780-1840), 6th Countess of Loudoun, married Francis Rawdon-Hastings in 1804 (see note below).

[158]Modern day Rajasthan, in northwestern India.

[159]Francis Rawdon Hastings (1754-1826), 2nd Earl of Moira and later 1st Marquess of Hastings, was appointed Governor-General of Bengal and commander-in-chief of forces in India on 18 November 1812, succeeding Lord Minto. He successfully waged a campaign to subdue the Ghorkas in Nepal, and for this service was created Viscount Loudoun, Earl of Rawdon, and Marquess of Hastings on 13 Febru-

who while he was in the upper Provinces wrote us word that he had been thinking that the instruction of the people of these Countries by setting up Schools in them would be the most likely method of curing them of their predatory habits, and gradually raising their character. He desired us to turn the matter over in our minds against his arrival at the Presidency. Soon after his arrival he invited us to dine with him (His country residence is just opposite our House on the opposite side of the River.) After Dinner he entered into a discussion of this matter with me; and committed the whole management of it to us, at the same time promising us a pretty long Subscription towards the beginning. He has since settled the amount of this Subscription 6000 Rupees, and has procured the consent of the Supreme Counsel to send my third son Jabez[160] (who arrived unexpectedly from Amboyna a few days before we dined with him) to *Ajmeere,*[161] at the expense of Government. The Schools, however, are not to be considered as government Schools, but as our private ones. My Son left us for that place a week ago. The journey will take four Months and a half. S.ʳ David Ochterlony[162] will direct him as to situations for Schools; we know him to be quite friendly to our plans.

The committing of this business to us may be considered as a memorable interposition of Divine Providence; We have commenced printing the Bible in all the Languages spoken in these parts, and were able to send the Gospel by Matthew in one or two of them. It is memorable that just at this time a Diocesan School Society was instituted, at the Head of which is the bishop of Calcutta. Another society, denominated the Calcutta School Society also was formed about the same time.

---

ary 1817. By the end of 1817, Hastings had established the supremacy of the British throughout India. As the *DNB* notes, "During the last years of his governorgeneralship Hastings devoted himself to the civil and financial duties of the administration with great ability and industry. In spite of the hostility of the directors [of the East India Company] he supported many useful measures for the education of the natives, and encouraged the freedom of the press."

[160]**Jabez Carey** (1793-1862), third son of William Carey and BMS missionary in Amboyna and India, 1814-1832.

[161]Ajmer, Rajputana (modern-day Rajasthan).

[162]Sir David Ochterlony (1758-1825) was a 1ˢᵗ Baronet and army officer in the East India Company, 1778-1826. In 1804 he became the resident commander in Delhi, but in 1806 was forced to give up his position to a civilian, Archibald Seton. He was promoted to major-general by Hastings in 1813. For his work in the Nepalese campaign in 1814-1815, Ochterlony was appointed a KCB and created a baronet. He was instrumental in bringing peace to the province of Rajputana and for his work was named by Hastings in March 1818 as resident and commissioner-general to the Rajput states. In December 1818 (one month after the date of the above letter) he would be appointed resident at Delhi, and in 1822 resident of Malwa and Rajputana.

Bro.ʳ Wards Nephew[163] is going to Sumatra with a Printing Press. Sʳ T. Raffles[164] wrote to us as soon as he arrived there; He is now in Bengal and lately spent a Day and Night with us. He is desirous of setting up Schools there, and would give all the protection he can to Missionaries. Young Mʳ Ward is very pious, and I trust will be of much use there. He goes in a few Days with Sʳ Thomas. Thus the Lord is enlarging our sphere of Action. May He now give that Spiritual prosperity without which outward advantage will be ineffectual.—We shall have occasion for large draughts upon the Liberality of the Christian public, and great need of help from above. I trust we shall not be forgotten in your prayers.

> I am, My Dear Sir,
> very truly yours
> W Carey

Serampore
21.ˢᵗ Nov.ʳ 1818

N.B. I have taken the liberty of consigning a box of Seeds and another of bulbs, to your care for M.ʳ J. Cooper, Gardener to Lord Molton, Wentworth Hills, near Rotheram, Yorkshire; I formerly sent them to M.ʳ Shepherd, of the Botanic Garden. M.ʳ Cooper is I trust a pious man, but he entertains suspicions of M.ʳ S. which I do not wish to perpetuate. These are sent by the [illegible word] Capt. Harris. I shall also consign to you two similar ones for the Hon.ᵇˡᵉ W.ᵐ Herbert, Spofforth near Wetherby, Yorkshire.[165] I have written to M.ʳ Cooper and M.ʳ Herbert to apply to you for them. I hope I am not presuming too much in doing

---

[163]Ward's nephew, **Nathaniel Ward**, along with Gottlob Brückner, worked in Sumatra until 1850, at which time the BMS mission ended, but not before completing a translation of the Java New Testament, undertaken at the behest of Sir Thomas Stamford Raffles. BMS missionaries **Charles Evans** and **Richard Burton** (see letter 129) had been asked by Sir Thomas Raffles, then governor of Sumatra, to open a station at Fort Marlborough, where the younger Ward was working the press he had brought with him, as mentioned in the above letter. See Cox, *History*, 1:354; "Calendar of Letters," *Baptist Quarterly* 7 (1934-1935): 45.

[164]**Sir Thomas Stamford Raffles** (1781-1826), director of Sumatra for the East India Company, 1813-1816, and governor, 1818-1824.

[165]William Herbert (1778-1847) was a naturalist, classical scholar, linguist, politician, and clergyman, noted primarily for his work on plant hybridization, which led to a correspondence with Charles Darwin. He was Rector of Spofforth, Yorkshire, 1814-1840, after which he became Dean of Manchester, 1840-1847. Shortly before the date of the above letter, Herbert had published *Musae Etonenses* (1817). He would soon follow that with *On the Production of Hybrid Vegetables* (1819). He also authored a short *Biographical Notice of the Rev. William Carey, D.D. of Serampore* (Newcastle, 1843).

thus. The Boxes for M.ʳ Herbert will be shipped on the Princess Charlotte, in which Bro.ʳ Ward goes to England, and by which I send this

125. *John Ryland, Reading, to Christopher Kitching,*[166] *Baptist minister, Kingston, Jamaica, 6 January 1819.*[167]

Reading Jan. 6. 1819

My dear Broʳ
 I had begun a Letter to you before I left Bristol, but in my hurry, I
left it behind; I can only write a few lines, we rejoice that God has preserved you on your voyage and continued your health. We trust he will
direct you in all respects, and make your way plain before you—
 Assure those who complain of the irregularities of the Negro Bʳ,
that we earnestly wish to correct them, and were anxious to send out
well instructed Missionaries, that they might be instructed more perfectly in the doctrines of Christianity. Tell them that we have given you
a very earnest charge never to intermeddle with any political concerns;
and always to inculcate on the slaves who profess to embrace Christianity, that they should pay the utmost regard to the Duties inculcated on
servants by the apostles; and to adorn the Doctrine of God their Savior
by their sobriety, honesty, diligence and fidelity. Broʳ Dyer[168] is writing
to Joseph Burns Esqʳ who was very friendly to Broʳ Coultart.[169]
 We hope that by this time you have obtained a licence, and therefore we think it wᵈ be better for you to remain at Kingstown till Mʳ
Coultart can return, and to let Godden[170] go to Spanish Town; our chief
reason for this is, that we fear it wᵈ be likely to make a bad impression
on the mind of the Kingston Magistrates, to give a licence to one, and
then soon after that to have to licence another for the same place— We
trust the Lord will find you a suitable station, and shall be sure to take
Care of you, if the Lord keeps you faithful to him. Only let us hear from
you as fully and particularly as you can, respecting your own attempts
to do good, and what you find of real piety in any of the Negroes. You
will doubtless need much patience, and prudence, and will find the example of the Apostle as recorded in I Thess. ii. 7, 8. and in Acts xx.24-28.
worthy to be kept in mind continually.

---

[166]**Christopher Kitching** (Ryland spells it variously "Kitchen" "Kitchin" and
"Kitching"), BMS missionary to Jamaica, 1818-1819.
 [167]MAM. PLP. 93.40.1, JRULM.
 [168]**John Dyer** (1783-1841), secretary of the BMS, 1818-1841.
 [169]**James Coultart** (d. 1836), BMS missionary to Jamaica, 1817-1836.
 [170]**Thomas Godden**, BMS missionary to Jamaica, 1818-1823.

You know who has said "If any one lack wisdom let him ask of God, who giveth liberally unto all men and it shall be given him." We trust that Integrity and Uprightness will preserve you, and when a man's ways please the Lord he will make his Enemies to be at peace with him. Trust in him at all times, pour out your heart before him, he will be a refuge for you. My Son[171] was at Bristol last week who left Dr Steadman very well—

If you have occasion to draw on me, you may be assured your Bills will be punctually paid; but you must draw at the usual term of ninety days

I am

Yours cordially

John Ryland

Jan. 6. 1819

We unite in kind Respects to Mrs Kitchen

---

126. Joseph Cottle,[172] [Bristol], to Thomas Raffles, Liverpool, 4 May 1819.[173]

Dear Sir:

I send you one line to request if you see Mr. C. you will *not* speak to him on the subject I lately spoke to you concerning; nor indeed to any one else, as our intentions are somewhat altered.

Pray accept the enclosed, as a small mark of respect, & believe me to be

Very sincerely yours,

Joseph Cottle

May 4, 1819

---

127. William Ward, Cheltenham, to John Nelson,[174] Church Street, 1 Oyer Court, Whitehaven, 5 August 1819.[175]

---

[171]**Jonathan Edwards Ryland** (1796-1866), son of John Ryland, Jr., and a popular writer and editor.

[172]**Joseph Cottle** (1770-1853), Baptist layman in Bristol and initial publisher of *Lyrical Ballads*, by William Wordsworth and Samuel Taylor Coleridge, in 1798.

[173]Eng. MS. 375, f. 470, JRULM.

[174]Ward traveled from India on the *Charlotte* with Mr. Nelson who, the letter suggests, was a Scotch Baptist. Ward spent much of 1819-1820 in England, leaving in October 1820 for a visit to America, before returning the next spring to England;

Cheltenham, Aug. 5, 1819

My dear Friend,

I received your letter yesterday, & thank you for it. I had been thinking about you, & resolving to write to you. I should have written sooner, but have been very ill one part of the time, & have been travelling so much the other part, that I have really had no time. But as I am come here to drink the water, I have now more leisure: this is the 26th letter I have written since I came here, & I have been here only 6 days

I was glad to find that you had left off wandering from the flock; & that you have been enjoying the comforts of home & of the house of God, our better home—

"There my best friends, my kindred dwell,
There God my Saviour lives."

I had heard something of the loss of the place, & the visiting of the Trustees; but am glad that you have found a place of refuge, & have obtained a Chapel which was before almost useless; & if the Scotch minister be a good man, then you can say with Paul, the afflictions which have befallen you have tended to the furtherance of the Gospel. Ah! my friend, "the Lord can clear the darkest skies; can give us day for night." When I left the ship my legs were much swelled as well as other parts of my body. I thought it was only the confinement, but when I got to Bristol, I found that I had a dropsy beginning to lay hold of me; & the D^r had some concern for my life; but these symptoms were soon removed; & I bless God that I am now much better, & hope that by remaining at this place for a week or two more I shall have gained a considerable degree of strength. I am glad to hear that you are so well, & that you appear to enjoy your Christian privileges: may you often be enabled to say "Verily God is in this place." I rejoice too, that you are trying to be useful. This, my friend, is the very means of gaining good, for even Christ, though his sufferings were so dreadful, shall see of the travail of his soul & be satisfied:

"There on a green & flowery mount
Our weary souls shall sit;
And with transporting joys recount
The labours of our God."

---

he finally arrived back in Serampore in the fall of 1821. For more on Ward's furlough, see Cox, *History*, 1 280-284.

[175]Raffles Handlist, fasc. 34, f. 20, JRULM. Ward's sermon of 23 June 1819, *From the Power of Satan unto God*, was preached at Zion Chapel and printed in the *Baptist Magazine* (1819): 305-307. On the day of the above letter, Ward spoke at Queen-Street Chapel, Lincoln's-Inn-Fields, London.

Go on, then, my dear friend, live very near to God in your closet & in your daily walk, & resolve, by teaching the young, by conversing with your ungodly neighbours, by assisting in every attempt to call sinners to repentance, resolve, I say, in the strength of God, that you will snatch one sinner from the [illegible word] & take one sinner with you to heaven, to be your eternal joy, & your crown of rejoicing in the day of the Lord Jesus. Wrestle with God to give you one sinner, & try to catch that one sinner, & I doubt not you will then save a soul from death, & even a multitude of sins.

Remember me to your Minister. May the Lord give him those seals to his Ministry that shall make him shine as the stars for ever & ever. Remember me also to your partner in life; & forget not to pray for
Your affectionate friend
& companion on board the Princess Charlotte,
W Ward.

---

128. F. A. Cox, Upper Homerton, [London], to Thomas Raffles at Mr. Bolton's, Great George Street, Liverpool, 30 August 1819.[176]

Upper Homerton
Aug.ᵗ 30. 1819

My dear Sir
I avail myself of the opportunity of M.ʳ Medley's visit to Liverpool, to say, that after using every effort to make satisfactory arrangements for my own journey thither in October, my Academical as well as Ministerial claims are so considerable, that I cannot possibly accomplish my wishes, & am therefore compelled, though reluctantly, to decline the proposed services at your Chapel in October. At the same time I propose visiting Liverpool about Christmas & hope then to be able to obtain contributions for our meeting-house.[177]
I remain
My dear Sir
Yours most truly
F. A. Cox

---

[176]Eng. MS. 375, f. 473c, JRULM.
[177]The Baptist meeting at Mare Street, Hackney.

129. Joseph Ivimey, London, to Thomas Raffles, Liverpool, 19 December 1819.[178]

London Dec[r] 19th 1819

My dear Sir,

I know you will excuse me for troubling you with this letter. My friend M[r] Richard Burton, who is a member with us, and M[r] Charles Evans, a member with M[r] Roberts of Bristol, are going as missionaries to the Island of Java.[179] They expect to sail on Wednesday next. I understand that you promised Bro Burton that you would give him a letter of introduction to the Governor. I shall feel exceedingly obliged, and you will greatly serve the Society by sending a letter for that purpose by return of post. I feel confident that you will be "happy thus to help them forward after a godly sort." I am, Dear Sir,

Yrs most respect[fully]
Joseph Ivimey

P.S. They go by the "London."

130. William Ward, [Liverpool], to Thomas Raffles, [Liverpool], Thursday morning [1819].[180]

Thursday morn.[g]

Rev. & dear Sir,

I have heard with much concern of your late accident, & of the present state of your health, & should have availed myself of your kindness in giving you a call this morning, but have been obliged to resort to medicine myself, & am now confined. I shall be happy to hear that you are better this morning; & hope you will soon be again in your delightful work. May you be long preserved & long prospered in it.

Governor Raffles was at Serampore a short time before I left home; both he & his lady: they were then well. They have since proceded to Darusslam.[181] My nephew is gone with Sir Tho[s] taking with him a print-

---

[178]Eng. MS. 379, f. 1056b, JRULM.

[179]**Richard Burton** (d. 1828) sailed with his fellow BMS missionary, **Charles Evans**, to Sumatra in 1820 (both men had been Bristol students). They would work for a time with Nathaniel Ward (see letter 124).

[180]Eng. MS. 386, f. 3015, JRULM. This letter was written while Ward was still on furlough in England.

[181]Darrussalam was located in the northern tip of the island of Sumatra, where Raffles was returning as governor.

ing press,— I hope he may be a blessing to the country, as he is a pious young man, & Sir Thoˢ enters into all his missionary plans.

Yʳˢ very very truly

W. Ward

Rev. T. Raffles.

Part Five

1820–1837

131. William Carey, Serampore [Bengal], to John Shepherd,[1] Curator of the Botanical Gardens, Liverpool, 29 January 1820.[2]

My Dear Sir,

By the Princess Charlotte, Capt Mc Kean,[3] I have the pleasure of sending you a Box of plants of which I enclose a list. I have tried a new method with some of them, and shall be happy to hear how it succeeds. I planted them in the Box, about two months before the dispatch, during that time I allowed them but little water that they might be brought as nearly as possible to the to the state of winter, I then filled up the Box with other plants, wrapped in moss or straw, and bent down the planted ones over them. I cannot tell whether this will succeed better than your method, but make the trial.

I wrote you word of the excellent state in which your last dispatch arrived, I am sorry however to say that not above four or five of the plants could be preserved; This makes me doubt whether shrubby plants can be transported so far with much hope of success. Of your former dispatch almost all the plants are doing well but they were plants of a different kind. I have no doubt but perennial plants with thick roots, or which grow in large tufts will come in good preservation, in the way you send them, as will all sorts of bulbs. It is the best way to send seeds of those plants which produce them. This I will do to you, and we must persevere in attempts to transport the other kinds till we finally succeed.

I have raised many valuable plants from the seeds you so kindly sent me; and one circumstance makes me think of another method which may be worth trial. I suppose that almost as many species of

---

[1] **John Shepherd** (1764-1836), Curator of the Liverpool Botanic Gardens, 1802-36, and correspondent of William Carey.

[2] Eng. MS. 374, f. 361b, JRULM. The above letter was postmarked from Calcutta General Post Office, 20 February 1820.

[3] The *Princess Charlotte* was a 22-gun ship built by the shipping firm of Thomas and Jonathan Brocklebank, Whitehaven. She was launched on 6 September 1815 for service in the East Indies. Captain McKean was the ship's initial captain, traveling mostly to Calcutta and Bombay until 1827.

plants as you sent, have sprung up spontaneously from the earth in which the plants were sent, from which I conclude that if bog or peet soil were mixed with as many seeds as one third of its bulk and nailed up in the manner you nail up your plants; and a list of the seeds sent, a greater proportion would grow then in any other way, I could spell out the plants when they come up. any small bulbs or tubes mixed among them might also succeed. I have a good number of ferns sprung up from your earth. some Galiums, and scabioses, with many other plants.

By desire of Loddiges & Sons Hackney[4] I sent them seeds packed in that way, which they inform me succeeded remarkably well. I think I sent you a Box packed in the same manner. I shall be glad to hear how they succeeded.

You can scarcely send me plants which are not new. I am particularly desirous to obtain bulbus plants and herbaceous ones or such as die down in winter, and shoot up again in the spring. You have furnished me with a good number of Irises, I still however want Pseudoacorus. —verna. —cristata. —ensata. —ventricosa. —stylosa. — Putescens. —flavissima. —anemia. —plicata. —Swertia. —gerania. — susianapersica. —tuberosa. —lusitanica. —mauritiana. —juncus.— alata. —scopioides, and Ruthenica. Irises come up well from seeds if they are new. I want all the Maricas[5] except paludosa. All the Trolliums. Colchicums. Anemones. Erythroniums, Tulips. — Hyacinths.—Of Bromalia we have only—ananas and karattas. All the *Pittisimmas* you sent are flourishing well. I still want—media.—bractiata.—and integrifolia. There is no Tillandsia in India. All the Massonias are wanting with us, as is also the Snow drop. Of Narcissus I still am desirous of obtaining—

---

[4]Conrad Loddige & Sons operated a large nursery in Mare Street, Hackney. Loddige opened his first nursery in Hackney in 1787; by 1842, William Robinson, a Hackney antiquarian, would declare that Loddige's nursery represented "the finest display of exotics ever collected in this country." By the date of the above letter, his nursery, later operated by his sons William and George, encompassed more than fifteen acres, where, Robinson writes, "productions from every part of the globe are cultivated, requiring a course of variety of temparature [sic]: for those from the tropical climates houses have been erected from twelve to forty feet in height. Of palms there are nearly *two hundred* species, and of orchiderus plants nearly *two thousand.*" Robinson adds, "The temperate houses extend upwards of 800 feet in length, and ample space is there devoted to *camelias* and plants from *South America* and *New Holland*, as well as *heaths* and multitudes of other plants from the *Cape of Good Hope.*" To Robinson, there was no possibility of Loddige's nursery ever "exhausting the countless wonders of nature." See *Pigot and Co.'s London & Provincial New Commercial Directory for 1827-8* (London: J. Pigot, [1827]) 187; William Robinson, *The History and Antiquities of the Parish of Hackney, in the County of Middlesex,* 2 vols. (London: John Bowyer Nichols and Son, W. Pickering, and Caleb Turner, 1842-43) 1:90, 91.

[5]Myricas.

poeticus.—angustifolius.—Pseudo Narcissus. Sibthorpia.—bicoler.—exignus.—moschatus.—nutens.—solatus, and inflatus. Of Pencratiums I want Mexicanum.—carolinianus.—verecundum, and calathinum. Of Amaryllis I require reticulata,— bivaginato.—advena.—corusca.—and stellaris. Bulbocodium [illegible word] is not in India. nor are any of the species of Uvularia, or Smilacina— Convallaria majalis, — verticillata.—latifolia. and bifolia are not yet in our collections nearly all the Lilies are wanting, and all the Fritillaries

I fear succulent plants can scarcely be sent so far, or I should beg some of them particularly Aloes, and the Custus flagella fennis. Seeds of Mesembryanthemum, and particularly of Pelargoniums, Fuchsias.—Ostens, Solidago, Cineraria, Coreopsis and Achilleas will be peculiarly acceptable.

Be informed, My Dear Sir, I shall use every effort to convey to you all that I can send either by seeds or in any other way.

I am, very truly yours

W. Carey

Serampore
29.th Jan.y 1820

132. William Ward, Bristol, to James Deakin, Glasgow, 12 April 1820.[6]

Bristol April 12, 1820.

My dear Sir,

Mr King of Birmingham, has communicated to me your very kind request that I should make your house my habitation while at Glasgow. Accept my very sincere respects, & best thanks. I feel rather doubtful, in consequence of the agitated state of your country whether this be the right time to visit Scotland; & I should be glad of a line from you or Br. Anderson of Edinburgh if you think my journey should be delayed. If I receive a line from you or him, I shall leave London for Edinburgh on the 3d or 4th of May, though I shall hardly arrive at your capital before the 20th through delays on the road. A line directed to No 60, Paternoster-Row, London, if delay be necessary will oblige. I shall go to Edinburgh first, to consult with Br. Anderson. Permit me to remain with very great respect, My dear Sir, Yrs very faithfully

W Ward

---

[6]Raffles Handlist, fasc. 34, f. 21, JRULM. This letter is written on a printed notice of letters from two missionaries—Adoniram Judson to **John Lawson**, and **William Robinson** to **John Ryland**. This fascicle also contains a printed letter by **John Dyer** of the BMS.

133. William Carey, Serampore [Bengal], sent via Capt. Chapman of the Ganges, to J[ohn]. Shepherd, Curator, Botanical Gardens, Liverpool, 27 October 1820.[7]

My Dear Sir

I only heard two days ago of the Ganges[8] being about to sail, and hear she sails tomorrow. I have therefore hastily filled you a Box of Plants, as [marked out word] the enclosed list; I could not possibly get seeds ready; I therefore only enclose one species in a full box. It is a new Canna, from Nepola.

Accept my best thanks for a parcel of Seeds which came without a letter, but undoubtedly from you.—My collection owes much to you.

If you could, and would send me a quantity of seeds of shrubs &c in Peet earth, well rammed down in a box or Cask—about twice or thrice as much earth as seeds, you would do me a great favour. We have no Peet Earth in Bengal, and Ericas, Rhododendra, Azaleas, and a hundred species more perish for want of it. The earth would therefore be as great a treasure as the seeds. I have occasionally received a small quantity in which these plants thrive prodigiously which we cannot preserve at all in our common soil. I just hint at a few Genera which might be sent that way with great hope of success. Viz. Syringa, Circaea, Veronica, Pinguicula, Monarda, Roseovarius, Salvia, Ancistrum, Collinsonia, Globularia, Scabrosa, Galium, Bouvardia, Cormus, Alchemilla, Ilex, Myosotis, Lythospernum, Anchusa, Cynoglossum, Pulmanaria, Symphaticum, Onosma, Eclium, [illegible word], Funicula, Dodecatheon, Lysimachia, Azalea, Phlax, Polemonium, Campanula, Phytuma, Lobelia, Lonicera. I am very desirous of our two most common species, Caprifolium and Periclymanum. Cestrum, ~~and~~ Viola, I long to see the sweet violet again.—But a list of these wants will only tire you to look it over. I should however feel much gratified by receiving a box or Cask of seeds thus packed in earth, it should not be quite dry, nor very moist. Bulbs are also very desirable. We have not the Snow drop, Tulip, Hyacinth, Erythroniums, nor many other species of bulbs, particularly Haemanthus and Massonia, scarcely any Lilies, or Fritillaries.

I am particularly desirous of obtaining succulent Plants, Cactus except the species in the Hortus Bengalensis,[9] Aloe, Stapelia, and Euphor-

---

[7]Eng. MS. 387, f. 20c, JRULM.

[8]This ship, based in Philadelphia, sailed regularly to Calcutta and Canton.

[9]A reference to the *Hortus Bengalensis: or Catalogue of Plants Growing in the Honourable East India Company's Botanic Garden at Calcutta* by **William Roxburgh**, which was printed by Carey at Serampore in 1814. Roxburgh had left the manuscript with Carey when he returned to England in 1813, along with his other important manuscript (also published by Carey at Serampore), *Flora Indica* (2 vols., 1820, 1824). See Farrer, *William Carey: Missionary and Botanist*, 96-97.

bia, will come well packed in Moss, and I should think Sempervirens, and Sedums might do so.

But I must conclude having two or three more letters to write and it is now Nine Oclock at night.

I am, My Dear Sir,

very truly yours

W Carey

Serampore.

27.th Oct.[r] 1820

M.[r] Roscoe[10] mentions your having some fine Cannas, pray send me seeds, also Maranta & Thalia.

I can spell out the plants when they grow, if you kindly add a list of the seeds mixed with the earth. The box is marked S. I. or rather was intended to be so, for the carpenter cut the I. so as to be like T turned upside down. It is S. I. you will I hope find it.

134. John Ryland, Bristol, to Thomas Raffles, Liverpool, 22 February 1821.[11]

Dear Sir

A few days ago M[r] Prust[12] applied to me saying you wish'd to collect some specimens of the hand writing of different Min[rs] and w[d] be glad if I could furnish you with Some. I certainly then felt fully disposed to do whatever was in my power to gratify you; and I have since been laid under an additional obligation, by your kind communication from Sumatra rec[d] on Saturday. But the difficulty lies in finding anything worth your acceptance, and yet what I could part with, which shall also not contain any confidential information relative to private concerns.

I also do not know whose hand writing which I have wou'd be most acceptable, I have found specimens of M[r] Newton, Fuller, R. Hall, S. Pearce, Foster, D[r] Carey, M[r] Scott.[13] If you will name any one else whose

---

[10]**William Roscoe** (1753-1831), Liverpool Unitarian, literary scholar, art historian, botanist, and M.P. in 1806.

[11]Eng. MS. 383, f. 1773e, JRULM.

[12]Probably the father of Edmund Thornton Prust (1808-1886), who was born in Bristol and educated at Mill Hill School and at Highbury, 1826-1829. He pastored the Independent congregation at Commercial Street in Northampton, 1829-1830.

[13]These individuals are John Newton, Andrew Fuller, Robert Hall, Samuel Pearce, John Foster, William Carey, and Thomas Scott, the Evangelical vicar of Olney. Some of the letters from these men that have already appeared in this book may have come to Raffles from Ryland's own collection.

writing I am likely to have, I will search my papers to try if I can serve you further.

Since I began this letter I have seen a very kind letter sent from Sir T. S. R. to Mr Dyer.[14] I shall be glad, if when you write to him, you will assure him that we feel our selves greatly indebted to him for his kindness. Being exceedingly hurried at this time, especially on acc^t of the approaching death of my dear Colleagues wife,[15] you will excuse my hastily subscribing myself,

Your cor^l & much obliged Bro^r

John Ryland

Feb. 22^d 1821.

135. Newton Bosworth,[16] Cambridge, to J. H. Wiffen,[17] Woburn Abbey, 25 October 1821.[18]

Cambridge, 25th October, 1821.

My dear Friend,

Allow me to thank you again and again for your very kind letter rec.^d yesterday, and especially for your prompt and explicit reply to my enquiries respecting Mr Salmon,[19] a reply which leaves me nothing to wish for as to the points I was desirous of ascertaining. Not knowing how I shall be situated tomorrow, when Dr Thackeray[20] is to pack up

---

[14]**Sir Thomas Raffles,** Rev. Raffles's cousin (see letter 124), and **John Dyer**, BMS secretary (see letter 125).

[15]Mrs. Crisp, wife of **Thomas Steffe Crisp** (1788?-1868), assistant pastor at Broadmead and tutor at Bristol Academy (he later served as Principal, 1826-1868), died on 26 February 1821. Her maiden name was Vipan, and she had been a member for several years of the Independent congregation at Broadmead. See Broadmead Independent Church, 1817-1834 (MS., Bristol Record Office, Bd/M1/4) f. 38-39.

[16]**Newton Bosworth** (1778-1848), Baptist educator and writer, operated boarding schools in Cambridge (1803-1823) and London (1823-1834) before emigrating to Canada.

[17]**Jeremiah Holmes Wiffen** (1792-1836), Quaker writer and educator in Woburn, Bedfordshire,

[18]Eng. MS. 373, f. 213a, JRULM.

[19]Most likely a reference to **Thomas Salmon** (1800-1854), Methodist evangelist and later missionary to India for the London Missionary Society.

[20]Frederic Thackeray, M.D. (1774-1852) was a prominent physician in Cambridge (he resided for many years in St. Andrew's Street) during the first half of the nineteenth century. In 1766, his father, Thomas Thackeray (1736-1806), became one of the first surgeons at Addenbrookes Hospital in Cambridge. Frederic's brother,

the books he is about sending to you, I obey the injunction—"*Carpe diem*"—to write to you a few lines, or words, as opportunity may be afforded to me, in reply to the remainder of your letter, and for the purpose of continuing a correspondence which I shall always be happy to maintain, as far as I can, with my good friend at Woburn Abbey.

I do not *usually* see the *Quarterly*;[21] but your information excited my curiousity to see the next N.º It has reached Cambridge, I find, but D.ʳ T., who has seen it, assures me that there is nothing in it about your translation of Tasso, the whole article being taken up with an account of M.ʳ Hunt's, so that you must wait awhile, which I trust you will do with exemplary patience, for the awful declaration of your sentence in that count.[22]

Friday evening—1/2 past 6.

It was well I began yesterday, tho' my pen was suddenly arrested in its progress. I have had no time till now to resume it; and I have just rec.ᵈ the D.ʳˢ summons to let him have my parcel by 7 o'clock. I am much interested in your reflections suggested by his marriage & your own experience & prospects. I must take another turn among "Aonian Hours," for the Tale, &c.[23] I should be happy to satisfy your enquiry about the Baptists; but I scarcely know, at the moment, what book to send you, as almost all their writings which explain any of their tenets, are written in defence of the practice by which they are designated, and by which *alone* (or nearly so) they are distinguished as a body from the Independent dissenters in general. With the one exception I have men-

---

William (1770-1849) was a prominent physician at Chester. Frederic succeeded his father at Addenbrookes Hospital in 1796. Frederic was apparently known to many members at St. Andrew's Street, including Robert Hall, for in 1804 he was the attending physician during Robert Hall's first mental breakdown. In 1817, Frederic became a member of the Cambridge County Club, the same club Robert Hall had joined in 1798. See Henry John Wale, *My Grandfather's Pocket-Book. From A.D. 1701 to 1796* (London: Chapman and Hall, 1883) 230; Timothy Whelan, "'I am the Greatest of the Prophets': A New Look at Robert Hall's Mental Breakdown, November 1804," *Baptist Quarterly* 42 (2007): 116-119.

[21]The *Quarterly Review* was one of the most important periodicals of its day, with William Gifford (1756-1826) serving as the initial editor, 1809-24. John Taylor Coleridge (1790-1876) was editor from 1824 to 1853.

[22]A reference to *Tasso's Jerusalem Delivered, an Heroic Poem*, translated by J. H. Hunt (1818), which was reviewed in the *Quarterly Review* in July 1821 (pp. 426-437). Wiffen had just published his *Jerusalem Delivered. Book the Fourth ... Being the Specimen of an Intended ... Translation in ... Spenserian Verse; With a Prefatory Dissertation on Existing Translations* (1821). His complete translation of *Jerusalem Delivered* would not appear until 1824.

[23]A reference to Wiffen's *Aonian Hours; and Other Poems* (London: Longman, Hurst, Rees, Orme, and Brown, 1819).

tioned, the *Particular* Baptists agree with the *Calvinistic Independents* in doctrine and discipline; and the *General* Baptists with the Arminian Dissenters. I venture to send you a Pamphlet, that I may not be negligent of your request, (tho not exactly what you wish for): it is the second in the bound volume. If you wish for any further information, I shall be happy to communicate it to you whenever you may express your desire to receive it. I enclose also, for your perusal, the Annual Report of the B. M. Soc[y], which I have this day rec.[d] In return may I ask you, in what publication the tenets of the 'Friends' are most correctly given, and whether you can favour me with the perusal of it?

My watch is within a minute of 7, and I have the parcel to make ready. So with every good wish, I conclude—hoping soon to write again, for which, however, I hope also you will not wait; but assure yourself that, whether in or out of course, a letter from you will always give great pleasure to, my dear friend,

Your's most sincerely,
N. Bosworth

Attached to the previous letter is a letter from J. H. Wiffen, Woburn Abbey, to T. H. Horne,[24] London, 19 February 1823.[25]

My dear Sir,

I have but a few moments to answer thy letter of yesterday morning. I by no means wished to insinuate that Mr Bosworth was not fully competent to give instruction in Writing & Arithmetic as well as the Classics.[26] Thou will form thine own opinion from the letter I send thee, which I judge likely to be more satisfactory than any opinion I should give upon the subject. The letter may be returned at any convenient opportunity, and with every wish for the welfare and success, believe me, with kind remembrances to Mr. Roy.

Thy sincere friend
J. H. Wiffen

Wob. Abb. Feb. 19th. 1823.

---

[24]**Thomas Hartwell Horne** (1780-1862), bibliographer, scholar, and prolific author.

[25]Eng. MS. 373, f. 213b, JRULM.

[26]Wiffen's letter to Horne was written shortly after Bosworth's removal to London, where he established a new school at Hackney (see letters 147 and 148).

136. Joseph Cottle, Bristol, to Thomas Raffles, Liverpool, May 29, 1823.[27]

My dear Sir

I send you one line just to say, that I have not yet been successful in my endeavour to obtain an Autograph of our poor unfortunate Chatterton. I have still one clue which may conduct to the desired result, but should any impediment arise in that quarter, why I will then, even filch a bit from my own continuous MS; so much is it my wish to comply with your request.[28]

Pray accept this as an apology for my not having returned an earlier answer, & however much you may have censured me in your heart,

---

[27]Eng. MS. 351, f. 49a, JRULM.

[28]Thomas Chatterton (1752-1770) gained considerable notoriety for his "Rowley Poems" (he began composing them when he was 12); he alleged that the poems were transcriptions of fifteenth-century manuscripts found at the Church of St. Mary Redcliffe in Bristol. He tried to sell his poems to various magazines in London, but to no avail. They were soon declared as forgeries; consequently, broken and impoverished, Chatterton committed suicide at the age of seventeen. Despite his unfortunate attempt at defrauding the public concerning the "genuineness" of the Rowley poems, many of the poems themselves were indeed brilliant adaptations of fifteenth-century poetry, revealing a remarkable genius in such a young poet. Chatterton later became a hero to many of the Romantic and Pre-Raphaelite poets. In 1802, Cottle, in collaboration with Robert Southey, published the complete edition of Chatterton's *Works* (3 vols) (see Cottle's reference to this in letter 263). Though no Chatterton letters exist in the Raffles Collection, Raffles continued to query Cottle for some time about a Chatterton autograph. The following letter by Cottle (MS. Eng. Lett. d. 455, f. 201, Bodleian Library, Oxford), dated 1 May 1828 and clearly written to Raffles (though unassigned), confirms this, as well as Cottle's decision not to "filch a bit" of Chatterton from his own collection.

Sir,

An opportunity offers of sending to Liverpool, free of expense, by which I avail myself of informing you, (and which I do, with much regret,) that I have none of Chatterton's writing by me, except such as is of a continuous nature, and which would be greatly injured by mutilation. Under other circumstances I should have felt pleasure in complying with your request.

I am Sir
very respectfully yours
Joseph Cottle

P.S. I have to return you many thanks for the interesting relict of that great Ornament of Human Nature, Wm Penn. Will you do me the favour to accept the enclosed. It becomes me to offer many apologies for not having returned an earlier reply.

for this unexplained delay, believe me still to be, with much respect for
your talents, and usefulness,

My dear Sir,

Yours with great sincerity

Joseph Cottle

Dr. Raffles   Liverpool

*137. John Ryland, Clifton, near Bristol, to John Sheppard,[29] Frome, 12
September 1823.[30]*

My dear Sir

    You w^d really oblige me greatly, if you would favor us with a Ser-
mon on Lord's Day Ev. next. If you will return with me to tea, after the
L. S.[31] you shall have my study to yourself. All the prime of tomorrow
morning will be occupied by my attendance on the funeral of a person
unknown. I shall have to preach in the aft^n and to administer the L. S. 2^y
Your Compliance will very much oblige myself and our friends, especially if you can let me know tomorrow that you will not refuse my request. I am   Dear Sir

Your's respectfully

John Ryland

*138. William Carey, [Serampore], to Mr. [Nathaniel] Wallich,[32] [Calcut-
ta], 17 November 1825.[33]*

My Dear Wallich,

    It is possible the expressions in my minutes may be too strong, and
it is not to be supposed that Major Campbell will retract his. I wish to
see you, but must return to Serampore this afternoon, as I am to be at
Bankura to morrow morning early. I have engaged to drive in town on
Friday. If therefore you could [come?] up on that day I shall be at liberty
from Two Oclock till Six, and we could talk over the whole.

I am, My Dear Wallich

Aff^y yours

W Carey

---

    [29]**John Sheppard** (1785-1879), Baptist writer and lay preacher from Frome,
Somerset.
    [30]Eng. MS. 861, f. 46, JRULM.
    [31]Lord's Supper.
    [32]**Dr. Nathaniel Wallich** (1786-1854), English botanist and horticulturalist
working Calcutta, India, 1807-1842.
    [33]Eng. MS. 861, f. 12, JRULM.

139. Robert Hall, Leicester, to Samuel Saunders,[34] Frome, Somerset, 16 December 1825.[35]

Rev & dear Sir

Having come to a decision to leave Leicester, it is natural for my friends to turn their attention to the means of procuring a successor, and having been informed that you have entertained thoughts of leaving Frome, have requested me to apply to you to know whether you will be so good as to pay a visit to Leicester. My family will probably not leave this place till the spring, previously to which, perhaps the congregation at Broadmead will expect me to spend some time with them; if they should you will greatly oblige my friends & myself by consenting to visit them during my absence. In case they should not, as I must remove by about Lady day,[36] may we beg the favor of your not engaging yourself to any other people, till you have seen Leicester.

If I should be under the necessity of visiting Bristol, I will take the liberty, as soon as the time of my visit is ascertained to acquaint you with it, hoping you may be able to supply for me during my absence.

From all I know or have heard, I cannot but believe your services will be highly acceptable, & I must be permitted to add that I should feel myself honoured by such a successor.

In speaking of a people to whom I have been affectionately attached for nearly twenty years, I may be expected to be partial, but justice compels me to say that their sentiments in religion are sober & correct, their disposition pious, & their behaviour to their minister kind and affectionate. Uneasinesses have arisen at different times, but I have never personally had occasion to complain of their treatment, & they are at present in a state of perfect peace. Imperfections, you my dear Sir, will know, will be found in every society, and trials in every place, but I flatter myself that a person of your talents & character will meet with as much esteem & affection from them, as you could reasonably wish. The congregation is large, & respectable, & the church numerous, though consisting for the most part of persons in the middle & inferior stations. On the whole should the great Disposer of events incline you to comply with our request, I indulge a pleasing hope that it will terminate in a union not unhappy to yourself, & eminently conducive to the spiritual advantage of a people, whose best interests will ever lie near the heart of Rev & dear Sir   Your affectionate Brother

Robert Hall

---

[34]**Samuel Saunders** (1780-1835), Baptist minister at Frome (1806-1826) and Liverpool (1826-1835). He would not take the position at Leicester.

[35]Eng. MS. 343, f. 27, JRULM.

[36]March 25.

140. MS. prospectus by F. A. Cox describing the curriculum and term schedule for his school at Hackney, January 1827.[37]

The Rev[d] F. A. Cox LL.D. proposes to take 3 or 4 young gentlemen into his house, for the purpose of extending their education beyond the general plan & period of Boarding-School instruction. The object will be to occupy advantageously the interval, or any portion of the interval between 14 or 15 & 20 years of age; not merely by accumulating knowledge, but by discovering & directing the bias & attitude of the mind, & forming the intellectual habits.

In addition to the Roman & Greek languages & literature, Mathematics & Science, D[r] Cox intends to pay particular attention to *English Composition* & to *general reading*, so as to form the taste, & point out the best methods of cultivating the mind in future. With this end in view courses in reading will be prescribed, & the merits & demerits of authors explained in connexion with the great subjects of History, Civil & Ecclesiastical, Moral Philosophy & Theology. Hebrew & Biblical Criticism will be incorporated into the system of instruction whenever it may appear practicable or desirable to the student.

D[r] Cox proposes commencing with this plan on Tuesday July 24th 1827. The terms, including every requisite accommodation & supply, excepting only Washing & Class Books will be 100 Guineas per annum. The gentlemen will have the use of a good library.

Further details may be the subject of conversation & correspondence.

Hackney   Jan[y] 1827

141. Robert Hall, Bristol, to Christopher Hill, Esq., Scarborough,[38] *19 February 1827.*[39]

19th Feb[y] 1827

Dear Sir

It would certainly give me much pleasure to visit Scarboro not only on account of the place (delightful as it is) but still more from the esteem I feel for you & your excellent companion. But, not to mention other objections, the distance for me ever to think of complying for the purpose of opening a meeting. Such occurrences are so multiplied that

---

[37]Eng. MS. 375, f. 473d, JRULM.
[38]**Christopher Hill**, deacon at Ebenezer Baptist Chapel, Scarborough.
[39]MAM. PLP. 48.25.4, JRULM. On the back is written in another hand, "An Autograph letter of the late Rob[t] Hall, M.A. written to C. Hill Esq. of Scarborough, declining an invitation to that town. Dated Feb[r] 19th 1827."

were I to lend myself to that kind of engagements, I might spend my whole summer in journeys. Indeed I have great doubts of the propriety of making any ceremony whatever of the opening of meetings. Nothing of that kind was done at Leicester or Cambridge. I am very happy however to hear that the cause is so flourishing as to demand a new & larger place. That it may daily flourish more & more, & that you my dear Sir may be long spared to adorn and support it is the sincere prayer of dear Sir

Your affectionate friend
R. Hall

P.S. I beg to be most affec^e remembered to dear Mrs Hill

142. Joseph Hughes, Battersea, [London], to Thomas Raffles, Liverpool, 7 May 1827.[40]

My Dear Sir,

Notwithstanding the bereaving dispensation with which it has pleased God to visit me,[41] I propose accompanying Mr Brandram[42] to Liverpool next week. But I wish to see you previously. Be so good as to furnish Mr Clayton[43] with your Town Address—or it will suffice for me to know that you will be at the Tract Annivery.[44]

I am My Dear Sir Your's Affec^y
J Hughes

Battersea
May 7 1827

---

[40]Eng. MS. 378, f. 1015a, JRULM.

[41]Hughes is referring to the recent death of his eldest son, Joseph Hughes, Jr., who committed suicide by drowning in the River Avon near Pershore, largely due to "an unexpected disappointment from a lady to whom he was much attached." Hughes wrote a touching poem on his son's death. A full account can be found in John Leifchild, *Memoir of the Late Rev. Joseph Hughes, A.M.* (London: T. Ward, 1835) 304-312 (quotation from page 304).

[42]Andrew Brandram (1791-1850) was Anglican secretary of the British and Foreign Bible Society, 1822-1850. Like Joseph Hughes, he traveled widely in assisting and organizing local auxiliaries.

[43]There are several possibilities for this individual: John Clayton, Sr. (1754-1843), minister at the King's Weigh House, London, 1779-1828; John Clayton, Jr. (1780-1865), the former's son, who served as a Congregational minister at the Poultry Chapel in London, 1818-1848; and George Clayton (1783-1862), another son of the elder Clayton, who ministered to the Congregational church at York Street, Walworth, 1804-1854, where at one time a young Robert Browning worshiped.

[44]Anniversary of the Religious Tract Society, founded 1799.

143. Joshua Marshman to Thomas Raffles, Liverpool, 10 December 1828.[45]

My dear Sir,
     Let me beg you to write to Felt[46] and tell him that I have a great de-sire to take him but cannot decide until I see him and know exactly the state of religion in his mind; that I wish him therefore to come over to Liverpool by this *day month*, bringing all things with him as if he were actually going, as he probably may—and if he should not go with me—back again to Hamburgh, in case he wishes to return   I am, in haste
                         Very affect^y yours
                                        J. Marshman

Decr 10th—1828

144. William Knibb,[47] *near Kingston, Jamaica, to Edward Knibb,*[48] *Liverpool, 10 December 1829.*[49]

                                              Savanna la Mar
                                        December 10th 1829

My dear Brother
     Since I sent you the Letter containing the order for the Testaments, drawn on the Revd Thos Burchell[50] I have heard that the Parcel I men-tioned as not received was at Kingston, and have received your Letter contain^g the Bill from Mr Marples.
     In my last I requested to know whether I could draw for the Sum of money due as left me by Mr Wilson,[51] deducting that part I gave to mother   If that be the case you will *please deduct the balance* I owe you, and inform me by the next packet, what may remain— My reason

---

[45]Eng. MS. 380, f. 1347, JRULM.
[46]Unidentified. Marshman was on furlough at this time in England.
[47]**William Knibb** (1803-1845), BMS missionary to Jamaica (1826-1845) and a leader in the effort to end slavery in the British Commonwealth.
[48]Edward Knibb (b. 1798), William Knibb's older brother, along with their sis-ter, Frances ("Fanny") (b. 1801) and Edwards wife, Elizabeth Hay (b. 1812) (both of whom are mentioned in the above letter—Elizabeth was pregnant at the time of this letter), were all members of Raffles's congregation in Liverpool. Edward Knibb appears in several letters in this collection. By 1846, not long after his brother's death, he was living in Jamaica.
[49]Eng. MS. 344, f. 77, JRULM.
[50]**Thomas Burchell** (1799-1846), BMS missionary to Jamaica, 1822-1846.
[51]**John Broadley Wilson** served as Treasurer of the BMS, 1826-1834.

of making this request is that at present I have no other means of settling that account, which I wish assuaged, no less for your welfare than
my own—My expenses of late have been very heavy, and I shall be
happy when I find that you and Mr Marples are paid—

I am much obliged by your kind sympathy under the persecutions
and slanders we have to endure they *are* painful, but a gracious God
has hitherto given strength equal to the day, and is continually showing
us that we are not labouring in vain—His smiles abundantly compen-
sate for the frowns of man

My health I am happy to inform you is better than it has been, so
that I am able to work in the service of my adorable master—It w^d afford both me and mine much pleasure to see you, but I can scarcely
hope for that enjoyment this side the grave—I *know* that I am in a dying
land, I *wish* to feel it, and daily prepare for that momentous change,
which awaits us all

Mary is daily expecting an addition to our family she is but poorly,
but I hope will have strength to bear the approaching season of trial,
and that a kind and covenant keeping God will appear as her succour
and Stay—The dear Children are well, you would much like little Catherine could you see her—I have some thought of sending M^r [Lance?] to
you, sh^d providence open a way   He is but sickly, and I think a change
would be beneficial to him[52]

You are aware I believe, that the station I am sent to occupy is entirely a new one   I have many encouragements, and some discourage-
ments—I hope the divine being will bless my labours, and grant me the
happiness of form^g a Church here for his glory. Breaking up fallow
ground is hard work, and requires patience, may the Lord give me
every needful grace. I have now 2 Stations, and another in the mountains— one here and one about 10 miles off. The one in the mountains
is 12—When you remember that *singing* and every other part of the
service falls upon me you will conclude I have not much spare time. I
am anxiously looking for another place to preach in, and hope I shall
succeed, when my hands and I hope my heart will be full—
The following will give You some idea of my miss^y work—

---

[52]Mary Watkins (b. 1799), formerly of the Broadmead church in Bristol, married William Knibb in October 1824. She died at Waldensia, Jamaica, in 1866.
Knibb's eldest son, William Christopher (b. 1825), died of fever at Refuge, in Tre-
lawney, Jamaica, on 25 July 1837. Ann Knibb (1830-1892), William Knibb's second
daughter, married the Rev. Ellis Fray, who pastored churches at Refuge and Kettering, Jamaica. His eldest daughter, Catherine (b. 1827), married a Capt. Milbourne in
1848. She died in Jamaica in 1858. Knibb's youngest daughter, Fanny (b. 1841), died
at Stewarton, Jamaica, in 1861. Several children born to the Knibbs died in infancy.
For more on the Knibb family, see letter 150. See also John Clarke, *Memorials of the
Baptist Missionaries in Jamaica* (London: Yates and Alexander, 1869) 100, 114-115.

Sav la Mar[53] Sabbath—Morning prayer meeting at 6. Service at 1/2 past 10 after this Catechise the Slaves from the country—talk with them separately in a plain manner which generally takes till 2 oclock—Service again at 1/2 past 6 in the even^g—We have a prayer meeting every even^g when I am home—Tuesday Ev^{ng} Singing and Pray^r meeting   Thursday Ev^g public worship—Saturday morn^g, preach in the mountains next Sabbath I am at my other Station called *Fullersfield*, Tis in the country surrounded by estates—but at crop time, I have many slaves come, but now they cannot come so well, as they have so much to do—In fine weather I preach here in the morn^g and return to Sav la Mar and preach in the even^g

These engagements, with meeting the sick, travelling and study, leaves me not many idle hours. Often do I think of you, with my other dear relatives when I am travelling through the beautiful and wild scenes of Jamaica and long that for a few hours I could converse with those I love   Here unknown and despised, my mind is sometimes dejected but feeling that I am in the path of duty, I am cheered by the knowledge that God is my protector and friend—He is graciously blessing my efforts, a little Church is already formed and others appear to have received the truth in the love of it—O that the Holy Spirit may descend, and breathe upon the dry bones that they may live

We are truly concerned to hear of the indisposition of your dear Wife—you mention that the cold of Liverpool is too much for her—Sh^d she be consumptive, a voyage here w^d do her good—Mary is, and she is much better here than when in England—Sh^d a change be needed I need not say how very happy we sh^d be to see her, or any other of the family—Kingston w^d be the place to come to, and from thence I could easily fetch her here—Fanny used to talk of coming   I wish there was a prospect of that being the case

Hoping that the divine blessing still assuages you, and with very kind love to you, your partner, Fanny &c in which M^{rs} K cordially joins

I remain dear Edward

Your most affectionate Brother

Wm Knibb

---

[53]Savannah la Mar, Jamaica.

145. Joseph Hughes, Battersea, [London], to Thomas Raffles, Liverpool, 22 April 1831.[54]

My Dear Sir,
    The Committee of The British & Foreign Bible Soc[y] direct me to request that you will take one of the resolutions to be proposed at the approaching Anniversary.
    Whether we are to have a controversial meeting or not, the day will declare.
    The Committee by no means wish to supply an occasion.
            I am, my Dear Sir,
                Yours affec[y]
                    Jos Hughes

Rev T. Raffles DD

146. A printed prospectus of Newton Bosworth's Academy at Bruce Lodge, near Tottenham, London, dated December 1831.[55]

PROSPECTUS
OF
MR. BOSWORTH'S ACADEMY,
BRUCE LODGE, NEAR TOTTENHAM.

The great object of Education is to impart knowledge, to inculcate principles, and to form habits; but, that Education may fulfil its high design and complete its perfect work, it is necessary that the knowledge be important, the principles sound, and the habits good. To these ends the efforts of the judicious Teacher will be constantly directed, and the most effectual means to secure them will be sought out and employed with incessant assiduity. The mental temperament and the moral inclination of the pupils will be attentively studied, and whatever general system be adopted, its application will be varied as individual circumstances and cases may require. Every occasion will be eagerly seized of drawing forth the juvenile intellect, of directing it to useful purposes and pursuits, and of gratifying the natural curiosity of youth by the communication of important facts and principles, in the way most likely to inform the understanding and affect the heart. While teaching the use of words and the nature of language, care will be taken to convey

[54]Eng. MS. 378, f. 1015b, JRULM.
[55]Eng. MS. 373, f. 213c, JRULM.

ideas to the mind of the student, so that he may be trained to think rationally, to judge correctly, and to act wisely.

In announcing my design to open an Academy for a small number of pupils, it will be expected that I describe the Course I intend to pursue in conducting it.

The pupil will be introduced to an acquaintance with the best portions of Greek and Roman literature, by means of that strict and careful system of imitation which has been well established; at the same time such modifications in detail, and such changes in principle, will be adopted, as appear to be real improvements—recommended either by the example and authority of the best and soundest Teachers, or by their obvious coincidence with the known principles of the human mind.

In every case, too, where such a process would be applicable (and the exceptions would be few), I would resort to Mathematical pursuits, especially Geometry and Algebra; the first, to exercise and invigorate the reasoning powers by the strictness of its logic; and the second, to excite the inventive faculties, and induce a habit of expertness, by the facilities it affords to investigation, and the variety of its resources.

The application of the Sciences to the Arts of Life, and especially to the improved state of our Machinery and Manufactures, and the results of Chemical Analysis, will also be frequently noticed; and every proper occasion seized of acquainting the pupil with the facts and principles of Astronomy, Geology, and Natural Philosophy in general.

Geography and History are too important to be overlooked: they will not only come frequently before the pupil in the course of his Classical studies, but will be continued as a separate pursuit, so as to comprehend the modern periods of the one, and the most recent discoveries of the other.

Arithmetic in all its branches, and especially its application to Commercial purposes and all practical computations, will have a portion of time and attention assigned to it commensurate with its obvious and acknowledged importance.

English Literature, in many cases too slightly cultivated, will be frequently brought before the notice of the pupils, as it richly deserves to be; and their attention will, from time to time, be called to the excellences of our best writers, and the discussions of our ablest reasoners. Themes, and other exercises of composition, will be enjoined, to call forth and establish their own powers, and to keep in proper and useful activity their faculties of thought, discrimination, and research.

It has long appeared to me highly desirable that the minds of youth should be furnished with the principal Evidences of Christianity, and the history of the Sacred Records in their transmission from age to age, their version into other languages, and their increasing circulation through the world. This information it will be my endeavour to supply.

Meanwhile, and above all, it would never be forgotten that the great business of this life is to prepare for a better; and hence I shall consider it my duty, and, I trust, find it my delight, to render my pupils familiar with the laws of Moral obligation and the principles of Scripture truth, and to inculcate upon them the necessity and advantage of remembering their Creator in the days of their youth, and of seeking salvation through the merits of Christ.

As the usefulness and comfort of future life are materially affected by the habits acquired in youth, much of my attention will be directed to the formation of *good* habits, both mental and moral: the former will be necessarily connected with the whole course of instruction, in which I shall endeavour to establish regularity, voluntary exertion, and perseverence; in the latter, it will be my invariable object to train my pupils to the exercise of humanity, benevolence, justice, veracity, and self-control.

In adhering to these principles, and acting upon them, I trust I shall be taking the most effectual means to promote my own success, as well as the present, permanent, and eternal interests of my pupils.

NEWTON BOSWORTH.

Tottenham, Dec. 1831.

Terms:

       For Board and Instruction in the whole of the preceding Course, or such parts of it as may be selected by the parents, or be deemed most suitable for the pupil,

FIFTY GUINEAS PER ANNUM.
Under Ten Years of age, FORTY GUINEAS PER ANNUM.

The pupils will live with the family, and be treated as members of it; and every attention will be paid to their exercise, health, and comfort. A quarter's notice to be given of removal.

147. Newton Bosworth, Brucelodge, Tottenham, to J. B. Brown,[56] Islington, 20 January 1832.[57]

Brucelodge, 20 Jan. 1832

My dear Sir,

Having removed hither, and occupying a house at much less expense than the one at Hackney, though just as convenient, I am enabled to make a little modification in my Terms, which may bring them more generally within the reach of my friends & connections. You will allow me to trouble you with a copy of my Prospectus,[58] not doubting that if you meet with any gentleman to whom the presentation of it may [paper torn], your aid will not be wanting.

I am sorry I have not yet been able to acquire the information I have sought, respecting the unsold copies of your life of Howard.[59] The person who gave me the former hint, does not feel himself quite at liberty from his Situation with regard to the bookseller, to push the enquiry further—at least in a direct manner. Perhaps a friend might easily ascertain the point by calling at the shop, buying some book[s], & turning the conversation to "Howard." I have just tho't of a friend who might do it; if I see him soon, or write to him, I will put him upon the enquiry. Perhaps, however, you have already obtained all you wish for. If you come near me, a call will give pleasure to, my dear sir,
Your's truly,
N. Bosworth.

148. Joseph Hughes, Battersea, to Rev. R[obert]. Littler, 31 July 1833.[60]

Dear Sir

I am willing, & desirous also, to employ the sabbath, time after time, in such manner as the friends among whom I travel, may deem

---

[56]**James Baldwin Brown** (1785-1843).

[57]Eng. MS. 373, f. 213d, JRULM.

[58]See previous letter.

[59]The reference is to Brown's *Memoirs of the Public and Private Life of John Howard, the Philanthropist* (1823). John Howard (1726-1790), a dissenter and former member of the Bunyan "Old Meeting" in Bedford, was held in great esteem for his advocacy of prison reform.

[60]Eng. MS. 386, f. 4062, JRULM. This letter is incorrectly attached in the Raffles Collection to a picture of the Rev. John Hughes and listed under the latter's name. Most likely it is addressed to Robert Littler, pastor at that time of the Matlock Bath Independent Chapel, Derbyshire.

most conducive to the best welfare of those around them; & therefore hope it will be in my power to comply with your request.

I am expected at Mansfield on the 16th of August, & at Eastwood or Grisby on the 19th—Again, I am expected at Chapel I think on the 23d, & at Bakewell, on the 26th—You can judge, from your knowledge of the County, which day it will be more convenient & economical for me to select; addressing a line to me, which will find me at Nottingham, on the 13th, or Newark the 15th, or Mansfield the 16th Be so good as to give directions for the route—with best wishes, & the hope of profitable interviews,

I am, Dear Sir,

Yours truly,

J Hughes

149. *William Steadman, Horton, Yorkshire, to James Dinwiddie, Pool, West Yorkshire, 27 February 1835.*[61]

My dear Sir

I have a favour to ask of you for a relative of mine, which I will just explain Letitia Webb, sister to my former wife,[62] married a M.r Isaacs[63] an Independent Minister, settled for some years at Godalmine in Surrey; but for upwards of 7 years has been laid aside through a complaint in his throat. That has reduced the family, consisting of 6 children, to great distress, and which is increased by the failure of her brother, which has deprived her of the proceeds of a legacy left by her father of 30 or 40£ anny—She wishes to get her second son, John Isaacs, about 9 years old into the Congregational School at Lewisham, near London To this school I am informed you are a subscriber, and my request is that you would be as kind as to give your vote for his admission. You doubtless know the whole routine of the admission of children. It is I apprehend by a majority of the votes of subscribers, sent up to J. Pitman's Esq. 35 Cumming Street, Pentonville, or 7 Castle Alley, Royal Exchange and to be decided at a half yearly meeting, I think about the middle of April. I am sorry to put you to this trouble, but the concern I feel for my relatives must plead my excuse—wishing you every blessing, I am, My Dear Sir

---

[61]Eng. MS. 384, f. 1909c, JRULM.

[62]Steadman married the sister of Joseph Webb during the former's tenure at Broughton in 1793.

[63]John Isaacs (1780-1840) was educated at Gosport under David Bogue; he pastored the Independent meeting at Harts-lane, Godalming, Surrey, 1819-1825. Shortly thereafter, his health failed and he was forced to resign. He died at Guilford in 1840 after 15 years of illness. See *Congregational Calendar* (1842): 115.

yʳˢ very sincerely
W Steadman

Horton, Feb: 27. 1835

I have scarce any personal knowledge of M.ʳ Isaacs, having never lived near him; but from all I can learn I have every reason to believe him to be a pious, upright man, & a useful minister, as long as his capacity for labour lasted.

150. William Knibb, Falmouthm [Jamaica], to Edward Knibb, Liverpool, 18 April 1835.[64]

Falmouth, April 18th 1835

My dear Brother
We were fully as happy to receive your epistle as you could have been to welcome my publication. I have this morning heard that a young Lady, the daughter of the Builder of my Chapel is about to sail to Liverpool and send by her a few hasty lines, though they must be but few. I baptized 92 yesterday in the Sea, when about 3000 spectators were present, and all behaved with the utmost decorum. Among them was a Wesleyan Preacher, and 4 able persons of that persuasion. I had full 2000 in and round the Chapel yesterday at least I think so, preached twice, received the members, and administered the Lords Supper to about 900 persons. This morning I am fully fatigued, and to morrow I start on a Missionary tour of 100 miles. I and [illegible word] Abbott[65] Dexter[66] are stationed near [each] other, and are building 4 Chapels in the Parish, so that my hands, my head, and my heart are full.

Send you a picture frame for yourself or Betsy, and a *Ruler* for good Dʳ Raffles. On walking over the ruins of my old Chapel in this Town, I found two or three old stumps of the Posts which had supported the Chapel I had them carefully dug up, for they were precious to me. One of my deacons named Andrew Dirpon has made them into a few very few frames and rulers—that is their history—So you and the worthy Dʳ, the first Preacher who welcomed me *home*, when you receive these, part of the only *relics* left of the destroyed Chapels in 1832. This wood

---

[64]Eng. MS. 379, f. 1157a, JRULM.
[65]**Thomas F. Abbott**, BMS missionary to Jamaica, 1831-1847. See letter 156.
[66]**Benjamin Bull Dexter** (d. 1863), BMS missionary to Jamaica, 1834-1853.

had been in the ground full 20 years, which will give you some idea of its durability.[67]

When you present it to the D[r], give him my very kind respects; I hope he will not refuse the present because it is so trifling, its the circumstance makes it valuable *to me*. On reaching the ruins of the Chapel at Rio Bueno, my mind was much pleased at seeing *the whole ruins covered over with a plant called the tree of life*. If I were a poet, I could make a poem on the subject perhaps the worthy D[r] *can*.[68]

We are all through mercy well. Mary I expect will write. I should be very glad of the money. Christopher and Mary and Ann[69] have when they can spare it, I wish it here, as I have since purchased a house for 1000 pounds our money, and when they can pay it, let it be paid into

---

[67]Knibb is referring to the riots instigated by the Colonial Church Union, a group formed by members of St. Ann's Militia, Jamaica, mostly white merchants and landowners who became violently opposed to the efforts of the missionaries to educate and inevitably promote abolition among the slaves. They supported the established church and the royal government's prerogative to maintain slavery in the colony. In January 1832, the Union members engaged in a series of assaults on the Baptist chapels scattered throughout Jamaica. By the time the rioting had ended, thirteen Baptist chapels had been burned to the ground, with losses totaling more than £100,000. See Cox, *History*, 2:130-131, 135, 155, 162, 205; Clarke, *Memorials*, 106; Philip Wright, *Knibb "the Notorious": Slaves' Missionary 1803-1845* (London: Sidgwick and Jackson, 1973) 92-111; for a history of the political efforts of the Baptist missionaries in ending slavery in Jamaica, see Alex Tyrrell, "The 'Moral Radical Party' and the Anglo-Jamaican Campaign for the Abolition of the Negro Apprenticeship System," *English Historical Review* 99 (1984): 481-502.

[68]Knibb arrived in Jamaica from a furlough in England on 25 October 1834. He made his way to Rio Bueno and thence to Falmouth by 4 November, where he visited the ruins of his former chapels destroyed during the riots of January-February 1832. His experience concerning the "tree of life" became known to the Sheffield poet James Montgomery, who responded with the following lines:

> When flames devoured the house of God,
> Kindled by hell, with heaven at strife,
> Up sprung spontaneous from the sod
> A forest of the tree of life;
> Meet emblem of the sanctuary
> Which there had been, and yet should be.
>   Now on the same thrice-hallowed spot
> In peace a second temple stands,
> And God hath said, "Destroy it not!"
> For lo! The blessing he commands,
> As dews as Hermon's hill of yore,
> Life, even life for evermore!

See Cox, *History*, 2: 226; Clarke, *Memorials*, 106-11.
[69]For the Knibb family, see letter 144.

the hands of Mr Dyer, and I can draw for it. If I could have half of it in 6 months from when this reaches you I should be thankful. Let me know whether this can be done.

With very kind love to you all
Remain
Yours very affectionately
William Knibb

Mr Edward Knibb

151. W. Holder, Police Office, Falmouth [Jamaica], to William Knibb, [Falmouth], 18 November 1835.[70]

Police Office Falmouth
18 Nov 1835

Sir,
    Your communication of the 11th Instant to the [illegible word] the Custos & Magistrates of this Parish "requesting the loan of the Court House for 2 or 3 weeks near the Christmas Holidays for the purpose of meeting your congregation" having been submitted to the Sitting Magistrate this day, I am desired to acquaint you that such permission has been granted for the following Sabbaths—namely the Sunday before Christmas Day—the Sunday after Christmas Day and the Sunday after New Year's Day. I remain, Sir,

Your obed Svt
W. Holder

To the Revd W Knibb
Falmouth

152. William Knibb, Falmouth [Jamaica], to Thomas Raffles, Liverpool, 13 September 1836.[71]

Falmouth Jamaica
Sept. 13. 1836

Revd and dear Sir

---

[70]Eng. MS. 387, f. 131, JRULM. Another instance in 1838 of Knibb's use of the courthouse to handle overflow crowds at special services can be found in Cox, *History*, 2:237.

[71]Eng. MS. 387, f. 130, JRULM.

At the request of my Brethren I write to solicit the following favour, which I hope will not be denied. We are about furnishing a small supplement of Hymns for the use of our Congregations, and we shall esteem it a peculiar favour if you will furnish one or two Hymns respect[g] their freedom, or connected remotely therewith which we can use with assurances of that day which in a few years will bring perfect and entire freedom. Should you kindly comply with the request, and will forward the same to the Revd Mr Willcocks, Baptist Minister Devonport,[72] we shall be truly obliged. My Brother has informed me that you have some pleasure in the Collection of Curious Letters, I therefore write on this, dear to me, and I think to you. In 1832 I was taken a prisoner and sadly aped in this Court House.

In the same year the Colonial Church (United) held its fall meet[g] in the same and declared that Baptists and especially W Knibb should never preach again in the Island

In 1834 Lord Mulgrave[73] first proclaimed freedom in the same Spot, and on the 3rd Anniversary of my being taken prisoner, I preached in it the unsearchable riches of Christ to nearly 2000 persons and made a Collection for my new Chapel, amount[g] to *£103.6.8*

Thought you would like to possess the document and I have therefore taken the liberty of securing it

Wish[g] you and your amiable lady and family every blessing and hop[g] to be favoured with a reply.

With all

Love & resp truly

William Knibb

Revd D[r] Raffles

---

[72]**Thomas Willcocks** (d. 1845), Baptist minister at Devonport, 1811-1837.

[73]Earl Mulgrave was the Royal Governor of Jamaica at the time of the emancipation of the slaves in 1834. His support for the missionaries and their desire to abolish slavery earned him the hatred of the slaveholders on the island, many calling him "the baptist-loving earl, the heartless whig, the namby-pamby novel-writer," among other epithets; yet, as Cox notes, he met these epithets with "a spirit of calm and dignified firmness, becoming his character and office." He signed the bill, ending slavery throughout the British colonies (the bill had been passed by parliament on 28 August 1833) on 12 December 1833. He remarked that "slavery, that greatest curse that can afflict the social system, has now received its death-blow." He returned to England in March 1834, just prior to the implementation of the abolition bill on 1 August 1834, and was succeeded by the Marquis of Sligo. See Cox, *History*, 2:205-206; 195-198; Clarke, *Memorials*, 110.

153. Olinthus Gregory, Royal Military Academy, Woolwich, to Thomas Raffles, Liverpool, 20 April 1837.[74]

Royal Mil.ʸ Academy
20 April 1837

My dear Sir
    I feel very desirous to meet your wishes with regard to John Bunyan's autograph; and yet I find it difficult to accomplish my desire. The book in which the bits and scraps of Bunyan's writing occur, in marginal pithy or pious notes or remarks, is the first edition of Isaac Ambrose's Prima. Since I gave one of these scraps to Mr. [Proudfit?], and sent one, by him, to my friend Dr. Sprague, I have had so many applications that the book is almost ruined on account of its numerous indentations. Being, however, desirous to testify my sincere respect and esteem for Dr. Raffles, I have tempted myself to cut out one more little slice from my poor volume; and I now enclose it. The passage in Ambrose against which this was attached, relates to "the joy unspeakable, the joy of the Holy Ghost." It is of this that Bunyan says, "but whethur thou shalt have it here," &c. The scrap at the back "all irregular means yⁿ must be avoyded," relates to such means as end in false joy or delusive peace.
    I have every reason to believe that the writing is really Bunyan's. The original owner of the book testifies it to be such. I have shown it to Mr. Hillyard of Bedford,[75] and have compared it with Bunyan's writing in the church book at Bedford—and cannot but think that the similarity is great.
    I hope you continue useful, healthy, and happy; and am,
        My dear Sir,
            Yours very sincerely,
              Olinthus Gregory

---

[74]Eng. MS. 347, f. 197, JRULM. This letter has been placed within the folio marked "John Bunyan," not under Gregory. T. J. Brown, in an article in *The Book Collector* (Spring 1960), p. 54, argues convincingly that the MS. Gregory is referring to above is not in Bunyan's hand.
[75]**Samuel Hillyard** (see letter 60).

Part Six

1841–1845

154. *Lewis P. W. Balch,*[1] *New York, to Rev. Dr. S. H. Turner,*[2] *Theological Seminary, or Rev*[d] *D*[r] *[Robert Alfred] Vaughn,*[3] *Morton Street, New York, 30 January 1841.*[4]

N. Y. Jan 30./41.

Rev[d] & d[r] Sir,

    M[r] Low[5] who will hand you this, is an Englishman, and in many respects an interesting character. His Parents were of the middle rank of

---

    [1]**Lewis Penn Witherspoon Balch** (1814-1875), Evangelical Rector at St. Bartholomew's Church (Episcopal) in New York City, 1838-1850.

    [2]**Samuel Hulbeart Turner** (1790-1861), theology professor at the General Theological Seminary (New Haven and later New York City), 1819-1861.

    [3]**Robert Alfred Vaughn** (1795-1868), prominent Congregational minister, eminent scholar, and prolific writer in England. He would return to England in 1841 and attended the BMS annual meeting in London that May, giving a stirring speech in support of the BMS's intention to establish a mission in Western Africa. Concerning Europe's role in the slave trade, he exclaimed: "Oh, who can estimate the guilt that the human mind has contracted in this course of proceeding! It is impossible that we should estimate it." See *Missionary Herald* (June 1841): 308.

    [4]MAW, Box 39, JRULM.

    [5]Edgar Anthony Low (he appears in several letters below) may have been a relation of James Low (d. 1863), papermaker, who served as treasurer of the Baptist Union, 1834-1847. At the time of the above letter, Low was an Anglican (though clearly an Evangelical); in April 1842, however, he was baptized and joined the Baptist congregation in Tottenham, under the ministry of **J. J. Davies**. In June 1842 Low applied to the BMS as a missionary to Africa. The BMS Committee minutes note that Low was to be meet with the Examination Subcommittee on 7 July. After that meeting, the Subcommittee announced that they were "not prepared to recommend him for the acceptance of the Committee at present." They suggested instead "that should he have an opportunity of spending six months in religious improvement the Committee should be open to an application from him again at the end of that time—Resolved that the same be received and acted upon as the Resolution of this Committee." Low must have taken the Subcommittee's advice, for he reapplied on 2 November 1842 (see letter 197), requesting the opportunity "to visit Africa as a Missionary Traveller," the Committee minutes noted on the following day. The Committee recommended that a "Subcommittee be appointed to confer with M[r] Low

life. Gave him a good plain Education with a trade. He however conceived a strong desire to penetrate the interior of Africa from the north east coast near Abysinia. To this he has devoted his life, and is apparently fully aware of all the perils he must encounter.

His object is twofold. First—to carry a knowledge of Xn^y where a white man has never yet been, and 2^d, to gain information. To effect the former he is desirous of studying the Arabic language and such words as will best qualify him to impart the elementary principles of religion. To accomplish the latter, he is now learning navigation &c—He applied to me for advice respecting the best mode of securing his 1st object and I felt it my duty to send him to you, as one able and willing to give such information.

I doubt not but that it will give you pleasure to aid in advancing an object wh[ich] may be the means under God, of promoting the interests of the Redeemer's Kingdom on earth. We are directed not to despise the day of small things and I confess any thing wh[ich] may contribute to the social or spiritual well being of [paper torn] Africa, always ~~holds~~ creates a deep interest in my heart.

> I am Rev^d & dr Sir,
> Faithfully & cordially yours
> Lewis. P. W. Balch

Revd Dr Turner

---

on this subject, & that it consist of Messrs Hinton, Steane, & Whitehorne, with the Treasurer & Secretary." The subcommittee reported on 8 December that despite having "received lengthened written communications" from Low, they could not "recommend him to the Committee in that character." Though he may never have been an official BMS missionary, Low nevertheless served in Africa and mantained a loose connection with the BMS, for on 26 September 1844 a letter by Low, dated July 7 (BMS No. 286), was placed before the Committee, reporting on Low's work in conjunction with the newly established mission post in Fernando Po. For James Low, see Ernest A. Payne, *The Baptist Union: A Short History* (London: Carey Kingsgate Press, 1959) 262; "An Index to Notable Baptists, Whose Careers began within the British Empire before 1850," *Baptist Quarterly* 7 (1920-1921) 216; for the references to E. A. Low, see BMS Committee Minutes, Vol. H (Oct. 1841-Dec. 1842), f. 142; ff. 147-148; f. 200; 214; Volume J (30 May 1844—29 July 1847), f. 46.

155. A card bearing the signatures of all the BMS missionaries in Falmouth, February 1841.[6]

Baptist Missionaries in Association Falmouth Feb[y] 1841[7]

Joshua Tinson	Samuel Oughton
James M. Phillippo	David Day
Thomas Burchell	Ebenezer Jo[s] Francies
William Knibb	Joseph Merrick
Tho.[s] F Abbott	Henry John Dutton
Walter Dendy	John Edw.[d] Henderson
John Kingdon	Benjamin Millard
Benjamin B. Dexter	Philip Henry Cornford
John Hutching	Edward Wholley
John Clark	John May

156. Edgar Anthony Low to Rev. Lewis Balch, New York, 6 July 1841 [copy].[8]

New York, July 6. 1841.

Rev[d] Sir

I waited on D[r] Turner at the Theological Seminary who informed me he could not give me any information with regard to the Arabic Language as he had not studied it but he referred me to D[r] ~~Robertson~~

---

[6]Eng. MS. 861, f. 33, JRULM.

[7]The above letter from Falmouth that bore the signatures of those who attended the February association meeting of the Baptist missionaries in Jamaica appeared in the *Missionary Herald* (May 1841): 257, along with a printed list of the signatories: **Joshua Tinson** (1794-1850), BMS missionary, 1822-1850; **Samuel Oughton** and his wife, Hannah (the niece of Mrs. Thomas Burchell), 1835-1866; **James Mursell Phillippo** (1798-1879), 1823-1879; **David Day**, 1837-1862; **Ebenezer Joseph Francies** (1815-1846), 1839-1846; **Joseph Merrick** (1818-1849), one of the first native missionaries with the BMS, 1839-1849; **Thomas Fisher Abbott**, 1831-1847 (see also letter 150); **Henry John Dutton**, 1839-1846; **Walter Dendy**, 1831-1881; **John Edward Henderson** (1816-1885), 1840-1881; **John Kingdon** (d. 1855), 1831-1850; **Benjamin Millard**, 1840-1872; **Philip Henry Cornford**, 1840-1850; **John Hutchins** (d. 1851), 1834-1851; **Edward Woolley**, 1840-1847; **John Clark** (arrived in Jamaica in 1835); **John May** (1814-1894), 1840-1852. The letter concerns the newly proposed BMS missionary enterprise in Western Africa (the missionaries at Falmouth sent a monetary gift) and the newly proposed academical institution in Jamaica, under the leadership of Joshua Tinson (see letter 219).

[8]MAW, Box 39, JRULM. A note affixed to the MS. reads, "Copy of a letter written to Rev[d] L[s] Balch then in New York."

Robinson[9] who has just returned from the "Holy Land" Dr Turner expressed his ~~satisfaction~~ approbation at the object I had in view which gave me great satisfaction as it will assist in strengthening that resolution requisite to enable me to surmount whatever obstacles should present themselves. I called on Dr Robinson yesterday evening who gave me much valuable information with regard to the Arabic Language, it seems that I shall not be able to procure the necessary books in New York—the spirit and kindness of his remarks which will be of great practical value to me—and the kind Christian wish he expressed for my success I shall never forget He mentioned that with regard to the exertions of the African Society of London which I was not aware of which combined with the greater facilities I should find there of procuring books and other things requisite and the making arrangements— causes me to have thoughts of going home which had previously presented itself to my mind from not having heard from them for some time.

Dr Turner observed that it would be unpractical to inculcate a knowledge of Christianity where I was not acquainted with the Language spoken alluding to the different tribes in central Africa how undoubtedly such would be impracticable—I explained to him that my object in acquiring a more intimate *and* familiar acquaintance with the Holy Scriptures was this

1st that it would enable me to undergo with more resolution the troubles and sufferings incident to such an undertaking, to endure "hardness as a good soldier in Jesus Christ," to have a strong faith in ~~that~~ the power and protection of the Almighty resulting from the conviction that worldly ambitions and human approbation are not the causes which prompt me to overcome all obstacles and eventually by his assistance to perform such an undertaking—

2^ndly that many opportunities would present themselves where a knowledge of Christianity would be attended with the happiest results—I may peradventure be detained in captivity so as to be able to acquire the language spoken by my captors—the great extent of country I shall pass through in a large part of which I shall no doubt find some persons conversant with the Arabic language. I allude to the different tribes in the Interior—where I may have the opportunity of spreading some seed which may be the means of spreading hereafter. And Sir I consider that such an undertaking being attempted by an Individual alive to the awful obligation the Interests of Christianity have upon its members—and possessing the high knowledge of knowing their redeemer that it is their bounden and solemn duty to impart it to

---

[9]**Dr. Edward Robinson** (1794-1863), biblical scholar, author, and professor at New York Theological Seminary, 1837-1863.

others. I know sir that such remarks may appear at variance with the doctrine of the Church I have the happiness and privilege to belong which only recognizes such obligations in those who have it delegated to them by their bishops—but I should consider myself ungrateful and indifferent to my Heavenly Father for such privileges and the connecting hopes of a blessed immortality if passing through a country immersed in all the devilish rites and heathenism—and the results arising from the unrestrained flow of evil passions—I did not make an humbler though determined attempt with the aid of the Holy Spirit to impart to them some knowledge of the one and some hopes of the other.

Many persons think that the resources and attainments I possess are not compellent for such an undertaking and that it is something like presumption in an humble individual like myself possessing no extraordinary abilities or powerful resources—making such attempts when so many individuals much more competent in both respects have lost their lives and expeditions failed in attempting the same—but how many persons do we see Sir risking their lives by outraging the laws of their country and Creator by a course of evil ways leading to the scaffold—and ought we to be despised when men can be found risking their lives for that which it is impossible they can approve and the end of which they shut their eyes to—that some individuals should also be found equally ready to work there for what they know to be right and the end they know to be equally clear and which instead of being opposed to all Laws Human or Divine is in strict accordance with both. With regard to the means I possess I have often wished they were greater and regretted this seeming want of adaptation to the end they are to achieve. But I am afraid that such wishes and regrets show a want of faith and reliance on Him who to doubt is to disbelieve and who often in his wise counsel and purposes achieves great ends by very small means. Who can read the 11th chap of S[t] Pauls Epistles to the Hebrews and not feel himself lifted up above the so called means of this world and possessing a strength sufficient to perform all things for his Redeemers Glory—and who is not aware of the humble Fisherman of Galilee who issued out of Judea and were the means of founding that faith which has spread with the exception of a few places throughout the world—and I think that after 19 centuries have passed over their heads it does behove [sic] them to make some attempt to carry the knowledge of that faith to those few places—for my own part it hath pleased the Almighty to give me great physical powers of endurance as well as resolution to overcome obstacles and they shall be devoted to his Interests How can a life of suffering ~~now~~ being tied to a sure and certain hope of a joyful resurrection be placed in the same scales with the pleasures and sins of a worldly life and doubtful hopes of Eternity. The one scale would rise to Heaven and the other would sink I would not say to Hell. It pleased the Almighty to convey Paul to Rome as a captive. I am thankful I shall not be carried to Zela in this capacity—The kindness and interest you have taken in the object I have so much at heart would naturally lead me to be governed by your advice with regard to my returning to England I Remain Revd Sir

With Respect Your Obliged,
Edgar Anthony Low

To the Revd L. P. Balch
Bartholomew Church

157. Rev. Lewis Balch, New York, to Rev. H. Southgate, Constantinople, 19 July 1841.[10]

New York July 19—/41

Rev^d & d^r Bro,

Let me introduce to y^r friendly regards Mr Low, an Englishman whose soul is heartily interested for Africa. He purposes penetrating the interior from the coast of Zela.[11] Any information or advice you can give w^h will further his plans, will be gratefully recd by him, and appreciated by very sincerely y^r friend and Bro in the Gosp[el]—

Lewis P W Balch

Revd H. Southgate

On the address page is this note from Low:

Cut open in consequence of the penalty of having sealed or closed letter in mailbag—but not looked at

E A Low
Feb 5/42

---

[10]MAW, Box 39, JRULM.

[11] Zela (Zile) was an ancient city in Pontus (Anatolia) in N.E. Asia Minor (modern-day Turkey), along the coast of the Black Sea.

158. Joseph Angus,[12] Baptist Mission House, London, to Rev. [Benjamin] Clough,[13] 14 September 1841.[14]

Baptist Mission House
6 Fen Court, London
Sept. 14. 1841

My dear Sir
We are anxious to know something of the Cinghalese Versions of the New Testament and as you are perfectly conversant with the language, we venture to trouble you in these matters. Perhaps you will kindly favour me with a reply.

1. Are there more than two translations—one executed by you & Mr Chater[15]—the other, that executed by the Church Missionaries.
2. We have by us a Cinghalese New Testament, with the dates 1780 and 1814. What can this be? The Church Mission versions made by the Old Propagation Society[16] or some other?
3. What are the honorific terms which your version contains & which the C. Mission version omits?
4. Are the words βαπτιζω & βαπτισμα[17] translated or transferred—This I ask to be able to answer others.

Trusting that you will excuse the trouble I thus give you
Believe me to be
Yrs very faithfuly
In Xt Jesus
Joseph Angus

Revd Mr Clough.

---

[12]**Joseph Angus** (1816-1902), BMS secretary (1841-1849) and President of Regent's Park College, London (1849-1893). The Baptist Mission House was located in Fen Court, in buildings owned by the Particular Baptist Fund. At the time of the above letter, Angus, then twenty-five, had been sole secretary of the BMS for about two months.

[13]**Benjamin Clough**, Methodist missionary in Ceylon since 1814.

[14]Eng. MS. 861, f. 3, JRULM.

[15]**James Chater** (1779-1829), BMS missionary in India, Burma, and Ceylon, 1806-1829. The source of the query by Angus in the above letter relates to a translation of the Bible into Singhalese by Abraham de Armour, James Chater, Benjamin Clough, and William Tolfrey, and published by the Wesleyan Mission Press in Colombo in 1819.

[16]The Anglican Church established the Society for Promoting Christian Knowledge in 1698 in order to combat vice and ignorance through education and the distribution of Christian literature.

[17]The words are "baptize & baptism."

159. Rachel S. Voigt,[18] *Serampore, to Joseph Angus, Secretary, Baptist Mission Society, 6 Fen Court, Fenchurch Street, London, 16 March 1842.*[19]

Serampore March 16th 1842

Sir

I trust you will pardon my taking the liberty to trouble you on a subject, so trifling perhaps as I need an apology for its introduction to your notice.

Towards the close of 1840, I observed in the Baptist Magazine for that year the entry of a Donation of one guinea to Serampore. And being Secretary to the Serampore Ladies Benevolent Society, whose object it is to aid the various Schools and other Institutions in this Town (particularly those founded by my now deceased Father D[r] Marshman and his beloved associates) I wrote to M[rs] Burgon of Bucklersbury requesting her to procure the above sum from M[r] Dyer and remitt to me in a manner I specified—

Of the result of her application to M[r] D, who was doubtless then suffering from the unhappy state of mind which is said to have been the cause of his melancholy end,[20] she thus writes— "I called several times

---

[18]Rachel Voigt was the daughter of Hannah and Joshua Marshman. She married the chief medical officer for Serampore and spent many years assisting in the educational work begun by her mother, who died in 1847. See W. H. Carey, ed., *Oriental Christian Biography,* 3 vols. (Calcutta: J. Thomas, Baptist Mission House, 1852) 3:487-488; Ernest A. Payne, *The First Generation: Early Leaders of the Baptist Missionary Society in England and India* (London: Carey Press, [1936]) 89.

[19]MAW, Box 39, JRULM.

[20]**John Dyer** (1783-1841), first full-time secretary of the BMS, experienced some mental instability at the end of his life, resulting in his death by drowning on 22 July 1841. In a box of autograph letters collected by Joseph Angus, now in the possession of the Angus Library, Regent's Park College, is a letter from **William Brodie Gurney** (see letters 172, 184, 215), treasurer of the BMS and Angus's father-in-law, addressed to Angus, at that time in Cornwall, dated 15 July 1841, just one week prior to Dyer's death. In the letter Gurney pleads for Angus to return to London because of Dyer's deteriorating mental condition:

You will wonder how I came to write but the fact is M[r] Dyer is so unwell as to be unfit for business—He is in a nervous fever. He was here but unfit to come into the Com[e] room and I had to go backwards & forwards to him. I think his mind is under some delusion which seems to haunt him *but I do not drop this* The medical man says nothing but complete rest will set him right as I have promised M[r] Steane who is the only one who has seen him besides myself & who agrees with me that he sh.[d] be released from business for a season that I would write to suggest whatever you can make any arrangement by which you can be dispensed with in Cornwall M[r] Sturgis says there is nothing of any im-

upon poor Mr Dyer and at last I saw him and ascertained that he had no money on behalf of the Serampore Mission in the name of Miss Angus"—You will find the entry in question in Page 219 of the Bap Mag for April 1840 placed among Receipts from Newcastle under the head of 'Contributions' thus "Miss Angus for Serampore 1£.1s.0d."

It is perhaps right to mention that I forwarded by M^r [Flaxman?] of Adelaide a report of our Society in 1839 to M^r G Angus[21] whom I knew to have been an old & dear friend of my late revered Parent—whence the Donation may have proceeded.

Should you on investigation deem me a just claimant I shall feel obliged by your forwarding the sum in question to my Sister Mrs Capt Havelock now in England who may be heard of at the Chambers of my brother Mr Marshman[22] 1 Inner Temple Lane

I am
Sir
Your obed^t Ser^t
Rachel S. Voigt
Secy S L B Soc^ty

---

160. *J. B. Titherington,[23] Honiton, Devon, to [Joseph Angus, Baptist Mission House, London,] 1 April 1842.[24]*

Honiton, April 1st/1842

Dear Sir,

I shall esteem it as a favour if you would be kind enough to give me a brief reply to a few queries as follow:—

---

portance claiming our attention here but still Mr Dyer will not stay away and the excitement is highly injurious to him— ... If Mr Dyer is not better and you are out I think I shall not leave him at present but become Deputy Sec^y

(Autographs: Book II, Angus Papers, shelfmark 24.h.33, Angus Library, Regent's Park College, Oxford.)

[21]**George Fife Angas** (1789-1878) was originally from Newcastle and the Baptist church under Richard Pengilly. He was instrumental in the founding of the Colony of South Australia, serving as a director for both the South Australian Company and the South Australian Bank. He eventually emigrated to South Australia in 1851.

[22]**John Clark Marshman** (1794-1877), son of **Joshua Marshman**, assisted for many years in the work at Serampore and became, like his father, a significant writer, linguist, and educator.

[23]Titherington served as pastor of the Baptist church at Honiton from 1840 to 1846; previously he had ministered at Liverpool and Wincanton (1835-1840). My thanks to Geoffrey Breed for information on Titherington.

[24]MAW, Box 39, JRULM.

Is there at present wanted a Minister at Graham's Town in Western Africa?[25]

If so, is it the intention of the Miss^y Comm^e to interest themselves in sending one out—and on what terms would they do it? And what might be the probable expence of the voyage—and from what quarter would his support there come? What is the nature of the labour—and what the extent and prospects of the field? As also, what the language used—According to information the climate on the whole is salubrious—

Hoping you will if occasion serves, give me a word of information on some or all of these points

I am sir—

With much respect

Y^rs truly

J. B. Titherington[26]

161. William Jeeves,[27] Hitchin, to Joseph Angus, Baptist Mission, 6 Fen Court, Fenchurch Street, London, 7 April 1842.[28]

---

[25]**George Aveline** (see letter 193) was serving as a BMS missionary at Grahamstown, in what is now South Africa, at the time of the above letter. William Miller established the first Baptist chapel among the English settlers there in 1823, remaining as pastor until 1825. William Davies was sent by the BMS to Grahamstown in 1832 to pastor the remnants of Miller's congregation. Davies died in 1837, and Aveline had taken over by the end of 1838, eventually opening a new chapel in Bathurst Street in 1843. A drawing of Grahamstown, with an accompanying note on the mission there, appeared in the *Missionary Herald* (April 1843): 217-218. While at Honiton, Titherington may have had a local connection with the work at Grahamstown, for William Davies's wife was the daughter of the Rev. John Cherry of nearby Wellington, Somerset (my thanks to John Briggs for this information).

[26]The majority of the letters in Box 39 are labeled on the top of the address page according to writer, location, and date. They were also given a number in the order in which they were received; the numbering began anew each year immediately after the BMS Annual Meeting held in late April. The number for the Voigt letter is illegible. The BMS number for the Titherington letter is 3040. The BMS Committee received between 3500 and 4000 letters each year during the 1840s. When these letters were presented before the Committee, the recorder of the minutes also included their number. Throughout this section, when identifying the shelfmark of each letter, I have included the BMS number (if available) in parentheses. Titherington's letter was read before the BMS Committee in London on 7 April 1842. See BMS Committee Minutes, Vol. H (Oct. 1841-Dec. 1842), f. 108.

[27]William Jeeves (1814-1894) was evidently a bricklayer by trade, for when the new chapel at Tilehouse Street was erected at Hitchin, Hertsfordshire, in 1844, Jeeves was paid £526 for "bricklaying, etc." His wife appears as a contributor to the BMS in 1841 (£10) and 1842 (£10). See *Missionary Herald* (April 1841): 207; *Baptist Magazine* 34 (1842): 121; G. E. Evans, *Come Wind, Come Weather: Chronicles of*

Hitchin, April 7th 1842

My dear Sir,

I am directed by Mr Brown[29] to forward you this notice—not know-ing how, or when, you, or the deputation—intend coming I think it right to say the earliest coach that arrives here on Monday is the Times, at 6 o'clock, it starts from the Peacock at Islington at 2 o'clock—there is also a coach passes through Stevenage on Monday at—12 o'clock called the Stamford; that Town is 4 miles distant—but if you think proper to come by that coach—I shall feel pleasure in sending my Chaise ~~for~~ to meet you—Only let me know previously

I am my dear Sir
Yours truly
Wm Jeeves

Rev. J. Angus

162. Undated, unsigned, and incomplete portion of a letter written by a female missionary [Martha Wilson] in Calcutta, c. December 1841.[30]

It is necessary now to mention some particulars relative to my leaving Solo which I did not before I very unwillingly yielded to the advice of friends to continue in Calcutta till after the rains. Early in October I had fixed for returning and had made every arrangement for so doing. Mrs Alexander was on her way to fetch me when I received a note from one of the ladies in answer to one I had written to her intimating the im-propriety of my return on account of my health. This startled me. I

Tilehouse Street Baptist Church 1669-1969 (London: Whitefriars Press, 1969) 41; Jean Laidlaw, *Hitchin, Hertfordshire. Monumental Inscriptions of Tilehouse Street Baptist Church, Hitchin* (Hertford: Hertfordshire Family and Population History Society, 1992) 10.

[28]MAW, Box 39 (BMS 62), JRULM. Letter is written on the back of the following poster: "MISSIONS to the HEATHEN. / THE / ANNUAL SERMONS / ON BEHALF OF THE / BAPTIST MISSIONARY SOCIETY, / WILL BE PREACHED (D. V.) / AT TILEHOUSE-STREET CHAPEL, HITCHIN, / On LORD'S DAY, APRIL 17TH, 1842, / BY THE / REV. EUSTACE CAREY, / LATE MISSIONARY IN INDIA / Divine Worship to commence at half-past Ten, half-past Two, and at Six o/clock. / / On MONDAY EVENING, April 18th, 1842, / Will be held at Tilehouse Street Chapel, the Annual / PUBLIC MEETING / Of the Hitchin Auxiliary to the Baptist Missionary Society, / at six o'clock / A Deputation from the Parent Institution, with neighbouring Ministers and Friends, have kindly promised their assistance. / Paternoster, Printer, Hitchin."

[29]Thomas Brown, a member at Tilehouse who died in 1849, aged 73. See Laid-law, *Hitchin, Hertfordshire*, 22.

[30]MAW, Box 39, JRULM.

could not understand what could be meant unless Dr Wise[31] had spoken to that effect to them when he had not to me. Another thought also suggested itself whether any cause of dissatisfaction had arisen and he had expressed the opinion of the sort. This I could scarcely bring my mind to believe as all had ever expressed themselves perfectly satisfied. This caused me much uneasiness which was not lessened by a circumstance which happened in the evening. I was drinking tea at Dr Duff's[32] and was asked by Mr Lacroix (a London Missionary now on his way to England)[33] in what ship I thought of returning he having heard I was going home I afterwards found this report had been partly freely circulated though I had never thought of such a thing. I then inquired of Mrs Chapman on further particulars but she seemed equally surprised with myself, and said I had better know the wishes of the Committee from the Secretary, saying it was not the wish of the Committee that I should return. Dr Wise thinking I should be less likely to keep my health in Kishnagur than in Calcutta they therefore advised my staying for a time at Central School. Though severely disappointed I should have felt satisfied with this decision had I not heard from good authority that the real cause was my religious sentiments which had not before been known by all. At this I felt much hurt having received so much kindness from so many in the Church who had known I did not expect such a result. I wrote to the Ladies stating what I had heard and assuring them my great object would ever be to make the children acquainted with the way of Salvation, and not to bring before them my peculiar views. At the same time I said if they had not full confidence in me to consent to my return I could not feel comfortable to continue my connexion with them. Their reply was the same not referring to this subject but my health. I saw Dr Wise after this and asked him if he thought I might safely return in a month or two if my health continued in its present state. His reply was in the affirmative and I once more wrote requesting to return upon this condition. Again they objected assigning the same reason—this would appear inexplicable, my health being now apparently as good as when I first landed, did I not know some *do* object most strenuously for the reason mentioned though the majority favored and wished my return and I concluded rather than have division among

---

[31]Dr. T. A. Wise (1801-1889) was a missionary educator in Calcutta and author of two works, *Commentary on the Hindu System of Medicine* (1845) and *Thoughts on Education in India* (1854).

[32]**Alexander Duff** (1806-1878), Scottish-born educator and missionary to India under the Church of Scotland. A discussion of his school in Calcutta appeared in the *Missionary Herald* (June 1841): 302.

[33]**Alphonse Francois Lacroix** (1799-1859), Swiss-born educator and missionary (Congregationalist) in India. The experience related in the above letter occurred just prior to Lacroix's departure from India in 1839 for furlough in England.

themselves adopted the other expedient. Thus situated I began to think of some other sphere and finding there was no school in which I could be employed by my Baptist friends turned my thoughts to Burdwan having heard a teacher was wanted there—M^r and Mrs Weitbrecht having about to return to England.³⁴ Mr Thomas had made known his wishes in Septr but I would not then think of it.³⁵ When these circumstances occurred I could not help thinking it seemed almost like an interposition of Divine Providence to bring it about; still I would not cherish it feeling determined to adopt a different course. Just after receiving the last communication from the ladies I was obliged to leave Central School—it being under repairs and having received an invitation from Mrs Yates³⁶ to stay with her I availed myself of the offer. Here I received a note from Mr Thomas entreating me to reconsider the subject, I did so I trust prayerfully but thought if Burdwan wanted assistance I ought to go there. I wrote an answer accordingly. A week passed before I heard from Mrs Weitbrecht she then called upon me and from what she said I thought I ought to go there and wished to decide at once but Mrs Yates urged me to leave it till the next day. I did so and wrote an early referral to Mr Thomas but two letters that day caused me to waver. Not having parents at hand I felt I ought to view D^r and Mrs Yates in that light, they entirely approved of the step and two days after a note came needing a reply I felt that I must decide.

---

³⁴**John James Weitbrecht** (1802-1852), originally from Germany, and his wife, **Mary Edwards Weitbrecht** (widow of LMS missionary Thomas Higgs), served as CMS missionaries in Burdwan, India, 1834-1852. The Weitbrecht's sailed for England on furlough in December 1841 (hence the dating of the above letter), returning to India in October 1844.

³⁵**James Thomas** (1799-1858), BMS missionary in India, 1826-1858. His wife died in September 1840 during childbirth, leaving him with seven young children. In 1842 he married Martha Wilson, a young woman who had been originally sent to India by the Society for Promoting Female Education in the East (see letter 171). It is likely that the "wishes" of Thomas that the writer mentions above, as well as the later statement that Thomas had written to her again "entreating [her] to reconsider the subject," concern Thomas's proposal of marriage to Miss Wilson, and that she is indeed the author of the above letter. The final sentences, though not completely clear, seem to suggest that, after consultation with Mr. and Mrs. Yates, Miss Wilson did indeed consider the "wishes" of Thomas, which led to their marriage that same year.

³⁶Martha Pearce, widow of BMS missionary **W. H. Pearce**; in 1841 she became the second wife of **William Yates** (1792-1845), BMS missionary, educator, and prolific translator with the Calcutta Mission. Yates first wife was **Catherine Yates** (1797-1838).

163. Alexander Saunders,[37] 170 Regent Street, London, to Joseph Angus, Fen Court, Fenchurch Street, London, 11 May 1842.[38]

170 Regent S[t]
11th May 1842

My Dear Sir

I am surprised to find that some at least of the Directors of the London Miss[y] S[y] consider themselves models of forbearance & Charity towards our Society, from w[h] delusion I have tried to remove them.

It is difficult as you know to get at anything definite, but I got hold in conversation with one of the Directors of these things, w[h] if you can spare time I should be glad to refute.

1st That M[r] Freeman[39] laid down the rule that one Soc[y] should not send agents where another Soc[y] had them & we refused to agree to that Rule.

2nd That we had sent missionaries to their Stations in the *East* Indies & of course produced confusion & every evil work.

3rd That M[r] Freeman had proposed to our Com[ee] for 6 of the Directors t̶o̶ from each Soc[y] to meet to adjust differences & we declined.

I would not trespass on your time, if I did not feel that the Answers you will enable me to give will do good to a good man, a lover of good men.   Yours respectfully

Alex Saunders

164. Sophia Parsons,[40] 19 Colet Place, Commercial Road, London, to Joseph Angus, Walworth, 22 May 1842.[41]

Dear Sir

The accompanying letter[42] was written whilst on my passage from India—and addressed to a dear relative. Its Contents by him to have

[37]**Alexander Saunders** (1805-1846), prominent layman and deacon in the Baptist church at Camberwell, under the ministry of Edward Steane. His residence was listed as 58 Strand, London, in 1838, and 170 Regent Street, London, in 1842.

[38]MAW, Box 39 (BMS 352), JRULM.

[39]**Joseph John Freeman** (1794-1851), educator and secretary of the London Missionary Society, 1839-1846.

[40]Sophia Rawlings Parsons, widow of **George Parsons**, BMS missionary to India, 1839-1840. He was the nephew of John Dyer, former BMS secretary. She contributed £16 for the work at Patna in September 1842. See *Missionary Herald* (November 1842): 614.

[41]MAW, Box 39 (BMS 438), JRULM.

been Communicated to the friends of this Mission—but before his arrival in England he had departed from this world; I then felt disposed to suppress it—but finding by a note from Mr Thomas[43] that he had sanctioned to you the request he made—that I would give some information respecting Patna.

I am induced to forward this letter without alteration

Believe me dear Sir

Very respectfully yours

Sophia Parsons

19 Colet Place
Commercial Road
May 22nd 1842

165. J[ames]. Peggs,[44] Ilkeston, Derbyshire, to Joseph Angus, Baptist Mission, Fen Court, Fenchurch Street, London, 3 June 1842.[45]

Ilkeston Derbyshire
June 3 1842

My dear Sir

This is the time that kings go forth to war & I am proposing to send about 150 books to different stations in the Bengal Boundary—I write to enquire whether if I send them per Nottingham Railway by the *end* of next week I shall be in time for your remittances on Missionaries going

---

[42]The letter, unsigned, appeared in the *Missionary Herald* (August 1842): 446-49, praising the activities of BMS missionary Henry Beddy in Patna. In 1842, over 1100 printed scriptures in Bengali were distributed in Patna by Beddy. The *Annual Report* noted that Beddy "labours not without success. The present number of members is twenty. Hindustani service is conducted in the chapel every morning; and, in addition to general prayer-meetings, one female prayer meeting is held. The boy's school has been relinquished for want of a teacher; but a Female Orphan Refuge has been commenced, as well as a Sunday School." See *Annual Report of the Committee of the Baptist Missionary Society* (London: J. Haddon, 1842) 19, 22.

[43]**James Thomas** (see letter 160).

[44]**James Peggs** (1793-1850) served under the General Baptist Missionary Society in India, 1821-1825; he later became a well-known missionary advocate, writer, and minister in England. At the time of the above letter, he was pastor of the General Baptist church in Ilkeston.

[45]MAW, Box 39 (BMS 520), JRULM. With this letter are two printed letters, one by Thomas Haswell at Manargoody, to James Peggs, Ilkeston, 24 December 1841, titled "British Connection with Idolatry in the Madras Presidency"; the other by James Peggs, dated 26 February 1842, originally printed in *The Friend of India*, titled "Human Sacrifices among the Khunds, in India."

to Calcutta—Can you get this Circular in the Baptist Mag[46]—I am sorry I could not get to Kettering[47]—I have just returned from Bedford etc
        Yours Sir
            J Peggs

166. Thomas Parkinson, basket maker, Worksop, Nottinghamshire, to [Joseph Angus, Baptist Mission House, London], 6 June 1842.[48]

Worksop June 6th 1842

Sir
    I hope you will excuse the liberty I ham takeing in writeing to you but I have a Brother a member of your Church in India and sometime ago he sent me two pounds and I received it through the medium of your Missions—and I received another letter from him in March which states that he had sent me two Pounds more but through what medium he did not state—and has it is now June and it has not yet arrived I have taken the liberty to ask you if you have heard any thing of it from any of your Missionarys And I shall be obliged to you for an answer as soon as possible for I ham anxious to write back to him please to

my Brothers name is   address to me

James Parkinson   Thomas Parkinson
Monghyr   Basket Maker
Bengal   Worksop Nott[s]

---

[46]An advertisement for Peggs's *Gems for Serious Christians* appeared in the *Baptist Magazine* 34 (1842): 482.

[47]The BMS held its Jubilee Meeting at Kettering, 31 May-2 June 1842. For an account of the meeting, see *Baptist Magazine* 34 (1842): 373-388. The Jubilee year, celebrating the fiftieth anniversary of the founding of the BMS, was primarily designed as a fundraiser for the financially strapped BMS (several letters below detail various fundraising efforts by Baptist churches and organizations in England as part of the Jubilee). More than £32,000 was raised, enabling the Society to erase its debt and begin construction of new headquarters in Moorgate. Nevertheless, the BMS experienced deficits every year between 1842 and 1849. See Brian Stanley, *The History of the Baptist Missionary Society 1792-1992* (Edinburgh: T. and T. Clark, 1992) 213-214; Payne, *First Generation*, 18-19.

[48]MAW, Box 39 (BMS 559), JRULM. Note Parkinson's spelling and usage errors.

167. T[homas]. Harjette,⁴⁹ the Reformer Office, Hertford, to Joseph Angus, Baptist Mission, 6 Fen Court, Fenchurch Street, London, 15 June 1842.⁵⁰

Reformer Office, Hertford
June 15ᵗʰ 1842

Dear Sir,

I have been informed by a friend that Mʳ Holmes, connected with the Stamps Office, in Calcutta, has arrived in England, and that, no doubt, you know where he is residing; If my information be correct, will you oblige me with his address, as also that of our Brother Ellis,⁵¹ who I perceive by the Magazine has arrived safe from Calcutta

Yours respectfully
T. Harjette

Rev. Mʳ Angus.

168. Joseph Soul,⁵² British and Foreign Anti-Slavery Society, 2 New Broad Street, [London], to Joseph Angus, Fen Court, Fenchurch Street, London, 28 June 1842.⁵³

2ⁿᵈ N Broad St
June 28 1842

Dear Sir

The Committee are about to send out to India a set of questions re East Indian Slavery &c which they are anxious to put into the hand of men of the right stamp. It is thought that your Missionaries would kindly furnish replies to these queries, they will therefore be greatly obliged to you if you will furnish me with a correct List of the *Stations* & *name* of these *Gentlemen, tomorrow* in order that they may be sent by the overland mail

Yours most truly
Joseph Soul

Rev J Angus

---

⁴⁹**Thomas Lawrence Harjette**, London printer, 1821-1842.

⁵⁰MAW, Box 39 (BMS 645), JRULM.

⁵¹**Jonathan D. Ellis** (d. 1845), BMS missionary to India, 1831-1841. Ellis left Calcutta in June 1841 and arrived in England on 2 December 1841. See *Missionary Herald* (January 1842): 47.

⁵²**Joseph Soul** (1805-1881), abolitionist leader and secretary of the Orphan Working School, North London.

⁵³MAW, Box 39 (BMS 802), JRULM.

169. *Henry Colenutt,*[54] *Lower James Street, Portsea, to [Joseph Angus, Baptist Mission, 6 Fen Court, Fenchurch Street, London], 29 June 1842.*[55]

Portsea June 29

Dear Sir

As secretary of Meeting House Alley Chapel Seminary School [I] shall feel obliged for any information you can afford respecting the Orphan School at Calcutta, having recently formed a Juvenile Aux^y Miss^y Soc^y among the children. I think it desirable that something tangible should be presented them as a stimulus, having seen a communication in a recent "Herald"[56] on the above subject I wish to know fully the nature objects & character of such school, and of its claims on British Children especially. An answer at your earliest convenience (having delayed writing you during the press of business arising out of the meetings at Kettering &c)[57] will particularly oblige

Yours Respectfully
H. Colenutt
L^r James' Street
Portsea

170. *J. D. Ellis, 2 De Crespigny Terrace, Denmark Hill, [London], to [Joseph Angus, Baptist Mission House, London], 6 July 1842.*[58]

J. D. Ellis
1 De Crespigny Terrace
Denmark Hill,
6th July 1842.

My dear Brother.

As I am not well enough to venture in town at the committee meeting to morrow, on the other side I have given an extract of a letter from

---

[54]Colenutt was a member of the Baptist church, Meeting House Alley, Portsea, where Charles Room ministered from 1837 to 1844. His church contributed £43.14.2 to the Jubilee Fund in December 1842. See *Missionary Herald* (January 1843): 68.

[55]MAW, Box 39 (BMS 792), JRULM.

[56]A reference to the *Missionary Herald*, a periodical published by the Baptist Missionary Society to promote Baptist missions throughout the world. The *Herald* began in 1819 and continued until 1911.

[57]The BMS Jubilee meeting (see letter 165).

[58]MAW, Box 39 (BMS 846), JRULM.

Arracan, which may be suitable for the Missionary Herald, if you will
kindly put it into the hands of the Editor,

obliging Yours affect^y

Jno. D. Ellis

Attached to Ellis's letter is the following extract (in Ellis's hand):

Extract of a letter from Rev. W. C. Comstock,[59] American Baptist Missionary, dated Ramree, Arracan, 15th April, 1842.

> "The work of the Lord still goes on powerfully among the Ka-
> rens. Brother Abbot of Sandoway, Arracan in a month's tour among
> them last cold season baptized 278 and I think the whole number
> he has baptized in the two years that he has been in Arracan must
> be about 500. Missionaries are still shut out from Burmah, and we
> know not when that empire will be opened to them again. The
> word of God is not, however, bound; but is having free course there
> especially among the Karens." To this, by way of explanation, we
> may add that the Karens are numerous interesting hill tribes, not
> Buddhists, (the general form of Burmese idolatry) who are thickly
> scattered over the highlands of Burmah, while many are found in
> Yehandwin and a few in Arracan, which two last mentioned are
> provinces on the sea coast of Burmah, ceded by the Burmese gov-
> ernment to the East India Company at the close of the last war with
> that country, and in which provinces is now located the American
> Baptist Mission to the Burmese, as its agents have long been pre-
> vented residing in Burmah proper.

171. H. Hope, Secretary of Society for Promoting Female Education in the East, [London],[60] to [Joseph Angus, Baptist Mission House, London], 14 July 1842.[61]

---

[59]**W. C. Comstock** (1809-1844), American Baptist missionary to Burma, 1835-
1844.

[60]The Society for Promoting Female Education in China, India and the East was
formed in 1834; its purpose was to send women teachers to various English schools
already established in India. These missionary teachers were contracted to work for
a minimum of five years; if not, they were obligated to repay certain expenses
related to their work. Six months' notice was required of an intention to quit, or, as
this letter reveals, a marriage (see letter 162). Miss Hope's letter to Angus is the
result of information she has learned from a letter by "Mrs Thomas," the former
Miss Wilson. Given the time that would elapse for a letter to travel to England from
India (as much as six months), we can assume that the marriage of Miss Wilson and
Rev. Thomas occurred shortly after the situation described at the end of letter 162,
thus ending Miss Wilson's fifteen months of service to the society. Miss Hope's letter

July 14.42

Revd Sir,

I am requested by Mrs Thomas, wife of your Missionary at Calcutta, to apply to you for payment of her debt to the Society for promoting Female education in the East. Before Miss Wilson was sent out as their agent she signed an engagement binding herself, in the event of her marriage within five years after her arrival at Calcutta to refund the sum expended by the Society, on her account a fifth part being deducted for every year that sh^d previously elapse—

The sum expended was £150, & she married Mr Thomas fifteen months after her arrival, consequently the sum due to the Committee is £82—May I request you to have the goodness to pay this sum to Messrs Williams Deacon & Co Birchin Lane, on account of the "Society for promoting female education in the East" & to address a line to our assistant secretary, Miss Webb, 61 Stafford Place, Pimlico, informing her of your having done so—she will then return to you Miss Wilson's bond—

I am Revd Sir
Yours truly
H. Hope. Sec^y

Attached to the above letter is a printed account of the History, General Regulations, Bye-laws and List of Subscribers to the Society for Promoting Female Education in the East, July 1842.

172. Samuel Giles,[62] *32 George Street, Manchester, to Joseph Angus ["to be opened by Mr Stanger*[63] *if M.^r A is from home"], Baptist Mission House, 6 Fen Court, Fenchurch Street, London, 23 July 1842.*[64]

Manchester
32 George St July 23/42

My dear Friend,

---

was read before the BMS Committee on 4 August 1842; a resolution was then passed requesting that Angus meet with Miss Hope and discuss the matter further. See *The History of the Society for Promoting Female Education in the East* (1847); also BMS Committee Minutes, Vol. H (Oct. 1841-Dec. 1842), f. 157.

[61]MAW, Box 39 (no BMS number), JRULM.

[62]**Samuel Giles** (b.1809), wealthy calico printer in Great Cheetham Street, Manchester. His brother, John Eustace (1805-1875), and his father, William Giles (1771-1845), were both Baptist ministers. Samuel's other brother, William (1798-1856), was a prominent schoolmaster.

[63]**William Wright Stanger, Jr.** (1809-1877), accountant for the BMS.

[64]MAW, Box 39 (BMS 944), JRULM.

Three young men who have served their Apprenticeship as letter-press printers & are now working as journeymen on 2 of our newspapers, influenced by the stirring appeals which Mr Moffat[65] made at one of the Missionary meetings, are desirous of going to some Missionary Station where they could obtain a livelihood and at the same time forward the cause of Xt.. Having heard from some quarter or other that the Baptist Mission was about to establish printing presses—either in India Africa or one of the West Indian Stations they applied to us for information & counsel how to proceed. I replied that I had not heard of such an intention, but that I would write you requesting to be informed. & if you can in any way forward their object & give me the requisite information I shall feel much obliged. One of them is a Teacher at Union Chapel School (Mr Tucker's)[66] another in Mr Fletcher's (Independent)[67]—of the third I know nothing—four of them have made a Profession of religion.

Should you require for any quarter of the World individuals in their Capacity, I think they will do credit to the appointments. Testimonials as to skill and character of course would be forthcoming if required—they understand *every* branch of the business—& would go to any quarter where they can be useful

Are you likely to come our way soon—if so we shall have a bed at your service & if M^rs A will accompany you it will much increase the pleasure

The Commercial state of Manchester is truly deplorable—& the prospects of the poor appalling. The work people out of employment are too much turned by want, and all but utter destitution to rise, but, were they as I have seen them in years past I am sure they would not be long in reversing the injuries under which they are groaning.

Please to present my kind respects to Mr Gurney[68] & his family & to your good lady in which Mrs Giles desires to unite—Begging the favor of an early reply   I remain,

My dear Friend
Yrs very sincerely
Sam. Giles

---

[65]**Robert Moffatt** (1795-1883), missionary to South Africa for the London Missionary Society, 1817-1870.

[66]**Francis Tucker**, former BMS missionary in India and, at the time of the above letter, minister at the Union Chapel, Oldham, near Manchester. The Sunday school at Union Chapel collected £22.19.6 for the BMS in November 1842. See *Missionary Herald* (January 1843): 58.

[67]**Richard Fletcher** (1800-1861), Independent minister at Grosvenor Street Chapel, Manchester, 1831-1853.

[68]**William B. Gurney** (1777-1855), successful shorthand writer for parliament and the Old Bailey, treasurer of the BMS (1835-1855), and father-in-law to Joseph Angus.

N.B. The young men are not needy adventurers out of Employment, but all of them I believe in good Situations with full worth. S.¹ G.

173. Joseph Clare,⁶⁹ Manchester, to Samuel Giles, Manchester, 1 August 1842.⁷⁰

Respected Sir

For the favor you have so kindly rendered to the individuals who waited upon you some few days ago, whose object was to ascertain whether they might be able to obtain under the Baptist Missionary Association a situation in some part of British India,—they doubtless are willing to show you their gratitude for the promptitude with which you so immediately acceded to their wishes in obtaining for them the required information and, Sir, though I was not among the number then present allow me to assure you that the information to me was equally gratifying and satisfactory when made acquainted with it, for which I venture to forward you my most sincere and heartfelt thanks—

In presuming to trouble you with these lines I wish to intimate that I was the first person who broached the matter (the purpose above stated) to the young man Nicholson⁷¹ who I presume must have mentioned it again to the persons who accompanied him to you: he not being in constant employment, and, consequently, having some loose time on his hands, I asked him to endeavour to obtain the required information, which of course you have very kindly given, in conjunction with Mr Angus, of London—Now, Sir, in order to show you and give you an idea of the cause which induced me to desire such information, and which has brought about the application made, I must state that at a meeting which took place some few weeks back, in the Corn Exchange, a brief report of which (enumerating the various objects which the Association wished to carry out) appeared in the paper on which I am regularly employed—that report gave me to understand that men in our business were (if not already would ere long be) wanted &c one of the objects stated was that it was intended to establish a Printing Establishment somewhere in India & I, consequently, was anxious to know something about the matter—you have afforded that informa-

---

⁶⁹Joseph Clare, letter-press printer at 23 Mottram Street, Salford, near Manchester. See *Pigot and Slater's Directory of Manchester and Salford*, 1:63.

⁷⁰MAW, Box 39 (BMS 986), JRULM.

⁷¹Two Nicholsons lived near Mr. Clare and the church in Liverpool Road, Manchester: a William Nicholson, joiner, at 16 Wellington Place, Liverpool Road, and a Henry Nicholson, carter, at 3 Manor Street, Liverpool Road. See *Pigot and Slater's Directory of Manchester and Salford*, 1:189.

tion, and gratified that desire; and as an individual who is at all times anxious and willing to serve and render all the good my humble means and capacity are capable ~~of benefitting~~, in any way, to fellow creatures, I could make up my mind to undertake a situation in that foreign country under the Missionary Society; but perhaps Sir, my family encumbrance might be an obstacle and objection it would not be so on the part of ourselves, ~~meaning~~ as my wife would willingly accompany me— I have 2 children—a boy and girl—and my wife is very near her confinement of another—however the society might not altogether object to the family—if so, it might be obviated in this way—if the Society were to advance the passage and traveling expenses it could be paid to them back by installments—say—so much per month which would willingly be done; though my wife might be able to do some little good in that country, as she had been for many years prior to her marriage a Sunday School teacher—It is also necessary that I should state my age—I am 30, until October next when I shall complete my 31st year— With regards to the practical acquaintance of my business I may mention that—after having served seven years apprenticeship since which I have worked in four different establishments each of which I left on my own account, and four years I occupied the situation of superintendent in an office at Stockport where reference might be made if necessary— however from my experience I consider myself competent to superintend and manage a Printing Establishment—with respect to religious experience I can only say that I am in the habit of frequenting a place of worship (in the neighborhood where I reside) Hope Street Chapel, Liverpool Road Oldfield Lane[72]—denominated *Independent* as to piety I think it would be indiscreet on my part to dwell, but I am fully conscious that the Lord's light has not stricken my heart with any other influence than merely ephemeral devotion Sabbath after Sabbath—I am very sorry that I cannot give a better account of my piety than already stated still were I to be engaged under that benevolent association I venture to guarantee my conduct and example would be such as to give all the outward and visible signs of submission and respect to my superiors and showing loving kindness and brotherly love towards all whom I shall have authority over—I may here mention that I have only been in Manchester close upon three years prior to that I resided [at]

---

[72]Hope Chapel began in 1837, but it did not officially open for worship until December 1838 (it was later enlarged in 1843). John Poore, from Highbury College, served as the church's first minister, 1838-1853. In 1853 he and Richard Fletcher, pastor at Grosvener Street Independent Chapel (see letter 172) left Manchester to work in Australia as missionaries with the Colonial Missionary Society. See Nightingale, *Lancashire Nonconformity*, 217-221; Albert Peel, *These Hundred Years: A History of the Congregational Union, 1831-1931* (London: Congregational Union of England and Wales, 1931) 199.

Stockport where I attended, as teacher, the Stockport Sunday School for all denominations some time; after which I frequented Rev. N. K. Pugsley's Chapel[73]—probably the School and the Rev. gentleman you are acquainted with. I don't know that I can add anything more that is really necessary unless I state that providing I should be thought worthy the society's observation I might as well say that I have a good and comfortable situation at present both as regards employment and situation in domestic life—a comfortable house and goods necessary—these of course I should sacrifice for the object which myself and the other individuals are seeking.

In conclusion I wish to ask M[r] Giles to be kind enough to intercede in my behalf, and if he should think fit to forward this or any portion of it (to M[r] Angus) it is quite at his will and pleasure so to do—With all due respect I beg to subscribe myself to Mr. Giles

Most humble and obedient Servant

Joseph Clare

174. Clara Vowell Ryley, Ashley Place, Bristol, to [Joseph Angus, Baptist Mission House, London], 20 August 1842.[74]

Ashley Place
Aug 20th 42

Sir

I have forwarded a Box to Fen-court today by Waggon; it contains garments for the African women such as were applied for some months ago, and is sent by the Broadmead Ladies. The Box is leaded.

I am Sir

Yours respectfully

Clara Vowell Ryley

---

[73]**Nathaniel Knight Pugsley** (1787-1868), then residing in Heaton Norris, was the minister at the Hanover Chapel (Independent), Manchester, 1821-1858.

[74]MAW, Box 39 (BMS 1127), JRULM.

175. William Tarn,[75] Religious Tract Society, 56 Paternoster Row, to Joseph Angus, Baptist Mission, 6 Fen Court, Fenchurch Street, London, 23 August 1842.[76]

Religious Tract Society
56 Paternoster Row
23rd Augt 1842

My dear Sir
Your application on behalf of a missionary going to India has been laid before our Committee, and a grant of Tracts voted him, which are herewith sent
We shall be glad to have the name of the Missy
Yours truly
Wm Tarn

Rev J Angus

176. Thomas Baker,[77] 15 John Street, Portwood, Stockport, Cheshire, to [Joseph Angus], Baptist Mission House, 6 Fen Court, Fenchurch Street, London, 6 September 1842.[78]

---

[75]William Tarn was the son of Joseph Tarn (1766-1837), deacon at Union Chapel, Islington, founding member of the Evangelical Tract Society, and business manager of the Religious Tract Society, 1810-1837. William's sister, Maria, married Samuel Dyer, CMS missionary to China; their daughter, Maria Jane, married J. Hudson Taylor, also a missionary to China. William Tarn served as Assistant Secretary and Cashier of the RTS from 1829 to 1849. See William Jones, *The Jubilee Memorial of the Religious Tract Society: Containing a Record of its Origin, Proceedings, and Results* (London: Religious Tract Society, 1850) 54.

[76]MAW, Box 39 (BMS 1146), JRULM.

[77]Thomas Baker, the uncle of BMS missionary **Nathaniel Ward**, was a schoolmaster in John Street, Portwood, near Manchester. Had Baker been reading the *Missionary Herald* more closely, he would have seen that a letter from Ward had appeared in the magazine the previous year, the editor noting that "various circumstances have combined to render our intercourse with Mr. Ward, of Padang, very infrequent and precarious." The BMS would not receive another letter from Ward until October 1844; the letter was dated 15 February 1844, from Pedang, Sumatra. He writes that although the Sumatran mission had been withdrawn by the BMS many years earlier, Ward had remained behind to pursue the language and produce on his own "an intelligible version of the scriptures, supporting [himself] by means of agriculture." He writes that he now has a "copious dictionary of the language ... and ample means" to complete a translation of the Bible. See *Pigot and Slater's Directory of Manchester and Salford*, 3:144; *Missionary Herald* (March 1841): 142-143; (October 1844): 537-539.

September 6th 1842
No 15 John Street in Portwood
in the Borough of Stockport

Reverend Gentlemen

Whereas, I Thomas Baker have been anxious of writing to you ever since the 20th September 1840, the day on which I obtained Directions by the Rev. Mr Baker of Zion Chapel, Greek Street, in Stockport, Cheshire[79]—I Thomas Baker am a Native of Derby, and I have been house-keeper in Stockport ever since September 1789—I think in the year 1812 I heard of the Rev William Ward having sent for my Sister's eldest son Nathaniel Ward to go to Serampore Mission House 9 Miles from Calcutta East India; I believe that Nathaniel Ward went to Serampore Mission House, East Indies.

I believe that I have Read in a printed book, that the "Rev William Ward died in the East Indies in the 54th year of his age,["] perhaps in the year 1823.

I think that in the Year 1834 I Thomas Baker was with my Sister M. Ward, then at No 17 Saint Hellen Street Derby; I do not recollect hearing any thing of Nathaniel Ward in 1834—

Within the time of the last 29 years I have heard of Nathaniel Ward Translating the New Testament into the Malay-language in East Indies, and also formed a new dictionary in Malay Language.

Reverend gentlemen...I do not want to ask such a question of you as would require the work of your pen to Ramble through the East Indies or other places to find an answer for me, but, my present question to you, will admit of an immediate answer   videlicet

I wish you to transmit by the Regular post a plain written letter in plain language, as full an account in writing of all that you know of the latest on Account or accounts both oral and written of and concerning my Nephew Nathaniel Ward what part of the world Nathaniel Ward was in, and is in, what, doing with his hands, pen, tongue and apparent tenor of actions and business in present life now is

If I have omitted anything herein which is necessary for an immediate answer to me, I shall expect you to fill up the [sentence not finished]

I am Your Humble Servant

the Author of Poems on Queen Victoria, viz Metropolitian [sic] Glory, and Epithalamium. Printed Copies thereof entered into London on

---

[78]MAW, Box 39 (BMS 1286), JRULM.
[79]**Charles Baker**, minister at Zion Chapel, Stockport, 1837-1845.

Monday 10th Feb 1840 and forwarded into "Stationers' Hall" London.[80] I have made a present of one printed Copy to Rev. C. K. Prescot, Rector.[81] One to Rev. T. Nolan, of Saint Peter's Church.[82] One to Rev Mr Jackson of St Thomas's Church,[83] and one to the Rev Mr Baker, Minister at Zion Chapel, Greek St Stockport one printed copy to Samuel Andrew Esq Stockport[84]—one copy to No 17 Saint Hellen Street Derby one printed copy to Ms Baker Silk-Throwster Derby—one printed Copy to Rev Mr Howell Curate,[85] one copy to Rev Mr N. K. Pugsley Minister at Hanover Chapel—one to Jesse Howard Esq[86] and 2 to Officers of Police Stockport several printed copies—To Watch Committee Captain one copy &c &c To Wm Baker Esq Mayor one—To superintender of Police one Copy

Direct to Thomas Baker—15 John Street
Portwood, in the Borough of Stockport Cheshire

177. Richard Johnson, 2 Rumford Street, [Liverpool], to Joseph Angus, [Baptist Mission House, London,] 8 September 1842.[87]

2 Rumford St
8 Sept 1842

My dear Sir,
Since I received your favour of the 29th, I have made enquiries about the Vessels to Africa, but am sorry to say that none are going just

---

[80]I have been unable to locate any extant copies of these poems by Baker; most likely they were privately printed.

[81]Rev. Charles Kenrick Prescot, Parsonage, Churchgate. Prescot took a B.A. and M.A. at Oxford (1808, 1810) and then succeeded his father as rector of Stockport, Cheshire, from 1820 until his death in 1875. See *Pigot and Slater's Directory of Manchester and Salford,* 3:153; John Venn, ed., *Alumni Cantabrigienses.* Part II: From 1752 to 1900, 6 vols. (Cambridge: Cambridge University Press, 1922-1954) 5:186.

[82]Rev. Thomas Nolan, Edgley. See *Pigot and Slater's Directory of Manchester and Salford*, 3:152.

[83]Rev. William Jackson, Lancashire Hill, Heaton Norris. See *Pigot and Slater's Directory of Manchester and Salford*, 3:150.

[84]Possibly Samuel Andrew, Esq., of Hall Street, Stockport. See *Pigot and Slater's Directory of Manchester and Salford*, 3:143.

[85]Rev. Edward Howell, Townend House, Lancashire Hill, Heaton Norris. See *Pigot and Slater's Directory of Manchester and Salford*, 3:150.

[86]Jesse Howard was a cotton spinner and manufacturer at 48 Fountain Street in Manchester and in Newbridge Lane, Stockport. See *Pigot and Slater's Directory of Manchester and Salford*, 1:135, 3:150.

[87]MAW, Box 39 (BMS 1305), JRULM.

at present, that you could send by to the friends at Fernando Po,[88] most of them only call there on returning from their voyages & the delay would be too great by them, & only one house here sends direct & I have got a friend to look out for his next vessel when we will try to get permission to send & I will also try to find a reputable captain who will leave letters at Bonny (about one day's sail of Fernando Po) but it will be some three weeks before I have even a chance, but I will keep a sharp look out, as there are several vessels now loading here for Africa & I need not assure you it will at all times give me the greatest pleasure to facilitate your communications to our dear Friends there & in the meantime believe me

My dear Sir
Yours very truly
Richd Johnson

To Rev^d J Angus A. M

---

[88]The BMS initiated an expedition to Africa in 1840, sending **John Clarke** and **G. K. Prince** to explore the possibilities of establishing a mission on the island of Fernando Po, off the coast of West Africa at the mouth of the Niger River. They arrived at Fernando Po on 1 January 1841, establishing a base station at Clarence as well as making significant contacts with tribal chiefs on the Cameroonian mainland. The operation garnered considerable attention in the pages of the *Baptist Magazine* during the last half of 1841. As the editor noted when presenting excerpts from several letters by Clarke during his travels to Africa in 1841, "Fernando Po has, however, occupied the greatest part of the attention of our brethren, it being, in their judgment, the spot on which it is desirable to commence operations. The situation of the island, in relation to the mouths of the Niger, and of other great rivers, the intercourse carried on between it and England, the readiness of the natives to listen to instruction, the facilities it affords for the acquisition of African languages, and the comparative salubrity of its climate, have recommended it to them as the spot where a station should first be formed, which may be a stepping-stone to other stations, and a general rendezvous from different parts of the main land. Here, they say, 'the field is white already to harvest.' They have made some essays, and the results are encouraging." Clarke and Prince left West Africa in the spring of 1842, making a stop at Jamaica before reaching England in September. For the remainder of 1842 and the first half of 1843, both men would travel widely across England, raising funds for the new BMS mission in Africa. One of the chief concerns of Clarke during his deputation work in 1842-1843 was the need for the BMS to purchase a boat that would enable the missionaries to travel along the coast of Africa and up the rivers into the inland. Many of the following letters in this section deal with various issues related to the acquisition of a boat. Richard Johnson of Liverpool, the writer of this letter, will figure prominently in these discussions. See *Baptist Magazine* 33 (1841): 466.

178. John Padwick, Chymist, East Street, Havant, Hampshire, to [Joseph Angus,] Baptist Mission Society, 6 Fen Court, Fenchurch Street, London, 12 September 1842.[89]

Havant Sept 12 1842

Respected & Dear Sir

Tho unknown I have presumed to address you an enquiry

An Indian Girl has lately been met with here & received into the Cottage of a poor man from being a common beggar—She declares herself from Norbe near Calcutta (abt 3 days journey) & as having been taught in the Sabbth School of a Mission Station, by a Mr Hellyer & Mrs Fletcher, there are 27 members & 63 scholars two other Missionaries Messrs Turner[90] & Green used occasionally to come up from Calcutta— her name is *Betsy Flory* & the mother of the same name was a *member* herself—the Girl is 14 yrs of age & left India May 1840 with her mother to escape a Mr Tusler who wanted to purchase her & on refusal threatened to take her by force—they left unknown to any but the father, not even the Missy (tho the Girl went to see him on leaving)—the Father is a Captain Flory (native infantry) & an Idolater—& they had money on arrival (a double handful of Gold) but were cheated by a Jew & obliged to beg, that is the Girl for the mother would not & by fatigue &c (as we imagine) the Mother died after being ill but 2 hours passing much blood from the Mouth

Such is the tale & we would not be sanguine from the frequent imposition but it comes in simplicity & without hesitancy or contradiction in minutiae of circumstance—The facts she gives of her mother are most satisfactory & evince strong enlightened & permanent piety & very valuable are the lessons she has given the daughter her death was peaceful & joyful

She says her mother died at Newby & on mentioning Newbury to her said yes that's the place but getting all we can from her & making every possible enquiry there can find no clue or possibility of its being Newbury

Enclosed is a stamp & may I beg you to reply & tell us if you have a station & Missionaries &c as herein stated as we are anxious to know the truth & write to the Father &c &c

---

[89]MAW, Box 39 (BMS 1335), JRULM.

[90]John Thomas Turner (1818-1866), an Anglican, was a CMS missionary in India. He baptized some 2000 converts and built over forty village churches during his tenure in India. His wife, Harriet, operated a large girls' school in the Tirunelveli District.

The Girl is in good keeping at this Cott^g & X^n friends have clothed
her &c & are seeking to instruct farther in holy things
I am a member of Mr Scamps[91] the Independent Church here & the
Girl is [in] my wife's Sab. School Class—

Y^r reply will oblige

Y^{rs} humbly in X^n Jesus

John Padwick   Chymist

East St^t Havant   Hants

*179. John Clarke,[92] Harvey Street School Room, Leicester, to [Joseph
Angus, Baptist Mission House, London], 20 September 1842.[93]*

My dear B^r
Will you supply by the Vessel now about to proceed to Fernando Po
the enclosed order for nails for the Chapel to be built at Clarence.[94]
I have had two letters from Friends there, & from Mr Sturgeon[95] the
enclosed order comes—

ever yours

John Clarke

Leicester
Harvey St School Room
Sep^t 20th 1842

*180. Joseph Fletcher,[96] Shooter's Hill, [London,] to Joseph Angus, Fen
Court, Fenchurch Street, London, 24 September 1842.[97]*

Shooters Hill

Septem 24 1842

My dear Sir

---

[91]**William Scamp** (1774-1860), Independent minister at Havant, 1803-1846.

[92]**John Clarke** (1802-1879), BMS missionary to Jamaica (1829-1839), West
Africa (1843-1847), and Jamaica once again (1852-1879).

[93]MAW, Box 39 (BMS 1396), JRULM.

[94]At that time, Clarence was the primary settlement on the island of Fernando
Po, with a population of about 700. A number of large houses there were owned and
occupied by the West African Company. Nearby was the village of Krou Town. See
Cox, *History*, 2:358.

[95]**Thomas Sturgeon** (d. 1846), BMS missionary to Fernando Po, 1842-1846.

[96]**Joseph Fletcher**, at this time treasurer of the Baptist Theological Education
Society and the Baptist Building Fund.

[97]MAW, Box 39 (BMS 1423), JRULM.

My good friend Colonel Nicholls[98] has Africa engraven on his heart and holds Fernando Po as an outwork for its defense. The knowledge he has of all that relates to that interesting quarter of the globe is far superior to that of most other men and I would not presume to question what he has recommended.

I may be excused for saying professionally that I do not approve and could not propose to any one to adopt the principle of the Archm[d] Screw[99] on a vessel whose services will be so essential as those you describe because it is at present a mere matter of experiment very partially tried and comparatively *not at all in use*

There is one serious objection worthy of peculiar consideration in your case, *the moving power is under water* and any injury it receives will require the vessel to be laid aground—the Colonel will tell you that the first sickness which eventually brought about the unhappy failure of the late expedition was occasioned by the ships being laid on shore to repair the keels of the rudders—in the common engine with paddle wheels—all the work is above water and can be repaired afloat the cost of such a vessel would be heavy and would depend as to its amount

---

[98]Lieut.-Col. Edward Nicholls became superintendent of Fernando Po in 1829, but his health soon deteriorated and he was forced to return to England. The British government withdrew officially from the island in 1834, turning control over to a couple of traders, John Beecroft and Richard Dillon. Nicholls was very supportive of the BMS and new mission at Fernando Po; he provided Clarke and the other missionaries with valuable information as well as letters of introduction to several native chieftains. Nicholls was also involved in the initial decision by the BMS to purchase an iron-clad schooner equipped with an Archimedes Screw. See Cox, *History*, 2:360; *Missionary Herald* (January 1843): 51; BMS Committee Minutes, Vol. I (Jan. 1843-May 1844), ff. 33, 35.

[99]The earliest type of pump was the Archimedes screw, first used by Sennacherib, King of Assyria, for the water systems at the Hanging Gardens of Babylon and Nineveh in the 7th century BC, and later described in more detail by Archimedes in the 3rd century BC. In the nineteenth century the device was also used on steam-powered ships. In this situation, however, the pump was usually powered by a small steam engine that used the steam produced by the boiler. According to one marine historian, "The substitution of the screw propeller for the paddle-wheel began to grow general about the period 1845-50. The screw propeller had been invented long before, but its practical utility had not been generally recognized, and it was still regarded as being in the experimental stage. The first notable experiments as to the comparative efficiencies of paddle-wheels and screw propellers were made in 1840, when the 'Archimedes,' with a screw propeller, beat the paddle-wheel boat 'Ariel' between Dover and Calais by five to six minutes under steam and sail." Other races during the next several years ended in "favour of the screw propeller." See Richard Sennett and Henry J. Oram, *The Marine Steam Engine: A Treatise for Engineering Students, Young Engineers, and Officers of the Royal Navy, and Mercantile Marine* (London: Longmans, Green, and Co., 1898) 6.

upon the nature and power of the engines which are the most costly part of the concern.

You must also weigh one fact that the expense of maintaining and working a Steam Boat is great and unremitting employed or not. The Engineer and his Men are unceasingly at work or the Engines will be destroyed. The cost of the coal would be according to the distance run but not to the labor. and when the depreciation is taken into the calculation you may reckon at least 20£ per annum but besides the impossibility or if not so the enormous expense of effecting repair which on Steam Boats is continually wanted

I consider that in Africa round Fernando Po that Government only holding the national purse can assure Steam navigation—A Company of Merchants trading in the River and on the Coast might find advantage in such Auxiliaries but Missionary funds are inadequate to such an expenditure.

I have written what has occurred to my mind in answer to your note   You will of course shew it to the Colonel. I know that a large ship built in Scotland is launched, fitted with the Screw and may shortly be expected in the River—she has been constructed by proprietors of the Archm^d patent and is a part of an experiment untried

I am my dear Sir
Sincerely yours
Joseph Fletcher

Rev^d J Angus

181. J. G. Pike,[100] Derby to [Joseph Angus, Baptist Mission House, London,] 28 September 1842.[101]

Derby Sep 28, 1842

My dear Sir

Once when I called on Mr Dyer & we were talking about the price of rupees I learned from him that you had some friend at the India house whose information had been a guide as to the time of buying bills—I forgot whether M^r D stated that thus guided he had bought before a rise in the state of exchange or had waited for a fall—Have you any friend from whom you could get information whether there is likely *soon* to be a fall? The rate is now high. When I bought for our spring remittance

[100]**John Deodatus Gregory Pike** (1784-1854), minister to the General Baptist church in Derby, 1810-1854, and secretary of the General Baptist Missionary Society, 1816-1854.

[101]MAW, Box 39 (BMS 1467), JRULM.

the rupee was 1s/11d it is now 2s/1d—Now if there be a likelihood of a *speedy* alteration I would delay our remittance to next month, otherwise of course we must send at the present terms—Can you learn this, without much trouble, and if so soon? If you can I should be obliged to you—I expect my brother will call on you tomorrow for an answer to this, if you go out would you have the kindness to leave a single line for him stating the result of my inquiry, addressed, Revd G. T. Pike

Believe me dear Sir
Yours paternally
J. G. Pike

PS You may tell Mr Belcher[102] to whom I wrote last week that my fears were realized & I was a prisoner at home all last Sabbath.

182. Sophia Parsons,[103] 19 Colet Place, [London], to [Joseph Angus, Baptist Mission House, London], 28 September 1842.[104]

Dear Sir

I called on Monday at Fen Court hoping to have an opportunity of representing to you the case of the Patna Orphan School—but I was disappointed in seeing you and I venture to address you on that subject by letter —You are aware that at the close of last year a Boarding School in connection with the Baptist Mission was commenced, for Native Female Orphans at Patna—It was commenced under a deep conviction of the necessity of such an Institution to afford a home for the destitute beings who deprived of their parents, generally become slaves in Native Families—and with the prayerful hope that the children thus gathered under Xtian instruction and influence with the superadded grace of God might hereafter become blessings in the midst of the Heathen— It was commenced without any definite means of support—and before any dwelling had been prepared for the accommodation of the Children. The liberality of Friends in the neighborhood has hitherto provided them with food and clothing—but they are accommodated rather inconveniently in a room at Mr Beddy's[105]—On the subject Miss Beddy

---

[102]**Joseph Belcher** (1794-1859), Baptist minister, author, and secretary to the Baptist Union, 1832-1840. He had just recently resigned from his church in Greenwich. See *Baptist Magazine* 34 (1842): 194.

[103]See letter 164.

[104]MAW, Box 39 (BMS 1468), JRULM.

[105]Henry Beddy and his wife were appointed in 1831 as BMS missionaries to India, working primarily in Patna; he retired in 1849. See letter 164, n. 41, for more on Beddy; also E. Daniel Potts, *British Baptist Missionaries in India, 1793-1837* (Cambridge: Cambridge University Press, 1967) 246.

who has the superintendence of the School there writes—May 30/42—
"Our 8 Orphan girls are making progress and in every respect afford satisfaction &c—I should feel quite happy on their account if a dwelling
were provided for them—they are now constantly in my room and the
heat is suffocating—but this is preferable to their sleeping in the small
room at first assigned them"—Since my return to England I have been
endeavoring to raise money for the erection of a building for them, and
the Xtian Native Female who instructs them in their domestic duties—
in the hope of its being completed this coming cold season to be ready
for their reception before the hot season again begins (which is as early
as the Month of March—) I have not succeeded in my attempt as I could
wish in Consequence of the extraordinary efforts made for the Jubilee
Fund this year—The Store I have collected does not exceed 20£'s—a
sum scarcely sufficient to authorise the commencement of a building
which it is estimated would cost between a 150 and 200£'s—In a letter
received by the last overland from Mr Beddy it appears that the trouble,
fatigue, and anxiety, necessarily connected with building in an Eastern
Clime might be dispensed with if money could immediately be obtained
He says "The Native Hospital to the north of my house is now for sale—
it would make in every respect a most desirable place for the Refuge
and having been offered the refusal I have made an offer under certain
reservations of 200£s for it, about 1 fourth its real value I have got no
definite answer but rather think they will not let it go for so small a
sum—"The House I remember it is near M^r B's—and is in every respect
well-suited to the purpose—being a plain airy building—standing in a
compound of considerable size—I once named it as a desirable abode
for the children but at that time there was little prospect of obtaining
it—it has been suggested to me that one object of the Jubilee Fund is to
aid in the Establishment of Schools wherever needed—and this has encouraged me to lay before you the claims of Patna and to entreat aid for
its orphan Institution from that Fund were it a subject that admitted of
delay I might have shrunk from making the appeal—but nothing has
yet been done to raise the Native Female fund in that part of Hindoos-
thum of which Patna is the Chief City—and an Institution of this kind is
the only means of promoting that object to any extent—The children
taught in this school may in all probability become teachers of those
who secluded in their own houses have not the opportunity of gaining
instruction—or hereafter at the heads of their own humble house-
holds—be patterns of domestic order and social enjoyment—a dwelling is at present the principal thing needed—their future support admits not of a doubt even should the children be multiplied to 10 times
their present number—Annual subscriptions have been charitably
promised toward the object from friends in this country but hitherto
they have been maintained without aid from England—That the Com-

mittee may be disposed to consider the case and generously to respond to the appeal is the sincere desire dear Sir of
Yours most respectfully
Sophia Parsons

Sep^tr 28/42
19 Colet Place

183. Elizabeth Ivimey,[106] 19 Great Coram Street, Brunswick Square, London, to [Joseph Angus, Baptist Mission House, London], 29 September 1842.[107]

E Ivimey
19 Great Coram Street
Brunswick Square
Sepr 29—1842

My dear Sir
Several friends to whom I spoke at the close of our meeting last night, expressed a desire to have copies of the letters which were read by Mr Clarke, and as I think they would be generally interesting to all who feel a desire for the enlargement of the Redeemer's Kingdom, especially in Western Africa, I venture to suggest the propriety of having them printed, with a short heading, stating the previous character of the Individual and the circumstance of his having received elementary instruction in reading and writing at Cape Coast Castle, under the superintendence of missionaries (*I suppose* though not of our denomination) I think they would find a ready sale, and the prospects would add a little to the Jubilee Fund.
Trusting that you will pardon the liberty I have taken in giving this *hint,* and praying that the efforts made by you and all who are engaged in the great work of sending the Gospel to those who are "sitting in darkness," may be owned and blessed by Him who has declared that "His word shall not return unto Him *void.*" I remain my dear sir
Yours respectfully
in Christian bonds
Eliz^h Ivimey

---

[106]Elizabeth Gratwick (1783-1850), a widow, married **Joseph Ivimey** in 1830; she was Ivimey's third wife. Ivimey pastored the Baptist church at Eagle Street, London, from 1805 until his death in 1834. See her obituary in the *Baptist Magazine* 42 (1850): 593-97.
[107]MAW, Box 39 (BMS 1488), JRULM.

Should you act on my suggestion I shall feel pleasure in promoting the sale as far as in my power.

184. William Colgate,[108] New York, to William B. Gurney, Esq.,[109] 6 Fencourt, Fenchurch Street, London, 7 October 1842 [duplicate].[110]

Duplicate of Letter by the British Queen
New York   Oct. 7th. 1842.

Wᵐ B. Gurney Esqʳ

Sir Enclosed we hand you Bank of Commerce Bill on Mess. Baring Bros. & Co. for Our Hundred & ninety eight pounds twelve shillings Sterling (£198.12.0) which at 8 1/4% Exchange you will find closes Ward's church account, after anticipating the November Quarter's dividend which we believe it is proper to remit Mr. J. C. Marshman for the Serampore College through you, if we understand the arrangement between the College and your Missionary Society. We have sent duplicate of the a/c to Wm. Thacker Esqr. to forward to J. C. Marshman.

We thank you Sir for the attention shewn the sons of our Wm. Colgate in England,[111] and who we expect about this time embarking for home with improved health.

Yours Respectfully
William Colgate

The New York State Stock is, in this community considered *undoubled*.

Dr Wᵐ Colgate in Int. a/c with the Fund left in the M. S.[112] by the late Rev. Wᵐ Ward for the Education of Hindoo Youth for the Ministry.

1841
Sept.   10   To Balance of Funds after purchasing
                      100 Shares of New York state Stock

                                                                    330.47

Nov.   1   Interest due this date on 100 shares of
                     New York State Stock or $10,000 at 5% per

---

[108]**William Colgate** (1783-1857), wealthy New York soap manufacturer and prominent Baptist layman. At the time of the above letter, he was in charge of collecting subscriptions in America to the BMS. See *Missionary Herald* (January 1843): 68.
[109]**William B. Gurney** (see letter 172).
[110]MAW, Box 39 (BMS 1735), JRULM.
[111]James Colgate (1818-1904) and his brother, Samuel (1822-1897).
[112]Missionary Society.

1842		Annum payable quarter yearly			125.00
Feb.	1	Do	Do	Do	125.00
May	1	Do	Do	Do	125.00
Augt.	1	Do	Do	Do	125.00
Nov.	1	Int in anticipation		Do	125.00
					$955.47

Second of Exchange drawn by Bank of Commerce
in N. York on Mess Baring Bros & Co. at todays
sight for £198.12 which at 8 1/4% [per annum] is $955.47

Duplicate of a/c sent by the British Queen

185. Selina Spurgin, Stratford St. Mary's, Suffolk, to Joseph Angus, Baptist Mission House, Fen Court, Fenchurch Street, London, 11 October 1842.[113]

Sir

With feelings of pleasure I have to inform you by the aid of a serv[t] of the Langham friends I have been able to get up a Box of useful, as well as fancy articles, which I intend for M[r] Knibb for South Africa.

I have made up many things I consider suitable for some of the Missionaries Wives, Children, and native teachers—which I hope will prove acceptable to our worthy & ever esteemed friend.

I shall feel much obliged by your informing me when you would like me to send up the Jubilee box and where to have it left, as I think of asking some friend to take charge of it to London who may be going up without any luggage In this case I would inform you by post the day it would be there—and then it would go free of all expense.

Waiting Your reply
I remain dear Sir
Yours very respectfully
Selina Spurgin

Stratford St Mary's
Suffolk
October 11th

---

[113]MAW, Box 39 (BMS 1621), JRULM.

186. J. M. Cramp,[114] *Hastings, to Joseph Angus, Baptist Mission, 6 Fen Court, Fenchurch Street, London, 15 October 1842.*[115]

Hastings
Oct. 15/42

My dear Brother

If I knew how the duties of the Secretary's office are to be divided, I should feel better able to answer your questions. A consulting Counsel is not always fit to take the circuit—and vise versa.

As to Brother Hewlett of Dover[116]—"*Prudent?*" I know nothing to the contrary. "*Practical?*" "*Business*-like?" These may be clasped together. He has not had much experience of public affairs, and I do not think he excels his brethren in the management of business. That is, I know many who are equal to him in that respect. "*Conciliating?*" I should think so: judging from his amiable temper, gentleness of manner, and pleasing address. "*While catholic-spirited, denominational too?*" That is rather doubtful. He is too catholic-spirited to be denominational enough for many in our Churches. This would not be an objection *to me*—but we must bow to public opinion.

---

[114]**John Mockett Cramp** (1796-1881), prolific author and Baptist leader, was at this time minister of the Wellington Square Chapel in Hastings.

[115]MAW, Box 39 (no BMS number), JRULM.

[116]**James P. Hewlett** served as minister to the Baptist congregation at Salem Chapel, Dover, 1839-1849. As the *History* of the Salem Chapel notes, "Mr. Hewlett was a man of fine ability and sterling character and it is impossible to estimate how much Salem owed to the Pastor who, under God, piloted her through the troubled seas of her early history, and who in 1842 declined what seems to have been a very tempting offer from a London Church." The "offer" cited by the writer may not have come from a church but from Angus and the Baptist Mission House. As a result of a subcommittee report in October 1841, the BMS committee decided to pursue the election of a cosecretary to assist Angus in the work of the Mission House. The subcommittee had considered several names, but due to various problems, they could not bring forward a name at that time. The full committee deliberated and asked William Brock of Norwich to consider the position. He would eventually decline. Between November 1841 and June 1843, the BMS Committee continued to search for an assistant to Angus, offering the position to Frederick Trestrail and J. E. Giles, but like Hewlett, they too rejected the offer. See *Missionary Herald* (November 1841): 587-590; Walter Holyoak, *Dover Baptists. A Brief History* (Dover: Dover Express Office, 1914) 19, 17-21; Frank Buffard, *Kent and Sussex Baptist Associations* (Faversham, Kent: E. Vinson, [1963]) 154; *Beechen Grove Baptist Church* (Beechen Grove: Printed for the church, [1947]) 10; Payne, *First Generation*, 18; Stanley, *History*, 213; BMS Committee Minutes, Vol. H (Oct. 1841-Dec. 1842), ff. 10, 30, 41; Vol. I (Jan. 1843-May 1844), f. 80.

I must honestly say that I do not think Brother Hewlett is the man you want. It strikes me that he is not an effective platform speaker; and that, I suppose, is a sure question. He is clear—correct—neat—and can elaborate a speech: but I question his skill at off-hand oratory. His addresses are rather pleasing than powerful.—Besides this, I am fully of opinion that your new Secretary should be a man of considerable standing in the Church—very generally known—and possessing the confidences of his brethren.

Last winter I had frequent conversations with Brother Ellis, late of Calcutta[117]—He used to maintain that you ought to have two foreign Secretaries associated with yourself; one for the East—the other for the West and Africa—yourself for home. His reasoning on this subject appeared to me forcible. The trains of management to our Jamaica brethren will slightly affect such a scheme; but I still think that it would materially conduce to the welfare of our foreign stations; and relieve the general Secretaryship, if some brother were appointed *Secretary for Indian Affairs*. India will now, I hope, obtain its proper share of attention. It is a vast field, and must be much better cultivated by all parties—our Missionaries there have long complained of the want of sympathy at home, and the scanty measure of regard which their stations have received. Let a brother take India under his charge—make himself thoroughly acquainted with all the stations and the missionaries, even to the minutest details—conduct the correspondences—study India's wants, capabilities, peculiarities, facilities &c &c—surely much good might result from such an arrangement. The general Secretaries cannot do all this. India deserves such a man. He should have nothing to do with any other department of the Mission; and he might be a pastor still. Yourself and your new colleague wholly devoted to the work, might divide your labour as you please: one taking W. Indies and Africa, with the Herald, and the other the Home Department, sharing some portion of the general business between you, and each of you taking occasional journies—

Excuse my ramble. May the Lord himself guide in these important affairs.

> Yours faithfully
> J. M. Cramp

Rev. Jos. Angus

---

[117]See letter 167.

187. Owen Johnson Birt,[118] *Bristol to his uncle [Joseph Angus, Baptist Mission House, London], 17 October 1842.*[119]

Bristol Oct 17 1842

My dear Uncle

On my Fathers return from London last Friday, I was informed by him of the opening which will occur in the Missionary field in the island of Ceylon, and also of the kind interest which you have taken in my case and prospects. For several years past I have been led to consider it my duty to become a missionary to the heathen, and, during the last few months, my mind has been especially directed to this object by the advice of Dr Prichard,[120] an eminent physician in Bristol, who considers that in a tropical climate I should enjoy robust health. The West Indies seemed to offer an attractive station, and Dr Prichard strongly recommended my going to Jamaica, or some other island there. Since my Fathers return however, and the views given me respecting Ceylon, I have thought incessantly on the subject, and have endeavoured to ascertain what is the will of God in my future lot. It now appears to me that as a more important work remains to be carried on in Ceylon than in Jamaica, should I be deemed qualified for the station, to that island I ought to go. Indeed it was, at first, my wish to be fixed in the East Indies because I thought labourers were more needed there.

In the present state of my affairs I did not think it right to decide until I had again consulted Dr Prichard and had asked his opinion of Ceylon as a place of residence. I had an interview with him this morning, when he expressed himself *very strongly* in favour of that island, saying that though he had no doubt I should enjoy very good health in the West Indies, it would be far better for my mind and body to go to Ceylon—that it was far more healthy, and, he believed, that there I should be quite strong and vigorous. This testimony I consider very satisfactory. After I left Dr Prichard I called on Mr Crisp,[121] who expressed

[118]Owen Johnson Birt was the son of **Caleb Evans Birt** (1795-1854), minister at Broadmead in Bristol. The younger Birt was appointed as a BMS missionary to Ceylon in October 1842 (see letters 188, 192), but unfortunately, he died in route on 15 March 1843. His wife, however, continued on to Ceylon. A letter from her appeared in the *Missionary Herald* (April 1844): 210-212. See BMS Committee Minutes, Vol. I (Jan. 1843-May 1844), f. 79.

[119]MAW, Box 39 (BMS 1716), JRULM. Birt's letter was presented to the Committee by J. H. Hinton on 20 October 1842. See BMS Committee Minutes, Vol. H (Oct. 1841-Dec. 1842), f. 191.

[120]**James Cowles Prichard** (1786-1848), Bristol doctor and author of several medical works.

[121]**Thomas Steffe Crisp** (1788-1868), Principal of Bristol Baptist Academy and assistant pastor at Broadmead.

his decided opinion that I was suited to the place and work, and that in terms so strong, that, whilst truly gratified for his kindness, I hardly like to repeat them. He said that he would write a letter of recommendation to the Committee if it were thought desirable.

The advice of my dear friends and that of my tutors being now in accordance with my personal wishes, I have decided, as I trust by the direction of the Spirit of God, to offer myself to the Committee of the Missionary Society as a candidate for the work in Ceylon and I am willing and ready to go at once should they think proper to accept me.

And now my dear Uncle, what steps do you advise me to take in this matter? How must I proceed? Can I offer myself to the Committee for this station through you? You have been so kind hitherto that I am sure now you will favour me with your advice. Will you be so kind as to send me a line, in answer to this, as soon as convenient. We are all anxiously expecting to hear how my dear Aunt is, and trust that she is better. Give my best love to her and my cousins.

My dear Father and Mother join with me in most affectionate regards to you and my dear Aunt.

I am, my dear Uncle
Your truly attached nephew
Owen J. Birt

On the back page Angus has written the following account of Birt's acceptance by the BMS Committee:[122]

22nd year
5 years since baptized.—

Gurney	recommend that Mr O. J. Birt be
Steane	accepted for Miss^y Service in
Hinton	Ceylon
Soule	Arrangements be made for M^r
Green	Birts leav^g as early as *possible* &

---

[122]The members of the Committee who signed the statement confirming Birt's assignation as a missionary were all Baptist ministers except for W. B. Gurney: **Edward Steane** (1798-1882), Baptist minister at Denmark Place Chapel, Camberwell, and secretary of the Baptist Union, 1835-1882; **J. H. Hinton** (1791-1873) at Devonshire Square, London, 1837-1863; **Israel May Soule** (1806?-1873) at Battersea, 1834-1873; **Samuel Green** (1796-1883) at Lion Street, Walworth, 1841-1849; **George Pritchard** (1773-1852) at Keppel Street, London, 1817-1837; **William Groser** (1791-1856), formerly at Maidstone (1820-1839) before removing to London in 1839 to become secretary to the Anti-Opium Society; and Joseph Angus. Birt was approved on 27 October 1842. See BMS Committee Minutes, Vol. H (Oct. 1841-Dec. 1842), f. 195.

Pritchard
Groser
Angus

that the usual allowances by
granted for his outfits & passage
[illegible] request friends at
Bristol & London.

188. Richard Johnson, 2 Rumsford Street, Liverpool, to Joseph Angus, Baptist Mission House, 6 Fen Court, Fenchurch Street, London, 27 October 1842.[123]

2 Rumsford Sᵗ
L[iver]pool
27 Oct 1842

My dear Sir

On receipt of your favour yesterday, I asked Mʳ Jackson (of Hamilton & Coʸ) about his Vessel & he said he would not go to Fernando Po until her return from other parts of Africa, but he told me that Horsfall [&] Son were likely & I find they do send one direct to Fernando Po, but the time is not fixed nearer than within the next three months, Mʳ Horsfall expressed himself friendly so far as to not to show any impediments in the way of their going on the same terms as other passengers, & he promises to send for me to see the Captain as soon as their arrangements are more matured, and also for this Captain to give me some information from Fernando Po which Mʳ Horsfall thinks may be useful to us, after which I will write you.[124]

& believe me
My dear Sir
Yours very truly
Richᵈ Johnson

Revᵈ J Angus A. M.

[123]MAW, Box 39 (BMS 1709), JRULM.

[124]The firm of Messrs. Horsfall & Son, Liverpool, would provide free passage for Merrick and his wife to Fernando Po the next spring. See BMS Committee Minutes, Vol. I (Jan. 1843-May 1844), f. 37.

189. Edward Foster,[125] *Thompson Lane, Cambridge, to Joseph Angus, Baptist Mission House, Fen Court, Fenchurch Street, London, 28 October 1842.*[126]

Thompson Lane
Oct 28 1842

My dear Sir,

I have been informed that if I directed a letter to you under cover to M[r] Clarke, Missionary to Africa, you would be so kind as to direct it for me and send it to him, as you are in possession of what place he may be at

Your attention to that effect will greatly oblige

Yours very truly
Edward Foster

190. Richard Johnson, Liverpool, to Joseph Angus, [Baptist Mission House, London,] 28 October 1842.[127]

L[iver]pool
28 Oct 1842

My dear Sir

I have seen the owners & Captain of the African Vessel & cannot arrange for the Missionaries to have a passage in her, they are not certain of going to Fernando Po direct from here; & I find the Cap[n] very much opposed to D[r] Prince[128] & M[r] Clarke on [account] of their interference with the Servants of the Western Africa C[o] in the case of the man who was immured in a Dungeon, I tried to reason with the Captain on the subject, but he was very warmly opposed to them & said there would be no security for either lives or property if such interference was al-

---

[125]Edward Foster contributed £20 to the BMS Jubilee Fund in December 1842. An "E. Foster, sen," contributed £100. This was most likely his father, Ebenezer Foster (1777-1852) of Anstey Hall, Trumpington, the founder of Foster's Bank and Mayor of Cambridge (1836-1837) and High Sheriff (1849). His father was Richard Foster (d. 1790), also of Cambridge and a deacon at St. Andrew's Street. Seven other Fosters contributed to the BMS at that time. Fosters had been leading members at St. Andrew's Street and prominent public figures in Cambridge for several generations by 1842. See *Church Book: St. Andrew's Street* 133, 142,173; *Missionary Herald* (January 1843): 67.

[126]MAW, Box 39 (BMS 1721), JRULM.

[127]MAW, Box 39 (BMS 1737), JRULM.

[128]**George K. Prince** (1800/01-1865), medical doctor from Jamaica who served as a BMS missionary with John Clarke at Fernando Po, 1840-1848.

lowed; the hope by this vessel of a passage having failed, I again applied to Messʳˢ Hamilton Jackson & Co & Mʳ Jackson promised to help us, & get a passage by the first vessel they send & perhaps it may be as soon as the other; If you see Dʳ Prince or Mʳ Clarke please tell them the reason Mʳ Jameson[129] is so much offended is owing to a *report* published in the West Indies & reported in some publication or Magazine, the name of which I have not yet got, which he considers contains an improper reflection on him, I am sorry to lose these two opportunities, especially the services of Jameson, as he trades direct, but have little doubt we shall find other channels of communication with the brethren there, & any letter you have for them I can send by Mʳ Horsfall's ship, & will advise you when I can get a package for them by some other & believe me

Yours vʸ truly

Richᵈ Johnson

To the Revᵈ J. Angus A. M.
London

191. *Edgar Anthony Low,*[130] *Union Street, [London,] to the Committee of the Baptist Mission Society, [Baptist Mission House, London], 2 November 1842.*[131]

To the Committee of the Baptist Mission Society

It having been intimated to me that a practicable Man for the penetration of Africa in connexion with their Mission at Fernando Po would have their serious consideration if it did not recieve [sic] their approbation and support, I respectfully submit the following to them. It is to endeavour to reach Kernuk on the Shary river, the chief town in the Kingdom of Loggun by proceeding in a North Easterly direction from the Old Calabar river, through the Mandara Kingdom, or up the Jehadda river, according as circumstances would permit

The objects which I should have in view are these.

I.   The opening a communication wherever practicable with the various places I should pass through for the establishment of Xtian mission stations and the reception of Native Teachers

---

[129]**William Jameson** (1807-1847), Scottish Presbyterian missionary in Jamaica, 1835-1847.

[130]Low (see letters 154, 156, 157), still pursuing his objective of becoming a missionary, had now become a Baptist.

[131]MAW, Box 39 (BMS 1759), JRULM.

II. The collecting information of the country for the purpose of drawing attention and exerting interest towards it.

III. The establishment of a Mission at Kernuk. I will take the liberty of offering a few remarks on the desirableness of selecting this part of the country and making Kernuk the object for a mission tho no doubt most of them will have already occurred or are known to the committee.

    I.   It is above 600 miles from the coast and yet places you almost in the heart of Africa.

    II. The following extracts from Major Denham's Travels in Africa[132] Speaking of the inhabitants of the Kingdom of Loggun he says "they are any one's people who can gain an influence over them and appeared to care as little about the Mohammedan form of religion as we did ourselves it is a very populous country—Kernuk has 15, 000 inhabitants at least. They have a metal currency. The first which he had seen in Negroland They are a much handsomer race than the Borneoese and far more intelligent. They are very industrious and labour at the loom very regularly—in one house I saw 5 looms at work. The market ~~which~~ is held every evening and well supplied with the necessaries of life for which they exchange their various manufactures. Kernuk itself is more healthy than any other part of the banks of the Shary—and in another place he says they are a remarkable healthy goodworking race and in the immediate neighbourhood of the great river (the Shary) some of the towns are extremely healthy."

    III. Its contiguity and communication with Begharmi. The language spoken being almost the same and one half the inhabitants natives of that Kingdom.

Some of the committee may think it too near the Mohammedan line of countries but even Fundah which is much more so is supposed by Mr Iain out of 36, 000 inhabitants to have 9/10ths pagans.

How is the country to be reached and the others passed through. So far as I have directed my attention to this subject, it will be necessary to form a small expedition of 3 or 4 persons acquainted with the language spoken of the countries we should pass through. The expedition to be prepared to travel by land or water as opportunity offered. The journey overland from Old Calabar to the Ichadda must be performed on foot as there are no means of conveyance—natives might be lured to convey whatever articles were required ~~to be taken to be used~~ as a medium of

---

[132]Dixon Denham (1786-1828) was the author of *Narrative of Travels and Discoveries in Northern and Central Africa: in the Years 1822, 1823, and 1824* (1826).

exchange, for food and other things we might require and should be able to procure—

When we reached the Ichadda the difficulties of conveyance would be very much diminished the river would afford one means by purchasing a strong large canoe or land traveling might be had recourse to if the advantages were found to be greater.

I may here say that in traveling through countries little known it is almost impossible to say how you are to do so till you arrive on the spot. When the best means of doing so which present themselves would have to be made use of—I respectfully refer the committee to the following Societies Individuals and papers

> the Royal Geographical Society
> African Civilization Society[133]
> Wesleyan Mission Society[134]
> Edward Robinson LLD of New York
> Rev[d] L. P. Balch of New York[135]
> Sir Fowler Buxton
> Col. Nicolls[136]
> Rev[d] Robert Moffat[137]

---

[133]The African Civilization Society was formed in 1840, largely due to the efforts of Thomas Fowell Buxton, (1786-1845), Anglican M.P., philanthropist, prison reformer, supporter of the Bible Society, and leader of the British abolitionist movement after Wilberforce. Buxton led an unsuccessful expedition into the interior of West Africa (Niger) in 1838-1839. Undeterred, he returned to England and published *The African Slave Trade* (1840), proposing an active role by the British in civilizing Africa as the best means of ending slavery, even recommending, among other things, that the British government purchase the island of Fernando Po. He described the African Civilization Society to an American abolitionist that same year as "instituted to cooperate in various ways, and under the protection of the Government with the ministry, for the deliverance, instruction, and elevation of the African race." Other abolitionist societies would soon eclipse Buxton's society, and by 1843 the African Civilization Society had dissolved. Buxton was supportive of the BMS's plan of acquiring a steam-powered schooner for the mission at Fernando Po, as his letter of 11 June 1843 to John Clarke reveals. It was published in the *Missionary Herald* (August 1843): 443, and was accompanied with a donation of £20. See also R. R. Gurley, *Mission to England, in Behalf of the American Colonization Society* (Washington DC: W. W. Morrison, 1841) 17.

[134]The missionary wing of the Methodist church was formed at Leeds in October 1813, largely as a result of the work of Dr. Thomas Coke, who died while leading the first Methodist mission to Ceylon in 1814. By the early 1840s, Methodist missionaries were working in India, South Africa, Australia, and along the western coast of Africa.

[135]For Robinson, see letter 156; for Balch, see letters 154, 156, 157.

[136]See letter 180.

[137]See letter 172.

to some letters and papers in the hands of our respectful Secretary the Rev J. Angus with two of the Revᵈ Balch's

With Xtian respect I remain
Edgar Anthony Low

Nov 2. 1842

P.S. The journies of Mʳ Campbell and Freeman[138] shew what may be done as regards the difficulty of traveling in Africa. The former is 700 miles from Cape Town—and both had their full share of difficulties.

192. Owen Johnson Birt, Bristol, to Mr. [[W. W.] Stanger, Jr., Baptist Mission House, Fen Court, Fenchurch Street, London, 3 November 1842.[139]

Bristol Nov. 3 1842

My dear Sir

I wrote to Mʳ Angus on Saturday last with a view to ascertain among other things, whether the papers were taken to Ceylon by the Sumatra. He wrote to me yesterday and kindly enclosed a list of the things needed for the outfit, nearly all of which I shall get in Bristol but did not mention the vessel. Now will you be so kind as to send me a line saying what has been done and any further particulars which you may be able to obtain respecting the time of sailing &c. I feel assured that I may rely upon your kindness to do this for me & also to attend to my wishes respecting the cabins nos 8 & 10 with which you are acquainted. I feel very anxious about it because, if you remember, Mʳ Tyndal only gave us till last Monday to decide. Mʳ Kidd is quite willing to give us his cabin to me, so there will be no trouble on that account. Trusting you are well

I am my dear sir
yours truly
Owen J Birt

---

[138]Low is referring to *Travels in South Africa, Undertaken at the Request of the Missionary Society* (1815) by the Scottish missionary, **John Campbell**. The other reference is to Thomas Birch Freeman (1809-1890), a pioneering Methodist missionary to Africa. He toured England in 1840 speaking of his travels and experiences within the interior of Africa, and that may be what Low is referring to here; however, Freeman's first published account of his travels, *Journal of Two Visits to the Kingdom of Ashanti, in Western Africa*, did not appear until 1843. He followed that with his *Journal of Various Visits to the Kingdoms of Ashanti, Aku, and Dahomi* (1844).

[139]MAW, Box 39 (BMS 1761), JRULM.

193. E. A. Claypole,[140] *Ross, Herefordshire, to [Joseph Angus, Baptist Mission House, London], 21 November 1842.*[141]

My dear Sir

In acknowledging the receipt of the money last week you say nothing in reply to my inquiry respecting Mr Aveline of Graham's Town.[142]—Can you take charge of a small packet which I will send to him from one of his relation? It will contain some articles wh[ich] belonged to his late father and which he will value very highly. Please also to mention when you will send to him if you know a [E A?] judge—

Yours sincerely

E. A. Claypole

Ross. Nov 21st 1843.

194. Henry Crasweller,[143] *36 Welbeck Street, [London], to Joseph Angus, [Baptist Mission House, London,] 24 November 1842.*[144]

36 Welbeck Stt
Novr 24—42

My dear Sir

A Friend of mine Mr Willm King is about to go to Ceylon for the purpose of establishing himself as a Coffee Planter and is desirous of obtaining a letter of introduction to the Revd Mr Daniel[145] at that place—may I beg the favor of a note from you to Mr Daniel—I shall esteem it a favor and am

Dear Sir
Yrs very truly
Henry Crassweller

Revd J Angus

---

[140]**E. A. Claypole**, Baptist minister at Ross-on-Wye, Herefordshire, c. 1828 to the late 1850s. His church made a contribution to the BMS in November 1841 of £24.2.11 and £19.18.3 in November 1842. See *Missionary Herald* (January 1842): 48; (January 1843): 57.

[141]MAW, Box 39 (BMS 1916), JRULM.

[142]**George Aveline**, BMS missionary to Grahamstown, South Africa, 1838-1843.

[143]**Henry Crassweller** (d. 1880), deacon in the Baptist church at Eagle Street, London, 1812-1880.

[144]MAW, Box 39 (BMS 1939), JRULM.

[145]**Ebenezer Daniel** (1784-1844), BMS missionary to Ceylon, 1830-1844.

195. Thomas Thompson,[146] *Turpentine Distiller, Bill Quay, near Gateshead, Durham, to the Committee of the Baptist Missionary Society, [London], 26 November 1842.*[147]

Bill Quay Nov[r] 26th 1842

Gentl[n]

Having recently heard that you contemplate the erection of a small steam ship, to convey the messengers of the glorious gospel of our Lord and Saviour Jesus Christ, along the banks of the Niger, and into the interior of Africa, the thought occurred to me that you might have some difficulty in getting an individual competent to manage the steam engine, and one that is willing to go to that unfavourable clime, I trust that I am enabled by the grace of God, after very serious consideration to say "here am I send me, should none more efficient be found willing to go." I esteem it a very great honour and privilege to be engaged in any humble way to promote the interests of Christ's Kingdom among men, how much more to be able to leave my native land, to be the humble instrument in the hand of God of conveying the heralds of salvation to the dark places of the earth which are full of the habitations of cruelty. My heart bleeds for Ethiopia & that she may soon stretch forth her hands unto God. But you will be wishful to know my capabilities as it respects steam engines, I have not served an apprenticeship to the erection of them. At the age of 17 I completed the erection of a small steam engine, which I sold. From 17 to 19, I had the charge of a low pressure steam engine, with the charge of the works and the machinery. From the age of 19 to 22, I had the charge of a high pressure steam engine between 30 & 40 Horse power, with machinery and hydraulic presses for the purpose of extracting oil from Linseed. From the age of 22 to the present period being 2 years I have had the management of a Turpentine distillery with machinery, which situation I now hold. The above situation I have filled under the same Comp[y] which I now serve. Should you determine upon me, please inform me as soon as convenient the

---

[146]**Thomas Thompson**, here offering his services to the BMS, would have to wait until 1845 before leaving for Fernando Po; he died there the next year.

[147]MAW, Box 39 (BMS 1980), JRULM. Thompson's letter was presented to the Committee on 1 December 1842. The Committee would not act upon Thompson's request for some time. Richard Pengilly would recommend Thompson in letters to Angus dated 11 January 1843 and 27 February 1843 (see letters 212 and 232), showing increasing frustration with the Committee's inaction. Finally, on 6 April 1843, the Committee voted to accept Thompson's request to work as an engineer on the new vessel that the Committee was preparing to purchase for work in Africa. See BMS Committee Minutes, Vol. H (Oct. 1841-Dec. 1842), f. 212; Vol. I (Jan. 1843-May 1844), f. 53.

conditions on which you would engage, also should it so happen in the Providence of God that I should fall a victim to the climate, whether my wife and two daughters the one nearly 3 years old, and the other 10 months, would in any way be provided for, also what articles we might be providing suitable to take out, also that I may give my present employers sufficient notice. I have a turning lathe and a good many tools suitable for machinery which will be at your service if they can be taken out.

I am your Ob^t Servt in Christ
Thos Thompson

To the Committee of the
Baptist Missionary Society

N. B.
Please direct for me
Thos Thompson
Turpentine Distiller
Bill Quay
near Gateshead
Durham

196. Edgar Anthony Low, 12 Union Street, Spitalfields, London, to [Joseph Angus, Baptist Mission House, London], 29 November 1842.[148]

Novr 29 1842

Reverend Sir
I have troubled you with this thinking the committee would like to know more fully the state of my mind in regard to remaining in Africa. The impression on my mind when asked if I were willing to remain was that it would be merely on my own account—for however confident and determined to convey the Gospel there as holding a communion direct from God—I feel much diffidence as to being a servant of the Society's. But knowing that the committee are much better able to judge what will be most for God's glory I wish to be altogether guided by their counsel so long as a great work is to be attempted; and there is to be no sparing of those who engage in it. They will never find me hang back to be unwilling to take up my cross and deny myself—But I take no credit to myself in this matter. It will be no cross to me to remain in Africa— thanks be to God who hath prevented me from conferring with flesh

---

[148]MAW, Box 39 (no BMS number), JRULM.

and blood—I can spend my life quite as happily in the service of God—
in the heart of Africa as if I were only 4 or 500 miles from the coast—
and from love to Christ would rather choose to be in the front of battle—I know full well how apt we are to choose ease instead of hard-
ships and for this cause would prefer to place myself in the situation in
which there is the least. I feel that I cannot do enough to show my love
to my savior and therefore the greater and harder the work the more
ready am I to engage in it. If I feel any doubt of being able to go through
with this work—and that what will result from its accomplishment viz
the calling sinners to repentance and upholding the cross of Christ in
defiance of at all its enemies and the feeling of who is sufficient for
these things comes across me—his words my grace is sufficient for
thee—and in my strength shall thy weakness be perfected is my supper
There is much of wrong impression to be done away with—as to the
nature of the interior of Africa—before Christians will become alive to
the facilities of carrying the Gospel thither—for instance [El Ranery?]
the sheik of Kornou—16 years ago—was very anxious that the English
merchants should reside at his place and that more especially they
were to have their wives with them that they might have no induce-
ments to leave—and it is well known that putting aside the existence of
slavery, the state of morals in regard to sexes is superior to what it is in
this and the other large cities of Europe—In answer to a question asked
me, viz whether I had any faculty in acquiring a language—if I remember aright I think I said that I had not—my wish has been not to speak
and think more highly of myself than I ought and in my communicating
with the Society to underrate rather than overate the talent God in his
mercy has bestowed on me. Yet having some knowledge of the Latin
and more lately gained some acquaintance with the New Test Dialect I
should hope (of course it would be my strenuous endeavour) with
God's blessing after a colloquial acquaintance with a dialect to be
enabled to translate some portion of the New Test into it—I am well
aware that the rules of grammar arise out of the construction of a language and that the English alphabet and mode of spelling may be
akd[149]—unless it be found desirable as might be the case at Loggun or
Begharmi to use the Arabic character—which I don't think there would
be any necessity for inasmuch as those who could read Arabic might
have the scriptures in that language—The Becker translation of part of
the New Test tho called an African Dialect is I believe a branch of the
Arabic—This is in the Arabic characters and spoken by the [illegible] or
Foulahs and an Arab tribe who are met with in various places of this
part of Africa in some places 1500 miles apart, so that in translating
part of the New Test into the Begharmi language the English characters

---

[149]awkward?

and the simplest mode of spelling would only require to be used—and which a good colloquial acquaintance of the language combined with perseverance I humbly and earnestly hope would enable me to accomplish—In regard to preaching too—what troubles me much is that I cannot. I do so experimentally so deeply of divine things as I could wish. I trust that by prayer and perseverance combined with the teaching of God's Holy Spirit I shall be enabled to do so. I cannot bear the thoughts of preaching myself instead of Christ—intellectually as it might be instead of in the power of God's Spirit—I have made some extracts from letters which I wrote soon after my conversion and from a journal I have been in the habit of keeping thinking that such would more fully shew the state of my mind at those times. I have also enclosed a [illegible] of my doctrinal view of the elements of Christianity—with one or two letters I thought you might like to look at—In what I have written and sent I have tried to avoid on the one hand the letting anything like [illegible] prevent me from putting that to paper which might be to God's glory and on the other any thing like carnal pride prompting me to send or write anything

"you may suppose that it has given me some concern the disappointment my hopes have met with in regard to this country—but there is one circumstance resulting from it which I trust will be to my future advantage—it has shewn me the vanity and vexation of this life. Man disquieteth himself in vain he heapeth up riches and cannot tell who shall inherit them—

I shall not trouble myself with such things for the future—but set my affections on higher things—do good eschew evil and do all to the Glory of God—"written Decr 1840—had my eyes opened to my sinful and lost state in the preceeding [sic] Oct^r

"I came here expecting to find this country one in which I could live peaceably quietly and comfortably instead of which I find I am drawn into a vortex of trouble and unpleasantness Nevertheless tho I have not found it in the way I wished still I have secured it. That it is not of this world—the ways of God are inscrutable and unfathomable who shall discover them better thought I while I was preparing to come to this country and anticipating so much pleasure and comfort that I should be disappointed—and yet not disappointed for if I have not met with that which I expected I have secured that which is much better—peace of mind and determination to do the will of Him who made me—for if you could have created a being would you not expect it to owe you some gratitude for such creation—does not ~~his~~ a person expect his dog to do what he is told which if he does not he is corrected—yet you gave it not life you merely take care of it—Now God has given us life with many other blessings therefore we ought to do His will."

"You may think it very doubtful (alluding to my going to Africa) but I do not despair of seeing you again there is a spirit in Man and I trust it is in me which will enable him when in the midst of danger and suffering to extricate himself trusting in God who has said I will never leave thee nor forsake thee—which if we believe the Bible to be the world of God—we believe those words for they are in the Bible—then if we fear to place ourselves in such a situation for the benefit of our fellow creatures and the Glory of God we are full of doubtings and believe not with all our hearts."   written from Guelph Feb. 1841.

"You may imagine that there is great reason to fear the not seeing me again. In fact that I may perish in the deserts of Africa—fear not the same being who sustained the Patriarch Joseph and other Holy men recorded in the Old Test^t and upheld and protected the Apostles and followers of our blessed Saviour through all their trials and wanderings will protect and sustain me for He knows what is the principal cause though mixed as with others less worthy which prompts me to such and undertaking. I intend wherever practicable to introduce the Christian Religion." April 1841

If I succeed in crossing Africa, I should go out again having made up my mind to assist in the utmost of my power in helping that unfortunate country to throw off the incubus of sin and misery which sits upon her, resulting from that ignorance of their Creator which binds Civilized and Christian Nations and beings one to the other. July 1841

May 1841 Left Guelph for New York on my way to Zela spent a religious and profitable evening with a friend previous to doing so the next morning—read some chap. from the Ps. (Fret not thyself) M^r [Lo?] offered up prayers to our Heavenly Father for mercy and more especially for my protection and support which I have experienced since I left had not such a trust in God's mighty protection as I should have had.

But feel more reliance on him now—found travelling exposes you to great worldly temptation—must let the interests of my father in heaven be more at heart and bear up against the influence of the world

On setting out from Guelph was much perplexed how I should proceed now that I am in New York clearly perceive that the finger of God has guided me I must trust in him humbly but with all my heart and He will ordain all for the best.

June 8/41 should endeavor to get now a course of reading of works useful in such an undertaking as mine but cannot see my way clear at present—and know not whether I should succeed in procuring the opportunity which my stay in New York will afford me if so it will be my duty so to regulate my time there—I may make the most of it for my own improvement now—for God's Glory hereafter—

June 15. M^r F to call on Mr Balch this mor[in]g but was taken ill I cannot see the future but my Heavenly Father can in a calm and holy frame of mind must leave all to him.[150]

June 21. Mr Fraser gone to another world whither we must also follow Grant Lord that many of us may see the error of our ways our pride vanity love of self and this world Indifference to Thy Interests—and that we may have the assistance of thy Holy Spirit—It is a good plan for a Xtian wishing to live in accordance with his Creator's Love every now and then to look into his own heart and discover what are his faults—to purge himself so that he may restrain those which are wrong and cultivate the particular form of Godliness he is most sufficient in—now it seems to me that I require a closer communion with God—more reliance on his mercy and protection with a stronger belief that He will give it to me that I am too much ashamed of his name in worldly company to be a good Xtian. The Lord grant me his Spirit to overcome such shame
    I also want a greater degree of courage to advance his interests and to fight the battle of the cross I ought to endure hardness as a good soldier of Jesus Christ being strong in faith. O most holy and blessed Savior our Lord Jesus help me with the Holy Spirit to have that courage and attain that strength. I possess too much vanity and love of approbation from my fellow worms instead of desiring it for my Creator.

Sepr It pleased my heavenly Father to impress on my heart a deep sense of his awful presence when retiring to rest—having been previously talking very warmly in defence of the poor suffering African which I pray ~~he will~~ him to contrive to me till it please him to take me to himself and O that I may never be ashamed to in thy defence in whatever company I may be give me strength O Lord and uphold me with thy Spirit—and shall we not risk our lives even

---

[150]See letter 156.

as our blessed leader did fighting valiantly for the faith—and now my God preserve me and extend his protection to me when in the desert—in suffering hunger and thirst—I faint.

And O that he will so warm my heart as to make it beat with high delight when I think of his goodness and mercy to us always

God be merciful to me a sinner

I will die in his service and I shall see his face when he is pleased in his good purpose to take me away—

April 1842 Yesterday I was baptized in the name of the father Son and Holy Spirit one God blessed for ever—and therein put on the Lord Jesus Christ—may the Holy Spirit enable me to walk worthy of my calling I can do nothing of myself—only through Jesus Christ I would much rather be in heaven now Nevertheless I desire to do God's work—rather than my own—only I am a sinful creature and so long as I remain on earth shall be one it grieves me very much to crucify our dear Lord again and to put him to open shame by my sins but I find in me the same that Paul did—a law in my members that warreth against the spirit

With my spirit I serve God but with my body Sin This is just my state now that I have been baptized and I had imagined much to my satisfaction and comfort that I should have been enabled to put away all sin and to have crucified myself with holiness to perfection that while we are in the flesh Sin will prevail—Jesus Christ is my refuge—I will never let go that steel anchor of my hope My Soul Trust thou in the Lord wait patiently faint not neither be weary but trust continuously in thy ~~Lord~~ Saviour

May the Holy Spirit sanctify my Spirit and enable it to compel my body since it will not give up its ~~vice~~ sins to suffer martyrdom for committing them—and may I thus glorify our Lord Jesus in dying—

Novr 2^d 1842 I rely entirely on the merits of my Savior for Salvation—pure simple faith is all that is necessary to the sinners part believe on the Lord Jesus Christ and ye shall be saved yet many experienced the goodness of ~~good~~ God I feel that if my heart believeth unto righteousness—if I really believe that Jesus Christ is the Eternal Son of God and came down from heaven to save me [from] eternal death my whole life must be a life of faith and so I have discovered this from studying the writings he has left us for that purpose whatever is written therein shall be my guide for the future— The more souls are saved the more Glory will accrue to God not by might nor by power but by my Spirit saith the Lord—I possess no might I possess no power Ask of me—saith another part of his word—the Holy Spirit and I will give it to thee—that is all I want and since it is to be had a free gift and God is willing to bestow it on those who seek for it I am determined not to rest content till I procure it—so that I may delight in Him and in the doing of his will

197. *George Alexander, Epsom, to [Joseph Angus, Baptist Mission House, London,] 1 December 1842.*[151]

Epsom 1st Decr 1842

Revd & Dear Sir—

On my return to London from India, I had hoped to have had the pleasure of waiting upon you on the subject of this communication—I would premise that I am in Honble Comy Civil Service & for some years have been in the Comee of the Calcutta Tract Socy[152] that for upwards of 2 years I was Cash Secy to the Socy & by God's blessing was enabled to increase the funds & operations of the same. On leaving India, I found the Socy in debt owing to the great increase of demand for Tracts which the Comee considered their duty to endeavor to meet; and without any prospect of such an income in India as would enable them to comply with the wants of the people & the calls of the several Missionaries—I may here mention that the Missn connected with yr Socy alone, stated that they could distribute 100,000 tracts during the Season

It was under these circumstances that I in Comee proposed to lay our necessities before the Parent Socy in England who have Missns in Bengal & Calcutta and I recd a letter & resol.n from the Calcutta Comee to represent them—that document I have forwarded to Mr Arundel[153] of the London Missy Socy—My object now is to represent to you, Sir, & y.r Committee that the Tract Socy is an all-important one now in India that the Missn could not progress in their great work without its aid & that should yr Comee be pleased to contribute annually or otherwise to the

---

[151]MAW, Box 39 (BMS 2001), JRULM. Alexander's letter was read before the Committee on 29 December 1842, after which the Committee decided "that the request be referred to such of our brethren in Calcutta as are members of the Calcutta Union." See BMS Committee Minutes, Vol. H (Oct. 1841-Dec. 1842), ff. 224-225.

[152]The Calcutta Tract and Book Society was formed in 1825 as the publishing and distributing arm of the Religious Tract Society in India. Like the RTS, the Calcutta Society received support from several denominations. During its first year, the Society distributed over 117,000 tracts in several languages. Other societies were formed in Bombay and Madras. See Jones, *Jubilee*, 420-431.

[153]Rev. John Arundel served as Secretary of the London Missionary Society from 1826 to 1841. He also served on the Committee of the Religious Tract Society, 1820-1824 and 1842-1843. See Jones, *Jubilee*, appendix iv.

Calcutta Tract Soc^y the money would I am persuaded be well bestowed & on a direct Miss^y object—I write now to each Miss^y body connected with the Bengal, viz the London—the Church—the General Assembly Church of Scotland & to yourself.[154] Should I be so happy as to receive contributions from you & the others I shall be glad to forward to the Treasurer of the Tract Soc^y in Calcutta. I may mention that formerly the Miss^y bodies in Calcutta subscribed for Tracts annually, but this has been abandoned and as the Miss^{ns} are so largely provided with our publications we look with confidence to the Parent Societies to help us in present difficulties—Hoping for a favourable reply I remain Dear Sir
Yours very truly in Xtian bonds
George Alexander

The Revd Mr Angus
&c &c &c

198. Frederick Trestrail,[155] Cork, to the Committee of the Baptist Mission, 6 Fen Court, Fenchurch Street, London, 3 December 1842.[156]

Cork: Decr 3rd 42

Dear Brethren
The tidings that the war in China—one of the most unjustifiable, bloody & atrocious wars w^h ever disgraced a civilized country—is happily ended have filled all X^n minds with joy. God will doubtless overrule this event for good; and it behoves that Church to meet the intimations of His Providence. As our Jubilee year is not yet closed, and not withstanding the pressure of the times, the fund will amount to much more than was expected, it has been deeply impressed on my mind, that a mission should be commenced for *China*! Nothing could be more delightful that the Jubilee year of Missions, should be connected not only with the termination of unprincipled wars, but with missions to those countries which our Nation's arms have spoiled & laid waste. I intrust you therefore, dear brethren, to take up this proposal. I doubt not that

---

[154]Low is referring to the London Missionary Society (1795), the Church Missionary Society (1799), the Church of Scotland Missionary Society (1824), and the BMS (1792).

[155]**Frederick Trestrail** (1803-1890), Baptist minister in London and Clipston (1831-1836) before serving as secretary of the Baptist Irish Society and the BMS (1849-1869).

[156]MAW, Box 39 (BMS 2026), JRULM. Trestrail's letter was presented before the Committee on 8 December 1842. See BMS Committee Minutes, Vol. H (Oct. 1841-Dec. 1842), f. 215.

others have suggested it, but should the same idea occur to many minds who have had no opportunity of concert in the matter, it will give to such a proposal a greater degree of interest, and render it more worthy of serious consideration.[157]

I am Dear B[n]

Your [illegible]

Fred Trestrail

To the Com[e] of the Baptist Mission

199. Samuel Tucker, Union Bank of Australia, 38 Old Broad Street, [London,] to [Joseph Angus, Baptist Mission House, London], 9 December 1842.[158]

Union Bank of Australia

38, Old Broad Street

9th December

Reverend Sir,

D[r] Steane[159] having mentioned to me that the Baptist Missionary Society were in want of two German Missionaries to proceed to India, I have mentioned the subject to M[r] Busche the bearer of this, who after having been five years in a Missionary Seminary, is now here for the purpose of obtaining an engagement. Referring you to him for further particulars, I am

Rev[d] Sir,

Yours sincerely

Samuel Tucker

---

[157]Enthusiasm for missionary activity in China ballooned after the Treaty of Nanking in August 1842. Now that foreigners could reside in five "treaty ports" in China, the call went out among the various missionary societies to send missionaries. The General Baptist Missionary Society decided to establish a mission in China in March 1843. The BMS, however, was slow to enter the enterprise, given the state of its indebtedness from its other missionary ventures. It was not until 1859 that the BMS, urged by Edward Steane, then secretary of the Baptist Union, resolved to open a China mission, led by Charles Hall and Hendrik Kloekers. See Stanley, *History*, 175-178.

[158]MAW, Box 39 (BMS 2092), JRULM.

[159]Edward Steane (see letter 187).

200. William Simpson, 22 Bartlett's Buildings, Holborn, [London], to Joseph Angus, Baptist Mission, Fen Court, Fenchurch Street, London, 9 December 1842.[160]

22 Barlett's Buildings
Holborn 9th Decem 1842

Revd and Dear Sir,

I sent in a few Days ago 2 copies of my little Private Journal of the "Niger Expedition"[161] as kept by myself which I request your acceptance of

And I now use the freedom to send in 4 additional copies of said little work which I should to be obliged if you could assist me in disposing of amongst the friends of Africa the price thereof is 5/- each, it is not advertised and I use this freedom thro you and some of my friends in announcing it; I trust you will excuse this liberty taken and Believe me to Remain

Revd Sir
yours faithfully
Willm Simpson

To the Revd Jo: Angus M.A.
Baptist Mission
Fen Court
Fenchurch St

P.S. I regret I did not see you when I called yesterday: but the Gentleman I saw in the office gave the liberty I now take

201. Miss Aveline, Mount Pleasant, Ross, Herefordshire, to [Joseph Angus, Baptist Mission House, London,] 10 December [1842].[162]

Miss A's address is Mount Pleasant
Ross Herefordshire
Decr 10th

[160]MAW, Box 39 (BMS 2170).

[161]William Simpson, *A Private Journal kept during the Niger Expedition: From the Commencement in May, 1841, until the Recall of the Expedition in June, 1842* (1843).

[162]MAW, Box 39 (BMS 2093), JRULM.

Miss Aveline will feel much obliged to Mr Angus if he will kindly forward the parcel to Mr Aveline at Grahams Town[163] by the first *safe* opportunity. Miss A will also esteem it a kindness if Mr Angus will acknowledge the receipt of this parcel by the first convenient post, it contains mementoes of a departed Parent which makes its safety a matter of anxiety

[unsigned]

202. J. D. Ellis, Lewes, Sussex, to Mr. W. Stanger, [Baptist Mission House, London], 16 December 1842.[164]

Lewes, Sussex
16th Dec 1842

My dear Sir,

I believe I am indebted to you for kindly sending on to me the Calcutta Missionary Heralds for August & September. Besides which I have received more from Calcutta since March last, so that I am still wanting in April, May, June and July of this year, and which have been possibly sent for me to Fen Court If so, may I trouble you to send them on [illegible word] under a cover just as you would a newspaper, for they come then postage free. I must also trouble you to enquire for me about the *Bengal* [illegible word] *Overland Summary* which is sent regularly for me to Fen Court; but in account of the uncertain state of my own health, it is addressed to Mr Tucker first. If on getting it monthly you will kindly see it addressed Rev. F. Tucker, at Oxford street, Manchester,[165] I shall be obliged, and it will be forwarded on to me. All papers from the British Colonies and India circulate *free*, so that they only require to be put in the post office. As to any letters or papers at any time for me please to address Lewes, Sussex. Through the kindness of God I am again improving in health, although slowly. With kind regards to Mr Stanger sen and Mr Smith[166] I am

Very sincerely yours
Jho. D Ellis

---

[163]See letter 193.

[164]MAW, Box 39 (BMS 2145), JRULM.

[165]Francis Tucker (see letter 172) went as a BMS missionary in 1839 to Calcutta, where Ellis served with him. Both men were present in Calcutta at the death of George Parsons in November 1840. See *Missionary Herald* (January 1841): 86-87.

[166]Possibly a reference to James Smith, at that time pastor of New Park Street Baptist Church, Walworth.

203. J. D. Ellis, Lewes, Sussex, to Joseph Angus, Baptist Mission, 6 Fen Court, Fenchurch Street, London, 16 December 1842.[167]

Lewes, Sussex 16th Dec 1842

My dear Brother,

I beg to thank you for forwarding to me the Calcutta Missionary Herald for Scholars, the interesting intelligence of which gave me feelings of great joy. And not only the accounts of the Jubilee meetings were so delightful, but in a letter to me Mr Thomas speaks confidently of the proposed union of Serampore College with the Society as having met the most cheerful ~~acceptance~~ approval of the brethren in Calcutta, and also of the union of the native churches in Bengal a thing which I think is of great promise. As to myself I have to thank the Father of mercies that I continue to improve, although slowly, and some of my symptoms are certainly better than at any period since I have been in England. My way has been indeed dark, and my mind would oftentimes have sunk had it not been for Divine support and the many precious promises of God's holy word. With kind Xtian regards to any enquiring friends, I am

Yours Affecty

Jho. D Ellis

204. Christopher Anderson, Edinburgh, to unnamed correspondent contemplating serving as a professor at Serampore College, 17 December 1842.[168]

My dear Brother

I wish much that I could help you to what you wish, but I possess no copy of the Charter, nor do I know that there is a copy in this country. I hope however that without the sight you will avail yourselves of the advantages it may present for the training of Native Ministers. Moreover should you inform me that you have been entertaining some thoughts as to whether you might not be useful, as the Professor there, drawing up the first seeds of India unto God, tell Mr Angus that I will cordially & with genuine heart felt interest say, *Go*, and may the good will of Him who dwelt in the Bush ever rest on you both. You know however that I say this even though you should tarry at home. Still were you there I should rejoice and remain

Ever yours affy

Christr Anderson

Edinb: 17 Dec 42

---

205. John Clarke, Berwick, to Joseph Angus, Baptist Mission, Fen Court, London, 24 December 1842.[169]

Berwick Dec[r] 24th 1842

My dear Bro,

I cannot recommend the going of M[r] & M[rs] Merrick in a Vessel to Cape Coast Castle. It is a most trying place at which to remain; and a twelvemonth might pass away before a single Vessel for Fernando Po, or any of the Rivers near, would call there—Ric[d] Johnson Esquire 8 Duke S[t] Edge Hill, Liverpool,[170] will do his utmost to find a Vessel for Bonny, Calebar, or Cameroons—and, for a vessel going to *one* of these Rivers, you sh[d] inquire; as very few Vessels, indeed, call at Fernando Po. But the Vessel taking them out ought to engage to land them at Clarence. North West Bay would not do—and any other place would risk their lives at the most dangerous time, most unnecessarily. *Far better* to wait for a proper Vessel, than to send them out in an improper one— and not only sh[d] the place of landing be well decided, but the character of the Captain, and state of the Vessel, and sort of supplies, for the Voyage, should be ascertained I need not say that some West African Captains are notorious for their harshness, and brutality, and it w[d] be [our] duty to avoid sending a young or an old Missionary with such—B[r] Hewett,[171] of St Tho[s] y[e] Vale wishes to have a good Schoolmaster immediately—will you keep this in mind—He says "My great object in writing is to ask you to get for the people at Jericho a good efficient Schoolmaster, a man who can preach, or at least conduct a service—the people are very anxious to have a good school, & so am I. You know what kind of a man we want—if the Committee will not send him out, why then the people will pay his expenses. We want him as early as possible—you will I know do this for the sake of people, whom you love so much, & who love you with equal affection"—I do not know of any proper person for this situation, I hope you do; and that you will be able to send one—but, I need not say, the people should pay the whole expense—they cannot better employ a part of their means—and too long they have looked upon education as a good they should have for nothing—Ever yours in warmest love,

John Clarke

---

[169]MAW, Box 39 (BMS 2230), JRULM.
[170]See letters 177, 188, 190.
[171]**Edward Hewett** (d. 1883), BMS missionary to Jamaica, 1842-1883.

206. John Clarke, Ford Forge, [Berwick], Northumberland, to Joseph Angus, 6 Fen Court, Fenchurch Street, London, 29-30 December 1842.[172]

Ford Forge, Northumberland
Dec[r] 29th 1842

My very dear Bro,

I have just replied to M[r] Tucker's Note, and shall tomorrow, I hope more fully answer yours—M[rs] Clarke on our return to Berwick will send the Specimens which you request to M[rs] Angus I have no idea of our little Steam Boat costing much annually, as our voyage will be so short—our rigging of the Vessel so simple—the sea except in Tornadoes so smooth—and every river we visit, at the first, so well known If we can obtain two men who understand sailing, and engineering, we shall be able to obtain black men at Fernando Po to work the Vessel under their directions. The wood for firing will cost us the price of the labourer generally, and seldom much more—

I hope it will prove no great annual expense to the Society ~~compared to~~ and the facility it will afford for our establishing Missionary Stations in many parts of the adjacent coast will I trust be very great—

I give on the opposite page a few observations on the necessity of having a Steamer, & hope to say more on the same subject, if time will allow, tomorrow[173] I remain
your affectionate B[r]
John Clarke

Observations on the Necessity of having the means of conveyance to, and from, different parts of the Island of Fernando Po, and the Rivers on the adjacent Continent.

1st It is an unnecessary exposure of life to go to any distant part of the island in a small Canoe, or in an open boat. Tornadoes are very common—frequently, when a strong sea breeze sets in, the sea is too

---

[172]MAW, Box 39 (BMS 2280), JRULM. Clarke's letter (as well as the letter by Edward Cowper of King's College [letter 213]) was read before the Committee 19 January 1843; a resolution was passed recommending Cowper's letter be passed along to Clarke. See BMS Committee Minutes, Vol. I (Jan. 1843-May 1844), f. 9.

[173]The following "observations" by Clarke appeared in the *Missionary Herald* (August 1843): 435-436, as part of a promotional account of the work at Fernando Po. The effect was profound, as letters in support of Clarke's proposal came from such prominent individuals as Thomas Buxton, Thomas Clarkson, Lt. Col. Edward Nicholls, and Macgregor Laird, the eventual builder of the schooner. The letters appeared in the *Missionary Herald* (August 1843): 443-445.

rough for such craft—the danger from exposure in them, to sun and rain, is always great.

The canoe in which I sailed was once upset. *Twice* (from the danger of going out from the shore) we struck upon rocks—For hours I have been compelled to continue wet[ting] my umbrella in the sea, to prevent a "coup de soliel"—Four Towns can be gone to, from Clarence, by land   these contain about 1200 Inhabitants—all the others must be gone to by sea—so that in order to be able to visit from 15 to 20 thousand Aboriginees, we must have the means of going by water to the different landing places

2nd There are no regular Traders from Fernando Po to the Continent—Vessels calling at Fernando Po on their way to the Rivers are few in number and uncertain In most of these it would be unsuitable for Missionaries to go on account of the common practices of many African Traders—In the first Voyage to the Continent, made by Dr Prince and myself, we ventured to cross to the River Cameroons in a small Boat. We were exposed to the sun and rain, and to a sea almost too high for our little vessel—Fever followed as a consequence, & we believed that for us to think of a repetition of such a Voyage would be nothing short of a tempting of the Lord God—

The Dr next went in a Schooner—The Captain was constantly in a state of intoxication—the Vessel was not seaworthy; and on her next voyage was wrecked; & several of the crew were drowned; and the rest were exposed to savage men near the Mouth of the New Calebar   In consequence of the state of the Vessel; and the bad accommodation, in the rainy season, the Doctor got fever; and, but for his speedy return to Fernando Po, must have fallen a sacrifice to his zeal—

3rd Missionaries should be placed in Fernando Po for "acclimating;" and when accustomed to the climate of Africa, some should be sent to Cameroons, Bimbia, Bonny, & Calebar—The coast near the Amboises, & the Rio del Ney, should be explored; as the land is high the country populous, and easy of access from the Island

Missionaries placed at the different stations shd be visited frequently *with supplies*—a sea voyage, and a change, should be practicable, when ill health requires them—and advice from Br Missionaries, it should be possible to obtain

A regular communication is, I think, absolutely necessary for the comfort of the Missionaries; & for the speedy, & permanent, success of the Mission To supply this a Steam Boat of about 50 Tons would be required; and by means of this, at all seasons, we could visit the different stations—impart aid by advice, encouragement, etc.—Remove a sick—

or unsuccessful, dissatisfied, or captious[174] Missionary—and so prevent quarrels with the natives; and do all that could be done for the quiet, & peaceful extension of the Gospel of Jesus—

The expense of such a Vessel, both original & permanent, would, I believe, be amply repaid by the great facilities it would give for the spread of the Gospel in Africa. The Engineer, should, if possible, be also a Missionary.

4th Missionaries should be kept entirely free from Trade, & Traders; and should,[175] on first visiting a place, not be compelled to apply for a lodging or Board and a ship, the Captain of which may have rendered himself obnoxious to the people on shore by his extortion, or cruelty—

We met with one who had fired upon a Canoe, and killed two black men in it—another, who tied those who brought him bad oil, up to the rigging; and flogged them nearly to death—almost all are Sabbath breakers, adulterers, swearers, and with such, I need not say, your Missionaries should have nothing to do, in the way of receiving hospitality; or introduction to the Natives upon the Coast—[176]

5th Missionaries should not be landed from a Canoe or Boat, at a Town, & cast upon the King, or Headman, for shelter, and food. Such was our situation when we reached Cameroons—we had not a small boat, or canoe, in which to land—we stood in our boat until a Captain took pity upon us, and came with his small boat, and took us on shore— [177] another Captain introduced us to King Bell—we were cast upon him for lodging, & for food—The most horrible things soon reached our ears—and we found out afterwards that we had been the guests, for a week, of a man who had murdered his fellow men to obtain a character as a King—whose courteousness, and voluptuousness were excessive— who received the hire of harlots—and those were among his own women & sisters—whose wives for the most part had before been the wives of his Father—who prayed, and made offerings, to his departed Parent & who in the pride of his heart, blasphemously, said that "he and God were all the same!"—

A steam boat, with moderate accommodation, would afford a sleeping place at first visits—our clothing & articles for barter, would be more secure on board our own Vessel; and in every point of view this means of conveyance would be economical, and useful—[178]

---

[174]These last two adjectives were deleted in the printed letter, as well as the remaining portion of the paragraph after the word "Missionary."

[175]This opening phrase was deleted in the printed letter.

[176]This paragraph was deleted in the printed letter.

[177]The remainder of this paragraph was deleted in the printed letter.

[178]The printed letter has inserted at this point a portion of Clarke's letter to Angus of 24 January 1843 (see letter 217).

To withhold this means would be to shut up Missionaries in Fernando Po; or to desert those who might occasionally obtain a passage to the Main Land—I could hope for no considerable success, unless the means of communication be afforded; and the various Stations, we hope to establish, be regularly visited, and watched over with devotedness, tenderness, and care.[179]

John Clarke

Berwick Decr 30th 1842—

207. William Fisher,[180] High Sotherby, to P. J. Saffery,[181] Waltham Abbey, Essex, 31 December 1842.[182]

High Sotherby Decr 31, 1842

My Dear Brother

I rec^d yours on Wedns enclosing the mission Cards with Mr Angus' Circular.

When I inform you that we made a collection at Bromley on Christmas day for this mission you will not I hope be disappointed if little more is done at present. Beside our friends at Bromley & elsewhere have had to make considerable effort lately in erecting a Chapel in the

---

[179]Clarke's letter ends here, but the printed letter closes with a paragraph apparently taken from another letter by Clarke to Angus, one that is not in this collection. The added paragraph aptly exhibits the colonial nature of the mission: "With the aid of such a vessel we should be able, in connexion with our higher object, to do much to promote civilization; and to open the way for legitimate trade from the Lagos to the Gaboon, and to an indeterminate extent up the numerous mouths of the Niger and other rivers in the Bights of Benin and Biafra; cultivation of the soil would no doubt follow, and soon we might hope that a supply of cotton and sugar would be furnished, and a wide field for our manufactures opened throughout this populous country."

[180]William Fisher (1789-1848) pastored at Bromley, Northumberland, for many years before removing to Padiham, where he remained until his death in 1848. See Samuel Couling. "A Biographical Dictionary of Baptist Ministers of Great Britain & Ireland Deceased from 1800 to the close of 1875" (MS., Angus Library, Regent's Park College, Oxford).

[181]**Phillip J. Saffery** (b. 1803), Baptist minister at Brown Street, Salisbury, 1826-1836. As this letter and the following letter reveal, as well as numerous instances in the *Missionary Herald*, Saffery was actively involved in the activities of the BMS during the 1840s, serving as the Society's agent for raising funds among the Baptist churches in the north of England. See *Missionary Herald* (July 1844): 383; BMS Committee Minutes, Vol. I (Jan. 1843-May 1844), ff. 73, 92, 176, 178.

[182]MAW, Box 39, JRULM.

neighbourhood where we have had a preaching station more than 20 years.

However I purpose to morrow taking the Cards to Bromley, & stating to our friends the substance of your letter, & if they cannot do any thing more at present they will have them on hand for a future & more convenient season. I hope that the Jubilee Fund is still being replenished, from the Xn liberality of our Churches; may it be increased a thousand fold! What a field for Miss^y enterprise is being opened in China! 300 & 50 millions of immortal beings enslaved by the god of this world & sunk in all the depths & degradation of idolatry, & awful thought, and no idolater hath any inheritance in the Kingdom of God. And a point will come up in Eternity when the misery of one of these lost spirits shall have exceeded all the completed misery of the whole human race! I wish my Dear Brother you could do any thing with our Society in reference to these perishing millions. I think if you could be an instrument in the hand of God of putting into operation means for the salvation of China it would add greatly to the splendor of your heavenly crown & afford you sublime satisfaction in a dying hour. I think [you] have it in your power sh^d the Society sanction such a means of deeply interesting the Xn public on behalf of the teeming millions of China I am sure you will not think me obtrusive in throwing out this hint. I have long less or more presented my feeble intercessions on behalf of this for distant & benighted land. Will you permit me to inquire if you could not find time to write an ~~paper~~ article for the Baptist Magazine on this subject! But I must conclude my Dear Brother with my best wishes & prayers that the Great Head of the Church may make you [an] eminent blessing Yours in Xn love

W Fisher

You need not trouble to return these letters.

P. J. Saffery

P. S. I sh'd have informed you that our young friends had Cards for the Jubilee, by which they collected several pounds.

208. Sarah Walker, 7 West Parade, Halifax, to Joseph Angus, Baptist Mission House, 6 Fen Court, Fenchurch Street, London, 2 January 1843.[183]

West Parade Halifax
January 2^d 1843

---

[183]MAW, Box 39 (BMS 2206), JRULM.

Sir,

In compliance with the request of Mr Saffery I forward the few garments my children have made for Africa and shall be glad if you can acquaint us with the probable time of Mr Clarke's departure for Africa as I hope with the aid of a few friends to furnish a Box of clothes or other articles for Fernando Po.

Esteeming it a great privilege to be engaged in this work & earnestly desiring that the blessings of the Lord may rest on our beloved Missionary friends I remain yours in Xtian regard

Sarah Walker

209. J. Peggs, Ilkeston, Derbyshire, to Joseph Angus, Fen Court, Fenchurch Street, London, 7 January 1843.[184]

Ilkeston, Derbyshire
Jan 7/ 43

My dear B^r

This is my *birth* day—*fifty* and I receive it as *a token* for good that I am favored to drop [along?] this parcel to my Miss. Brethren—There are 144 books & Pamphlets Please to forward the Packet for *Moffat* to the London Mission House *directly* Write me by *return of post* that my Parcel has reached you I send you my last Literary Child—-*The Gems for Schools*[185]—Treat it kindly for its father's sake

Yours sir

J. Peggs

210. J. Peggs, Ilkeston, Derbyshire, to Joseph Angus, Mission House, Fen Court, Fenchurch Street, London, 11 January 1843.[186]

Ilkeston, near Nottingham, Derbyshire
Jan 11 1843

My dear Friend

---

[184]MAW, Box 39 (BMS 2339), JRULM. Accompanying this letter is a printed letter, taken from the *Baptist Magazine,* by A. Sutton in Cuttack, India, to the Rev. J. Peggs at Ilkeston, Derbyshire, 13 June 1842, titled *British Support of Juggernaut's Temple*. Peggs would continue his attack on the Juggernaut for some time. See "Government Grant to Juggernaut's Temple," *Baptist Magazine* 37 (1845): 45-46.

[185]I can find no record of this title. Peggs may be referring to *Gems for Serious Christians,* which he published in 1842.

[186]MAW, Box 39 (BMS 2258), JRULM.

On Saturday I sent a large Parcel by Postman from Nottingham for the West Indies &c—I have not heard yet of its arrival—I hope to hear today—if you have not written then do write per *first* post—Your predecessor in Office introduced me to M[r] Poynder[187] & you must help me all [you] can in my poor efforts for India—I write now to request you to procure for me—"Correspondence between this Governor General of India the Court of Directors &c in reference to the abolition of certain Pilgrim Taxes." Ordered to be presented Aug 11. 1840—M[r] Poynder writes me these *Parliamentary Papers* may be obtained from the—*Journal Office* Abington St, Westminster Please to procure me these Papers, they are not copious & *send them*—I cannot rest till our Govt. remove this grant of 60.000 rupees per ann. to Juggernaut's Temple.

I wish you would ascertain Lord *Aucklands Address* & send him my letter This is for *another* Document—I tell you in confidence & propose to address a public Letter to Sir R. Peel[188] upon this matter—but I must have the *facts of the case*—

Your early attention will help

Yours &c

James Peggs

Read Lord Aucklands *Letter*[189]

---

[187]**John Poynder** (1779-1849) was a successful London lawyer and supporter of missions in India; his partner was **William Alers Hankey** of Fenchurch Street, who was also actively involved in numerous evangelical associations during his lifetime (see letter 240). Hankey, a Congregationalist, served as chair of a subsidiary meeting at Finsbury Chapel, London, during the annual gathering of the London Missionary Society, 12 May 1842. Hankey had published a pamphlet in 1840 condemning the British government's support of the Juggernaut through certain tax collections, the same topic being raised by Peggs in the above letter. Hankey had argued that the Brahmins often raised the issue of British support for idolatry in India as a reason for their rejecting Christianity. He writes, "'Why,' say they, 'do you find fault with our religion, when your own government openly supports it?' The Mahomedan rebuke is still more pungent, 'You may pile up your arguments from earth to heaven, they will never make me a Christian. You are idolaters, and we hate idolatry. We serve one God: you pretend to serve one God, and yet support idolatry. Since you ruled this country you have always paid for the support of idolatry; we never did. And you can support idolatry, and yet be Christians?'" See *Baptist Magazine* 34 (1842): 308; *Missionary Herald* (March 1848): 148-150.

[188]Robert Peel (1788-1850) was one of the leading English politicians of this period. He served many years as leader of the House of Commons before becoming Prime Minister briefly in 1835; he served again as Prime Minister from 1841 to 1846.

[189]George Eden (1784-1849), Earl of Auckland, a Whig politician in parliament for many years, served as governor-general of India from 1836 to 1842, succeeding Lord William Bentinck. His uncle was Lord Minto, a former governor-general of India. The latter reference here is most likely to Auckland's *India Revenue Letter*,

211. George Venables and the Rev. C. Venables, Wooburn, to Joseph Angus, Baptist Mission House, London, 11 January 1843.[190]

Rev Sir

As on other side is today sent to Mr Southgate Packer [illegible] change with directions "to pack & forward" the same by 1st Ship to

"Rev^d J Thomas"
"Baptist Mission House"
"Calcutta"

Hoping the same will be found correct & satisfactory I rem[ain] Revd Sir
Yrs very respe^y
George Venables
Rev C. Venables

212. Richard Pengilly,[191] *Newcastle-on-Tyne, to Joseph Angus, Secretary, 6 Fen Court, Fenchurch Street, London, 11 January 1843.*[192]

My dear Bro^r

My young friend Thos Thompson (a very worthy & pious young man, son of Henry Thompson of Paradise) who some time ago offered himself for the African Mission in the Capacity of a Engineer, or manager of the Engine of the Contemplated Steamer, is very desirous of knowing from you whether his services are *likely to be required*. If you would be so kind as just state *what you think of it* it would be very interesting to him and his friends.[193]

We sh^d also be glad if you would inform us whether Dr Prince is likely to be passing this way and when. It would be very desirable for him to spend an Evening here and another at Durham, if possible: one at least.

I would also thank you to give me the address of my old friend Mr Phillippo. United by my diminished family circle in love to you and yours I am yrs truly

Richd Pengilly

Newcastle Jany 11 1843

---

which was dated 15 March 1839 and published that same year. The earlier reference to an "Address" may be to this same *Letter.*

[190]MAW, Box 39 (BMS 2355), JRULM. Postmarked "Beaconsfield."

[191]**Richard Pengilly** (1782-1865), Baptist minister at Tuthill-stairs, Newcastle, 1807-1845.

[192]MAW, Box 39 (BMS 2378), JRULM.

[193]See letter 195.

213. Edward Cowper,[194] King's College, London, to [Joseph Angus], Secretary of the Baptist Mission [London,] 12 January 1843.[195]

To the Secretary of the Baptist Mission

King's College London
Jany 12 1843

Sir

Having attentively considered your letter, & the letter of Mr Gurney Esq & also the letter of your Missionary at Fernando Po relative to the communication from the Island to the Continent I am of opinion, that the various desiderata of—Sailing Power—Internal Power—Ease of management —safety—comfortable dwelling for the missionary & 10 or 12 persons beside—& facility of removal form a hostile position—will be best attained by,

An Iron Steam Boat about 70 or so feet long—with small Paddle wheels, capable of being disconnected from the Engine—A high Pressure *turbulated* (ie locomotive) Boiler—& a Single Engine of 20 Horse Power—& the boat be rigged for sailing & the Steam Power *subsidiary* to the Sailing Power—

Such a Boat & Engine well made (& no other ought to be ventured) would cost from 1500 to 2000£—the "Locomotive" Steam boat on the Thames cost 2000£ but your boat would not require so much power but would have rigging, which the "Locomotive" has not—

The Engine would occupy about 20 Feet having a good Cabin at each end of 25 or 30 feet, to which the Missionary might not only *retire* in case of annoyance, but in which he might *reside* while sojourning at any particular place—

An Iron Boat is preferable to wood in every respect, & I should strongly advise against a smaller boat, the missionary should have every physical comfort that the elasticity of his mind may be always ready for the great object of his heart, & for the same reason it might never to be his permanent duty to attend to the Engine although with instruction he might undertake the management occasionally—The Engine would require an Engineer & a Stoker—

---

[194]Edward Shickle Cowper (1790-1852) served for many years as head of the Department of Engineering at King's College, London. In cooperation with his brother-in-law, Augustus Applegath, he developed significant improvements in the newspaper printing press. His son, Edward Alfred Cowper (1819-1893), became one of the leading mechanical engineers of his day, supervising the redesigning of the Crystal Palace, 1852-1854. Cowper's recommendations, given in this letter, mirror almost exactly the specifications and design of the original *Dove*, the schooner purchased by the BMS in 1843 (see letter 239).

[195]MAW, Box 39 (BMS 2361), JRULM.

Sincerely wishing success to the cause you have at heart
I remain Sir
Yours respectfully
Edwd Cowper

214. J. M. Trew,[196] *African Civilization Society, 15 Parliament Street, to Joseph Angus, Fen Court, Fenchurch Street, London, 16 January 1843.*[197]

15, Parliament Street,
16th Jany 1843

Reverend Sir,
I am directed by the Vice Chairman of this Society to solicit the favour of your attendance at a Committee to be held at this Office on Wednesday the 25th instant at one o'clock precisely, on most important business.
I am Reverend Sir
Your very Obed^t Servt
J. M. Trew

Revd Joseph Angus Sec^y

215. George Bayley,[198] *[London], to William Gurney, Esq., Camberwell, 18 January 1843.*[199]

Dear Sir
Excuse me for troubling you once more with a line or two on the subject of a Baptist Mission to China[200] and first allow me to thank you

---

[196]John McCannon Trew (1792-1869) composed several pamphlets about African missions, including *Africa Wasted by Britain, and Restored by Native Agency, in a Letter to the Right Honorable and Right Reverend the Lord Bishop of London* (1843) and previously, *An Appeal to the Christian Philanthropy of the People of Great Britain and Ireland in behalf of the Religious Instruction and Conversion of Three Hundred Thousand Negro Slaves* (1826).

[197]MAW, Box 39 (BMS 2408), JRULM.

[198]**George Bayley**, Esq., Baptist layman from Camberwell and member of the Committee of the Baptist Building Fund and the Baptist Theological Education Society, as well as ship inspector ("surveyor") for Lloyd's Register of London.

[199]MAW, Box 39 (BMS 2420), JRULM.

[200]The request being put forth in this letter led to a donation of £500 in 1843 from the BMS Jubilee Fund to the American Baptist Foreign Missionary Society's operation in Hong Kong, proposed to the BMS Committee by Edward Steane of Camberwell on 22 March 1843. See Stanley, *History*, 175-178; BMS Committee Minutes, Vol. I (Jan. 1843-May 1844), f. 44.

for your prompt answer to my note of enquiry. I feel the force of your reasons as to the desirableness of keeping up the present stations at the same time I do think the interest that is now felt in China is such as would justify an attempt to raise a separate fund to support *one* missionary at Hong Kong. Who can baptize that mighty nation except Baptists!—shall Independents *sprinkle* their tens of thousands and shall not the Baptists immerse their thousands!—Honestly, my dear Sir, I think we *dare* not withold our missionaries from China.

As to morrow is the meeting of the Baptist Association at Park St could not the question be put to the meet'g in the following form—"Will you support one mission'y to China?" The Church to which I belong I feel some would contribute £20 pr anm to that object and I will undertake to collect it—will not *M*[r] *Steanes*[201] contribute another 20—*Park St*[202] another *Church St*[203] another—Lion St another[204]—Eagle St another[205] Devonshire Square[206] another?—I verily believe that were the question put that the several Pastors would pledge themselves to raise that sum without drawing one farthing from the funds of the Bap. Mission.

Only let the effort in collecting be quite *seperate* [sic] and specific and a commencement will be made immediately.

Could not a miss[y] be sent out with M[r] Dyer[207] to study the language at Hong Kong?—leaving this matter with You and earnestly hoping that at least an attempt will be made to support *one* miss[y] amongst the teeming mill[ns] of China   I am dear Sir
Yours truly

G B

---

[201]Steane's congregation at Denmark Place, Camberwell.

[202]New Park Street was formerly located in Carter Lane, where John Gill and John Rippon had previously pastored. Joseph Angus succeeded Rippon in 1836; James Smith followed Angus, ministering from 1841 to 1850. See Godfrey Holden Pike, *The Metropolitan Tabernacle; Or, An Historical Account of the Society* (London: Passmore & Alabaster, 1870) 138; W. T. Whitley, *The Baptists of London 1612-1928* (London: Kingsgate Press, 1928) 128.

[203]The Baptist church at Green Street (founded in 1785 by James Upton) moved to Church Street, Lambeth, Southwark, in 1801. At the time of the above letter, the pastor was George Cole, who came from Evesham and served at Church Street from May 1842 to July 1848. See Seymour J. Price, *Upton: The Story of One Hundred and Fifty Years 1785-1935* (London: Carey Press, 1935) 94-95.

[204]Lion Street Church was located in Southwark; the pastor was **Samuel Green**.

[205]Eagle Street, London, was led at this time by **Robert William Overbury** (1812-1868), minister from 1834 to 1853.

[206]Devonshire Square was pastored at this time by **J. H. Hinton.**

[207]**Samuel Dyer** (1804-1843), Congregationalist missionary to Malay, China, and Hong Kong, 1828-1843.

216. C. E. Birt, 10 Cave Street, Bristol, to [Joseph Angus, Baptist Mission House, London], 23 January 1843.[208]

10 Cave Street Jany 23rd

My dear Brother

I feel greatly obliged by your favor received yesterday and must cordially concur in your proposal of substituting specimens of the recent editions of the New Testament from our own press for the Wesleyan copy of the Cingalese Bible.

From the rank that Dr Richard holds not only professionally but as a Scholar I should be gratified by knowing that the illuminati might discover in his library proofs of the excellency attained in the Translation department of our Mission.

We have not heard from our dear Owen since the pilot left the ship. The few lines which he brought on shore and posted at Ryde were indeed most satisfactory but unless they meet a vessel in the way, there is now no expectation of hearing from them again till they have reached Ceylon—The late gales have tried our faith though we cherish the hope that the Sumatra may have got beyond their range.

There is one point which I undertook to ascertain from you in confidence as he felt fettered in it and that is whether the expenses of his journey to Portsmouth may be legitimately deducted from the twenty five pounds put into his hands as a provision for the voyage—This question I trust my dear friend you will accept as it is confidingly proposed and tell me most cordially what is the proper view of it—

I trust your health holds out under your abundant labors and with a grateful sense of your personal kindness and attention I am

My dear brother
Yours most sincerely
C. E. Birt

217. John Clarke, Irvine, [Ayrshire], to [Joseph Angus, Baptist Mission House, London], 24 January 1843.[209]

Irvine
Jany 24th 1843

My dear Bro,

---

[208]MAW, Box 39 (BMS 2456), JRULM.

[209]MAW, Box 39 (BMS 2504), JRULM. Apparently this is Clarke's second letter to the BMS concerning Cowper's comments about the steam vessel. According to the Committee's minutes, Clarke first letter was numbered 2473, but the letter is no longer extant. See BMS Committee Minutes, Vol. I (Jan. 1843-May 1844), f. 14.

The letter from Mr Cowper[210] is important as far as the sort of Boat most suitable for Africa is in consideration; but I think two very powerful objections arise against the size—The *first* is the difficulty of carrying such a Boat safely over the shallow bars,* & up the narrow rivers— the *second* is the expense such would annually entail on the society—all I could advise would be a Boat of 50 Tons; with a well constructed "*Low* Pressure" Engine—There is too much put upon the Boiler in the high pressure ones; and the danger of bursting is certainly greater—If I am not mistaken the construction of the "low pressure" Engine is more simple—more easily understood, and less liable to disarrangement—I however submit this opinion to those who are better acquainted with the matter than I am—The horse power should be suited to the size; and kept rather beyond than below, on account of our going against the stream when ascending the River—The London was sometimes useless on account of the weakness of her horse power which propelled her only about 5 miles, when she had sometimes a current of 7 miles per hour against her—I think, if there are strong doubts about the untried "*screw*,"[211] the paddle wheels should be preferred—Let us go on *surely* in a matter of such great importance—The advantage I have seen to the screw is simply for the sailing—paddle wheels must of necessity impede the progress a little—The screw is apt in Rivers where weeds abound to become entangled—this is perhaps the only real objection to its use—

In haste I remain yours very respectfully & affectionately
John Clarke

P.S. It is just post time & I hasten to close—alter the lines on the third page & improve them if you please I hope to be in London on Tuesday if well, but I am suffering again from a cold—

*The idea of a large boat impelled by oars is out of the question altogether. The Boat in which we went to Cameroons & Bimbia was of 15 Tons, & had oars, but they were comparatively useless. And indeed the hands could scarcely be prevailed upon to use them. The amount of labour of this kind is too great for a hot climate; and the difficulty of obtaining labourers to pull at such oars is always ~~impossible~~ very great. The shelter in such a boat would be of no value, & it would be useless, as a place to sleep in by night at the Towns we might visit—all these considerations combine to shew that a large boat impelled by oars is quite unsuitable for the work we contemplate in Africa
J. C.

---

[210]See letter 213.
[211]See letter 180.

218. Robert Gay,[212] *on board the barque* Hindoo, *in the Downs, London, to [Joseph Angus, Baptist Mission House, London], 28 January 1843.*[213]

Barque Hindoo
Downs Jan 28th 43

Dear Sir

I write as well as the rolling of the vessel will allow to inform you that we are now at Anchor off Deal with a strong gale from the N.W. but our confidence *good* in the skill of our Captain and the efficiency of the crew we meet with good treatment and are all as well as can be expected myself perhaps the best Mr and Mrs Hands[214] have retired to rest Mr and Mrs G. likewise the latter suffers more we expect to remain here if our anchor prove strong enough till we get a fair winds which I hope will not be long—all desire an interest in your prayers and to be affectionately remembered to the friends at the mission house.

I am Dear Sir
Your Obedt Servant
Robert Gay

Sat Eveng 7 oclock

219. Josiah Fletcher,[215] *Norwich, to unnamed correspondent, 2 February 1843.*[216]

Norwich, Feby 2nd. 1843

Dear Sir

I find from your Letter to Mr Gurney that I omitted to say that the Set of his works and 6 West Indies been sent for Bapt Theolog. Institution in consequence of an application signed I think by Mr Tinson—[217]

Your letter to Mr Gurney dated Jan 30 has been forwarded to me and Mr Gurney desires me to say you are at liberty to devote the 2 West

---

[212]**Robert Gay** (d. 1865), BMS missionary to Jamaica in 1842-1856.

[213]MAW, Box 39 (BMS 2508), JRULM.

[214]**Thomas F. Hands** (d. 1870), BMS missionary to Jamaica, 1842-1852.

[215]**Josiah Fletcher**, bookseller, publisher, and deacon in the Baptist church at St. Mary's, Norwich.

[216]MAW, Box 39 (BMS 2534), JRULM.

[217]A reference to the new educational institution at Calabar, Jamaica, organized by **Joshua Tinson** during his furlough in England, 1842-1843. His mission was a success; the school opened in October 1843.

Indies as you propose and direct me also to send Biblical & Notes 8vo &
Evags 8vo which I will do first free conveyance.
Y^rs respectfully
Josiah Fletcher

**220. *George K. Prince, Isleham, to Joseph Angus, Baptist Mission, 6 Fen
Court, Fenchurch Street, London, 8 February 1843.*[218]**

Isleham—8th Feb^ry 1843—

In the persuasion, Beloved Sir, that the Lord has guided me to the
decision, I have now liberty to inform you that I am willing to return to
Western Africa according to the desire of the Managing Committee of
our Missionary Society—My design is to serve my Heavenly Master by
making Him known to the Heathen & by rendering service to my Brothers in that peculiar calling in which he has called me—

One of the tokens of the divine pleasure concerning me in this matter, is the self denying obedience wrought by ~~Him~~ the Lord in the mind
of my very dear wife; she has freely offered herself a willing sacrifice, &
has laid down her material affections, & personal considerations upon
the altar of the Lord our Righteousness, by whose mercies to her own
soul she is constrained to present herself bodily, a lovely sacrifice unto
Him who will recompense her abundantly—Unitedly we commit ourselves into his hands as into those of a faithful Creator, & trust that that
Commitment is now made, & will be continually renewed, in well doing,
to the praise of Him who looketh effectually in those called according to
his purpose in Christ Jesus—

Our consideration of the arrangements preliminary & necessary to
the fulfillment of the service now agreed to may be postponed till I ~~shall~~
can have the satisfaction of conferring with you: Meanwhile I take
pleasure in relieving your mind of the anxious expectations in which
you have with so politely & practically awaited the decision of your
much obliged

Geo. K Prince

To Revd Jos. Angus—
Secretary to Baptist Miss^ry Soc^ty, London

---

[218]MAW, Box 39 (BMS 2576), JRULM.

221. Richard Johnson, Liverpool, to Joseph Angus, [Baptist Mission House, London,] 9 February 1843.[219]

Liverpool
9 Feb 1843

My dear Sir

I should have replied to y[r] favour sooner, but have been unable to ascertain any thing positive about the vessels for Africa Mess Fitzhugh Walker & Co's memorandum was a copy of our L'pool trade list & thus could only refer me to it.

The John Campbell & another called the Windermere, are suitable ships & do not sail for a month yet, but I cannot yet ascertain whether they will land passengers at Fernando Po, but hope to have their reply in a few days & will again write you, the "Martha" the vessel we wanted the Capt[n] to alter, only got away on Tuesday, she had been a little damaged in the late gales; I suppose it is still a Missionary & *Wife*, my difficulty is on account of the Lady, & please to say if they would go provided they had to land at Bonny & run the risk of being taken f[m] thence to Fernando Po, in the meantime believe me

Yours very truly
Rich[d] Johnson.

To Rev[d] J Angus A M

222. Richard Johnson, Liverpool, to Joseph Angus, Baptist Mission, 6 Fen Court, Fenchurch Street, London, 11 February 1843.[220]

L[iver]pool 11 Feb 1843

My dear Sir

I received y[r] favour this morning & now enclose the reply from Mess Maxwell's and as I have no idea what sum you will give for the passages to Africa, you had better inform me, & I will make as good bargain as I can, she is a fine vessel & hope there will be time enough for the Missionaries to get ready, but Mess M— could not determine sooner to send her first to Fernando Po, as it depended on their taking kroomen to the Coast, which I suppose now they do not, at all events it seems a favourable opportunity if there is time believe me

Yours very faithfully
Rich[d] Johnson

To Rev[d] J Angus A M

[219]MAW, Box 39 (BMS 2584), JRULM.
[220]MAW, Box 39 (BMS 2604), JRULM.

223. John Clarke, Penzance, to Joseph Merrick (care of the Rev. W. G. Lewis, Cheltenham[221]), 13 February 1843.[222]

Penzance
Feb[y] 13th *1843*

My dear Br & Friend,

I am rather taken by surprise in hearing of your expected departure for Africa—I had hoped we should in the end have gone out together; but God our Father knows what is best—His will be done—

I know not that I can advise you much respecting what you should take. I see no use at all for another Tent; as you are not likely to travel, I suppose, as we did, for some time—If you could take Pitch Pine Framing for a small House it might be serviceable but unless the Vessel is to call *positively* at Clarence Cove, you could do nothing with this at all. Bed-stead—Mattress etc.—a few hard wood chairs—plates etc. Hardware of all household sorts would be necessary—you can buy ship chairs and have Tables, & common bed steads made there, if you choose, but all are dear, & not very well made—The Table you might get there better than any other thing perhaps—you had best consult with M[r] W[m] Stanger,[223] & take care that he gives you plenty of paper, I shall never forget the distress I was in for want of writing paper—

You should have a good supply of flour, Sago, arrowroot—Salt, Candles—Lamp oil—a good lamp, a stove for drying the house in rainy weather—Coffee—Cocoa—Tea—Sugar—all the things they gave us when we went out—and a double supply, if possible that M[r] Sturgeon[224] may share with you—take a good dress each of Blanket clothing. Don't be afraid of its thickness—you will both of you want it in the rainy weather—Take a few pairs of shoes—one pair thick soled for the rains—good silk umbrellas—Light hats—Plenty of nails for Building of Locks &c a few—I shall bring more I hope with me when I come. Take some common knives, not clasp ones; and some "*Remnants*" for barter. I hope to see you ere you go—In the mean time write me to Plymouth, I shall be there again soon after the next Sabbath—If you write before Friday address me at Falmouth—

On Tuesday 21st I shall be at S[t] Anstell—then go to Plymouth for about a week or more. Thank you for the letters. M[rs] Clarke will send them to you when she has read them. I wish you had reminded me of

---

[221]**William Garrett Lewis** (1797-1865), Baptist minister at Cheltenham, 1842-1864.

[222]MAW, Box 39 (BMS 2650), JRULM.

[223]See letters 192, 202.

[224]See letter 179.

the Heb. Bible at Berwick—I have written Mrs Clarke to send it to Fen Court for you—

I am sorry to hear of your Boils, I hope you are now better—My work here is very hard, I have very little time for any thing, but travelling & speaking

I remain with warmest love to you & dear Mrs Merrick, your ever affectionate B^r & Friend

John Clarke

224. John Clarke, Falmouth, to Joseph Angus, 6 Fen Court, Fenchurch Street, London, 16 February 1843.[225]

Falmouth
Feby 16th 1843

My dear Brother,

I have too long omitted to acknowledge the kindness of many dear Friends who have deeply interested themselves on behalf of Africa— The only excuse I can offer is my perpetual traveling and engagements in ~~behalf~~ furtherance of their object, which is ever dear to me; and for the advancement of which I cheerfully offer myself to God, to live, to labour, and to die on the plains, or mountains, of Ethiopia—

I have ~~first~~ to acknowledge, with much gratitude, a valuable assortment of Nails, Screws, Padlocks, Tools, Ship implements, Knives, Plates, Frame,[226] Ironmongery of various sorts—Stationary—Bags, Neckerchiefs—Shawls—Prints (Cotton) Cloth Pinafores, & various Fancy & useful articles—Buttons—a Bag of Building Nails, (from Mr Miles of Henley in Arden) and various other articles, through our kind, and devoted Friend, Miss Morgan of Birmingham[227]—The Promise of a second supply of Needles from our venerable friend the Rev^d J Smith of Astwood[228]—Various presents of pen knives—pocket-knives, scissors &c from friends at Sheffield—the present of a Bible from a little girl who could not retain in her possession two Bibles while so many of her fellow creatures were without one—two testaments at Hook Norton for the children of our friend J. W. Christian & one from a friend at Berwick

---

[225]MAW, Box 39 (BMS 2691 1/2), JRULM. This letter appeared in the *Missionary Herald* (April 1843): 228-229.

[226]Printed letter has "pans."

[227]Possibly a relation of **Thomas Morgan** (1776-1857), Baptist minister at Bond Street in Birmingham, 1823-1853. Another possibility is that she was related to the Thomas Morgan who served as a BMS missionary in India, 1839-1882.

[228]**James Smith** (1770-1850), Baptist minister at Astwood, Worcestershire, 1813-1850.

to be given to some African who can read the word of God. A present of Books, & various other valuable articles, to Mrs Clarke, myself, & daughter from our liberal and devoted Friend, R Sherring Esq^e of Bristol.[229] Five Pounds for the purchase of Books, for my personal library, from our respected Friend, Mrs J. L. Angas of Newcastle[230]—valued personal presents from M^r & Mrs Prowse of Exeter—several Volumes of useful works for Africa, from Friends at Berwick—a Book on Africa from a Friend at Leeds—And to these favours I ought to add the universal interest, which has every where been manifested, towards the African Mission; and the great kindness which christian friends have been pleased to bestow upon myself—for these I am sincerely thankful to God, & to those dear B^{rs} & Sisters in Christ Jesus, among whom I have gone, and whose faces in the flesh I expect to see *no more*—If I live to reach the Mountains of Fernando Po, I shall reflect upon their kindness with deep gratitude, & interest; & there, as well as here, I shall pour out my heart in prayer to God, that prosperity of soul may ever attend all who feel for the Heathen, & seek to glorify God, and extend the dominion of Jesus, by sending among them the Gospel of his grace—As many inquiries are made respecting the articles most useful for Africa—I may add to the "Hints for clothing societies," already sent you, the following list as descriptive of the things which w^d be of greatest use to us in that Land—

Nails of all descriptions, for erecting Houses—Shingle Nails, etc. Carpenter's tools—Cooper's adzes—a turning lathe—Drilling tools—A large supply of axes, & hatchets—Fish hooks—lines—Cord etc. Common halfworn table knives are highly valuable—Strong Hoes, & Cutlasses, for agricultural labour—small grind stones, & sharping stones. Bill hooks; & Chisels, for digging up yams, as used in the West Indies— Looking glasses—~~magnifying & multiplying glasses~~—Caps— umbrellas—shoes—Cups—Tin plates—Iron pots &—Nets—& large lines for fishing in the sea. Writing paper, Memorandum Books, etc. Ink—Steel pens—Books in any of the languages of Africa; & Books on African History—Friends who may feel disposed to supply any of these articles for the benefit of the African Mission, w^d need to lose no time in forwarding them to Fen Court as M^r & Mrs Merrick are likely to sail for

---

[229]**Richard B. Sherring** was a prominent Baptist layman and member at Broadmead, Bristol; he was a generous benefactor of the BMS, contributing nearly £2000 in 1842-1843.

[230]Mary Angas (1775-1850) was the wife of John Lindsey Angas (1776-1861) and sister-in-law to **George Fife Angas** (1789-1878) (see letter 159). All were members of the Baptist church at Tuthill Stairs, Newcastle (the printed letter in the *Herald* spells her name "Angus"). She and her husband made a pledge of £100 to the Jubilee Fund in August 1842. See *Missionary Herald* (October 1842): 564.

Africa in a few weeks, & I do not expect to remain in England beyond the month of May—[231]

Mr. Sherring has been most liberal and kind. He has added to his former presents to me, the following, Hall's Works, in russia, Hall's Fifty Sermons, Doddridge's Works, and Expositor, complete in russia, Fuller's Works, ditto, Cuvier's Works, 11 guineas, Pritchard's Works, to include a volume in the press, Howe's Blessedness of the Righteous, a large bible, and several smaller works, all in russia, and in good binding.[232]

That the blessing of God may rest upon our efforts for His Glory, & that "Ethiopia may soon stretch out her hands unto God" is the prayer of my dear Brother, yours, most respectfully and sincerely,

John Clarke

225. W. R. Maxwell, King Street, [Liverpool], to Messrs. R. & R. Johns[t]on, Rumford Street, [Liverpool], 16 February 1843.[233]

Gent[n]

With reference to your Enquiry as to whether either of our Ships for Africa w[d] call at Fernando Po we have to say that the Windemere intended to sail in a week will do so— Passengers however being rather unusual to that quarter we are unable to name any rate but should your friends wish to go we doubt not an arrangement can be made—

We remain Gent[n]
Your [most] obt[t]
W. R. Maxwell

King St
16 Feb[y] 1843
Mess[rs] R & R Johnston   Rumford St.

226. A. Tidman,[234] Blomfield Street, London, to Joseph Angus, [Baptist Mission, 6 Fen Court, Fenchurch Street, London], 21 February 1843.[235]

---

[231]The Merricks would not sail until June 1843, with Clarke following close behind in August. The phrase "as M[r] & M[rs] Merrick are likely to sail for Africa in a few weeks" was deleted in the published letter.

[232]This paragraph is not in the autograph letter, but does appear in the printed letter, another example (see letter 206) of Angus lifting a passage from one letter and inserting it into another.

[233]MAW, Box 39 (no BMS number), JRULM.

[234]**Arthur Tidman** (1792-1868), Congregational minister who served in the office of the Foreign Secretary of the London Missionary Society, 1833-1868.

Blomfield St Feb 21

My dear Sir

I have much pleasure in sending the inclosed. You should have had it earlier but it was adopted only *last* Ev^g.

Yours very truly

A Tidman

Revd J Angus.

Our Petitions will be presented by the Marquis of Landsdown & Sir George Grey

Accompanying this letter is a MS. copy of a petition by the Directors of the London Missionary Society to the House of Commons, undated; Angus has marked through references and statements related to the LMS and replaced them with statements and figures relative to the BMS. Angus's additions to the text appear in {}.[236]

To the Honorable the Commons of the united Kingdom of Great Britain and Ireland in Parliament Assembled

The Petition of the undersigned the ~~Directors~~ Committee of the ~~London~~ Baptist Missionary Society Humbly Sheweth,

That your Petitioners are entrusted with the direction and management of an Institution, formed in London in the year 179~~5~~2, for the ~~sole object of spreading of Christ among heathen and other unenlightened nations'~~ diffusion of he Kingdom of Jesus Christ thro the heathen world, and that for the accomplishment of this benevolent and sacred design, the generous contributions of the Members of the Society, now exceed £80,000 per Annum.

That in addition to extended operations in the ~~Islands of the South Pacific Ocean, Africa and the West Indies~~ West Indies and Africa, the Society has prosecuted Missionary labors *in India* for more than ~~five and forty~~ 50 years, and that it has at present in that Country (including the Honorable Company's Territory and the protected States,) ~~51~~ 24 Missionaries, ~~373~~ 83 Europeans and Native Assistants, who occupy upwards of ~~120~~ 40 Stations; and that with these there are connected

---

[235]MAW, Box 39 (BMS 2687), JRULM.

[236]This petition was the result of a Proclamation by Lord Ellenborough concerning the restoration of the gates of the temple at Somnauth, which was laid before the BMS Committee on 16 February 1843. The Committee resolved that day to prepare a "Petition be prepared to be presented to each House of Parliament, expressing the views of this Committee, & praying that measures may be taken to counteract the effect of such Proclamation, & to prevent the recurrence of similar proceedings." See BMS Committee Minutes, Vol. I (Jan. 1843-May 1844), ff. 25-26.

nearly ~~500~~ 100 Schools, in which instruction is gratuitously afforded to ~~many~~ some thousands of the native population.

That encouraged by the measure of success which, under the blessing of God, has attended the various labors of the selfdenying and devoted Agents of ~~the Society~~ this and other kindred Societies, your Petitioners confidently anticipate, from the ~~unrestricted~~ general application of the same scriptural means, the gradual improvement of the Natives in knowledge, and in social habits; and the ultimate triumph of the Christian faith over the absurdities and abominations of ~~Idolatry~~ Heathenism.

That your Petitioners deeply sensible of the serious obstruction to the propagation of Christianity in India, which heretofore existed in the connection of the British Government with the idolatrous rites and ceremonies of the natives, have regarded the various measures adopted by Her Majesty's Government, and the Honorable the Court of the Directors of the East India Company, for the removal of this evil, with pleasure and thankfulness.

That under the influence of these feelings your Petitioners have read with deepest regret, and the most painful apprehensions the proclamation of the Right Honorable the Governor General of India, addressed to the Hindoo Chiefs and People, in which they are congratulated, in the strongest terms, on the victorious removal, by the united British and Native Army of the gates of an ancient Idol Temple [notorious for cruelty and licentiousness] from the Tomb of a Mussulman Conqueror at Ghuznee,[237] ~~accompanied by~~ while directions {are given} for the transmission of 'these trophies with all honor to the restored Temple of Sournanth.'[238]

That while your Petitioners abstain from pronouncing {an opinion} on the impolicy of ~~these measures~~ this measure, ~~and while they are unwilling to condemn the motives of His Lordship the Governor General in adopting such proceedings,~~ they entertain the strongest conviction that {{}by the native population of India{}}, ~~they~~ it will be regarded as {an} ~~expressions~~ of the highest honor, from the Representative of a Christian Nation to their false Gods, and that by ~~their~~ its direct tendency ~~they~~ it will operate as a formidable obstruction to the labors of the Christian Missionary, by strengthening the prejudices of the Mahometan and confirming the blind confidence of the {Hindoo} Idolater.

Your Petitioners therefore most earnestly pray that your Honorable House will adopt such measures as may be best calculated to counteract the influence of ~~these~~ this illjudged ~~measures~~ proclamation, and

---

[237]A reference to the battle between the combined British-Indian forces and the Afghans at Ghuznee on 23 July 1839 in the First Afghan War.

[238]Probably a reference to The Temple of Sarnath in Veranasi, northeast India, the place where Buddha delivered his first sermon.

to prevent the recurrence of proceedings so dishonorable to our character and so injurious to our influence as a {professedly} Christian Nation.

And your Petitioners will ever pray &c

227. John Clarke, Grampound, Cornwall, to Joseph Angus, 6 Fen Court, Fenchurch Street, London, 22 February 1843.[239]

Grampound, Cornwall
February 22ᵈ, 1843

My dear Bro,

The services at Plymouth, & in that quarter, continue until the 2ᵈ of March—The Bristol Friends say they wish a meeting on my return—I shall write to say that, if they continue to think this necessary, they must correspond with you on the subject—Will you bear in mind that I wish my Daughter placed at Walthamstow[240] next month, if proper—and think it right, & *necessary*, that I should go to Berwick to bring up Mʳˢ Clarke & Child—I wish Mʳˢ C— to see Margᵗ several times at Walthamstow ere we embark for Africa; and wish the poor child to be acquainted there, ere she is finally separated from her Mother—

I wish also to obtain, either for a personal or a Station Library, the Tract Society's works—& should thank you, or some other friend, to give me a list of Books *beyond*: which you might think necessary for my use in Africa—of course, if Mʳ Hewett[241] will send the money in time, I shall be able to pay for all, from the sale of my Books in Jamaica—

I paid to Mʳ Stanger a Bill of from £3 to £4—for Books sent to Bʳˢ Oughton & Dendy in Jamaica—These were a present from me for their kindness in affording me so much hospitality & kindness in that Land—the Books were on Africa; & will, I hope, do good, in imparting light respecting Africa to these Bʳⁿ &c who may read them

I remain yours very respectfully, & affectionately,

John Clarke

P.S. Will you apply to the secretaries of the different Missionary Societies, who have [paper torn] in Africa, for a set of their Books in African languages and for any Reports giving information on the state & manners of the Natives of those tribes among whom Missionaries labour:

---

[239]MAW, Box 39 (BMS 2716), JRULM.

[240]Walthamstow was home to the school for the children of missionaries led at this time by Joseph John Freeman (see letter 163).

[241] Edward Hewett (see letter 205).

Please to include South, & East African dialects; and refuse nothing that pertains to *any* part of Africa.

J. C.

228. C[harles]. Kirtland,[242] Newark, to Joseph Angus, [Baptist Mission House, London,] 24 February 1843.[243]

Newark Feb[y] 24th 1843

My Dear Bro[r]:

The accompanying parcel from M[rs] Kirkland and female friends is for M[r] Merrick to take to Africa. They would have been sent before but we have been waiting for several of the garments & did not get them until Wednesday. I am sorry we could not send more, but our friends are able to do but little, still though ~~it is~~ we know, it is a willing offering and will help to clothe a few of the naked daughters of Africa. I hope our dear brother will have a safe passage and meet with a cordial reception among the sable tribes. I have thought much, very much on this deeply interesting mission and shall not cease to pray for its success

Sincerely yours
C Kirkland

The following is a list of the articles. 3 gowns—5 Frocks—2 Aprons. 2 Womens under garments—5 childrens do—3 Pinafore's—6 Handkerchiefs—1 Pair Stockings—1 Pair Shoes—2 Fanny bags. In all 30 articles. Please to acknowledge the receipt of them in the Herald—

229. John Clarke, Plymouth, to Joseph Angus, 6 Fen Court, Fenchurch Street, London, 24 February 1843.[244]

Plymouth—Feb[y] 24th *1843*

My dear Bro[r]

---

[242]**Charles Kirtland** (1811-1886), Baptist minister who worked with the London City Mission in Holborn, the Norwich City Mission, and the Baptist Home Missions in Nottingham and Newark, 1835-1846. A letter from Kirtland to Angus, dated 17 November 1841, from Newark, detailing his work in home missions, appeared in the *Quarterly Register of the Baptist Home Missionary Society* (December 1841): 681-683.
[243]MAW, Box 39 (BMS 2794), JRULM.
[244]MAW, Box 39 (BMS 2733), JRULM.

Your arrangements please me well, as I see Berwick is in them—Mʳ Sherring[245] presses hard for my return by Bristol—Is this possible? I refer him to you for an answer—He offers to send the £50 by me to your hand—

The long letter from Jameson[246] I left in your hand, with the request that you wᵈ send a copy of it to Edinburgh—The people there are quite impatient about it—I hope you will find it and send a copy without delay—The letter of acknowledgments I wrote as soon as even I obtained half a day's leasure [sic] to find the necessary information—I sent it without regard to the time of the coming out of the Herald, to appear, simply, *as soon as possible*—I do not yet know whether any use has been made of my letter upon "Clothing Societies"—It is called fondly for by those to whom I read it in Edinburgh, & looked for by others—My letter of acknowledgments will not be fully understood unless that on "Clothing Societies" appears first—

I decidedly think that if the Houses belonging to the W. A. Company[247] at Clarence can be bought for £1500 it should be done—But bear in mind that althoʰ the houses &c are well worth this sum to us—they are in a Miserable state, & will need sums paid out in their repair—I mean 4 of them out of the five—Let no claim be Paid to the Town itself, except with the determination to do justice to all the people who have homes there, by giving them a title to them—This they shᵈ have had; *but have not* at present—It will do us immense good to begin our work with this act of justice—More of this when I see you—

I am taken by surprise about the Schooner—while I do not wish to take the responsibility of being the *alone* adviser for a steamer, yet my mind after a night's reflection comes to the same conclusion as before, that only by means of a small steamer—I care not how small (if she will live in a Tornado) can our work be begun on the Continent of Africa—To lie for days in a Schooner becalmed, when a few hours would take us to our desired Port, will be a great loss of time—to say nothing of other inconveniences—I think the great error we are likely to fall into is in

---

[245]See letter 224.

[246]William Jameson (see letter 190).

[247]The West African Company of London was one of the primary agents in the economic development of Fernando Po between 1836 and 1843, when it withdrew and sold its properties to the BMS as part of a program to help freed slaves from the West Indies to resettle in Africa (see letters 236 and 242). This program, however, was stalled by the takeover of the island by the Spanish, who would eventually expel the BMS from the island. Clarke's letter was read before the BMS Committee on 2 March 1843, after which the Committee authorized Angus to propose the sum of £1500 for the purchase of the property. See Martin Lynn, "Commerce, Christianity and the Origins of the 'Creoles' of Fernando Po," *Journal of African History* 25 (1984): 258-259. BMS Committee Minutes, Vol. I (Jan. 1843-May 1844), f. 33.

having a Vessel which on account of size will not answer our purpose for going up Rivers & Creeks to the various Towns we desire to visit— Still if it is really so that a Vessel of 70 Tons is large enough to navigate the Atlantic—(Mr Wheeler's was 100 Tons) then such a Vessel could be procured, & might go once or so, to Cameroons, Calabar, & Bonny, & other navigable Rivers, & if she was found almost useless for our purpose, afterwards she might be sold; & perhaps at some distant time the required Vessel might be got—but I quite see that we could not do so much good by means of a Schooner in making the Gospel known in many parts; or in visiting, regularly, our B^{rs} stationed in untried fields— I still doubt exceedingly whether a Schooner of 70 Tons could carry provision, water, etc. etc. for the supply of 20 passengers, or more, and Crew—The matter is a difficult one, and much wisdom is required: for the salvation of many souls, humanly speaking, depends upon the plan we shall pursue—I shall be glad to hear of Mr Merrick & of his prospects of going, *or not*, before us—I hear Dr Prince now agrees to go[248]

Ever yours in affectionate love

J C

230. John Clarke, Plymouth, to W. W. Stanger, 6 Fen Court, Fenchurch Street, London, 27 February 1843.[249]

Plymouth
Feby 27th 1843

My dear Brother,

The interest you take in African affairs I shall ever remember with much feeling, and do, & ever shall, rank you among the sincere friends of that dark land—I am of opinion that we may begin missions on some of the rivers by means of a Schooner, but am also convinced that no regular means of communication can be kept up with these stations without a Steam Boat—I really do not care how small the Steam Boat might be, nor how slow its progress, when compared with larger ones—all I desire is power to go to the Rivers regularly; and around the Island when it might be found necessary to do so—I have no objection to a Schooner to take Missionaries from Jamaica; but I think a small Steamer ought not to be given up—I know the Committee will start at the idea of having both—but if the Schooner was not required for keeping up a regular communication with Jamaica, she could be sold to good

[248]Prince returned to Fernando Po in the spring of 1843, several months ahead of Clarke and Merrick.
[249]MAW, Box 39 (BMS 2750), JRULM.

advantage, I dare say, in Africa, or in the West Indies—If we don't attempt great things, we need not expect them—I expect much from Jamaica, & hope that no such excessive expense is to be incurred, as has been in the case of the Cambden—

We have two men who are Practical Engineers—one at Newcastle,[250] another in Mr Horton's Church at Devonport[251]—what then stands in the way of taking out a small Iron Steam Boat in parts, & having her put together there; and engaging these two men as Missionaries, as well as Engineers for Africa?—

I have seen the difficulties in the way from the first, but do not think them insurmountable—I hope soon we shall find a place for the Ark, on the Mountains of the Cameroons & then our way into the vast Interior will gradually open—

I remain your ever affectionate
B^r & Friend
John Clarke

P.S. Love to your Father, Mother, and dear Family
P.S. The Engineer here is employed in the Government dock yard, & would give up all immediately to go to Africa—Mr Horton speaks very highly of him—Another fine young man in the same Church wishes to go as a Missionary to Africa—

231. John Clarke, Plymouth, to Joseph Angus, 6 Fen Court, Fenchurch Street, London 27 February 1843.[252]

Plymouth
Feby 27th/43

---

[250]Thomas Thompson (see letters 195, 212).

[251]**Thomas Horton** (1796-1877), Baptist minister at Morice Square, Devonport, 1820-1850. The "engineer" Clarke is referring to in the above letter is **Alfred Saker** (1814-1880), who later became an important BMS missionary at the Fernando Po mission in Africa. Letters from Thompson and Saker were placed before the Committee on 9 March 1843; recommendation letters from Pengilly and Horton were presented on 16 March. In June, Saker wrote to the Committee recommending a Mr. Benson, "a coloured man" from America, as a sailor for the new Mission vessel to be employed in Africa. In late July, Saker and Thompson were asked to meet with the Committee in London, with Saker being required to pass a physical examination. Saker did so and sailed for Jamaica and then Africa, along with John Clarke, on the *Chilmark* the next month. See BMS Committee Minutes, Vol. I (Jan. 1843-May 1844), ff. 36, 40, 89, 98, 101, 107.

[252]MAW, Box 39 (BMS 2755), JRULM.

My dear Bro,

I should greatly delight in seeing you, and also Mr Hanson for an evening in London, but it seems impossible at present—I hope Mr Hanson will not have left ere I return to London in April—My views about the Steamer I have given hastily to Mr W. Stanger—I have [an] interesting letter from Mr Clark of Brown's Town, & from Mr Francies, but hear nothing at all from Mr Hewett—My mind is very uneasy on account of his conduct—not so much on account of the matters themselves, as on account of the view it gives me of character, but I must not judge too hastily—

The conduct of the Presbyterians & Independents is disgraceful in the extreme—Mr Jameson of Goshen has published a letter in Jamaica newspapers giving up his connection with the Af. Civ. Society, because they offer to encourage our Mission at Fernando Po, when I have so rashly baptised in 13 months 13 persons, & allow these to do what they can to bring others to Jesus!! What does such a man say of the conduct of Andrew & of Philip? & of Jesus himself in sending the cured demoniac to his father's house!!!

In haste I remain your affectionate B^r
John Clarke

P.S. I had four engagements yesterday & was most excessively tired, & worn out in mind—I feel a little recovered today—I stop at Mrs Ignare's—Miss E. Ignare is a devoted friend to the Missionary Cause—

232. Richard Pengilly, Newcastle-on-Tyne, to Joseph Angus, Baptist Mission, 6 Fen Court, Fenchurch Street, London 27 February 1843.[253]

Newcastle on Tyne
Feby. 27. 1843.

My dear Bro.^{r}

I am not quite sure that it would be deemed presumptive in Country Brethren if they were to suggest any thing to London Committees in the direction of our Missionary Institutions. If you know it would be so, then the following suggestion you will not allow to go beyond yourself.

I have thought that if a Steamer sh.^{d} be resolved upon for the African Coast & Rivers in connexion with our Mission, requiring those persons who may be engaged to take charge of the working of her, to be constantly on board, or in attendance upon her,—As the vessel would not be every day, or every week, required in the service of the Mission, *she might be frequently employed in the common use of Steam vessels, in*

---

[253]MAW, Box 39 (BMS 2771), JRULM.

conveying Passengers or goods from one Port or place to another, and thereby work for her own support, and of course prevent any expense on the Funds of the Society, and yet as *fully serve* her original purpose as if not so employed.

I leave the suggestion with you, to state it to the Committee, or not, as you think proper.

My young friend, Tho.ˢ Thompson, has not received any communication as was promised. If you write to him perhaps you had better enclose it to me as his residence (3 miles down the Tyne) might occasion difficulty to the Post office

I am glad you have booked Mr Phillippo for us at the close of the Summer.   I am

Affect^{ly} yours
Richd Pengilly

Our circle & yours are all pretty well. Deo gratia!

233. John Clarke, Plymouth, to Joseph Angus, 6 Fen Court, Fenchurch Street, London, 28 February 1843.[254]

Plymouth
Feb. 28th/43

My dear Bro,

I have rec^d a request from Bristol to attend meetings in May—I hope you will not, *on any account*, engage me for a date beyond the London Meetings in April—as it will then be full time for me to rest a few days in quiet to prepare for a speedy departure to the *proper* sphere of *my* labours—I wish to write you at great length about the Steamer, could I find time—I am afraid all is going wrong in this matter, and that a plan is about to be adopted which will prevent thousands from hearing the Gospel for many years to come—

My opinion is that a ship could be freighted to go by Jamaica for the first Missionaries, far cheaper than to buy one for this purpose—Indeed if you do not keep such a Vessel as the Schooner you propose constantly going to Jamaica and England I do not see what we can do with her in Africa—for next to a little 30 Tons steamer, a sort of Gravesend boat would be the only thing we could well manage in the Rivers we wish to visit—But ~~every~~ a common sailing boat, or Schooner must have great disadvantages connected with Navigation in the part of the world for which ~~they~~ we require it—The risk of life is such that you out [ought]

254MAW, Box 39 (BMS 2777), JRULM.

not to lose sight of this point—risk from getting sick in long calms—risk from not being able to remove soon an invalid to a more healthy spot—risk in getting aground near dangerous tribes at a distance from large & frequented Towns—Excuse this hasty scrawl—I have scarcely had time today to withdraw to write it—I have written to Mr Winter[255] to say I cannot engage for May but will see him on the 9th—

ever yours in love

John Clarke

234. George Bayley,[256] 1 Addington Place, Camberwell, to Joseph Angus, Walworth, 7 March 1843.[257]

1 Addington Place Camberwell

March 7, 1843

My Dear Sir

Having to leave town in the morning for Yarmouth I shall not be able to meet you at Fen Court on the African Mission as I fully intended to have done—However, as you are already aware of my opinions upon the relative advantages and disadvantages of the two kinds of vessel proposed to be employed—it is perhaps undesirable for me to trouble you with any further remarks on the subject than to say subsequent reflection upon the various points which came under discussion at your house, have only confirmed me in the opinion I here expressed.—viz.

That looking to the practicable means at the disposal of he Committee—a sailing vessel will be the least costly in the first purchase, less expensive ~~in~~ to maintai~~ning~~ in an efficient state, and not so liable to be put *hors de combat*[258] as a Steam vessel—

On the other hand, a Sailing vessel will not move from place to place against contrary winds and currents with the same facility as a Steam Vessel.

With respect to the communication with the West India Islands from Fernando Po—the distance is too great to be attempted with the slightest chance of success by a Steam Boat of the Size and Build adapted for the African Rivers.—If therefore a Steam Boat he decided

---

[255]**Thomas Winter** (1790-1863), Baptist minister at Counterslip, Bristol, 1823-1860.

[256]See letter 215.

[257]MAW, Box 39 (BMS 2826), JRULM.

[258]The phrase means "out of action."

upon for the Rivers, a Sailing vessel must be provided for the communication with Jamaica.—if that connection is to form part of the plan—

Bear in mind, that the annual cost of maintaining a Steam Boat of the size and accommodation required for the Rivers & the Island will be from £800 to £1000 P.ʳ Annum—with the constant danger of injury and loss that is irreparable in Africa.—

A Sailing vessel, can always be manned by natives some of whom are already well known as useful & efficient Seaman—and the probable injuries are all reparable with the means and materials at nearly all times within reach of her crew,—

I send with this a drawing of a Steam Boat of 97 Tons—by which you will see that even by putting in a short compact Boiler not more than 20 feet of available length can be obtained for cabins—and when the Steam is high those cabins must be extremely hot.—

The drawing you will have the goodness to keep in your own possession and return to me after the meeting.—

I am Dear Sir
Yours Truly
George Bayley

Revᵈ J Angus—

235. Andrew Armstrong, Stirling, to [Joseph Angus, Baptist Mission House, London], 7 March 1843.[259]

Stirling 7 March 1843

Dear Sir

I have a nephew, a promising young lad going out to Columbo in Ceylon, as a clerk to a mercantile house there, and wish to introduce him to Mr Daniell[260] though I am not personally acquainted with the latter, but think I have seen in a late Herald that Mr D. might be under the necessity of coming home in bad health, would you suppose that he may have left that by 3 or 4 months—if so would you favor me with the name of any other Baptist Missionary there to whom I may introduce my friend it may be an advantage to him—I regret Mʳ Harris' return;[261] you must just send out more—I am Dear Sir very cordially yours

Andrew Armstrong

---

[259]MAW, Box 39 (BMS 2850), JRULM.
[260]See letter 194.
[261]**Joseph Harris**, BMS missionary to Ceylon, 1837-1843.

P. S. I have been a Baptist for upwards of 30 years Mr Daniell's name is familiar to me through the Bap.^t Mag.^e before he left England—

A A

236. D. W. Witton, Vice Chairman, West African Company, Levant House, St. Helens Place, London, to Joseph Angus, Baptist Mission, 6 Fen Court, Fenchurch Street, London, 9 March 1843.²⁶²

Levant House, St Helens
9th March 1843

My dear Sir,
I have laid before the Committee of Management of the West African Company, your two letters (addressed to me) of the 3^d in^st and this day respectively, the former offering on behalf of the Baptist Missionary Society the sum of £1500 for the Company's Possessions in the Island of Fernando Po.²⁶³
In reply, I am desired respectfully to inform you, that the Committee decline accepting the offer in question.

I remain
My dear Sir
Yours very truly
W. Witton
Vice Chairman

Revd Joseph Angus
Secre^ty to the Baptist Missionary Society

A note in pencil, opposite the signature, in an unknown hand, reads:

I fear that the Government are likely to offer. I have not however seen Mr Witton.

237. William Brown,²⁶⁴ 5 Standishgate, Wigan, to [Joseph Angus, Baptist Mission House, London,] 14 March 1843.²⁶⁵

---

²⁶²MAW, Box 39 (BMS 2852 1/2), JRULM. Witton's letter was read before the Committee on 22 March 1843. Within six weeks, however, Witton and the West African Company would change their mind and agree to the purchase price of £1500. See BMS Committee Minutes, Vol. I (Jan. 1843-May 1844), ff. 42-43; 67.
²⁶³See letter 229.
²⁶⁴**William Brown**, founding member in 1827 of the Baptist church at Wigan.

Wigan Mar 14 1843
5 Standishgate

Rev Sir

I hope you will excuse the liberty I take, in requesting you to furnish me with the address of some Missionary, or Mission Agent, or pious individual at Madras; who would be likely to procure for me, some information, of the circumstances attending the death of a younger brother; who, though having two diplomas as a Surgeon and Apothecary, threw up his prospects; and, following the bent of his depraved nature, and his fondness for intoxicating drinks, entered the service of the East India Company, and died a gunner at Madras. Trusting your Christian kindness will excuse my freedom

I am Rev Sir
Yours faithfully
William Brown

238. F. Allport,[266] *98 Gracechurch Street, London, to Joseph Angus, Baptist Mission, 6 Fen Court, Fenchurch Street, London, 17 March 1843.*[267]

98 Gracechurch St
17th March 1843

Dear Sir

You will perceive by the above that I have embark'd on a business in which your kind recommendation may at times be of much service & I hardly need add that I would do my best to deserve it—

I have started with Captn Wimble (formerly of the "London" and "Maidstone") as Ship and Insurance Brokers & although we have just at present only *East* India Ships—yet we are prepared to do our best for any friends that may give us an opportunity with reference to any part of the World.

---

[265]MAW, Box 39 (BMS 2938), JRULM.

[266]Allport, as this letter reveals, had recently partnered with a Capt. Wimble in forming a shipping business at the corner of Gracechurch Street and Leadenhall Street. Allport's letter to Angus was written on company stationary advertising six ships that had been built by Messrs. Wigram of Blackwall, all departing from Gravesend bound for Madras or Calcutta, with shipping operations being conducted by Allport's firm. One of the ships is the *Maidstone* (1000 tons), mentioned in this letter.

[267]MAW, Box 39 (BMS 3066), JRULM.

I enclose Cards of our India Ships & shall feel obliged by your placing [them] any where under the notice of those who may by any probability be looking thitherward.

May I request the favor of your handing the accompanying note to my kind friend Mr Gurney—just stating the substance of the above

With respects to M^rs A.

I am My dear Sir

Yours faithfully

F. Allport

Revd J. Angus

239. G. K. Prince, Bridgwater, to Joseph Angus, [Baptist Mission House, London], 21 March 1843.[268]

Bridgwater—21 Mar. 1843

My dear Sir—

I hope Mr Evans[269] will be at liberty to preach at New Park St & that his promise to have a farewell at John S^t for the Afr. Miss^ies has gratified you—he expressed himself much pleased on Thursday even^g & several of his people were pleased to Manifest their interest in this Mission, & of the ladies some mean to prepare a box for F^do Po—he thinks the members will be glad to correspond with us abroad and will have their sympathies quickened by the Connexion.

Mr Crowther, the black Catechist who accompanied Mr Schou from the Coast with the Niger Vessels to Fer^do Po is ab^t to be ordained for Afr.[270] & I think it more than likely that there is some intended connexion between that purpose & the one wh: Mr Trew is urging for adoption in his pamphlet addressed to Bishop of London, for a Normal institution in *our* island—I daresay (for I have not had the opp^ty for read^g it) your attention wo^d not be ill bestowed by a perusal of "Africa wasted by Britain & restored by Native Agency"—[271]

I have taken fright at a favorable notice of it in a provincial paper, which hopes that the Ch. Of Engl^d will *lead the way* in the island of F. Po.

---

[268]MAW, Box 39 (BMS 3030), JRULM.

[269]**James Harington Evans** (1785-1849), minister at John Street Chapel in London, 1818-1848.

[270]**Samuel Ajayi Crowther** (c.1807-1891) would later serve as bishop of Western Africa for the Anglican Church, 1864-1891.

[271]*Africa Wasted by Britain, and Restored by Native Agency, in a Letter to the Right Honorable and Right Reverend the Lord Bishop of London* (London: J. Hatcherd, 1843).

& take [illegible] possession, else some others will, & thus deprive it of that honor! I have a thought of open^g the Eyes of that Editor of limited Mis^{ry} information

As soon as I finish the Somersetshire tour, I should like to be at liberty (if the occasion sho^d be still existing) to go to Liverpool to provide for & to inspect accommodations for Sea—& from thence I cou^d go to Edin^h where I have business to transact before my final departures—

The Glentaura is advertised as having arrived on the 17th at Livrp^l from Bonney & Ferd^o Po—last the 25th Decr so I hope the W Afr Co have intelligences that may help to close our business with them, & that you have been put in possession of fresh & welcome news from Mr & Mrs Sturgeon.

I trust that the business upon which our quarterly Com^{ee} will deliberate tom^w will issue to the promotion of this Afr. Mission.

I shall lament if the Steamer be vaporised & our hopes be made visionary—Mr Simpson in his brief acc^t of the Niger Expedition ~~says~~ reports many things favorable to our Mission at F. Po—& has a striking paragraph expressive of the desires of King Agua at Cameroons[272] for religious instruction, tis most impressively in unison with Christian's report to this same effect of his visit to Agua's people. Oh I trust the Spirit will give faith to our Managers to observe practically ~~what~~ the recorded saying which the Soc^{ty} has borrowed for a motto one of its earliest & most revered originators—[273]

----

[272]For Simpson and his *Private Journal kept during the Niger Expedition*, see letter 200. Agua was one of the chieftains of the Cameroons to whom Clarke and Prince were given letters of introduction by Col. Nicholls in 1840. See Cox, *History*, 2:360.

[273]Clarke would partially win this battle with Angus and the Mission Committee, which chose to purchase, not a sailing schooner, which he feared they would do, but rather a seventy-ton ironclad steam-powered schooner, the *Dove*, complete with an Archimedes screw (see letter 180) to be used for the transportation of missionaries to Jamaica and West Africa. The ship was built by John Laird of Birkenhead in 1843 at a cost of £2,140. An engraving of the ship appeared in the *Missionary Herald* (October 1843): 541, with a detailed description on the following page. An announcement of the launch of the *Dove* from the shipyard in Liverpool on 11 November 1843 appeared in the *Missionary Herald* (December 1843): 683; in the brief notice, a writer for the *Liverpool Standard* was quoted as saying, "We do not remember to have seen a vessel of more beautiful model, or one more likely to be found a good sea boat in a gale, and swift sailer under ordinary circumstances." Such was not the case, however, for by the end of January 1844, the BMS Committee declared the Dove "not seaworthy for both sailing & steaming purposes." An agreement was reached between Laird and the Committee, in which a new boat would be built, using the engines and paddles from the old boat. The cost of the boat (now 90 feet in length) was valued at £1300 and would be ready in four months. Half the loss of the first boat would be covered by the BMS, and the other half by Laird, who was also responsible for removing and transferring the engines to the new boat. In August 1844 a subcommittee was formed "to ascertain the qualities of the 'Dove' as

Please oblige me with some succinct references to the very interesting objects upon wh. I have touched, as soon after they have been
deliberated upon as you can & to the care of Mr Baynes, Wellington[274]

I am Dear Sir, with much esteem,

Yrs   Geo. K. Prince

*240. J. Peggs, Ilkeston, Derbyshire, to Joseph Angus, Baptist Mission, 6
Fen Court, Fenchurch Street, London, 21 March 1843.*[275]

Ilkeston Derbyshire
March 21. 1843

My dear Sir

---

a sea-going vessel, & to report thereon to the Committee." The next month Laird's
new ship was tested by Captain Walters (the Dove's first captain who resigned
shortly before the ships maiden voyage), who "fully approved of her qualities as a
sea-going Boat." Shortly thereafter George Bayley, the ship inspector for Lloyd's
Register, gave his approval to the ship. The ship was completed and sailed for
London in December 1844 while final arrangements for its purchase were being
carried out between Laird and the BMS Committee. In January 1845 the BMS
Committee announced that they were "fully satisfied" with the "fitness" of the *Dove*
"for the service for which she is designed, and of her sailing qualities." On 27 January
1845, a dedication service was held on board the *Dove* and on 4 February it left
Gravesend for Cowes where the missionaries would embark and sail from thence to
Fernando Po. The pilot (Thomas Milburn) wrote that "a finer vessel cannot be:
indeed I cannot say too much for her qualifications. She is uncommonly stiff under
canvas." By 1847, Clarke had come to believe the ship was not fulfilling its original
design and urged the BMS to sell it. As these letters reveal, Clarke had wanted a
steam-powered boat small enough to be effective in the rivers of West Africa. The
BMS opted for a boat large enough to handle the Atlantic Ocean, but one, they
thought, small enough to maneuver along the African rivers; that apparently was not
the case. It may also be that the maintenance costs of the boat played just as large a
role in its demise. In February 1850, a BMS sub-committee report noted that "owing
to the expense attendant upon the maintenance of the Dove . . . immediate steps
[should] be taken to bring her home or to dispose of her in Africa." In 1853 the *Dove*
was sold for £300 to a local trader in West Africa. For a drawing of the *Dove*, see
Baptist Magazine 35 (1843): 541; *Missionary Herald* (January 1845): 48; (March
1845): 158-59; Geoffrey R. Breed, "The *Dove*," *Baptist Quarterly* 40 (2004): 440-42;
Payne, *First Generation*, 79. (f. 188); BMS Committee Minutes, Vol. H (Oct. 1841-Dec.
1842), ff. 192; Vol. I (January 1843-May 1844), ff. 9, 14, 27, 29-30, 33, 35, 64, 70,
182, 186-88, 201; Vol. J (May 1844-July 1847), ff. 8, 28-29, 40, 43.

[274]**Joseph Baynes** (1795-1875), Baptist minister at South Street, Wellington,
Somersetshire, 1820-1861.

[275]MAW, Box 39 (BMS 3049, JRULM.

When I returned from Chesterfield I found your letters—These printed letters may serve your purpose. But I have the pleasure to inform you that through your *valuable* favor of Lord Aucklands Dispatch I have addressed a *printed* Letter to Sir Robt Peel B^t.[276] on the present note of British Connexion with Idolatry in India & Ceylon &c—

It is printed by *Snow*.[277] Paternoster Row £50 price 1/— Please to send to *Snows* for two or three copies to be forwarded to *your* correspondent at *Poynder, Hankey*[278] &c— N. pp. 8, 9 and 45—you will see *recent* information about the [illegible word] festival.—

The enclosed was returned to me addressed to Mr Davis. Please send me the names of some of your active men in *British America* that I may send some parcels of my books to them & to the [Donnia?] library. You have not acknowledged my books in the *Herald*; Peels Pamphlets costs me £20. Help me to circulate it, and to pay for it too. One friend has sent me £5. He lives near *Peterboro*—a strong eccentric man.—*T. B. Ward Esq.*[279] Stand ground—Apply to me for your objects

Yours &c—

J. Peggs

241. T. R. Williams, Merryvale, near Narberth, Pembrokeshire, to [Joseph Angus, Baptist Mission House, London], 21 March 1843.[280]

Merryvale
Near Narberth
-    March 21st 1843

Reverend Sirs

The relations of the Revd Richard Williams Baptist Missionary at Agra[281] in the East Indies received a letter from his wife dated 17th June

---

[276]See letter 210.

[277]John Snow was a printer at 35 Paternoster Row. See *Hodson's Booksellers Publishers and Stationers' Directory for London and Country* (London: W. H. Hodson, 1855) 74.

[278]For Poynder and Hankey, see letter 210.

[279]Ward was probably a General Baptist, but he would have had little to cheer about at that time in Peterborough. By the time of the above letter, the General Baptist minister at Peterborough, Samuel Wright, was nearing the end of a lengthy pastorate that had seen a steady decline in the church membership. When he died in 1845, the church had dwindled to five members. A new chapel, however, was built in the early 1850s, and under the leadership of Thomas Barrass, church membership rose to nearly 700 by the end of the century. See *Three Hundred Years of Free Church Life. Tercentenary 1953, Park Road Baptist Church, Peterborough* (Peterborough: n.p., [1953]) 8-10.

[280]MAW, Box 39 (BMS 3071), JRULM.

last and they have heard that he was at Calcutta last November on his way home, but not having heard a word since they are afraid that he is dead and are in much trouble

Shall I beg you will be so good as to drop a line to say if you know any thing of him

If he sailed homeward, have you heard in what vessel, I mean can you give any information that will give his relatives some hope to see

I remain Revd Sir

Your most ob^t Servant

T. R. Williams

Narberth

Pembrokeshire

242. D. W. Witton, 2 Crosby Square, London, to Joseph Angus, [Baptist Mission House, London,] 22 March 1843.[282]

2 Crosley Square

March 22.nd 1843

My dear Sir,

I yesterday brought again before the Committee of Management of the West African Company, the offer made by you, on behalf of the Baptist Missionary Society, for the purchase of the Company's Possessions at Fernando Po, and I regret to add, that the offer has been again declined—It will be very agreeable to me, to have some conversation with you at your convenience, upon the Subject in question—I remain

My dear Sir

Yours very truly

D. W. Witton

Revd Mr Angus—

---

[281] Richard Williams (see also letter 243) was appointed a BMS missionary in 1839, serving until 1859, much of the time in Agra. He died in India in 1880. A letter from Williams concerning his work in Agra appeared in the *Missionary Herald* (February 1841): 92-93. A notice of his arrival in England on 17 April appeared in the *Missionary Herald* (May 1843): 285.

[282] MAW, Box 39 (BMS 3039), JRULM.

243. J. Longbourne, Bonvilles Court, [London], to Joseph Angus, Secretary, Baptist Society, London, 22 March 1843.[283]

Bonvilles Court [?]
22 March 1843

Sir

I received and thank you for your note in reply to my enquiry respecting the period of departure of the Rev.[d] Richard Williams from Calcutta.

The information contained in your note relieved the feelings of distress under which Williams's family were suffering respecting him, but a Letter just received from M[rs] Williams gives reason to apprehend that her Husband must have left Calcutta in October. I beg to send herewith a note I found here on my return home last night, and hope you will be able to give some satisfactory information, and remove the apprehensions which the writer entertains of his relation having suffered in one of the recent Gales.

I remain Sir
Your obed.[t] S[t]
J. Longbourne

Rev.[d] [Joseph Angus]
Secretary Baptist Society

244. William Brock,[284] *[Norwich], to unnamed correspondent, undated, but late 1843.*[285]

My dear friend,

My engagements for 1843 are already made, so made that I am not able to comply with your request for Burton.[286]

Albeit I am your debtor for some week evening service or services which I will undertake as early as my circumstances in 1844 will allow.

---

[283]MAW, Box 39 (BMS 3072), JRULM.

[284]**William Brock** (1807-1875), Baptist minister at St. Mary's, Norwich (1833-1848), and Bloomsbury Chapel (1848-1872).

[285]Eng. MS. 861, f. 6, JRULM. Also included are two portraits of Brock.

[286]Given the opening sentence of Brock's letter, which links the recipient of his letter with Burton [Bourton?], this could be James Hannan (1808-1872), who pastored the Baptist church at Bourton, Somerset, 1833-1850. Other possibilities include a Mr. W. Hood, minister at a Home Missionary Chapel at Great Bourton, near Banbury. See Couling; *Baptist Magazine* 17 (1825): 432. My thanks to John Briggs for this information.

We are very anxious about our new committee men for the "Literary" Institution. Mʳ Alexander[287] and myself think of Messr.ˢ Reed,[288] Brooke,[289] Bidwell,[290] J. Geldart Junʳ,[291] G. Groat,[292] E. Blakely[293] J. B. Taylor or exactly such men.[294] Will you think often of them also?

Yours in kind regards to Mʳˢ H

In much mercies

William Brock

---

[287]John Alexander (1792-1868) attended Hoxton Academy, 1814-1817, after which he commenced a long career as pastor of Princes Street Independent Chapel, Norwich, 1819-1866. See *Congregational Yearbook* (1869): 234.

[288]**Andrew Reed** (1817-1899), minister at the Old Meeting (Independent), Norwich, 1840-1855.

[289]William Brooke, master of Priory School, King Street. See *Pigot and Co.'s Royal National and Commercial Directory and Topography of the Counties of Bedford, Cambridge, Essex, Herts, Huntingdon, Kent, Middlesex, Norfolk, Suffolk, Surrey and Sussex* (London: Pigot, 1839) 489.

[290]Probably Joseph Bidwell, engraver and copper-plate printer in Bethel Street, or Henry Bidwell, linen and woolen draper, at 17 Gentleman's Walk. See *Pigot and Co.'s Royal National and Commercial Directory*, 495, 497.

[291]Geldart contributed £20 to the BMS Jubilee Fund in 1843. See *Missionary Herald* (January 1843): 60.

[292]Groat, of Groat and Co. (and later of Willett and Groat), was a silk manufacturer in Lower Westwick Street. See *Pigot and Co.'s Royal National and Commercial Directory*, 491.

[293]This could be Edward Blakely, furrier, in London Street, Norwich. He was possibly a relation of John Rix Blakeley, a former midshipman who was converted though the ministry of James Browne, pastor of the Congregational church at North Walsham, near Worstead. Blakely soon developed questions about baptism, and to resolve his doubts, traveled to Norwich to study Greek and Hebrew under Kinghorn. He eventually accepted believer's baptism and joined Kinghorn's congregation at St. Mary's in April 1814. He returned home and joined the Baptist church at Worstead, working as a schoolmaster, teaching in the Sunday school, and conducting village preaching. In 1832 he became pastor at Worstead, but his service was short-lived; he died in 1837 at the age of forty-eight. See *Pigot and Co.'s Royal National and Commercial Directory*, 495; *Baptist Magazine* 30 (1838): 77, 415-420, 462-466; Maurice F. Hewitt, "Early Days at Worstead," *Baptist Quarterly* 11 (1942-1945): 172-174.

[294]Groat and Taylor (of Youngman, Beare, and Taylor) were Norwich manufacturers and laymen in Brock's congregation at St. Mary's. They (and possibly some of the other laymen mentioned in the above letter from St. Mary's as well as the two Independent churches) met regularly at this time at the Old Meeting Book Club, a gathering of ministers, lawyers, doctors, merchants and manufacturers for the purpose of discussing and circulating printed materials. See Charles M. Birrell, *The Life of William Brock, D.D.* (London: James Nisbet and Co., 1878) 128-129.

245. William Knibb, Jamaica, to Thomas Raffles, Liverpool, 7 August 1844.[295]

Rev[d] and dear Sir

I feel confident that no apology is necessary for my now addressing you.

I believe that [it] is customary with many churches in England now and then to address those of their members who tarrie in distant places, and as my Brother Edward is still in connexion with your Church I think a letter of advice would be of much service. God has [illegible word] smiled upon his efforts; and I fear that it is engendering a love of the world, which is so awfully destructive of real piety. It will *be well* that the effect may be the better that he should not know that I have written any thing at all the nearness of the relationship prevents my speaking to him on these matters as I could wish, and surrounded as he is by temptations on every hand, a letter from the Church, such a one as I am sure you would write, might bring to remembrance those things which immersed in worldly cares, we are all so apt to forget.[296]

It has pleased our heavenly father to afflict us with a very severe drought and the poverty and distress it has produced are distressing, while the Mission has been seriously crippled in its resources. Well the Lord reigneth, and if these causes are all but sanctified, they will prove universal blessings.

It will give you great pleasure I am sure to learn that the breach between ourselves and our Independent Brethren is fast healing. M[r] Barrett[297] preached some time ago in our Chapel at Kingston. I expect to meet him there next week when I shall invite him to Falmouth.

Nothing has given me so much pain, as this aberration [sic] in speach [sic] among brethren. M[r] Freemans[298] visit did unusual good. A visit now and then from a father in the Gospel would cheer our hearts.

These are necessary when the Missionary needs all the support and council that can be given. What a mercy that there is one ever at hand to impart it.

with sincere respect
I am
William Knibb

---

[295]Eng. MS. 379, f. 1157b, JRULM.

[296]William Knibb would die in 1845, and within a year his brother Edward would be living in Jamaica.

[297]**William Garland Barrett**, LMS missionary to Jamaica, 1835-1848.

[298]Joseph John Freeman (see letter 163), who visited Jamaica on behalf of the LMS in 1842-1843.

246. Joseph Angus, Baptist Mission House, London, to Thomas Raffles, Liverpool, 28 November 1844.[299]

My dear Sir,
    You were kind enough last year to hold out the hope of your being able to preach one of our Anniversary Sermons next Spring, & by a Resolution passed at our Meeting today I have now the pleasure to ask whether you can take our Morning Sermon. The time is some day in the last week in April & the place the Poultry Chapel I sincerely hope you will be able to gratify us in this particular
                    & am My dear Sir,
                            very sincerely Yours,
                                    Joseph Angus

Rev. D[r] Raffles.

247. Joseph Angus, Baptist Mission House, London, to Thomas Raffles at Liverpool, 20 March 1845.[300]

My dear Sir,
    You have kindly consented to preach for our Society on the 30.th of April at the Poultry Chapel. Your kindness in complying with our request evidences us to hope that you will not refuse another. It is to speak at our Annual Meeting at Exeter Hall on the following day, May 1. This request I send in compliance with a vote adopted unanimously at our Committee Meeting of today.
        Believe me to remain
                    very sincerely Yours,
                            Joseph Angus

Rev. D.[r] Raffles.

248. Joseph Angus, Baptist Mission House, London, to Thomas Raffles, Liverpool, 24 March 1845.[301]

My dear sir,
    I have much pleasure in enclosing a brief History of our Mission, & am greatly obliged by what I take to be a kind consent to speak at our

---

[299]Eng. MS. 372, f. 47a, JRULM.
[300]Eng. MS. 372, f. 47b, JRULM.
[301]Eng. MS. 372, f. 47c, JRULM.

morning meeting.[302] If you will favour me by leaving the other points touched on in your note till I can forward you a Resolution, I will take care & let you have it early.

Believe me to be

very sincerely Yours,

Joseph Angus

Revd Dr Raffles

---

[302]Thomas Stamford Raffles, in his *Memoirs* of his father, notes that the elder Raffles preached at the 30 April 1845 meeting of the Baptist Missionary Society at the Poultry Chapel, but he did not preach at the annual meeting the next day. The former meeting was primarily for purposes of fund-raising. The Annual Public Meeting involved various speeches, lectures, and the passing of resolutions. See Thomas Stamford Raffles, *Memoirs of the Life and Ministry of the Rev. Thomas Raffles, D.D., LL.D.* (London: Jackson, 1864) 381.

Part Seven

Undated Letters

249. Richard Ashworth[1] to a Mr. Jatron[?], undated and without location.[2]

My friend,

In compasion to the many vacant meetings especially about you, & in consideration y^t Harry gives me very acceptable asistance, and often preaches to the good likeing of divers of our people, but thro' age & Infirmity is not able often to go out, we think it proper to excuse you at present from any stated day of service, except occasionally or by way of Exchange when some particular matter or occasion may fall out. Every one's talents & capacity is both the Reason & rule of their service, and none should hide their Lord's Mony. Nor be found Solo at his Coming. I am longing to hear how Armystid goes on w^h Romaine's prayers[3] [illegible word] Love & [illegible word] and am Yours

Rd Ashworth

250. Andrew Fuller to unnamed correspondent, undated [c. 1784].[4]

Dear Bro^r

I see you have next you Claudes 1st Vol.[5] —Respecting your objection I must say it seems to me a very obscure one— "If Adam had eter-

---

[1]**Richard Ashworth**, Baptist minister at Rossendale, 1715 to 1751.

[2]Eng. MS. 369, f. 6, JRULM. This letter, given Ashworth's dates, is most likely c. 1740s.

[3]**William Romaine** (1714-1795), evangelical Calvinistic vicar at St. Anne's, Blackfriars, London, 1766-1795. The work referred to in the above letter is most likely Romaine's *Duty of Praying for Others: Enforced by Some Arguments taken from the Success of Those Prayers, which the Church made for St. Peter's Deliverance from Prison* (1757).

[4]Eng. MS. 369, f. 50a, JRULM. Given the reference to "Mrs. M." at the end of the letter, as well as the reference to a minister's meeting of the Northamptonshire Association, it is highly probable this letter was addressed to J. W. Morris at Clipston. Morris's church was a member of the Northamptonshire Association. This letter expounds on Fuller's ideas of grace and faith as expressed in his *The Gospel Worthy of All Acceptation* (1785). See Clipsham, "Andrew Fuller and Fullerism," 214-222.

nal life dwelling in his soul as a natural principle (as I think you affirm)"—I affirmed that eternal life (or blessedness) was *promised* in the covenant of works, and would have been *enjoy'd* if Adam had obey'd, w^h I supposed inferable f^m Matt.19.17. And this Mr Brine grants—tho' he denies that the life promised in the Cov^t of works was the *same* with that promised by the covenant of grace, yet he grants they were alike in duration. Consequently, both were *eternal lif*e. Motives to L. & U. p. 25.[6] But as to my affirming that "eternal life dwelt in his soul as a natural principle," I think I never did say any such thing either of his soul or of that of believers. Tho' I believe that grace in ye Saints is glory begun, and as it were, a well of water springing up into everlasting life—yet I do not think this is owing to the *nature* of ye principle, but to the continual influence of God's Holy Spirit. I suppose if God were this moment to leave me utterly as to his gracious influence, the *nature* of my principle of love to him is not such as would keep alive, but I should utterly apostatize. There seems therefore no propriety in saying of even a believers principle that eternal life *naturally* dwells in it, w^h I take to be your meaning. True it is *eternal life begun*, but that is owing to the engagements of God who has promised to keep this spark alive rather than to its being *in its own nature* necessarily eternal. God did not engage to keep it alive in Adam, but he has in believers. What absurdity would follow affirming that if Adam had stood, his children would have been born after his likeness, and that was in the image of God. The *flesh* in Jn. 3.6. denotes the state of man as *corrupted*, and not as innocent. As to "the first Adam being made equal to the second" He was equal to him considering Xt as *man*, in the *moral state of his mind*. The Superiority of the 2nd Adam to ye first lay not in his being more holy, or the principles of his mind being of ano^r nature, but in his being *God*, and so an honor derived to all he did, and upon the individual of human nature w^h he assumed. And what absurdity follows my say^g that "the Second Adam is to have the honor of doing that for us w^h the first did not chuse to perform"? Is not this the fact? Did he not *obey the law* w^h Adam did not chuse to obey? Y^n does he not stoop lower than that, to stand in our place as well as Adams, and bear our griefs & carry our sorrows! To do that for us w^h was wickedly refused to be done by Adam, and even to

---

[5]A reference to Robert Robinson's two-volume translation of *An Essay on the Composition of a Sermon* (London, 1782), by the Frenchman Jean Claude (1619-1687). Morris notes that Claude's *Essay* was one of the first books that Fuller read and emulated as he began his ministry, which would date this letter c. 1784. See Morris, *Memoirs*, 69-74.

[6]**John Brine** (1703-1765), High Calvinist Baptist minister at Curriers' Hall, Cripplegate, London, 1730-1765. Fuller is referring here to Brine's *Motives to Love and Unity Among Calvinists who Differ in Some Points . . . Wherein is Contained an Answer to Mr. Alverey Jackson's Question Answered . . .* (1753).

atone by his death for him & our defects no way detracts f^m Xts honor, but rather speaks his infinite *humiliation*. Your last sentence shocks me— "But in this Adam seems to discover a greater regard for the honor of Xt (shall I say) than my Bro^r Fuller, for sooner than he would rival his maker of that glory w^h is due to his name only, would rather forego his present honor & happiness and thereby give an opportunity for that glory to be manifested w^h we now behold in the person of Xt Jesus!" A fine apology indeed for the fall of man! And so a state of innocence stood in the way of Gods glory, and Adam was so humble that rather than do that he would sin against God & so give him at least an occasion of glorifying himself! Truly I tho't the motive leading to mans apostasy had been *pride*, and not *humility*; aspiring to be as a God, instead of giving place to God! According to this mode of reasoning man did better in sinning much better than angels who kept their first estate! But I hope this was merely a slip.—Dr Bro^r if I can receive any additional knowledge f^r your objections, or be convinced of any thing, or afford any assistance to you, I shall be glad of the opportunity—Our Ministers Meeting is on *Wednesday* the 28th Ins^t ano^r at Northampton on the Friday. Shall be glad to see you.

With respects to Mrs M. I am d^r Bro^r

Y^rs affectionately

A Fuller

N.B. I think in representing the principle of innocence in Adam as the same *in nature* with that in believers, we do not degrade either Xt or believers but rather by the contrary we degrade the *image of God* in w^h we were originally created. See Gen^s 1.27 comp^d with Ephe. 4.21. "After God" there certainly means after the likeness of God—Quere, Can there be two essentially different images of the one unchangeable God?

P.S. Have sent you *Beart*.[7] He was an Independent Minister of *Bury* Suffolk about 70 or 80 years ago—There is I think a great deal of good sense and good divinity.

---

[7]A reference to *Truth Defended: or, A Vindication of the Eternal Law and Everlasting Gospel* (1707-1708), by John Beart (1673-1716), which was reprinted in London in 1779. Beart also authored *Divine Breathings* (1716).

251. Rowland Hill[8] to John Rippon [London], undated [c. 1791?].[9]

I thank you for you kind offer of assistance on Tuesday next but as I find I am at liberty to stop a day or two longer than I expected you will do me a much greater favor if you give me a sermon on that day sennight the 12th instant as I shall not have returned from Glostershire [sic] til the latter end of that week

I do not lament the side you and I took at the Committee of the book society[10]   I find matters have given universal disgust as we supposd woud be the case.   I am ashamd to see my name as chairman on that business   I shall be there on Wednesday morn tho I must afterwards leave town   I am affraid we shall have warm work. M[r] Taylor[11] by the rules of the society is actually ineligible   well we must get thro the mistakes of others as well as we can

Y[rs] Sincerely

R Hill

Sat Eve
By favor of M[rs] [Applegath?]

---

[8]**Rowland Hill** (1744-1823), popular evangelical minister at the Surrey Chapel, London, 1783-1823.

[9]MAM. PLP. 53.49.13, JRULM.

[10]This is a reference to a Book Society founded in London in 1750 for promoting religious knowledge among the poor. The society was founded by a Mr. Benjamin Forfitt, a member of the Independent congregation at the Weigh-house under William Langford and John Clayton. Rowland Hill preached the annual sermon for the Society in 1791, so he may have been the Society's secretary that year as well, but that is not clear. Among the ministers who preached annual sermons for the Society were Samuel Stennett (1755), Samuel Medley (1789), and John Rippon (1796 and 1803). Baptists who served as stewards included John and Joseph Flight, Robert Keene, John Collett Ryland, James Davidson, Bannister Flight, Benjamin Tomkins, Samuel Beddome, Joseph Gutteridge, Henry Keene, William Lepard, John Pelly Lepard, John Hemming, Boswell Beddome, Henry Smithers, Joseph Wickenden, John Cowell, John Foster, Samuel Medley, Jr., and Benjamin Lepard. For more on the Book Society, see John Rippon, *A Discourse on the Origin and Progress of the Society for Promoting Religious Knowledge among the Poor, From It's Commencement in 1750, to the year 1802 ... To which is added A Complete List of the Treasurers and Other Officers, as well as of the Ministers who have Preached the Annual Sermons, and of the Gentlemen who have Served the Office of Stewards* (London, [1803?].

[11]Possibly a reference to **Dan Taylor,** General Baptist minister at Mile End, London.

252. John Ryland, Northampton, to John Sutcliff, Olney, undated [c. July 1792-December 1793].[12]

Dear Bro.[r]

I thank you for your Note & Bro[r] Dent thanks you too—He will be glad to see you, etc. & has sent Word to M[r] Heighton[13] of what you propose—I shall be glad to see you there, & believe M[r] Trinder[14] & M[r] Wykes[15] will meet us also there—

Have rec.[d] an unanimous Invit.[n] from both Ch[s] at Bristol[16]—But neither think myself fit for that Post nor am willing to leave my own—Yet am concerned for them—& fear they will be much at a loss for a middle aged orthodox Man of some Learning, unless they are allowed to move some one who is now settled—and even if they were at liberty to pick they [sic] kingdom I know none who w.[d] be best for them—I think we ought to pray for them—But we will talk more of this when I see you— perhaps my Ans[r] need not go till after that time—

I am

Y[rs] affect.[ly]

J. Ryland

---

[12]Eng. MS. 371, f. 107f, JRULM. This letter was written during the period of Ryland's candidacy at Broadmead, which occurred between April 1792 and December 1793. The letter is one of the earliest responses by Ryland to a matter that would prove to be very difficult for him. After supplying early in 1792, the Broadmead church extended a call to Ryland on 22 April 1792. In a letter to the Broadmead church, dated 18 May 1792, Ryland declared that he would most likely remain at Northampton. Nevertheless, Broadmead extended a second call to Ryland on 24 June 1792. He preached again at Broadmead in August and September, after which Broadmead extended a third call to him. Whether it is this third call that Ryland and his ministerial friends have been contemplating in the above letter, or the first call in April that led to his letter of 18 May, is unclear. Ryland would eventually accept the call to Broadmead and left Northampton in December 1793. See Grant Gordon, "The Call of Dr. John Ryland, Jr.," *Baptist Quarterly* 34 (1992): 214-227.

[13]**William Heighton** (1752-1827), Baptist minister at Roade (see letter 35).

[14]**Thomas Trinder** (1740-1794), deacon at College Lane, Northampton, 1777-1794.

[15]A Thomas Wykes, woolstapler, lived in Northampton at that time. He joined the church at College Lane in 1771 and became a deacon; he died on 24 November 1795. He may have been related to a former tutor at J. C. Ryland's Academy, William Wykes (d. 1785), who pastored the Baptist meeting in Kingsbridge, c. 1770-76. See *Universal British Directory*, 4:89; College Lane Church Book, f. 12; W. T. Adey, *The History of the Baptist Church, Kingsbridge, Devon* (Kingsbridge: n.p., 1899) 12-18; Rippon, *Baptist Annual Register*, 2:299, 4:984.

[16]Between 1753 and 1853, the Broadmead church consisted of two congregations—one Particular Baptist and the other Independent (often called the "Little Church")—worshiping under one pastor but maintaining separate Church Books (held now at the Bristol Record Office).

253. A portion of one of John Ryland, Jr.'s, miniscule sermon notes.[17]

254. A facsimile of one of John Ryland, Jr.'s, tiny sermon notes, from Prov. 6.22, preached in 1789 and 1805.[18]

255. Abraham Booth, London, to Joseph Jenkins,[19] *London, undated.*[20]

> A. Booths respects to Dr. Jenkins—Here sends the Memoranda he mentioned; some few of which, he thinks, may be applied with advantage against Mr. Edwards,[21] but leaves them entirely to Dr. Jenkins's discretion; not wishing that any one of them should be used if he do not consider it proper to be.
>
> A. Booth intends to leave the little Parcel, on Monday morning, at Mr. Cowells[22] & to inquire for a Parcel there directed for himself. Intends taking the first opportunity of looking over the *first Letter* against Mr. Edwards, & of returning it with a line. Desires his kind remembrance to Mrs. Jenkins, & sincerely prays that God would bless the affliction under which Dr. Jenkins at present labours, & effectually remove it.
>
> Saturday Even^g

256. Rev. James Burgess to Arthur Clegg,[23] *Manchester, 7 February [179]'9.*[24]

---

[17]Eng. MS. 861, f.45, JRULM.

[18]Eng. MS. 383, f. 1773a, JRULM.

[19]**Joseph Jenkins** (see letter 21) came to London from Wrexham in 1793, ministering at Blandford Street (1793-1798) and Walworth (1798-1819).

[20]Eng. MS. 861, f. 5, JRULM. This autograph (c. 1795) was presented at a later date to a Mr. Everett, apparently by Booth's son, most likely Isaac (1761-1840), then living at Mansfield. The younger Booth was a clerk in the Bank of England and later a deacon at the Baptist church in Little Prescot Street, London. See his obituary in the *Baptist Magazine* 33 (1841): 128-129.

[21]A reference to **Peter Edwards**, former Baptist turned Independent minister at Portsea. This letter can be dated c. 1795-1796.

[22]**John Cowell**, a member at Carter Lane, 1774-1802, after which he removed to the Baptist church at Potter Street, Harlow.

[23]The Cleggs of Manchester maintained a Baptist identity for some time. In 1804 Arthur Clegg, Esq., of Manchester, most likely Burgess's correspondent in the above letter, subscribed £3 to the Baptist Missionary Society. For more on the Cleggs, see letter 6. See also *Periodical Accounts*, 3:145.

[24]Eng. MS. 369, f. 21, JRULM. This letter appears in Nightingale, but numerous changes have been made and the P.S. has been left out. It was written sometime the emergence of the *Evangelical Magazine*, which first appeared in 1793. See Nightingale, *Lancashire Nonconformity*, 3:327.

Dear Sir

Ever since You gave your very friendly and beneficial assistance in yᵉ sale of my timber at Milhouses I have retained a gratefull sense of the greatness of yᵉ favor & the chearful manner in which you confer'd it, have also waited for an opportunity of making something more than a mere verbal acknowledgment of it. Consequently I here with send you gratuitously some small fruit of my ministerial labours since declining nature & a thorn in the flesh disabled me for stated pulpit work. As my life has been prolong'd & my faculties continued in some degree far beyond what I or any of my acquaintances expected, and finding that the spiritual life within has not in this last period of my life decayd with yᵉ decays of my outward man but rather the contrary; I have been as diligent in my good Master's work, (according to my lesser abillities [sic]) as I was when I had a whole flock of Christ's sheep to tend & feed. When my lungs & lips faild me both head heart and hand have been for the most part employd in the delightful work of the ministry. And tho' after I retird into private life I have been often sollicited to strike into trade I could never reconcile my unwilling mind unto it: much less to resemble my successor at Hatherloe who I find has made shift to join yᵉ sacred calling of yᵉ minster with yᵉ worldly calling of a cotton Tradesman (tho he has no child). But indeed religion, I have been informed, runs very low at Hatherloe. During my Ministry there we had a very full Congⁿ of hearers, besides four prayer meetings of men, and one of women. But yᵉ introduction of instrumental music, which had neither New Testament precept or precedent threw yᵉ Congⁿ into Confusion & drove away their Minister; & I believe a general deadness prevaild & diminution succeeded &c.

The Exposition and Select Meditations,[25] which you was so obliging as to subscribe for, were all, excepting about three, soon passd off. The like quick sale my next piece had. What will be yᵉ fate of this my last publication which I now make a present of to you time will discover, but not during my own life time. For, excepting a Sum sent to the Printer of the Evangelical Magazine at L—n & two shops in your town, yᵉ chief part are to be reservd to yᵉ time of my interment, when a smallish number are to be given by way of dole to the pious poor of those congrˢ where I oftenest officiated during my ministry. I shall only add that this my last piece has now an addition which is not in any of those few already sent to Booksellers; indeed it was not added before last week It bears this title A Prospect of near approching [sic] death prompts the author to gird on his Xᵃⁿ Armor. That part I lately transcribd from my diary of experiences which I have kept above 50 years.

---

[25] I have not been able to locate an extant copy of this work.

P.S. If after a perusal of this Book you so far approve of it as to think it may be useful to some of your religious Friends I shall be beholden unto you to lend or recommend [sic] it to y^m to become subscribers to it, & to permit me to reap ye profits which Booksellers claim. I take the price to be very moderate viz 1^s-10 merely. I now find both head & hand fail me in writing, (which I need not wonder at, because in my 80th year) I must abruptly conclude with my best respects to you & Mrs Clegg—As your Friend Ed. Clegg[26] sent for me to visit him, ye latter visit was to day when I found him weakening apace; but quite sensible, thankful for prayer & religious advice. His attendants informed me y^t there is a great alteration in him for ye better. Farewell[27]

J. Burgess   Feb. 7 '9

257. Facsimile of Samuel Pearce's handwriting: A poem, "On being prevented by sickness from attending on Public Worship."[28]

The fabric of Nature is fair
But fairer the temple of grace
To Saints 'tis the joy of the Earth
The most glorious, and beautiful place
To this temple I once did resort
With crowds of the people of God
Enraptur'd we enter'd his courts
And hail'd the Redeemer's abode
The father of mercies we prais'd
And prostrated low at his throne
The Savior we lov'd and ador'd
Who lov'd us, and made us his own
Full oft' to the message of grace

---

[26]This may be the same Edmund Clegg who pastored a High Calvinist church at Shudehill, 1762-1781. He is described by Burgess as Arthur Clegg's "Friend," but they may have been relations as well. See "The Johnsonian Baptists," *Transactions of the Baptist Historical Society* 3 (1912-1913): 56.

[27]Nightingale lists Burgess's death as May 1804, which he took from Powicke. Urwick, however, states that Burgess died shortly after leaving Hatherlow in 1776, but that is clearly incorrect. If Burgess was around thirty when preaching at Whitworth in the late 1740s (see letter 12), and has been preaching for fifty years, then the date of Burgess's birth would be c. 1719/1720, making the date of the above letter February 1799. See Nightingale, *Lancashire Nonconformity*, 3:327; William Urwick, *Historical Sketches of Nonconformity in the County Palatine of Chester* (London: S. Fletcher, 1864) 327; Frederick James Powicke, *A History of the Cheshire County Union of Congregational Churches* (Manchester: T. Griffiths, 1907) 191.

[28]Eng. MS. 371, f. 97b, JRULM. This poem appears in the *Baptist Annual Register*, 3:432-433.

To sinners addres'd from the sky
We listen'd extolling that grace
Which set us—once rebels—on high
Faith clave to the crucified Lamb
Hope, smiling, exalted its head
Love warm'd at the Saviors dear name
And vow'd to observe what he said
What pleasure appear'd in the looks
Of the brethren and sisters around
With transport all seemd [sic] to reflect
On the blessings in Jesus they'd found
Sweet Moments! If aught upon earth
Resembles the joys of the skies
It is thus when the hearts of yᵉ flock
Conjoin'd to the shepheard arise
But Ah! These sweet moments are fled
Pale sickness compels me to stay
Where no voice of the turtle is heard
As the moments are hasting away
My God!—Thou art holy and good
Thy plans are all righteous & wise
O help me submissive to wait
Till thou biddest thy servant arise
If to follow thee here in thy Courts
May it be with all ardor & zeal
With success & increasing delight
Performing the whole of thy will
Or shoulds't thou in bondage detain
To visit thy temples no more
Prepare me for mansions above
Where nothing exists to deplore
Where Jesus, the sun of the place
Refulgent incessantly shines
Eternally blessing his saints
And pouring delight on their minds
There—there are no prisons to hold
The captive from tasting delight
There the day never is clos'd
With shadows, or darkness, or night
There myriads & myriads shall meet
In our Saviors high praises to join
Whilst transported we fall at his feet
And extol his redemption divine
Enough then—my heart shall no more

Of its present bereavements complain
Since er'e long I to glory shall soar
And ceaseless enjoyments obtain.

258. A portion of a letter from Robert Hall, [Leicester], to a Mr. Alexander, Esq., Blackheath, near London, undated.[29]

. . . With respect to Mr Don, it would gratify me much to have him for a time in our neighbourhood. Were it not for the distraction of a young family I would be most happy in offering him any Room under my roof. But the noise of children would not suit. If you will [illegible word] him upon the proposal & hear information whether he is willingly disposed to come into Leicestershire, I will make all the enquiry in my town for a suitable situation. But I know not well how to set about it untill I have some assurance of his readiness to accept it. Those to whom I might find it proper to reply would probably feel themselves to be [illegible word] unless I could make them a more specific proposal, I'm sorry that [illegible word] of Mr Fosters resignation. He is a wonderfull man, but not at all [illegible word] to the common people. I am yours most sincerely

Robert Hall

259. A brief MS. in an unknown hand about the Serampore Trio (Carey, Marshman, and Ward), c.1810.[30]

"The Mission at Serampore is almost a new thing in the earth for purity of Doctrine, Zeal, good order, and wise management. Three such men as Carey, Marshman, and Ward, are seldom to be found united together. They compose a threefold cable not to the broken. Their Qualities unite well. Mr Carey is firm, prudent, and persevering. Mr Marshman abounds in the rare grace of Zeal, which surmounts all obstacles, and keeps all alive, and in motion. Mr Ward's solid judgment and personal Religion give stability and beauty to the Union. They are as devoted, and active as men can be. The other Brethren of the Mission are worthy to be followers of these three first, though they may not attain unto the first three."

---

[29]MAM PLP 48.25.3, JRULM. This letter can be dated c.1810, not long after the birth of Hall's daughter and about three years after John Foster's resignation at Frome.

[30]Eng. MS. 387, f. 20d, JRULM.

260. William Steadman, Bradford, to Isaac Mann,[31] *Shipley, (undated), on a Friday evening.*[32]

My d.ʳ brother

I received your parcel just after M.ʳ Davies had let out & will attend to your suggestions.

On account of the Market on Thursday it will be necessary to have the Association on Tuesday & Wednesday. I will thank you to inform M.ʳ Lister.[33]

With respects to M.ʳˢ Mann &c I am

My d.ʳ brʳ

Yʳˢ affˡʸ

W Steadman

Friday evᵍ

261. William Carey to unnamed correspondent [probably Mr. Shepherd of the Liverpool Botanical Gardens], undated.[34]

A portion of a letter in which Carey is requesting various seeds of plants and flowers to be sent by ship to India.

Desiderata

Iris germanica
___ pseudoacorus
___ orientalis
___ virginica
___ foetidissima
Cyclomon coum
___ europaeum
___ hederifolium
___ persicum
Galanthius nivalis (common Snowdrop)
Leucojum or Snow flake
___ vernum

---

[31]**Isaac Mann** (1785-1831), Baptist minister at Burslem, Staffordshire; Shipley, Yorkshire; and Maze Pond, Southwark.

[32]Eng. MS. 861, f. 66, JRULM. Letter is written c. 1814-1816, during Mann's tenure at Shipley.

[33]**James Lister** (d. 1851), Baptist minister at Lime Street (later Hope Street), Liverpool, 1803-1847.

[34]Eng. MS. 343, f. 38, JRULM. Most likely Carey's correspondent is **John Shepherd**, curator of the Liverpool Botanical Gardens, c. 1820.

___ aestivalis[35]
___ autumnale
Narcissus
___ poeticus
___ augustifolius
___ Psuedo Narcissus
___ major
___ minor
___ bulbocodium
Lilium
___ bulbiferum
___ aurantium[36]
___ pomponium
___ martagon
Erythronium
__ dens canis
Convallaria
___ majalis
___ polygonatum
___ verticillata
Comfrey or Symphitum officinale

Also Seeds of Primulas, viz: Cowslips, Oxlips, Polyanthus—Phlax of different sorts—Dianthus or Pinks of different species. Mesenbryan-themums of different species. Roses. Cistus. Thalictrum, Rananculus, Anemones, Aquilegia or Columbines, Geranium, Erodium, Pelargonium, Passiflora, Aster, Coreopsis, Rudbeckia, Soldago, Buphthalmum, Helianthus, and Centauria.

The best way of sending them is to mix the Seeds with Peat Earth, about three or four times as much earth as seeds, and put them into a box so as compleatly to fill it, and then nail it down. A list of the Seeds should be sent by the Ship on which they arrive, with a letter to advise of their being shipped. The Roots may be put into the same box, but should be labelled that they may be distinguished.

W Carey

---

[35]aestivum?
[36]auratum?

262. Christopher Anderson, Liverpool, to Thomas Raffles, [Liverpool], undated.[37]

Rev.[d] Christopher Anderson, Edinburgh
Liverpool
Friday Morning

Dear Sir

I intend calling this forenoon but may not be so fortunate as to find you at home, and therefore write these few lines before going out. From the enclosed Note you will see how I have been and am now situate; and in such circumstances I hope it will not appear intrusive if I take the liberty to circulate a few of these circulars among some of our people. Before sending one to any of them I am desirous of acknowledging you in the matter, and, if not asking too much, of receiving your total sanction.

I am Dear Sir in the best bonds
Yours most faithfully
Christ.[r] Anderson

Hope Street[38]

263. MS. Autobiographical Sketch of Joseph Cottle, Bristol.[39]

Mr. Joseph Cottle was born in Bristol, March 9, 1770. C. is understood not to have received the advantages of a Classical Education. His thirst for reading, however, was conspicuous, from early life, which was doubtless strengthened by his having been the pupil ~~from the age of 8 to 10~~, and subsequently the personal friend of the late celebrated John Henderson, of Pembroke College, Oxford, one of the strongest minds of modern times, and a memoir of whom, Mr. C. has published, in the 3rd Edition of his Poems (now out of print.)

In the year 1791, Mr. Cottle began the business of a Bookseller, in Bristol, which he relinquished in the year 1798, since which time he has been unconnected with business, except for a short period, when he purchased a share in a Printing Concern where he was an inactive partner.

When a Bookseller Mr. Cottle was surrounded by a Constellation of Geniuses, such as Bristol is not likely soon again to Witness. In this

---

[37]Eng. MS. 372, f. 44b, JRULM.

[38]Most likely, Anderson was staying in the home of William Hope, who built the first house in Hope Street, Liverpool (see letter 121).

[39]Eng. MS. 351, f. 49b, JRULM. The sketch is in Cottle's hand.

number were many Young Men who have since distinguished them-selves; such as Mr. Coleridge, Mr. Southey, Mr. Wordsworth, Mr. Lloyd,[40] ~~Mr. Lovell, Mr. C. F. Williams~~, Mr. Davy (now Sir Humph-rey)[41]—Counsellor Gilbert[42]—Dr. Beddoes[43] etc. etc.   Mr. Cottle was rendered remarkable, from having been the Original Publisher of the Poems of Messrs Southey—Coleridge—& Wordsworth—three men who do honour to the literature of their country, and who derived their first encouragements from a Brother Bard.[44]

It has come to the Editor's knowledge, that Mr. Coleridge presented Mr. Cottle with a copy of the 1st Edit. of his Poems, on the blank leaf of which he wrote the following: a circumstance which reflects as much credit on the writer as on the receiver.

> Dear Cottle, on the blank leaf of my Poems, I can most appro-priately write my acknowledgment to you for your too disinte-rested conduct in the purchase of these [poems]. Indeed if ever they should acquire a name and character, it might be truly said that the world owed them to you. Had it not been for you, none perhaps of them would have been published, and many not written. God bless you! Your obliged & affectionate Friend.

April 15, 1796   S. T. Coleridge

---

[40]Charles Lloyd (1775-1839) joined with Charles Lamb in publishing a book of poems titled *Blank Verse* (1798); that same year Joseph Cottle published Lloyd's novel, *Edmund Oliver.*

[41]Sir Humphrey Davy (1778-1829), noted chemist, began his career at the Pneumatic Institution in Clifton, near Bristol, under Thomas Beddoes, before achiev-ing considerable fame in London at the Royal Institution.

[42]The brilliant but eccentric William Gilbert (1760?-1825?) was the author of the poem, *The Hurricane: A Theosophical and Western Eclogue. To Which is Sub-joined, A Solitary Effusion in a Summer's Evening* (Bristol, 1796). His father, Natha-niel Gilbert, was a plantation owner in Antigua. In 1787 William was placed in Ri-chard Henderson's asylum at Hanham, near Bristol. Henderson's son, the brilliant scholar John Henderson (1757-1788), introduced Joseph Cottle to Gilbert, referring to the latter as the "Young Counsellor," from which Cottle has attached the same appellation in the above letter. See Joseph Cottle, *Reminiscences of Samuel Taylor Coleridge and Robert Southey* (London: Houlston and Stoneman, 1847) 42-43.

[43]Thomas Beddoes (1760-1808) was a physician and scientific writer who, af-ter completing his M.D. at Oxford in 1786, became a reader there from 1788 to 1792, when he resigned his position due to conflicts over his support of the French Revo-lution. In 1798 he established a Pneumatic Institution for treating disease at Clifton, near Bristol. He also wrote a number of political pamphlets between 1795 and 1797.

[44]Cottle published Coleridge's *Poems* in 1796, as well as the initial copies of the first edition of Coleridge's and Wordsworth's *Lyrical Ballads* in 1798.

Mr. Cottle, in conjunction with his friend Mr. Southey, published in 1802, the complete edition of Chatterton's Works, in 3 Vols. 8mo, for the benefit of Mrs. Newton, Chatterton's Sister; from the profits of which work she received between two and three hundred pounds; a sum which rendered the latter part of her life comfortable. Till this time Chatterton's family had never derived any pecuniary advantage from the publication of "Thomas Chatterton's Poems." The Illustrative Essays, in this work, were written exclusively by Mr. Cottle (bearing the initials J. C.) and in which he appears completely to have settled the Rowley Controversy, by proving, to a moral demonstration, that the whole of the poems ascribed to "Thomas Rowley," were written by "Thomas Chatterton." A Publication of this nature came well from Mr. Southey and Mr. Cottle, as they are both (as was Chatterton) Natives of Bristol.

Mr. Cottle's various poems were published in the following order.

> Poems, 12mo 1795—2nd Edit, 1796—3rd Edit, 1802—Malvern Hills 4th 1798-Alfred, an Epic Poem, 1 Vol, 4to, 1800—2nd Edit, 2 Vols 12mo, 1804—3rd Edit, 2 Vols 12mo 1816—A New Version of the Psalms of David 12mo 1801—2nd Edit 1805—The Fall of Cambria, 2 Vols 8vo 1808—2nd Edit, 2 vols 8vo, 1811.—Messiah 1 Vol. (part 1st) 1816—Part 2, 1819.—Epostulatory Epistle to Lord Byron, 1820—and Dartmoor, a Descriptive Poem, 1822.

Attached is also a MS. of Cottle's poem, "Juvenile," in Cottle's hand.

264. Newton Bosworth to a Mrs. Greene, location unknown, returning a manuscript, with complements, etc. undated.[45]

D.r Madam,

I am obliged, after all, to return the MS. without giving them the reconsideration they deserve. My time has been very much occupied, and I find, from some engagements which did not occur to my recollection yesterday, I shall not have any time at my command, till it will be too late to undertake the examination. Some friends will be here, and I am very fearful of trusting to any intervals I may be able to snatch away. However, I have looked through as much as I could, a second time, and am quite of the same opinion, as to their value, that I was yesterday. I am sure M.r Brown ought, and I have no doubt he will, consider them as contributing very materially to the perfection of his plan.

---

[45]Eng. MS. 373, f. 213b, JRULM.

You will see I have furnished the references to the texts from which 2 of M.ʳ H's[46] funeral sermons were preached, and have altered the first word of that from the Acts.

I am, Dear Madam,
With great Respect (in haste)
yʳˢ sincerely,
Newton Bosworth.

P.S. I must not forget to *thank* you for the favour of dispensing your manuscripts, and for the pleasure and interest with which that perusal has been attended.

265. John Foster, [Stapleton, near Bristol],[47] to Josiah Wade,[48] Esq., Rownham Place, Clifton, [Bristol],undated.[49]

My dear Sir,
Here is a delectable task for your eyes, and trial for your patience— a trial which would have gone hard with that of Job.—I would see that old fellow thrashed, and indeed every other villanous bad penman. It is a grievance which no man has a right to inflict on his correspondents. I have nearly made out but not all the contents of the sheet. There seems an obligation to send it to Mʳ Cottle, after you, and Mʳ Roberts have seen it, if indeed he will task himself to decypher it. If you hand it to him,

---

[46]John Howard, prison reformer. The Mr. Brown mentioned here is **James Baldwin Brown** (1785-1843). The MS. Bosworth has shared with Mrs. Greene apparently formed a part of Brown's *Memoirs of the Public and Private Life of John Howard, the Philanthropist* (1823), which would date the above letter c. 1822.

[47]**John Foster** (1770-1843), Baptist minister at Downed, near Bristol (1800-1804) and Frome (1804-1806) before devoting himself to a successful career as a journalist and writer.

[48]**Josiah Wade** (1760/61-1842), longtime attendant at the Baptist meeting in the Pithay, Bristol, and close friend of Cottle, Foster, and Samuel Taylor Coleridge.

[49]Eng. MS. 376, f. 692, JRULM. The letter that Foster has received and is sharing with Cottle and the others concerns Carey's horticultural garden at Serampore and some other recent events, including the death of Carey's third wife. The letter may have been written by Joshua Marshman, who frequently corresponded with Foster. The above letter was obviously written not long after the death of Carey's third wife in 1835. Grace Hughes (1777?-1835) married William Carey in 1822. Though not the equal of his second wife, Charlotte von Rumohr (she died in 1821), Grace nevertheless faithfully cared for Carey during his latter years. As a result of the numerous bank failures in India during 1831-1833, Grace Carey lost the £3000 inheritance she had received from her first husband.

have the goodness to require his speedy return of it to you, to be sent by post to Mʳ C. *Carleton Place, Bedminster.*⁵⁰

As to Dʳ Carey's great *botanical garden,* one could almost be sorry that they, not having the same decided taste for such a thing, should be under the permanent charge of keeping it up, since they probably cannot turn its productions to any profitable account. At the same time it really speaks well for Dʳ C. that his mind, so variously and intensely occupied, had yet taste enough to take an interest in the productions of oriental Nature.

We had not previously heard of the decease of his widow.—She was no friend to the Marshman family.—one therefore the less regrets her removal, and the cessation of the claims she would have had on their hard-pressed friends.

I remain, my dear Sir

Yours very truly

J. F.

*266. John Greene,⁵¹ No. 2 Peel St., Toxteth Park, [Liverpool], to Thomas Raffles, Liverpool, Sunday morning, undated (c. 1839).*⁵²

My dear Sir

I have taken a House as above chiefly for Mʳˢ Greene's health.

I enclose for your perusal incidental testimonials from our mutual friend the Revᵈ Timothy East⁵³ who has promised to spend a week with us before winter and has given me a charte blanche to preach a Sabbath for you when agreeable.

---

⁵⁰In his later years, Cottle lived with his sister and her husband, the wealthy merchant John Hare, in their home in Bedminster, where they worshiped at Zion Independent Chapel, which was built almost exclusively from donations by Mr. Hare.

⁵¹A shop man and a linen draper while he lived in Cambridge, John Greene would later publish *Reminiscences of the Rev. Robert Hall, A. M. Late of Bristol, and Sketches of his Sermons Preached at Cambridge Prior to 1806* (1832). At some point he removed to Birmingham, where he died in 1844. See *Church Book: St. Andrew's Street Baptist Church, Cambridge 1720-1832* (London: Baptist Historical Society, 1991) 144, 150, 154.

⁵²Eng. MS. 377, f. 814, JRULM.

⁵³**Timothy East** (1783-1871) ministered to churches in Somerset, Birmingham, Yorkshire, and Devon, 1805-1864.

If other motives for removal from Edgbaston were wanting the recent awful disturbances in Birmingham[54] would supply them, where I had a narrow escape for my Life.

I am my d^r Sir

Y^{rs}respec^y

John Greene

formerly of Cambridge

267. William B. Gurney, London, to unnamed correspondent [Rev. William Gurney, Rector of St. Clement's in the Strand], undated.[55]

Rev^d & Dear Sir

Being well assured of your readiness to assist in every attempt to promote the glory of God & the Salvation of Sinners, I beg leave to lay before you, & earnestly intreat your full consideration of the inclosed Case; and I entertain no doubt of obtaining from you that liberal aid to the Cause which has not hitherto been denied where the means were in possession. I would suggest in addition to what the printed Paper states that the Rent goes to 12 poor Widows, and is raised from the Gallery Pew-Rents before the Minister receives any thing for his Labours.

I am

Your faithful Servant

W Gurney

Brompton Villa
Old Brompton

Among your Congregation, by small sums, if you can raise 5£—or even one—it will be of great service as this Letter will be widely circulated. The cause is a peculiar one, it being the only Chapel & school on such a place.[56]

---

[54]A reference to the riots that erupted in Birmingham in 1839 over unrest caused by the lack of political reform and the rise of the Chartist movement.

[55]Eng. MS. 377, f. 848, JRULM.

[56]A note written to the side of the letter identifies the correspondent as "The Rector of St Clement's in the Strand   A well known character." The Rector was William Gurney (1785-1843), who served at St. Clement Danes, Westminster, from 1807 until his death in 1843. He died at Great Canfield vicarage, where the rector was John Phillips Gurney; whether these Gurneys were relations of William B. Gurney is unclear. The rector was a supporter of various evangelical causes, even allowing the use of the church at St. Clement's as part of the 34th annual meeting of the London Missionary Society in May 1828. See *Evangelical Magazine* 36 (1828): 263; Venn, *Alumni Cantabrigienses*, 3:176-177.

Biographical Index[1]

Abbott, Thomas Fisher—Abbott, a member of the Particular Baptist church at Taunton, arrived in Jamaica in 1828 for reasons of health, not as a missionary. He soon joined William Knibb's congregation at Falmouth, a decision that cost Abbott his job as a wharfinger. Shortly thereafter, Abbott applied to the BMS and was set apart as a missionary at Montego Bay in April 1831. The Montego church suffered considerable damage during the riots of 1832, and Abbott was briefly imprisoned in 1833 and 1834. After his release, he established several new churches between 1835 and 1840. Abbott removed to Falmouth after Knibb's death in 1845, but poor health forced his return to England in 1847, at which time he retired from the BMS. See Clarke, *Memorials,* 148-152.

Adam, William (1710-82)—Adam ministered to Independent congregations at Painswick (1734-50), Bedworth (1751-62), and Soham (1763-82). Josiah Thompson described Adam as "the best scholar and the most intelligent independent minister in the country." He married a second time in old age to a young wife and had a second family, which greatly impoverished him, forcing him in his last years to obtain relief from several neighboring churches. At the time of his death, his congregation consisted of only three female members and a few hearers. See Josiah Thompson, "The State of the Dissenting Interest in the Several Counties of England and Wales . . . The First Part, c. 1774" (MS., Dr. Williams's Library, London); "Statistical View," 814 (the author incorrectly identifies him as Thomas Adam).

Addington, Stephen (1729-96)—After completing his studies at Philip Doddridge's Independent academy at Northampton, Addington began ministering at Spaldwick, Huntingdonshire, in 1750, before removing to Market Harborough in 1752, where he remained until 1781. That year he became minister of the Independent congregation at Miles Lane in London (until 1795) as well as tutor at the Mile End Academy, 1783-1791. Among his works are *A Dissertation on the Religious Knowledge of the Antient Jews and Patriarchs, Containing an Enquiry into the Evidences of their Belief and Expectation of a Future State* (1757); *The Christian Minister's Reasons for Baptizing Infants* (1771); *The Life of Paul the Apostle* (1784); and *A Letter to the Deputies of Protestant Dissenting Congregations, in and about . . . London and Westminster on their Intended Application to Parliament, for the Repeal of the Corporation and Test Acts* (1787). An affectionate history of Addington can be found in Wilson, *History and Antiquities,* 1:499-518.

---

[1]Information on some of the entries below has come from Donald M. Lewis, ed., *The Blackwell Dictionary of Evangelical Biography: 1730-1860,* 2 vols. (Oxford: Blackwell, 1995) [cited as *DEB*]; *The New Oxford Dictionary of National Biography*; and the Surman Index, Dr. Williams's Library, London.

Anderson, Christopher (1782-1852)—Anderson, a banker's clerk, was converted through the ministry of James and Robert Haldane in 1799. He became a Baptist and planned to join Carey in India as a BMS missionary but poor health would not allow him to do so. He turned to the ministry instead, studying at Bristol Academy and with John Sutcliff at Olney. He eventually settled in Edinburgh where he organized a small congregation along Baptist lines in 1808. He would remain with that congregation until shortly before his death. He was a staunch supporter of the BMS, especially William Carey and the Serampore Mission. He helped to form an Itinerating Society of preachers, both in Scotland and Ireland, which later became a part of the Baptist Home Missionary Society. He founded the Edinburgh Bible Society and was involved in the formation of the Edinburgh Gaelic School Society. During the years of the split between the Serampore Mission and the BMS, Anderson served as one of the chief negotiators for Carey and Marshman. See Derek B. Murray, "Christopher Anderson (1782-1852)," ed. Haykin, in *The British Particular Baptists*, 3:171-179; Donald E. Meek, ed., *A Mind for Mission: Essays in Appreciation of the Rev. Christopher Anderson (1782-1852)* (Edinburgh: Scottish Baptist History Project, 1992); *DEB*.

Andrews, Mary (d. 1795)— Mary Andrews and her husband, William, were members of the Baptist congregation at Olney and were instrumental in bringing Sutcliff to Olney. William Andrews died on 8 February 1787. Sutcliff lived in the Andrews's home until his marriage in 1795, just after Mrs. Andrews's death on 9 March 1795 (see letter 42). See Olney Church Book, ff. 17, 19; "Character and Death of Mrs. Andrews," *Evangelical Magazine* 3 (1795): 292; and Haykin, *One Heart*, 87-91, 238-241.

Angas (Angus), George Fife (1789-1878)— Angas, along with his brother John Lindsey Angas (1776-1861) and John's wife Mary (1775-1850), were all members of the Baptist church at Tuthill Stairs, Newcastle, where John served for many years as a deacon. Richard Pengilly arrived as pastor in 1807, the same year George Angas organized the church's first Sunday school. A lifetime supporter of the BMS and other evangelical missionary societies, George moved to London in 1832 and was instrumental in the founding of the Colony of South Australia, serving as a initial director for both the South Australian Company and the South Australian Bank. He eventually emigrated to South Australia in 1851. Another George Angus (1725-1815) served as a deacon in the church at Hamsterley/Rowley, near Newcastle-on-Tyne, for many years. He farmed at Styford, on the north side of the Tyne, near Hexham; late in life he retired to Broomley, at which time his son-in-law, John Angus, took over the farm. These Anguses were relations of Joseph Angus, BMS secretary, as well as William Henry Angus (d. 1832), who served as a missionary with the BMS in the 1820s to seamen in seaports throughout Europe. See Walter D. Potts, "A Record of the Baptist Sunday School, Founded at Tuthill Stairs, Newcastle, April, 1807," in *Souvenir of the Sunday School Centenary Celebration 1807-1907* (Newcastle-upon-Tyne: Newcastle and Gateshead Baptist Council, 1907) 7; Angus Watson, *The Angus Clan (Years 1588 to 1950)* (Gateshead: Angus Watson, 1955) 93-106; John Bradburn, *The History of Bewick Street Baptist Church* (Newcastle-on-Tyne: n.p., 1883) 8; Richard Pengilly, with Henry Angus Wilkinson, "The Pedigree of the Angus Family" (MS., Angus Library, Regent's Park College, Oxford); J. D. Bollen, "English-Australian Baptist Relations 1830-1860," *Baptist Quarterly* 25 (1973-1974): 303-304, n. 63; David Douglass, *History of the Baptist Churches in the North of England, from 1648 to 1845* (London: Houlston and Stoneman, 1846) 258-259, 272, 277-279.

Angus, Joseph (1816-1902)—Originally from Newcastle, Angus, after completing his studies at Stepney College and Edinburgh University, succeeded John Rippon as pastor at New Park Street, Southwark (formerly Carter Lane) in 1838. In 1840 he became co-secretary of the BMS, and in 1841, after the death John Dyer, sole secretary, a position he held for the next eight years. In 1841 he married Amelia Gurney, daughter of William B. Gurney, then treasurer of the BMS. He left the BMS in 1849 to become president of Stepney College, moving the college to Regent's Park in 1856, where it became affiliated with the University of London. He remained with the college until his retirement in 1893. He served as editor of the Baptist newspaper, *The Freeman,* and authored numerous works in theology, biblical studies, and English literature. See Payne, *First Generation*, 13-25; R. E. Cooper, *From Stepney to St Giles': The Story of Regent's Park College 1810-1960* (London: Carey Kingsgate Press, 1960) 60-80; Stanley, *History*, 212-214; *DEB.*

Armitage, William (1738-1794)—Armitage was born at Huddersfield, Yorkshire, and studied under James Scott at the Heckmondike Academy. He served as an Independent minister at Horton, Yorkshire (1765-1769), and Delph (1769-1772) before removing to the Independent meeting at Chester, where he served from 1772 until his death in 1794. He married the sister of Abraham Greenwood, Baptist minister at Oakham. See Miall, *Congregationalism in Yorkshire*, 251; notices of Armitage also appeared in the *Evangelical Magazine* 1 (1793): 255; and 2 (1794): 265-270.

Ashworth, James (d. 1802)—Ashworth was baptized by his uncle, Thomas Ashworth (see next entry) at Gildersome in 1759. In 1770 he succeeded his uncle as pastor at Gildersome, being ordained there on 8 August 1770. The church flourished and several men were called into the ministry as a result of his preaching, including Luke Heywood in 1776 and Joseph Asquith and John Ross in 1777. While at Gildersome, Ashworth helped found the Yorkshire and Lancashire Association of Baptist Churches in 1787. Along with John Fawcett, Ashworth preached the dedication service for Thomas Langdon's chapel in Leeds in July 1781. Ashworth remained at Gildersome for 26 years, leaving in June 1797 to become pastor at Farsley. When the church split in 1801, he and some members formed a new meeting at Horsforth; he died there the next year. For more on Ashworth, see John Haslam, *History of the Baptist Church at Gildersome, in the County of York* (Leeds: Walker and Laycock, 1888); *Baptists of Yorkshire*, ed. Shipley, 41-77.

Ashworth, Richard—Ashworth ministered to the Cloughfold Baptist Church in Rossendale from 1705 to 1751. He was the father of Thomas Ashworth, who succeeded him as pastor at Rossendale in 1751 (Thomas would later serve as pastor at the Baptist church at Gildersome from 1755 until his death in 1769). Richard Ashworth's grandson was James Ashworth (see previous entry), who succeeded his uncle Thomas at Gildersome from 1771 to 1797. Another son of Richard Ashworth was Caleb Ashworth (1722-1775), who studied under Philip Doddridge at Northampton and was a correspondent of the Baptist poet, Anne Steele. When Doddridge died in 1751, the academy moved to Daventry and was headed by Caleb Ashworth, who had become an Independent in 1746 and was then ministering to the Independent congregation in Daventry. According to Theo F. Valentine, Caleb Ashworth was "a man of outstanding ability and it seems a great pity that the Baptists of his day did not take advantage of his scholarship." See Valentine, *Concern for the Ministry*, 37; James S. Hardman, "Caleb Ashworth of Cloughfold and Daventry," *Baptist Quarterly* 8 (1936-1937): 200-206.

Aveline, George—Aveline was sent out from the church at Maidstone as a BMS missionary to Grahamstown (in what was then known as the Cape Colony) South Africa, in 1838. He opened a new chapel there in Bathurst Street on 14 March 1843 (an account of the service appeared in the *Missionary Herald* [August 1843]: 436-438). He returned to England later that year, however, ending his work as a missionary. During his time at Grahamstown, Aveline established two schools, educating some 150 scholars by the time he left. The Grahamstown church, though an anomaly for the BMS at that time, was nevertheless supportive of the work of the Society, contributing a sum of £417 to the BMS Jubilee Fund in 1843. Letters from Aveline to friends in London concerning his Jubilee fundraising efforts appeared in the *Missionary Herald* (December 1842): 687-688, and (February 1843): 124-125. Writing to William Groser on 24 June 1842 (letter appeared in the *Missionary Herald* [October 1842]: 560), Aveline reminded his correspondent that he had always been supported by his congregation at Grahamstown or other private means, noting that "since I left England, I have never drawn sixpence form the Society's funds, and I have now the animating hope of annually contributing to their increase." He added, "I seem to have led a sad idle life in England compared with my now constant and multiplied engagements." See also Cox, *History*, 2:395, 400; *Baptist Magazine* 33 (1841): 73; *Missionary Herald* (March 1843): 180; Sydney Hudson-Reed, *By Taking Heed: The History of Baptists in Southern Africa 1820-1977* (Roodepoort, South Africa: Baptist Publishing House, 1983) 15-17; Stanley, *History*, 215.

Bagster, Samuel (1772-1851)—Educated at J. C. Ryland's academy at Northampton in the early 1780s (when George Dyer, the Romantic poet and antiquarian, was an usher), Bagster began his bookselling and publishing business in the Strand, London, in 1794. In 1816 he moved to Paternoster Row. Bagster (along with his sons) became best known for his publication of a Polyglot Bible as well as many other Bibles of outstanding scholarship and detail in numerous languages, both biblical and European. He was a member of the Baptist church in Keppel Street, London. See Samuel Bagster, *Samuel Bagster of London 1772-1851: An Autobiography* (London: Samuel Bagster and Sons, 1972); Ernest A. Payne, "John Linnell,

The World of Artists and the Baptists," *Baptist Quarterly* 40 (2003): 24; *DEB*.

Baker, Charles—Baker removed from Boston, Lincolnshire, in December 1837 to begin working with the fledgling Particular Baptist congregation in Stockport. Not long after his arrival, many who attended the Stockport Sunday School began to attend his ministry, and by September 1838, the church had been formally organized and Baker ordained as minister. The congregation soon purchased a building from the Socialists of Stockport, and after considerable renovations, the chapel was opened in May 1840, seating 750. Baker remained as pastor of Zion Chapel until 1845, enjoying considerable success. See Urwick, *Historical Sketches*, 308-309.

Baker, Moses (1755-1822)—Baker came to Jamaica from New York in 1783 as free black and worked in Kingston as a barber. Converted under the ministry of George Liele (1750?-1828), he soon began preaching in a house in Kingston and formed the first Baptist church there. He would later found the second Baptist church in Jamaica at Crooked Spring, on the estate of I. L. Winn, a Quaker. Winn's estate was later purchased by Samuel Vaughan, who was sympathetic to Baker's ministry (see letter 107). Thomas N. Swigle (see biographical entry below), like Baker, a black preacher who ministered in Kingston for many years, described Baker's work in a letter to John Rippon, published in the *Baptist Annual Register* in 1797: "Moses Baker [is] a free brown man, who is also one of our brethren, and now resides on Stretch and Sett sugar estate, in the parish of Saint James, about 140 miles westward from Kingston; he is employed there by Isaac Lascelles Winn, Esquire, to preach to his negroes on that property; and another gentleman —Vaughan, Esq. of that parish, who has a great number of slaves on his estate, has also employed brother Baker for that purpose; and allows him a compensation. And on those sugar estates, where permission is not granted, their slaves hungering after the good word of God, come of their own accord to brother Baker, at his place of residence, to be instructed by him: so he has in number abut one thousand brethren there; and the greater part of the hearers are converted souls." In 1802 new regulations passed by the authorities in Jamaica prohibed Baker from preaching to the slaves on the plantations, a ban which lasted for several years. During that time Baker became a correspondent of Rippon and Ryland, pleading for the cause of the slaves and for a white preacher to come and minister to them. Ryland struggled for several years to find a candidate to assist Baker, finally sending John Rowe (1788-1816) to Jamaica in 1814. See John Ryland's accounts of Baker in the *Evangelical Magazine* 11 (1803): 365, 550; and 12 (1804): 469; Christopher Brent Ballew, *The Impact of African-American Antecedents on the Baptist Foreign Missionary Movement: 1782-1825* (Lewiston [NY]: Edwin Mellon Press, 2004); *Baptist Annual Register*, 3:212-214; Edward A. Holmes, "George Liele: Negro Slavery's Prophet of Deliverance," *Baptist Quarterly* 20 (1963-1964): 340-351; 361; Cox, *History*, vol. 2; Clarke, *Memorials*, 18-30; Brooke 13-14; *DEB*.

Balch, **Lewis Penn Witherspoon** (1814-1875)—After serving briefly as an assistant minister at St. Andrew's Church, Philadelphia, Balch became the second rector at the newly-formed St. Bartholomew's Church (Episcopal) in New York City in October 1838. Originally from Virginia, Balch graduated from Princeton in 1834; he then studied for two years at the General Theological Seminary in New York City. He was one of many evangelical ministers who formed a prominent group within the Episcopal Church in America in the 1830s. Upon his arrival at St. Bartholomew's, however, Balch discovered that the diocese was markedly High Church. He maintained his evangelical position (as his letters in this collection on behalf of Low and the BMS suggests), even weathering the trial and suspension of his Bishop, Benjamin T. Onderdonk, for his Anglo-Catholic tendencies. Not long after his arrival at St. Batholomew's, Balch organized a Sunday school, doubling the church's membership in his first year; by 1844 the church had grown from 56 communicants to over 400. In 1839 Balch married the granddaughter of John Jay, first Chief Justice of the United States. He remained at St. Bartholomew's until 1850, during which time he published several editions of Edward Bickersteth's *A Treatise on the Lord's Supper* (1845, 1849, and 1855), and at least one original work, *God in the Storm: A Narrative . . . Prepared on Board the* Great Western, *after the Storm Encountered on her Recent Voyage* (1846). See E. Clowes Chorley, *The Centennial History of St. Bartholomew's Church in the City of New York, 1835-1935* (New York: n.p., 1935) 69-82.

Bamford, Charles (1727-1804)—Bamford was born at Whitworth, near Rochdale, Lancashire, and was converted through the preaching of William Grimshaw of Haworth. He joined the Independent meeting at Whitworth under James Burgess (see letter 6) in 1748, but eventually adopted Baptist views and was baptized at Bacup in March 1755. He joined the church there and began preaching in homes. His first ministerial position was at Pellon Lane Church, Halifax (1755-1760), followed by a term at Machpelah, Oakenshaw, where he remained until 1774. In 1775, Bamford preached for a time to the congregation at Higher Lane, Haslingden, near Accrington, and then at Tottlebank. He returned to Haslingden, then came back once again to Tottlebank for a three year trial, "but the church did not accept him, it is supposed owing to his certifying the christening of an infant, which was contrary to Baptist doctrine." Robert Wylie writes: "Leaving there, he declined preaching for a time until a newly-formed interest at Pole-Moor in Yorkshire again called him forth to labour, and there he preached with considerable success for several years." Bamford served the Baptist church at Pole Moor, or Slaughwaite, near Huddersfield, Yorkshire, from 1793 to 1804. The *Baptist Annual Register* noted of the church at Pole Moor: "... the meeting-house is built on the common, a mile north of the village of Slaughwaite, six miles from Halifax, and three from Sallendine Nook. The number of members about sixty. A pleasing and an increasing congregation.—'The good old pastor is more popular than ever.'" See *Baptists of Yorkshire,* ed. Shipley, 216, 233; Robert J. V. Wylie, *The Baptist Churches of Accrington and District* (Accrington: W. Shuttleworth, Wellington Press, 1923) 33, 34; *Baptist Annual Register,* 3:39.

Barclay, George (1774-1838)—Born into a dissenting family in Kilwinning, Ayrshire, Barclay was apprenticed at thirteen to a cabinet-maker. About 1790 he was converted and shortly thereafter was called to preach. He married in 1796 and left for Paisley, where he prepared for the Congregational ministry. Encouraged by Robert Haldane, Barclay entered an academy established by the Haldanes at Dundee in late 1799, but the next spring moved to Glasgow to study under Greville Ewing. In April 1802 he began ministering in Kilwinning as part of a mission effort to the outer areas of Scotland. During his first year at Kilwinning, he became an immersionist and in December 1803 formed a Baptist church, independent of all other Baptist churches in Scotland or England. Established as an "English" Baptist church (he did not follow the Scotch Baptist model), his church nevertheless reflected the influence of the Haldane congregational model. His interest in the Baptist movement and the missionary effort brought him into close contact with Andrew Fuller, John Ryland, John Sutcliff, and Christopher Anderson, becoming "their companion and aid when they visited the north on behalf of the Mission." As Hugh Anderson writes, "Their letters to him, of which there are many among his papers, breathe the warmth, and generous nature of their Christian friendship. He was also the correspondent of *Carey*, and *Marshman*, and *Ward*, and *Judson*; and in all the trials and triumphs of the Baptist Mission he ever took the deepest interest." He played an important part in the reunification of the BMS and the Serampore Mission in 1837-1838 (his son, a BMS missionary, had died in Calcutta in 1837). Along with Christopher Anderson, Barclay helped establish an itinerant society for Scotland in 1807 and regularly conducted preaching tours of western Scotland, using the tour also as a means of promoting the work of the BMS. Barclay traveled to Ireland with John Saffery of Salisbury in July-August 1813 on behalf of the BMS. See Anderson, *Letters*, 48; John Leechman, "Memoir of the Late Rev. George Barclay," *Baptist Magazine* 31 (1839): 1-5; Derek B. Murray, "Christopher Anderson and Scotland," in *A Mind for Mission: Essays in Appreciation of the Rev. Christopher Anderson (1782-1852)*, ed. Meek, 4, 6; D. W. Bebbington, ed., *The Baptists in Scotland: A History* (Glasgow: Baptist Union of Scotland, 1988) 33-35; Talbot, *Search for a Common Identity*, 109, 115, 123; *DEB*.

Barrett, William Garland—Barrett was one of six LMS missionaries who came to Jamaica in 1835, four settling in the south and two in the north. Barrett was stationed at Four Paths, in Clarendon. According to Bryan Stanley, not long after their arrival, Barrett and other non-Baptist missionaries in Jamaica became critical of the BMS missionaries, alleging the phenomenal growth of the Baptist churches was at the expense of "spiritual discipline and purity." Their chief complaint centered upon the practice by some of the Baptist missionaries of selling "tickets" each quarter to the communicant members of the various Baptist churches as a means of controlling current members and new communicants. The phenomenal growth of the Baptist churches in Jamaica in the 1830s required such a method (which the Baptists actually borrowed from the Methodists). Although subject to occasional abuse, the chief cause of the "breach" between the Baptist and non-Baptist missionaries in Jamaica may have been the overwhelming success of the Baptist interests in relation to the efforts made by the LMS missionaries. Samuel Green argued in 1842 that Barrett's complaints were "purely retaliatory." Patricia T. Rooke takes a similar line, describing Barrett as "a highly strung man, given to hysterical malice and suffering some personal and nervous strain not assuaged by the lack of success of his mission in Jamaica." Barrett returned to England in 1848 due to poor health and settled in Hertfordshire, becoming pastor of an Independent chapel at Royston. His son, William Fletcher Barrett (1844-1925) became a pioneer in the area of psychical research. See Clarke, *Memorials*, 231; Stanley, *History*, 85; Samuel Green, *Baptist Mission in Jamaica: A Review of W. G. Barrett's Pamphlet entitled A Reply to the Circular of the BMS Committee* (London: Houlston and Stoneman; and G. and J. Dyer, 1842) 5; *Baptist Magazine* 34 (1842): 586; Patricia T. Rooke, "Evangelical Missionary Rivalry in the British West Indies: A Study in Religious Altruism and Economic Reality," *Baptist Quarterly* 29 (1981-1982): 348; Richard Noakes, "The 'Bridge which is between Physical and Psychical Research': William Fletcher Barrett, Sensitive Flames, and Spiritualism," *History of Science* 42 (2004): 419-423.

Bayley [Bailey], George—Bayley was a Baptist layman living in Camberwell, London. Like Joseph Fletcher (see entry below), he was serving at various times on the Committee of the Baptist Building Fund and the Baptist Theological Education Society. Bayley collected £1.9 for the BMS in November 1840, and paid £1.1 for his annual subscription to the BMS in February 1841 and March 1842. He may be the same Mr. Bailey who, along with a Miss Bailey, contributed £5 each to the Jubilee Fund in December 1842 as part of the donations from members of the Baptist church in Eagle Street, London. By trade he was a ship inspector for Lloyd's Register (the title page for his 1844 book listed him as "surveyor to Lloyd's Register of Shipping"), a company founded in 1760 to examine merchant ships and classify them according to the sea-worthiness (Lloyd's Register should not be confused with Lloyd's of London, the famous insurance company, though both originated from the same coffee house). Because of his expertise, Bayley played an important role for the BMS Committee in the acquisition of the *Dove* between 1842 and 1844. When John Clarke first proposed the purchase of a steam vessel for the BMS work at Fernando Po, a subcommittee was formed and was immediately asked "to confer with Mr Bayley, of Lloyd's, more specially in reference to the probable annual cost of such vessel" (f. 27). Bayley proposed that the cost of a steamer would be between £800 and £1000 a year; he thus recommended instead that the Committee purchase a 70-ton schooner, which would only cost between £300 and £400 per year. Bayley would continue to serve as the advisor to the subcommittee that would eventually opt for a sailing schooner equipped both with a steam engine and an Archimedes screw. Bayley was involved in making judgments about the *Chilmark*, as well as the second version of the *Dove*, which was purchased in late summer 1844 and finally sailed for Africa in 1845. Bayley granted the ship a Certificate of Lloyds, describing it to the

BMS Committee as "the first description of the First Class." He authored *Tables Showing the Progress of the Shipping Interest of the British Empire, United States, and France* (London: Smith, Elder, and Co., 1844). See *Baptist Magazine* 33 (1841): 59; 35 (1843): 535; 36 (1844): 656, 663; *Missionary Herald* (January 1841): 45; (April 1841): 207; (May 1842): 270; (January 1843): 52; BMS Committee Minutes, Vol. I (Jan. 1843-May 1844), ff. 27, 29-30, 33, 94; Vol. J (May 1844-July 1847), ff. 40, 43, 74.

Baynes, Joseph (1795-1875)—Baynes first came under the influence of Thomas Spencer, Independent minister in Liverpool, when he was fourteen; at sixteen, however, he was baptized and joined the Baptist church in Lime Street, Liverpool, led by James Lister. In 1815 Baynes entered Bristol Academy and later studied at Glasgow. In 1818 he became William Winterbotham's assistant at Shortwood, Gloucestershire, and in 1820 pastor of the church in South Street, Wellington, Somerset, where he remained for 41 years. He retired in 1861, occasionally preaching in and around Bristol.

Beatson, John (1743-1798)—Born into an Anglican family near Leeds, as a young man Beatson joined the Independent church at White-Chapel in Leeds. His first pastorate was at the Independent church at Cleck-heaton, but during his year there he became a Baptist. He was baptized by William Crabtree at Bradford in December 1767, and shortly thereafter accepted a call to the Baptist church at Sutton-in-Craven, where he remained until 1770. Beatson ministered to the Baptist meeting at Salt-house Lane, Hull, from 1771 to 1794. He had a very successful ministry at Hull; besides the two works mentioned in letter 20, Beatson also published a political sermon, *On the Duty and Interest of Men as Members of Civil Society* ([[Hull], 1778); a sermon on the slave trade, *Compassion the Duty and Dignity of Man, and Cruelty the Disgrace of his Nature* (1789); and a posthumous work titled *The Divine Right of a Christian to Freedom of Enquiry and Practice in Religious Matters. To which are prefixed Brief Memoirs of the Life, Character and Writings of the Author* (Hull, 1799). John Hindle succeeded Beatson at Hull. See *Baptists of Yorkshire*, ed. Shipley, 67, 95; John Beatson, *The Divine Right of a Christian to Freedom of Enquiry and Practice in Religious Matters*, 2nd ed. (Hull: W. Cowley, [1799]) iii-xvi.

Beck, Thomas (1755?-1844)—Beck was born at Southwark and ministered at Whitefield's Tabernacle, Moorfields, and in Kennington before serving as pastor at Hermitage Street in Wapping, 1776-1777. He then supplied at various places before ministering at Princes Street, Gravesend, 1780-1788. He returned to London and pastored the Independent congregation at Bury Street, St. Mary Axe, London, from 1788 to 1825, living in Deptford.

Beddome, Benjamin (1717-1795)—Beddome, the son of John Beddome (see below), was a well known Baptist minister and hymnodist. After studying at Bristol Academy and in London, he was baptized at Goodman Fields in 1739 and admitted to the Baptist Board in 1740. He began supplying at Bourton-on-the-Water that same year and was ordained there in September 1743, where he remained until his death. He composed some 800 hymns in his lifetime, most of which were published posthumously in 1817 in *Hymns Adapted to Public Worship*. See Michael A. G. Haykin, "Benjamin

Beddome (1717-1795)," ed. Haykin, in *The British Particular Baptists*, 1:167-182; Hayden, *Continuity and Change*, 224; *DEB*.

Beddome, John (1674-1757)—In 1697 Beddome, a member of the Baptist meeting in Horsleydown, Southwark, moved to Alcester, Warwickshire, where he assisted John Willis, pastor of the Alcester Baptist church. While in Alcester, Beddome founded a school at nearby Henley. He took over as pastor in Alcester upon Willis's death in 1705, and in 1711 invited Bernard Foskett, then living in London, to become his assistant; the two men thereafter remained lifelong friends and colleagues. Foskett left Alcester in 1720 to become pastor at Broadmead in Bristol and Principal of the Bristol Academy. In 1724 Beddome followed his friend to Bristol, succeeding Emmanuel Gifford at the Baptist meeting in the Pithay, first as assistant pastor to William Bazley from 1725 to 1736, and then as pastor until his death in 1757, when he was replaced by John Tommas. Foskett would live in Beddome's home in Bristol for nearly 40 years. See Jacqui Snowdon, *The Alcester Baptist Story 1640-1990* (Alcester: Warwick, 1990) 18-19; Robert W. Oliver, *The Strict Baptist Chapels of England: The Chapels of Wiltshire and the West* (London: Fauconberg Press, 1968) 100; Hayden, *Continuity and Change*, 64-67.

Belcher, Joseph (1794-1859)—Originally from Birmingham, Belcher was a prolific author, producing numerous biographies of evangelical figures from the late 18th and early 19th centuries. An active leader within the Baptist Home Missionary Society, he ministered to churches at Somersham, Folkestone, Chelsea, and Greenwich from 1818 to 1842. From 1832 to 1840 he served as Secretary to the Baptist Union. He emigrated to America in 1844 and died in Philadelphia in 1859. He published brief biographies of George Whitefield, Isaac Mann, and William Carey, as well as a history of the Baptist Irish Society in 1845. See *DEB*.

Belsham, Thomas (1750-1829)—After completing his studies at the Independent Academy at Daventry, Belsham remained for the next seven years as an assistant tutor (see letter 11) before beginning his pastoral career at Worcester. He returned to Daventry three years later to become Headmaster of the Academy. He remained there until 1789, when he resigned to become a Unitarian minister. He assisted Joseph Priestley in the formation of a Unitarian college at Hackney, and then, after Priestley's emigration to America in 1794, became pastor of the Unitarian congregation at Gravel-Pit in Hackney. In 1805 he succeeded John Disney at Essex Street (Unitarian) Chapel, London, where he remained until his death in 1829. His first work, *Review of Mr. Wilberforce's Treatise Entitled Practical View* (1798), created considerable controversy. His most popular work was *A Summary View of the Evidence and Practical Importance of the Christian Revelation* (1807). He was a frequent contributor to the *Quarterly Review*, *Gentleman's Magazine*, and the *Monthly Repository*.

Bevan, Joseph Gurney (1753-1814)—The son of a chemist/druggist in Lombard Street, London, Bevan was the cousin of Joseph John Gurney and Elizabeth Gurney Fry, both well known Quaker activists. He took over his father's business in 1784, and retired ten years later. He became a Quaker at seventeen, and remained a steadfast follower, refusing to supply armed ships with drugs from his firm. He began writing for an almanac published by the Quaker printer, James Phillips, in 1794, and wrote for four years, contributing numerous poems. He moved to Stoke Newington in 1796, where he published *Refutation of the Misrepresentations of the Society of Friends, Commonly called Quakers, with a Life of James Nayler; also a Summary of the History, Doctrine, and Discipline of Friends* (1800). In 1802 he published his *Appeal to the Society of Friends*, in which he showed that Quakers were not and had never been Unitarians. *Thoughts on Reason and Revelation* appeared in 1805. He was considered by many to be one of the ablest of the Quaker apologists. See *DEB.*

Bicheno, James (1752-1831)—As a teenager, Bicheno joined the Baptist congregation at St. Andrew's Street in Cambridge. He entered Bristol Academy in 1776, and began his pastoral ministry at Falmouth in 1778. Between 1780 and 1807, Bicheno ministered to the Baptist congregation at Newbury, where he also operated a school. He continued as a schoolmaster in Newbury until 1811, when he removed to Coate [Cote]. He returned to Newbury in 1819 and served once again as pastor of the Baptist church from 1820 to 1824. He suffered from paralysis after 1824, being unable to speak or move. His chief concern was biblical prophecy (as letter 109 demonstrates), especially in regard to European events from 1789 through the Napoleonic Wars, as evidenced in such publications as *Signs of the Times* (1793); *A Word in Season: Or, a Call to the Inhabitants of Great Britain, to Stand Prepared for the Consequences of the Present War* (1795); and *The Probable Progress and Issue of the Commotions which have Agitated Europe since the French Revolution, argued from the Aspect of Things, and the Writings of the Prophets* (1797). See John Oddy, "Bicheno and Tyso on the Prophecies," *Baptist Quarterly* 35 (1993-1994): 81-89; *Church Book: St. Andrew's Street*, 52-53, 56-57, 134-135; Hayden, *Continuity and Change*, 225; *DEB.*

Biddulph, Thomas Tregenna (1763-1838)—An evangelical Anglican, Biddulph graduated from Queen's College, Oxford, with a B.A. in 1784 and an M.A. in 1787. After a series of curacies in Padstow, Ditcheat, St. Mary-le-Port, Wansborough and Bengeworth (1793-1803), he became curate of St. James, Bristol, and Dauston in 1799, positions he held until his death in 1838. He was active in the Sunday school movement, the Tract Society, and the Church Missionary Society from their inceptions, as well as the British and Foreign Bible Society. He helped found the periodical *Zion's Trumpet* (later *The Christian Guardian*) in 1795. He was a strong Church and State man, opposed to Roman dogma and Catholic Emancipation as well as parliamentary reform. See *DEB.*

Birley, George—Birley was raised in the General Baptist congregation at Ashford, Derbyshire. In 1765 he removed to Birchcliff, Yorkshire, to assist Dan Taylor as a tutor in his academy there. In 1768 he left Taylor's school and became a tutor at J. C. Ryland's academy in Northampton, although he retained his membership in Taylor's church at Birchcliff. While at Northampton, Birley preached frequently to Baptist congregations in Moulton,

Spratton, Burton-Latimer, and Stony-Stratford. The General Baptist meeting at St. Ives, which had long been without a stated minister, invited Birley to preach for them in the early 1770s, and he supplied regularly for several years before moving there in 1777, at which time he commenced regular preaching duties. Birley was not officially ordained as pastor of the congregation at St. Ive's until 1786; Dan Taylor of London, his close friend, and Robert Robinson of Cambridge performed the service. In 1789 Birley led the congregation into membership in the New Connection of General Baptists. Birley's wife died in 1782, with Taylor preaching her funeral sermon. Birley was still ministering at St. Ive's in 1818, subscribing that year to Adam Taylor's *The History of the English General Baptists* (2 vols; 1818). A collection of letters between Birley and Dan Taylor, composed between 1771 and 1808, resides at the Angus Library, Regent's Park College, Oxford (D/Hus 1/6), as well as letters between Birley and the Rev. William Thompson of Boston, Leicestershire (D/Hus 1/7).

Birt, Caleb Evans (1795-1854)—The son of Isaiah Birt (see below), C. E. Birt studied law at Cambridge but did not graduate (due to his dissenting status and refusal to subscribe to the Thirty-Nine Articles). In 1813, he was baptized by his brother, John Birt, at that time the Baptist minister at Hull. Shortly thereafter he entered Bristol Academy, and later (1816) completed an A.M. in theology at Edinburgh University. He served as pastor of the Baptist congregation at Agard Street, Derby, for the next ten years before removing to the church in Meeting-house Alley, Portsea, Hampshire, where he ministered from 1827 to 1837. He was President of the Baptist Union in 1836 and in 1837 became pastor at Broadmead, Bristol, where he remained until 1844. His final ministry was at Wantage in Berkshire, 1844-1854.

Birt, Isaiah (1758-1837)—After completing his studies at Bristol Academy, where he became a lifelong friend of Robert Hall, Birt became co-pastor of the Baptist congregation at Plymouth in 1781, preaching in the meeting house at Liberty Fields, now Pembroke Street, Dock. Samuel Pearce was converted in 1783 through the preaching of Birt. In 1789 the meeting at Dock organized as an autonomous church, with Birt as pastor. He remained there until 1813, first at Liberty Fields and then in the new chapel at Morice Square, Dock. Birt also preached in Saltash, where a separate church would eventually be formed. In 1798 William Steadman became his assistant pastor. Steadman would later become pastor of the congregation at Liberty Fields, with Birt remaining at Morice Square. During the early 1790s, Birt, like many Baptists, was an active supporter of the French Revolution and an opponent of the war with France, especially Pitt's policies that seemed to infringe on the constitutional rights of Britons. Birt's aggressive church planting in neighboring villages created enough clerical hostility that he was forced to defend himself in his *Vindication of the Baptists, in Three Letters, Addressed to a Friend in Saltash* (Bristol, 1793). In 1813 he accepted the pastorate of the Baptist congregation at Cannon Street in Birmingham, where he served until 1827, at which time he retired to Hackney. See Henry M. Nicholson, *A History of the Baptist Church Now Meeting in*

George Street Chapel, Plymouth, from 1620 (London: Baptist Union Publications, 1904) 83-85; Hayden, *Continuity and Change*, 225; *DEB.*

Biss, John (d. 1807)—The Bisses, along with their daughter, Mary, were members of the Baptist church at Plymouth Dock under Isaiah Birt. Biss studied for the ministry under John Sutcliff at Olney. The Bisses, along with Joshua Rowe, Richard Mardon, William Moore, and their families, sailed from Bristol for Serampore (via America) in December 1803. Biss's health deteriorated quickly upon his arrival in Bengal in 1804; he was forced to return to England, but never arrived, dying on board the *Bremen* in February 1807. Hannah Biss later married her fellow traveler William Moore (now a widower himself) in 1813. She died in 1843. See Cox, *History,* 2:151, 168; "Sutcliff's Academy at Olney," *Baptist Quarterly* 4 (1928-1929): 277; *DEB.*

Bland, Francis—Bland ministered to the Baptist congregation at Soham, where Andrew Fuller had formerly served as pastor. Bland was originally a member of the Soham church and studied at Bristol Academy from January 1787 until July 1788, at which time he was called to the Soham church, where he remained until 1802. See *Baptist Annual Register,* 1:4.

Blundel, Thomas, Sr. (1752-1824)—Blundel was admitted to Bristol Academy from Andrew Fuller's church at Kettering in 1790. He left Bristol in 1791 and began supplying for the Baptist meeting at Arnsby, where Robert Hall, Sr. had ministered. After a year and a half of trial ministry, Blundel was ordained at Arnsby on 3 April 1793, remaining there until the spring of 1804, when he removed to Luton. During his tenure at Luton, he published a volume of sermons as well as *An Essay on Revelations* (1810). He was excluded at Luton for adultery, but remained in the ministry. His final pastorate was at Keighley (1812-1823), after which, due to ill health, he returned to Luton, where he died in 1824. Like his father, Thomas Blundel, Jr. (1786-1861), also studied at Bristol Academy (1804-1809). Upon leaving there in 1810, he became pastor at College Lane in Northampton, where he remained until 1824. He formed the College Lane Sunday School in 1810. The younger Blundel was a member of the BMS committee (1815-1828), secretary of Stepney College (1827-1828), and chaplain of Mill Hill School (1821-1831). He later opened his own school at Totteridge and ended his days, strangely enough, as an Anglican clergyman. See Fuller to Ward, 4 February 1812 (BMS Archives, I); *Baptists of Yorkshire,* ed. Shipley, 188; John T. Godfrey and James Ward, *The History of Friar Lane Baptist Church, Nottingham* (Nottingham: H. B. Saxton, 1903) 177-179; Hayden, *Continuity and Change,* 226; Payne, *College Street Church, Northampton*; *DEB.*

Booth, Abraham (1734-1806)—Booth was born at Blackwell, near Alfreton, Derbyshire, where he worked as a farm laborer throughout his youth. Though he never received a formal education, he acquired enough learning to open his own school at Sutton-in-Ashfield in 1758, shortly after his marriage. He had been baptized in 1755 and became associated with the Baptists in Nottinghamshire. He switched from an Arminian position to a strict Calvinistic one, and in 1768 published his famous work, *The Reign of*

Grace. Shortly after this, the church at Little Prescot Street, Goodman's Fields, London, called Booth to be their pastor, and he was ordained on 16 February 1769, remaining there until his death in 1806. Among his other published works are *An Apology for the Baptists* (1778), *Paedobaptism Examined* (1784), *Essay on the Kingdom of Christ* (1788), *Commerce in the Human Species* (1792), *Glad Tidings to Perishing Sinners* (1796), and *Pastoral Cautions* (1805). See Ernest A. Payne, "Abraham Booth, 1734-1806," *Baptist Quarterly* 26 (1975-1976): 28-42; Robert W. Oliver, "Abraham Booth (1734-1806), ed. Haykin, in *The British Particular Baptists*, 2:31-55; *DEB*.

Bosworth, Newton (1778-1848)—Bosworth arrived in Cambridge in 1799 as Olinthus Gregory's assistant in his day school. Shortly thereafter he joined St. Andrew's Street, commencing a lifelong friendship with Robert Hall. When Gregory left for Woolwich in January 1803, Bosworth took over as headmaster of the school, a position he maintained for the next twenty years. He married Catherine Paul of Cambridge in July 1805, and two years later moved to Northampton Street, where he opened a boarding school. In 1811, Bosworth was elected a deacon at St. Andrew's Street. In the summer of 1823, he moved to London, settling at Tottenham, where he opened another boarding school (see letter 147). In 1834 he left England for Canada, where his family had emigrated the year before. While in Canada, Bosworth was instrumental in the formation of the Canada Baptist College in 1838; he also ministered to several congregations in Upper Canada, helping to form the Canada Baptist Union in 1843. He authored several works, including articles in *Pantologia* (1808-1813); *The Accidents of Human Life* (1813); *Hochelaga Depicta* (1839), and a history of Montreal. See *Church Book: St. Andrew's Street*, 166-167.

Botsford, Edmund (1745-1819)—Botsford was born in Woburn, Bedfordshire, and grew up in the local Baptist church. In 1765 he immigrated to Charleston, South Carolina, and was baptized into the Baptist church there in March 1767. In 1769 he began studying for the ministry, receiving his license to preach in 1771. He ministered to a group of Baptists at Tuckseeking, Georgia (about 40 miles from Savannah), and was ordained by the Charleston church in March 1772, but by the end of 1772 he had left Tuckseeking. At that time Botsford and Daniel Marshall were the only two ordained Baptist ministers in Georgia. In 1773 he organized a Baptist church in Burke County, Georgia, the second Baptist church to be established in that state. He ministered there until 1779, when he returned to South Carolina as a result of the British control of Georgia during the Revolutionary War (Botsford, like most Baptists in America, was a strong supporter of the American cause). He soon became minister of the Baptist church at Welsh Neck in Orange County, South Carolina, a part of the Bethel Baptist Association. In 1780, however, he was forced to flee once again, this time to Virginia, returning to South Carolina in December 1781. While ministering at Welsh Neck, he began preaching often in Charleston, rebuilding the pastorless church there. In 1786 the church was restored to a sufficient capacity to call Richard Furman as pastor. Botsford's congregation at

Welsh Neck was a large one, numbering some 167 members in 1790, according to John Asplund. Botsford corresponded with a number of English Baptists, sending Sutcliff an account of his wife's death in 1790 and of his church's efforts in joining with Sutcliff and the English Baptists in forming a regular monthly prayer meeting (Botsford's sister married a Mr. Hinton of Upton, a relation of James Hinton, Baptist minister at Oxford). See John Asplund, *The Annual Register of the Baptist Denomination, in North-America; to the First of November, 1790* (Southampton County VA: J. Asplund, 1791) 43; *Baptist Annual Register*, 1:104-108; Charles D. Mallary, *Memoirs of Elder Edmund Botsford* (Charleston: W. Riley, 1832); also James Hinton to Edmund Botsford, 8 November 1787 (MS., copy at Bristol Baptist College, Misc. Letters, G96, Box 7).

Bradburn, Samuel (1751-1816)—Born in Gilbralter, Bradburn became one of the leading Methodist ministers of his day. He was called the "Methodist Demosthenes" for his oratorical skills. He began itinerating in 1774 in the Liverpool circuit and was a close friend of John and Charles Wesley. He came under fire in Bristol for disturbing the peace of the society by favoring ordination and opening the Portland chapel during regular church hours and administering the sacraments. He usually supported the people against the "High Church bigots." He was ordained in 1792 and published shortly thereafter a pamphlet, *The Question, Are the Methodists Dissenters?* He was one of the nine who drew up the compromise Plan of Pacification in 1795 and was elected Methodist Conference President in 1799. See *DEB*.

Brine, John (1703-1765)—Brine was originally from Kettering (as was his close friend and fellow High Calvinist, John Gill). He served as pastor of the Baptist congregation at Curriers' Hall, Cripplegate, London, 1730-1765. Gill, Brine, and other High Calvinists refrained from offering their hearers an *open* invitation to accept Christ. Fuller, Ryland, Sutcliff and other Baptist ministers would eventually reject this position in favor of a more moderate, evangelical Calvinism; the writings of Gill and Brine, nevertheless, remained highly influential in their defense of Calvinism and Baptist distinctives. Brine's major works include *A Defence of the Doctrine of Eternal Justification* (1732); *Remarks upon a Pamphlet, intitled, Some Doctrines in the Superlapsarian Scheme Impartially Examin'd by the Word of God* (1736); *The Certain Efficacy of the Death of Christ* (1743); *An Antidote Against a Spreading Antinomian Principle* (1750); and *A Vindication of Divine Justice* (1754). See Hayden, *Continuity and Change*, 175-194; *DEB*.

Brock, William (1807-1875)—After serving an apprenticeship to a watchmaker, Brock worked as a journeyman tradesman before becoming a ministerial student at Stepney College in 1830. He began his pastoral career at the Baptist church at St. Mary's, Norwich (1833-1848), before removing to the newly established Bloomsbury Chapel in London, where he remained as pastor until 1872. Brock became one of the most prominent Baptists of his day, noted for his outreach programs to young people and the disadvantaged, as well as his support for foreign and home missions, including the YMCA. He was actively involved in youth and adult education during his time in Norwich (which may explain the reference to a "Literary" Institution in letter 244). He served as president of the Baptist Union in 1869. For more on Brock, see Birrell, *Life of William Brock*; Faith Bowers, *A Bold Experiment: The Story of Bloomsbury Chapel and Bloomsbury Central Baptist Church 1848-1999* (London: Bloomsbury Central Baptist Church, 1999); *DEB.*

Brook, Benjamin (1776-1848)—Born near Huddersfield, Yorkshire, Brook spent his early years attending the Independent congregation at Holmfield, under the ministry of Robert Gallond. In 1797 Brook entered Rotherham College as a ministerial student, leaving in 1801 to assume the pastorate of the Independent congregation at Tutbury, where he would remain until 1830. He then retired to Birmingham, and spent his remaining years in literary and historical endeavors. His major academic interest was Puritan and nonconformist history, which led to his most important publication, *The Lives of the Puritans: Containing a Biographical Account of Those Divines who Distinguished Themselves in the Cause of Religious Liberty, from the Reformation under Queen Elizabeth, to the Act of Uniformity in 1662* (3 vols, (1813). He also published *Appeal to Facts to Justify Dissenters in their Separation from the Established Church* (1806; 3rd ed. 1815) and *Memoir of the Life and Writings of Thomas Cartwright* (1845). At his death he was working on a history of the Puritans in New England.

Brooksbank, Joseph (1762-1825)—Originally from Yorkshire, Brooksbank was educated at Homerton Academy, 1780-1785. He preached at Haberdashers' Hall, London, from 1785 to 1825, eventually uniting his Independent church with the Baptist congregation at Broad Street. In 1801 he served on the committee of the Religious Tract Society. See *Baptist Annual Register*, 3:543.

Brown, James Baldwin (1785-1843)—Brown began practicing law at the Inner Temple in 1816, traveling for a time on the northern circuit and the Lancashire sessions. His wife was the sister of Thomas Raffles, Independent minister in Liverpool. Brown's son was the Rev. James Baldwin Brown (1820-1884), a leading nineteenth-century Congregationalist minister. Brown was widely known for his *Memoirs of the Public and Private Life of John Howard, the Philanthropist* (1823). Previously, along with Thomas Raffles and Jeremiah Holmes Wiffen, he contributed to a work entitled *Poems by Three Friends* (1813).

Brown, John (d. 1800)—Brown began his ministry at the Baptist meeting at Kettering in 1751 and was involved in the formation of the Northamptonshire Association. After a dispute over the church's management of a friendly society for poor people, Brown left the church on 24 January 1771 and formed a new meeting in Kettering, which survived until 1786. He died in London in 1800. See Gladys M. Barrett, *A Brief History of Fuller Church, Kettering* (St. Albans: Parker Bros., 1946) 5.

Brown, William—Brown was a founding member in 1827 of the Baptist church at Wigan, which first met at Commercial Hall under Benjamin Millard. The church moved to King Street in 1854. Brown became the first superintendent of the church's Sunday school, formed in September 1826. By the mid-1830s, the school was instructing over 300 pupils. However, the church remained small for many years. A David Brown, probably a relation, was also a founding member of the church. See J. H. Malins Johnson and James Starr, *One Hundred Years: A Brief History of King Street Baptist Church, Wigan. 1826-1926* (Wigan: J. Starr and Sons, 1926) 8-11; Ian Sellers, *Pathways to Faith: A History of Wigan Baptist Church 1796-1996* (Wigan: n.p., 1996).

Brunsdon, Daniel (1777-1801)—Originally from Pershore, Brunsdon was baptized by John Ryland, Jr., and trained for the ministry by John Sutcliff at Olney. John Chamberlain was his fellow student at that time. Brunsdon sailed for India in 1799 with his new wife (a Miss Hirons of Fairford, Gloucestershire), the Marshmans, William Grant, and William Ward. His ministry in Serampore was short-lived, unfortunately, for he died of an enlarged spleen and mercury poisoning in July 1801. His wife later married James Rolt, a builder and lay worker in India in 1803; she returned to England in 1810. See Cox, *History*, 2:76; *DEB.*

Bull, William (1738-1814)—Born near Wellingborough, Northamptonshire, Bull entered Daventry Academy in 1760, where many students had already adopted Arianism. He remained a decided Calvinist his entire life, however. In 1764 he succeeded James Belsham as pastor of the Independent congregation at Newport Pagnell. Shortly after his arrival there, he opened a small academy and soon became friends with John Newton, then vicar at Olney. With the help of Newton and some of his Evangelical friends, such as William Wilberforce and Henry Thornton, Bull expanded his small school into an Academy for training ministers in 1783. His circle of Anglican Evangelicals expanded to include Zachary Macaulay, Thomas Babington, and many others, a group that later became known as the "Clapham Sect." Bull served from 1797 to 1814 as the first President of the Bedfordshire Union of Christians. His wife, Hannah (d. 1814), was the sister of Mrs. Mary Andrews of Olney, in whose house John Sutcliff lived between 1775 and 1795. See Josiah Bull, *Memorials of the Rev. William Bull of Newport Pagnell* (London: Nisbet, 1865); Haykin, *One Heart*, 115.

Bunting, Jabez (1779-1858)—The son of a Manchester tailor, Bunting was originally trained to be a doctor. In 1794, however, he underwent a Methodist conversion and by 1799 had become a Wesleyan itinerant preacher. After a couple of short ministries, he came to London in 1803 and began working with foreign missions and publishing for the Methodists. He would remain a key player in the Wesleyan hierarchy thereafter, helping to form the Methodist Missionary Society in 1813. He was keen on administration, which eventually led to his decline in preaching. He served as President of the Methodist Conference in 1820, 1828, 1836, and 1844, as well as Conference Secretary on many occasions. See *DEB.*

Burchell, Thomas (1799-1846)—Burchell was converted in the Baptist church at Nailsworth in 1816. After his marriage in 1822 and completion of his studies at Bristol Academy, he sailed for Jamaica, settling at Montego Bay early in 1824. Ill health forced his return to England in 1826, at which time he made known his views on slavery in a public letter. When he returned to Jamaica in 1827 he was sent to court because of the letter. He traveled to

England for a short visit in 1831, but returned to Jamaica during the middle of the slave revolt in early 1832. He was arrested, but escaped to England, still advocating abolition. He returned once again to Jamaica in 1834 and continued to be an important leader for the BMS. Numerous references to Burchell appear in Cox, *History,* vol. 2, and in Clarke, *Memorials;* see also Gordon A. Catherall, "Thomas Burchell, Gentle Rebel," *Baptist Quarterly* 21 (1965-1966): 349-363; Catherine Hall, *Civilizing Subjects, Metropole and Colony in English Imagination, 1830-1867* (Cambridge UK: Polity, 2002) 84-209; *DEB.*

Burder, George (1752-1832)—During his time as Independent minister at Coventry (1783-1803), Burder became a leader in the Sunday School movement, assisting also in the founding of the London Missionary Society (1795), the Religious Tract Society (1799), and the British and Foreign Bible Society (1804). He moved to Islington in 1803 to become secretary of the London Missionary Society, a post he held until 1827. During this time he ministered to the Independent congregation at Fetter Lane, London. He authored several works of note during the last quarter of the eighteenth century, including *Early Piety, or, Memoirs of Children Eminently Serious Interspersed with Familiar Dialogues, Emblematical Pictures, Prayers, Graces, and Hymns* (1776), *A Collection of Hymns, from Various Authors, Intended as a Supplement to Dr. Watts's Hymns and Imitation of the Psalms* (1784), and his most famous work, *Village Sermons; Or ... Plain and Short Discourses on the Principal Doctrines of the Gospel; Intended for the Use of Families, Sunday Schools, or Companies Assembled for Religious Instruction in Country Villages* (7 vols, 1798). See *DEB.*

Burgess, James (d. 1804)—Burgess ministered to a small Independent congregation at Whitworth, Lancashire, for many years. Powicke notes that by 1770 Burgess was preaching at Hatherlow, but returned to Whitworth in 1776 because of "his opposition to those who were for introducing musical instruments, and to those that were of the free will." He was best known for his sermon *Beelzebuub Driving and Drowning his Hogs* (London, 1770), delivered while serving as minister of Haugh-Fold chapel in Lancashire. He also authored *The Reconciler* (Manchester, 1794). Other works attributed to Burgess include *A Proverbial Catechism for Youth, The Pilgrim's Travels from Mount Sinai to Mount Zion,* and *Exposition and Select Meditations,* although I have not been able to locate any extant copies of these three works. See Powicke, *History,* 191; Urwick, *Historical Sketches,* 328.

Burls, William (1763-1837)—A wealthy London merchant from Lothbury, Burls joined John Rippon's congregation at Carter Lane, Southwark, on 1 March 1795, and became a deacon in 1802. He was a significant supporter of the BMS, serving as a trustee and the Society's London agent and treasurer for many years, often allowing the missionaries to draw their bills on his own name and account. He personally collected over £1000 for the Serampore Mission after the 1812 fire. He presided at the Birmingham meeting when the BMS was reorganized after Andrew Fuller's death in 1815. Among the other Londoners who were BMS committee members at various times with Burls were Joseph Gutteridge (1752-1844) (deacon at Little Prescot Street, Goodman's Fields), Benjamin Shaw, M.P., F. A. Cox of Hackney, Joseph Ivimey of Eagle Street, and William Newman of Stepney. Burls was also the first treasurer of the Baptist Union. See Horsleydown and Carter Lane Church Book, f. 67; "Calendar of Letters," *Baptist Quarterly* 7 (1934-1935): 40; Ernest A. Payne, *The Excellent Mr. Burls* (London: Kingsgate Press, 1943).

Burton, Richard (d. 1828)—Originally a member of Joseph Ivimey's congregation at Eagle Street, London, Burton was appointed as a BMS missionary in 1820 and sailed that year with Charles Evans (of the Pithay church in Bristol) to Sumatra (both men had been Bristol Academy students). They were joined the next year by William Robinson (1784-1853) of Olney, who had been working in Java since 1812. Evans and Burton had been asked by Sir Thomas Raffles, then governor of Sumatra, to open a station at Fort Marlborough, assisted by Nathaniel Ward, William Ward's nephew. Burton began his work in Sebolga, a Batta village in the bay of Tappanooli, learning the language and working with an orphan institution. During the insurrection in Sumatra in 1825, the Burtons, along with a number of girls from the orphanage, fled to Calcutta. They then took over the mission at Digah, where Joshua Rowe had laboured, assisting now in the education of over 250 children. Burton's wife died in 1826, and he followed not long afterwards, in September 1828. As Cox writes of Burton, "He was a diligent and faithful missionary, and he had many seals to his ministry among the European soldiers and others. He had applied himself zealously to the acquisition of the language, but he was not permitted to realise his devout expectations of labour and usefulness." See Cox, *History*, 2:353; 1:416.

Butfield, William (d. 1776)—Butfield served for many years as the Baptist minister at Thorn, Bedfordshire, where he was succeeded by Robert Faulkner (see letter 34). Butfield was a boyhood friend of Edmund Botsford (see entry above). See Mallary, *Memoirs*, 15-17.

Butterworth, John (1727-1803)—Butterworth served as minister of the Particular Baptist church at Cow Lane, Coventry, 1753-1803. He was originally from a prominent Baptist family in Rossendale, Lancashire. His *Serious Address* (1790), signed "Christophilus," was written in opposition to the Unitarianism of Priestley. He also produced a concordance and Bible dictionary. Three of his brothers were Baptist ministers as well: James at Bromsgrove, Henry at Bridgnorth, and Lawrence (1740-1828) at Evesham. John's son, Joseph (1770-1826), became a Methodist and a significant publisher (primarily works of law) in London; he also served as M.P. for Coventry (1812-1818) and later for Dover, and was a leading prominent Evangelical and friend of Wilberforce. See Clyde Binfield, *Pastors and People: The Biography of a Baptist Church, Queens' Road Coventry* (Coventry: Queens' Road Baptist Church, 1984) 20-28; *DEB*.

Button, William (1754-1821)—Button was raised in London and attended the Baptist meeting at Unicorn Yard, where William Clarke (1732-1795) preached from 1762 to 1784. After completing his studies at J. C. Ryland's academy in Northampton, Button returned to London for further study under Clarke and was called to the ministry by the congregation at Unicorn Yard on 15 August 1773. In May 1775 he became the initial pastor for the newly formed Baptist meeting at Dean Street, Southwark, where he remained until 1815. Besides his pastoral duties, Button also operated a successful printing business (and later with his son, Samuel). His major publications were *Remarks on a Treatise, entitled, The Gospel of Christ Worthy of All Acceptation; or, The Obligations of Men Fully to Credit and Cordially to Approve Whatever God Makes Known, by Andrew Fuller. Wherein the Nature of Special Faith in Christ is Considered, and Several of Mr. F.'s Mistakes Pointed Out, in a Series of Letters to a Friend* (1785); and *National Calamities Tokens of the Divine Displeasure: A Sermon Preached at the Meeting House Dean Street, Tooley Street, Southwark, on February 28, being the Day Appointed for a General Fast* (1794). See Unicorn Yard and Carter Lane Church Book, ff. 219, 224, and 230.

Campbell, John (1766-1840)—One of Scotland's most notable missionaries in the early years of the nineteenth century, Campbell was born in Edinburgh and became active in evangelistic efforts while working as a hardware merchant; he organized several Sunday schools in Edinburgh in the late 1780s and early 1790s. He began his ministry as a Congregationalist, working with James Haldane and others in forming an itinerant preaching society across Scotland. In the late 1790s he became director of the Scottish branch of the London Missionary Society. He was involved with bringing 24 children from Sierra Leone to Scotland to receive an education, but due to certain difficulties, the children were educated at Battersea, London, with Joseph Hughes superintending the work and John Foster serving as a tutor. Campbell removed to Hackney in 1804 to begin his ministry at the Independent Chapel, Kingsland Road. For a time he served as editor of the *Youth's Magazine*. In June 1812 he was sent by the London Missionary Society to tour portions of South Africa on behalf of the Society, returning in 1814 and publishing *Travels in South Africa, Undertaken at the Request of the Missionary Society* (1815). He made a second tour of the same region between 1818 and 1821. He was also the founder of the Tract Society of Scotland. See Robert Philip, *The Life, Times and Missionary Enterprises of the Rev. John Campbell* (London: Snow, 1841); William Robinson, *The History and Antiquities of the Parish of Hackney, in the County of Middlesex.* 2 vols. (London: John Bowyer Nichols and Son, W. Pickering, and Caleb Turner, 1842-1843) 2:252-254; *DEB.*

Carey, Eustace (1791-1855)—The son of Thomas Carey, William Carey's brother, Eustace was baptized by John Ryland, Jr., in Northampton in 1809. He began his studies at John Sutcliff's academy at Olney later that year. In 1812 he entered Bristol Academy and in February 1814 sailed for India. He settled in Calcutta, where he ministered to a small congregation and assisted in the work of the BMS mission. In 1815 relations between the Calcutta mission and the Serampore Mission began to deteriorate over issues that would eventually separate the latter mission from the BMS in 1827. As a result, Eustace Carey formed a separate missionary union at Calcutta, an action that seriously strained relations with his uncle and the other missionaries at Serampore. He was forced to leave Calcutta in 1824 due to poor health. He returned to England to serve as a deputation director for the BMS, publishing the first biography of William Carey for the BMS in 1836. See *DEB.*

Carey, Jabez (1793-1862)—He was the third son of William Carey. Originally trained to be a lawyer, he was appointed as a BMS missionary in 1814, working as a teacher in Amboyna. Soon he was operating schools with over 300 students, while completing a translation of Isaac Watts's *Catechism* into Malay. After the colony was returned to the Dutch, he returned to India in 1818 (see letter 124), organizing a "Lancastrian" school in Ajmeer, Rajistan, in an effort to civilize the native populations. He retired from the BMS in 1832 and became a successful judge in Calcutta. See Cox, *History,* 2:241-242, 314; *DEB.*

Carey, Mary (1765-1839), and **Ann Carey Hobson** (1763-1843)—Both women were sisters of William Carey. Ann married William Hobson (1756-1826), a Cottesbrooke farmer. Mary (often referred to as "Polly" by Carey) never married and lived with the Hobson's for much of her life. Both sisters were ardent supporters of Carey's work in India. After becoming speechless and paralyzed (except for the use of one limb) in 1789, Mary spent the last fifty years of her life bedridden. Nevertheless, she managed to maintain a correspondence with Carey and other BMS leaders. Several letters of William Carey to his sisters, as well as from Mary to William, can be found in the BMS Archives at the Angus Library, Regent's Park College, Oxford. For more on the Careys, see Terry G. Carter, ed., *The Journal and Selected Letters of William Carey* (Macon GA: Mercer Press, 2000) 197; Mary Drewery, *William Carey: A Biography* (Grand Rapids MI: Zondervan, 1979) 72-73; Timothy George, *Faithful Witness: The Life and Mission of William Carey* (Birmingham AL: New Hope Press, 1991) 100-103; Carey, *William Carey,* 152, 239; *DEB.*

Carey, William (1761-1834)—A shoemaker by trade, Carey became a Baptist in his teens. His first pastorate was a small congregation at Moulton. In 1789 he removed to Harvey Lane in Leicester, where Robert Hall would later pastor. For several years Carey had been developing a strong sense of the need for Baptist missions to foreign lands; he spoke on the subject at a Northamptonshire association meeting on 30 May 1792, shortly after he had published his famous discourse, *An Enquiry into the Obligations of Christians to Use Means for the Conversion of the Heathens* (1792). He and several other ministers formed the Baptist Missionary Society in October 1792, and on 13 June 1793 Carey and his family, along with Dr. John Thomas, sailed for India, where Carey remained until his death in 1834. After spending some years doing missionary work while operating an indigo plantation near Mudnabatty and later at Kidderpore, conditions required that Carey move the mission to Serampore, Bengal, about fifteen miles from Calcutta and at that time under the control of the Danes. Late in 1799, Joshua Marshman and William Ward joined him, and together they formed the "Serampore Trio." In India, Carey became one of the leading linguists in the world, translating the Bible into Bengali, Oriya, Sanskrit, Hindi, Assamese, Marathi, and other languages, as well as numerous texts from those languages into English. In 1801 he was appointed professor of Bengalee and Sanscrit at the College of Fort William, and in 1818 founded Serampore College. He also became a renowned horticulturalist as well, establishing an Agricultural and Horticultural Society at Serampore around 1820. See Carter, ed., *Journal and Selected Letters*; Drewery, *William Carey*; Carey, *William Carey*; F. D. Walker, *William Carey, Missionary, Pioneer, and States-man* (Chicago: Moody Press, 1951); George, *Faithful Witness*; idem, "William Carey (1761-1834)," ed. Haykin, in *The British Particular Baptists*, 2:143-161; Farrer, *William Carey: Missionary and Botanist*; *DEB*.

Chamberlain, John (1777-1821)—Originally from Welton, Northamptonshire, Chamberlain was baptized at Guilsborough in 1796. He spent a year at Olney with Sutcliff (1798), followed by pastoral training at Bristol Academy (1799-1802), during which time he kept a diary, which was later used extensively by William Yates in his *Memoirs of Mr. John Chamberlain, Late Missionary in India* (1824). Chamberlain met Hannah Smith, a member of Sutcliff's church, during his year at Olney. She was born at Walgrave, in Northamptonshire, in 1779, where her father was a deacon in the Baptist church. They were married on 29 April 1802, and on 15 May they set sail for America and then India. Hannah Chamberlain died there on 14 December 1804. A second wife died in 1806, as well as his three children by 1812. He first worked in Catwa, supporting himself as a cloth merchant. He then opened northern India to the BMS, becoming the first Englishman to preach the Gospel in Delhi. On several occasions he was forced to return to Serampore, finally settling at Monghyr. He died after just three weeks at sea on his way to England in 1821. See Joshua Marshman's "Account" of Mrs. Chamberlain's death, as well as two letters by Hannah Chamberlain to John Sutcliff, in the *Periodical Accounts*, 3:66-77 and 3:78-82; see also Payne, *The First Generation* 90-96, Cox, *History*, 1:105-136, 207; Yates, *Memoirs of Mr. John Chamberlain*; *DEB*.

Chater, James (1779-1829)—Chater, along with William Robinson, came to India as a BMS missionary on board the *Criterion* in August 1806. The two men, however, were ordered to leave during a crackdown on missionary activity by the representatives of the East India Company. Chater, along with Richard Mardon, was commissioned to develop a mission in Burma in 1807, but Chater left that country in 1811, leaving the work with Felix Carey, who later turned it over to Adoniram Judson and the American Baptist Mission. In 1812, Chater settled in Columbo, Ceylon (Sri Lanka), where he remained until his death in 1829. See Stanley, *History*, 54-55, 168; Gravett, *Three Hundred Years of God's Grace*, 27; Cox, *History*, 1:156, 167, 191-192, 202; *DEB*.

Clark, John (1809-1880)—Clark worshiped in Baptist churches in Thrapston, Devonshire Square in London, and at the Old Bunyan Meeting in Bedford before accepting an appointment as a BMS missionary to Jamaica in 1835, assisting John Coultart at St. Ann. His fiance, a Miss Spiller, arrived in early July 1836, and they were married on 12 July, the same day Coultart and Nichols (at Torquay) died. Clark helped open a chapel at Brown's Town in

1836, which was enlarged in 1838. In the next four years he opened chapels in Sturge Town, Bethany, Clarksonville, and Salem. Besides church
planting, Clark also started a number of schools in Jamaica and founded ten
villages. Along with fellow missionaries Walter Dendy and James Phillippo,
Clark published *The Voice of Jubilee: A Narrative of the Baptist Mission,
Jamaica, from its Commencement; with Biographical Notices of its Fathers
and Founders* (London: J. Snow, 1865). See Clarke, *Memorials*, 170-171;
DEB.

Clarke, Adam (1760?-1832)—Clarke was a Wesleyan preacher, Biblical
commentator, theologian, linguist, and scholar. After his conversion to
Methodism in 1778, John Wesley sent Clarke to the Kingswood School
(near Bristol) for training, after which he was assigned to the Bradford-on-
Avon, Wiltshire, circuit in 1782, followed by a stint in Cornwall and the
Channel Islands (he could speak French fluently). Later he was sent to
Liverpool, where he served from 1793 to 1795. In 1795 he left Liverpool
for London, where he would spend the majority of the rest of his life, be-
coming proficient in such languages as Hebrew, Syriac, Arabic, Persian,
Sanscrit, Armenian, Coptic, and Ethiopic, as well as Greek and Latin. He was
a regular contributor to the *Eclectic Review*, and worked often with the
British and Foreign Bible Society. He received an M.A. from King's College,
Aberdeen, in 1807. He was elected president of the Wesleyan Conference in
1806, 1814, and 1822. He also composed and published extensive biblio-
graphies of classical literature, as well as works on missions and his celebrated *Bible . . . with Commentary and Critical Notes* (8 vols; 1810-1825).
See *DEB.*

Clarke, John (1802-1879)—Clarke joined the Baptist church at Berwick-on-
Tweed, Northumberland, in 1823 and within a few years began to think
seriously about going to the mission field. In 1829 he was approved by the
BMS to begin work in Jamaica, where he ministered to various churches
among the slave population for the next ten years. In October 1840, while
on furlough in England, he was appointed, along with Dr. G. K. Prince of
Jamaica, to conduct a missionary expedition in West Africa. In 1841-1842,
the two men surveyed the island of Fernando Po and some surrounding
areas along the coast of West Africa. Clarke and Prince returned to England
in 1842 to promote the new venture for the BMS. Clarke sailed for Jamaica
on the *Chilmark* in August 1843, taking with him Alfred Saker of Devonport,
along with Saker's wife, Helen, to recruit Jamaican missionaries to West
Africa. The *Chilmark* arrived at Fernando Po in February 1844. After three
years, Clarke left for England due to ill health. He returned to Jamaica in
1852, and remained there until his death in 1879. His major writings include *Memorials of the Baptist Missionaries in Jamaica* (1869), a life of John
Merrick, and two works on West African dialects—*Introduction to the
Fernandian Language*, and *Specimens of Dialects . . . in Africa*. See F. W. Butt-
Thompson, "A Voyage to Fernando Po," *Baptist Quarterly* 15 (1953-1954):
82-87, 113-121; *DEB.*

Claypole, E. A.—He was the minister of the Baptist church at Ross-on-Wye,
Herefordshire, c. 1828 to some time in the late 1850s. From 1861 to at least

1867 he ministered at the Third [Baptist] Church in Wallingford, Berkshire. See *Evangelical Magazine* (1831): 154; *Baptist Handbook*, 1861-1867.

Clegg, Arthur—J. C. Ryland, in his MS. book entitled "The Society for Christian Improvement and Good Works" (MS., Bristol Baptist College Library), which he began in October 1759, listed "Arthur Clegg" as the Baptist minister in Manchester. That entry may have been added after 1759, for it is more likely Clegg was affiliated with Caleb Warhurst and the dissenting chapel in Cold House Lane in 1759. In 1762 the paedobaptists withdrew, led by Warhurst, to form a new Independent congregation in Cannon Street. According to Ashton, Edmund Clegg (Arthur's relation?—see letter 256 for more on the Cleggs) took a small group of High-Calvinists from the congregation at Coldhouse and formed a new meeting at Shudehill, which he ministered until c.1781, at which time he left and the congregation rejoined Coldhouse. Whether Arthur Clegg left with the group that went to Cannon Street or the High Calvinist group at Shudehill is unclear. See Ralph Ashton, *Manchester and the Early Baptists: Being a Sketch of the Origin and Growth of the Particular Baptist Church Worshipping in Gadsby's Chapel, Rochdale Road, Manchester* (Manchester: n.p., 1916) 21; Urwick, *Historical Sketches*, 293; Kenneth Dix, *Strict and Particular: English Strict and Particular Baptists in the Nineteenth Century* (Didcot, Oxfordshire, UK: Baptist Historical Society, 2001) 30-66.

Clough, Benjamin—Clough was a Wesleyan missionary in Ceylon for many years. With the assistance of Abraham de Armour, James Chater, and William Tolfrey, Clough produced a Singhalese edition of the New Testament that was issued by the Wesleyan Mission Press in Colombo in 1819. Along with Tolfrey, he published *A Compendious Pali Grammar* in 1824. Clough also compiled, under the patronage of the government of Ceylon, *A Dictionary of the English and Singhalese and Singhalese and English Languages* (Colombo, 1821-1830).

Coke, Thomas (1747-1814)—Coke completed his B.A. at Jesus College, Oxford, in 1768 and an M.A. in 1770 before serving as curate at South Petherton, Somerset. He met John Wesley in 1776 and decided to become a Methodist; before long he had become Wesley's chief assistant. He was instrumental in the creation of the Deed of Declaration (1784) that gave legal status to the Methodist Conference after Wesley's death. In 1784 he was set apart by Wesley as the Superintendent of American Methodism and was soon joined as "Bishop" by Francis Asbury. After Wesley's death, Coke was actively involved in the transformation of Methodists into a separate denomination, being elected President of the Methodist Conference in 1797 and in 1805. Beginning in the 1780s, he was instrumental in creating a Methodist mission overseas, from the West Indies to Sierra Leone to India in 1813. After the renewal of the East India Charter in 1813 and its greater acceptance of missionaries, Coke led the first group of Methodist missionaries to India, but he died at sea enroute. Some Methodists, both in England and America, however, resented Coke for his sense of superiority and his ambition to control the Conference. He authored *A Plan of the Society for the Establishment of Missions Among the Heathens* (1783-4); *The Life of John*

Wesley [with Henry Moore] (1792); *A Commentary on the Holy Bible* (6 vols; 1801-03); and *A History of the West Indies* (3 vols; 1808-11). See *DEB*.

Coles, Thomas (1779-1840)—Coles was born at Rowell, Gloucestershire, and at the age of four moved to Bourton, were he grew up under the ministry of Benjamin Beddome and his assistant, William Wilkins. He became a member of the Baptist church in Bourton in 1795, and immediately left for Bristol Academy. In 1797 he was a Ward's scholar in Aberdeen. After completing his M.A. in 1800, he accepted a position as assistant at Little Prescot Street, under Abraham Booth. One year later, and after much debate on Cole's part, he became pastor of the Baptist church at Bourton-on-the-Water, where he remained until his death in 1840. See Thomas Brooks, *Pictures of the Past: The History of the Baptist Church, Bourton-on-the-Water* (London: Judd and Glass, 1861); Henry Coles, ed., *Letters from John Foster to Thomas Coles, M.A.* (London: H. G. Bohn, 1864).

Coles, William (1735-1809)—Coles was born at Daventry, Northamptonshire, of dissenting parents; in his late teens he was converted and soon after called to the ministry. He first went to Coventry to attend the ministry of John Butterworth, and then to Northampton and J. C. Ryland in 1756. After preaching in churches near Northampton for a year, he began ministering to the Baptist congregation at Newport-Pagnell in July 1758, where he remained for 10 years. He then removed to the church at Maulden, Long Buckby, in October 1758, preaching there until his health forced him to resign in 1805. Coles's daughter became Andrew Fuller's second wife in December 1794. See *Baptist Magazine* 9 (1817): 122-127.

Colgate, William (1783-1857)—Colgate was born in Hollingbourne, Kent, the son of a farmer who imbibed strong republican, pro-American, pro-French sentiments. In 1798 the Colgates emigrated to Maryland. In 1804, William moved to New York City, where he was apprenticed to John Slidell, a soap-maker. After three years Colgate started his own company, manufacturing various soap and petroleum products, eventually becoming one of New York City's most prosperous and influential citizens. He was first affiliated with the Presbyterian Church (his father had been an Arian Baptist), but in 1808 he was baptized and joined the First Baptist Church of New York. In 1811 he moved his membership to the congregation at Oliver Street and in 1838 to the Tabernacle, for which he had donated huge sums for its construction. He was a major supporter of Baptist schools and Baptist missionary enterprises, as well as the American Bible Society. In 1827 he helped found the American and Foreign Bible Society (largely a Baptist group initially). He also assisted in the founding of the American Bible Union in 1850. His sons, James (1818-1904) and Samuel (1822-1897), continued his legacy of involvement in higher education and, as a result of their generous endowments to Madison University (originally the Hamilton Institution), the school was renamed Colgate University in 1888. See William Brackney, ed., *Historical Dictionary of the Baptists* (Lanham MD: Scarecrow Press, 1999) 108; William Cathcart, *The Baptist Encyclopedia* (Philadelphia: L. H. Everts, 1881) 249-250.

Collins, Luke (d. 1805)—Collins pastored the Baptist meeting at Bethel Chapel, Shipley, 1769-1770. He then became an Independent, ministering at Horton-in-Craven, Yorkshire (1771-1793); Lowther Street in Kendal (1794-1802); and Ulverston, Lancashire (1802-1805). See *Bethel Church, Shipley, 1758-1958* (Shipley: n.p., 1958); James Miall, *Congregationalism in Yorkshire: A Chapter in Modern Church History* (London: J. Snow, 1868) 284; Benjamin Nightingale, *Lancashire Nonconformity; Or, Sketches, Historical and Descriptive, of the Congregational and Old Presbyterian Churches in the County. Churches of Manchester, Oldham, Ashton, etc.*, 6 vols. (Manchester: John Heywood, [1890-1893]) 1:260, 287.

Comstock, W. C. (1809-1844)—The son of a New York Baptist minister, Comstock worked as an attorney before becoming an American Baptist missionary. He spent one year at the Hamilton Literary and Theological Institution (now Colgate University) and then sailed with his wife for Burma, arriving in early 1835. They settled in Arracan, establishing churches and schools until his death in 1844 as a result of cholera. See Carey, *Oriental Christian Biography*, 3:374-376.

Cooke, Stephen—A prominent merchant in Kingston, Jamaica, Cooke began corresponding with John Rippon in the early 1790s concerning the black Baptist minister, George Liele, and his work among the slaves on that island. Cooke continued to correspond with Rippon and various leaders of the Baptist Missionary Society for many years. His first letter to Rippon, dated 26 November 1791, appeared in the *Baptist Annual Register*, 1:338-339.

Cornford, Philip Henry—Cornford was a student at Newport Pagnel Academy before becoming a BMS missionary in October 1840, working at Rio Bueno and Stewart Town. His wife died during their first year in Jamaica. He remarried in 1842 and began preaching at Montego Bay, where he ministered for five years. In 1847 he moved to the Jericho church in St. Thomas-in-the-Vale. He returned to England in 1850, ministering to Baptist churches at Ramsey, Huntingdonshire, and Luton, Bedfordshire, for ten years before emigrating to New Zealand in 1860. See Clarke, *Memorials*, 183.

Cottle, Joseph (1770-1853)—Cottle grew up in the Baptist congregation at the Pithay, Bristol. James Newton, the assistant pastor at the Pithay and a tutor at the Baptist Academy, lived in the Cottle home for nearly thirty years before his death in 1789. Cottle was also a frequent attendant at the Baptist church in Broadmead and was for over forty years a member of the Committee of the Bristol Education Society, which oversaw the work of the Academy. In November 1800, after the death of his father, Robert Cottle, a deacon for many years in the church at the Pithay, Joseph, along with his mother and sisters, left the Pithay church and became members of the Baptist and Independent congregations at Broadmead. In March 1830, when a separate church record book was begun for the Independent congregation at Broadmead, Joseph Cottle was listed as one of the deacons (the initial pages of the MS. are in Cottle's hand). In December 1832, however, after many years at Broadmead, Joseph and his sister Mary were dismissed to the Zion Chapel (Independent) in Bedminster, where they were living at that time. Joseph's brother, Thomas, lived for a while at Bath and then moved to London, where he subscribed to the BMS in 1800-1801 and in 1804-1805. Joseph Cottle is best known for publishing Samuel Taylor Coleridge's first book of poems in 1796, early volumes of Robert Southey poems, as well as the initial copies of Wordsworth's and Coleridge's *Lyrical Ballads* in 1798. A voluminous poet himself, Cottle is best known for his *Early Recollections; Chiefly Relating to the Late Samuel Taylor Coleridge, during his Long Residence in Bristol* (2 vols; 1837), and his slightly revised version, *Reminiscences of Samuel Taylor Coleridge and Robert Southey* (1847). See *Baptist Annual Register*, 3:306; *Periodical Accounts*, 2:204; 3:132; Timothy Whelan, "Joseph Cottle the Baptist," *Charles Lamb Bulletin*, N.S. 111 (2000): 96-108; *DEB*.

Coultart, James (d. 1836)—Coultart was from Holywood, near Dumfries, Scotland, and studied at Bristol. He was approved as a BMS missionary in 1816, along with his wife, the former Mary Ann Chambers. They sailed for Jamaica on 14 March 1817 and landed on 9 May. He quickly got a license to preach, incorporating a group of members from George Lisle's congregation. His wife died that September. Coultart's health was not good either, and he returned to England in 1818 and was present at the ordinations of Christopher Kitching and Thomas Godden that March. He remarried and returned to Jamaica and commenced building a chapel in Kingston (Kitching had already died). The chapel was opened on 27 January 1822 and accommodated 2000 people. He resigned from the Kingston church in 1829 and removed to Mount Charles; he was replaced by Joseph Burton (1803-1860) in Kingston. Coultart traveled to England several times due to health reasons, returning once again to Jamaica in 1834 with James Phillipo. He preached at St. Ann's Bay until his death in 1836. See Cox, *History*, 2:24, 234.

Cowell, John—Cowell became a member at Carter Lane, Southwark, in 1774. In 1778, while living in Gravel Lane, Southwark, he subscribed to J. C. Ryland's *Contemplations*. He was also a subscriber to the Baptist Missionary Society, donating £1.1 in 1800 and in 1804. A later entry in the Carter Lane church book notes that Cowell and his wife, also a member, were dismissed "to the church at Potter Street, near Harlow, Essex under the Pastoral care of Mr Brown" at a Church meeting on Monday, 20 December 1802. According to the church records at Potter Street, on 31 March 1811 it was proposed at a church meeting that messengers from the church visit Cowell concerning his absence from church and the Lord's Supper and church meetings. On 26 May two messengers were appointed to visit Cowell. On 30 June they reported that Cowell had told them he was not attending because neither "he nor his family could profit by the ministry of" Rev. Bain. To Cowell, "every thing was carried at them according to the will of the pastor and that he absented himself from church meetings for the sake of peace but that he wished to hold communion with us as a church in the way he had done for a long time past. That he did not wish to hold his subscription or any pecuniary aid needfelt. The church admitted his reason for not attending regularly the public means of grace as it was not their business to search the heart. Nor to say who or where he should hear, every one having a public right to seek spiritual profit where they may find it. His second reason they could not admit as it was one principle part of his office to attend church meetings. It was agreed to present to him by the reporting messengers the church's respects & request him to attend at church meetings and that they fully comply with his request to continuance on communion." He left Harlow and joined a dissenting congregation at Ware in 1822. See Horsley-down and Carter Lane Church Book, f. 41; "List of Subscribers," Bristol Baptist College Library, shelfmark G97a.Ah.33; *Periodical Accounts,* 2:204; 3:132; Stephen Hulcoop, *Extracts from the Minute Book of Potter Street Baptist Church Harlow Relating to Discipline of Members by the Church Meeting Covering the Period 1776-1827* (Harlow: S. H. Publishing, 2001) 21-22.

Cox, Francis Augustus (1783-1853)—Cox studied at Bristol Baptist Academy and Edinburgh University (M.A.) before commencing his pastoral career. After two years as pastor of the Baptist church at Clipston, Northampton-shire (1804-1806), and two years at St. Andrew's Street, Cambridge (1806-1808), following Robert Hall's resignation (letter 81 denotes the beginning of Cox's ministry at St. Andrew's Street), Cox returned for a time to Clipston before accepting the pastorate at Mare Street in Hackney, where he re-mained for more than forty years. He was actively involved in Baptist affairs throughout the first half of the nineteenth century, working on the BMS committee and supporting the Baptist Home Missionary Society, helping to create the *Baptist Magazine,* assisting in the founding of the Baptist Irish Society, and serving as a part-time tutor at Stepney College from 1813 to 1822. He served as secretary to the General Body of Dissent-ing Ministers, supported the Anti-State Church Association, and, like Joseph Hughes, was instrumental in the founding of London University, becoming its first librarian. He represented the Baptist Union in 1835 on a tour of America, after which he, along with James Hoby, authored *The Baptists in America.* He is best known for his *History of the Baptist Missionary Society, from 1792 to 1842* (2 vols; 1842). Cox was thrice chairman of the Baptist Union. See J. H. Y. Briggs, "F. A. Cox of Hackney: Nineteenth-Century Baptist Theologian, Historian, Controversialist, and Apologist," *Baptist Quarterly* 38 (1999-2000): 392-411; *DEB.*

Crabtree, William (1720-1811)—Crabtree was for many years the Baptist minister at Bradford. He was born c. 1720, and began ministering at Brad-ford in 1753, where he would remain thereafter. Isaac Mann wrote a short life of Crabtree in 1815. A number of letters to and from Crabtree can be found in the Isaac Mann Collection, National Library of Wales. See *Baptist Annual Register,* 1:13.

Cramp, John Mockett (1796-1881)—Cramp was educated at Stepney College, 1814-1818. He pastored at Dean Street, Southwark, 1818-1825; assisted his father at St. Peters Baptist Chapel (St. Peters, England), 1827-1825; and pastored at Wellington Square Chapel in Hastings, 1842-1844. He was editor of the *Baptist Magazine,* 1825-1828; served on the BFBS committee,

1820-1844; and from 1844-1849 was President of the Canada Baptist College in Montreal. In 1851 he became President of Acadia College in Wolfville, Nova Scotia, where he retired in 1869. He was a prolific author, including *Baptist History from the Foundation of the Christian Church to the Close of the Eighteenth Century* (1868). See *DEB*.

Crassweller, Henry (d. 1880)—Crassweller was a deacon at the Baptist church at Eagle Street in London from 1812 to 1880. A letter from Crassweller, dated 3 December 1841, from 36 Welbeck Street, London, appeared in the *Baptist Magazine* 34 (1842): 31. He was a generous giver to the BMS, contributing £50 to the Jubilee Fund in December 1842. He also collected another £1.16 for the Fund. His son, Harris (1827-1905), completed his studies at Stepney College in 1854 (he earned a B.A. as well from London University). He ministered to Baptist congregations at Leominster (1854-1856), Woolwich (1856-1864), St. Mary's Gate, Derby (1864-1871), and Cross Street, Islington (1871-1887). Edward Whymper, a member at Maze Pond, Southwark, mentions in his diary that he heard the younger Crassweller preach once at Maze Pond in 1856, noting that the sermon was "very good in matter, but dreadful bad in style." See *Missionary Herald* (January 1843): 52; Seymour J. Price, "Maze Pond and the Matterhorn," *Baptist Quarterly* 10 (1940-1941): 202-208; F. G. Hastings, "The Passing of St. Mary's Gate, Derby," *Baptist Quarterly* 9 (1938-1939): 45-49; *Baptist Handbook* (1906): 433-434.

Crisp, Thomas Steffe (1788-1868)—Crisp was originally from Suffolk. After taking his degree at Glasgow University in 1809, he ministered to the Independent congregations at Southwold, Suffolk (1810-1811), and at St. Ives, Huntingtonshire (1811-1818). He came to Broadmead and the Baptist Academy in June 1818, replacing Henry Page, who had resigned the previous year. Upon Robert Hall's arrival as pastor at Broadmead in 1826, Crisp was appointed Principal of the academy and assistant pastor at Broadmead, positions he maintained until his death at the age of 80 in 1868. See C. Sidney Hall and Harry Mowvley, *Tradition and Challenge: The Story of Broadmead Baptist Church, Bristol, from 1685 to 1991* (Bristol: Broadmead Baptist Church, 1991) 44, 54, 57, 62-63; *DEB*.

Crowther, Jonathan (1794-1856)—The son of a prominent Methodist minister, Crowther was born in Cornwall and educated at Kingswood School. After completing his studies at Woodhouse Grove, Crowther was ordained and became a headmaster at Woodhouse (1814-1816) and at Kingswood (1823-1825). He then served as a circuit preacher and a follower of Jabez Bunting. From 1837 to 1842 he served as superintendent of the Methodist mission in India (Madras). He returned to England and in 1849 was appointed classical tutor of the Northern branch of the Theological Institution at Manchester and Didsbury. Though loyal to the Methodist Conference, Crowther was nevertheless a supporter of women's preaching, allowing Sarah Boyce and Martha Gregson to preach in Methodist chapels in Birmingham during his tenure on that circuit (1829-1831). Among his published works are *A Sermon on the Death of the Rev. D. McAllum, M.D.: Preached in New-Street Chapel, York, July 23, 1827* (York, 1827); *A Defence* of the Wesleyan Theological Institution (1834); and *Sermons* (1839). For Crowther, see Biographical Index, Methodist Archives, JRULM.

Crowther, Samuel Ajayi (c.1807-1891)—Born in Western Nigeria, he was sold into slavery when about thirteen, but was eventually freed when the Portuguese ship on which he had been bound was captured by the British and the slaves taken to Sierra Leone. Three years later he became a Christian and renamed after a prominent leader in the Church Missionary Society. He was one of the first students at Fourah Bay College, Freetown, specializing in linguistics. After serving a time as a schoolmaster, he was chosen to be the interpreter for Thomas Buxton's unsuccessful Niger Expedition (see letter 191). Crowther's abilities did not go unnoticed, however, and he came to England with the remaining leaders of the Expedition to seek ordination in the Church of England. He returned to his original homeland and joined the Anglican mission near Abeokutu, Nigeria. He journeyed to England in 1851, speaking throughout the country and meeting Queen Victoria and Prince Albert. He published a number of grammar texts in African languages and was one of the earliest scholars of the Igbo language. In 1864 he was appointed bishop for Western Africa; in 1889 dissention arose among a group of white clergy in Western Africa that led to a splitting of the black and white leadership in Western Africa. When he died two years later, Crowther was replaced by a white bishop. See John Flint, "Crowther, Samuel Ajayi," *Oxford Dictionary of National Biography* (Oxford: Oxford University Press, 2004); David Killingray, "The Black Atlantic Missionary Movement and Africa, 1780s-1920s," *Journal of Religion in Africa* 33 (2003): 3-31.

Daniel, Ebenezer (1784-1844)—Daniel joined the Baptist church at Burford, Oxfordshire, when he was seventeen. After studying at the Bristol Academy, he ministered to Baptist congregations in Brixham (1808-1812) and Luton (1812-1830) before seeking appointment as a BMS missionary to Ceylon, replacing James Chater. Daniel and his family left England in May 1830; during the next fourteen years he would be the driving force behind the Cingalese Baptist Mission. His wife died on her return to England in 1838. After her death, Daniel was aided by two new BMS missionaries, Joseph Harris and C C. Dawson. In his last years he helped establish a missionary academy at Colombo. He died in Ceylon on 2 June 1844. Shortly before his death, he published a small volume titled *Reminiscences of Two Years' Missionary Labours in the Jungles of Ceylon*, a portion of which appeared in the *Baptist Magazine* 35 (1843): 491-496; 545-550. See Carey, *Oriental Christian Biography*, 3:289-293.

Darracott, Richard (1751-1795)—Darracott attended Daventry Academy, under Caleb Ashworth, and began his ministry at Bridge Street Meeting, Walsall, Staffordshire, in 1770. In 1773 he became pastor to two congregations, one at Fulwood and the other at Bishops Hull, Somerset, remaining at the latter until 1793. He died at Taunton in 1795. He was the son of Risdon Darracott (1717-1759), a student of Doddridge at Northampton. The elder Darracott ministered at Chulmleigh, Devon, and at Penzance, Cornwall, 1738-1739, before removing to Barnstaple and then to Wellington, Somerset, where he ministered to the Independent congregation from 1741 to 1759. Risdon Darracott was affectionately known as "the Star of the West." He was also the author of *Scripture Marks of Salvation, Drawn up to Help Christians to Know the True State of Their Souls* (1756). See *Evangelical Magazine* 3 (1795): 305; *Protestant Dissenter's Magazine* 2 (1795): 216.

Davies, John Jordan (d. 1858)—Davies, originally from Wales, was raised in the Church of England, but adopted Baptist views and attended Bristol Academy. After preaching for a time at Bath, he removed to Tottenham in 1828 where he was ordained on 12 June of that year, remaining as minister there for the next seventeen years. His final ministry was at Park Street, Luton, 1849-1857. See *Baptist Magazine* 20 (1828): 375; my thanks to John Briggs for information on Davies.

Davis (Davy), Henry (1700-1780)—Davis became a deacon in the small Strict Baptist congregation at Northampton in 1743, an elder in 1744, and pastor in 1748, with John Gill giving the charge and John Brine the sermon. Davis was the father of the Independent minister at Wigston, Leicstershire. John Ryland, Jr., would later write, "Mr. Davis was a very worthy man, a plain, serious preacher; but the church gradually dwindled, till at last they broke up, and sold the place to the Wesleyan Methodists. After this, Mr. Davis preached for some time in his own house at Harlestone, four miles from Northampton, till he became quite infirm with age. He died in 1780, aged 80, and was buried in College-lane meeting yard." See John Ryland, "History of the Baptist Churches at Northampton," *Baptist Annual Register*, 4:772.

Day, David (d. 1862)—After spending several years as a pastor in Speen, near Newbury, Day was appointed as a BMS missionary to Jamaica in November 1837. His wife died during their first year in Jamaica. Day then married the niece of J. M. Phillippo and remained in Jamaica for the next twenty-two years, working mostly in churches in the parish of St. Mary until his death in 1862. See Clarke, *Memorials*, 175-176.

Dendy, Walter (d. 1881)—Dendy was appointed as a BMS missionary in 1831 from the church in Salisbury, under the ministry of P. J. Saffery (Dendy's brother-in-law). The Dendy's sailed for Jamaica with the Burchells in 1831. Like many of the Baptist missionaries in Jamaica, Dendy was imprisoned in 1833; upon his release he took over William Knibb's church at Falmouth. In 1835 he removed to the church at Salter's Hill, the church originally formed by Moses Baker. During the time of martial law, government forces killed twenty-one of his members. Dendy sailed for England (with two of his deacons) in March 1841, returning to Jamaica in November of that same year. He would remain with the BMS until his death in 1881. Along with John Clark and James Phillippo, his fellow missionaries in Jamaica, Dendy published *The Voice of Jubilee: A Narrative of the Baptist Mission, Jamaica, from its Commencement; with Biographical Notices of its Fathers and Founders* (London: J. Snow, 1865). See Clarke, *Memorials*, 159-166; *Baptist Magazine* 34 (1842): 397-398.

Dent, Joseph—Dent was from Milton, Northamptonshire, and was baptized on the same day as John Ryland, Jr. (13 September 1767). Dent married Elizabeth Ryland, John Ryland's sister, who was described by James Culross as "comely in appearance and gracious in spirit." Dent was "a man of genuine piety, solidity of thought, and promptitude of action—qualities that served him well in his long diaconate" at College Lane, which began in 1777. After Ryland left in 1793, Dent was one of the chief leaders of the church during its next six years when it remained without a pastor. In 1812 he served on the BMS Committee. In the summer of 1825, Dent was instrumental in forming a Baptist church at Milton, consisting of members from College Lane in Northampton and William Heighton's congregation at Roade. See James Culross, *The Three Rylands: A Hundred Years of Various Christian Service* (London: Elliot Stock, 1897) 24; Cox, *History*, 2:221; Payne, *College Street Church, Northampton*, 15.

Dexter, Benjamin Bull (d. 1863)—After finishing his studies at Stepney College, Dexter was set apart as a BMS missionary at Olney on 21 January 1834. He arrived in Jamaica on 1 April 1834, ministering initially at Montego Bay and Salter's Hill for a time, than at Rio Bueno and Stewart Town, laying the foundation stones for new chapel buildings at each place on 23 May 1835. He retired from the mission field in 1853 and returned to England, where he died in 1863. See Clarke, *Memorials*, 167-168; Cox, *History*, 2:207-209.

Dore, James (1763/64-1825)—Dore studied at Bristol Academy (1779-1782) and then succeeded Benjamin Wallin as pastor at Maze Pond in 1783, with Robert Robinson of Cambridge delivering the introductory discourse at Dore's ordination service on 25 March 1784. Dore would remain at Maze Pond until 1815. Of the congregation at Maze Pond, Walter Wilson noted, "the church has long been in a flourishing state, and may vie with the most respectable congregations of the same persuasion." Dore's most significant publication was his sermon, *On the African Slave Trade* (1788). He was the younger brother of William Dore, Baptist minister at Cirencester. See *Three Discourses Addressed to the Congregation at Maze-Pond, Southwark, on Their Publick Declaration of Having Chosen Mr. James Dore their Pastor, March 25th, 1784* (Cambridge: F. Archdeacon, 1784); Wilson, *History and Antiquities*, 4:286; Hayden, *Continuity and Change*, 230; *DEB*.

Dracup, John (1723-1795)—Dracup ministered to the Independent meeting at Steep Lane, Sowerby, Yorkshire, 1755-1772; he then joined the Baptists and preached at Rodhill End, near Todmorden, Lancashire, and at Rochdale, 1772-1783. He returned to Steep Lane in 1784 as a Baptist, and the church joined the denomination at that time. Dracup remained there until his death in 1795.

Duff, Alexander (1806-1878)—Duff, a Scottish-born educator and missionary, attended St. Andrew's University, 1821-1829, where he came under the influence of Thomas Chalmers. He was sent to India by the Church of Scotland in 1829 as an educator. He taught in English, and was instrumental in the Indian government's decision in 1834 to make English the language of higher education in the country. In the 1830s and '40s he was one of the more controversial European figures in Calcutta. He was not popular initially with the East India Company (he violated their policy of non-interference in matters of religion) nor with the Home Mission Board. He spent 1834-1839 in Scotland defending himself and his educational policies in India. In 1843 he left the state church and joined the Scottish Free Church; the next year he published his important treatise, *Female Education in India.* He continued to serve tours of missionary duty in India until 1863, at which time he returned to Edinburgh and taught at New College while also working as mission director for the Free Church. See *DEB.*

Dunscombe, Thomas (1748-1811)—Dunscombe came from Tiverton to the Bristol Academy in 1770. His brother, Samuel, was the Baptist minister at Cheltenham, 1768-1797, during which time the latter became a close friend of Robert Robinson. Samuel was also one of the signatories at the founding of the Bristol Education Society in 1770. Thomas Dunscombe supplied at Coate in 1772, where he was ordained in 1773. He itinerated in chapels at Buckland and Bampton in Oxfordshire, and at Farringdon between 1773 and 1797. He preached the sermon for the annual meeting of the Bristol Education Society in 1792. In 1797 he married the poet Mary Steele and moved to Yeovil for a time before returning to Broughton. He died at Farrington, near Coate, in 1811, shortly after preaching at James Bicheno's installation service at Coate. See Case, *History of the Baptist Church in Tiverton*, 40; Coate Church Book, 1684-1885 (MS., Angus Library, Regent's Park College, Oxford); Hayden, *Continuity and Change*, 230.

Durrant, Timothy—A farmer from Lesiate, Durrant joined the nearby congregation at King's Lynn in 1790 and began assisting William Richards in preaching and conducting some of the affairs of the church. In 1800 the management of the church fell primarily into his hands. He would serve as pastor until 1808, during which time a new chapel was built. After his resignation, he remained a deacon in the church until 1812. See *The Baptists in King's Lynn* (King's Lynn: n.p., 1939) 13-14.

Dutton, Anne (1692-1765)—Early in her life, Dutton joined a Calvinist church in Northampton and never departed from those beliefs. Her second husband, Benjamin Dutton (d. 1747), served as pastor to the Baptist congregation at Great Gransden, 1733-1747. During her life, Dutton composed over twenty-five works, some concerning assurance of salvation and genuine evangelical piety (printed forms of spiritual autobiography), and some more polemical in nature, patterned after the thought and style of several Calvinistic preachers of the Great Awakening she admired and with whom she corresponded, especially George Whitefield (see letter 4). She was an ardent opponent of Wesley's Arminianism. She was also instrumental in the call of Robert Robinson to St. Andrew's Street in Cambridge in 1759. Robinson wrote an admiring account of his visit with Dutton shortly before her death in a letter to John Robinson of Eriswell on 30 November 1766, now in the Crabb Robinson Correspondence, Dr. Williams's Library, London. Among her writings are *A Narration of the Wonders of Grace, in Verse* (1734), *Letters on Spiritual Subjects, and Divers Occasions* (1747), and *A Brief Account of the Gracious Dealings of God with the Late Mrs. Anne Dutton* (1750). See JoAnn Ford Watson, *Selected Spiritual Writings of Ann Dutton*, 6 vols. (Macon GA: Mercer University Press, 2003-2009); J. C. Whitebrook, "The Life and Works of Mrs. Ann Dutton," *Transactions of the Baptist Histor-*

ical Society 7 (1920-1921): 129-146; Timothy Whelan, "Six Letters of Robert Robinson from Dr. Williams's Library, London," _Baptist Quarterly_ 39 (2001-2002): 355-356; _DEB._

Dutton, Henry John (d. 1846)—After completing studies at Stepney College, Dutton was appointed a BMS missionary to Jamaica in October 1839. He arrived in Jamaica in February 1840, working mostly in Brown's Town. His wife, who was pregnant, remained in England, but she died while giving birth in June 1840. Dutton remarried in July 1841 and returned to England on furlough in 1843. On his return to Jamaica he was chosen to assume control of the church at Jericho, but those plans never came to fruition, for he died in November 1846. See Clarke, _Memorials_, 178-179.

Dyer, John (1783-1841)—The son of a Baptist minister, Dyer was the first full-time secretary of the BMS. He was influenced as a teenager by William Steadman, both at Broughton and Plymouth, and began preaching in Plymouth and later at Reading. He was elected to the BMS Committee in 1812 and in 1818 became the BMS Secretary, moving (though not without some controversy) the headquarters to London. Shortly thereafter, however, difficulties developed between the Home Office and the Serampore Mission concerning the management of funds and various other matters of jurisdiction. A split occurred between the two groups in 1827, a rift not remedied until 1838. Dyer was very much a centralized bureaucrat, never visiting any of the foreign missions. He died on 22 July 1841, and was succeeded by Joseph Angus as Secretary of the BMS. See Payne, _First Generation_, 120-126; idem, "The Diaries of John Dyer," _Baptist Quarterly_ 13 (1949-1950): 253-259; _DEB._

Dyer, Samuel (1804-1843)—Dyer served as a Congregationalist missionary to Malay, China, and Hong Kong under the auspices of the London Missionary Society from 1828 until his death in 1843. Educated at Woolwich and Cambridge, he studied for the ministry at Gosport under David Bogue and at Homerton Academy under John Pye Smith. As a missionary, he was primarily employed with the mission press; he was instrumental in developing moveable metal type for Chinese script. His daughter married the famous missionary to China, J. Hudson Taylor. _DEB._

East, Timothy (1783-1871)—East, a Congregationalist, was originally from Berkshire and received his education at Gosport Academy. He served as pastor at Zion Church, Frome, Somerset, 1805-1818; at Ebenezer, Steelhouse-lane, Birmingham, 1818-1843; at Providence, Ovenden, Yorkshire, 1855-1857; and at Paignton, Devon, 1859-1864. He authored a series of tracts entitled _The Evangelical Rambler_ (1822-1825) as well as _A Series of Discourses on the Proper Deity of the Son of God, and the Primary Design of his Mission_ (1843) and _Christianity Contrasted with Hindooism. A Sermon Preached before the London Missionary Society, at the Tabernacle, on Wednesday Evening, May 8, 1822_ (1822).

Edmonds, John (d. 1823)—John Edmonds and his two brothers, Edward and Thomas, were called to the ministry out of the Baptist church in Cannon Street in Birmingham. Edward (c.1750-1823), after a short stint as pastor at Wooton-under-Edge, moved to the church in Bond Street, Birmingham, in 1785, where he remained until his death in 1823 at the age of 73. His son, George Edmonds (1787?-1868), gained notoriety in Birmingham for his radical, "popular" politics. Thomas Edmonds served as pastor of Baptist congregations at Sutton-in-the-Elms (1786-1794), Upton-on-Severn (1794-1806), Bridgnorth (1806-1813), and Leominster (1813-1834). John Edmonds came to the Baptist church at Guilsborough shortly after a new chapel was built in 1781. As a result of the church's success, coupled with the general distrust that developed in late 1792 by conservative advocates of the established church who sought to link all religious dissenters with republican politics, Edmonds and his congregation experienced persecution and the destruction of their building by a mob in late December 1792. John Rippon provided the following account of the ordeal: ". . . but after many virulent expressions which had dropt from individuals in various companies, and after part of a brick wall belonging to the meeting-house had been outrageously pulled down, of which these innocent people took no notice: on Dec. 25, 1792, they were alarmed at the cry of *fire*, and soon discovered that *their place of worship was in flames*: they made immediate efforts to extinguish them, but the thatch on the roof rendered their efforts ineffectual. They advertized *fifty guineas* reward for the apprehension of the incendiary or incendiaries, and his *Majesty* and the ministers of state offered *two hundred pounds* more, but in vain." John Edmonds remained at Guilsborough until at least 1811. In 1823 he was serving as pastor at the Long Buckby church, not far from Guilsborough. See *Baptist Annual Register*, 2:9; my thanks as well to John Briggs for information on the Edmonds.

Edmonds, Thomas (1784-1860)—Edmonds was the son of John Edmonds, Baptist minister at Guilsborough (see above). After completing his studies at Bristol Academy and Marischal College, Aberdeen (M.A., 1806), the younger Edmonds served for a time as minister at Clipston before removing to Exeter in 1809. He assumed the pastorate at St. Andrew's Street in Cambridge in 1812, remaining in that capacity until 1831. His publications included *The Gospel Committed to Faithful Men: A Sermon Delivered in London, on Thursday, June 20, 1816, Before the Subscribers and Friends of the Stepney Academical Institution* (1816); *Christian Missions Vindicated and Encouraged: A Sermon Preached on Behalf of the Baptist Mission, at Queen's Street Chapel, Lincoln's Inn Fields, on Wednesday morning, June 23, 1819* (1819); and *Christian Union: A Circular Letter Addressed to the Ministers and Churches of the Cambridgeshire Association* (1834). See the entry on Edmonds in E. J. Tongue, "Dr. John Ward's Trust," *Baptist Quarterly* 13 (1949-1950): 267-275; *Baptist Handbook* (1861): 98.

Edwards, Jonathan (1745-1801)—Son of the famous leader of the American Great Awakening, Jonathan Edwards (1703-1758), the younger Edwards in 1794, shortly before being dismissed from the Whitehaven Congregational Church of New Haven, Connecticut, sent John Ryland, Jr., a box of religious pamphlets from America (now at Bristol Baptist College Library, shelfmark G97A). These pamphlets may have been in response to the pamphlets sent by Ryland that are mentioned in letter 34. Edwards would later serve as President of Union College, New York. See *DEB*.

Edwards, Peter—After ministering to the Baptist meeting at White's Row, Portsea, 1785-1794, Edwards resigned and became an Independent minister. Shortly thereafter he published *Candid Reasons for Renouncing the Principles of Antipaedobaptism* (1795), which was answered that same year by Joseph Jenkins, at that time pastor of the Baptist church at Blandford Street, London, in *A Defence of the Baptists Against the Aspersions & Misrepresentation so Mr. Peter Edwards . . . in his Book, entitled Candid Reasons, for Renouncing the Principles of Antipaedobaptism. In a Series of Letters.* See "Calendar of Letters," *Baptist Quarterly* 6 (1932-1933): 180.

Ellis, Jonathan D. (d. 1845)—Ellis and his wife were appointed as BMS missionaries to India in 1831. He came out of the church at Maze Pond, Southwark, having been trained as a printer before arriving in India. He worked initially at Chitpore, superintending the men's department of the Native Christian Boarding School, while Mrs. Ellis worked with the women. Ellis soon organized a small church, but poor health forced him to remove to Howrah in 1838. The Ellis's moved again late in 1838, this time to Intally. In March 1841, Mrs. Ellis returned to England, with her husband following her that June. When he arrived in England, he learned that his youngest child had died at sea and that his wife had just died in Exeter. Devastated, he retired to Exeter to regain his health, remarrying briefly before his death on 9 February 1845. During his final illness in 1843-1844, the BMS paid his medical bills, including £185 Ellis requested for 1844. See Carey, *Oriental Christian Biography,* 3:78-79; Potts, *British Baptist Missionaries,* 246; BMS Committee Minutes, Vol. I (January 1843-May 1844), ff. 174-175.

Etheridge, Samuel—Etheridge was a deacon for many years at the Baptist church at Little Prescot Street, in Goodman's Fields. He was the uncle of Samuel Jackson of the Baptist congregation at Unicorn Yard (see letter 28). Etheridge was a great benefactor of Baptist causes. In 1784 he gave a bequest of £100 to the Particular Baptist Fund. In 1805 the Sunday School Society of the church received a legacy of £50 from Etheridge, the bequest reading, "To a Society who meet at Mr. Booth's Meeting House to teach young girls to read, Fifty pounds in aid of their benevolent design." See Ernest Kevan, *London's Oldest Baptist Church* (London: Kingsgate Press, 1933) 94, 101.

Evans, Caleb (1737-1791)—Baptized at Little Wild Street in London in 1758, Evans assisted Josiah Thompson at Unicorn Yard, Southwark, for a year, then came to Broadmead in Bristol in 1759, first as assistant then later as co-pastor to his father, Hugh Evans. After his father's death, Caleb Evans served as senior pastor at Broadmead from 1781 to 1791. He became involved with the work of the Academy as well, helping to found the Bristol Education Society in 1770. In 1779 he was named Principal of the Academy, a post he held until his death. Evans read widely in the Puritans and the classics and was an evangelical Calvinist (like his friend Robert Hall, Sr.), passing that tradition on to the young preachers he trained at Bristol. He also had a keen interest in itinerant preaching and evangelism. His writings include numerous sermons, as well as some controversial political tracts, such as *A Letter to Mr Wesley* (1776), concerning the American war; also a

Collection of Hymns Adapted to Public Worship (1769), with John Ash. See Norman S. Moon, "Caleb Evans, Founder of the Bristol Education Society," *Baptist Quarterly* 24 (1971-1972): 175-190; idem, *Education for Ministry*, 10-26; Kirk Wellum, "Caleb Evans (1737-1791)," ed. Haykin, in *The British Particular Baptists*, 1:213-233; Hayden, *Continuity and Change*, 123-141; *DEB*.

Evans, Charles—Evans (of the Pithay church in Bristol) sailed with Richard Burton in 1820 to Sumatra (both men had studied at Bristol Academy). They were joined the next year by William Robinson (1784-1853) of Olney, who had been working in Java since 1812. Sir Thomas Raffles, then governor of Sumatra, had requested Evans and Burton to open a station at Fort Marlborough, where they were assisted by Nathaniel Ward, William Ward's nephew. According to Cox, Evans, "finding himself unequal to the combined exertion of conducting the school, and acquiring the native language, removed to Padang." After the insurrection in Sumatra in 1825 and the new restrictions imposed upon missionaries there, Evans was forced to retire from Padang. Suffering now from ill health, he returned to England. See Cox, *History*, 1:353.

Evans, Hugh (1712-1781)—Baptized at Broadmead by Bernard Foskett in 1730, Evans became Foskett's assistant in March 1733/4 and co-pastor in February 1739/40, eventually becoming senior pastor and principal of the Academy, 1758-1781. In 1756, as evidence of his tolerant approach to communion and fellowship among believers, Evans organized some sixty paedobaptists who regularly worshiped at Broadmead into an Independent congregation within the larger Broadmead congregation, serving as pastor of both congregations. The Independent congregation (what became known as the "little church") remained a part of the Broadmead church until the mid-nineteenth century. He was also instrumental in the formation of the Bristol Education Society in 1770, attempting to provide the Particular Baptist churches of England and Wales with qualified ministers. As Roger Hayden has noted, "Hugh Evans successfully continued Foskett's work with students, nurtured the Welsh links, and after the appointment of Caleb [Evans], worked with him to put the students programme on a denominational basis, while retaining control within it. Upon this foundation Hugh and Caleb built up the concept of an educated, able and evangelical Baptist ministry which would be vital for the missionary expansion of the denomination at home and overseas." See Moon, *Education for Ministry*, 10-24; Hayden, *Continuity and Change*, 116, 119; *DEB*.

Evans, James Harington (1785-1849)—Evans was the minister at John Street Chapel in London, 1818-1848. He was educated for the Anglican ministry, but left the established church in 1815 and began preaching in London in a Swiss church. He moved to the new chapel in John Street in 1818, but for many years refused to consider himself a part of any denomination. By the late 1830s, however, John Street, and Evans himself, had clearly moved into the Baptist denomination. Evans became a strong supporter of the BMS, publishing *A Sermon on Behalf of the B.M.S.* in 1837. See *DEB*.

Evans, John—Evans studied at Bristol Academy before serving as pastor of the Baptist congregation in Foxton, Northamptonshire, 1751-81. He was one of the founders of the Northamptonshire Baptist Association, composing the first circular letter in 1765; he was also moderator of the Association meeting and writer of the circular letter in 1774. He retired to Northampton in 1782. See *Baptist Annual Register*, 2:428; Payne and Allan, *Clipston Baptist Church,* 12; Arthur S. Langley, "Baptist Ministers in England about 1750 A.D," *Transactions of the Baptist Historical Society* 6 (1918-1919): 150.

Ewing, Greville (1767-1841)—Originally a minister in the Church of Scotland, Ewing took an active role in the formation of the Edinburgh Missionary Society in 1796, serving as its first secretary and editor of the *Missionary Magazine* from 1796 to 1798. He became a Congregationalist minister in Glasgow in 1799, remaining in that capacity until 1836. Ewing, along with the Haldane brothers and Ralph Wardlaw, was instrumental in bringing Congregationalism and home missions into Scotland. He would later break with the Haldanes when they became Baptists, remaining loyal to his congregationalism. Ewing played a leading role in the formation of the Congregational Union of Scotland in 1812. At the time of letter 96 (1811), he was also serving as a tutor at the Glasgow Theological Academy, a Congregationalist school he helped found in 1809. Despite his affiliations, Ewing was a solid supporter of the BMS, collecting subscriptions and donations on the part of the Serampore Mission to replace the contents lost in the fire of March 1812 (see letter 99). Among his publications are *A Defence of Itinerant and Field Preaching: A Sermon Preached before the Society of gratis Sunday Schools, December 24, 1797, at Lady Glenorchy's Chapel, Edinburgh* (1799) and *The Duty of Christians to Civil Government* (1799). See Talbot, *Search for a Common Identity*, 90-98; *DEB.*

Eyre, John (1754-1803)—Eyre was an Evangelical Anglican clergyman who studied at Trevecca College in Wales and then performed itinerant preaching in Cornwall, 1774-1778. He became curate of Weston in 1779 and later held curacies at Lewes (Sussex), Reading, and Chelsea. In 1785 he removed to the Episcopal chapel at Homerton where he remained until his death. He was a founding member of the London Missionary Society, Village Itinerancy, and, along with Samuel Greatheed and others, one of the first editors of the *Evangelical Magazine*. See *DEB.*

Fawcett, John (1740-1817)—Fawcett, a Yorkshire resident all his life, was converted through the ministry of George Whitefield, and after a brief stint as a Methodist preacher, was ordained a Baptist minister in 1765. He began his ministry at Wainsgate before moving the church to Hebden Bridge in 1777, where he remained (living at Ewood Hall) until his death in 1817. Though twice offered pastorates outside Yorkshire, he chose to remain with his people there. Though self-educated, Fawcett was a man of culture and a leader in providing education for young ministerial students in the north of England. He was instrumental in the founding of Horton Academy at Bradford (later Rawdon College), and kept a private academy for many years. He was an active supporter of the BMS and the British and Foreign Bible Society, a hymn writer, occasional author, and leading figure in the

Baptist Evangelical revival of his day. See John Fawcett, Jr., *An Account of the Life, Ministry, and Writings of the Late Rev. John Fawcett, D.D* (London: Baldwin, Cradock, and Joy, 1818); *DEB.*

Fenn, John—Fenn was a hosier at 78 Cornhill, London. He may have been the father of Joseph Fenn [Finn], who became a missionary to India for the Church Missionary Society. In 1799 Fenn took on a new partner in his business, Joseph Wickenden. Wickenden joined James Dore's congregation at Maze Pond in August 1799, having been in business previously in Portsmouth and a member of the Baptist church there. Both Fenn and Wickenden were supporters of the BMS, subscribing £2.2 each in 1800-1801 and 1804-1805. Wickenden became a deacon at Maze Pond in 1800, and also served as an associate member of the Particular Baptist Fund in 1804-1805. See *Universal British Directory*, 1/2:142; *Periodical Accounts*, 2:204, and 3:132, 137; Maze Pond Church Book (MS., Angus Library, Regent's Park College, Oxford) 2: ff. 20,184, 189, and 194; Valentine, *Concern for the Ministry*, 48.

Fernandez, Ignatius (1757-1830)—Fernandez was born in Portuguese Macao, and was trained for the priesthood by an Augustinian monk. He grew skeptical of "Rome's image-worship," however, and declined the priesthood. He traveled to Bengal in 1774, where he eventually built a large wax-candle factory and an indigo plantation. He was converted through the work of the BMS missionaries in 1796, baptized in 1801 and ordained in 1804. Thereafter he became a true friend of the mission, ministering to the church at Dinagepore for many years and organizing several schools. Carey once sent him to England to buy "works of good philosophy and divinity, not in antiquated language!" Fernandez is first mentioned in a letter of Carey to Fuller on 22 June 1797. William Yates, in his *Memoir* of John Chamberlain, includes a long letter by Chamberlain to John Ryland, dated 3 September 1804, in which Chamberlain informs Ryland that he and his wife had recently stayed with Fernandez in Dinagepore. To Chamberlain, Fernandez was a man whose "heart is warm with the love of Christ, nor has he greater pleasure than when he is telling the good news of salvation to poor sinners. He supports a school, consisting of about thirty boys, some of whom could read the Scriptures, say the catechism, and sing several hymns . . . Brother Fernandez's situation is solitary, but far from discouraging. He preaches every Lord's day to his servants, and sometimes others attend; besides which, he has many opportunities of speaking to people about their spiritual concerns." William Carey, writing to either William or Samuel Hope of Liverpool shortly after the death of Fernandez, recalled his first meeting with Fernandez in 1796: "He was then building a dwelling-house at Dinagepore, which, he said, he intended for the worship of God, and invited brother Thomas and myself to preach at the opening of it, which we soon after did. From that time till this there has been preaching in it; and our late brother was the instrument of collecting the largest church in Bengal. It now consists of nearly one hundred members, and when we take into account those who have died in the Lord, the number must amount to one hundred at least. These will be his crown of joy in the day of the Lord

Jesus." See Carey, *William Carey,* 170; Eustace Carey, *Memoir of Dr. Carey,* 2nd ed. (London: Jackson and Walford, 1837) 308; Yates, *Memoirs of Mr. John Chamberlain,* 1:388-389; S. Powell, "Account of Mr. F—," *Baptist Annual Register,* 3:405-407; *DEB.*

Fishwick, Richard (1745-1825)—Fishwick was possibly the leading Baptist layman in the north of England during the last quarter of the eighteenth century. He spent his early years in Hull, where he and his family worshiped in the local Baptist church. He was baptized by John Beatson in 1777, and the next year removed to Newcastle to join with another Baptist layman from Bishop Burton, Archer Ward (1753-1800), and his partner Samuel Walker of Rotherham, in forming the Elswick White-Lead Works. He enquired about the Baptists, only to discover that the congregation at Tuthill-stairs had recently been split by a Socinian wing, led by Caleb Alder and his son-in-law, William Robson. They would eventually form the Pandon-bank chapel, with Edward Prowitt, a former student at Bristol Academy, as their first minister (Prowitt had also briefly pastored at New Road, Oxford, 1784-1786, but resigned because he had already "adopted heterodox views"). Fishwick reinvigorated the small meeting at Tuthill Stairs, at that time led by Henry Dawson, who was succeeded in 1781 by William Pendered. Fishwick and Ward laboured incessantly for the next eighteen years in building a Baptist work in Newcastle, which culminated in the completion of a new chapel at Tuthill-stairs in 1798. That year Fishwick was chosen treasurer of the newly formed Northern Evangelical Society. He spent considerable sums of his own money helping to build Baptist chapels throughout the north of England. Both Fishwick and Ward were close friends and correspondents of David Kinghorn, Baptist minister at Bishop Burton, and his son, Joseph, once an apprentice to Ward and Fishwick and later Baptist minister at Norwich. In fact, Fishwick paid the majority of Joseph Kinghorn's educational expenses during his time at Bristol Academy. Fishwick was a strong supporter of the BMS in the north, subscribing £5 to the Baptist Missionary Society in 1804-1805. Fishwick's final years were not so glorious, however. Unwise speculations led to the loss of much of his fortune, and he moved to London in 1806 in greatly reduced circumstances. He joined John Rippon's congregation at Carter Lane and died at Islington in 1825. See Douglass, *History,* 218-219, 240-241, 243-244; Bradburn, *History of Bewick Street,* 5; Frank Beckwith, "Fishwick and Ward," *Baptist Quarterly* 15 (1953-1954): 249-268; Philip Hayden, "The Baptists in Oxford 1656-1819," *Baptist Quarterly* 29 (1981-1982): 130; *Periodical Accounts,* 3:142.

Fletcher, Joseph—Fletcher was a Baptist layman, serving as treasurer at this time of the Baptist Theological Education Society and the Baptist Building Fund. His address is listed both as Shooter's Hill and the Union Docks, Limehouse—the former may have been his private residence and the latter his business residence, for he was involved in the shipping trade and was active in assisting the BMS Committee and its missionaries in matters pertaining to ships and passages to various destinations. When Edward Hewett (see below) was approved as a missionary in 1842, the BMS Committee granted £140 to outfit him and send Hewett and his wife to Jamaica; the Committee minutes also noted that "Joseph Fletcher Esq (in whose vessel they were likely to sail) had given up the Owners' Share of the Passage Money." As the letters in Part Six reveal, Fletcher was involved in the procurement and testing of the *Dove* as a suitable vessel for the BMS, contributing not only advice on the vessel but also £400 towards its purchase in 1844. For his help in this matter, the Committee thanked him "for the full & very important suggestions with which he has favoured them." See *Baptist Magazine* 33 (1841): 408; 34 (1842): 664; 35 (1843): 265-266, 587, 654-655; 36 (1844): 583, 657; 38 (1846): 306, 522, 705-706; BMS Committee Minutes, Vol. H (Oct. 1841-Dec. 1842), f. 75; Vol. I (January 1843-May 1844), f. 188; Vol. J (30 May 1844—29 July 1847), ff. 7, 9, and 43.

Fletcher, Josiah—Fletcher was a deacon for many years in the Baptist church at St. Mary's, Norwich, during the pastorates of Joseph Kinghorn (1789-1832) and William Brock (1833-1848). Fletcher was a printer, bookseller, and bookbinder by trade, with offices in Upper Haymarket Street. He published, along with his fellow church member, Simon Wilkin, the *East Anglian, Norfolk and Suffolk and Cambridgeshire Herald* in Norfolk. In 1845 a new paper was begun, the *Norfolk News*, of which six of the founding proprietors were Baptists, including Fletcher, who printed the paper. See Charles Boardman Jewson, *The Baptists of Norfolk* (London: Carey Kingsgate Press, 1957) 99-102, 119; George Gould, *Open Communion and the Baptists of Norwich* (Norwich: Josiah Fletcher, 1860) lvii; *Pigot and Co.'s Royal National and Commercial Directory and Topography of the Counties of Bedford, Cambridge, Essex, Herts, Huntingdon, Kent, Middlesex, Norfolk, Suffolk, Surrey and Sussex* (London: Pigot, 1839) 492.

Fletcher, Richard (1800-1861)—Originally from Newcastle-upon-Tyne, Fletcher entered the Independent college at Rotherham in 1819. After ministering at Ebenezer Chapel, Darwen, Lancashire, 1823-1831, he moved to Manchester, succeeding the popular William Roby as pastor of the Grosvenor Street Chapel. He remained there until 1853, when he and John Poore, minister at Hope Chapel, Manchester, were persuaded by the London Missionary Society to serve as missionaries in Australia following the gold rush. Fletcher ministered at St. Kilda, Victoria, Australia, 1853-1861. He was the father of William Roby Fletcher (1833-1894), prominent Congregational minister in Australia, 1858-1894. See *Congregational Yearbook* (1863): 225-228.

Flight, Thomas (1726-1800)—In 1783, after serving many years as the London agent for the Worcester China Factory, Thomas Flight purchased the factory, placing primary operations of the Worcester branch into the hands of his two sons, Joseph (1762-1838) and John (1766-1791). They opened a retail shop at 45 High Street, Worcester, in July 1788. The next month they wer visited by George III, a visit that resulted in the factory receiving a royal patent. By 1790 Flight and his sons were operating a china factory in London (22 Bread Street), one in Worcester, and the Worcester China Warehouse at 1 Coventry Street in the Haymarket, London, selling primarily French porcelain that John Flight had purchased for purposes of imitation during his frequent visits to France between 1785 and 1791. After Flight's untimely death in 1791, Martin Barr (former business partner of Thomas Gillam, the father of John Flight's young widow), a devout Calvinist and member of the Independent congregation at Angel Street in Worcester, became Thomas Flight's new partner. By 1800 the business was listed as "Flight & Barr, Worcester China Warehouse," in the Haymarket. Tom Flight, as well as his sons, Joseph and John, and a third son, Bannister, all attended the Baptist congregation at Maze Pond, Southwark. Tom Flight joined the church in 1756 and served as a deacon for nearly 27 years. On many occasions he served as the messenger of the church to the Particular Baptist Fund and the Body of Protestant Dissenting Deputies. He was a wide supporter of Baptist causes throughout the kingdom, as well as the more ecumenical aims of the Sunday School Society, to which he generously subscribed £21 in 1789. Like many Baptists in the late 1780s and early 1790s, Flight was an active supporter of the French Revolution and the efforts to enact political reform in England. Among his close friends was the radical editor of the *Cambridge Intelligencer*, Benjamin Flower (see entry below), at that time a member of Robert Hall's congregation at St. Andrew's Street in Cambridge. In his will Flight left £200 to the church for the relief of the poor. See Maze Pond Church Book, 2: ff. 118,190, 192; *The Merchant and Tradesman's London Directory for the Year 1787* (London: R. Shaw and W. Lowndes, 1787) 60; *Universal British Directory*, 1/2:146; *Kent's Directory for the year 1800* (London: Richard and Henry Causton, 1800) 69; *Plan of a Society Established in London,* Anno Domini *1785, for the Support and Encouragement of Sunday-Schools in Different Counties of England* (London: Sunday School Society, 1789) 25; "A Diaconal Epistle, 1790," *Baptist Quarterly* 8 (1936-1937): 216.

Flower, Benjamin (1755-1829)—Flower was raised in Edward Hitchin's Independent congregation at White Row, Spitalfields, London, where Benjamin's father, George Flower, was a deacon. After working six years as the European agent for a manufacturer in Tiverton, Flower became the first and only editor of the *Cambridge Intelligencer*, which he published from 1793 to 1803. He removed to Harlow in 1804, where he operated a printing business until 1815. In 1819, he retired with his two daughters, Eliza and Sarah, to Dalston, Hackney, where he died in 1829. While in Cambridge he was an attendant (and occasionally the hymn leader) of Robert Hall's congregation at St. Andrew's Street from 1793 to 1798, having been a friend and ardent admirer of Hall's predecessor, Robert Robinson. In 1799 Flower spent six months in Newgate prison for libeling the Bishop of Llandaff in an editorial in the *Intelligencer*. While in prison, he met his future wife, Eliza Gould (1770-1810). She grew up in Bampton, Devon, where her father was a deacon in the local Baptist church. In 1799 (when she met Flower) she was living in London in the home of Joseph Gurney (1744-1815), a deacon at Maze Pond and the father of William B. Gurney (see letter 267). During their years at Harlow, the Flowers attended the Baptist meeting at Fore Street; Flower, his wife, and two daughters are all buried in the Baptist cemetery in Foster Street, Harlow. Among his publications are

The French Constitution: With Remarks on Some of its Principal Articles ... and the Necessity of a Reformation in Church and State in Great Britain, Enforced (1792); *National Sins Considered, in Two Letters to the Rev. Thomas Robinson ... to Which are Added a Letter from the Rev. Robert Hall, to the Rev. Charles Simeon ...* (1796). See Timothy Whelan, *Politics, Religion, and Romance: The Letters of Benjamin Flower and Eliza Gould Flower, 1794-1808* (Aberystwyth: National Library of Wales, 2008) xiii-xlvii.

Forsaith, Robert (1749-1797)—An Independent minister, Forsaith was originally from Sleaford, Lancashire, and entered Hoxton Academy in 1765, studying under Savage, Kippis, and Rees. He assisted at Norwich from 1770 to 1782, apparently creating a schism, which forced his separation from the church. He pastored at Oundle, Northamptonshire (1783-1785), and then became classical tutor at Daventry Academy (1785-1789), before returning once again to Northampton (1790-1797). He subscribed to Habakkuk Crabb's *Sermons* in 1796 (printed by Benjamin Flower in Cambridge). See *Protestant Dissenter's Magazine* 4 (1797): 280.

Foster, John (Baptist essayist) (1770-1843)—Born near Hebden Bridge, not far from Halifax, Yorkshire, Foster was raised in a strict dissenting home and attended John Fawcett's congregation at Wainsgate. When he was seventeen the church set him apart for the ministry, and four years later (1791) he matriculated at Bristol Academy, under the immediate supervision of Joseph Hughes, then classical tutor at the Academy and assistant pastor at Broadmead. During his year at Bristol, Foster met Joseph Cottle, a member at the Pithay church as well as a frequent attendant at Broadmead and soon to be member of the Committee of the Bristol Education Society. Foster left Bristol on 26 May 1792 to pastor the struggling congregation at Tuthill Stairs at Newcastle. After about a year, he left for Dublin, where he preached occasionally and taught in an academy. While in Ireland, Foster embraced radical politics, associating with some "violent Democrats" and helping to form a society called the "Sons of Brutus," which, he says, "exposed me at one period to the imminent danger, or at least the expectation, of chains and a dungeon." Foster returned to England in 1796, pastoring a General Baptist congregation in Chichester for two and half years before moving to Battersea, near London, to assist his old tutor and friend Joseph Hughes (now pastoring the Baptist congregation there) in instructing a class of twenty young Africans from Sierra Leone as part of a civilizing missionary outreach. Between 1800 and 1804, Foster ministered to a small congregation of Baptists at Downend, near Bristol. In 1804 he removed to the Baptist congregation at Sheppard's Barton, Frome, and shortly thereafter published his famous *Essays in a Series of Letters* (1805), which went through thirty-five British and American editions between 1805-1920. Two of these essays, "On the Application of the Epithet Romantic" and "On Some of the Causes by which Evangelical Religion has been rendered less Acceptable to Persons of Cultivated Taste," were Foster's first critical essays on literature and aesthetics. He resigned his pastorate in 1806 and commenced a connection with the *Eclectic Review* that would last until 1839, contributing 185 articles during those years. He returned to Downend in

1817, and in 1821 removed to Stapleton, three miles from Bristol, where he lived until his death in October 1843. Throughout his life he was an advocate for political reform and a staunch Nonconformist with a strident belief in freedom of conscience along with the need for greater education among the masses. See J. E. Ryland, *Life and Correspondence of John Foster*, 2 vols. (London: H. G. Bohn, 1852) (quotation above found on 1:26); Timothy Whelan, "John Foster and Samuel Taylor Coleridge," *Christianity and Literature* 50 (2001): 631-656; *DEB*.

Foster, John (of Biggleswade) (1765-1847)—A prosperous merchant, Foster was treasurer of the Bedfordshire Union of Christians, 1797-1847. He was a prominent member of the Baptist church at Biggleswade for over fifty years, joining in 1788, becoming a trustee in 1790, and a deacon in 1799. Related to the Fosters who attended St. Andrew's Street, Cambridge, John Foster served as a lay preacher in the Biggleswade meeting from 1816 to 1818 (as well as 1836) and in several village congregations surrounding Biggleswade. He was also a supporter of the BMS, subscribing £1.1 in 1800-1801. See John Brown, *The History of the Bedfordshire Union of Christians* (London: Independent Press, 1946) 87; *Biggleswade Baptist Church 1771-1971* (Biggleswade: [n. p.], [1971]) 39-40; *Periodical Accounts*, 2:205; C. H. Chaplin, *History of the Old Meeting Baptist Church, Biggleswade* (Biggleswade: C. Elphick, 1909) 27-29.

Fountain, John (1766-1800)—Fountain joined the Baptist church at Eagle Street in London in 1794. In January 1796 Andrew Fuller and the BMS committee agreed to take him under the direction of the Society. That April he sailed on board the American ship *Elizabeth*, arriving in India on 16 September 1796. He applied himself to the language and eventually assisted in translation work at Mudnabatty, as well as preaching at Dinagepore and Rungpore and working with the school there. Fuller chastised him for his political outspokenness, but Carey consistently defended him. He moved with Carey to Kidderpore when Carey purchased a small factory there, but left in 1799 to help the new missionaries—Marshman, Ward, Brunsdon, and Grant—who had just arrived in Calcutta. When they decided to make Serampore the mission headquarters, he settled there in November and soon married a Miss Tidd of Oakham, who had arrived with the new missionaries. He decided to return to Dinagepore in the spring, but took ill and died in August 1800 at the age of 33. See Eagle Street Church Book, London, Vol. 1, 1737-1785 (MS., Angus Library, Regent's Park College, Oxford) f. 133; Carey, *Oriental Christian Biography*, 3:332-336; *DEB*.

Fownes, Joseph (1715-1789)—Originally from Andover, Fownes was educated at a Presbyterian academy in the early 1730s. He began his ministry with the Presbyterian congregation at Cradley in 1736, and was ordained there in April 1743. He then removed to the Presbyterian congregation at High Street in Shrewsbury, first as assistant, then co-pastor (1748-1765) with Job Orton, and finally as pastor, 1765-1789. He authored *An Enquiry into the Principles of Toleration* (Shrewsbury, 1773).

Francies, Ebenezer Joseph—Francies was the son of George Francies, Baptist minister at Colchester and later at Lambeth, Surrey. After completing his studies at Stepney College, he was appointed as a BMS missionary to Jamaica in May 1839. He worked in the Hanover parish until 1844, when he was forced to remove to the island of St. Vincent for health reasons. After a furlough in England, he and his wife began a new work in Haiti in December 1845; however, their time in Haiti was short-lived, for Francies died of a fever in July 1846. His wife died in Falmouth, Jamaica, the next year. See Clarke, *Memorials*, 177-178.

Francis, Benjamin (1734-1799)—After studying at Bristol Academy, Francis, a Welshman, ministered initially at Chipping Sodbury (1756-1759) before settling at Horsley, where he remained the rest of his life. He was a noted hymn writer, and was unanimously called to replace John Gill at Carter Lane in London in 1772, but decided to remain at Horsley. See Brown, *English Baptists of the Eighteenth Century*, 94; Michael A. G. Haykin, "Benjamin Francis (1734-1799)," ed. Haykin, in *The British Particular Baptists*, 2:17-29; Hayden, *Continuity and Change*, 55-57, 128-131, 175-194, 234; *DEB.*

Freeman, Joseph John (1794-1851)—Freeman served as Secretary of the London Missionary Society from 1839 to 1846. Educated at Hoxton Academy (1812-1816), he ministered to Independent churches in Chelmsford, Dawlish, Westbury and Kidderminster between 1816 and 1826. From 1827 to 1835 he served as an LMS missionary to Madagascar. When he returned to England in 1837, he assumed the pastorate of the Independent church at Walthamstow, where he assisted in the founding of the Walthamstow School for Missionary Children (later Walthamstow Hall, Sevenoaks). He also began working for the LMS at that time. In 1842-1843, he visited the West Indies on behalf of the LMS, examining the working conditions among the blacks on the islands after emancipation. He was most impressed with their generosity, claiming that the former slaves in British Guiana and Jamaica had contributed a quarter of a millions pounds to the work of their churches and missions. During 1848-1851, he visited mission stations in Madagascar and South Africa; he died at Hamburg, Germany, in September 1851, on his return to England. See Richard Lovett, *The History of the London Missionary Society, 1795-1895* (London: H. Frowde, 1899) 681-710.

Fuller, Andrew (1754-1815)—Baptized into the Baptist congregation at Soham in 1769, Fuller soon found himself involved in a High Calvinist controversy that eventually placed him in the role of pastor at a very young age. His study of scripture and his reading of Jonathan Edwards and others led him to an evangelical Calvinist position, and his influential work, *The Gospel Worthy of All Acceptation* (1785) was the fruition of that study (and the subject of letter 27). He subsequently influenced numerous ministers among the Particular Baptists to follow his evangelical emphasis, a movement that became known as "Fullerism." He left Soham in 1782 for the Baptist church at Kettering, where he remained the rest of his life. He became one of the leaders of the Northamptonshire Association, along with Robert Hall, Sr., John Ryland, Jr., and John Sutcliff. With these men and others, he founded the BMS in 1792, and became its first secretary, a post he held until his death. Despite devoting much of his time and effort to the work of the BMS, Fuller, through his pen, was a key defender of orthodox Calvinism against the claims of High Calvinism, Antinomianism, Socinianism, and infidelity, most notably in his major work, *The Calvinistic and Socinian Systems Examined and Compared as to Their Moral Tendency* (1793). Without question, Fuller was one of the leading evangelicals of his day and his legacy in regards to the BMS remains to this day. See Morris, *Memoirs*; Ryland, *The Work of Faith*; Clipsham, "Andrew Fuller and Fullerism"; Peter J. Morden, *Offering Christ to the World: Andrew Fuller (1754-1815) and the Revival of Eighteenth Century Particular Baptist Life*. Studies in Baptist History and Thought, vol. 8 (Carlisle: Paternoster Press, 2003); Tom J. Nettles, "Andrew Fuller (1754-1814)," ed. Haykin, in *The British Particular Baptists*, 2:97-141; *DEB*.

Gamby, William (1790-1813)—Gamby came from Southill, Bedfordshire, where his father, John Gamby (1730-1802), served as minister of the Baptist meeting, 1787-1802. The younger Gamby was apprenticed in Leicester and attended the ministry of Robert Hall. He was baptized in 1810 and recommended as a missionary on 1 October 1811. He studied under Sutcliff at Olney in 1812, but his health deteriorated, resulting in his untimely death the next year. See Gravett, *Three Hundred Years*, 28; "Sutcliff's Academy," 277; *Baptist Annual Register*, 4:1074; *Baptist Magazine* 6 (1814): 200-02.

Gay, Robert (d. 1865)—Gay, from Hastings, was appointed a BMS missionary to Jamaica in 1842, working with Knibb in the publication of the *Baptist Herald* and the *Friend of Africa*; he also supervised Knibb's schools. He later ministered to the Falmouth church, 1847-1856. He retired from the mission field in 1856 and returned to England, where he ministered to the Baptist church at Little Kingshill until his death in 1865. In letter 219, Gay was just commencing his voyage to Jamaica. See Clarke, *Memorials*, 185.

Geard, John (1749-1838)—Originally a member of the Baptist church at Montacute, Somerset, Geard was one of the first students to enter Bristol Academy after the formation of the Bristol Education Society in 1770. While at Bristol, he supplied the fledgling Falmouth and Chacewater meetings in 1773. He began his official ministry as the successor to Samuel James at Tilehouse Street, Hitchin, Hertfordshire, in 1774; he was ordained in April 1775, and remained at Hitchin until 1831. He was a strong supporter of the BMS as well as a pioneer in village preaching in such places as Shillington, Bendish, Breachwood Green, and Langley. Geard, like many of his Baptist brethren in the late 1780s and early 1790s, was not averse to politics. The church book notes that in 1788, on the centenary of the Glorious Revolution, a collection of £1.15 was taken for the building of a memorial pillar to Runnymede. When that scheme fell through, the money was sent instead to the Abolitionist Society in London "that this nation which boasts so much of liberty may not expose itself to the reproach of the inconsistency as well as the cruelty of enslaving others." Geard was a strong supporter of the BMS from its inception in 1792, as well as Sunday schools, which began at Tilehouse in 1812. Geard's last seven years were spent in retirement. See James McCleery, *The History of Tilehouse Street (Salem)*

Baptist Church, Hitchin (Hitchin UK: Carling and Hales, 1919) 30-35; David Watts, *A History of the Hertfordshire Baptists* ([Hertfordshire]: Hertford-shire Baptist Association, 1978) 14; Hayden, *Continuity and Change*, 234.

Gentleman, Robert (1746-1795)—Gentleman was born at Shrewsbury and studied at Daventry Academy. He kept a boarding school while serving as pastor of the Independent congregation at Swan Hill, Shrewsbury, 1767-1779. He then ministered at Lammas Street, Carmarthen, where he was also a tutor in the Carmarthen Academy, 1779-1784. His last pastorate was at the New Meeting, Kidderminster, 1784-1795. See *Protestant Dissenter's Magazine* 2 (1795): 312.

Giles, Samuel (b.1809)—Giles was a calico printer in Great Cheetham Street, Manchester. His father, William Giles (1771-1845), was a Baptist minister at Dartmouth (where Samuel was born), Lymington, Chatham, and Preston (Lancs.) from 1833 to 1842. Rev. Giles spent most of 1842 in Manchester, then preached at Ashton-under-Lyne, Lancashire, in 1843-1844 just before his death in 1845. Samuel was educated at John Hinton's academy at Ox-ford; his brother, John Eustace (1805-1875), would gain considerable recognition as pastor of the Baptist congregation at South Parade, Leeds, 1836-1846, followed by pastorates at Bristol, Sheffield, and at Clapham Common. Samuel's oldest brother, William Giles, Jr. (1798-1856) would become a schoolmaster at Chatham, 1817-1821, where Charles Dickens was one of his students. Giles, Jr., would move to Lancashire in the early 1830s, where he operated schools at Barton Hall and Patricroft; he also ministered to the Baptist meeting at Barton Lane, Eccles. He later opened a school at 38 Ardwick Green, Manchester, c. 1837, but in 1842 resigned from the church at Eccles and moved his school to Seacombe House, Ash-ton, Cheshire. He served as pastor of the Baptist church there from 1843 to 1845. In 1848, he moved again, this time to Netherleigh House, Chester, continuing as both a schoolmaster and pastor until his death in 1856, by which time he had become F.R.G.S. For a brief time during 1842 (the date of letter 172), all three Giles—William, Sr., William, Jr., and Samuel—lived in or near Manchester. In fact, in 1843, William, Jr., and Samuel entertained Dickens at William's home at Ardwick Green. See "Giles, Father and Sons," *Baptist Quarterly* 4 (1928-1929): 333-336; *Pigot and Slater's Directory of Manchester and Salford,* 3 vols. (Manchester: Pigot and Slater, 1841) 1:104; *DEB.*

Gill, John (1697-1771)—Gill was introduced to High Calvinism as a young student in Kettering by John Skepp, whose influence marked the works and ministry of Gill thereafter. In 1719 Gill assumed the pastorate of the Baptist congregation at Horsleydown in Southwark, not far from his High Calvinist friend, John Brine, at Cripplegate. Gill remained with the Southwark con-gregation until his death in 1771. Like Brine and others who followed the High Calvinist model, Gill was constrained by his theology to refrain from offering any of his hearers an unrestricted invitation to accept Christ. The High Calvinism of some of Gill's followers was probably greater than his own, but his works abound in close defenses of a system that a later gener-ation of evangelical Calvinists would view as arid, narrow, and stifling in regard to evangelism. Nevertheless, Gill was a profound scholar and voluminous writer and defender of orthodox Calvinism against the early inroads of Socinianism and Antinomianism. Gill's biblical and doctrinal studies were standards for many students and ministers during the eighteenth and early nineteenth centuries, especially his three-volume *A Body of Doctrinal Divinity*, which earned him an honorary D.D. from Aberdeen in 1748. See George M. Ella, *John Gill and the Cause of God and Truth* (Eggleston: Go Publications, 1995); Robert W. Oliver, "John Gill (1697-1771)," ed. Haykin, in *The British Particular Baptists*, 1:145-165; *DEB*.

Gill, John (d. 1809)—He was the nephew of the legendary John Gill. The former came to St. Albans from his uncle's congregation at Carter Lane, Southwark, in 1758 and in 1768 the St. Alban's church joined the Northamptonshire Association. Two annual meetings of the Association took place at St. Albans in 1783 and 1795, with Andrew Fuller preaching at the latter. During Gill's ministry, which lasted until his death in 1809, the church remained relatively small, with a membership of under 50. See Watts, *History of the Hertfordshire Baptists,* 13.

Godden, Thomas (d. 1824)—Along with Christopher Kitching, Godden was set apart as a missionary to Jamaica at Frome in March 1818. He came out of James Bicheno's congregation at Newbury. In October 1819, not long after he commenced his work at Spanish Town, his wife died. He did not remain long in Jamaica, retiring in 1823 due to poor health; he died in November 1824. See Cox, *History,* 2:25-32.

Grant, William (d. 1799)—Grant, along with Joshua Marshman and Daniel Brunsdon (at that time all three were members of the Broadmead congregation in Bristol), sailed with William Ward for India in 1799. Grant had been converted by means of Latin lessons given by Joshua Marshman in Bristol. Grant's subsequent decision to become a missionary was instrumental in Marshman's decision to go to India. Shortly after his arrival, however, Grant died, never meeting William Carey.

Greatheed, Samuel (d. 1823)—Originally from London, Greatheed served in the British Army during the American War. He became an assistant tutor at William Bull's Academy at Newport Pagnell in 1786; he later supplied as minister of an Independent congregation at Woburn, Bedfordshire, 1789-1791. He then accepted the pastorate and remained there until 1797, after which he retired to Bishops Hull, Somerset. He was one of the first editors of the *Evangelical Magazine*, as well as one of the founders of the London Missionary Society (1795) and the Bedfordshire Christian Union (1797). His major publication was *Memoirs of the Life and Writings of William Cowper, Esq.* (1814). See *Congregational Magazine* 2 (1819): 56.

Green, Samuel (1796-1883)—The son of a Baptist minister in Norfolk, Green entered Stepney College in 1816 and in 1820 began his ministerial career at Falmouth, where he remained for four years. He then preached at Faringdon, Berkshire, for one year before removing to Thrapstone, Northamptonshire. He came to the Baptist church in Lion Street, Walworth, as assistant to John Chin, in 1834, becoming a member of the London Baptist Board in 1835. He served as senior pastor at Lion Street from 1841 to

1849, before retiring to Hammersmith in 1855. Among his publications is *The Biblical and Theological Dictionary* (1841). At various times he served as secretary to the Baptist Irish Society and Stepney College. See Whitley, *The Baptists of London*, 143; Couling, "Biographical Dictionary, 1875-1889."

Greenwood, Abraham (1749-1827)—Greenwood, originally from Barnoldswick, became one of John Fawcett's first ministerial students at Wainsgate. Greenwood married Alvery Jackson's daughter and became the first pastor at Rochdale in 1775. He removed to Dudley in 1780 and later to Oakham, where he ministered from 1787 to 1796. He then removed to South Killingholme, Lincolnshire, serving as pastor of the Baptist church there until his death in 1827. He was one of a select group of pastors who was present at the formation of the Baptist Missionary Society at Kettering in 1792. He was probably the son of John Greenwood, a deacon in the Baptist church at Barnoldswick. See Arthur S. Langley, "Abraham Greenwood, 1749-1827," *Baptist Quarterly* 2 (1924-1925): 84-89; E. Winnard, *The History of the Baptist Church, Barnoldswick, 1500-1916* (Burnley: [n. p.], 1916) 61.

Gregory, Olinthus (1774-1841)—At the age of nineteen, Gregory, from Yaxley, Huntingtonshire, published *Lessons Astronomical and Philosophical* (1793), an early indicator of his future prominence in the field of mathematics. Before he commenced his career as a mathematics teacher, however, he spent several years in Cambridge, arriving in 1796 to work as sub-editor of Benjamin Flower's *Cambridge Intelligencer*. He attended at St. Andrew's Street and was baptized there, becoming a close friend of Robert Hall. He also operated a bookshop and a school, during which time he hired Newton Bosworth as his assistant. In 1803 he was became an instructor of mathematics at the Royal Military Academy at Woolwich, leaving Cambridge and turning his school over to Bosworth. In 1821 he was appointed professor of mathematics, having established himself as a preeminent authority by that time. By the time he retired in 1838, he had composed several scientific treatises, written about half the scientific articles for the encyclopedic work, *Pantalogia* (1808-1813), served as a member of numerous philosophical and scientific societies, and become widely known for his writings in Christian apologetics, such as *Letters on the Evidences of Christianity* (1811). For many years Gregory worshiped with the Baptist church at Maze Pond, Southwark. As the writer of his obituary in the *Baptist Magazine* writes, though Baptist tenets "were immovably fixed in his creed, and adopted after most extensive research and patient thought, yet no man ever held them with more pure and genial catholicity of feeling." He frequently attended Anglican services in his later years, but was always an adherent of the principles of civil and religious liberty. He was widely known for his edition of *The Works of Robert Hall* (6 vols; 1832). Along with Joseph Hughes, F. A. Cox, and others, he was instrumental in the founding of University College, London University. See *Baptist Magazine* 33 (1841): 129-130, 268-273; *DEB*.

Groser, William (1791-1856)—The son of the Baptist minister at Watford, Groser entered the ministry in 1813 at Princes Risborough, followed by a long tenure at Maidstone (1820-1839). He removed to London in 1839 to become secretary to the Anti-Opium Society, for which he contributed a number of printed tracts. In 1838 he became editor of the *Baptist Magazine*; he would later serve as a member of the committee of the Baptist Irish Society, the London Baptist Board, the BMS, and the Religious Tract Society. He was also an early supporter of the Baptist Union. See Price, "The Early Years of the Baptist Union," 127; *DEB*.

Grunden (Grindon), Richard (d. 1814)—He served 28 years as pastor of the Baptist meeting at Sharnbrook, Bedfordshire. He removed to the Baptist meeting in Ringstead, Northamptonshire, in 1798, where he remained until his death on 9 August 1814. See *Baptist Annual Register*, 1:3; 3:4; *Baptist Magazine* 6 (1814): 425.

Gurney, William Brodie (1777-1855)—Gurney succeeded his father, Joseph (1744-1815), as shorthand writer for the Old Bailey and for parliament; his older brother, John (1768-1745) (later Sir John Gurney) became a leading London lawyer, judge, and eventually Baron of the Exchequer in 1832. Between 1770 and 1816, the Gurneys were staunch Particular Baptists, first under Thomas Craner at Red Cross Street and then under James Dore at Maze Pond, Southwark. One of the leading Baptist layman of his day, W. B. Gurney helped form a Sunday school at Maze Pond in 1801 and in 1803 the London Sunday School Union, of which he was at various times secretary, treasurer, and president, remaining a part of the organization until his death. For many years he served as editor of *The Youth's Magazine*, a cheap periodical devoted to religious concerns. He was involved with the British and Foreign Bible Society, treasurer of Stepney College (1828-1844), the Baptist Missionary Society (1835-1855), and the Particular Baptist Fund. He authored *A Lecture to Children and Youth on the History and Characters of Heathen Idolatry. With Some References to the Effects of Christian Missions* (1848), and edited the 15th and 16th editions of Thomas Gurney's *Brachygraphy* (1824, 1835). Gurney's daughter, Amelia, married Joseph Angus in 1841. Gurney's son, Joseph (1804-1879) (who was for over 50 years a member of the committee of the Religious Tract Society and later treasurer of Regent's Park College) succeeded his father as shorthand writer for parliament in 1849, remaining in that position until his retirement in 1872. At that time, his nephew, William Henry Gurney Salter, took over, continuing more than 100 years of service by members of the Gurney family as shorthand writers for parliament and the Old Bailey. See William Henry Gurney Salter, ed., *Some Particulars of the Lives of William Brodie Gurney and his Immediate Ancestors. Written Chiefly by Himself* (London: Unwin, 1902); A. C. Underwood, *A History of the English Baptists* (London: Baptist Union Publications Department, 1947) 146-147; *DEB*.

Guy, William (1739-1783)—Guy came to the Baptist meeting at Sheepshead, Leicestershire, in 1774, where he remained until his death in 1783. He immediately led the church into a revival; Sutcliff visited Guy in the autumn of 1774 to witness the revival for himself. John Ryland, Jr., preached Guy's funeral sermon, *Seasonable Hints to a Bereaved Church: And the Blessedness of the Dead, Who Die in the Lord* (1783). See Haykin, *One Heart*, 83-84.

Hague, William (1736-1831)—Originally a Methodist, Hague was a native of Scarborough. He was baptized by Joseph Gawkrodger at Bridlington, and soon began preaching. He founded the Ebenezer church at Scarborough in 1771, a congregation in which both Baptists and Independents worshiped together. A chapel was built in 1777, with a gallery added in 1790. A letter from the church to John Rippon, dated 26 June 1796, noted that Hague was "advancing in years and almost blind." A second letter, dated 20 June 1798, commented that Hague had "a wife and three children at home," living on a salary of only £30, a figure that, the letter surmises, "as our congregation increases, we hope it will be better." Apparently, it did, for Hague would remain at Scarborough another 21 years. His financial situation may have improved as well, or he may have exemplified great generosity in his poverty, for in 1804-1805 he subscribed £1.8 to the Baptist Missionary Society. See *Baptist Annual Register*, 3:39; *Periodical Accounts*, 3:144; Ernest A. Payne, "A Yorkshire Story," *Baptist Quarterly* 19 (1961-1962): 366-369.

Haines, George (d. 1780)—Haines, originally from Gloucester, was called into the ministry through the influence of Benjamin Francis at Horsley. Haines would serve as minister at Bethel Chapel (Baptist) in Shipley from 1771 until his death in 1780. Earlier ministers at Shipley included Joseph Gawkrodger (1758-1767) and Luke Collins (1769-1770). Under Haines's leadership, the chapel was enlarged. He was succeeded briefly by Robert Gaze (1781-1782) and then by John Bowser (1782-1812). Eventually, Isaac Mann would pastor at Shipley, 1814-1826. See *Bethel Church, Shipley, 1758-1958* (Shipley: n.p., 1958) 4-5, 20.

Haldane, Robert (1764-1842)—Along with his brother James (1768-1851), Robert Haldane was a leading figure in the evangelical revival of Scotland in the late 1790s and early 1800s. Originally a seaman, he retired early from his commission and used his wealth and estate to preach, train ministers, and establish evangelical churches throughout Scotland. Encouraged by their contacts with a number of English evangelical ministers, both Anglican and Nonconformist, in 1797 the two brothers founded the Society for the Propagation of the Gospel at Home, evangelizing primarily in the Highlands of Scotland. In 1798 James became pastor of a independent Congregational church (in many respects, a "nondenominational" church, as Brian Talbot describes it) in The Circus in Edinburgh, which shortly thereafter moved into a new building (seating 3200) called the Tabernacle Church. Robert purchased another Circus in Glasgow and converted it into a church as well. Fuller and Sutcliff preached to 4000 in Edinburgh and 5000 in Glasgow on a BMS tour of Scotland in October 1799. In 1808 he led his congregation into adopting Baptist polity, initiating a significant revival of Baptist work in Scotland through his preaching, philanthropy and publications. Robert Haldane served many years as minister of the Baptist church at Airdrie. See George Yuille, *History of the Baptists in Scotland from Pre-Reformation Times* (Glasgow: Baptist Union Publications Committee, 1926) 55-60; Lawson, "Robert and James Haldane," *Baptist Quarterly* 7 (1934-1935): 276-285; George McGuiness, "Robert (1764-1842) and James Haldane (1768-1851)," ed. Haykin, in *The British Particular Baptists*, 2:219-

235; Bebbington, ed., *Baptists in Scotland*, 9-47; Talbot, *Search for a Common Identity*, 73-114; for Fuller's discussion of the Haldanes, see Fuller to William Ward, 23 May 1801, MSS. BMS, vol. 1, Angus Library, Regent's Park College, Oxford. *DEB.*

Hall, Robert (1764-1831)—Raised under the tutelage of his father, Robert Hall, Sr., in the Baptist church at Arnesby, the younger Hall showed a remarkable precocity as a child. After a brief stay at John Collett Ryland's academy in Northampton, he entered Bristol Academy at the age of 14. He eventually completed his A.M. at Aberdeen in 1785 while serving as classical tutor and assistant pastor to Caleb Evans at Broadmead and the Academy. After tensions developed between the two men in 1790, Hall preached that fall for two months in Cambridge, then for the first six months of 1791 before finally accepting the call to succeed Robert Robinson at St. Andrew's Street in Cambridge in July of 1791. For most of that decade Hall would continue Robinson's liberal tradition of freedom of conscience, allowing numerous Arians to remain within his congregation, all the while developing a ministry that would prove of great importance to himself and his denomination, both politically and ecclesiastically. Like Robert Robinson, Joseph Priestley, Richard Price, and his former Bristol mentor Caleb Evans, Hall bore an outspoken allegiance to the fundamental principles of political dissent, as his pen soon demonstrated, resulting in two classics of dissenting literature from the 1790s, *Christianity Consistent with a Love of Freedom* (1791) and *An Apology for the Freedom of the Press* (1793). His radical positions altered in the late 1790s (as did many reformers), and he turned his focus toward the threat of infidelity in his most famous publication, *On Modern Infidelity* (1800). He resigned from St. Andrew's Street early in 1806 after a second mental breakdown; he quickly recovered, however, and in 1807 accepted the pastorate of William Carey's former church in Leicester. He remained there until 1826, at which time he returned to Bristol to succeed John Ryland, Jr., as pastor at Broadmead and president of the Academy. He remained at Broadmead until his death in 1831. He argued in print with Joseph Kinghorn in 1816 about the terms of communion, and boldly defended the Framework Knitters Fund of Leicestershire in 1819. His most lasting notoriety during his lifetime, however, involved his preaching, which to many observers was unmatched by any other minister of his day. Olinthus Gregory published Hall's *Works*, along with a *Memoir*, in 1832. See "Memoir" of Robert Hall in vol. 6 of Olinthus Gregory, ed., *The Works of Robert Hall, A. M.*, 6 vols. (London: Henry G. Bohn, 1834); Timothy Whelan, "Coleridge and Robert Hall of Cambridge," *Wordsworth Circle* 31 (2000): 38-47; idem, "Robert Hall and the Bristol Slave-Trade Debate of 1787-1788," *Baptist Quarterly* 38 (1999-2000): 212-224; idem, "'I have *confessed myself a devil*': Crabb Robinson's Confrontation with Robert Hall, 1798-1800," *Charles Lamb Bulletin, New Series* 121 (2003): 2-25; *DEB.*

Hall, Robert, Sr. (1728-1791)—Originally from Newcastle-upon-Tyne, the elder Robert Hall was baptized and joined the congregation at Hexham in 1752, after which he entered the ministry and pastored at Arnesby from 1753 until his death in 1791. He was one of the leaders in the movement against High Calvinism in favor of a more evangelical ministry, which he set forth in his influential work, *Help to Zion's Travellers* (1781). See Michael A. G. Haykin, "Robert Hall, Sr. (1728-1791)," ed. Haykin, in *The British Particular Baptists*, 1:203-211.

Hands, Thomas F. (c.1817-1870)—Hands came from the church in Cannon Street, Birmingham. After studying at Bristol Academy, he and his wife were appointed as BMS missionaries to Jamaica in December 1842. He worked at Staceyville, Mount Angus (with David Day), Yallahs, and beginning in 1847, at the second Baptist church in Montego Bay. In 1852, he returned to England, where he ministered to Baptist congregations at Salisbury (1853-1856) and Luton (1857-1869) as well as serving for a time as traveling secretary for the Bible Translation Society. He died in 1870 at the age of 53. See Clarke, *Memorials*, 194.

Hankey, William Alers—Hankey, a Congregationalist, was like his colleague John Poynder, a businessman actively involved in numerous evangelical associations during his lifetime. He worked closely with the Religious Tract Society for many years, assisting in the production of an early tract, *Scripture Extracts*. He devoted considerable volunteer time to proofreading tracts written in various languages, including Spanish, which he mastered during his later adult years. Hankey also served as treasurer of the Protestant Union in 1843. See Jones, *Jubilee Memorial of the Religious Tract Society*, 60; *Baptist Magazine* 35 (1843): 658.

Harjette, Thomas Lawrence—Harjette was a printer in London, initially at Burlington Arcade, Piccadilly (1821), and then at 29 Bedford Street, Covent Garden (1822-1828). He was listed as Harjette and Savil, 107 St. Martin's Lane, Charing Cross, 1828-1832, and closed his printing career at 10 Craven Buildings, Drury Lane in 1843. Most likely he was a Baptist, for among his list of printed works (1822-1843) are circular letters of the Essex Baptist Association, sermons by Baptist ministers (at least one by Isaac Mann), and the 8th, 9th, and 10th *Annual Report of the Baptist Society for Promoting the Gospel in Ireland* (1822-1824). He also printed pamphlets for the American Colonization Society (involving Liberia), the first five volumes of the *British Magazine*, as well as an edition of the writings of George Washington. See William B. Todd, *A Directory of Printers and Others in Allied Trade, London and Vicinity 1800-1840* (London: Printing Historical Society, 1972) 90.

Harmer, Thomas (1714-88)—Born at Norwich, Harmer was educated at Moorfields and immediately began his ministry as pastor of the Independent Church in Wattisfield in 1734, remaining there until his death in 1788. He compiled a detailed history of the Congregational churches & most of the dissenting churches in Norfolk & Suffolk up to the year 1774, a manuscript now at Dr. Williams's Library, London. He was succeeded by Habbakuk Crabb, son of a deacon in the church and a native of Wattisfield (and the uncle of Henry Crabb Robinson, the famed diarist). See Harmer's obituary in the *Gentleman's Magazine* (1788), Part 2:1127.

Harris, John (1727?-1801)—Harris joined Broadmead in 1745, and served as a deacon from 1760 to 1801. For many of those years he served as chairman of the deacons. He wife was a cousin of Hugh Evans, his pastor for many years at Broadmead. Harris was a prominent merchant (a sugar refiner in Lewin's Mead) and alderman for the City of Bristol, serving twice as Sheriff (1776, 1778) and once as Mayor (1790). John Ryland said of Harris, "When he was chief magistrate of this city in 1790, he was enabled to discharge the duties of that office with great fidelity and respectability, and ever since he maintained the highest character for diligence and uprightness in his civil capacity." As a sugar refiner, he was closely connected to the West Indies market, fueled in Bristol by the slave trade. As a result, he eventually opposed his pastor, Caleb Evans, during the slave trade debate in Bristol in the late 1780s. See "Sketch of Dr. Ryland's Sermon, preached at Broadmead, Bristol, May 31, 1801; Occasioned by the Decease of John Harris, Esq. One of the Aldermen of that City," *Baptist Annual Register* 4:609; Timothy Whelan, "Robert Hall and the Bristol Slave-Trade Debate of 1787-1788," *Baptist Quarterly* 38 (1999-2000): 212-224; Roger Hayden, "Caleb Evans and the Anti-Slavery Question," *Baptist Quarterly* 39 (2001-2002): 4-14; Hall and Mowvley, *Tradition and Challenge*, 40.

Harris, Joseph—Harris and his wife were appointed as BMS missionaries to Ceylon in 1837. After working with Ebenezer Daniel for a time at Columbo, Harris removed to Kandy, where he was joined by C. C. Dawson and his wife. The two missionaries planted churches and schools throughout that region of Ceylon, as well as establishing a printing press. Harris retired from the BMS in 1843 (note reference in letter 235) and returned to Great Britain. Carey, *Oriental Christian Biography,* 3:292; Cox, *History,* 2:322-324; 2:402.

Hartley, William (1740-1822)—Born in Wadsworth, Heptonstall, near Halifax, Yorkshire, Hartley was influenced early in life by his mother, a Methodist, and regularly attended Society meetings. Richard Smith, who preceded John Fawcett at Wainsgate, was another early influence upon Hartley. Shortly after his marriage to a Miss Halliwell in 1761, Hartley heard Dan Taylor, a General Baptist, preach a sermon that awakened him to an experiential awareness of his sin. He joined Taylor's congregation, but his own reading of the Bible led Hartley to a Calvinist position. He left Taylor's society and returned to John Fawcett's at Wainsgate, where he was baptized and joined the church. Under Fawcett, Hartley was called to the ministry, and in 1771 removed to Halifax, where he faced many "unhappy circumstances" during his tenure there, including the death of his wife in December 1771. He was ordained in August 1772, and within a few years proposed to a woman in the church, but his choice of companion did not suit many in the church, and he was forced to resign. According to an anonymous obituary in the *Baptist Magazine*, "This interference, especially when the person he chose was an approved member of the church, was culpable in the highest degree." He left in August 1776, and remarried that October. He removed to Bingley in late 1779, and in 1790 accepted a call to the church at Tuthill-stairs, Newcastle-upon-Tyne. Before officially settling there, however, he returned once again to his old church at Halifax. He removed to Lockwood in 1795, and remained there ten years, before finally assuming the pastorate of the Newcastle church, which was once again destitute. After one year at Newcastle, he removed to Stockton-on-Tees, where he ministered until his death in 1822. As the obituary in the *Baptist Magazine* noted, "Ministers who pass through the world with less trial and affliction than the subject of this Memoir, may learn from his case, to whom they are to attribute their superior comforts. A more holy man than our deceased friend is probably not to be found on earth." See *Baptist Magazine* 14 (1822): 500, 504.

Haweis, Thomas (1734-1820)—Originally from Redruth, Cornwall, Haweis was an Anglican evangelical, serving as rector at All Saints, Aldwincle, Northamptonshire, chaplain to Selina, Countess of Huntingdon (1774), and as joint founder, along with John Eyre and David Bogue, of the London Missionary Society (1795). He was widely known for his commentary, *The Evangelical Expositor* (2 vols; 1765-1766), and his *Translation of the New Testament from the Original Greek* (1795). See *DEB.* ·

Heighton, William (c.1752-1827)—Heighton was called into the ministry under Andrew Fuller at Kettering. He ministered to the Baptist meeting at Roade (a church in the Northampton Association) from 1786 until his death in 1827 at the age of 75. He was one of the original Northampton-shire ministers involved in the formation of the Baptist Missionary Society in 1792. See Payne, *College Street*, 12-17; idem, *Roade Baptist Church 1688-1938* (London: Kingsgate Press, 1939).

Henderson, John Edward (1816-1885)—Henderson studied at Stepney College before becoming a BMS missionary in July 1840. He began his work in Kingston, Jamaica, and later at Waldensia and Hoby Town. Henderson suffered from periods of poor health, spending considerable time in America in the 1850s. He remained a BMS missionary until 1881. See Clarke, *Memorials*, 180-181.

Hervey, Thomas (1741-1806)—A controversial Anglican evangelical clergyman, Hervey began his career as a curate at Rapside and then at Underbarrow near Kendal, where he was also a schoolmaster. He published a work on shorthand but gained considerable recognition for his work, *Elementa Christiana*, an exposition of the Thirty-Nine Articles. He was at one point (as letter 14 demonstrates) accused by some of his fellow clerics before his Bishop of being too evangelical. See *DEB.*

Hewett, Edward (d.1883)—Hewett studied at Stepney College before he and his wife, Eliza, were appointed as BMS missionaries to Jamaica in 1842. During the next forty years he would pastor churches at Jericho, Mount Hermon, Mount Carey, the Second Baptist Church in Montego Bay, and Bethel Town. His first wife died in 1846; he next year he married Estheana Burchell (daughter of Thomas Burchell). Hewett died in 1883; his second wife in 1903. See Clarke, *Memorials*, 191-192.

Hewlett, James P.—The son of an Anglican minister, Hewlett was the initial pastor at the Baptist congregation at Salem Chapel, Dover, which formed in October 1839. Hewlett completed his ministerial studies at Rawdon College, Bradford, in 1835. He ministered at Kingsbridge, Devon, before accepting the call to Dover late in 1839. The church immediately organized a

Sunday school and began supporting the BMS, contributing £25.11 its first year. In 1841 the church joined the East Kent Association of Baptist Churches, with Hewlett serving as moderator that year and as general secretary from 1842 to 1849. During his tenure at Dover, the church grew considerably and expanded its ministries with the addition of a choir, a Tract Society, a Sunday school library, as well as an itinerant preaching ministry among various nearby villages. Hewlett retained some vestiges of his Anglican upbringing during his ministry at Dover, even wearing a Genevan gown in the pulpit. In 1842 he was sought by Baptist leaders to serve as Joseph Angus's assistant at the Baptist Mission House, but he declined (see letter 186). He remained at Dover for ten years before removing to the Beechen Grove Baptist Church in Watford in December 1849, where he continued his practice of wearing the Geneva gown, as well as expanding the service of praise (an organ was introduced in 1852) and moving the church from open communion to open membership. After nine years, he became a District Secretary for the British and Foreign Bible Society. He retired in 1874 to Wiltshire. See Buffard, *Kent and Sussex Baptist Associations*, 154; *Beechen Grove Baptist Church*, 10; Holyoak, *Dover Baptists*, 17-21; Payne, *First Generation*, 18; Stanley, *History*, 213.

Hill, Christopher—Hill was a deacon at the Ebenezer Baptist Chapel, Scarborough, where William Hague ministered from 1773 to 1824. In 1804, Hill subscribed to two BMS collections, one for Hull (£1.1) and one for Scarborough (£2.2.) In 1826, Benjamin Evans (1803-1871) commenced his distinguished pastorate at Ebenezer Chapel, marrying Hill's daughter, Sarah, in 1828. See *Periodical Accounts*, 3:143, 144; Christine Paine, "Benjamin Evans of Scarborough 1803-1871," *Baptist Quarterly* 21 (1965-1966): 174.

Hill, Rowland (1744-1823)—He was the 6th son of Sir Rowland Hill of Hawkstone Park, Shropshire. Sir Richard Hill (1732-1808) was his elder brother and influenced Rowland toward spiritual concerns at an early age. After receiving his early education at Shrewsbury and Eton, he entered St. John's College, Cambridge, in 1764. He graduated in 1769 and wanted to take orders in the church, but was refused by six bishops because of his irregular preaching habits. He was finally ordained in 1773 by the Bishop of Bath and Wells, and took a curacy at Kingston, Somerset. He continued to preach as an evangelist, and as a result was turned down for the priesthood. He became immensely popular among the people, however, and a chapel was erected for him in Wotton, Gloucestershire, and another in 1783 in London (Surrey Chapel), which became his preaching home for the rest of his life. He published his *Village Dialogues* in 1810 and was a promoter of many of the evangelistic endeavors of the day, such as being first chairman of the committee for the Religious Tract Society as well as a member of the British and Foreign Bible Society and the London Missionary Society. See *DEB*.

Hillyard, Samuel (1770-1839)—Minister at the Old Meeting at Bedford, 1790-1839, Hillyard was one of the early leaders of the Bedford Sunday School Union and Bedfordshire Union of Christians. John Brown considered Hillyard (often called the "Nonconformist Bishop of Bedfordshire") to be "the animating spirit of the [Sunday school] movement from the beginning." The son of Thomas Hillyard (1746-1828), minister of the Independent church at Olney (1783-1828), Samuel first preached at Bedford in late 1790, while completing his studies at William Bull's academy at Newport Pagnall. He was ordained at Bedford in June 1792. Because he was an Independent, a number of the Baptist members (the Old Meeting had been a mixed con-gregation since Bunyan's days) left to found the Third Church of Bedford in Mill Lane in 1793. Nevertheless, Hillyard developed close ties with Robert Hall of Cambridge and Andrew Fuller of Kettering, demonstrating a keen interest in the affairs of the BMS. Like his friend Samuel Greatheed, Hillyard was one of the founders of the Bedfordshire Union of Christians in 1797. The following letter from Fuller to Hillyard, dated 21 August 1798 (MS97:13, Spencer Research Library, University of Kansas), demonstrates Hillyard's ecumenical view of missions:

My d[r] bro.[r]

I sh.[d] be obliged to you if you c.[d] drop a line on Saturday, your Market day, if you have no opportunity before, to Bro.[r] Dickens of Keysoe, to inform him that I mean to call and spend a night with him, viz Friday Sep 7. and that if agreeable to him and his friends shall have no objection to giving them a Sermon that Evening. I knew of no method of conveying a Letter besides, or I w.[d] not have troubled you. To repay you for this trouble I will tell you a few particulars of a Letter f[m] Carey dated at different times f[m] June 22.97 to Jan.[y] 9.98 w[h] I rec.[d] last week. And I dare say our good friend M[r] Livius w.[d] like to see it. They and their families are well, except that Fountain has been very ill of a fever & flux, of w[h] he was hardly recoverd. The natives of whom they have entertained hopes still persevere, tho' not so zealous as at first. A new door has been opened for preaching the word at Dinagepore, the chief city in those parts of Bengal. At that place there lives a Portuguese gentleman, a M[r] Fernandez, originally designed for a popish priest, but who as he came to years of maturity c.[d] not approve of the ido-latry of popery. Of late having heard of our friends, he sent to them for some books. They sent him Newton on the prophecies &c and afterwards visited him. He heard M[r] Thomas preach, and entered so heartily into the doctrine as soon after to build them a place of worship at Dinagepore. It was publickly opened by Carey Thomas & Fountain in November last. They have engaged to preach there one Lords day in every month. It was Careys turn to be there on L[ds] day Jan.[y] 7. 98. It was the time of the Assizes. He preached in English one part of the day, & in Bengalee the other. Nearly all the Europeans in the City came to hear; among whom were the three Judges. They attended both parts of the day, & invited M[r] Carey to dine with them. They had much conversation on the gospel, par-ticularly the Mission. They appear to have known all our proceed-ings. A Period.[l] Acc.[t] or else a *Register* had been sent over to India

& handed about among the higher Circles. They appeared amicable. Some of the Interior Magistrates favour the translation of the scriptures.

A box of books w^h we sent out in 94 and had almost given up for lost, and w^h included a Polyglot bible, is now safe at Mudnabatty. A fount [sic] for types of the Country languages has been set up at Calcutta. Mr Carey conceiving that by this means a press might be set up at Mudnabatty, proposed it to Mr Udney, who highly approved of it, and gave orders for its being constructed. Powell is making the press, & men may be had fm Calcutta to work it.

Mr Udney understands Persic, as do most of the higher orders of people in India. On his looking over the Polyglot he found the Persic translation of the Pentateuch and four gospels. He immediately set some copyists to work to transcribe it for the press.

If a press can be established at Mudnabatty under Careys eye it will be a great object. We must appoint a banking house in London on which he may draw for Money, & then the generous benefactions of our friends will soon come into action. Upwards of 500£ has lately been received f^m Scotland unsolicited.

Affec.^y y.^rs A. Fuller

See Brown, *History*, 77, 78; Tibbutt, *Bunyan Meeting Bedford*, 43-44.

Hindle, John (d. 1798)—Hindle was trained at Wainsgate by John Fawcett. After preaching for a time at Bingley, Hindle removed to the church at Pellon Lane, Halifax, where he ministered from 1779 to 1789, succeeding William Hartley. During Hindle's time at Pellon Lane, the chapel was enlarged, the membership grew, and his salary was doubled. Unfortunately, Hindle's personality clashed with many in the congregation, and "his irritable disposition led to his removal" in 1789, according to a church historian. He followed this with pastorates at Blackley (1791-1793) and Salt-house Lane in Hull (1794), where he succeeded John Beatson. He remained only one year and by 1798 was ministering at Cannon Street in Manchester, succeeding John Sharp. His tenure was short-lived, however, for he died that same year. See *Baptists of Yorkshire,* ed. Shipley, 68, 94, 101, 216; T. Michael, *A Brief Historical Account of the First Baptist Church, Halifax* (Halifax: S. N. Whitaker, 1890) 13; Dix, *Strict and Particular*, 34n.16.

Hinton, James (1761-1823)—After completing his studies at Bristol Academy, Hinton became pastor of the mixed congregation at Oxford in 1787, where he would remain until his death in 1823. Due to a poor salary, he was obliged to operate a school as well. Despite poor health and a divided, often contentious, congregation, during Hinton's ministry the church grew into a solid Baptist church (celebrating an open communion); the building was enlarged twice during his tenure at Oxford. He practiced his evangelical Calvinism not only within his own congregation, but also throughout the countryside by means of itinerant preaching. Unruly undergraduates frequently interrupted his services in Oxford, and in 1792 Dr. Tatham, Rector of Lincoln College, attacked Hinton in a pamphlet. He was also attacked by a mob and nearly killed by soldiers while preaching at Woodstock in 1794.

Though accused of radicalism, he was a moderate Whig, supporting the Volunteers during the invasion scare of 1798, and in his later years becoming decidedly pro-government in the Napoleonic wars. He remained active in Baptist affairs, including support for the BMS, and was instrumental in the early formation of the Baptist Union. See R. Chadwick, ed., *A Protestant Catholic Church of Christ: New Road Baptist Church, Oxford* (Oxford: New Road Baptist Church, 2003) 107-136; *DEB.*

Hinton, John Howard (1791-1873)—The son of James Hinton of Oxford, J. H. Hinton served as pastor of the Baptist congregation at Devonshire Square in London from 1837 to 1863, after which he retired to Bristol. From 1841 to 1866 he served as secretary of the Baptist Union, and was president in 1837 and 1863. See *DEB.*

Hirst, John (1736-1815)— Hirst was born in Rochdale and converted through the preaching of the Methodists. He eventually adopted Calvinism and was brought by the Rochdale Methodists before John Wesley for preaching "erroneous sentiments respecting justification." Having lost his home among the Methodists, Hirst took up with the Baptists at Accrington, who quickly set him apart as a preacher. He preached for the church at Bacup during the illness of their pastor, Joseph Piccop, in 1772. A few months later Piccop died and on 31 December 1772 Hirst was installed as pastor; he would remain at Bacup until his death in 1815. His ministry was successful and a new chapel was opened in 1777 and enlarged in 1783, only to give way to an even larger chapel in 1812. A Sunday school was formed in 1811. Hirst was not averse to politics at times, for he noted in the church book on 4 September 1790, "Ask them [the deacons] how the money in the hands of George Hargreaves is to be disposed of, whether to the poor stock, or to be reserved for the colection [sic] respecting the repeal of the Test and Corporation Acts." The Baptist minister James Hargreaves published a biography of Hirst. See Overend, *History of the Ebenezer Baptist Church, Bacup*, 160-185.

Hoby, James (1788-1871)—The son of George Hoby, a boot maker and deacon at Andrew Gifford's congregation at Eagle Street in London, the younger Hoby was trained at Bristol Academy, after which he served as assistant pastor at Maze Pond, Southwark, and as pastor at Weymouth, Birmingham (Graham Street), and Twickenham. Along with F. A. Cox, Hoby traveled to America in the 1830s to promote Baptist causes and the abolition of slavery, a trip that resulted in the publication of *The Baptists in America* (1836). He was actively involved with the BMS and served as chairman of the Baptist Union in 1851 and 1854.

Hope, Samuel (1760-1837)—Hope was a prominent banker in Liverpool, active philanthropist, and a member of the Baptist congregation at Byrom Street. He founded the first Baptist Sunday school in Liverpool and the Liverpool Sunday School Union in 1815. A strong supporter of the BMS, he subscribed £5.5 to the support of the Society in 1804-1805. He also served for a time as the treasurer in England of the Serampore Mission. John Dyer described him as the "great stay of the Serampore Mission." See *Periodical Accounts*, 3:145; J. Hughes, *Liverpool Banks and Bankers 1760-1837* (London: H. Young & Sons, 1906) 212; N. P. Hancock, "Healing the Breach: Benjamin Godwin and the Serampore 'Schism,'" *Baptist Quarterly* 35 (1993-1994): 127; E. A. Payne, "The Necrologies of John Dyer," *Baptist Quarterly* 13 (1949-1950): 309; *DEB.*

Hope, William—Like his relation Samuel Hope, William Hope of Liverpool was an active supporter of the Baptist Missionary Society, serving for many years as the director of the Yorkshire and Lancashire Auxiliary Society of the BMS. According to the list of monies received by the Treasurer of the BMS, collected from 1 May to 1 August 1819, William Hope collected £269.18. Carey wrote to Hope in 1830, informing him of the death of Ignatius Fernandez. Hope and his wife served as superintendents of the Byrom Street Sunday School in 1819, which ministered that year to over 400 children and some 30 adults. See letter 25 for a reference to William Hope of Pool Lane, which may be his father, for in 1804 a William Hope, Sr., subscribed £5.5 to the Society, with another £2.2 coming from William Hope, Jr. See *Baptist Magazine* 11 (1819): 411; Cox, *History*, 1:388-389; Evan Owen, "A History of the Liverpool Baptists" (MS., Angus Library, Regent's Park College, Oxford); *Periodical Accounts*, 3:125.

Horne, Melville (1761-1841)—Horne was an Anglican clergyman who played a prominent role in the beginnings of the missionary movement in England in the late eighteenth and early nineteenth centuries. He joined the Methodists in 1784 and the next year began preaching in Chester, where John Fletcher, vicar of Madeley, was superintendent. Horne was ordained in 1786 and became curate at Madeley after Fletcher's death; the next year Wesley appointed Horne superintendent for the new Wolverhampton circuit, which he maintained until 1791. In 1792 he became the second chaplain to the new colony in Sierra Leone; he did not stay long, however, returning to England in 1793. He quickly published *Letters on Missions* (1794), a work that advocated direct involvement by evangelicals in overseas missions. From 1796 to 1799 he was the vicar at Olney (where Newton had been), after which he served at Macclesfield, 1799-1811. In 1809, Horne, who had not preached in a Methodist meeting since 1792, came into conflict with Jabez Bunting, a future leader of the Methodists, which resulted in a controversial pamphlet by Horne, *An Investigation of the Definition of Justifying Faith* (1809). His career demonstrated the difficulties many individuals faced after 1800 in attempting to be both Anglican and Methodist. His later curacies were in Essex, Cornwall, and Salford. See *DEB.*

Horne, Thomas Hartwell (1780-1862)—Bibliographer, scholar, and prolific author, Horne was a lifelong resident of London. His first publication, *A Brief View of the Necessity and Truth of the Christian Revelation*, appeared in 1800, after which he joined the Methodists and became a bibliographer, primarily at the British Museum. He also served as a private clerk to Joseph Butterworth, M.P. for Coventry (1806-1809) and son of John Butterworth (1727-1803), Baptist minister at Coventry. Horne's *An Introduction to the Critical Study and Knowledge of the Holy Scriptures* (1818) went through eleven editions by 1860. He became a curate in the Anglican Church in

1819, and eventually served as Prebend of St. Paul's Cathedral from 1831-1862. See *DEB*.

Horton, Thomas (1796-1877)—After studying at Bristol Academy, Horton preached briefly at Devizes before assuming the pastorate of the Baptist church at Morice Square, Devonport, where he ministered from 1820 to 1850. After his resignation, he remained in Devonport, eventually helping to found Hope Baptist Chapel, which opened in 1855. He retired in 1870. See Couling, "Biographical Dictionary, 1875-1889."

Hughes, John—Hughes came to Brassy Green from the church at Wrexham in 1775. While at Brassy Green he also ministered to the small congregation of Baptists in Chester, where William Hartley was supplying in 1779. He suffered a stroke in 1777 and never regained his health, dying in 1783 at the age of 38. During his illness the church suffered considerably. See Margaret F. Thomas, *Brassey Green & Tarporley: A Baptist History* (n.p., 1984) 8.

Hughes, Joseph (1769-1833)—Born in Yorkshire and trained as a youth at John Fawcett's academy at Hebden Bridge, Hughes received his formal training at Bristol Baptist Academy, at King's College, Aberdeen, and at Edinburgh University. From 1791 to 1796 he was classical tutor at Bristol, replacing Robert Hall; Hughes also served also as assistant pastor at Broadmead with Caleb Evans and John Ryland, Jr. He left Bristol for the Baptist church in Battersea, where he ministered from 1797 until his death. His greatest achievements lay outside his pastorate, however, providing the primary impetus and leadership in the founding of the Religious Tract Society in 1799 and the British and Foreign Bible Society in 1804. He served as a secretary for both societies for the remainder of his life. He also played a role in the founding of London University. See Leifchild, *Memoir of the Late Rev. Joseph Hughes*; *DEB*.

Huntington, William (1745-1813)—Huntington was a controversial High Calvinist preacher in London, first at the Providence Chapel (1782-1810) and later at the New Providence Chapel (1811-1813). A former coalheaver with little formal education, Huntington (his original name was "Hunt," and he later added "S.S." ["Sinner Saved"] to his new name) and his network of chapels would prove extremely problematic for London's moderate Calvinists. A "self-called" minister, Huntington came to London from Kingston in 1782 and soon commenced construction of the Providence Chapel in Tichfield Street. He preached to upwards of 3000 hearers, earning an exorbitant annual income that approached £2000. He would later build other chapels in the London area, ministering to all simultaneously. He attracted large numbers of Baptists to his meetings, as well as Independents and followers of the Countess of Huntingdon, despite the fact that his hearers had to purchase a ticket in order to enter his chapels. His early life was full of scandals, and his ministry was plagued with controversy, primarily over his Antinomian tendencies. He was despised by the Particular Baptists and entered into pamphlet wars with Rowland Hill, Caleb Evans, John Ryland, Jr., and the Baptist poet and polemicist, Maria de Fleury. Despite his fervent denials, Huntington's opponents accused the controversial preacher of being a High Calvinist antinomian. Though conversion by grace alone was a fundamental belief of all Calvinists, including antinomians, Huntington also contended that believers under the dispensation of grace were free from the requirements of the law. To de Fleury and other evangelical Calvinists, Huntington preached a gospel of "easy" grace which absolved the Christian of any obligation to obey God's moral law, thereby granting the believer unlimited liberty in his or her behavior, a liberty evangelical Calvinists were convinced would inevitably lead to licentiousness. Nevertheless, Huntington's antinomianism enticed large numbers of hearers away from London's morally strict Baptist and Independent congregations and into his Providence Chapel, as well as his other chapels in Monkwell Street and Horsleydown. Though moderate Calvinists consistently attacked Huntington as a heretic and proselytizer, his influence remained strong as large numbers attended his services. See T. Wright, *The Life of William Huntington, SS.* (London: Farncombe, 1909); John Mee, "Is There an Antinomian in the House? William Blake and the After-Life of a Heresy," *Historicizing Blake*, ed. Steve Clark and David Warrall (Houndsmills, Basingstoke: Macmillan, 1994) 43-58; Dix, *Strict and Particular*, 6-29; Timothy Whelan, "'For the Hand of a Woman, has Levell'd the Blow": Maria de Fleury's Pamphlet War with William Huntington, 1787-1791,'" *Women's Studies* 36 (2007): 431-454; *DEB.*

Hutchins, John (d. 1851)—After studying at Stepney College, Hutchins was set apart as a BMS missionary at Bedford in February 1834, arriving in Jamaica that April, where he began working at Savannah-la-Mar and Fuller's Field. His wife died in 1838; he died as a result of a cholera epidemic in Jamaica in 1851. See Clarke, *Memorials*, 168-170.

Ivimey, Joseph (1773-1834)—Baptized by John Saffery at Wimborne, Dorset, Ivimey began as an itinerant preacher in Portsea before becoming pastor of a congregation at Wallingford. From 1805 to 1834 he ministered to the Baptist church in Eagle Street, London. He was instrumental in the founding of the Baptist Union in 1812, serving as secretary the remainder of his life. He also worked with the Baptist Irish Society, Stepney College, the *Baptist Magazine,* and the BMS. His chief publication was his four-volume *History of the English Baptists* (London: J. Ivimey, 1811-1830). See J. C. Doggett, "Joseph Ivimey (1773-1834)," ed. Haykin, in *The British Particular Baptists*, 3:113-131; *DEB.*

Jackson, Alvery (1700-1763)—Jackson was converted through the ministry of Thomas Dewhurst and baptized at Sutton-in-Craven in 1715. He later attended Baptist churches at Heaton and Rawdon. In 1718 he began ministering at Barnoldswick, where he was an early advocate of hymn singing. During his years at Barnoldswick, three men were called into the ministry: Abraham Greenwood, John Tommas, and Richard Smith. He gained some notoriety for his involvement in a pamphlet war between some "evangelical" Calvinists and High Calvinists, 1737-1753. Participants in this debate (what was termed by them "The Modern Question") included Matthias Maurice, Abraham Taylor, and Jackson, all promoting an evangelical emphasis within their Calvinism; John Brine and John Gill led the High Calvinists. Jackson's contribution was *The Question Answered* (1752). He remained at Barnoldswick until his death in 1763. See Winnard, *History*, 49-50; 60-61; Hayden, *Continuity and Change*, 186-188; *DEB*.

Jackson, Samuel (1755-1836)—He was a currier and leather cutter in Little Windmill Street, London. He served as a deacon in the Baptist meeting at Unicorn Yard, Southwark, from the early 1780s until 1811. He audited the church's financial accounts in 1785, and served as a Protestant Dissenting Deputy as well as a Messenger to the Particular Baptist Fund in 1807. He was a subscriber to the BMS in 1800-1801 and 1804-1805, at that time living in Hackney. In 1813 he served as a lay representative from Unicorn Yard to the first Committee in London of the newly established Baptist Union. Bristol Academy has a photocopy of a letter from Jackson, then living at 68 Lombard Street, London, dated 28 May 1795, to the Rev. Richard Furman, Baptist minister in Charleston, South Carolina (shelfmark G96, Box T). See *Universal British Directory*, 1/2:191; Unicorn Yard Church Book, f. 262r, 333r; *Periodical Accounts*, 2:205; 3:134; Price, "The Early Years of the Baptist Union," 121-122; Payne, "Necrologies of John Dyer," 308-309.

Jameson, William (1807-1847)—Jameson arrived in Jamaica in 1835 as part of a contingent of missionaries sent out by the United Secession Presbyterian Church (Scotland). A presbytery was formed in 1836, and in 1841 a school for training ministers was opened in Goshen, directed by Jameson until 1846, when he departed for the new mission being started by the Presbyterians in Old Calabar, West Africa. He died there in 1847. That same year the Scottish Missionary Society transferred all its missionaries in Jamaica to the United Secession Church, which then became the United Presbyterian Church in Jamaica. John Clarke, who would later assist Jameson on his arrival at Fernando Po in January 1847, offers considerable praise for the Presbyterians and their work in Jamaica, despite his problem with Jameson in letter 231. See Clarke, *Memorials*, 225-230; Alexander Robb, *The Gospel to the Africans: A Narrative of the Life and Labours of the Rev. William Jameson in Jamaica and Old Calabar* (Edinburgh: A. Eliot, 1861) 263.

Jarman, John (1774-1830)—Jarman was originally from Clipston, the son of a tailor. In 1801, he moved to Oakham and joined the local Baptist church. He soon began lay preaching in Nottingham and Biggleswade, and in January 1804 the church at Biggleswade offered a trial pastorate to Jarman, but he declined in favor of accepting a call to the Friar Lane congregation at Notthingham. He arrived in Nottingham in April 1804, remaining as pastor until his death in 1830. His only publication was *The Duties of the Office of Deacons Explained and Enforced* (1828). Jarman conducted a Sunday school for many years at Nottingham and often brought in other ministers to preach benefit sermons for the school. On 13 August 1809, Robert Hall preached the sermon. Jarman was successful during his tenure at Nottingham, and in August 1815 a new chapel was opened in George Street. Jarman also served on the BMS Committee in 1812. See John T. Godfrey and James Ward, *The History of Friar Lane Baptist Church, Nottingham* (Nottingham: H. B. Saxton, 1903) 39, 47, 56, 199-203; Sydney F. Clark, "Nottingham Baptist Beginnings," *Baptist Quarterly* 17 (1957-1958): 162-169; Cox, *History*, 2:221.

Jenkins, John (1656?-1733)—The grandfather of Joseph Jenkins (see below), John Jenkins was the primary minister of the Baptist congregation at Rhydwilym from 1689 until his death in 1733. By the turn of the century, Jenkins had become one of the leading Baptist ministers in Wales, acquiring some notoriety from his dispute with John Thomas, Independent minister at Llwyn-y-grawys, Llangoedmor, in 1691 over the question of baptism. Jenkins is believed to be the first minister to receive assistance from the Particular Baptist Fund in 1718. See *Dictionary of Welsh Biography*.

Jenkins, Joseph (1743-1819)—The son of a Baptist minister (Evan Jenkins) from Wrexham, Joseph Jenkins was educated in London and eventually studied at Aberdeen as a Ward scholar. He was baptized by Samuel Stennett at Little Wild Street Church in 1766. After a brief pastorate in an Independent church in Chester, he served for several years in London, tutoring ministerial students under the auspices of the Baptist Education Fund. He participated in the ordination of Abraham Booth at Little Prescot Street on 16 February 1769. He commenced his ministry as pastor of the Old Meeting (Baptist/Independent) in Wrexham in 1773. In 1793 he removed to Blandford Street, London, and in 1798 succeeded Joseph Swain at Walworth, remaining there until his death in 1819. He was awarded an honorary D.D. from Edinburgh in 1790. Among his publications are *The Orthodox Dissenting Minister's Reasons for Applying Again to Parliament* (1772); *The Christian's Strength: A Sermon Preached at Wrexham, in Denbighshire* (Shrewsbury and London, 1775) (mentioned in letter 21); *The National Debt, Considered in a Sermon, Preached at Wrexham in Denbighshire, February 21, 1781. Being the Day Appointed for a General Fast* (Shrewsbury, 1781). See Kevan, *London's Oldest*, 90; *DEB*.

Johns, William—A chemist and surgeon by trade, Johns was attending Carter Lane in Southwark at this time, although he did not become a member until 7 October 1804. He left England for India in 1810 with John Lawson to join William Ward at Serampore, raising £1200 for the Serampore Mission during their stay in America before arriving in India in 1813. He was to become the medical officer at Serampore during Nathaniel Wallich's furlough in England; however, his application to the East India Company for residence in India was rejected, the last missionary to be so treated before the renewal of the Company's charter that same year. He was forced to return to England immediately, and in December 1813 sent a letter to the *Baptist Magazine* about a service he attended during his brief stay at Serampore. In January 1814, he participated in the designation service of Eustace Carey at Northampton. He also published the first pamphlet in England on the practice of the *sati* (*suttee*), titled *A Collection of Facts and opinions relative to the Burning of Widows with the dead bodies of their husbands, and to other destructive customs prevalent in British India* (1816). He eventually returned to Serampore as a civilian and, like several of the other junior members working in Serampore, became disenchanted with the work of the Mission there, especially disliking the Marshmans. After failing to establish a medical practice at Serampore, coupled with poor health and the deaths of his wife and son, he returned to England in 1819. He published an account of his experiences in India, *The Spirit of the Serampore Mission,* in 1828, a work that contributed greatly to the split between the BMS and the Serampore group. His wife was Mary Blakemore, the sister of Martha Pearce, who was the wife of William Hopkins Pearce, the son of Samuel Pearce and BMS missionary in Calcutta. See letter 110; *Baptist Magazine* 6 (1814): 124-125; "Calendar of Letters," *Baptist Quarterly* 7 (1934-1935): 42; R. W. Butt-Thompson, "The Morgans of Birmingham," *Baptist Quarterly* 1 (1922-1923): 267; *DEB.*

Johnson, John (1706-1791)—Raised a General Baptist in Cheshire, Johnson became a High Calvinist Baptist and controversial founder of his own sect. After some very successful itinerant preaching among the Particular Baptist churches in the North West of England, Johnson accepted the call of the Byrom Street Chapel in Liverpool in April 1740. His increasing High Calvinism (and some Sabellian beliefs) began to stir dissension within the congregation, and when he returned from a tour of duty as a volunteer during the 1745 rebellion, a split occurred in the church. In 1747 Johnson took his followers and opened a new chapel in Stanley Street, becoming known as Johnsonian Baptists. Despite his High Calvinism, he remained busy as an evangelist and published a number of pamphlets, including *The Faith of God's Elect* (1754), *Evangelical Truths Vindicated* (Liverpool, 1758?), and *The Election of God Undisguised* (1759). See Owen, "History of the Liverpool Baptists"; *DEB.*

Jones, David (1741-1792)—Jones was converted through the ministry of Howel Harris, a leading Welsh Calvinistic Methodist. Jones, however, soon joined the Particular Baptists at Pen-y-garn and in 1773 was ordained as assistant to Miles Harry. Jones would generally be associated with Pontypool. He published his first work in 1758, and in 1777 produced an elegy on Harris. Jones's second wife owned property at Dol-goch, Newcastle Emlyn, and in 1785 he removed there, joining the Baptist meeting at Graig, Newcastle, and becoming co-pastor. He continued to maintain close ties, however, with the Calvinistic Methodists, especially Peter Williams and David Morris. In 1786 Jones began working with Williams on a Welsh edition of John Canne's "pocket bible," which had been widely used in its English form by Howel Harris and Miles Harry in the 1730s and '40s. The efforts of Jones and Williams were widely supported by the Baptist Association in 1787 (not so by the Methodists, who expelled Williams in 1791). The work was finally published by the two Welshmen as *Y Bibl Sanctaidd: Sef Yr Hen Destament a'r Newydd* (1790), complete with glosses along each column. This is the work by Jones that John Ryland refers to in letter 34 as "Good News from Wales." See *Dictionary of Welsh Biography.*

Jones, Noah (1725-1785)—Jones was born in Wales and studied at the Carmarthen Academy, c. 1742-1745. In 1745 he began his ministry at Newtown, Wales, before moving to the Pensnet Meeting in Cradley, Staffordshire, in 1748, where he remained until 1762. His final ministry was at Walsall, Staffordshire, from 1762 to 1784. See George Eyre Evans, *Vestiges* *of Protestant Dissent* (Liverpool: F. and E. Gibbons, 1897) 247; idem, *Midland Churches: A History of the Congregations on the Roll of the Midland Christian Union* (Dudley: "Herald" Printing Works, 1899) 91.

Jones, William (1762-1846)—Jones was the Liverpool publisher of Archibald McLean's *A Defence of Believer-Baptism, in Opposition to Infant Sprinkling.* Originally from Denbighshire, Jones grew up in Cheshire, where he received a classical education. He was sent to Chester in 1780, working as an apprentice to a wine merchant. In the early 1780s he began worshiping with a group of Baptists that had recently begun meeting at Common-Hall Lane in Chester. In 1782-1783, however, Jones left for London, eventually working as a clerk for a Mr. Elderton (a Socinian) in Cheapside. During his stay in London he usually attended the ministry of Abraham Booth at Little Prescot Street. After only one year, however, he returned to Chester to work for a Mr. Thomas Crane, a member of the Baptist meeting there. In January 1786 he married Crane's daughter. In October 1786 McLean preached for five weeks in Chester, staying with Jones and baptizing him and several others, moving the small Baptist congregation into the fold of the Scotch Baptists, which at that time could claim only one other congregation in England. In March 1793 Jones purchased a bookseller's business, previously owned by his brother-in-law, in Castle Street, Liverpool, and began holding Sunday meetings in his home, although he may have occasionally attended Byrom Street under Samuel Medley. Sometime in 1796 or 1797, McLean came to Liverpool and, with the help of John Jones of Ramoth, helped organize a congregation of Scotch Baptists in Lord Street, with David Stewart Wylie and Jones as elders. During the next few years Jones edited two periodicals, *The Theological Repository* (1800) and *The Christian Advocate* (1809). In 1812 Jones removed to London, where he joined the Scotch Baptist congregation, first at Red Cross Street and later in Windmill Street, Finsbury, serving as an elder. While in London he continued his work in the book trade, serving also as editor of the *New Evangelical Magazine* (1815-1824), *The New Baptist Magazine* (1825), *The Baptist Miscellany and Particular Baptist Magazine* (1827), and *The Millennial Harbinger* (1835). He authored several works during these years, including *A History of the Waldenses* (1811), *A Dictionary of Religious Opinions* (1815), *The Biblical Cyclopoedia* (1816), *Christian Biography* (1829), and *The Works of Mr. Alexander McLean* (1823). See William Jones, *Autobiography of the Late William Jones, M.A.* (London: J. Snow, 1846); *Dictionary of Welsh Biography*; Owen, "History of the Liverpool Baptists"; Wilson, *History and Antiquities,* 3:325-326; R. Taylor, "English Baptist Periodicals 1790-1865," *Baptist Quarterly* 27 (1977-1978): 50-82; *DEB.*

Keith, George (d. 1782)—Keith joined John Gill's congregation at Carter Lane, Southwark, in 1756. He was a bookseller and printer, first in Cheapside (1749-1753) and then at several locations in Gracechurch Street (1753-1782). He married John Gill's daughter, and published many of Gill's most important works. In 1774 (after Gill's death), Keith and Joshua Warne, his friend and fellow deacon, both holding High Calvinist views, left Carter Lane and its new pastor, John Rippon, and joined William Button's new congregation in Dean Street, Southwark. See Horsleydown and Carter Lane Church Book, ff. 22, 27.

Kilham, Alexander (1762-1798)—Founder of the Methodist New Connection, Kilham became one of Wesley's traveling preachers in 1785 and handled several circuits in Lincolnshire and the East Riding of Yorkshire in the following years. After Wesley's death in 1791, Kilham's independent streak and anti-establishment thinking left him at odds with many in the Methodist hierarchy, and he was banished in 1792 to the Aberdeen circuit for his support of allowing non-ordained itinerant preachers to conduct the Lord's Supper. He soon formed a group of Methodists (later called "Kilhamites") who sought to break all ties with the Established church. The issue reached a crisis with Kilham's publication in 1795 of *The Progress of Liberty Amongst the People called Methodists*, which advocated a greater voice for the laity than the movement was willing to allow. At the Methodist Conference in 1796, Kilham was expelled for his "seditious" publication. He kept up his attack during his preaching tour of the north of England that year, as well as in his periodical, the *Methodist Monitor* (see letter 53). Kilham proposed some reform measures at the Methodist Conference at Leeds in 1797, but failed again, at which time he and a large group separated to form the Methodist New Connexion on 9 August 1797. About 5000 joined the first year, all from the north of England, comprising some 66 societies. Kilham was appointed the first secretary and established himself in Sheffield. In 1798 he moved to Nottingham to continue his duties as secretary, but on an itinerating trip he developed a cold and died. See *DEB*.

Kilpin, Samuel—Kilpin came out of the Old Meeting at Bedford, the same church from which his relation, William, had been called out in 1789. William was ordained at Bedford on 20 October 1790 and served as pastor of the congregation at Cotton-end in Bedford until his untimely death on 20 March 1791 at the age of 28. Samuel's father, John Kilpin, was a member at the Old Meeting for more than fifty years, serving as a deacon for thirty years. At the time of letter 54, Samuel was still a student at Bristol Academy under John Ryland, but he was already doing supply preaching. He officially began his ministry at Leominster in 1801. From 1812 to 1829, he ministered to the Baptist congregation at South Street in Exeter, where Joseph Stennett had once served. Kilpin was a faithful supporter of the Religious Tract Society and the Baptist Missionary Society. See H. G. Tibbutt, *Cotton End Old Meeting, 1776-1962* (Bedfordshire: Cotton End Baptist Church; Rushden: S.L. Hunt, 1963) 15; Arthur Gabb, *A History of Baptist Beginnings with an Account of the Rise of the Baptist Witness in Exeter and the Founding of the South Street Church* (Exeter: Horsham, 1952) 36-37, 45; *Memoir of Rev. Samuel Kilpin of Exeter, England; with Some Extracts from His Correspondence, to which is added His Narrative of Samuel Wyke Kilpin* (New York: American Tract Society, [1835?]).

King, Thomas (1755-1831)—A grocer and chandler, King succeeded Reynold Hogg as treasurer of the BMS in 1795. He was a member at Cannon Street in Birmingham for forty-eight years and a deacon for forty years. He would remain treasurer of the BMS until 1821, when William Burls, a member at

Carter Lane, Southwark, succeeded him. King continued to serve on the BMS committee until his death in 1831. See Payne, *First Generation,* 60-67; *DEB.*

Kingdon, John (d.1855)—Originally from Devizes, Kingdon studied at Bristol Academy and began his work as a BMS missionary in Jamaica in 1831, serving initially at Savannah-la-Mar. Like many of the other BMS missionaries in Jamaica, he too was imprisoned in 1832-1833. Afterwards, he labored mostly in Machioneal until 1845, when he returned to England. He later served in Belize and Liberia (in collaboration with the Southern American Missionary Society), where he died in 1855. See Clarke, *Memorials,* 156-159.

Kinghorn, Joseph (1766-1832)—Shortly after he was baptized at seventeen by his father, David Kinghorn (a Baptist minister in Yorkshire), Joseph entered Bristol Academy. After a short stint at Fairford in Gloucestershire, he began his ministry at the Baptist meeting at St. Mary's, Norwich, in 1789 and remained there until his death in 1832. He was involved in the local campaign to repeal the Test and Corporation Acts in 1790, and was troubled over England's involvement in the war with France. Like numerous other Baptist ministers of his day, Kinghorn, an excellent scholar, also kept a school to train young men for the ministry. During his years in Norwich, Kinghorn was a member of the Speculative Society, a group of intellectuals (dominated by local Unitarians) devoted to the free inquiry of ideas. Though not a High Calvinist, Kinghorn was, however, a believer in closed communion, becoming embroiled in a controversy with Robert Hall in 1816 over the practice of open communion. Though not a prolific writer, Kinghorn still contributed a number of articles to the *Baptist Magazine*, the *Eclectic Review*, and the *Evangelical Magazine.* He was also a firm supporter of the BMS, speaking and traveling widely on its behalf. He played an active role in the effort to keep the Serampore Mission unharmed during the parliamentary debate in 1813 over the renewal of the East India Company's charter. See M. H. Wilkin, *Joseph Kinghorn of Norwich: A Memoir* (Norwich: Fletcher and Alexander; London: Arthur Hall, 1855); Charles B. Jewson, "St. Mary's, Norwich," *Baptist Quarterly* 10 (1940-1941): 340-346; Dean Olive, "Joseph Kinghorn (1766-1832)," ed. Haykin, in *The British Particular Baptists*, 3: 81-111; *DEB.*

Kirtland, Charles (1811-1886)—Born an Anglican, Kirtland became a Baptist during his youth in Oxfordshire. He went into Christian work in the mid-1830s, working with the London City Mission in Holborn. He then worked for the Norwich City Mission for a time, before becoming the agent of the Baptist Home Mission for Nottingham, followed by a short term in a similar position in Newark. He also ministered to a Baptist congregation in Newark during the early 1840s, at one point seeking guidance from Joseph Angus about the possibility of foreign service, which did not materialize. He later preached at Sabden, Lancashire (1846-1851), before removing to Canterbury (1851-1865). From 1865 to 1874 he served as secretary of the Baptist Irish Society. He closed his career as minister of the York Road Baptist Chapel in Battersea, 1874-1883. See *DEB.*

Kitching, Christopher (d. 1819)—After his baptism in 1814, Kitching (John Ryland spells it variously "Kitchen," "Kitchin," and "Kitching") became a student of John Trickett at Bramley before studying at Horton Academy under Steadman and Isaac Mann. He was apparently the first student to enter the foreign service from that school, being set apart, along with Thomas Godden, at Frome in March 1818. He and his wife sailed from Falmouth on 30 July 1818, reaching Jamaica on 18 September 1818; unfortunately, he died that December. Mrs. Kitching returned to Yorkshire, where she would marry Isaac Mann. Two letters by Kitching from Jamaica appeared in the *Baptist Magazine* 11 (1819): 47, 410; see also Cox, *History,* 2:79-80.

Knibb, William (1803-1845)—Originally from Kettering, Knibb, along with his older brother, Thomas, moved to Bristol in 1816 to work with J. G. Fuller (Andrew Fuller's son). The Knibb brothers joined the church at Broadmead and became Sunday school teachers. William was baptized there in 1822. Shortly thereafter, Thomas Knibb became a BMS missionary in Jamaica, but he died within a few months of his arrival. William promptly volunteered to take his place, sailing with his wife, Mary, for Jamaica in 1825. He first ministered at Savanna-la-Mar, then at Falmouth, from which the majority of his anti-slavery activities were conducted. Though discouraged by the BMS in London, Knibb was openly vocal in his opposition to slavery, and undoubtedly his activities were instrumental in provoking the Jamaica slave revolt of 1831-1832. Many of his followers were persecuted and imprisoned as a result of the uprising. After being held prisoner by the government, Knibb was released in February 1832, his chapels having suffered considerable damage. The criminal cases at Montego Bay against Knibb and his coworkers Thomas Burchell, Thomas Abbott, Walter Dendy, and Francis Gardner were eventually dropped. Knibb returned to England and, along with Burchell and James Phillippo, spoke in churches and meetings across England, advocating the end of the persecution of the missionaries and slavery in Jamaica. His efforts led to the abolition of slavery throughout the British Commonwealth in 1834. He stated in June 1845 that the membership in his church at Falmouth was 1280; at Refuge, 780; Rio Bueno, 315; Waldensia, 746; Stewart Town, 813; Unity, 340; and Kettering, 200. See J. H. Hinton, *Memoir of William Knibb* (London: Houlston and Stoneman, 1847); Cox, *History,* vol. 2; Clarke, *Memorials,* 99-114; Tyrrell, "Moral Political Party," 481-501; Wright, *Knibb "the Notorious"*; Gary W. Long, "William Knibb (1803-1845)," ed. Haykin, in *The British Particular Baptists,* 3:211-231; *DEB.*

Knight, James—Knight began his ministry at the Independent congregation at Bridewell Alley in 1791, succeeding John Rogers. In 1793 he moved to the Independent meeting in Nightingale Lane, London. He was formerly a member of the Independent church at the Weigh-house, and studied at Homerton Academy. He was a successful London minister for many years. Among his publications are *The Utility of Seminaries for Religion and Learning: With a View to the Christian Ministry . . .* (1801); *Christian Courtesy: A Sermon, Delivered at a Monthly Association of Congregational Ministers and*

Churches in Connexion with the Old College, Homerton, at Dr. Collyers's Meeting House, Peckham, April 6, 1815 (1815); and *Voluntary Subjection to God, the Genuine Liberty of a Rational Creature* (1816). See *Evangelical Magazine* 2 (1794): 30.

Lacroix, Alphonse Francois (1799-1859)—Originally from Switzerland, Lacroix served in Napoleon's army for a time, but was converted and commissioned in Rotterdam as a missionary of the Netherlands Missionary Society, after which he was sent to the mission at Chinsurah, Bengal, where he arrived in March 1821. In 1825 Lacroix joined the London Missionary Society, working in villages in the south of Calcutta. He moved to Bhowanipore in 1837 to concentrate on native evangelism. He was a close friend of Alexander Duff, even though he disagreed with the latter's promotion of English as the language of education. Lacroix spoke fluent Bengali and was an impressive figure among the missionaries in India in his day. See Lacroix's memoir, *Missionary Devotedness: A Brief Memoir of the Rev. A. Lacroix, of Calcutta, Thirty-Nine Years a Missionary to the Heathen* (London, 1860). *DEB.*

Lancaster, Joseph (1778-1838)—Lancaster was born in Southwark, the son of a shopkeeper. In his early teens he became convinced he should serve as a missionary in Jamaica, and removed to Bristol, but was unable to afford the fare to Jamaica. He remained for a time in Bristol and eventually joined the Society of Friends. He returned to London in 1798 and opened a small school in Southwark that was to be free of charge, with payment strictly optional. The school became quite popular, but Lancaster found it difficult to employ teachers because of the unpredictability of funds. He then adopted the monitorial system used by another educator, Andrew Bell, in Madras, India, which eased his problem considerably. Lancaster developed an elaborate system of punishments designed to encourage the students through means of shame, but without corporal punishment. Within a few years Lancaster's school had over 1000 pupils and began to receive national attention and financial support. In 1808, due to increasing debts, Joseph Fox, a dentist and member of the Baptist congregation at Carter Lane in Southwark, and William Allen, a Quaker, along with Samuel Whitbread, M.P., took over the management of the school. They proceeded to form the Royal Lancastrian Society, whose aim was to create similar non-sectarian schools throughout England, none of which were to be controlled by the Church of England. By 1810, fifty schools had been formed, educating over 14,000 pupils. In 1816 a disagreement between Lancaster and his trustees led to a separation and the formation of a separate school by Lancaster in Tooting. The school failed and Lancaster, now bankrupt, emigrated to America, where he continued to form new schools, some as far away as Canada and Venezuela, all of which were unsuccessful. He died in New York in 1838. Among his writings are *Improvements in Education, as it Respects the Industrious Classes of the Community* (1803), *Instructions for Forming and Conducting a Society for the Education of the Children of the Labouring Classes of the People, According to the General Principles of the Lancastrian or British Plan* (1810), as well as *The British System of Education Being a*

Complete Epitome of the Improvements and Inventions Practiced by Joseph Lancaster . . . (1810). See Carl F. Kaestle, *Joseph Lancaster and the Monitorial School Movement; A Documentary History* (New York: Teachers College Press, 1973).

Langdon, Thomas (1755-1824)—Originally from Devon, Langdon attended Bristol Academy, after which he worked a short time as an assistant to Daniel Turner at Abingdon before assuming the pastorate of the Baptist church at Leeds in 1782. He remained there the rest of his life, operating a school for most of those years. He was influenced theologically by Andrew Fuller and Robert Hall, the latter his friend and fellow student at Bristol in the late 1770s. He published a sermon on church constitution and terms of communion in 1790 and wrote a circular letter for the Yorkshire association in the summer of 1791. In March 1790 Langdon received an invitation from the Rev. J. Biggs, Baptist minister at Swift's Alley, Dublin, to preach for the Dublin General Evangelical Society, the object of which was "to prevail upon, and defray the expenses of, such ministers as should be approved, to make visits to that country, to preach under their directions, whenever it should be thought practicable, either in town or country, with the hope of stirring up the people to regard their immortal interests." In November 1790, after Biggs's sudden death, the church at Swift's-Alley sent a letter by William Allen to Langdon asking him to become their pastor, but Langdon declined. He was an ardent abolitionist and political reformer in the late 1780s and early 1790s, serving on the Yorkshire committee of Dissenters for the Repeal of the Test and Corporation Acts as well as assisting William Wilberforce in sending petitions from northern England to parliament in 1791 to protest the continuation of the slave trade. Langdon published *The Obligations of Christians to Support a Conversation Becoming the Gospel* in 1795. He was also a bookseller during much of the 1790s, and during 1795-1797 served as the distribution agent in Leeds for Benjamin Flower's newspaper, the *Cambridge Intelligencer*. Langdon would also be instrumental in the formation of the Northern Education Society in 1804. See Mary Langdon, *A Brief Memoir of the Rev. Thomas Langdon, Baptist Minister, of Leeds* (London: Simpkin and Marshall, 1837) 21, 23, 44-47; F. W. Beckwith, "The First Leeds Baptist Church," *Baptist Quarterly* 6 (1932-1933): 72-82; Hayden, *Continuity and Crisis*, 237; *DEB*.

Lawson, John (1787-1825)—Lawson moved to London at sixteen to become a wood engraver and artist. He attended the Baptist meeting at Eagle Street and through the preaching of Joseph Ivimey was called to be a missionary. He left London in 1808 to study with Sutcliff in Olney. He returned to London and joined the Baptist church in Eagle Street, serving an apprenticeship with a Mr. Colwell in an effort to become a miniature painter. He also published some poetry during this time (see letter 90). After his marriage to Frances Butterworth (she was a member at Devonshire Square), Lawson and his new wife sailed for Calcutta, accompanied by William Johns and a Miss Chafin, early in 1811. After a considerable stay in America, the new BMS missionaries arrived in India on 10 August 1812. Lawson was to begin working with the printing department at Serampore, cutting types, Johns to assist Wallich, the medical doctor (see Johns above). The East India Company rejected Johns, but Lawson was allowed to stay, primarily because Marshman intervened on his behalf, claiming his skills were needed in creating Chinese fonts. Lawson would eventually leave the Serampore group and join the other junior BMS missionaries in Calcutta—Eustace Carey, William Yates, James Penney, W. H. Pearce, and William Adam. Lawson spent most of his time there as co-pastor (along with Eustace Carey) of the Baptist church in Calcutta, and later as pastor of the second Baptist church on Circular Road. He was also involved with the school in Calcutta, run by his wife and Mrs. Pearce, providing instruction in writing, grammar, composition, geography, and drawing. An excellent musician and poet, Lawson was best known for his work in perfecting certain fonts used in publishing Bengalee and Chinese works. In a letter to Joseph Ivimey, dated 30 July 1813, Lawson states that since his arrival in India he had been principally engaged as an artist, teaching drawing in the school at Serampore and even being offered money by the local Europeans for his work. See Lawson's letters in the *Baptist Magazine Baptist Magazine* 6 (1814): 172-173; 11 (1819): 134-137, 541-544; also Cox, *History,* 1:225, 233-324, 333-335; *DEB.*

Leland, John (1754-1841)—A Baptist from Massachusetts, Leland was inspired by the ministry of Elhanan Winchester. Leland preached throughout Virginia from 1773 to 1790, baptizing over 600 persons. He returned to Massachusetts in 1791 and devoted himself primarily to his writing. He was an outspoken advocate of religious liberty, freedom of conscience, and separation of church and state. He was an admirer of Thomas Jefferson, and is thought to have influenced James Madison's political understanding of the separation of church and state. His *Virginia Chronicle, with Critical Remarks under 24 Heads*, was advertised in the *Baptist Annual Register*, 1:324. Among his other notable publications are *The Rights of Conscience Inalienable* (1791) and *The Government of Christ a Christocracy* (1804). See Brackney, ed., *Historical Dictionary*, 255; *DEB.*

Lepard, John Pelly (d. 1796)—Lepard worked with his father, William Lepard, as a London stationer, rag merchant and paper maker. The elder Lepard operated shops in Tooley Street, Upper Thames Street, Southwark, and at 26 Newgate Street from 1784 to 1788, at which time the younger Lepard joined the firm. John Pelly Lepard moved to 91 Newgate Street in 1789, and his father joined him there in 1792. After the younger Lepard's death in 1796, his father moved the firm to 103 Shoe Lane. James Smith, a deacon at Little Wild Street and a messenger for many years to the Particular Baptist Fund, along with his son, John James Smith, were both watchmakers in Bunhill Row. He is probably the same James Smith who joined with William Lepard in 1792 in operating a printing and bookselling business at 14 Bridges Street, Covent Garden, remaining with Lepard until 1798. William Lepard, Sr., John Pelly's grandfather, joined Carter Lane, under John Gill, in 1717 and died in 1799, aged 99; William, Jr., joined in 1755. Among the junior Lepard's earliest printing jobs (1758-1766) were various works by Gill. All three Lepards were prominent members of Carter Lane, Southwark.

See *Universal British Directory*, 1/2:211; Horsleydown and Carter Lane Church Book, 1719-1808 (MS., Metropolitan Baptist Tabernacle, London) ff. 22, 27, 33-35; Maxted, *London Book Trade*, 137, 208; Christopher Woollacott, *A Brief History of the Baptist Church in Little Wild Street, Lincoln's-Inn Fields, from 1691 to 1858* (London: Houlston and Wright, 1859) 41.

Lewis, William Garrett (1797-1865)—Lewis was born at Margate; he first began preaching at Sandwich, Kent, and in 1824 became pastor of the Baptist church at Chatham, where he remained for 18 years. In 1842 he succeeded James Smith as pastor at Cheltenham, remaining there until 1864, when he retired to Weston-super-Mare. While at Cheltenham, a new chapel (Salem Chapel) was built.

Lindsey, Theophilus (1723-1808)—After resigning his living in the Church of England following the failure of the Feathers Tavern Petition in 1772, Lindsey became one of the leading Unitarians of his day and founder of an influential Unitarian congregation in Essex Street in London, where he ministered from 1778 to 1793, when he was succeeded by John Disney. He wrote numerous defenses of Unitarianism, including *A Historical View of the State of the Unitarian Doctrine and Worship from the Reformation to Our Own Time, with Some Account of the Obstructions it has met with at Different Periods* (1783) (a reply to Robert Robinson's *Plea for the Divinity of Christ*). He also wrote *An Apology on Resigning the Vicarage of Catterick, Yorkshire* (1774) and its sequel in 1776, mentioned in letter 21. See G. M. Ditchfield, *Theophilus Lindsey: From Anglican to Unitarian* (London: Dr. Williams's Trust, 1998).

Lister, James (c.1779-1851)—Originally from Glasgow, he served as pastor of the first "English" Baptist church in Scotland, formed in Glasgow in 1801, with James Deakin (see letters 98 and 133) as one of his deacons. In 1803 Lister removed to the newly formed Baptist church in Lime Street (the result of a split in the congregation at Byrom Street after the death of Samuel Medley), where he would remain until 1847, by which time the church had moved to a new chapel in Hope Street. Thomas Raffles preached his funeral sermon on 30 November 1851. See Yuille, *History*, 60-61; "Calendar" 138; Halley, *Lancashire: Its Puritanism and Nonconformity*, 535-536; Bebbington, ed., *Baptists in Scotland*, 33; Talbot, *Search for a Common Identity*, 118, 122; Thomas Raffles, *"The Perfect and Upright Man": A Funeral Sermon for the Rev. James Lister delivered in Myrtle Street Baptist Chapel, Liverpool, on Sunday Morning, Nov 30, 1851* (Liverpool: Egerton Smith, 1851).

Llewelyn, Thomas (1720?-1793)—A Welshman, Llewelyn studied at Bristol Academy and Homerton Academy, London, prior to his ordination at Little Prescot Street, Goodman's Fields, c. 1747. He chose to establish himself in London as a teacher of ministerial students, becoming the primary tutor for the newly founded London Baptist Educational Society (1752-1759). His immediate successors were Joseph Stennett, Joseph Jenkins, and William Clarke of Unicorn Yard. He continued to support the LBES, leaving £100 to the Society at his death. He bequeathed his library, however, to Bristol Academy. Llewelyn's main achievements were his important historical studies of Welsh versions of the Bible and his work with the Society for the Propagating of Christian Knowledge (and other groups) in distributing Welsh Bibles. See Arnold H. J. Baines, "The Pre-History of Regent's Park College," *Baptist Quarterly* 36 (1995-1996): 193-196; Hayden, *Continuity and Crisis*, 238; *DEB.*

Lowell, Samuel (1759-1823)—Lowell was born in Birmingham and trained to be an engraver, but as a young man was called to be a Methodist itinerant preacher. He first preached in the Methodist connection in Yorkshire at Stainland (1781-1786) and Brighouse (1786-1789), where he was ordained in 1786. In 1789 he became a Calvinist, ministering to the Independent meeting at Woodbridge, Suffolk, from 1789 to 1799. While there, his preaching became "attractive and popular ... and soon became known beyond the sphere of his immediate ministrations." After some preaching engagements at the Tabernacle in Bristol in 1798, he was invited to preach for a season at Bridge Street, where he formally commenced his pastorate in the summer of 1799, remaining there until his death in 1823. The church experienced considerable growth under Lowell's leadership. In 1801 he published *Sermons on Evangelical and Practical Subjects, Designed Chiefly for the Use of Families*, and in 1802, at the cessation of the war with France, *The Blessings of Peace*, a sermon preached in Bristol on the national day of thanksgiving. John Leifchild succeeded Lowell at Bridge Street. The following excerpt from a letter by the Rev. David Edwards of Ipswich to Samuel Lucas (see below) at Shrewsbury, dated 9 March 1790, notes Lowell's removal to Woodbridge:

> Mr Lowell from Halifax succeeds Mr Palmer at Woodbridge. He was formerly in Mr Wesley's connection, but saw reasons to join the congregational churches—is a lively preacher and an agreeable talent at extempore preaching, lively and conversible in company—I was, at what is call^d, his settlement in Novr last—There was a large and a respectable congregation—your friend Waldegrave preach^d or rather went into the pulpit to laugh at us, or to make folks laugh; but, I assure you I was very serious, and often vex^d—He took a noble text viz. To me who am less than the least of all saints &c—We expected to hear something of the unsearchable riches of the gospel, but we had very little of that—It was the most crude and undigested discourse as I have heard for many years—However there were some useful sentences deliver^d now and then—His attempts at being witty were like Solomon's fly in the ointment. But I would not be too severe—Our Christian tempers sh^d be like the windows narrow without, but very wide within. (Eng. MS. 369, f. 40, JRULM)

See also M. Caston, *Independency in Bristol: With Brief Memorials of its Churches and Pastors* (London: T. Ward, 1860) 102-111.

Lucas, Samuel (1748-1799)—Originally from Bury St. Edmunds in Suffolk, Lucas was educated at Mile End and Homerton Academy between 1768 and 1773. He began his ministry at Walsall in 1773 before removing to the Independent chapel at Swan Hill, Shrewsbury, in July 1779. He would remain there as pastor until a paralytic seizure led to his retirement in May

1797 and his death in 1799. See Ernest Elliot, *A History of Congregational-ism in Shropshire* (Oswestry: Woodall and Minshall, 1898) 24.

Mack, John (1797-1845)—Originally from Scotland, Mack was educated at Edinburgh University and Bristol Academy. Recruited by William Ward during Ward's furlough in England in 1819-1820, Mack was eventually appointed as a BMS missionary in 1821. He became a professor of science at the newly founded Serampore College in November 1821, and in 1824 the Serampore Press issued his highly regarded *Principles of Chemistry*, the first modern science text in an Indian language. Mack also taught Greek, Latin, and Hebrew, as well as mathematics and natural sciences. Mack and Marshman produced the periodical, *The Friend of India,* in 1835. He served as Principal of Serampore College from 1837 to 1845. See Cox, *History,* 1:355-366; *DEB.*

McLean, Archibald (1733-1812)—McLean, a Scotsman originally trained to be a printer, first came under the influence of the Sandemanian John Glass, and retained some of his principles throughout his ministry. He came to Baptist convictions c.1763-1764 and was baptized by John Gill in London in May 1765. In 1768 McLean moved to Edinburgh and became an elder in a Scotch Baptist church there. In 1785 he entered the ministry full-time, and traveled widely in an effort to increase the Baptist witness in Scotland and elsewhere. Through his efforts, the Scotch Baptist Connexion came into being. His writings were influential in the Scotch Baptist cause as well, especially his *The Commission Given by Jesus Christ to his Apostles, Illustrated* (1786). He also wrote the first work on believer's baptism in Scotland (mentioned in this letter) and generally maintained a strict rigidity in his doctrinal views that often led him into disputes with other Baptist ministers. Despite his differences, McLean was a strong supporter of the BMS in its early years. See "The McLeanist (Scotch) and Campbellite Baptists of Wales," *Transactions of the Baptist Historical Society* 7 (1920-1921): 147-181; *DEB.*

Madgwick[e], William—Baptized at Broughton, along with Thomas Purdy, in 1769, Madgwick later studied at Bristol Academy. His first preaching experience was at Unicorn Yard, which he supplied after the departure of William Clarke in 1784. According to the Unicorn Yard Church Book, Madgwick preached for five Sundays, after which the church met on Sunday, 22 January 1786, and invited him to preach again in June. Madgwick preached for five Sundays that summer, but the church decided not to pursue him as a candidate any longer. An entry in the Church Book notes, "it being observed by the repeated absence of both members & hearers; not with that satisfaction to the Church or congregation as could be wished—the Sentiments of the Brethren & Sisters present being taken & being nearly unanimously returned to be that Mr Madgwicks ministry had not been acceptable not being useful—agreed that the above be conveyed him in the most tender & respectful manner by the Officers of the Church who are also directed to present him with the Churches most affectionate wishes." Joseph Jenkins turned down an offer from the church during this time. Daniel Williams left his church in Preston and assumed the pastorate at

Unicorn Yard in January 1787. Madgwick then went to Foulmire [Fowl-mire], Cambridgeshire, where a dissenting congregation was formed in 1781. Joseph Harrison came to preach to them in 1782, but some problems in his ministry led to a group leaving and forming a Baptist meeting at Harston, which Harrison led. After Harrison's removal, the church at Foulmire called Madgwick in 1787 as pastor. He was replaced by Thomas Smith of Bedford in 1795. While at Foulmire, Madgwick subscribed to Robert Robinson's *Ecclesiastical Researches* (1792). See Broughton Church Book, Angus Library, Oxford; Unicorn Yard Church Book, ff. 265-69; "Statistical View" 504.

Mann, Isaac (1785-1831)—Born at Bridlington, Yorkshire, Mann was the first student trained at Horton Academy, Bradford. He was ordained at Halifax in 1809. After two years, he resigned and removed to the Baptist meeting at Burslem, Staffordshire. After that he pastored at Shipley, not far from Bradford. He returned to Horton as classical tutor in 1816, becoming joint secretary of the Northern Education Society in 1822. In 1826 he accepted the call of the congregation at Maze Pond, Southwark, where he remained as pastor until his death in 1831. A significant collection of his letters resides at the National Library of Wales. See "Calendar of Letters"; *DEB.*

Mardon, Richard (1775-1812)—Mardon and his wife Rhoda were appointed as BMS missionaries to India in 1803. Like the Bisses, the Mardons had been members at Plymouth Dock, and Mardon had likewise studied under Sutcliff at Olney. The Mardons, along with Joshua Rowe, John Biss, William Moore, and their families, sailed from Bristol for Serampore (via America) in December 1803. Mardon worked briefly with Chater in Rangoon, but by February 1808, due to health reasons, he had removed to Malda in Bengal. Mrs. Mardon died in India in 1811; Richard Mardon died in Burma in 1812. See Cox, *History,* 1:137, 224-325; "Sutcliff's Academy," 277; *DEB.*

Marshman, John Clark (1794-1877)—Educated at Serampore and later in Europe, J. C. Marshman returned to Bengal to assist his father, Joshua Marshman (see below), and William Ward in the printing of periodicals at Serampore. In 1827-1828 the younger Marshman published his *Dictionary of the Bengalee Language*, establishing his reputation as an Oriental scholar. In 1835 he revived the *Friend of India*, and in 1840 founded the *Bengal Government Gazette*. After the death of his father, the younger Marshman, along with John Mack, took over the operations of Serampore College. In 1848 he published his famous *History of Bengal*. He retired to England in 1855, where he published his *Life and Times of Carey, Marshman, and Ward* (1859) and his *History of India* (1863-1867). In 1868 he was awarded the Star of India by Queen Victoria. See *DEB.*

Marshman, Joshua (1768-1837)—Originally a weaver, Marshman left that trade as a young man to teach at the Broadmead charity school in Bristol; he would become a student at Bristol Academy in the late 1790s. Influenced by Carey's writings on India, Marshman and his wife, Hannah (1767-1847), sailed with Ward, Brunsdon, and Grant in 1799 for Bengal, where Marshman became a valuable part of the Serampore Trio. Though not a great preacher, he was an excellent organizer, becoming the Mission's chief secretary in dealing with the East India Company. He also became the chief developer of the various educational wings of the Mission, helping to found Serampore College in 1818 as a place where nationals could be trained to replace missionaries. Marshman developed a keen interest in the Chinese language and wrote several important works in Chinese, including a translation of the Bible that was completed in 1822. He was also involved with Ward in numerous publishing ventures of the Mission. Not always easy to get along with, Marshman's personality led some younger missionaries to associate more with Eustace Carey and the Calcutta Mission after 1818. While on furlough in 1827-1828, Marshman, along with Christopher Anderson of Edinburgh, superintended the separation of the Serampore Mission from the BMS, a rift not healed until 1838. See A. Christopher Smith, "Joshua (1768-1837) and Hannah Marshman (1767-1847)," ed. Haykin, in *The British Particular Baptists*, 2:237-253; *DEB.*

May, John (1814-1894)—May was ordained to the ministry at the Baptist church at Saltash, Cornwall, in 1837; in 1840 he was appointed as a BMS missionary to Jamaica. May and his wife initially worked in the mountain station at Bethsalem, but in 1844 moved to the church at Lucea in the Hanover parish. The Mays returned to England for health reasons in 1852, with May once again ministering to the Baptist church at Saltash. See Clarke, *Memorials*, 182-83.

Medley, Samuel (1738-99)—Medley spent his early years in Warwick, where his father served as an assistant at J. C. Ryland's academy. Converted after a period as a wartime sailor, Medley was baptized in 1760 and soon after began his ministry as pastor of the Baptist congregation at Watford (1762–1772) before moving to Byrom Street in Liverpool, where he remained until his death. The congregation experienced considerable growth during Medley's tenure. Medley was noted for his preaching abilities, as well as his numerous hymns. See B. A. Ramsbottom, "Samuel Medley (1738-1799)," ed. Haykin, in *The British Particular Baptists*, 1:235-49; *DEB.*

Medley, Samuel, Jr. (1769-1857)—Son of Samuel Medley of Liverpool (see previous entry), the younger Medley became a noted painter. He entered the Royal Academy in London in 1791 (he was a student at one point of Sir Joshua Reynolds) and first exhibited the following year. Initially he painted religious and historical subjects, but later became known primarily for his portraits. By 1805 his health precluded his continuing his painting full-time, and he turned to the stock exchange, from which he would maintain a comfortable living the remainder of his life. He was a member at Carter Lane under John Rippon between 1798 and 1812, and thereafter worshiped at Hackney under F. A. Cox. He was an active participant in the early years of the Baptist Union and supporter of the BMS from its earliest days. Along with Cox, Joseph Hughes, and many other prominent London Nonconformists and Anglicans, Medley was instrumental in the founding of University College, London, in 1826. In 1818, he married Elizabeth Smallshaw (his second wife), daughter of John Smallshaw of Liverpool (see letter 39). See Price, "The Early Years of the Baptist Union," 121-123; Horsleydown and Carter Lane Church Book; *DNB.*

Merrick, Joseph (1818-1849)—Merrick and his father, Richard (1790-1841), were the first native missionaries to work with the BMS, being set apart during a special service in February 1839 at the Baptist church in Jericho, Jamaica. Both father and son desired to go with John Clarke to West Africa, but the death of Richard precluded that event. Nevertheless, Joseph Merrick sailed for England in August 1842 to make preparations for the new work in Fernando Po. From August 1842 through May 1843, Merrick traveled across England promoting the West African mission. On 14 June 1843, he and his wife, along with Dr. Prince and his wife, joined Alexander Fuller on a ship bound for Fernando Po, arriving there on 6 September 1843. Merrick began his work in Bimbia, establishing a printing press in Jubilee Town in 1845, from whence he published portions of the Bible in several native dialects. Poor health forced his return to England in October 1849. Unfortunately, he died on board ship on 22 October 1849. See Clarke, *Memorials*, 204-210; David Killingray, "Black Baptists in Britain 1640-1950," *Baptist Quarterly* 40 (2003): 69-89; *DEB*.

Millard, Benjamin (d. 1875)—After studying at Stepney College, Millard arrived in Jamaica in November 1840. He initially worked with Thomas Abbott at St. Ann's Bay, and after 1846, at Falmouth and several surrounding churches. He remained with the BMS until 1872. See Clarke, *Memorials*, 181-182.

Moffatt, Robert (1795-1883)—Moffatt served as a missionary to South Africa for the London Missionary Society, 1817-1870. He returned to England on furlough in 1839, at which time he supervised the printing of the New Testament and Psalms into the Sechwana language. He traveled and preached throughout England 1840-1842, meeting a young David Livingstone in the process. He sailed for South Africa on 30 January 1843, remaining there until 1870, when he returned to England in retirement. In 1857 he completed the translation of the Old Testament in Sechwana. See Albert Peel, *A Hundred Eminent Congregationalists 1530-1924* (London: Independent Press, 1927) 84-85; *DEB*.

Moore, William (1776-1844)—Moore and his wife, Eleanore, were members of the church at Stogumber (at that time known as Stoke Gomer), Somerset, under Robert Humphrey. Moore studied for a time at Sutcliff's academy at Olney before completing his training at Bristol Academy. He and his wife were appointed as BMS missionaries to India in 1803, along with the Rowes, Bisses, and Mardons. They all sailed to Serampore from Bristol (via America) in December 1803. After working in Serampore and Bankipore (near Patna), the Moore's settled at Digah in Bihar, were they formed a new church in March 1812. Mrs. Moore (the former Eleanor Hurford of Taunton) died in August 1812, after which William Moore married Hannah Biss (d. 1818), whose husband, John, had died in 1807. Moore retired in 1839 and died in 1844. See Cox, *History,* 1:137, 150-151; "Sutcliff's Academy," 277; *DEB*.

Morgan, Thomas (1776-1857)—Originally from Crinow in Pembrokeshire, Wales, Morgan entered Bristol Academy in 1792. He succeeded Samuel Pearce as minister at Cannon Street in Birmingham in 1802, remaining as pastor until 1811. He married Ann Harwood, daughter of John Harwood (d. 1792). The elder Harwood moved to Birmingham from London in 1778, becoming a successful grocer and chandler in partnership with Thomas King (1755-1831). Both men served many years as deacons in the Baptist church at Cannon Street. Morgan resigned in 1811 due to poor health, but in 1815 became the afternoon lecturer at the Baptist church in Bond Street, Birmingham. He became co-pastor with Edward Edmonds in 1820 and served as pastor from 1822 to 1846. He spent his final years in retirement at Church Hill, Handsworth. See Arthur S. Langley, *Birmingham Baptists Past and Present*, 34-35, 129-130; Butt-Thompson, "The Morgans of Birmingham," 263; *Baptist Annual Register*, 1:495-496; Couling, "Biographical Dictionary, 1800-1875."

Morris, John Webster (1763-1836)—A printer by trade (a vocation he maintained throughout his ministry), Morris began preaching at Clipston in 1785, not far from Carey's church in Moulton. He joined the BMS committee in 1793, and later edited and printed the BMS's *Periodical Accounts* from 1798 to 1809. In 1803 he removed to the Baptist church in Dunstable, Bedfordshire. After the death of his wife, he developed personal problems mostly as a result of substantial indebtedness. He left the pastorate in 1810, but continued to write and print religious works, as well as preaching on special occasions, much to Fuller's dismay. Fuller wrote to William Ward on 16 July 1809 that "Poor Morris ... is ruined. His pride and extravagance since he has been at D. is beyond anything. He must have sunk the greater part of £1000 in those few years ... And now he acts dishonourably to his creditors ... and yet goes about preaching!" Among his publications are the *Memoirs of . . . Andrew Fuller* (1816) and *Biographical Recollections of the Rev. Robert Hall* (1833). See Payne and Allan, *Clipston Baptist Church*, 10-12; Fuller to Ward, MSS. BMS, vol. 1, Angus Library, Regent's Park College, Oxford; *DEB.*

Morse, Jedediah (1761-1826)—Morse ministered for many years to the Congregational Church in Charlestown, Massachusetts. He was an ardent Federalist, evangelical, and religious writer, assisting in the founding of Andover Seminary, the American Tract Society, and the American Bible Society. He authored America's first geography, *The American Geography; Or, A View of the Present Situation of the United States of America* (1789), and in 1790 came out with his important *History of America*. One of his sons was Samuel F. B. Morse, inventor of the Morse code. See *DEB.*

Mullett, Thomas (1745-1814)—Mullett was initially a prosperous papermaker and stationer in Bristol at 18 Bristol-back. He married Mary Evans (1743?-1800), the daughter of Hugh Evans (and Sarah Browne) and sister to Caleb Evans, ministers at the church in Broadmead. At some point in the late 1780s or early 1790s, Mullett removed to London, where he began operating as an American agent in partnership with his wife's nephew and his son-in-law, Joseph Jeffries Evans (1768-1812). At the time of Mullett's death in 1814, he was residing in Clapham; he was buried at Bunhill Fields, with John Evans, General Baptist minister at Worship Street, London, delivering his funeral sermon. During his time in London, Mullett and his son-in-law, J. J. Evans, became close friends with the diarist Henry Crabb Robinson. Mullett and Evans appear frequently in the early volumes of Robinson's diary.

Originally a Quaker from Taunton, Mullett became a member at Broadmead on 9 May 1769. He soon joined with a select group of men in Bristol and the West Country in founding the Bristol Education Society on 7 June 1770; he served as the Society's secretary from 1770 to 1778. The Broadmead Subscription Book for 1772-1813 notes that Thomas Mullett paid his pew rents regularly until 1788. Mullett, like Caleb Evans, Robert Hall, and many other members at Broadmead in the 1780s and '90s, was an ardent advocate of political reform in England and the revolution in America, where he visited on three occasions and met numerous individuals of "high respectability," including a meeting with General Washington at Mount Vernon in 1783. As his obituary in the *Gentleman's Magazine* notes (an excerpt taken from John Evans's *Address, on the Resurrection of Christ, Delivered in Bunhill-fields, Wednesday, November 23, 1814 at the Interment of Thomas Mullett*), during Mullett's years in Bristol he was heavily involved in the Whig political reform movement. "Few understood better than did Mr Mullett the rights of the subject; none advocated with more manly firmness the principles of civil and religious liberty, which he knew included in all their ramifications the prosperity of mankind. His intellectual powers were of a superior cast . . . Having taken a comprehensive view of what was offered to his consideration, his mind was not harassed by any puerile vacillations; but, conscious of the firmness of the ground on which he stood, he prosecuted his object till it was accomplished. Hence it was that he was looked up to by a number of respectable characters, and not unfrequently, occupied in matters of arbitration between his fellow-citizens in the commercial world."

During the late 1760s, Mullett became friends with General Horatio Gates, famed military commander for the American forces during the Revolutionary War, when Gates resided in Bristol, 1766-1770. Four letters from Mullett to Gates, written between 1791 and 1794 and now in the possession of the New York Historical Society, reveal Mullett's passion for parliamentary reform in England and his sympathy with the French Revolution. Mullett (who apparently served as Gates's business liaison in England) writes to Gates, at that time living in America, on 17 September 1791, "You'll be happy to hear that the French Revolution is Compleat, by the Kings having adopted the Revisd Constitution and declaring that he will maintain and defend it against all *domestic* or foreign foes—That Paris shall be his Residence as he is at length Convinced it is the wish of the Nation that the reform should be as universal as the National Assembly have made it. A decision this, that is full of mortification to the Aristocrats, and death to all hopes they had so long Cherishd of a Counter Revolution. In addition I suppose all the Kings in Europe are in Secret Mourning!" He then adds, "We have had a revival of the old Cry of Church & King, and down with the Dissenters—and this fury has been Cherishd by the Clergy in many furious pulpit harangues and pamphlets—the disorder broke out at Birmingham, but has been very much check'd by the hangmen at Warwick and Worcester, who were immediately applied to on this Occasion, and who administered with their usual alacrity." Mullett writes again to Gates on 24 November 1791, informing Gates about the latest meeting of the London Revolution Society, a meeting Mullett attended. After relating details of some business with a Mr. Jones and Charles Harford, two former friends of Gates who were now, according to Mullett, "infected with the . . . Contagion" of Toryism," Mullett provides a fascinating account of the current political scene from the eyes of an optimistic, reform-minded Baptist dissenter. France, he says, "is progressing to the perfect establishment of a System that has dethrond despotism, and which has conveyd a Shock to the heart of every tyrant in this quarter of the Globe. *Our Court* looks with a proportion of Astonishment, and *coldly* expresses their acquiescence in the French Kings Acceptance of the New Constitution. They also tremble at the idea of reform—they know it is necessary, but fear to begin, uncertain of the Event. In the present reign it *may* be force—in the Next it may be more gradually accomplishd. There is an encreasing Spirit of approbation of the French—and a visible decay of Old prejudices. You would have felt an elevation at the Revolution Society at the London Tavern on the 4th November. 300 set down in the great Room to dinner; amongst them some of the ablest, and most distinguished of *the last* National Assembly, particular *M.r Pethion*, who is just elected successor to M.r Bailly Mayor of Paris. He made a short speech of Congratulation to Englishmen on the examples they had often given the World of a hatred of Tyrants; he spoke with all the plainness, and firmness of a Republican, and with all the dignity of a Man. Common Sense *Paine* was invited—his health was drank, with thanks to him for his able defence of the Rights of Man; on which he thankd the Society, & proposd as a toast—the Revolution of the World! The Republic of North America, and its first Citizen, was amongst the most applauded toasts; and Connected with one expressive of a Wish, that "Revolutions may never Cease—while the Cause of them exists!" I attended on an invitation of an Old Acquaintance, and Member of the Society, and have never witnessd a popular Assembly of more decorum, or with so much of the "feast of reason, and the flow of Soul." A Variety of letters, and addresses, from Societies, in France, were read, and Conveying such general information, and expressing such sentiments, as prove in my Opinion, that a people so well informd on the principles of freedom, and who have so gloriously asserted them, Cannot again degenerate into Slaves! I intended you half a [Sheet] as this, but you will be tird with a whole one. The subject must be my Apology—You, my dear Sir, have felt the inspiration of it. May you live to enjoy much of that felicity in the Western World, which your efforts contributed to obtain, as well as to hear of, and to applaud that spirit which is extending the freedom & happiness of Europe. See "Memoirs of Mr. Thomas Mullett, by the Rev. John Evans," *Gentleman's Magazine* 85 (1815, Part 1): 83-85; *Sketchley's Bristol Directory, 1775* (Bristol: James Sketchley, 1775) 68; "Alphabetical List of Members in 1802," f. 31; Broadmead Subscription Book, no. 3; *Account of the Bristol Education Society*, 24; Moon,

Education for Ministry, 7, 137; Horatio Gates Papers, New York Historical Society, microfilm edition, 1979.

Newman, William (1773-1835)—Newman was heavily influenced by John Collett Ryland while serving as a tutor at Ryland's Academy at Enfield. In 1792 Newman was baptized and two years later ordained as a Baptist minister. He assumed the pastorate of the Baptist congregation at Old Ford, Bow, that same year and remained there until his death in 1835. Like so many other Baptist ministers, he too doubled as a schoolmaster, both at Bow and Bromley, Essex. In 1810 he was appointed President of the newly formed Stepney College, a position he held until 1827. Among his publications are *A Manual for Church Members* (1825) and *Rylandia* (1835). See Cooper, *From Stepney to St. Giles*, 26-59; *DEB*.

Newton, James (1733-1790)— Originally from the Maze Pond church in Southwark, Newton became the assistant pastor to John Tommas at the Baptist congregation in the Pithay, Bristol, in early 1758, where he would remain until his death in 1790. He also served for many years as the classical tutor at Bristol Academy. During his time in Bristol, Newton boarded in the home of Robert Cottle, Joseph Cottle's father. Cottle considered him his "most revered and honoured friend," a scholar whose "learning was his least recommendation." "Many an evening," Cottle remarks in his *Reminiscences*, "do I recollect to have listened in wonderment to colloquisms and disputations carried on in Latin between Mr. Newton and John Henderson." Newton was also Hannah More's private instructor in Latin and assisted in editing of many of her works. He willed his library to the Museum at the Baptist Academy. He also composed a number of hymns. See Joseph Cottle, *Reminiscences of Samuel Taylor Coleridge and Robert Southey* (London: Houlston and Stoneman, 1847) 53; Henry Sweetser Burrage, *Baptist Hymn Writers and their Hymns* (Portland, ME: Brown, Thurston, and Co., 1888), pp. 64-65; *DEB*.

Newton, John (1725-1807)—Newton was originally a sea merchant trafficking in the slave trade. He was converted during a storm on a voyage in 1748; however, for a number of years he continued to captain slave ships. From 1755 to 1760 he was surveyor of the tides in Liverpool and began to exercise his spiritual gifts in meetings in his home, even entertaining George Whitefield. Newton became a Calvinist at this time, but was friendly to John Wesley, numerous dissenters, as well as his Anglican evangelical friends. Newton tried to obtain orders in the church but was rejected; he contemplated becoming a dissenter, but eventually attained the curacy at Olney in 1764. During his years in Olney, Newton became friends with the poet William Cowper (they collaborated on the *Olney Hymns* in 1779) and John Ryland, Jr., one of his favorite correspondents. In 1780 Newton became curate of St. Mary Woolnoth in London, remaining there until his death in 1807. He influenced a number of Anglican evangelicals, including Charles Simeon, Hannah More, and William Wilberforce. His autobiography, *An Authentic Narrative* (1764), was immensely popular, as well as his hymn, "Amazing Grace." See L. G. Champion, "The Letters of John Newton to John Ryland," *Baptist Quarterly* 27 (1977-1778): 157-163; *DEB*.

Nichols, William—A hosier by trade, Nichols had once been a deacon in the Baptist church at Friar Lane in Nottingham. In 1807 he became pastor of the Baptist congregation at Collingham, replacing Thomas Latham. He remained as pastor until his death in 1835. During his time at Collingham he assisted in the formation of the Baptist meeting at Sutton-on-Trent, and preached regularly at Besthorpe and Girton. The Collingham church hosted several meetings of the Baptist Missionary Society during Nichols's tenure, with sermons preached there by John Sutcliff, Robert Hall, and William Steadman. The Collingham Church Book notes that Nichols discharged his duties "faithfully and affectionately" and was always "ready to employ his efforts in promoting the cause of Christ both in this and other places, assisting in the support of most religious institutions, and owning a readiness to help neighbouring churches who stood in need of his aid, and to whom it pleased God to grant a considerable portion of success during his ministry among us, and was the principal cause of establishing the Baptist interest in Sutton-on-Trent, and which cause was chiefly supported by him for more than twenty years." See F. M. W. Harrison, *The Story of the Collingham Baptist Church in the County of Nottinghamshire* (Newark: Collingham Baptist Church, 1970) 10-11.

Okely, Francis (1719-1794)—Okely was born at Bedford and educated for the Anglican ministry at Cambridge. After leaving Cambridge, he founded a religious society in Bedford, initially associating with the Baptists, but by 1743, through the influence of John Cennick, he had joined the Moravians and removed to Germany. He returned to England and preached in Bristol for a while, and later in Manchester, Ashton, and Stockport. In 1757 he returned to Bedford and became affiliated with the Methodists again, but by 1767 he was preaching once again in a Moravian church in Northampton. During his years there (at which time John Ryland, Jr., became acquainted with him), Okely translated numerous works by German writers, including Boehme, Engelbrecht and Hiel. He eventually rejected trinitarianism and the atonement, and came to believe in continued prophetic revelation. See *Protestant Dissenters Magazine* 1 (1794): 336; *DEB.*

Oughton, Samuel—Oughton and his wife, Hannah (the niece of Mrs. Thomas Burchell), were appointed as BMS missionaries to Jamaica in 1835, where they initially worked with the Burchells in the parish of Hanover. In 1840 the Oughtons removed to Kingston. Like Tinson, the Oughtons were also in England on furlough in 1843. Mrs. Oughton died in 1862; Samuel Oughton labored in Jamaica until 1866, after which he retired to Brighton, England. See Clarke, *Memorials*, 171-174.

Overbury, Robert William (1812-1868)—Overbury studied at Stepney College c. 1830-1833, after which he co-pastored with Joseph Ivimey at Eagle Street in London for one year before assuming the pastorate in 1834, a position he retained until 1853. He later ministered at Morice Square, Devonport (1853-1856), and Salem Chapel, Morice Town, Devonport (1856-1859). He served for many years as a member of the committee of the Baptist Union and the London Baptist Board; he was also a co-founder of the Baptist Tract Society. See *Baptist Magazine* 33 (1841): 636; *DEB.*

Page, Henry (1781-1833)—Page served as assistant pastor at Broadmead as well as secretary and tutor at Bristol Academy from 1802-1817. He was the son of John Page, Esq., a prominent member of the Broadmead church and sheriff of Bristol in 1795, the same year Henry was baptized and joined the church. After studying at Bristol for a time, he took an M.A. at Marischal College, Aberdeen, in 1800. He married Ann Selfe in 1802; they had three sons and seven daughters. After his departure from Bristol, Page served as minister of the Baptist church in Worcester until 1827, when he left for the Continent, leaving behind his wife and children. He died in France in 1833. See Hall and Mowvley, *Tradition and Challenge*, 43-44.

Palmer, John (1768-1823)—Originally trained in medicine, Palmer succeeded William Smith as pastor of the Baptist congregation at Shrewsbury in 1794, remaining in that capacity until 1822. He worked on several occasions for the Particular Baptist Case Committee and the Committee for Village Preaching in the 1790s. His account of a tour to Ireland appeared in the *Baptist Annual Register,* 4:656-659.

Parker, John (1725-1793)—Converted under the preaching of William Grimshaw of Haworth, Parker spent several years as a teaching elder of the church at Barnoldswick under Alvery Jackson. Upon Jackson's death in 1763, Parker succeeded him as pastor, remaining at Barnoldswick until 1790. He removed to Wainsgate, but after one year as minister of the Baptist meeting there, his health failed and he died in 1793. See Winnard, *History*, 61-62; *Evangelical Magazine* 2 (1794): 392-394; J. H. J. Plumbridge, "The Life and Letters of John Parker," *Baptist Quarterly* 8 (1936-1937): 111-122; John Parker, *Letters to his Friends, by the Rev. John Parker ... with a Sketch of his Life and Character, by John Fawcett* (Leeds: Thomas Wright, 1794).

Parsons, George—In August 1838, two weeks after his ordination, George Parsons (from Laverton, near Frome) married Sophia Rawlings of London. They soon departed for Calcutta as BMS missionaries on the *Moira*, arriving there in late February 1839. His health was poor from the beginning, and in October 1839 the Parsons removed to Monghyr, where he applied to the BMS board for permission to have his brother, John, a village preacher in England at that time, join him at Monghyr. The Parsons brothers were nephews of John Dyer, BMS secretary. George Parsons was apparently gifted in language acquisition, for he was preaching in the native language within one month. His health, however, continued to decline, and he died at Calcutta on 13 November 1840. John Parsons married Jane Rawlings (Sophia's sister?) and sailed for India in July 1840; they arrived in Calcutta one week after the death of George Parsons. John Parsons served the BMS in India until 1869. Sophia Parsons returned to England in 1842, and did not return to India. See *Baptist Magazine* 33 (1841): 472; Carey, *Oriental Christian Biography*, 2:344-356; Ernest A. Payne, "The Journal of Jane Parsons," *Baptist Quarterly* 23 (1969-1970): 266-267.

Patrick, Joseph—Patrick was originally from Andrew Fuller's church at Kettering. He began ministering at Southill, Bedfordshire, in April 1804, but his pastorate was troubled from its early days. According to the "Memorials" of the church written by John Warburton, minister at Southill from 1846 to 1892, "there was a great disturbance among the people" during Patrick's ministry. "It was considered by the major part of the people that Mr. Patrick had swerved from the principles he professed when he first came among them. Some took part with Mr. Patrick, thus causing disquiet among them." Two deacons, Warburton notes, "one Sunday afternoon, stood at the bottom of the pulpit stairs to prevent Mr. Patrick going up, telling him he had departed from the truth, and that he should not enter the pulpit. This caused an uproar." Most likely, Patrick was too moderately Calvinistic for the tastes of many within the congregation. During his time at Southill, however, many were added to the church and a new chapel opened in 1805. Patrick would leave Southill in 1811 and remove to the Baptist congregation at Fenny Stratford, Bucks., becoming their first official pastor. William Heighton of Road, Northampton, preached that day, among others. The church had been formed in 1805 and at the time of Patrick's ordination consisted of 28 members. For Warburton's history, see *Strict Baptist Chapel Southill* (n.p., 1993), 5-6; *Baptist Magazine* 4 (1812): 128.

Pearce, Samuel (1766-1799)—Converted as a teenager in the Baptist church at Portsea, Pearce soon committed himself to the ministry. He began his studies at Bristol Academy in 1786, and in 1790 became pastor of the Baptist congregation at Cannon Street in Birmingham. He immediately became involved with the political reform movement, publishing a radical pamphlet titled *The Oppressive, Unjust, and Prophane Nature, and Tendency of the Corporation and Test Acts, exposed, in a sermon preached before the Congregation of Protestant Dissenters, meeting in Cannon-Street, Birmingham, February 21, 1790.* He was an ardent evangelical Calvinist, devoting himself to itinerant preaching and the establishing of Sunday schools around Birmingham. He was one of the founders of the BMS, assisting Andrew Fuller in editing the *Periodical Accounts* and in fundraising. He studied Bengali in the hope of joining Carey in India, but the BMS committee decided that he should remain in England. Though his health declined after 1796, he still remained active in promoting Baptist causes throughout England, Ireland, and Asia, as letters 52 and 57 attest. See Arthur Mursell, *Cannon Street Baptist Church, Birmingham. Its History from 1737 to 1880* (London: n.p., 1880); Tom Wells, "Samuel Pearce (1766-1799)," ed. Haykin, in *The British Particular Baptists*, 2:183-199; *DEB*.

Pearce, William Hopkins (1794-1840)—The son of Samuel Pearce (see above), W. H Pearce was trained as a printer at the Clarendon Press at Oxford before arriving in India as a BMS missionary in 1817 to join William Ward at the Serampore Press. Before he left for India, however, he joined with William Johns (see above) in publishing the first tract in England on the subject of the *sati* [*suttee*], titled *A Collection of Facts and opinions relative to the Burning of Widows with the dead bodies of their husbands, and to other destructive customs prevalent in British India* (1816). In 1818 he joined William Yates and the younger group at Calcutta, where he worked with the Calcutta Education Press and the Baptist Mission Press until his death. He served for a time as pastor of the Baptist church at South Colings, and was a leader in the area of native female education in India. He authored a Bengali textbook titled *Geography*. See Cox, *History*, 2:286-293; *The Bengal Obituary* (Calcutta: Holmes and Co.; London: W. Thacker & Co., 1851) 254; *DEB*.

Peggs, James (1793-1850)—Peggs was one of the first missionaries sent to India by the General Baptist Missionary Society, serving in Orissa from 1821 to 1825, when ill health forced his return to England. Previously he had ministered to a congregation in Norwich. After his return, he served as pastor of General Baptist congregations at Coventry (1828-1834), Bourne (1834-1841), Ilkeston (1841-1846), and Burton (1846-1850). He became best known for his philanthropic activities, especially in distributing printed religious materials paid for by subscriptions, as letters 166, 210, and 211 demonstrate. He published more than thirty titles and distributed more than 30,000 copies of his pamphlets. He contributed a history of the General Baptist mission in India to the second volume of F. A. Cox's *History*. See "An Index to Notable Baptists, Whose Careers began withing the British Empire before 1850," *Baptist Quarterly* 7 (1920-1921): 224; *DEB*.

Peirce, James (1673-1726)—Peirce came from a Nonconformist family in London. He lost his parents at an early age and was taken in by his minister, Matthew Mead, who eventually sent him to the University of Utrecht and then to Leyden. After five years of study, he returned to London, preaching occasionally at Miles Lane. He was ordained in 1699 and two years later began his ministerial career, first in a mixed dissenting congregation in Cambridge (1701-1706) and then in a Presbyterian chapel in Newbury (1706-1713) before coming to the James' Presbyterian meeting in Exeter in 1713. A few years after his arrival in Exeter, a controversy erupted within the congregation over Peirce's growing Arianism, much of which derived from the influence of the Cambridge minister William Whiston. In March 1719, he and his associate minister, Joseph Hallett II, were expelled from the church in Exeter for failing to subscribe to orthodox trinitarianism. Immediately, a new church was formed at the Mint in Exeter (some 300 attendants came with Peirce from the James' Meeting). See Murch, *History*, 421-431; Allan Brockett, *Nonconformity in Exeter 1650-1875* (Manchester: Manchester University Press, 1962) 69-95; 156-157.

Pengilly, Richard (1782-1865)—Originally from Cornwall, Pengilly became a Baptist in 1802, part of a small group that formed a Baptist church in Penzance. He studied at Bristol Academy (1803-1807) before accepting the pastorate of the Baptist church at Tuthill Stairs, Newcastle, where he was ordained on 12 August 1807. He remained there until April 1845, when he became chaplain for the Penzance Workhouse, a position he retained until 1857. He spent his final years at Croydon. His publication, *Scripture Guide to Baptism*, went through numerous editions in his lifetime. See Douglas, *History*, 298; *DEB*.

Phillippo, James Mursell (1798-1879)—Phillippo was from Norfolk and trained for the ministry at Horton Academy, Bradford. He arrived in Jamaica as a BMS missionary in 1823, working at Spanish Town, planting churches and establishing schools. During his ministry in Jamaica, which lasted more than fifty years, he baptized over 5000 people and educated about the same number in his schools. He worked closely with William Knibb and Thomas Burchell in leading the fight for the abolition of slavery throughout the British Commonwealth in the early 1830s. He also had plans for a university in Jamaica patterned after University College, London. See E. B. Underhill, *Life of James Mursell Phillippo* (London: Yates and Alexander, 1881); *DEB.*

Pike, John Deodatus Gregory (1784-1854)—Pike was born at Edmonton, Middlesex, and studied for the ministry at Wymondley. He pastored the General Baptist church in Derby, 1810-1854, which, at the time of letter 182, had just opened a new chapel in St. Mary's Gate. When the General Baptist Missionary Society was formed in 1816, Pike became the first secretary, a position he held until his death in 1854. He also edited the *General Baptist Repository and Missionary Observer.* His best-known publication was *Persuasives to Early Piety* (c.1820). His son, James Carey Pike (1817-1876), who studied at Stepney College, succeeded him as secretary of the GBMS. See John Baxter Pike and James Carey Pike, *A Memoir and Remains of the Late Rev. John Gregory Pike, Author of "Persuasives to Early Piety"* (London: Jarrold and Sons, 1855); Payne, *First Generation,* 133-140; "The Origin of the General Baptist Missionary Society," *Baptist Quarterly* 1 (1922-1923): 270-275 (a transcription of Pike's account of the origin of the GBMS); G. P. R. Prosser, "The Formation of the General Baptist Missionary Society," *Baptist Quarterly* 22 (1967-1968): 23-28; *DEB.*

Poynder, John (1779-1849)—Poynder was a successful London lawyer. Raised an evangelical Anglican, he served as a solicitor for Bridewell Prison and Bethlehem Hospital for almost forty years. During that time he also published *Literary Extracts* (1844), displaying his interest in English literature. Poynder, like his friend William Alers Hankey (see above), served on numerous committees for evangelical organizations, including the Church Missionary Society, the Reformation Society, and the Protestant Association. He took an active interest in Indian affairs, especially the efforts to abolish the practice of *sati* [*suttee*], which finally occurred in 1829, as well as the practice of the British government in allowing portions of tax revenues to support the Juggernaut. See *DEB.*

Prichard, James Cowles (1786-1848)—Prichard studied medicine at Bristol in 1802 and later at St. Thomas's Hospital and Edinburgh University, where he took an M.D. in 1808. He began his medical practice in Bristol in 1810, focusing on ethnology and insanity. His research led to his first publication, *Researches into the Physical History of Man* (1813). He was originally a Quaker, but became an Anglican later in life. He may have been a Unitarian at some point, for in 1811 he married Anne Maria Estlin, daughter of John Prior Estlin, who ministered at the Unitarian chapel at Lewin's Mead in Bristol from 1771 to 1817. Among Prichard's other publications are *An Analysis of the Egyptian Mythology* (1819); *Treatise on Diseases of the Nervous System* (1822); *Treatise on Insanity and Other Disorders Affecting the Mind* (1835); and *Natural History of Man* (1843).

Priestley, Joseph (1733-1804)—Probably the most famous scientist, philosopher, and Unitarian minister of his day, Priestley was educated at Daventry Academy. He then ministered to Independent congregations at Needham Market, Suffolk, and at Nantwich between 1755 and 1761. After a period where he served as a tutor at Warrington Academy in Lancashire, he assumed the pastorate at Mill Lane in Leeds in 1767. He resigned in 1772 to accept a position under the sponsorship of William Petty, 2nd Earl of Shelbourne, for the purpose of devoting himself to scientific experiments. In 1780, now espousing Unitarian doctrines, he returned to the ministry, this time at the New Meeting in Birmingham. Tragically, his home, along with his manuscripts and scientific apparatus, was burned during the Birmingham Riots in July 1791. He removed to London, but emigrated to America in 1794, where he died in Northumberland, Pennsylvania, in 1804. Among his numerous philosophical, scientific, and religious works was *The Doctrine of Philosophical Necessity Illustrated* (1777), referred to by Joshua Toulmin in letter 22.

Prince, George K. (1800/01-1865)—A English medical doctor in Jamaica and active supporter of the BMS work there, Prince traveled with John Clarke in 1840 to Fernando Po, West Africa, to determine its feasibility for a BMS mission. After considerable expeditions in the area, they left Fernando Po in the summer of 1842 and arrived in England that September. After several months of speaking engagements and fundraising, Clarke returned to Jamaica in August 1843 to gather recruits for Fernando Po before continuing on to Fernando Po; Prince, however, returned directly to West Africa from England in the late spring, 1843. In 1848 he and his wife (a native of Jamaica) left West Africa, and later emigrated to America, where he died at Davenport, Iowa, in 1865. See *DEB.*

Pritchard, George (1773-1852)—After holding pastorates in Colchester and at Shouldham Street, London, Pritchard removed to the Baptist church at Keppel Street, London, in 1817, becoming at the same time a member of the London Baptist Board. He remained at Keppel Street until 1837. At the time of letter 188, he was residing in Pentonville. He authored biographies of William Newman, Joseph Ivimey, James Smith of Ilford, and John Chin. See Whitley, *Baptists of London,* 128; *Baptist Magazine* 33 (1841): 636; Couling, "Biographical Dictionary, 1800-1875."

Pugsley, Nathaniel Knight (1787-1868)—Pugsley was originally from Kentisbeare, Devon. He was educated at Hoxton Academy (1812-1815) and commenced his ministry at the Orchard Street Congregational Church in Stockport in 1815. He resigned, however, in 1819 and, with a group from Orchard Street, organized a new congregation at Hanover Chapel, which officially opened in October 1821. Pugsley remained at Hanover until 1858, maintaining an active involvement in the Stockport Sunday School. See Urwick, *Historical Sketches,* 306-307.

Pyne, John—Pyne ministered to the Particular Baptist congregation at Shrewsbury from 1762-1773, after which he and a group of members succeeded from the church to form another Baptist congregation in Shrewsbury. Sutcliff briefly followed Pyne as minister to the former congregation in the summer of 1774 before he removed to Olney in 1775. Pyne assumed the pastorate of the Baptist church in Bewdley in 1781, remaining there until 1788, when he removed to Bristol due to a lack of financial support. See Haykin, *One Heart*, 64-65; *Claremont Baptist Church, Shrewsbury*, (Shrewsbury: n.p., 1920) 7; A. J. Klaiber, "Baptists at Bewdley, 1649-1949," *Baptist Quarterly* 13 (1949-1950): 120.

Raffles, Thomas (1788-1863)—Raised a Wesleyan Methodist, Raffles studied at Homerton Academy, 1805-1809, after which he began his long career as a Congregational minister, first at Hammersmith for three years, then at Great George Street in Liverpool, 1812-1863. One of the leading Congregational ministers of his day, he was a noted preacher, pastor, educator, and antiquarian. He was involved with the formation of Blackburn Academy (later Lancashire Independent College) in 1816, where Joseph Fletcher and William Hope served as tutors. Raffles was also chairman of the Congregational Union in 1839, and authored several books, including *Memoirs of the Life and Ministry of the Late Rev. Thomas Spencer, of Liverpool* (Liverpool, 1813). His massive collection of autograph letters and portraits is now held by the John Rylands University Library of Manchester, from which the majority of the letters transcribed in this book were taken. See Raffles, *Memoirs of the Life and Ministry of the Rev. Thomas Raffles*; *DEB*.

Raffles, Sir Thomas Stamford (1781-1826)—Raffles began working for the East India House as a clerk and was eventually appointed secretary to the office in Penang, Sumatra, in 1805. He became fluent in Malay and in 1807 became secretary to the governor. He served as lieutenant governor of Java in 1811 and director of Sumatra from 1813 to 1816. Due to poor health, he returned to England in 1816 and published his *History of Java*, for which he was knighted in 1817. He returned to Sumatra as governor in 1818, establishing schools and importing missionaries. The directors in England, however, became disenchanted with Raffles over his reformist ideas. On his return to England in 1824, his ship caught fire and all his papers and belongings, valued between £20,000-30,000, were lost. His difficulties with the Directors increased as well, and he died shortly thereafter of apoplexy in 1826.

Ransford, Thomas—A hat manufacturer in Wine Street, Bristol, Ransford lived at 8 Orchard Street. He was a leader in the Broadmead church, as was his father, Edward Ransford (1738-1813), who served as a deacon for the last 23 years of his life and left a legacy to the church (see letters 107 and 123). The younger Ransford married Ann Gay, a member of Broadmead, but she died in 1793. There was also an Edward Ransford, Jr., in the church, who was approved for baptism and membership on 9 October 1788. See *Matthew's Bristol Directory for 1794*, 68; Broadmead Church Book, 1779-1817, ff. 57, 60.

Reed, Andrew (1817-1899)—Reed was the son of Andrew Reed, Sr. (1787-1862), an Independent minister. He studied at Mill Hill Academy before commencing his career at the Old Meeting, Norwich, where he ministered from 1840 until 1855. He later ministered to Independent churches in Middlesex, London, Lancashire, and Sussex, from 1855 to 1881. His brother, Charles Reed (1819-1881), became well known for his work on the London School Board and the Sunday School Union as well as serving as M.P. for Hackney (1868-1874) and St. Ives (1880-1881). See *Congregational Yearbook* (1900): 211.

Reyner, Joseph (1754/5-1837)—Originally from Yorkshire, Reyner was a lifelong Independent, though very friendly with such Baptists as the Haldanes of Scotland and Fuller of Kettering. He was a successful cotton importer and shipper, with offices at 11 Philpot Lane, Fench Street, then later in Duck's Foot Lane and Old Swan Stairs, London. Reyner served many years as a deacon and trustee of Kingsland Chapel. His business partner was Joseph Hardcastle, another evangelical leader. Reyner was the first treasurer of the Religious Tract Society (1799-1827) and chaired its annual meetings from 1800 to 1825. He also assisted Joseph Hughes in the founding of the British and Foreign Bible Society in 1804, and was active in the London Missionary Society, among other philanthropic ventures (he was a member of nineteen religious and philanthropic societies). He supported the BMS as well; his firm, Hardcastle and Reyner, subscribed £10.10 in 1800-1801. *Universal British Directory*, 1/2:266; *Periodical Accounts*, 2:205; *DEB*.

Rhees [Rhys], Morgan (1760-1804)—Rhees was born in Wales and admitted to Bristol Academy in 1786. He was ordained at Pen-y-garn in 1787 and became an itinerant minister. He was an admirer of the French Revolution, even opening a meetinghouse in Boulogne and founding a society for distributing the New Testament to French citizens in the early 1790s. When he returned from France he immigrated with a colony of Welsh people to America in 1794. William Rogers welcomed Rhees to Philadelphia, where his eloquent preaching attracted great crowds. He traveled widely in America, preaching wherever he went. In connection with Dr. Benjamin Rush, he purchased a tract of land in Pennsylvania, which he called Cambria, and formed a church there. Later he removed to Somerset, Pennsylvania, where he died in 1804. He was buried in Philadelphia. He married a daughter of Col. Benjamin Loxley, a distinguished officer of the Revolution. Like his countryman, Iolo Morganwg, Rhees promoted the recovery of the ancient Welsh bardic tradition. As Gwyn Williams describes him, Rhees was the "hammer of slavery, preacher of Sunday and Welsh schools, promoter of the John Canne Bible, missionary to the French, [and] editor of Wale's first political journal in its own language." See Cathcart, *Baptist Encyclopedia*, 977; Gwyn A. Williams, *The Search for Beulah Land: The Welsh and the Atlantic Revolution* (New York: Holmes & Meier, 1980) 53-80 (quotation above taken from p. 72); *DEB*.

Richards, William (1749-1818)—Born into a Baptist family in Wales, Richards attended Bristol Academy in 1773, after which he commenced his pastoral ministry at Pershore in 1775. He left the next year for King's Lynn, where he remained the rest of his life as minister to the Particular Baptist congregation there. His health, however, began to fail in 1795, and he spent most of the next three years in Wales, returning again to Wales in 1800 and 1801. He did not preach in King's Lynn after 1802, although he never formally dissolved his pastoral position. After his wife's death in 1805, Richard's spent the next seven years largely in seclusion. During his career he moved away from strict Calvinism and Trinitarianism, endorsing Arianism and Sabellianism. The *Unitarian Biographical Dictionary* identifies him as an avowed Unitarian. He was an admirer of the political system of America and its tolerance of religion, eventually receiving an honorary degree from Rhode Island College. During the 1780s and '90s he was a political radical and reformer, opponent of the slave trade, admirer of the French Revolution, and supporter of Catholic Emancipation. High Calvinists dominated his congregation at King's Lynn, however, a situation that eventually created considerable problems for Richards as he espoused an Arian position. Among his publications are *Reflections on French Atheism and on English Christianity* (1794); *Food for a Fast-Day; or, A Few Seasonable Hints for the Use of Those Good People who Believe in the Propriety and Efficacy of Public Fasts* (1795); *A Word in Season: or a Plea for the Baptists* (1804); *The History of Lynn, Civil, Ecclesiastical, Political, Commercial, Biographical, Municipal, and Military, from the Earliest Accounts to the Present Time* (1812); and *Plain Hints and Brief Observations on Primitive Christianity in Some of its Leading Objects and Characteristic Bearings* (1818). See John Evans, *Memoirs of the Life and Writings of the Rev. William Richards, LL.D.* (Chiswick: Charles Whittingham, 1819); *The Baptists in King's Lynn* (Kings Lynn: [n.d.], 1939) 10, 12; George Carter, *Unitarian Biographical Dictionary* (London: Unitarian Christian Publishing Office, 1902) 103-104; John Oddy, *The Reverend William Richards (1749-1818) and his Friends: A Study of Ideas and Relationships* (Nottingham: [n.d.], 1973); idem, "The Dissidence of William Richards," *Baptist Quarterly* 27 (1977-1978): 118-127; *DEB*.

Riland, John (1736?-1822)—Riland was an Anglican evangelical minister at St. Mary's, Birmingham, and author of *Extracts from Various Devotional Writings of Joseph Hall* (Birmingham, 1784). Some letters that passed between Riland and the Rev. Francis Blick were attached to *A Sermon on John VII: 17: Delivered in the Parish Church of Sutton Coldfield, January 30, 1791* (Birmingham, 1791). An interesting letter to Riland appeared in the *Protestant Magazine* (February 1782), in which the writer questions statements made by Riland in a recent publication in which he argued that England's laws were "inadequate" to protecting women and preventing lewdness, especially prostitution. Riland was a major factor in the formation of the Birmingham Sunday School Society in the mid-1780s. On 4 July 1791, at a meeting of the Birmingham chapter of the Committee to Promote the Abolition of the Slave Trade, Riland appears among the individuals receiving public thanks from the Committee (a printed copy of the resolutions passed that day can be found in the William Smith Papers, VI, Duke University). Whether this "Riland" was a relation of John Ryland, Jr., is unknown. See Thomas Walter Laquer, *Religion and Respectability: Sunday Schools and Working Class Culture, 1780-1850* (New Haven and London: Yale University Press, 1976) 27.

Rippon, John (1751-1836)—Born into a Baptist family in Tiverton, Rippon arrived at the Bristol Baptist Academy in 1769 and three years later replaced the legendary John Gill as pastor of the Baptist church at Carter Lane, Southwark, where he remained the rest of his life. Unlike Gill, however, Rippon was an evangelical Calvinist after the model of Andrew Fuller and John Ryland, Jr. He became one of the leading Baptist figures in London during his long tenure at Carter Lane, which eventually relocated to New Park Street in 1833, where C. H. Spurgeon would later preach. One of Rippon's early achievements was his work as editor of the *Baptist Annual Register* from 1790 to 1802, the first periodical to chronicle the activities of the Particular Baptists and their involvement in the evangelical revival in England and America, as well as in India and Sierra Leone through the work of the BMS. Rippon was also a well known hymn writer, with his *Selection of Hymns* (1787) going through twenty-seven editions in his lifetime. He was the Baptist Union's first chairman in 1813, and was a consistent advocate of Baptist unity. He also published a work on the life of John Gill (1838), as well as a short history of Bristol Academy. See Ken R. Manley, *Redeeming Love Proclaim: John Rippon and the Baptists*, Studies in Baptist History and Thought, vol. 12 (Carlisle: Paternoster, 2004); Sharon James, "John Rippon (1751-1836)," ed. Haykin, in *The British Particular Baptists*, 2:57-75; *DEB*.

Roberts, Thomas (1780-1841)—Roberts attended Bristol Academy, 1798-1799. He eventually succeeded John Sharp as pastor of the Baptist congregation in the Pithay in Bristol in 1807 and remained there the rest of his life, moving the church to King Street in 1817. He was an immensely popular preacher and a favorite of Samuel Taylor Coleridge. As J. G. Fuller writes, "On Mr. Robert's settling in Bristol, it very soon appeared that he was quite adequate to the position to which he had been called. The congregation very quickly increased, until at length it was usual for the meetinghouse to be crowded to overflowing, every standing-place even being occupied. Neither did his preaching please the majority merely. As a striking instance in proof of the contrary, it may be mentioned that the late highly-gifted and accomplished Mr. Coleridge, being repeatedly a hearer, more than once expressed the high admiration which he felt, assuring a gentleman from whom we had the fact, that Mr. Roberts was the only extemporary preacher he had ever listened to with pleasure . . ." See J. G Fuller, *A Memoir of the Rev. Thomas Roberts, M.A. Pastor of the Baptist Church in King Street, Bristol: With an Enlarged History of the Church* (London: Houlston and Stoneman, 1842) 27-28.

Robinson, Edward (1794-1863)—Robinson was a prominent biblical scholar and prolific author. A graduate of Hamilton College in 1816, he began his academic career as an instructor of Hebrew at Andover Theological Seminary (1823-1826). After four years of study abroad, mostly in Germany, he returned to Andover, becoming founding editor of the *Biblical Repository*. He came to New York in 1837 as the chair of biblical studies at the newly formed New York Theological Seminary (now Union Theological Seminary). Among his works are *A Harmony of the Gospels in Greek* (1834); *A Greek and English Lexicon of the New Testament* (1850); and *Biblical Researches in Palestine, Mount Sinai, and Arabia Petraea* (1841), for which he had taken an extensive leave of absence from the seminary in 1838, returning to New York in the fall of 1840. He also published an American edition of *Calmet's Dictionary of the Holy Bible* (1832) and the posthumous *Physical Geography of the Holy Land* (1865). Robinson was the first American scholar to achieve an international reputation in biblical studies. See Robert T. Handy, *A History of Union Theological Seminary in New York* (New York: Columbia University Press, 1987) 11-14.

Robinson, John—Robinson was a Baptist bookseller, first at Horsleydown, then at Shad, Thames, from 1765-1772. In 1765 he published John Gill's *Baptism a Divine Commandment*, which he followed with a second edition in 1766. He also sold Samuel Stennett's funeral sermon on the death of John Gill (1771). He was a member at Carter Lane and was for many years an officer of the Particular Baptist Fund. See Horsleydown and Carter Lane Church Book, f. 22.

Robinson, Robert (1735-1790)—By the late 1770s, as a result of the popularity of his writings, Robinson (Baptist minister at St. Andrew's Street, Cambridge, 1759-1790) had become one of the more influential and controversial Baptist ministers in England, both in matters of church polity and political dissent. His close friendships in the 1780s with Cambridge Socinians William Frend and Robert Tyrwhitt (both of Jesus College) and the former Particular Baptist turned Unitarian George Dyer of Emmanuel College, as well as his appreciation of the brilliant Unitarian Joseph Priestley, led many Baptists and former Evangelical friends of Robinson to consider him dangerously close to adopting a Unitarian position on the nature of Christ and man. An outspoken political reformer, Robinson was a founding member of the Society for Constitutional Information (1780), an important arm of the radical reform movement in England. Among his writings are *Arcana: or the Principles of the Late Petitioners to Parliament for Relief in the Matter of Subscription* (1774), *A Plea for the Divinity of our Lord Jesus Christ* (1776), *A Plan of Lectures on the Principles of Nonconformity* (1778), *Christian Submission to Civil Government* (1780), and *The Doctrine of Toleration* (1781), and *Slavery Inconsistent with the Spirit of Christianity* (1788). See Stephen Bernard Nutter, *The Story of the Cambridge Baptists and the Struggle for Religious Liberty* (Cambridge: W. Heffer and Sons, 1912); L. G. Champion, "Robert Robinson: A Pastor in Cambridge," *Baptist Quarterly* 31 (1986-1986): 241-246; *Church Book: St. Andrew's Street*; *DEB*.

Robinson, William (1784-1853)—Robinson and James Chater (1779-1829) arrived as BMS missionaries in India on board the *Criterion* in August 1806, but were ordered to leave during a crackdown on missionary activity by the representatives of the East India Company. Robinson and his wife were originally from Olney. He studied under Sutcliff from June 1804 to July 1805. After working for a time in Dacca, he settled in Bhutan, Bengal, in March 1810. The Robinson's left there in 1813, assisting for a time in the missions in Java and Sumatra. Eventually, Robinson returned to Bengal. By the late 1820s he had lost BMS support, but he continued to promote Baptist missions, working in Dacca until 1839. He buried four wives during his time in Sumatra. Apparently Robinson was too political for Fuller's taste in the tense years prior to the renewal of the East India Charter in 1813. Writing to William Ward on 10 June 1810, Fuller says of Robinson, "His democratical notions of I know not what liberty & equality are utterly unsuitable for a christian missionary." See Stanley, *History*, 54-55, 168; Gravett, *Three Hundred Years*, 27; Cox, *History*, 1:156, 167, 191-192, 202; Fuller to Ward, MSS. BMS, vol. 1, Angus Library, Regent's Park College, Oxford; *DEB.*

Rogers, William (1751-1824)—Born in Rhode Island, Rogers was the first student at College of Rhode Island (now Brown University), studying under James Manning. After his graduation in 1769, he served for a time as principal of an academy at Newport, Rhode Island. In December 1771 he succeeded Morgan Edwards as pastor of the First Baptist Church in Philadelphia, where he was ordained on 31 May 1772. He resigned in 1775 and the next year became a chaplain in the American army, a position he retained until 1781. He preached occasionally and served in various societies, but never served as pastor again. In 1789 he was appointed professor of oratory and English literature at the College of Philadelphia, and in 1792 to its successor, the University of Pennsylvania, where he remained until his retirement in 1811. In 1790 he served as vice-president of the Pennsylvania Society for the Abolition of Slavery. During his years in Philadelphia, he was active in evangelism, politics, and missions, serving in 1816-1817 as a delegate to the Pennsylvania State General Assembly. He served as vice president of the General Missionary Convention and was instrumental in the founding of the American Baptist national organization. Rogers was a frequent correspondent of John Rippon, William Carey, and Samuel Pearce, doing much to promote the Serampore Mission within the Philadelphia Baptist Association and among Baptists throughout America. Rogers welcomed Morgan Rhees to Philadelphia and introduced him to Isaac Backus in June 1795 as "one of our ministers from Wales." Rogers's wife, Hannah, a former member of the society of Friends, died on 10 October 1793, a victim of the yellow fever epidemic in Philadelphia that year. See *Act of Incorporation and Constitution of the Pennsylvania Society, for Promoting the Abolition of Slavery ... Also, a List of Those who have been Elected Members of the Society* (Philadelphia: Merrihew & Thompson, 1860), 16; Hayden, "Kettering 1792 and Philadelphia 1814," 9-11, 17-18; Hywel Davies, "The American Revolution and the Baptist Atlantic," *Baptist Quarterly* 36 (1995-1996): 141-142, 146; *Baptist Annual Register,* 2:57-61; Brackney, ed., *Historical Dictionary*, 357-358; *DEB.*

Romaine, William (1714-1795)—Like Augustus Toplady and John Newton, Romaine was an evangelical Calvinist minister in the Church of England. Influenced by the preaching of George Whitefield in the 1750s, he soon faced significant opposition to his preaching among his fellow Anglican ministers, resulting in the loss of several of his pulpit ministries because of his religious "enthusiasm." He finally settled as vicar of St. Anne's, Blackfriars, in London, in 1766, and remained there until his death in 1795. Romaine joined with John Newton (after his arrival in London in 1780) to become one of the leading voices of the evangelical revival among Anglicans in London. Newton, however, never advocated the more extreme Calvinism that Romaine preached. Among Romaine's writings are *The Life of Faith* (1763), *The Walk of Faith* (1771), and *The Triumph of Faith* (1795). See *DEB*.

Roscoe, William (1753-1831)—Roscoe was born at Mt. Pleasant, Liverpool, and became well known as a literary scholar and art historian. He also possessed a keen interest in botany, specializing in the study of one particular group of plants, the *Scitamineae*. Regarding this species, he was "the first to bring order out of chaos"; as a result, a new order of plants was named after him—*Roscoea*. Roscoe published his researches in *Monandrian Plants of the Order Scitamineae* (1828). He was one of the founders of the Liverpool Botanic Gardens in 1802 and was elected a fellow of the Linnean Society in 1804. Roscoe was also actively involved in the radical politics of the 1790s, maintaining an ardent opposition to the slave trade. He served one year as an M.P. for Liverpool in 1806. He was also one of the founders of the Athenaeum, the Library, and the Royal Institution at Liverpool. He died at Toxteth Park, Liverpool, in 1831. He and Carey corresponded about plants and other matters for a number of years. Their letters, written between 1820 and 1827, can be found in the Liverpool Public Library; copies can also be found in the S. Pearce Carey Collection at the Angus Library, Regent's Park College, Oxford. See H. Stanfield, *Handbook and Guide to the Herbarium Collection in the Public Museums, Liverpool* (Liverpool: The Museum, 1935) 59; Farrer, *William Carey: Missionary and Botanist*, 92.

Rowe, John (1788-1816)—Rowe, from Somersetshire, was baptized at Yeovil in 1807 and entered Bristol Academy in 1810. John Ryland struggled for several years to find a candidate to assist Moses Baker in Jamaica. At the base of a letter from William Wilberforce to Ryland, 19 November 1807, he writes in reference to Jamaica, "I cannot but think it is of great importance for us to send out some one speedily. *I have waited with great anxiety several years for some one to send.*" He would find his man in Rowe. As the Broadmead Church Book notes on 8 December 1813: "John Rowe, a member of the church at Yeovil, late a student in the Academy, who married Sarah Gundry, one of our members, was ordained in our Meeting House by prayer and laying on of hands, in order to his going as a missionary to Jamaica." The Rowes sailed on 31 December 1813 and arrived in Jamaica on 23 February 1814; his ministry, however, was short-lived, as he succumbed to a fever on 27 June 1816. Baker would later say of Rowe, "Though at a place where the most minute parts of his conduct were liable to the severest scrutiny, he conducted himself with such prudence and meekness as, at length, to gain the confidence and respect of the most prejudiced." See Wilberforce-Ryland Correspondence, MS. G.97a., Bristol Baptist College Library; Broadmead Church Book, 1779-1817, f. 345; *Periodical Accounts*, 6:72-73; Clarke, *Memorials*, 18-30; Leslie Brooke, *Baptists in Yeovil: History of the Yeovil Baptist Church* (Bath: Ralph Allen, 2002) 13-14; *DEB*.

Rowe, Joshua (1781-1822)—After his baptism by John Saffery in Salisbury in 1800, Rowe was accepted by the BMS as a missionary to India. After studying at Bristol Academy, he sailed with Richard Mardon, William Moore, and John Biss and their families on 3 January 1804 for India. He worked as secretary to the Serampore Mission for several years, but never mastered Bengali and was eventually removed to make way for J. C. Marshman. He did learn Hindi and some other languages, however. Rowe, along with Eustace Carey and others, supported the BMS in its controversy with the Serampore Mission; his son, Joshua, was nevertheless educated at Serampore College and eventually joined the staff there in 1830. See Cox, *History*, 1:137; *DEB.*

Rowe, William H. (1777-1817)—After completing his studies at Bristol Academy, Rowe was ordained at Redruth in 1803. He itinerated in Cornwall for many years, and was greatly interested in the India missions, naming his son after William Carey. He died in 1817. His final pastorate was at Weymouth, Dorsetshire. A letter from Rowe to his friend, John Saffery, 24 August 1799, written shortly after his arrival as a student at Bristol and Saffery's marriage to Maria Grace Andrews, can be found in the Reeves Collection, R/11/14, Angus Library, Regent's Park College, Oxford. See also *Baptist Magazine* 9 (1817): 186; 10 (1818): 1-9.

Ryland, Benjamin (d. 1832)—Ryland was originally from London and associated in his early days with the Baptist meeting at Cripplegate (under John Reynolds) and the Independent congregation at White Row, Spitalfields (under Edward Hitchin). At some point in the 1780s, he moved to Cambridge and attended St. Andrew's Street, under the ministry of Robert Robinson. In 1791 he removed to Biggleswade, Bedfordshire, where his brother-in-law, James Bowers, had become pastor of the Baptist congregation in November 1786. Robert Robinson delivered Bower's ordination sermon; one of Robinson's members, Richard Foster, had become involved, along with some of his relations, with the Baptist church in Biggleswade the previous year. After settling in Biggleswade, Ryland developed a successful business of general stores (mostly drapery and tailoring) and within a short time became a trustee of the Baptist church. He apparently had absorbed the reform-minded politics of Cambridge associated with St. Andrew's Street for Ryland became a distributor of Benjamin Flower's radical newspaper, *The Cambridge Intelligencer,* in 1793 (Ryland may have known Flower previously, for both would have attended at White Row, Spitalfields, in the 1770s). Apparently, Ryland and Bowers did not agree, and eventually Ryland left the Biggleswade meeting and began attending the church at Potton, under the Rev. R. Whittingham, a curate of the evangelical vicar, John Berridge. Bowers left Biggleswade in 1794 to pastor an Independent congregation in Haverhill, Essex. He was succeeded at Biggleswade by Thomas Mabbott. Ryland may have eventually moved toward Unitarianism, for he subscribed to Mrs. Alice Flowerdew's *Poems* in 1803 (Flowerdew was a member of John Evans's General Baptist congregation at Worship Street). Whether he was a relation of John Ryland, Jr., is unknown. His descendant, Henry Ryland (1856-1924), gained fame as a Pre-Raphaelite painter. See *Universal British Directory*, 2:379; *Baptist Annual Register*, 2:1; Chaplin, *History*, 20-25.

Ryland, John Collett (1723-1792)—Raised in Bourton-on-the-Water and baptized into the Baptist congregation there by Benjamin Beddome, Ryland received his pastoral training at Bristol Academy, 1744-1745. He then spent the next thirteen years as minister of a Baptist congregation at Warwick. In 1759, he moved to Northampton, serving both as pastor of the Baptist church at College Lane and headmaster of the academy. Ryland left Northampton in 1786, turning the church and school over to his son, John Ryland, Jr., and taking up residence in Enfield, where he operated another dissenting academy until his death in 1792. Ryland authored numerous publications during his years in Northampton and Enfield, both in religion and education, including *Essay on the Dignity and Usefulness of Human Learning, Addressed to the Youth of the British Empire in Europe and America* (1769), *Contemplations on the Beauties of Creation (1777), The Character of the Rev. James Hervey, A. M. late rector of Weston Favel in Northamptonshire* (1790), *A Body of Divinity in Miniature, Designed for the Use of the Youth of Great Britain and France* (1790), and *An Address to the Ingenuous Youth of Great-Britain* (1792). For more on J. C. Ryland, see Bagster, *Samuel Bagster of London*; William Newman, *Rylandiana: Reminiscences Relating to the Rev. John Ryland, A.M. of Northampton* (London: G. Wightman, 1835); Stephen Albert Swaine, *Faithful Men; or, Memorials of Bristol Baptist College, and Some of Its Most Distinguished Alumni* (London: Alexander and Shepheard, 1884); Culross, *The Three Rylands*; W. T. Whitley, "J. C. Ryland as Schoolmaster," *Baptist Quarterly* 5 (1930-1931): 141-144; Peter Naylor, "John Collett Ryland (1723-1792)," ed. Haykin, in *The British Particular Baptists*, 1:185-201.

Ryland, John, Jr. (1753-1825)—Trained at the academy in Northampton by his father, John Collett Ryland, the younger Ryland became one of the leading figures among the Particular Baptists of his generation, helping to move most of the denomination into the kind of evangelical Calvinism promoted by his own preaching as well as that of Robert Hall, Sr., Andrew Fuller, and John Sutcliff. Ryland was a precocious student as a child and maintained a keen interest in theological scholarship throughout his life. He succeeded his father as pastor of the church in Northampton in 1785, and in December 1793 moved to Bristol to assume the pastorate of the two congregations at Broadmead, as well as the presidency of the Baptist Academy there. He was one of the founders of the BMS and, after Fuller's death in 1815, became a joint secretary. Through his role as pastor and teacher at Bristol, Ryland became one of the most influential figures in the lives of scores of ministers and missionaries who trained at the Academy. He was also a close friend of two leading evangelical Anglicans of his day who ministered at different times in Olney during his years at Northampton, John Newton and Thomas Scott. Besides his important memoir of Andrew Fuller, Ryland authored numerous short works, sermons, and books, such as *The Duty of Ministers to be Nursing Fathers to the Church* (1796); *The Partiality and Unscriptural Direction of Socinian Zeal* (1801). See J. E. Ryland, *Pastoral Memorials: Selected from the Manuscripts of the late Rev.ᵈ John Ryland, D.D. of Bristol: with a Memoir of the Author*, 2 vols. (London: B. J. Holdsworth,

1826); Grant Gordon, "John Ryland (1753-1825)," ed. Haykin, in *The British Particular Baptists*, 2:77-95; *DEB*.

Ryland, Jonathan Edwards (1796-1866)—The son of John Ryland, Jr., J. E. Ryland served a number of years as a tutor under William Steadman at Horton Academy. He later became well known for his editions of the works of various writers, such as *Pastoral Memorials* (2 vols; 1826-1828), a collection of the writings of his father, John Ryland, Jr.; *The Life and Correspondence of John Foster* (1852); *Memoirs of John Kitto* (1854); and various works by August Neander, Johann Peter Lange, August Tholuck, and Ernst Wilham Hengstenbert.

Saffery, John (1763-1825)—An active supporter of the BMS and popular hymn writer, Saffery served as pastor of the Baptist church at Brown Street, Salisbury, 1790-1825, succeeding Henry Phillips (1720-1789). He was originally from Portsea. His first wife was Elizabeth Horsey, daughter of Joseph Horsey, Baptist minister at Portsea. After her death in 1798, he married Maria Grace Andrews (1772-1858), poet, novelist, and hymn writer, the following year. Saffery was succeeded at Brown Street by his son, Philip (see next entry). See G. A Moore and R. J. Huckle, *Salisbury Baptist Church 1655-2000* (Salisbury: n.p., 2000) 21-27; Brian Talbot, "John Saffery (1763-1825)," ed. Haykin, in *The British Particular Baptists*, 3:43-83; *DEB*.

Saffery, Phillip J. (b. 1803)—P. J. Saffery succeeded his father as pastor of the Baptist church in Salisbury, serving from 1826 to 1836. He may have ministered to a church near London after leaving Salisbury before joining the Baptist church at Waltham Abbey in the early 1840s. About this time he became the field representative for the BMS for the north of England, and in 1843 moved to Leeds, joining the church at South Parade under the ministry of J. E. Giles. As letter 207 demonstrates, Saffery traveled extensively throughout the north of England in the 1840s raising funds for the BMS. Saffery removed to Hammersmith in the early 1850s. Shortly thereafter he ended his relationship with the BMS and became a field representative for the Religious Tract Society. No obituary appeared after his death, the date of which is unknown, but it is sometime in the 1870s, as evidenced by the dates of letters between Saffery and his mother and sister, which can be found in the Saffery Papers, Angus Library, Regent's Park College, Oxford. See W. T. Whitley, ed., *A Baptist Bibliography*, 2 vols. (London: Kingsgate Press, 1916-1922) 2:242; W. Jackson, *One Hundred and Fifty Years of Baptist History at Waltham Abbey* (London: Elliot Stock, [1880]) 15, 17; John Julian, *A Dictionary of Hymnology* (London: John Murray, 1908) 112, 986-997.

Saker, Alfred (1814-1880)—Saker worked as a draughtsman in the Admiralty dockyard at Devonport and was a member of Thomas Horton's congregation. He answered the call to the African Mission after hearing John Clarke and Dr. Prince speak at Horton's church during their tour of England in 1842-1843. Saker and his family sailed, along with Clarke and several other missionaries, on board the *Chilmark* in July 1843, stopping first in Jamaica before reaching their final destination at Fernando Po. Saker would become one of the BMS's more celebrated missionaries of the nineteenth century. He died at Peckham, near London, in 1880. See Payne, *First Generation*, 76-78; Stanley, *History*, 106; *DEB*.

Salmon, Thomas (1800-1854)—Salmon was originally from Norfolk. He served as a Methodist evangelist from 1821 to 1824, after which he became a missionary for the London Missionary Society in Surat, India, from 1825 to 1833. He then returned to England and ministered to Independent churches at Wheathampstead, Hertfordshire (1835-1838) and Coleshill, Warwickshire (1838-1842), before removing to New York, where he died in 1854.

Sandys, John (d. 1803)—Sandys came from the Baptist congregation at Tottlebank. He was a student at J. C. Ryland's Academy at Northampton in the late 1760s and studied in London under William Clarke (with assistance from the Particular Baptist Fund) before entering the ministry. While in London, he attended Clarke's congregation at Unicorn Yard. According to the Unicorn Yard Church Book, he joined on Monday, 11 March 1771, signing the Church Book on 25 June 1772 and on 25 March 1773. He left shortly afterwards to serve as a tutor in John Fawcett's school at Hebden Bridge before supplying as interim pastor for the Baptist congregation in Shrewsbury, just prior to the arrival of John Sutcliff in the summer of 1774. Many in the congregation, however, remained loyal to Sandys, and by January 1775 Sutcliff had resigned. Sandys was then called as pastor early in 1777. An entry in the Unicorn Yard Church Book for 6 April 1777 adds some details concerning Sandys's call: "The Church being stay^d after the Celebration of the Supper a Letter received from the Church, at Shrewsbury, requesting the Dismission of Bro^r John Sandys with a View to take the pastoral care of them was read & assented to & a Letter dismissing him from us then being drawn up & read was sign^d by each Bro^r Present." Sandys remained at Shrewsbury until 1781, erecting a new meetinghouse in Dog Lane while he was there. Sandys did not leave on the best of terms, for some members of his church (in league, unfortunately, with some other Baptist ministers) accused Sandys of improper conduct regarding a £50 note which had been stolen from him during a trip to Birmingham in the fall of 1780. Left destitute by the theft, Sandys received £25.5 from his friend Robert Mosely, a deacon at Cannon Street in Birmingham. Mosely told Sandys to use the funds however he wanted. Sandys inquired of William Clarke, his former tutor in London, if he was responsible for repaying the £50 note to the Shrewsbury church, and Clarke told him he was not. As a result, Sandys, whose salary at Shrewsbury was only £34 a year, used the money for himself, which angered many of his members who believed the money belonged to the church. For the next two years, accusations of impropriety continued to plague Sandys (who was considered as a replacement for James Turner at Cannon Street in Birmingham in 1781). He applied to several London ministers, who, in collaboration with Mosely, cleared Sandys of any misuse of funds, an action that supposedly satisfied the Shrewsbury church. In the meantime, Sandys assisted in churches in Colchester and Adelphi. From 1786 to 1791 he served as pastor of the

Baptist church in Beechen Grove, Watford, Hertfordshire. In 1791 Sandys became Isaac Gould's assistant at Fore Street, Harlow. Not long after his arrival in Harlow, new accusations concerning the Mosely affair surfaced once again, creating an unwelcome distraction for Sandys. In 1793, John Martin, Baptist minister at Grafton Square (later Keppel Street), London, published several letters by Mosely and John Harwood (also a deacon at Cannon Street), as well as letters by Martin himself to Henry Keene, a deacon at Maze Pond, in an effort to clear Sandys's name once and for all. After the death of Isaac Gould in November 1794, Sandys took over pastoral duties at Fore Street, but, as Finch notes, his temperament did not suit many in the congregation; he stayed for less than a year before removing to Hammersmith, where he began a new work at Brentford Park in June 1799. By 1802 he was no longer pastor, which may have been due to declining health, for he died c. 1803. See Unicorn Yard Church Book, f. 214r, f. 219r, f. 222r, f. 237v; Jones, *Autobiography,* 13; Whitley, *Baptists of London,* 108; Thomas Finch, *Brief Biographical Memorials, of the Ministers and Proceedings of the Protestant Dissenting Congregation, of the Baptist Denomination, Harlow, Essex* (Bishop's Stortford: W. Thorogood, 1820) 41-42; G. H. Young and J. W. Barker, *A Short History of Harlow Baptist Church 1662 1962* (Harlow: Harlow Baptist Church, 1962) 10-11; Haykin, *One Heart,* 85-86, 90; *Claremont Baptist Church, Shrewsbury,* 4; Edward Spurrier, *Memorials of the Baptist Church Worshipping at Eld Lane Chapel, Colchester* (Colchester: F. Wright, 1889) 37, 40; R. F. Skinner, *Nonconformity in Shropshire 1662-1816* (Shrewsbury: Wilding & Son, 1964) 25-28; *Baptist Annual Register,* 3:23; John Martin, *The Case of the Rev. John Sandys, a Dissenting Minister, at Harlow, Essex. In Four Letters to Henry Keene, Esquire* (London: J. Martin, Jr., and William Button, 1793); Congregational Library, DWL, MSS. ii. c. 5 and MSS. ii. A. 10, ff. 31-41, for letters by J. C. Ryland and John Sandys, concerning Sandys's application to the Particular Baptist Fund in 1769-1770 for financial assistance during his time of study with William Clarke in London.

Saunders, Alexander (1805-1846)—Saunders was a Baptist layman in London whose brother, John (1806-1859) (after ministering to some churches in London) served as a missionary in Australia, 1834-1848, in loose conjunction with the BMS (he provided his own financial support), the Society being reluctant at that time to sanction mission work among the "non-heathen." The younger Saunders opened the first Baptist chapel in Sydney on 23 September 1836 and the church was constituted that December. Always ecumenical in his approach to missions, Saunders also served as the ministerial agent for the LMS in Sydney from 1838 to 1840, which possibly provides some poignancy to his brother's letter to Angus (see letter 163). In the early 1820s, both brothers became members of the Baptist church at Camberwell, under the ministry of Edward Steane. Letters between the two brothers can be found in the Saunders Letterbook, Mitchell Library, State Library of New South Wales. One letter from Alexander to John, dated 17 February 1838, appealing for funds for Baptist churches in Australia, appeared in the *Baptist Magazine* 30 (1838): 127-128. A letter from John in Sydney appeared in the *Missionary Herald* (May 1843): 284-285. Saunders had sent £50 from his church for the Jubilee Fund, proposing that "by this act the chain of love is made to encircle the globe: Australia, the last link is enwreathed with Africa, either India, America, and all-beloved home." Alexander Saunders collected £18 for the BMS in November 1840 and contributed £5 in April 1841. He served as a deacon in the church at Camberwell, an officer for the Bath Society for Aged Ministers, and secretary and treasurer of a fund formed for promoting the sell of the *Selection Hymn Book*, produced for the benefit of widows and orphans of Baptist ministers. In 1844 the proceeds enabled Saunders to transfer £180 to the fund. See *Baptist Magazine* 34 (1842): 665; 35 (1843): 655; 38 (1846): 236; 36 (1844): 423; *Missionary Herald* (January 1841): 45; (July 1841): 371; J. D. Bollen, "English Australian Baptist Relations, 1830-1860," *Baptist Quarterly* 25 (1973-1974): 292-296; B. G. Wright, "Saunders, John (1806-1859)," ed. Douglas Pike and John Ritchie, in *Australian Dictionary of Biography*, (Melbourne: Melbourne University Press, 1967), 2:418; Ken R. Manley, *From Woolloomooloo to "Eternity": A History of Australian Baptists*, 2 vols. Studies in Baptist History and Thought, vol. 16.1-2 (Milton Keynes UK: Paternoster Press, 2006) 1:23-35.

Saunders, Samuel (1780-1835)—Saunders spent his early years in Clapham; he was baptized in a Baptist church there (under the ministry of John Ovington) in 1801. He soon entered Bristol Academy (with the assistance of Joseph Hughes at Battersea) and in 1803 was ordained at Penzance, Cornwall. He did not stay long at Penzance, however, for after the death of John Kingdon, the church at Badcox Lane in Frome called him in 1806 to be their minister. Saunders left Frome in 1826 to become pastor of the Baptist church at Byrom Street in Liverpool, remaining there until his death in 1835. See Charles M. Birrell, "Memoir of the Late Rev. Samuel Saunders," *Baptist Magazine* 32 (1840): 1-5.

Savage, James (d. 1796)—Savage was the BMS's India House counselor. He also was the Secretary of the Good Samaritan Society in Shoe Lane for many years, and as a result was instrumental in the calling and placing of John Fountain as a missionary for the BMS in India. As S. Pearce Carey writes, "[John] Fountain, an eager helper of his Social Mission in Shoe Lane, off Fleet Street, had so impressed him by his versatile vivacity that he [Savage] offered to send him to India as a lay helper to Carey, to which Fountain eagerly agreed. Alas! it was all frustrated by Mr. Savage's sudden death" (in 1796—see letter 52). See Carey, *William Carey*, 168.

Scamp, William (1774-1860)—Scamp was originally from Devonport, Devon. After studying with David Bogue at Gosport, he came to Havant, where he was ordained in 1803 and remained as pastor of the Independent church there until his death in 1846.

Scott, James (1710-1783)—Born in Berwickshire, Scott attended Edinburgh University, 1728-1729, after which he served as a private tutor for several years. He began ministering to Independent congregations in 1739, first at Stainton, Westmoreland, then at Horton-in-Craven, Yorkshire (1741-1751), Tockholes, Lancashire (1751-1754), and lastly at the Upper Meeting at Heckmondwike (1754-1783). He was also the tutor at the Academy there (the leading institution of the Northern Education Society) from 1756-1783. Some of Scott's early students at Heckmondwike were Thomas Waldegrave, Timothy Priestley, and Richard Plumbe. According to Josiah Bull's biography of John Newton, "In the year 1756, at the suggestion, and through the influence of some friends of the gospel truth in London, who were anxious to stay the progress of Socinian and Arian opinions then prevailing in Yorkshire, Mr. Scott was led to superintend the studies of pious and orthodox young men, who might thus be prepared for the work of the ministry in that part of the country. Labouring in this good work till the year 1783, when he died, Mr. Scott was the means of introducing more than sixty ministers into the church of Christ. The institution thus originated still continues, and flourishes at the Rotherham College." See Josiah Bull, *John Newton of Olney and St. Mary Woolnoth: An Autobiography and Narrative* (London: Religious Tract Society, 1868) 96; Miall, *Congregationalism in Yorkshire*, 146-157, 273, 284, and 346; Nightingale, *Lancashire Nonconformity*, 2:1289; *DEB.*

Sharman, Edward—In September 1781, Sharman, along with William and Andrew Pell, formed a new Baptist church at Guilsborough, northwest of Northampton. Later, Sharman ministered at the Moulton church in the 1790s after Carey's removal to Leicester. He signed the minutes of the Northamptonshire Association for 31 May 1792, the meeting at which Carey preached his famous sermon on missions. Carey and Sharman had also worked together on the Leicestershire Committee of Protestant Ministers for the repeal of the Test and Corporation Acts in 1789-1790. Sharman was preaching at Moulton in 1794 but by 1798 he had been replaced by John Barker and was no longer a Particular Baptist. Andrew Fuller, writing to William Carey in Bengal on 2 May 1796, notes that Sharman, now at Cottesbrooke, had become a Unitarian and recently published a pamphlet against the divinity of Christ; he had also influenced several other Baptists friends known to Fuller and Carey. Fuller writes, "I reckon, though, it be a blundering performance, it must be answered, and if it be we will send you the book & its answer together, He has lately lost his wife. Some think him touched with insanity." See *Baptist Annual Register*, 2:10; 3:28; Fuller Correspondence, 1793-1815, MSS. BMS, Vol. 1, Angus Library, Regent's Park College, Oxford.

Sharp, John (1741-1805)—After ministering to Baptist congregations in Oakam (1770-1785) and Manchester (1785-1797), Sharp assumed pastoral duties at the Baptist meeting at the Pithay in Bristol on 21 April 1797, first as co-pastor with John Tommas until the latter's death in August 1800, and then as senior pastor until his own death in November 1805. See *DEB.*

Shepherd, John (1764-1836)—Shepherd came to Liverpool from Manchester, where he had been working as a horticulturalist. He was a close friend of Dr. John Bostock (see letter 119) and William Roscoe. In 1800, Dr. James Currie (1756-1805) and Dr. John Rutter, along with Roscoe and Bostock, formed a committee for establishing the Liverpool Botanic Gardens, and in 1803 the Garden officially opened, with Roscoe as president and Shepherd as curator. Widely known as an expert cultivator, Shepherd would remain curator until his death in 1836. The Liverpool Botanic Gardens became a model emulated from Philadelphia to St. Petersburg. Shepherd and William Carey corresponded for over 20 years, exchanging plants on a regular basis. "By 1820," Stanfield argues in his book on the Liverpool museums, "Carey had made large contributions to the Botanic Garden. Carey and Roscoe were also friends and exchanged plants." At one point (c. 1820) Shepherd sent Carey over 1000 grafted fruit trees, all of which survived. The Garden also contains collections sent by William Roxburgh (1751-1815), another friend of Carey. F. A. Cox quotes from a paper by Jonathan Carey, appended to Eustace Carey's *Memoir* of William Carey, in which Jonathan writes of his father's passion for plants: "In objects of nature, my father was exceedingly curious. His collection of mineral ores and other subjects of natural history, was extensive, and obtained his particular attention in seasons of leisure and recreation. The science of botany was his constant delight and study; and his fondness for his garden remained to the last. No one was allowed to interfere in the arrangements of this his favourite retreat, and it is here he enjoyed his most pleasant moments of secret devotion and meditation. The garden formed the best and rarest collection of plants in the east, to the extension of which, by his correspondence with persons of eminence in Europe and other parts of the world, his attention was constantly directed; and in return, he supplied his correspondents with rare collections from the east. On this science he frequently gave lectures, which were well attended, and never failed to prove interesting. His publication of 'Roxburgh's Flora Indica' is a standard work with botanists." See Stanfield, *Handbook*, 39; Cox, *History*, 1:377; Annie Lee, "John Shepherd," *Lancashire and Cheshire Naturalist* 17 (1925): 157-160, 198-200; Farrer, *William Carey: Missionary and Botanist*, 91.

Sheppard, John (1785-1879)—Sheppard was a significant Baptist author and layman from Frome, Somerset, where Sheppards had lived since the late 17th c. After finishing school in 1800, he began working in the woolen trade (his family were prosperous factory owners and merchants) and in 1806 he, along with his widowed mother, joined the Baptist congregation at Sheppard's Barton, Frome, where many of his relatives worshiped. At that time the church was led by John Foster (1770-1843), who had succeeded Job David as pastor in 1804. Foster and Sheppard would maintained a life-long friendship. Sheppard inherited enough of a fortune from his uncle to cease working and enroll at the University of Edinburgh, where he studied medicine, philosophy and Hebrew. While at Edinburgh, he became friends with Thomas Chalmers and Pinkerton the antiquary. In 1816 and 1817, he toured parts of Europe and studied briefly at Gottingen. From 1823 until his death he devoted himself to religious writing, lay preaching, and foreign travel. He died at Frome on 30 April 1879. His major works include: *Athaliah*, translated from Racine (1815); *Letters on a Tour of France* (1817); *Thoughts Preparative to or Persuasive to Private Devotion* (1823; *An Autumn Dream* (a long poem) (1837); *A Cursory View of the State of Religion in France* (1838); *On Dreams* (1847); *On Trees, their Uses and Biography* (1848); *The Foreign Sacred Lyre* (1857); and *The Christian Harp*

(1858). See T. G. Rooke, "Memoir of John Sheppard," in *Thoughts Prepara-tive to or Persuasive to Private Devotion,* by John Sheppard, 5-34 (London: Religious Tract Society, 1881); Ryland, *Life and Correspondence;* Timothy Whelan, "Thomas Poole's 'Intimations of Immortality' in a Letter to John Sheppard, February 1837," *Romanticism* 11 (2005): 199-223; *DEB.*

Sherring, Richard B.—A man of considerable wealth, Sherring, along with his wife, Hester, joined Broadmead Baptist Church in Bristol on 6 January 1820; by 1825 he had become a deacon. He was a prominent Baptist lay-man in denominational affairs and a generous benefactor of the BMS, contributing £100 in April 1842, another £100 in November of that year to the Kettering collection of the Jubilee Fund, and £1000 to the Bristol collec-tion that same month. At a Jubilee meeting in Bristol in June 1842, in which William Knibb was the featured speaker, Sherring pledged £500 toward the new mission in Western Africa. In September 1842, he gave £150 for the purchase of the proposed schooner for the work in Fernando Po. At anoth-er meeting in London in January 1843, Sherring further donated another £100, for a total in less than one year of £1950. He recognized literary greatness as well, for in 1844 he also donated to the BMS a bust of Robert Hall and John Foster, the complete works of Milton, and two volumes from the library of Samuel Taylor Coleridge. He served on the committee of the Bath Society for Aged Ministers in 1844 as well as that of the Baptist Col-leges and Educational Institutions. As late as 1857 he was serving as an honorary member of the BMS Committee. See *Missionary Herald* (July 1842): 402; (August 1842): 453; (November 1842): 615; (January 1843): 60; (March 1843): 180; (August 1844): 439; *Baptist Magazine* 36 (1844): 658, 659; 49 (1857): 803. Some letters between Sherring and Andrew Leslie can be found at Bristol Baptist College Library, shelfmark Z.c.29. (My thanks to Roger Hayden for information on Sherring's Broadmead mem-bership.)

Short, Charles (d. 1802)—Short was an agent for the East India Company at Debhatta, about forty miles from Calcutta. Upon Carey's arrival in India, Short offered the group his home as a temporary habitation. Short would later marry Dorothy Carey's sister, Catherine Plackett (who had traveled with the Carey's to India), on 15 November 1794. Though a Deist when he met Carey, Short would later be converted and spend his remaining years assisting in the work of the BMS in India. He and his wife left India in 1798, due to Short's declining health, but he returned, much to Carey's surprise, in 1801, only to die the next year. Catherine Short returned from India and settled at Clipston, remaining there until her death. See Payne and Allan, *Clipston Baptist Church,* 11.

Simmons, John—Simmons ministered for a time in Wigan, Lancashire, then at Braunston, Northamptonshire, throughout the 1790s. He was instrumental in bringing the Braunston church into the Northamptonshire Baptist Asso-ciation in 1790. His son, John Edmund Simmons, studied at Bristol and eventually ministered at Stoney Stratford, Buckinghamsire, from 1823 to 1830, and then at the Union Chapel, Bluntisham, Huntingtonshire. He wrote the circular letter for the Northamptonshire Association in 1823, 1843, and

1857. See *Congregational Magazine* (1831): 818; *Congregational Magazine* (1835): 817; T. S. H. Elwyn, *Northamptonshire Baptist Association* (London: Carey Kingsgate Press, 1964) 102-104; *A Brief Record of the Stony Stratford Baptist Church, 1767-1957* (Northampton: n.p., 1957) 16.

Skinner, William (d. 1834)—Skinner was a prominent banker in Stephen Street, Bristol, residing for many years at Ashley Place. He was a leading member of the Independent congregation (the "Little Church") that worshiped with the Baptist congregation at Broadmead (see letter 80). He signed as one of the Brethren of the Independent congregation in the calling of Robert Hall as assistant minister to Broadmead on 12 October 1783. Mary Skinner, his wife, signed as one of the "sisters." Many years later, when the congregation at Broadmead during the ministry of Robert Hall decided to organize more completely as a separate church body, the members of the Independent congregation met together on 20 January 1830 and chose two deacons—William Skinner and Charles Reed. A later entry, for 24 June 1834, reads: "Died Mr Wm Skinner an aged and highly respected Deacon of this Church, who after a long and exemplary Christian course, was gathered like a shock of Corn, fully ripe for his Masters use" (f. 22). Skinner was a solid supporter of the BMS, joining with two other men in January 1809 to provide funds for three missionaries independently of the Society. See Broadmead Church Book, 1779-1817, f. 38; Broadmead Independent Church Book, 1830-1853 (MS., Bristol Record Office, Bd/M2/2), f. 3; Cox, *History*, 1:181, 227, 299-300; see also a letter from Kreeshnoo in Calcutta to Skinner in Bristol, June 1812, in *Periodical Accounts*, 5:110-113.

Smith, James—Smith became a deacon at the Baptist meeting at Little Wild Street, Lincoln's-Inn Fields, London, in 1773, becoming a leading figure in the church and serving for many years as one of the treasurers of the Baptist Fund. See Woollacott, *Brief History*, 41.

Smith, James (1770-1850)—A native of Cornwall, Smith was called to the ministry at seventeen. After studying at Bristol Academy, he began his pastoral work at Pershore, Worcestershire. After a brief stint at Alcester, Warwickshire, he removed to Astwood, Worcestershire, in 1813, where he remained the rest of his life. An entry in the BMS Committee Minutes on 17 February 1842 notes that Smith contributed £50, but that was probably from a collection in his church. In February 1844, his contribution was only £1. See BMS Committee Minutes, Vol. H (Oct. 1841-Dec. 1842), f. 78; *Missionary Herald* (April 1844): 220.

Smith, James (1781-1839)—Smith was the third itinerant minister hired by the Essex Baptist Association for Home Missions (formed in 1796). The first two itinerants were James Pilkington at Rayleigh and William Bolton at Thorpe le Soken. Smith began his work at Bures in 1802, and then spent some time at Rochford Hundred, Great Wakering (where he opened a day school), Barling (where his preaching led to a mob scene instigated by the local magistrate), and finally at Ilford in 1808, a church founded in 1801 by members of the Harlow and Mile End congregations. Smith replaced John Hutchings and remained at Ilford until 1834. At the time of his arrival in Ilford, no established Anglican work existed, causing fears among some that all of Ilford might become overwhelmingly Baptist due to Smith's efforts. His practice of open communion, however, led some members to succeed and form the Ebenezer Strict Baptist Church. For the most part, though, Smith's ministry at Ilford was successful, with membership reaching nearly 100 by 1830. Smith was also engaged in considerable village preaching while at Ilford, assisting in the founding of the Loughton church, led by one of Smith's members, John King. In 1834, Smith removed to the Ebenezer Chapel, Shoreditch, London (in 1836 it became the Providence Chapel, Hackney Road), where Smith preached until his death in 1839. See Doris Witard, *Bibles in Barrels: A History of Essex Baptists* (N.p.: Essex Baptist Association, 1962) 57; Frank H. Smith, *The Story of Ilford (High Road) Baptist Church 1801-1951* (Ilford: C. W. Clark, [1951]) 10-11; Couling, "Biographical Dictionary, 1800-1875."

Smith, John—A student of John Sutcliff at Olney, Smith ministered to the Baptist church at Burton-on-Trent, Staffordshire, not far from Tutbury. Smith joined the Olney church on 16 April 1807, coming from the Baptist church at Boston (at that time dissolved). He was dismissed to the church at Burton-on-Trent on 23 February 1809 (see letter 80) and ordained on 20 May 1809. He is probably the same John Smith who ministered to the Baptist church at Ecton, Northamptonshire, from 1827 to 1835 (and possibly longer). See *Baptist Magazine* 1 (1809): 341; 27 (1835): 549-561; Olney Church Book, ff. 97, 101.

Smith, Opie—A wealthy brewer of "porter, beer, and brandy" in Horse Street, Smith was a member of the Particular Baptist congregation at Somerset Street in Bath for some fifty years and a deacon for more than thirty years, serving under the ministries of Robert Parsons (1752-1789) and John Paul Porter (1791-1832). He was a great benefactor of churches in Cornwall and assisted for many years with the financial support of the Western Baptist Association and its efforts to send itinerant preachers into Cornwall, especially Redruth, Penzance, and Helston. In 1803 he purchased Saffron Court in Falmouth, reviving the nearly defunct Baptist interest there and providing the stimulus for a new chapel, which was completed in early 1804. Thomas Griffin, an open communion Baptist, was called to be its first pastor. Robert Redding, at that time the Baptist minister at Truro and a closed communionist, had assisted the congregation prior to Griffin. Griffin remained at Falmouth until 1814. See *Universal British Directory*, 2:108; Fereday, *Story of the Falmouth Baptists*, 65-69; *The Case of the Baptist Church, Meeting in Somerset Street, Bath* (London: n.p., 1829) 13-14; Price, "Early Years of the Baptist Union," 171.

Smith, Thomas—After ministering to the Baptist church at Shipston-on-Stour, Worcestershire, Smith pastored the Baptist congregation at Tiverton, 1807-1812. While at Tiverton, he commenced the *Baptist Magazine* in 1809, which eventually led to his removal to London in 1812, where he continued for some time as editor of the *Magazine*. His interest in the BMS and missions in general was reflected in *The History and Origin of the Missionary Societies: Containing Faithful Accounts of the Voyages, Travels, Labours, and Successes of the Various Missionaries who have been sent out, for the Purpose* *of Evangelizing the Heathen, and Other Unenlightened Nations, in Different Parts of the Habitable Globe* (London: Printed for Thomas Kelly & Richard Evans by Charles Baynes, 1824-1825).

Soul, Joseph (1805-1881)—Soul was a leader within the abolitionist movement of the mid-nineteenth century. In 1840 he addressed an important convention of the Anti-Slavery Society and was included in Benjamin Robert Haydon's famous portrait of that event. Besides his duties with the British and Foreign Anti-Slavery Society, he served for more than thirty years as secretary of the Orphan Working School, Haverstock Hill, North London. See *Missionary Herald* (December 1843): 658.

Soule, Israel May (1806?-1873)—After studying at Stepney and ministering for a time at Lewes, Sussex, Soule succeeded Joseph Hughes as pastor of the Baptist church at Battersea in 1834. He remained there until his death in 1873. He became a member the London Baptist Board in 1838. See *Baptist Magazine* 33 (1841): 636; Couling, "Biographical Dictionary, 1800-1875."

Stanger, Jr., William Wright (1809-1877)—The son of William Stanger and grandson of the Rev. John Stanger (1743-1823), Baptist minister at Bessels Green (1766-1823), W. W. Stanger was a member of William Newman's congregation at Bow. During the mid-1840s, Stanger served as the chief accountant for the BMS (which explains his presence in several letters in Part Six of this volume). Stanger was also active in the work of the Bible Society. See J. H. Y. Briggs, "Chapel-goers, Chapels and the Local Community," *Baptist Quarterly* 33 (1989-1990): 61; Minutes of the BMS Committee, vols. H-J (1841-1847), Angus Library, Regent's Park College, Oxford.

Steadman, William (1764-1837)—Raised in Shropshire, Steadman, after completing his studies at Bristol Academy, became pastor of the Baptist congregation at Broughton, Hampshire, in 1789. During his time at Broughton, he developed a close friendship with John Saffery, pastor at Brown Street in Salisbury. In 1797 the two men itinerated throughout the West Country, primarily in Cornwall, as part of a new home missionary effort by the Particular Baptists. Steadman left Broughton for Plymouth Dock in 1798. In 1805 he removed to Bradford, Yorkshire, to become the first president of the new academy at Bradford and pastor of the Baptist congregation there. Though his heart lay with missions and the work of the BMS, Steadman's eyesight and domestic situation would never have allowed him to serve in that capacity. He became secretary of the Yorkshire and Lancashire Association, and actively supported the BMS and the Bible Society. During his tenure at Horton Academy, over 150 students entered the academy. He was awarded an honorary D.D. by Brown University in 1815. See Steadman, *Memoir of the Rev. William Steadman*; Walter Fancutt, "William Steadman's Hampshire Years," *Baptist Quarterly* 16 (1955-1956): 365-369; Sharon James, "Revival and Renewal in Baptist Life: The Contribution of William Steadman (1764-1837)," *Baptist Quarterly* 37 (1997-1998): 263-282; idem, "William Steadman (1764-1837)," ed. Haykin, in *The British Particular Baptists*, 2:163-181; *DEB*.

Steane, Edward (1798-1882)—In 1823 Steane began his long pastorate of the Baptist congregation at Denmark Place Chapel in Camberwell, where W. B.

Gurney was a member. After serving as one of the editors of the *New Baptist Miscellany*, Steane served as secretary of the Baptist Union from 1835 to 1882 and as President in 1860. He was instrumental in the founding of the Evangelical Alliance in 1846, serving as the first editor of its periodical, *Evangelical Christendom*. He published numerous sermons and other works during his long ministry at Camberwell, including *Constitutional Principles of the Christian Church* (1838); funeral sermons on W. H. Pearce, BMS missionary in India, and the Rev. John Dyer, Secretary of the BMS; and *Memoir of the Life of Joseph Gutteridge, Esq. of Denmark Hill, Surrey* (1850). See J. H. Y. Briggs, *The English Baptists of the Nineteenth Century* (Didcot: Baptist Historical Society, 1994) 233-234; *DEB*.

Stennett, Joseph (1692-1758)—The eldest son of Joseph Stennett (1663-1713), influential pastor of the seventh-day Baptist congregation at Pinners' Hall, London, the younger Stennett, after a time as pastor of the Baptist meeting in Exeter, came to the congregation at Little Wild Street in 1737, where he remained until his death. His son, Samuel Stennett (1727-1795), succeeded him as pastor. See B. A. Ramsbottom, "The Stennetts," ed. Haykin, in *The British Particular Baptists*, 1: 133-143.

Stennett, Joseph (d. 1824)—The son of Samuel Stennett (see above), Joseph was raised in his father's congregation at Little Wild Street in London. He attended Bristol Academy in 1780 before becoming a Ward Scholar at Aberdeen (1781-1784). He assisted in his father's church at Little Wild Street until 1798, when he became pastor of the Baptist congregation at Coate, Wiltshire, succeeding Thomas Dunscombe. He left Coate in 1810 to pastor at Calne; he retired to Bristol in 1824. See B. A. Ramsbottom, "The Stennetts," ed. Haykin, in *The British Particular Baptists*, 1:133-143.

Steevens, Thomas (1745-1802)—Steevens was a native of Northampton, but was baptized at Devonshire Square in London in July 1771 by John McGowan. He came to Colchester in late December 1773, and was ordained there in August 1774, remaining as pastor until his death in 1802. During his tenure the church absorbed the General Baptists and the Sabbatarians in the area. In September 1791 the Colchester church consisted of 112 members. See Spurrier, *Memorials*, 28-38, 49.

Stevens, John (1776-1847)—Stevens, originally from Northamptonshire, came to St. Neots in 1799 after preaching at Oundle for two years. On 1 October 1800 a church was formed with 13 members. He resigned in 1805 and removed to the Baptist church in Boston, Lincolnshire (see letter 80). In 1811 he moved to London to pastor a Strict Baptist congregation meeting in Grafton Street. Stevens moved his congregation to York Street, Westminster, in 1813, and in 1824 to a new building in Meard's Court off Wardour Street, following a split in his congregation at York Street. He subscribed to the BMS in 1804-1805. As John Briggs notes (from private correspondence with this writer), Stevens's career, in which he moved from his origins among the Particular Baptists to a position adhering to the principles of the Strict Baptists, is a good illustration of how the Strict Baptist position came to be defined within the denomination during the first half of the nineteenth century. See *Biblical Magazine* 3 (1811): 460; *Periodical Accounts*,

3:137; *Manual of the Baptist Denomination for the Year 1848* (London: Houlston and Stoneman, 1848) 45; Whitley, *Baptists of London*, 134.

Stillman, Samuel (1737-1807)—Originally from Philadelphia, Stillman pastored the First Baptist Church in Boston, 1765-1805. He was instrumental in the formation of Rhode Island College in 1764, as well as an organizer and officer of the Massachusetts Baptist Missionary Society, the first such society in America. In 1788 he served as a representative from Boston to the Constitutional Convention, and in 1799 was invited to give the eulogy at George Washington's funeral. Among his publications are *Thoughts on the French Revolution* (1794) and *Select Sermons on Doctrinal and Practical Subjects* (1808). See *DEB*.

Stuart, Charles (1746-1826)—A parish minister in the Church of Scotland at Cramond, Stuart resigned over doctrinal differences in the late 1770s and joined the Scotch Baptist congregation in Edinburgh. He was greatly influenced by reading Archibald McLean's *Defence of Believers' Baptism*, and later became a close friend of Andrew Fuller and an active supporter of the BMS. He edited the *Edinburgh Quarterly Magazine* from 1798 to 1800. In 1800-1801 he subscribed £2.2 to the BMS, and in 1804-1805 was heavily involved in procuring funds in Scotland for the translation work at Serampore. See Yuille, *History*, 49, 306; *Periodical Accounts*, 2:207; 3:147; *DEB*.

Sturgeon, Thomas (d. 1846)—Sturgeon joined the Baptist church at Waltham Abbey in 1829. For about ten years he was a faithful layman, working with the Sunday school and house-to-house visitation. He removed to Bilston in 1840 to become master of the British school there. After one year, he resigned to accept an appointment as a BMS missionary to the new mission at Fernando Po, sailing on the *Palmyra* on 2 December 1841 and arriving in West Africa in April 1842. The *Missionary Herald* published numerous letters by Sturgeon in 1842-1844, in which he detailed the progress of the mission at Fernando Po. He quickly established a school, educating approximately seventy scholars by the end of 1842. Sturgeon died, however, after serving just four years in Africa. See *Missionary Herald* (August 1842): 452-453; *Missionary Herald* (October 1842): 558-559; (February 1844): 105; Cox, *History*, 2:379, 395.

Summers, William—A London tinman, Summers became a close friend and correspondent of Samuel Pearce in the 1780s, accompanying him in 1796 on his preaching tour of Ireland for the Evangelical Society. This was the last of many preaching tours that Pearce engaged in, often for the purpose of collecting money for the BMS. Summers was a steady supporter of the BMS, subscribing £1.1 in 1800-1801 and in 1804-1805. See *Periodical Accounts*, 2:207; 3:136; *Universal British Directory*, 1/2:303.

Sutcliff, John (1752-1814)—Born in Yorkshire, Sutcliff was influenced as a young man by John Fawcett and Dan Taylor. He studied at Bristol Academy, 1772-1774, serving as a supply preacher at Trowbridge during part of his time at Bristol. After preaching at Shrewsbury for six months and Cannon Street, Birmingham, for another six months, he accepted the pastorate of the Baptist congregation at Olney early in 1775, remaining there until his death in 1815. Influenced, as were so many other English Baptist ministers at this time, by the writings of Jonathan Edwards, he reprinted Edwards's *Humble Attempt* (Northampton, 1789) and led the effort to promote an evangelical Calvinism among the Particular Baptist churches of the Midlands. He was a founding member of the BMS Committee, which explains why so many of his letters in this collection involve BMS matters, especially the letters from Andrew Fuller and John Ryland, Jr. He had a large library of his own and was actively involved in promoting printed Baptist materials throughout the world. He kept a "residential academy" for many years at Olney, much like Fawcett's in Hebden Bridge. See *Sutcliff Centenary. Baptist Chapel, Olney, June 22nd, 1914*, (Northampton: n.p., 1914; Michael A. G. Haykin, *One Heart*; idem, "'A Habitation of God, through the Spirit': John Sutcliff (1752-1814) and the Revitalization of the Calvinistic Baptists in the late Eighteenth Century," *Baptist Quarterly* 34 (1991-1992): 304-319; idem, "John Sutcliff (1752-1814)," ed. Haykin, *British Particular Baptists*, 3:21-41; "Sutcliff's Academy at Olney," *Baptist Quarterly* 4 (1928-1929): 276-279; Hayden, *Continuity and Crisis*, 246; *DEB*.

Swain, Joseph (1761-1796)—Originally from Birmingham, Swain came to London as an apprentice to his brother, an engraver. He was baptized by John Rippon at Carter Lane on 11 May 1783, and shortly thereafter called to the ministry, organizing the Baptist meeting at Walworth in late 1791. He was ordained there on 8 February 1792. The church grew considerably and the chapel was enlarged three times during his short tenure, increasing from 27 to over 200 members. He was the author of several works, including *Experimental Essays on Divine Subjects, in Verse and Prose, and Hymns for Social Worship* (1791); *Walworth Hymns* (1792); and *Redemption: A Poem* (1797). See *DEB*.

Swigle [Swiegle], Thomas Nicholas (d. 1811)—Swigle was a black Baptist minister in Jamaica who preached to a congregation of 700 near Kingston, laboring for many years in association with Moses Baker and some other black preachers in Jamaica before the arrival of the BMS missionaries. Swigle had been baptized by George Liele and began as his assistant and deacon. In 1797 he was being assisted in his church-planting work in Kingston by two of his own members, James Pascall and John Gilbert. Several letters by Swigle to Rippon were printed in the *Baptist Annual Register* between 1793 and 1802. In 1802 Swigle was prohibited for a time from preaching by the passage of a bill in Jamaica that made it illegal, under penalty of hard labor and flogging, for dissenters to instruct any person in a state of slavery. Eventually, the bill was overturned. See *Baptist Annual Register*, 3:212-214; Cox, *History*, 2:18-19; Clarke, *Memorials*, 30-31; Ernest A. Payne, "Baptist Work in Jamaica before the Arrival of the Missionaries," *Baptist Quarterly* 7 (1934-1935): 23-24.

Taylor, Charles (1756-1823)—Taylor became well-known for his edition of *Calmet's Great Dictionary of the Holy Bible* (1797), which went through numerous English and American editions, including an edition in Charlestown, Massachusetts, printed and sold by Samuel Etheridge, Jr. He also authored *Fragments, being Illustrations of the Manners, Incidents, and Phraseology, of Holy Scripture . . . Intended as a Continued Appendix to Cal-*

met's *Dictionary of the Holy Bible* (1799-1803) as well as *Concluding Facts and Evidences on the Subject of Baptism* (1815). His brother, Isaac Taylor (1759-1829), was an Independent minister and engraver at Colchester (1796-1810) and Ongar (1810-1829).

Taylor, Dan (1738-1816)—Taylor grew up in a small Yorkshire village, hearing the likes of William Grimshaw of Haworth, George Whitefield, and John Wesley as a boy, and consequently adopted Methodism. In the 1760s he became a Baptist, but because he still held Arminian views, he could not find a home among the Particular Baptist congregations of Yorkshire and was baptized at Gamston General Baptist Church, Nottinghamshire. He eventually formed his own General Baptist congregation at Wadsworth, near Birchcliffe, late in 1762. Appalled at the lack of evangelical fervor and orthodox beliefs among so many of the General Baptists, Taylor was instrumental in forming the "New Connection" in 1770. He served as chairman of this group repeatedly and as president of its academy from 1798 to 1812, as well as editor of the *General Baptist Magazine* from 1798 to 1800. He removed to Halifax in 1783 and then to the General Baptist congregation at Church Lane, White Chapel, London, in 1785. Along with his pastoral and teaching duties, Taylor also operated a bookshop in White Chapel for many years. A tireless itinerant preacher and voluminous writer, Taylor fought continually against the Arian, Socinian, and Unitarian influences within the General Baptist churches of his day. Though he disagreed with their Calvinism, Taylor was on good terms with many Particular Baptists, especially John Sutcliff. A collection of letters between Taylor and George Birley (see entry above), composed between 1771 and 1808, can be found at the Angus Library, Regent's Park College, Oxford (D/Hus 1/6). See also *Baptists of Yorkshire,* ed. Shipley, 104-197; Frank Beckwith, "Dan Taylor (1738-1816) and Yorkshire Baptist Life," *Baptist Quarterly* 9 (1938-1939): 297-305; Frank Rinaldi, *The "Tribe of Dan": A Study of the New Connexion of General Baptists 1770-1891* (Winona Lake: Paternoster, 2006); *DEB.*

Taylor, Henry (d. 1789)—Taylor ministered to the Baptist congregation at Crawshawbooth, Lancashire, before succeeding James Turner as pastor at Cannon Street in Birmingham in 1782. David Crosley trained both Taylor and Turner for the ministry in Rossendale. Taylor would maintain a successful ministry at Cannon Street until 1789, when Samuel Pearce succeeded him. He resigned, however, in order to return to the Methodists, from whom he had originally belonged. He drowned, not long after leaving Birmingham, during a crossing to Ireland. See Langley, *Birmingham Baptists*, 32; Mursell, *Cannon Street Baptist Church*, 9.

Thomas, James (1799-1858)—The son of Thomas Thomas (see below), James Thomas served as a BMS missionary to India, 1826-1858. His wife died in September 1840, leaving him with seven young children. His second wife was Martha Wilson, who was sent to India in 1839 by the Society for Promoting Female Education in the East to teach in English schools (see letters 162, 171). His letters from Calcutta appeared frequently in the pages of the *Missionary Herald* throughout the 1840s.

Thomas, John (1757-1801)—Originally from Gloucestershire, Thomas was converted under the ministry of Samuel Stennett at Little Wild Street, London. He was trained as a surgeon and served a brief term as a missionary in India in the 1780s, during which time he acquired considerable proficiency in Bengali. His inability to remain financially stable forced his return to England in 1792, after which he met Carey, with whom he returned to India in 1793 under the auspices of the BMS. Financial difficulties continued to plague Thomas, forcing both Thomas and Carey, through the assistance of Robert Udney, an indigo agent for the East India Company, to become managers of indigo plantations at Mudnabatty, Malda. Thomas died shortly after he and Carey moved to Serampore to establish the new mission there. Before his death, however, Thomas was instrumental in the conversion of Krishna Pal, the first Hindu convert for the mission. See *DEB.*

Thomas, Thomas (1759-1819)—The son of Timothy Thomas of Abderduar, Thomas Thomas attended Bristol Academy, 1778-1780. He served as the Baptist minister at Pershore (1781-1789) and Mill Yard (1789-1799) before becoming a schoolmaster (and itinerant preacher) at Peckham. In 1813 he became one of the first secretaries of the Baptist Union. See Ernest A. Payne, *The Baptist Union: A Short History* (London: Carey Kingsgate Press, 1959) 24, 26; C. M. Hardy, "Former Secretaries of the Baptist Union," *Baptist Quarterly* 1 (1922-1923): 219; Hayden, *Continuity and Crisis*, 247.

Thomas, Timothy (1753-1827)—Thomas, whose wife was the sister of Caleb Evans of Broadmead in Bristol, pastored the Baptist congregation at Devonshire Square, London, from 1781 until his death in 1827. For many years he also conducted a school in Islington (see letter 91). His father, Joshua Thomas (1719-1797), pastored the Baptist meeting at Leominster, 1753-1797. The latter was a Baptist historian of some note, publishing *A History of the Baptist Association in Wales from . . . 1650* in 1795. Like his cousin, Thomas Thomas, Timothy also attended Bristol Academy. See "Dissenters' Schools, 1660-1820," 227; Hayden, *Continuity and Crisis*, 247.

Thompson, Josiah (1724-1806)—Born at Shrewsbury, Thompson was ordained in February 1746 at the Baptist church in Unicorn Yard, London. He resigned in 1761 (he had been assisted by Caleb Evans from 1757-1759) and removed to Bury Street, where in 1764 he succeeded Thomas Porter as the afternoon preacher in the Independent church in Bury Street. After a few years, he retired to Clapham, where he lived off a considerable inheritance until his death in 1806. He did not preach much after his move to Clapham, but was asked three times to present addresses before the King on behalf of the Protestant Dissenting Ministers. His chief work, which was never published but exists in manuscript at Dr. Williams's Library, was "The State of the Dissenting Interest in the Several Counties of England and Wales . . . The First Part, c. 1774." In this work Thompson acquired information on over 600 dissenting congregations in England and Wales at the time of the application to parliament in 1772 for the relief of dissenting ministers (see letter 11). See Wilson, *History and Antiquities*, 1:326; 4:236.

Thompson, Thomas (d. 1846)—Thompson was appointed in December 1843 as a BMS missionary to Fernando Po. He and Thomas Milburn [Milbourne], (the latter married Catherine Knibb), were set apart for mission work by the church at Tuthill Stairs, Newcastle, in October 1843, a notice of which appeared in the *Missionary Herald* (December 1843): 683-684. He would sail in February 1845 from England to Cameroons on the maiden voyage of the *Dove*, an ironclad sailing schooner purchased by the BMS to transport missionaries to and from England and West Africa and the West Indies. An account of a portion of the maiden voyage, written by Thompson, appeared in the *Juvenile Missionary Herald* (1845): 155-156. Sadly, Thompson did not serve long in West Africa, dying there on 13 March 1846. See Breed, "The *Dove*," 441-442.

Tidman, Arthur (1792-1868)—Tidman served many years as minister of the Congregational Church at the Barbican, London; he was one of many who pressed for the founding of the Congregational Union in 1831, serving as one of its first secretaries. He resigned as secretary in 1833 to begin his work with the LMS, assisting William Ellis for two years before sharing the office of Foreign Secretary with Joseph John Freeman, 1841-1846. Between 1846 and 1865, Tidman served alone as Foreign Secretary for the LMS. His final three years he shared secretarial duties with Joseph Mullens. See *Congregational Year Book* 24 (1869): 281-285; Lovett, *History of the London Missionary Society*, 647.

Tinson, Joshua (1794-1850)—Tinson was sent by the Baptist church at Shortwood to study with Joseph Kinghorn in Norwich in 1817. A year later, he entered Bristol Academy. He was set apart as a BMS missionary to Jamaica in 1822, preaching primarily at Hanover Street, St. Thomas Parish, until his death in 1850. While on furlough in England, from August 1841 to January 1843, he completed plans with the BMS for the opening of a college at Calabar, Jamaica, which commenced under Tinson's leadership in October 1843 with eight students (see letter 219). Tinson served as principal at Calabar until 1850. See Clarke, *Memorials*, 82-85; H. O. Russell, "A Question of Indigenous Mission: The Jamaican Baptist Missionary Society," *Baptist Quarterly* 25 (1973-1974): 88; *DEB*.

Tommas, John (1723/1724-1800)—Born near Skipton, Yorkshire, Tommas was raised by parents who were originally Anglicans but became dissenters, eventually joining the Baptist church at Barnoldswick, during the ministry of Alvery Jackson, under whom Tommas was converted, baptized and educated. Tommas was called out to the ministry in 1745 and ordained at Gildersome in 1747, his first pastorate. He came to the church in the Pithay in Bristol in 1753, replacing the aged John Beddome, and remained there until his death in 1800. See "Sketch of the Life of the Late Rev. John Tommas, Pastor of the Baptist Church in the Pithay, Bristol," *Annual Register* 3 (1798-1800): 313-319.

Tooke, Horne (1736-1812)—Initially a minister in the Church of England, Tooke entered the political scene as a result of his support of the controversial populist John Wilkes during the famous Middlesex election of 1768. By 1771 Tooke's support of Wilkes had lessened considerably, and he and several other former associates of Wilkes formed the first Constitutional Society. His subsequent public quarrels with Wilkes resulted in Tooke's loss of church preferment and popular support. He spent a year in jail for his opposition to the war with the American colonies, and after repeated failed attempts to gain entrance to the bar, he received an inheritance from his father that enabled him to live somewhat comfortably. He remained a political agitator, however, joining the Society for Constitutional Information (the successor to his earlier Constitutional Society) in 1780, pushing relentlessly for a reform of parliament and the protection of the rights of citizens and the curtailment of aristocratic privilege. He lost to Charles James Fox in the election for Westminster in 1790, but continued to attend the meetings of the Society, which openly sympathized with the French Revolution. He was arrested in May 1794, along with John Thelwall, Thomas Hardy, and several others, for treason, but was acquitted in December of that year. He served as an M.P. briefly in 1801-1802 before retiring to his house in Wimbledon, where he died in 1812.

Toulmin, Joshua (1740-1815)—Toulmin was trained for the ministry as an Independent, and though he had already adopted some heterodox opinions, he still began his ministry at Colyton in a Calvinistic church. After only a year, though, he removed to the General Baptist chapel at Taunton, where he remained for forty years, becoming a leading Unitarian minister and author. He was an active political reformer during the 1780s and '90s. In 1814 he became senior pastor, working with John Kentish, at the New Meeting, Birmingham, Joseph Priestley's former congregation. Toulmin published over sixty books and numerous periodical pieces. See David L. Wykes, "Joshua Toulmin (1740-1815) of Taunton: Baptist Minister, Historian and Religious Radical," *Baptist Quarterly* 39 (2001-2002): 224-243.

Towgood, Micaiah (1700-1792)—Towgood was born in Axminster, Devon, and educated at Taunton. He began his pastoral work at the Cross Chapel, Moretonhampstead, Devon, in 1722. In 1736 he removed to Crediton, Devon, and in 1749 came to George's Meeting, Exeter, where he remained as pastor until 1782, also serving for many years as tutor at the Exeter Academy. He espoused Unitarian beliefs for most of his ministerial career. Among Towgood's numerous publications are *A Dissent from the Church of England Fully Justified* (1753) and *A Calm and Plain Answer to the Enquiry, Why are You a Dissenter from the Church of England? Containing Some Remarks on its Doctrine, Spirit, Constitution, and Some of its Offices and Forms of Devotion* (1772).

Townsend, George (1744-1783)—Townsend was from the parish of Halifax, Yorkshire, and was one of four original students to attend John Fawcett's academy, where he was baptized and admitted to Fawcett's congregation at Hebden Bridge. He was invited by the Accrington church for a trial ministry in 1775, and soon became the regular minister, remaining there until his death in 1783. John Fawcett preached his funeral sermon. See Wylie, *Baptist Churches of Accrington*, 36-38.

Trestrail, Frederick (1803-1890)—Baptized at Falmouth as a teenager, Trestrail left for Bristol Academy in 1827, during Robert Hall's tenure as president of the Academy and pastor of Broadmead. He pastored briefly at Little Wild Street in London in 1831, and at Clipston for four years, before moving to Newport, Isle of Wight, for reasons of health. He later served as secretary of the Baptist Irish Society (1844-1849), secretary of the BMS (1849-1869), and president of the Baptist Union (1880). He also pastored the Baptist church in Newport for twelve years before retiring to Bristol. He is mainly known for his *Reminiscences of College Life in Bristol* (1879). See *DEB*.

Trinder, Thomas (1740-1794)—Trinder came to Northampton from Gloucestershire in 1762 to work as an usher in Ryland's academy. After joining the congregation at College Lane, however, he removed to London in April 1764, where he joined Edward Hitchin's Independent congregation at White Row, Spitalfields. He soon returned to Northampton and in 1768 married Martha Smith, a member of the College Lane church and governess of a girl's boarding school at Northampton, 1765-1789. Trinder did not rejoin the church at College Lane, however, until 1775, and was not baptized until 1783. In 1777, he and Joseph Dent (who married John Collett Ryland's daughter, Elizabeth) were made deacons. Trinder died in 1794, leaving £500 to the church at Northampton to be distributed among the poor. His spiritual autobiography appeared in the *Baptist Annual Register*, 2:286-303. See also the College Lane Church Book, ff. 43, 190; Payne, *College Street Church, Northampton*, 19; Elwyn, *Northamptonshire Baptist Association*, 26-27; *Baptist Annual Register*, 1:135-142.

Trowt, Thomas (1784-1816)—Trowt, a native of Kingsbridge, Devon, joined the Baptist church in How's Lane, Plymouth (at that time pastored by John Dyer) in December 1811. After spending several years working in Kingsbridge and Plymouth, Trowt answered the call to the mission field, entering Bristol Academy in August 1813. He was set apart by the Pithay congregation in Bristol as a BMS missionary in April 1814, arriving in Java on 16 September 1814. Before he left Bristol, he married John Dyer's sister-in-law, Eliza Burnell. John Ryland, who spoke at Trowt's dedication service, observed that "since Mr. Trowt came to Bristol ... at the expense of the Baptist Missionary Society, he has discovered much ardent piety, and remarkable diligence in the acquisition of learning." Trowt's service in Java, however, was short-lived; he died from dysentery at Samarang in October 1816. See *Periodical Accounts*, 5:295-296 (for Ryland's quotation above); 6:355-396 ("Memoir of Mr. Thomas Trowt"); *Baptist Magazine* 6 (1814): 256-58; Cox, *History*, 1:253, 310-311; Carey, *Oriental Christian Biography*, 2:368-372. Some letters to Trout by Fuller, Carey, Marshman, and others, can be found at Bristol Baptist College Library.

Tucker, Francis—Tucker was set apart at Stepney as a BMS missionary to Calcutta in 1839. He ministered for a time at the Circular Road Chapel in Calcutta, where he was warmly received. His health declined, however, forcing his return to England in December 1840. He settled in Manchester and was instrumental in the formation of the Union Chapel, Oxford Street, Manchester, serving as the church's first pastor. By February 1842 he was no longer receiving pecuniary support from the BMS. He attended a Jubilee meeting of the BMS in Manchester on 7 June 1842, and brought forth many of the resolutions at the Annual Public Meeting of the BMS in London on 1

May 1845. He would later serve as pastor of the Camden Road Baptist Chapel, Camden Town, London. Union Chapel in Manchester would continue to prosper, however, largely due to the popular ministry of Alexander Maclaren (1826-1910). Tucker was in close fellowship in London with the Congregationalists, attending and even speaking during the annual meeting of the London Missionary Society in May 1860. He was the father of Leonard Tucker, BMS missionary to India and Jamaica. See Cox, *History,* 2:307, 400; Nightingale, *Lancashire Nonconformity,* 250; Payne, "Journal of Jane Parsons," 267, 322; Sellers, "Other Times, Other Ministries," 187; *Baptist Magazine* 33 (1841): 35; 34, 138, 140; (1842): 400; *Missionary Herald* (1845): 83ff; *Missionary Magazine and Chronicle* (June 1860): 473-477; BMS Committee Minutes, Vol. H (Oct. 1841-Dec. 1842), f. 83.

Tuppen, Thomas (1742-1790)—Tuppen was from Brighthelmstone, Sussex, and became a preacher in Whitefield's Connexion, supplying at Whitefield's Tabernacle in London and in Sussex and other places. He preached in the Portsea Tabernacle, Hants., between 1768 and 1785 (he was ordained there in 1769). His final pastorate was at Bath from 1785 to 1790. See *Evangelical Magazine* 2 (1794): 517.

Turner, James (1726-1780)—Turner came from Bacup to the Baptist congregation at Cannon Street in Birmingham in 1755, and was ordained there that year. At that time, the church numbered about 40 members, but under Turner's ministry the church greatly prospered, and in 1763 the chapel was enlarged, with another enlargement set to begin at about the time of his death in 1780, when membership was over 150. The tablet erected in his memory in the church notes that "he was a clear, judicious, acceptable, and successful preacher and he was a defender of all the doctrines of the everlasting Gospel." Henry Taylor succeeded Turner in 1782. Taylor was followed by Samuel Pearce in 1789. For more on Turner, see J. E. Hale, *Cannon Street Baptist Church, Birmingham. Its History from 1737 to 1880* (London: n.p., 1880).

Turner, Samuel Hulbeart (1790-1861)—After graduating from the University of Pennsylvania in 1807, Turner became an ordained priest of the Episcopal Church in America in 1814. After serving five years in Chestertown, Maryland, he returned to Philadelphia for a year as a superintendent in a theological school before being appointed professor of Historic Theology at the General Theological Seminary of the Episcopal Church in 1819. After a year in New Haven, Connecticut, the seminary relocated to New York City in 1821, with Turner now serving as professor of Biblical Learning and Interpretation of Holy Scriptures, a position he held until his death in 1861. Among his numerous published writings are a translation of Johann Jahn's *An Introduction to the Old Testament* (1827); *The Claims of the Hebrew Language and Literature* (1831); *A Companion to the Book of Genesis* (1846); and *Thoughts on the Origin, Character, and Interpretation of Scriptural Prophecy in Seven Discourses* (1851).

Ustick, Thomas (1753-1803)—Ustick graduated from the Baptist College in Rhode Island (now Brown University) in 1771, after which he pastored Baptist churches in Connecticut and Massachusetts before settling in Philadelphia in 1782, where he served as senior pastor of Philadelphia's First Baptist Church from 1782 until his death in 1803. He also operated a bookshop and was a librarian. From 1784 to 1791 he served in an *ex officio* capacity as a trustee of the College of Philadelphia (later the University of Pennsylvania). Like his friend William Rogers (see letter 51), he also was a member of the Pennsylvania Society for the Abolition of Slavery. See *Act of Incorporation and Constitution of the Pennsylvania Society*, 23.

Vaughan, Robert Alfred (1795-1868)—Vaughan was a prominent Congregational minister, eminent scholar, and prolific writer. He was privately educated by William Thorpe in Bristol, after which he pastored churches in Worcester and Kensington (1819-1833) before becoming professor of modern history at University College, London, in 1834. He left in 1843 to assume the presidency of Lancashire Independent College, Manchester. In 1857 he returned to London, ministering for a time at Uxbridge before retiring. He was one of the founding editors of the *British Quarterly Review* (1845-1886), remaining with the journal for twenty years. Among his publications are *Religious Parties in England: Their Principles, History, and Present Duty (*1839); *Congregationalism: or, The Polity of Independent Churches Viewed in Relation to the State and Tendencies of Modern Society* (1842); *The Modern Pulpit Viewed in Relation to Society* (1842); and *The Age of Great Cities; or, Modern Society Viewed in its Relation to Intelligence, Morals, and Religion* (1843), which was reviewed in the *Baptist Magazine* 35 (1843): 302-306. His edition of Milton's *Paradise Lost* was reprinted numerous times in the last half of the nineteenth century. See Albert Peel, *The Congregational Two Hundred* (London: Independent Press, 1948) 149; *DEB*.

Vaughan, Samuel—Vaughan was the proprietor of the estate at Flamstead where Moses Baker preached regularly to a large congregation of slaves. Vaughan allowed Baker much freedom in ministering to the slaves in the early 1800s, except in the area of marriage, to which Vaughan had to give his assent. Vaughan received much criticism from other slave-owners about what was occurring on his estate, but he allowed it nevertheless. He wrote in 1802, "The labours of Mr. Baker have been pursued nearly eight years, viz. from the 15th of October, 1794, and with increasing advantages to the property and to the negroes." Vaughan assisted in protecting Thomas Burchell from angry mobs in March 1832 during the riots directed at the missionaries and their chapels. For Vaughan's statement on Baker, see Clarke, *Memorials*, 29; also Cox, *History*, 2:117.

Vernor, Thomas (d. 1793)—Vernor opened his first bookshop at 31 Newgate Street, London, in 1766, later operating shops in Ludgate Hill and Bishopsgate Street. According to the Eagle Street Church Book, in 1767, Vernor, "stationer on Ludgate Hill, gave a satisfactory account of a work of God on his soul while destitute of ye means of grace at Gibralter & was accepted" as a member of the church, then under the ministry of Andrew Gifford. Vernor moved his shop to St. Michael's Alley, Cornhill, in 1772 and then to Birchin Lane in 1786. He died in 1793 and the firm was taken over by Thomas Hood, also a dissenter, who operated the business, then known as Vernor and Hood, until his death in 1811. See Eagle Street Church Book, f. 120v; John Nichols, *Literary Anecdotes of the Eighteenth Century*, 9 vols. (London: J. Nichols, 1812-16) 3:665; Henry Robert Plomer, et. al., *A Dictionary of the Printers and Booksellers who were at Work in England, Scotland and Ireland from 1726 to 1775* (London: The Bibliographical Society, 1968) 251.

Wade, Josiah (1760/61-1842)—Wade was an attendant at the Broadmead church, where he paid for pew subscriptions in 1787, 1788, and 1790, and later at the Baptist meeting in the Pithay, where he worshiped with Joseph Cottle. Wade was especially devoted to the ministry of Thomas Roberts during his tenure as pastor at the Pithay. He came to know John Foster and Samuel Taylor Coleridge in the 1790s as well. During the summer of 1794, shortly before Coleridge's initial visit to Bristol with Robert Southey, both Cottle and Wade contributed monies to rebuild the Baptist meeting house in Salisbury. Coleridge lived with Wade during his visit to Bristol in 1813-1814, when Coleridge was attempting to control his opium addiction. Two letters of Coleridge, both written from Bath in December 1813—one to Josiah Wade and the other to Thomas Roberts (1780-1841), graduate of the Academy in Bristol—provide a telling look at Coleridge's opium addiction as well as Coleridge's longstanding connections with prominent Baptist figures. In the letter to Wade, dated 8 December 1813, Coleridge writes: "Pray for my recovery—and request Mr. Robarts's [sic] Prayers—but for my infirm wicked Heart, that Christ may mediate to the Father to lead me to Christ, & give me a living instead of a reasoning Faith!—and for my Health as far only as it may be the condition of my Improvement & final Redemption." More information on Wade and Coleridge comes from a letter by John Foster to the Rev. Josiah Hill, dated May 1842, in which Foster writes:

> You have heard mention of Mr. Wade, near the Hotwells, Coleridge's friend. I attended his funeral on Monday morning ... [Foster had visited him during his last sudden illness] I thought he recognized me just for a moment; as indicated by a slight transient smile. I do not remember how or when I became acquainted with him, many years since. I had always found him extremely kind and hospitable. For years I had dined with him about once a month, usually in the company of Roberts, to whom he had been a faithful friend, and an attendant on his ministry. A few months before his death he made me a present of a very splendid set of engravings which had cost him thirty pounds. His age was eighty-one. He was not a literary nor properly speaking an intellectual man; it having been from mere generous good-will to a man floating loose on society, that he had, some forty years since, put his house and purse at the free service of Coleridge, and partly his associates ... He did not make formally what we denominate a profession of religion, but there were favorable indications in the manner in which he expressed himself in his illness.

The letter reveals an interesting linkage between Foster, Cottle, Wade, and Roberts and the activities of the BMS in India. See Broadmead Subscription Book, no. 3, 1772-1813; for Cottle's and Wade's signatures in the collection book for Salisbury, see Saffery-Whitaker Papers, acc. 180, B/4, Angus Library, Regent's Park College, Oxford; E. L. Griggs, ed., *Collected Letters of Samuel Taylor Coleridge*, 6 vols. (Oxford: Oxford University Press, 1956-1971) 3:462; Ryland, *Life and Correspondence*, 2:275-276 (for Foster letter quoted above); Whelan, "John Foster," 644-646.

Wake, Thomas—Wake began his ministry as pastor of the Baptist church at Smarden, Kent. In 1794 he removed to the Baptist meeting at Leighton Buzzard, where he remained until 1827; his final ministry was at Kislingbury, Northamptonshire, 1827-1831. In 1797 he assisted in the formation of the Bedfordshire Union; he was also active in village preaching. See *Baptist Annual Register*, 2:2; *Baptist Magazine* 27 (1835): 160-164, 203-207.

Waldegrave, Thomas (1732-1812)—Waldegrave was originally from Norwich and a Catholic by birth. He became a dissenter after attending the Old Meeting (Independent) in Norwich as a teenager and hearing Whitefield preach. In 1756 he became one of the first students to attend James Scott's Heckmondwike Academy. While at Heckmondwike, Waldegrave began preaching at nearby Tockholes, and (as letter 6 suggests) was ordained there in 1762. He remained at Tockholes until 1771, when he moved to the Independent meeting at Whiting Street, Bury St. Edmunds. A young Henry Crabb Robinson heard Waldegrave preach on many occasions, but was largely unimpressed with the evangelical Waldegrave, describing him some years later as "an ignorant, noisy, ranting preacher." Around 1800 Waldegrave's mental faculties began to fail and Charles Dewhirst, a student from Hoxton Academy, replaced him on 28 May 1801. See *Evangelical Magazine* 22 (1814): 262-267; J. Duncan, "History of the Congregational Church in Bury St. Edmunds (Its First 150 Years)" (Typescript, Dr. Williams's Library, London, 5106.5K.39); Thomas Sadler, ed., *Diary, Reminiscences, and Correspondence of Henry Crabb Robinson*, 3rd ed., 2 vols. (London and New York: Macmillan, 1872), 1: 5; Clyde Binfield, "Six Letters of Robert Robinson: A Suggested Context and a Noble Footnote," *Baptist Quarterly* 40 (2003): 51-54.

Wallich, Nathaniel (1786-1854)—Wallich, like William Carey, was a well-known botanist and horticulturalist. He sent numerous specimens of plants from India back to the Botanic Gardens in Liverpool. Originally from Copenhagen, he went to India in 1807 as surgeon to the Danish Settlement at Serampore. When the East India Company took over Serampore in 1813, Wallich became the surgeon for the Mission Station at which Carey was superintendent. On the death of Dr. William Roxburgh in 1815, Wallich became curator of the Botanic Garden in Calcutta. In 1828 he brought over 8000 specimens of plants with him to England; the next year he was elected a fellow of the Royal Society. He continued to work in India between 1835 and 1842 before returning to England in retirement in 1847. The 1825 *Report of the Botanic Garden* noted "the kindness and assiduity of our friends and correspondents there [India], amongst whom there are none that have conferred upon us such signal and long continued favours, as the Rev. Dr. Carey, of Serampore, and Dr. Wallich, who may truly be said to have vied with each other, in the joint and friendly interest they have taken in supplying us with every valuable and curious plant which that country, so rich in its vegetable productions, could afford" (quoted by G. H. Parry, chief librarian, Liverpool Public Libraries, in a letter to S. Pearce Carey, 9 March 1933, in the S. Pearce Carey Collection, Angus Library, Regent's Park College, folder marked "Botanical Carey"). See also Stanfield, *Handbook and Guide*, 46-47; Farrer, *William Carey: Missionary and Botanist*, 100-108.

Wallis, Beebe (1735-1792)—Wallis was a deacon in the Kettering church for twenty-four years, serving as interim minister for five years at one point. He was baptized by John Brown in 1768 and would later serve as treasurer of the Northamptonshire Baptist Association Fund. As J. W. Morris writes in his biography of Andrew Fuller, Beeby Wallis's father "was a respectable member of the same community. His grandfather, Thomas Wallis, was pastor at the time the learned Dr. Gill and Mr. Brine were members of the church, and were called to the ministry during his presidency. His great-grandfather, Mr. William Wallis, was the first minister and founder of the church at Kettering, in the year 1696. His grandfather, Thomas Wallis (d. 1726), succeeded his father as pastor, during which time both John Brine and John Gill were called to the ministry from the Kettering church. Mr. Beeby Wallis died without issue, and only collateral branches of his family exist. . . . About six months after the death of this valuable man, the Baptist Missionary Society was formed under the roof of his hospitable mansion, and warmly patronised by his pious widow." See "Mr. Beeby Wallis, A Deacon of the Church at Kettering," *Baptist Annual Register*, 1:488-491; Andrew Fuller, *The Blessedness of the Dead, Who Die in the Lord. A Sermon Delivered at Kettering, in Northamptonshire, at the Funeral of Mr. Beeby Wallis* (London: Collis, 1792); Morris, *Memoirs*, 45-46; W. T. Whitley, "The Wallis House, 1792," *Baptist Quarterly* 1 (1922-1923): 167.

Ward, Nathaniel (b. 1798)—BMS missionaries Charles Evans and Richard Burton had been asked by Sir Thomas Raffles, then governor of Sumatra, to open a station at Fort Marlborough to begin work on a translation of the Java New Testament. William Ward's nephew, Nathaniel, from Derby, had arrived in Sumatra with his printing press in April 1819 (see letter 124). The younger Ward worked along with Gottlob Brückner in Sumatra for many years before the BMS closed its mission there. Ward remained behind on his own, sustaining himself through agriculture while continuing to work on a translation of the Bible. Andrew Fuller visited Derby in 1812, mainly for the purpose of meeting the then fourteen-year-old Nathaniel, at that time apprenticed to a Mr. Smith, carpenter and joiner. Fuller describes the meeting in a letter to William Ward at Serampore on 15 July 1812: "The boy has a fine open countenance, and apparently heatlthy constitution. He bears a great resemblance to what I can conceive my dear brother Ward to have been at his age." See Cox, *History*, 1:354; "Calendar of Letters," *Baptist Quarterly* 7 (1934-1935): 45.

Ward, William (1769-1823)—Born and raised in Derbyshire, Ward became editor of the Derby *Mercury* in the late 1780s; he later edited the Staffordshire *Advertiser* and the Hull *Advertiser*, displaying throughout his brief career in journalism a strong affinity for radical reform politics. After his baptism at Hull in 1796, he abandoned politics and newspapers and entered John Fawcett's academy at Wainsgate to study for the ministry. Apparently he was still involved enough in civil matters, however, to publish a pamphlet titled *The Abolition of the Slave Trade, Peace, and a Temperate Reform Essential to the Salvation of England* (1796). In 1797 he began assisting the ailing Samuel Pearce in Birmingham, but his mind had for some time been focused on Carey's mission in India. Ward had met Carey at Carter Lane in London on 31 March 1793; five years later, in October 1798, Ward wrote to Carey, informing Carey that he was coming to India. With Joshua Marshman and several others, Ward arrived at Serampore on 13 October 1799, and would soon join with Carey in building the work of the Serampore Mission. His main work involved the Mission Press, considered by many as the most important press in Asia in the nineteenth century. His *Account of the Writings, Religion, and Manners, of the Hindoos* (Serampore, 1811), was considered well into the twentieth century as the standard guide to Bengal. He married the widow of John Fountain in 1802. He also founded the first western-style newspaper in an Indian language, the *Samachar Darpan*. While on furlough in England in 1819-1821, Ward helped found the British India Society. He died of cholera shortly after his return to India in 1823. See Eustace Carey, *Memoir*, 85-86, 282; S. Pearce Carey, *William Carey*, 112, 172; A. Christopher Smith, "William Ward, Radical Reform, and Missions in the 1790s," *American Baptist Quarterly* 10 (1991): 218-244; idem, "William Ward (1769-1823)," ed. Haykin, in *The British Particular Baptists*, 2:255-271; *DEB*.

Warhurst, Caleb—He was ordained in 1756 and began to assist James Winterbottom at the Baptist meeting at Coldhouse, in Manchester. Upon Winterbottom's death in 1759, Warhurst, an Independent and friend of John Newton, became pastor, remaining there until April 1762, when a group of Independents broke from the Baptists at Coldhouse and formed a new meeting in Cannon Street, with Warhurst as pastor. John Byrom of Manchester records in his diary that Newton, then worshiping mostly with the Independents, came to the opening of the Cannon Street chapel on 20 April 1762. Warhurst died in 1765. A letter from Titus Knight (and nine other members of the church at Halifax) to Caleb Warhurst at Manchester, 3 June 1763, requests that Warhurst visit Halifax to assist a Bro. Edwards in ordaining a Mr. Knight (MS., Congregational Library, MSS. II. Misc. Letters 1669-1819, a. 40, f. 13, Dr. Williams's Library, London). Warhurst was succeeded at Cannon Street by Timothy Priestley, brother of Joseph Priestley, the Unitarian. See Halley, *Lancashire: Its Puritanism and Nonconformity*, 519; Urwick, *Historical Sketches*, 293.

Warne, Joshua—Warne was a deacon at the Baptist meeting at Carter Lane, Southwark, during the ministry of John Gill. Warne, along with George Keith, Gill's son-in-law, would leave Carter Lane after Gill's death and join the new Baptist congregation at Dean Street in January 1774. Warne served as secretary of the Particular Baptist Fund, 1774-1783. See Horsleydown and Carter Lane Church Book, ff. 22-27.

Webb, Joseph (1779-1814)—Originally from Andover, Hampshire, Webb attended the Baptist church at Broughton, first under Josiah Lewis, then William Steadman. In 1793 Steadman married Webb's sister. Webb was baptized in 1796 and became a member of the church at Broughton, and in April began to reside with Steadman as one of his pupils. He accompanied Steadman and Saffery on their first itinerating tour of Cornwall in July and August 1797, preaching his first sermon at that time. He entered Bristol Academy in August 1797. In February and March 1801, Webb supplied at Cannon Street in Birmingham. After completing his studies at Bristol in the summer of 1801, he was called to the Baptist congregation at Tiverton, where he was ordained. That same year he married Christiana Jones, daughter of a Mr. Jones of Wilder Street, Bristol, a member of the church in Broadmead. The Tiverton church was greatly reduced in numbers when Webb went there, but within a short while the attendance had increased to more than 400 and side galleries were added to the chapel. In July 1804, due to health reasons, Webb left Tiverton and returned to Bristol. In 1806 he removed to Birmingham and in 1807 began teaching students in his home. His health remained poor, however, and he never resumed preaching. A letter from Webb to F. A. Cox, dated 5 February 1801, from Bristol, was printed in the *Baptist Magazine* 7 (1815): 413-415. See W. H. Rowe, "Memoir of the Rev. Joseph Webb," *Baptist Magazine* 7 (1815): 221-231.

Weitbrecht, John James (1802-1852)—Originally from Germany, Weitbrecht and his wife, Mary Edwards Weitbrecht (widow of LMS missionary Thomas Higgs) served as CMS missionaries in Burdwan, India, 1834-1852. The Weitbrecht's sailed for England on furlough in December 1841, returning to India in October 1844. Weitbrecht gained some recognition for his publication, *Protestant Missions in Bengal Illustrated* (1844). Mrs. Weitbrecht continued in India long after her husband's death, publishing some important works on the role of women in Indian missions and on the condition of women in India, especially those who were under the restrictive isolation of the *zenana*. She writes in *The Women of India and Christian Work in the Zenana* (1875) that "everywhere [*zenana*] means the same thing, namely, that women are not to be trusted, but must be shut up as birds in a cage—must be hidden from the sight of all but their own husbands ... Yet it is only lately that we have begun to realise, even in the faintest degree, the thickness of the gloom in which these poor women have been for so many long centuries simmered." She died in Notting Hill, London, in 1888, aged 79. Among Mrs. Weitbrecht's publications are *Female Missionaries in India: Letters from a Missionary's Wife Abroad to a Friend in England* (1843); *Missionary Sketches in North India with References to Recent Events* (1858); and a *Memoir* of her husband (1857). See Frederic Boase, *Modern English Biography*, 6 vols. (New York: Barnes and Noble, 1965) 6:819; Anna Johnston, *Missionary Writing and Empire, 1800-1860* (Cambridge: Cambridge University Press, 2003) (quotation from Mrs. Weitbrecht above taken from p. 88); *DEB*.

Welsh [Welch], Thomas—Welsh was originally from Folkestone and was trained as a businessman. He began studying with Sutcliff in Olney in 1810 and in June 1811 left for King's Lynn to become the minister at the Baptist church there. He was ordained on October 1811, but resigned in February 1813, "owing to dissatisfaction on the part of some members" (the church under its former pastor, William Richards, had acquired a substantial number of Arians). He then moved to the Baptist congregation at Newbury, where he was ordained in August 1813 (see letter 108). Welsh was present at the death of John Sutcliff in Olney on 22 June, hearing Sutcliff's last words. Welsh would remain at Newbury until 1839. See *Baptists in King's Lynn*, 15; *Sutcliff Centenary*, 7; B. R. White, "Samuel Whitewood, 1794-1860, at Andover," *Baptist Quarterly* 25 (1973-1974): 232.

Whitford, John—Like William Hague (see entry above), Whitford was originally a Methodist preacher affiliated with both John Wesley and George Whitefield (James Ashworth notes in letter 18 that Whitford came to Yorkshire "16 years since," which would have been 1759, while he was serving as a Methodist minister). Whitford eventually became an Independent minister, first at Clockheaton, Yorkshire, 1762-1766 (where he also conducted a school), then at Thornton, Bradford, and Kipping, 1766-1775. Unfortunately, at the latter place his "resignation became a necessity." He also had a short stay at the Independent congregation at Duke's Alley, Bolton, in Lancashire, 1775-1776. He then became a Baptist under the influence of John Allen from Bewdley, ministering at Bicester, Oxfordshire, in the 1780s. He continued to preach, planting churches and supporting missions, until 1821. See Miall, *Congregationalism in Yorkshire*, 234, 249; Nightingale, *Lancashire Nonconformity*, 3:19.

Wiffen, Jeremiah Holmes (1792-1836)—A Quaker from Woburn, Bedfordshire, Wiffen opened a school in 1811 at Woburn. In 1813 he published, along with Thomas Raffles and James Baldwin Brown, *Poems by Three Friends*, followed by *Elegiac Lines* (1818) and *Aonian Hours* in 1819. Wiffen's collection of poems, *Julia Alpinala* (1820) included a poetic tribute to Wordsworth titled "Sonnet to W. Wordsworth, Esq." In the summer of 1821 Wiffen was appointed librarian at Woburn Abbey. His translation of Tasso's *Jerusalem Delivered* appeared in 1824. Near the end of his life he published *Historical Memoirs of the House of Russell* (1833). See Samuel Rowles Pattison, *The Brothers Wiffen: Memoirs and Miscellanies* (London: Hodder and Stoughton, 1880).

Wilks, Mark (1748-1819)—Wilks was born at Gilbralter, the son of an army officer. He moved with his family back to Birmingham in 1756 and later was apprenticed as a button-maker. In his early twenties he left the Anglican Church and was baptized and admitted to the Baptist church at Cannon Street in Birmingham, under the ministry of James Turner. He was also greatly attracted to the Methodists at this time. He was invited by the Countess of Huntingdon to study at her college at Trevecca, eventually becoming one of her ministers in 1776 at the Tabernacle in Norwich. After he married in 1778, he was forced to leave the Countess's connexion, and a group pulled out of the Tabernacle and formed St. Paul's Chapel, a Calvinistic Methodist church, in 1780, with Wilks as founding pastor. In 1788, he constituted the church as a Particular Baptist church, at which time many of his followers deserted him. He would remain at St. Paul's until his death in 1819. To help support himself, he turned to farming at Costessey for the next ten years, taking no salary from the church. After that, he received £50 per annum. In the early 1790s, Wilks became actively involved in the movement for political reform, an interest that led to two significant publications, *The Origin and Stability of the French Revolution. A Sermon Preached at St. Paul's Chapel, Norwich, July 14, 1791* (Norwich, 1791); and *Athaliah, or The Tocsin Sounded by Modern Alarmists. Two Collection Sermons Towards Defraying the Expense of the Defendants in the Late Trials for High Treason, Preached on the 19th of April, 1795 in St. Paul's Chapel, Norwich* (Norwich, 1795). As his daughter notes in her "Memoir" of Wilks, "It is indeed alleged that a Christian minister ought not to interfere with the politics, either of his own or any other nation—that it is his duty to attend to the spiritual instead of the temporal interests of his fellow creatures. But can it be said that the one is not dependent on the other, and that where a nation is enchained by slavery and despotism, religion, if it can at all survive in a soil so unpropitious, will not partake of its sterility, and be feeble and unhealthy?" The church at St. Paul's grew, and in 1814 they moved into a new chapel in Colegate, St. Clement's. Wilks was also an early and avid supporter of the BMS throughout his ministry. See Sarah Wilks, *Memoirs of Rev. Mark Wilks. With an Appendix* (London: Francis Westley, 1821); Harold F. Oxbury, *From St. Paul's to Unthank Road* (Norwich: n.p., 1925) 11-15.

Wilks, Matthew (1746-1829)— The brother of Mark Wilks (see previous entry), Matthew Wilks was an Independent minister for most of his life, first at the Moorfields (built by George Whitefield) and later at the Tottenham Court Road Chapel. He was also involved in the creation of the *Evangelical Magazine* (1793), the London Missionary Society (1795), the Religious Tract Society (1799), the Irish Evangelical Society, and the British and Foreign Bible Society (1804). He was an active supporter of itinerant preaching, serving for twenty-five years as the honorary secretary of the Village Itinerancy. He vehemently opposed Lord Sidmouth's bill in 1811 for the licensing of non-conformist chapels. His son, John (a radical MP for Boston in the 1830s), was the first secretary of The Protestant Society for the Protection of Religious Liberty, an organization that fought for the repeal of the Test and Corporation Acts in 1828. His other son, Mark, was a Congregational minister in London. See *DEB*.

Willcocks, Thomas (d. 1845)—Willcocks studied at Homerton Academy in 1810 before assuming the pastorate of the Baptist church at Pembroke Street in Devonport in 1811, where he remained until his retirement in 1837. He authored three works late in life: *Moral and Sacred Poetry* (Devonport, 1829), with Thomas Horton; *History of Russia, from the Foundation of the Empire, by Rurik, to the Present Time* (Devonport, 1832); and *Psalms and Hymns for Public and Private Worship* (Devonport, 1839).

Williams, Edward (1750-1813)—Williams was a Welshman who served as an Independent minister at Ross-on-Wye, Herefordshire (1776) and Oswestry (1777-1791), keeping an academy during much of that time. Like Ryland, Fuller, and Sutcliff, Williams was a committed evangelical Calvinist. In 1792 he removed to Birmingham to pastor the Carrs Lane Independent church, at which time he was awarded an honorary D.D. from Edinburgh University. His most important publication was *An Essay on the Equity of Divine Government and the Sovereignty of Divine Grace*, which Edwards proposed for publication by subscription in an advertisement in February 1792. He also published that same year *A Discourse on the Christian's Reasons for Glorying in the Cross of Christ, Containing a Vindication of Christian Societies and Ministers who Insist on the Importance of Preaching Christ Crucified* (Shrewsbury, 1792).

Williams, Thomas (1755-1839)—Willliams was a London Calvinistic preacher (Independent), writer, and bookseller, operating from 10 Stationer's Court, Ludgate Street, London, from 1800 to 1818. In 1793 he was one of the founding editors of the *Evangelical Magazine*. In 1794 he published a stinging attack on Thomas Paine entitled *The Age of Infidelity: In Answer to Thomas Paine's Age of Reason, Part 1*. The following year William Button published Williams's *The Age of Credulity*, as well as his *An Historic Defence of Experimental Religion; in which the Doctrine of Divine Influences is Supported by the Authority of Scripture, and the Experience of the Wisest and Best Men in all Ages and Countries* (2 vols; (1795). Williams followed this in 1796 with *The Age of Infidelity: Part II. In Answer to the Second Part of The Age of Reason* (also printed by Button). He should not be confused with another London bookseller by the same name who, in 1797, was tried for sedition for printing Paine's *Age of Reason*. In 1801 Williams was serving as the depository for the Religious Tract Society. He consistently maintained close ties with Particular Baptists, especially Andrew Fuller, J. W. Morris, and William Newman. In 1804-1805 Williams was a subscriber to the Baptist Missionary Society. See *Baptist Annual Register*, 3:543; *Periodical Accounts*, 3:137.

Wilson, John Broadley (1765-1835)—Baptized by Isaiah Birt in Plymouth, Wilson was for many years an official in the ordnance department at Devonport dockyard after his removal to Clapham. He served as treasurer of the BMS from 1826 to 1834 (see letters 83 and 146); he was also elected the first treasurer of the London Baptist Building Fund in 1824. He worshiped for many years at Rowland Hill's Surrey Chapel. See Stanley, *History*, 210; Seymour J. Price, "The Centenary of the Baptist Building Fund," *Baptist Quarterly* 3 (1926-1927): 86; *DEB*.

Wilson, Thomas (1764-1843)—A London silk merchant who attended the Tabernacle in London (founded by George Whitefield), Wilson was the son of Thomas Wilson (1731-1794). The elder Wilson helped build a dissenting chapel at Derby in 1784. The younger Wilson succeeded his father as treasurer of Hoxton Academy in 1794, and remained so until his death. He retired from business in 1798, living then at 16 Artillery Place, near Finsbury Square. In 1799 he was instrumental in building a new chapel at

Hoxton (opened 24 April 1800) and gave the ground for the Hoxton Academy when it moved to Highbury in 1826. After 1804 he often served as a lay preacher and was instrumental in building numerous chapels around London and in other cities and locations in England. He became one of the first directors of the London Missionary Society in September 1795 (he later served as treasurer of the LMS from 1832 to 1843); he served as treasurer of the British and Foreign Bible Society, the Religious Tract Society, the Congregational Library; and he was one of the founders of the University of London. Mrs. Elizabeth Wilson (to whom letter 61 is addressed) was the daughter of Arthur Clegg, timber merchant and founding member of the Mosley Street Chapel (Independent) in Manchester (see letter 6). The Wilsons were married in 1791. Thomas Wilson was, like many dissenters in the 1790s, a strong advocate for political reform and the rights of the people; he was also opposed to England's war with France in 1793. As letter 61 reveals, Wilson maintained close connections with Independents and Baptists, subscribing in 1804-1805 to the Baptist Missionary Society. His son, Joshua Wilson, was also a major figure in British Congregationalism. See Joshua Wilson, *Memoir of the Life and Character of Thomas Wilson, Esq., Treasurer of Highbury College* (London: John Snow, 1849); *Periodical Accounts*, 3:137; *DEB*.

Winter, Thomas (1790-1863)—Winter joined the Baptist church at Wellington in 1806. He was ordained in 1814 and began ministering at Saltash, Cornwall. In 1816 he removed to the church at Beckington in Somersetshire, and in 1823 became pastor of the Baptist church at Counterslip, Bristol, where he remained for 37 years. He baptized over 2000 persons in his ministerial career.

Woodman, Isaac (1715-1777)—Woodman attended Bristol Academy, 1738-1740, after which he served as pastor of the Baptist church at Warwick from 1740 to 1746. In 1749 (ordained in 1753) he began a long ministry at Sutton-in-Elms, Leicestershire, remaining there until his death in 1777. He was awarded an A.M. from Rhode Island College in 1770. He was a founding member of the Northamptonshire Baptist Association in October 1764, signing the first Circular Letter in 1765. Woodman also wrote Circular Letters in 1771 on "Original Sin" and in 1775 on "Perseverance." John Rippon would later publish "Twelve Directions for a Christian's Holy Walking" by Woodman in the *Baptist Annual Register*, 3:113-117. See Elwyn, *Northamptonshire Baptist Association*, 11-13, 99; Langley, "Baptist Ministers," 148-149; Hayden, *Continuity and Crisis*, 249.

Woolley, Edward—Woolley studied at Stepney College before being appointed a BMS missionary in November 1840. After seven years in Jamaica, however, he left for America, where he died c. 1860 in one of the Western states. See Clarke, *Memorials*, 183-184.

Yates, Catherine (1797-1838)—Originally from Bristol, she was the daughter of William Grant, BMS missionary who died in India in 1801. Her mother then married John Chamberlain, but she died in 1806. Catherine was raised primarily by Hannah Marshman in Serampore. She married BMS missionary William Yates (1792-1845) in 1816 in India. In 1821 she established, along with several other missionary wives, the Calcutta Female Juvenile Society for the Education of Native Females, and served as superintendent for many years. See Carey, *Oriental Christian Biography*, 3:148-152; 1:29-48.

Yates, William (1792-1845)—After serving an apprenticeship to a shoemaker, Yates studied at Bristol Academy and then sailed for India as a BMS missionary, arriving in 1815, the first missionary to settle in India after the passage of the new charter for the East India Company in 1813. He was not willing to submit to the Serampore Mission's rules of conduct, and so he broke with Carey, Marshman, and Ward, setting up a separate mission in Calcutta, along with James Penney, John Lawson, Eustace Carey, and W. H. Pearce. Yates, a skilled linguist, published a number of textbooks in the native languages of India. After the death of his wife, Catherine, in 1839, he married Martha Pearce, the widow of his colleague, W. H. Pearce, in 1841. Yates's health declined and he was told to return to England in 1845, but he died on the journey and was buried at sea on 3 July 1845. See Carey, *Oriental Christian Biography*, 3:148-152; 1:29-48; *DEB*.

Bibliography

Primary Sources

Act of Incorporation and Constitution of the Pennsylvania Society, for Promoting the Abolition of Slavery: and for the Relief of Free Negroes Unlawfully Held in Bondage, and for Improving the Condition of the African Race: Also, a List of Those who have been Elected Members of the Society. Philadelphia: Merrihew & Thompson, 1860.

"Alphabetical List of Members in 1802." Broadmead Church, Bristol. Bristol Record Office, Bd/R/1/4d.

An Account of the Bristol Education Society Anno 1770. Bristol: M. Ward, 1776.

Annual Report of the Committee of the Baptist Missionary Society. London: J. Haddon, 1842.

Anderson, Hugh. *Letters of Christopher Anderson.* Edinburgh: W. P. Kennedy, 1854.

Asplund John. *The Annual Register of the Baptist Denomination, in North-America; to the First of November, 1790.* Southampton County VA: J. Asplund, 1791.

Bagster, Samuel. *Samuel Bagster of London 1772–1851: An Autobiography.* London: Samuel Bagster and Sons, 1972.

Baptist Annual Register. 4 vols. London: Dilly, Button, Thomas et al., 1790–1802.

Baptist Handbook. London: Carey Kingsgate Press, 1906.

Baptist Missionary Society, Committee Minutes. Vols. H-J (Oct. 1841–July 1847). BMS Archives, Angus Library, Regent's Park College, Oxford.

Beatson, John. *The Divine Right of a Christian to Freedom of Enquiry and Practice in Religious Matters.* 2nd ed. Hull: W. Cowley, [1799].

Birrell, Charles M. *The Life of William Brock, D.D.* London: James Nisbet and Co., 1878.

_____. "Memoir of the Late Rev. Samuel Saunders." *Baptist Magazine* 32 (1840): 1-5.

Broadmead Subscription Book, no. 3, 1772–1813. Bristol Record Office, Bd/A2/2.

Broadmead Church Book, 1779–1817. MS., Bristol Record Office, Bd/M1/3.

Broadmead Independent Church, 1757–1818. MS., Bristol Record Office, Bd/M2/1.

Broadmead Independent Church, 1817–1834. MS., Bristol Record Office, Bd/M1/4.

Broadmead Independent Church, 1830–1853. MS., Bristol Record Office, Bd/M2/2.

Bull, Josiah. *John Newton of Olney and St. Mary Woolnoth: An Autobiography and Narrative*. The London: Religious Tract Society, 1868.

_____. *Memorials of the Rev. William Bull of Newport Pagnell.* London: Nisbet, 1865.

Burls, Robert. *A Brief Review of the Plan and Operations of the Essex Congregational Union.* Maldon: [n.p.], 1848.

Carey, Eustace. *Memoir of Dr. Carey.* 2nd ed. London: Jackson and Walford, 1837.

Carey, W. H, ed. *Oriental Christian Biography, Containing Biographical Sketches of Distinguished Christians who have Lived and Died in the East.* 3 vols. Calcutta: J. Thomas, Baptist Mission House, 1852.

The Case of the Baptist Church, Meeting in Somerset Street, Bath. London: [n.p.], 1829.

Caston, M. *Independency in Bristol: With Brief Memorials of its Churches and Pastors.* London: T. Ward, 1860.

"Character and Death of Mrs. Andrews." *Evangelical Magazine* 3 (1795): 292.

Church Book: St. Andrew's Street Baptist Church, Cambridge 1720–1832. English Baptist Records, vol. 2. Gen. ed. Roger Hayden. London: Baptist Historical Society, 1991.

Clark, John, Walter Dendy, and James Mursell Phillippo. *The Voice of Jubilee: A Narrative of the Baptist Mission, Jamaica, from Its Commencement; with Biographical Notices of Its Fathers and Founders.* London: J. Snow, 1865.

Clarke, John. *Memorials of the Baptist Missionaries in Jamaica.* London: Yates and Alexander, 1869.

Coate Church Book, 1684–1885. MS., Angus Library, Regent's Park College, Oxford.

Coles, Henry, ed. *Letters from John Foster to Thomas Coles, M.A.* London: H. G. Bohn, 1864.

College Lane Church Book, Northampton, 1781–1801. MS., Northamptonshire Record Office, CSBC 48.

Cottle, Joseph. *Reminiscences of Samuel Taylor Coleridge and Robert Southey.* London: Houlston and Stoneman, 1847.

Couling, Samuel. "A Biographical Dictionary of Baptist Ministers of Great Britain & Ireland Deceased from 1800 to the close of 1875." MS., Angus Library, Regent's Park College, Oxford.

_____. "A Biographical Dictionary of Baptist Ministers of Great Britain & Ireland Deceased from 1800. Second Series 1875 to 1889." MS., Angus Library, Regent's Park College, Oxford.

Cox, F. A. *History of the Baptist Missionary Society, from 1792 to 1842.* 2 vols. London: T. Ward, and G. and J. Dyer, 1842.

Douglass, David. *History of the Baptist Churches in the North of England, from 1648 to 1845.* London: Houlston and Stoneman, 1846.

Duncan, J. "History of the Congregational Church in Bury St. Edmunds (Its First 150 Years)." Typescript, Dr. Williams's Library, London, 5106.5K.39.

Eagle Street Church Book, London. Vol. 1, 1737-1785. MS., Angus Library, Regent's Park College, Oxford.

Evans, John. *Memoirs of the Life and Writings of the Rev. William Richards, LL.D.* Chiswick: Charles Whittingham, 1819.

Fawcett, John, Jr. *An Account of the Life, Ministry, and Writings of the Late Rev. John Fawcett, D.D.* London: Baldwin, Cradock, and Joy, 1818.

Finch, Thomas. *Brief Biographical Memorials, of the Ministers and Proceedings of the Protestant Dissenting Congregation, of the Baptist Denomination, Harlow, Essex.* Bishop's Stortford: W. Thorogood, 1820.

Fuller, Andrew. *The Blessedness of the Dead, Who Die in the Lord. A Sermon Delivered at Kettering, in Northamptonshire, at the Funeral of Mr. Beeby Wallis.* London: Collis, 1792.

Fuller, J. G. *A Memoir of the Rev. Thomas Roberts, M.A. Pastor of the Baptist Church in King Street, Bristol: With an Enlarged History of the Church.* London: Houlston and Stoneman, 1842.

Gould, George. *Open Communion and the Baptists of Norwich.* Norwich: Josiah Fletcher, 1860.

Green, Samuel. *Baptist Mission in Jamaica: A Review of W. G. Barrett's Pamphlet entitled A Reply to the Circular of the BMS Committee.* London: Houlston and Stoneman; and G. and J. Dyer, 1842.

Gurley, R. R. *Mission to England, in Behalf of the American Colonization Society.* Washington DC: W. W. Morrison, 1841.

Hinton, J. H. *Memoir of William Knibb.* London: Houlston and Stoneman, 1847.

Hodson's Booksellers Publishers and Stationers' Directory for London and Country. London: W. H. Hodson, 1855.

Holden's Triennial Directory. 2 vols. London: W. Holden, 1805, 1809, 1811.

Horsleydown and Carter Lane Church Book, 1719–1808. MS., Metropolitan Baptist Tabernacle, London.

Ivimey, Joseph. *A History of the English Baptists.* 4 vols. London: J. Ivimey, 1811–1830.

Jones, J. A., ed. *Bunhill Memorials, Sacred Reminiscences of Three Hundred Ministers and Other Persons of Note, who are Buried in Bunhill Fields.* London: J. Paul, 1849.

Jones, William. *Autobiography of the Late William Jones, M.A.* London: J. Snow, 1846.

Jones, William. *The Jubilee Memorial of the Religious Tract Society: Containing a Record of its Origin, Proceedings, and Results.* London: Religious Tract Society, 1850.

Kent's Directory for the year 1800. London: Richard and Henry Causton, 1800.

Langdale, Thomas. *A Dictionary of Yorkshire: Containing the Names of All the Towns, Villages, Hamlets, Gentlemen's Seats, &c. in the County of York.* Northallerton: J. Langdale, 1822.

Langdon, Mary. *A Brief Memoir of the Rev. Thomas Langdon, Baptist Minister, of Leeds.* London: Simpkin and Marshall, 1837.

Leechman, John. "Memoir of the Late Rev. George Barclay." *Baptist Magazine* 31 (1839): 1-5.

[Lincoln, Rev.] *The Voice of Years, Concerning the Late Mr. Huntington, Being an Impartial Recollection of his Ministerial Character and Conduct, Humbly Designed to Excite Imitation and Caution . . . By a Disciple of Jesus.* London: A. Maxwell, 1814.

"List of Persons Dead Among the Congregation of Dissenting Baptists in Olney, Bucks 1775–1835." MS., Angus Library, Regent's Park College, Oxford.

"List of Subscribers." Bristol Baptist College Library, shelfmark G97a.Ah.33.

Mallary, Charles D. *Memoirs of Elder Edmund Botsford.* Charleston: W. Riley, 1832.

Manual of the Baptist Denomination for the Year 1848. London: Houlston and Stoneman, 1848.

Martin, John. *The Case of the Rev. John Sandys, a Dissenting Minister, at Harlow, Essex. In Four Letters to Henry Keene, Esquire.* London: J. Martin, Jr., and William Button, 1793.

Matthew's Bristol Directory for 1794. Bristol: Matthews, 1794.

Maze Pond Church Book, vol. 1, 1744–1783; vol. 2, 1784–1821. MS., Angus Library, Regent's Park College, Oxford.

Memoir of Rev. Samuel Kilpin of Exeter, England; with Some Extracts from His Correspondence, to Which Is Added His Narrative of Samuel Wyke Kilpin. New York: American Tract Society, [1835?].

"Memoirs of Mr. Thomas Mullett, by the Rev. John Evans." *Gentleman's Magazine* 85 (1815, part 1): 83-85.

The Merchant and Tradesman's London Directory for the Year 1787. London: R. Shaw and W. Lowndes, 1787.

Morris, J. W. *Memoirs of the Life and Writings of the Rev. Andrew Fuller.* 2nd ed. London: Wightman and Cramp, 1826.

Murch, Jerom. *A History of the Presbyterian and General Baptist Churches in the West of England.* London: Hunter, 1835.

Newman, William. *Rylandiana: Reminiscences Relating to the Rev. John Ryland, A.M. of Northampton.* London: G. Wightman, 1835.

Nichols, John. *Literary Anecdotes of the Eighteenth Century.* 9 vols. London: J. Nichols, 1812–1816.

Olney Church Book, 1752–1854. MS., Angus Library, Regent's Park College, Oxford.

Owen, Evan. "A History of the Liverpool Baptists." MS., Angus Library, Regent's Park College, Oxford (unpaged).

Parker, John. *Letters to his Friends, by the Rev. John Parker ... with a Sketch of his Life and Character, by John Fawcett.* Leeds: Thomas Wright, 1794.

Pengilly, Richard, with Henry Angus Wilkinson. "The Pedigree of the Angus Family." MS., Angus Library, Regent's Park College, Oxford.

Periodical Accounts Relative to the Baptist Missionary Society. 6 vols. Clipston: J. W. Morris; London: Burdett and Morris, 1800–1817.

Philip, Robert. *The Life, Times and Missionary Enterprises of the Rev. John Campbell.* London: Snow, 1841.

Pigot and Co.'s London & Provincial New Commercial Directory for 1827–1828. London: J. Pigot, [1827].

Pigot and Co.'s Royal National and Commercial Directory and Topography of the Counties of Bedford, Cambridge, Essex, Herts, Huntingdon, Kent, Middlesex, Norfolk, Suffolk, Surrey and Sussex. London: Pigot, 1839.

Pigot and Slater's Directory of Manchester and Salford. 2 vols. Manchester: Pigot and Slater, 1841.

Pike, John Baxter, and James Carey Pike. *A Memoir and Remains of the Late Rev. John Gregory Pike, Author of "Persuasives to Early Piety."* London: Jarrold and Sons, 1855.

Plan of a Society Established in London, Anno Domini *1785, for the Support and Encouragement of Sunday-Schools in Different Counties of England.* London: Sunday School Society, 1789.

Powell, S. "Account of Mr. F_____." *Baptist Annual Register,* 3 (1798–1800): 405-407.

Raffles, Thomas. *"The Perfect and Upright Man": A Funeral Sermon for the Rev. James Lister delivered in Myrtle Street Baptist Chapel, Liverpool, on Sunday Morning, Nov 30, 1851.* Liverpool: Egerton Smith, 1851.

Raffles, Thomas Stamford. *Memoirs of the Life and Ministry of the Rev. Thomas Raffles, D.D., LL.D.* London: Jackson, 1864.

Robinson, William. *The History and Antiquities of the Parish of Hackney, in the County of Middlesex.* 2 vols. London: John Bowyer Nichols and Son, W. Pickering, and Caleb Turner, 1842–1843.

Rogers, H. "The Late Samuel Fletcher Esq." *Good Words* 5 (1864): 520-529.

Rooke, T. G. "Memoir of John Sheppard." In *Thoughts Preparative to or Persuasive to Private Devotion,* by John Sheppard, 5-34. London: Religious Tract Society, 1881.

Rowe, W. H. "Memoir of the Rev. Joseph Webb." *Baptist Magazine* 7 (1815): 221-231.

Ryland, J. E. *Life and Correspondence of John Foster.* 2 vols. London: H. G. Bohn, 1852.

_____. *Pastoral Memorials: Selected from the Manuscripts of the late Rev.[d] John Ryland, D.D. of Bristol: with a Memoir of the Author.* 2 vols. London: B. J. Holdsworth, 1826.

Ryland, John. "History of the Baptist Churches at Northampton." *Baptist Annual Register* 4 (1801–1802): 713-720; 769-772; 983-986.

_____. *The Work of Faith, the Labour of Love, and the Patience of Hope, Illustrated; in the Life and Death of the Rev. Andrew Fuller.* London: Button and Son, 1818.

"Sketch of Dr. Ryland's Sermon, preached at Broadmead, Bristol, May 31, 1801; Occasioned by the Decease of John Harris, Esq. One of the Aldermen of that City." *Baptist Annual Register* 4 (1801–1802): 603-610.

"Sketch of the Life of the Late Rev. John Tommas, Pastor of the Baptist Church in the Pithay, Bristol." *Baptist Annual Register* 3 (1798–1800): 313-319.

Sketchley's Bristol Directory, 1775. Bristol: James Sketchley, 1775.

"Statistical View of Dissenters in England and Wales." *Congregational Magazine* 2 (1819): 183-185, 315-317, 371-375, 437-440, 501-505, 630-632, 696-698, 759-762, 813-714.

Steadman, Thomas. *Memoir of the Rev. William Steadman, D.D.: Pastor of the First Baptist Church, Bradford, Yorkshire, and President of the Northern Baptist Education Society.* London: Thomas Ward, 1838.

Surman, Charles. "Index of Ministers." Dr. Williams's Library, London.

"Text Book John Ryland, D.D. 1766–1825." MS., Northamptonshire Record Office, MS. CSBC2.

Three Discourses Addressed to the Congregation at Maze-Pond, Southwark, on Their Publick Declaration of Having Chosen Mr. James Dore their Pastor, March 25th, 1784. Cambridge: F. Archdeacon, 1784.

Thompson, Josiah. "The State of the Dissenting Interest in the Several Counties of England and Wales . . . The First Part, c. 1774." MS., Dr. Williams's Library, London.

Tottlebank Church Book. MS., Angus Library, Regent's Park College, Oxford.

Underhill, E. B. *Life of James Mursell Phillippo.* London: Yates and Alexander, 1881.

Unicorn Yard Church Book, 1719–1820. MS., Angus Library, Regent's Park College, Oxford.

The Universal British Directory. 5 vols. London: Printed for the Patentees [Peter Barfoot and John Wilkes], and sold by Champanye and Whitrow, Jewry Street, Aldgate, 1791–1798.

Urwick, William. *Historical Sketches of Nonconformity in the County Palatine of Chester.* London: S. Fletcher, 1864.

Wale, Henry John. *My Grandfather's Pocket-Book. From A.D. 1701 to 1796.* London: Chapman and Hall, 1883.

Wilkin, M. H. *Joseph Kinghorn of Norwich: A Memoir.* Norwich: Fletcher and Alexander; London: Arthur Hall, 1855.

Wilks, Sarah. *Memoirs of Rev. Mark Wilks. With an Appendix.* London: Francis Westley, 1821.

Wilson, Joshua. *Memoir of the Life and Character of Thomas Wilson, Esq., Treasurer of Highbury College.* London: John Snow, 1849.

Wilson, Walter. *The History and Antiquities of Dissenting Churches and Meeting Houses, in London, Westminster, and Southwark; Including the Lives of Their Ministers, from the Rise of Nonconformity to the Present Time.* 4 vols. London: W. Wilson for W. Button, 1808–1814.

Yates, William. *Memoirs of Mr. John Chamberlain, Late Missionary in India.* Calcutta. Calcutta: Baptist Mission Press, 1824.

Secondary Sources

Adey, W. T. *The History of the Baptist Church, Kingsbridge, Devon.* Kingsbridge: [n.p.], 1899.

"Andrew Fuller and James Deakin, 1803." *Baptist Quarterly* 7 (1934–1935): 326-333.

Ashton, Ralph. *Manchester and the Early Baptists: Being a Sketch of the Origin and Growth of the Particular Baptist Church Worshipping in Gadsby's Chapel, Rochdale Road, Manchester.* Manchester: [n.p.], 1916.

Baines, Arnold H. J. "The Pre-History of Regent's Park College." *Baptist Quarterly* 36 (1995–1996): 191-201.

Ball, Bryan. *Seventh Day Men: Sabbatarians & Sabbatarianism 1600–1800.* Oxford: Clarendon Press, 1994.

Ballew, Christopher Brent. *The Impact of African-American Antecedents on the Baptist Foreign Missionary Movement: 1782–1825.* Lewiston NY: Edwin Mellon Press, 2004.

The Baptists in King's Lynn. King's Lynn: [n.p.], 1939.

Barrett, Gladys M. *A Brief History of Fuller Church, Kettering.* St. Albans: Parker Bros., 1946.

Bebbington, D. W., ed. *The Baptists in Scotland: A History.* Glasgow: Baptist Union of Scotland, 1988.

Beckwith, Frank W. "Dan Taylor (1738–1816) and Yorkshire Baptist Life." *Baptist Quarterly* 9 (1938–1939): 297-305.

_____. "The First Leeds Baptist Church." *Baptist Quarterly* 6 (1932–1933): 72-82.

_____. "Fishwick and Ward." *Baptist Quarterly* 15 (1953–1954): 249-268.

Beechen Grove Baptist Church. Beechen Grove: printed for the church, [1947].

The Bengal Obituary. Calcutta: Holmes and Co.; London: W. Thacker & Co., 1851.

Bethel Church, Shipley, 1758–1958. Shipley: [n.p.], 1958.

Biggleswade Baptist Church 1771–1971. Biggleswade: [n.p.], [1971].

Binfield, Clyde. *Pastors and People: The Biography of a Baptist Church, Queens' Road Coventry.* Coventry: Queens' Road Baptist Church, 1984.

_____. "Six Letters of Robert Robinson: A Suggested Context and a Noble Footnote." *Baptist Quarterly* 40 (2003): 50-60.

Biographical Index. Methodist Archives, JRULM.

Boase, Frederic. *Modern English Biography*. 6 vols. New York: Barnes and Noble, 1965.

Bollen, J. D. "English-Australian Baptist Relations 1830–1860." *Baptist Quarterly* 25 (1973–1974): 290-305.

Bowers, Faith. *A Bold Experiment: The Story of Bloomsbury Chapel and Bloomsbury Central Baptist Church 1848–1999*. London: Bloomsbury Central Baptist Church, 1999.

Boxall, Lizzie, ed. "Portraits and Autographs Collected by the Rev. Thomas Raffles." Manchester: John Rylands University Library of Manchester, 1991.

Brackney, William H. *Historical Dictionary of the Baptists*. Historical Dictionaries of Religions, Philosophies, and Movements, vol. 25. Lanham MD: Scarecrow Press, 1999.

Bradburn, John. *The History of Bewick Street Baptist Church*. Newcastle-on-Tyne: [n.p.], 1883.

Breed, Geoffrey R. "The Dove." *Baptist Quarterly* 40 (2004): 440-443.

A Brief Record of the Stony Stratford Baptist Church, 1767–1957. Northampton: [n.p.], 1957.

Briggs, J. H. Y. "Chapel-goers, Chapels and the Local Community." *Baptist Quarterly* 33 (1989–1990): 53-62.

_____. *The English Baptists of the Nineteenth Century*. Didcot: Baptist Historical Society, 1994.

_____. "F. A. Cox of Hackney: Nineteenth-Century Baptist Theologian, Historian, Controversialist, and Apologist." *Baptist Quarterly* 38 (1999–2000): 392-411.

Brockett, Allan. *Nonconformity in Exeter 1650–1875*. Manchester: Manchester University Press, 1962.

Brooke, Leslie. *Baptists in Yeovil: History of the Yeovil Baptist Church*. Bath: Ralph Allen, 2002.

Brooks, Thomas. *Pictures of the Past: The History of the Baptist Church, Bourton-on-the-Water*. London: Judd and Glass, 1861.

Brown, John. *The History of the Bedfordshire Union of Christians*. London: Independent Press, 1946.

Brown, Raymond. *The English Baptists of the Eighteenth Century*. London: Baptist Historical Society, 1986.

Buffard, Frank. *Kent and Sussex Baptist Associations*. Faversham, Kent: E. Vinson, [1963].

Burke, Bernard. *Peerage and Baronetage*. 104th ed. London: Burke's Peerage, 1967.

Burrage, Henry Sweetser. *Baptist Hymn Writers and their Hymns*. Portland, ME: Brown, Thurston, and Co., 1888.

Butt-Thompson, R. W. "The Morgans of Birmingham." *Baptist Quarterly* 1 (1922–1923): 262-268.

_____. "A Voyage to Fernando Po." *Baptist Quarterly* 15 (1953–1954): 82-87, 113-121.

"Calendar of Letters, 1742–1831." *Baptist Quarterly* 6 (1932–1933): 138-140, 173-186, 218-226, 277-283, 319-322, 373-379; 7 (1934–1935): 39-46.

"A 'Carey' Letter of 1831." *Baptist Quarterly* 9 (1938–1939): 239-241.

Carey, S. Pearce. *William Carey, D.D.* London: George H. Doran, 1923.

Carter, George. *Unitarian Biographical Dictionary.* London: Unitarian Christian Publishing Office, 1902.

Carter, Terry G., ed. *The Journal and Selected Letters of William Carey.* Macon GA: Mercer University Press, 2000.

Case, H. B. *The History of the Baptist Church in Tiverton 1607–1907.* London: Baptist Union Publishing Department, 1907.

Cashin, Edward J. *Beloved Bethesda: A History of George Whitefield's Home for Boys, 1740–2000.* Macon GA: Mercer University Press, 2001.

Cathcart, William. *The Baptist Encyclopedia.* Philadelphia: L. H. Everts, 1881.

Catherall, Gordon A. "Bristol College and the Jamaican Mission: A Caribbean Contribution." *Baptist Quarterly* 35 (1993–1994): 294-302.

_____. "Thomas Burchell, Gentle Rebel." *Baptist Quarterly* 21 (1965–1966): 349-363.

Chambers, Ralph F. *The Strict Baptist Chapels of England: The Chapels of the Industrial Midlands.* London: Fauconberg Press, 1963.

Champion, L. G. "The Letters of John Newton to John Ryland." *Baptist Quarterly* 27 (1977–1978): 157-163.

_____. "Robert Robinson: A Pastor in Cambridge." *Baptist Quarterly* 31 (1986–1986): 241-246.

Chadwick, R., ed. *A Protestant Catholic Church of Christ: New Road Baptist Church, Oxford.* Oxford: New Road Baptist Church, 2003.

Chaplin, C. H. *History of the Old Meeting Baptist Church, Biggleswade.* Biggleswade: C. Elphick, 1909.

Chorley, E. Clowes. *The Centennial History of St. Bartholomew's Church in the City of New York, 1835–1935.* New York: [n.p.], 1935.

Claremont Baptist Church, Shrewsbury. Shrewsbury: [n.p.], 1920.

Clark, Sydney F. "Nottingham Baptist Beginnings." *Baptist Quarterly* 17 (1957–1958): 162-169.

Clipsham, E. F. "Andrew Fuller and Fullerism: A Study in Evangelical Calvinism." *Baptist Quarterly* 20 (1963–1964): 99-114; 146-154; 214-15; 268-176.

Cooper, R. E. *From Stepney to St Giles': The Story of Regent's Park College 1810–1960.* London: Carey Kingsgate Press, 1960.

Culross, James. *The Three Rylands: A Hundred Years of Various Christian Service.* London: Elliot Stock, 1897.

"A Diaconal Epistle, 1790." *Baptist Quarterly* 8 (1936–1937): 216.

Davies, Hywel. "The American Revolution and the Baptist Atlantic." *Baptist Quarterly* 36 (1995–1996): 132-149.

Ditchfield, G. M. *Theophilus Lindsey: From Anglican to Unitarian.* London: Dr. Williams's Trust, 1998.

"Dissenters' Schools, 1660–1820." *Transactions of the Baptist Historical Society* 4 (1914–1915): 220-127.

Dix, Kenneth. *Strict and Particular: English Strict and Particular Baptists in the Nineteenth Century.* Didcot, Oxfordshire, UK: Baptist Historical Society, 2001.

Doggett, J. C. "Joseph Ivimey (1773–1834)." In *The British Particular Baptists 1638–1910*, 3 vols, edited by Michael A. G. Haykin, 3:113-131. Springfield MO: Particular Baptist Press, 2003.

Drewery, Mary. *William Carey: A Biography.* Grand Rapids MI: Zondervan, 1979.

Ella, George M. *John Gill and the Cause of God and Truth.* Eggleston Co. Durham: Go Publications, 1995.

Elwyn, T. S. H. *Northamptonshire Baptist Association.* London: Carey Kingsgate Press, 1964.

_____. "Particular Baptists of the Northamptonshire Baptist Association as Reflected in the Circular Letters 1765–1820." *Baptist Quarterly* 36 (1995–1996): 368-381; 37 (1997–1998): 3-19.

Evans, G. E. *Come Wind, Come Weather: Chronicles of Tilehouse Street Baptist Church 1669–1969.* London: Whitefriars Press, 1969.

Evans, George Eyre. *Vestiges of Protestant Dissent.* Liverpool: F. and E. Gibbons, 1897.

_____. *Midland Churches: A History of the Congregations on the Roll of the Midland Christian Union.* Dudley: "Herald" Printing Works, 1899.

Fancutt, Walter. "William Steadman's Hampshire Years." *Baptist Quarterly* 16 (1955–1956): 365-369.

Farrer, Keith. *William Carey: Missionary and Botanist.* Kew, Victoria, Australia: Carey Baptist Grammar School, 2005.

Fereday, Leonard Alfred. *The Story of the Falmouth Baptists, with Some Account of Cornish Baptist Beginnings.* London: Carey Kingsgate Press, 1950.

Field, Clive. "Preserving Zion: the Anatomy of Protestant Nonconformist Archives in Great Britain and Ireland." *Archives* 33 (2008): 14-51.

_____. "Sources for the Study of Protestant Nonconformity in the John Rylands University Library of Manchester." *Bulletin of the John Rylands University Library of Manchester* 71/2 (1989): 103-139.

Flint, John. "Crowther, Samuel Ajayi." *Oxford Dictionary of National Biography.* Oxford: Oxford University Press, 2004.

Gabb, Arthur. *A History of Baptist Beginnings with an Account of the Rise of the Baptist Witness in Exeter and the Founding of the South Street Church.* Exeter: Horsham, 1952.

George, Timothy. *Faithful Witness: The Life and Mission of William Carey.* Birmingham AL: New Hope Press, 1991.

——. "William Carey (1761–1834)." In *The British Particular Baptists 1638–1910*, 3 vols, edited by Michael A. G. Haykin, 2:143-161. Springfield MO: Particular Baptist Press, 2003.

"Giles, Father and Sons." *Baptist Quarterly* 4 (1928–1929): 333-336.

Godfrey, John T., and James Ward. *The History of Friar Lane Baptist Church, Nottingham.* Nottingham: H. B. Saxton, 1903.

Gordon, Grant. "The Call of Dr. John Ryland, Jr." *Baptist Quarterly* 34 (1991–1992): 214-227.

———. "John Ryland, Jr. (1753–1825)." In *The British Particular Baptists 1638–1910*, 3 vols, edited by Michael A. G. Haykin, 2:77-95. Springfield MO: Particular Baptist Press, 2003.

Godfrey, John T., and James Ward. *The History of Friar Lane Baptist Church, Nottingham.* Nottingham: H. B. Saxton, 1903.

Gordon, Grant. "The Call of Dr. John Ryland, Jr." *Baptist Quarterly* 34 (1991–1992): 214-227.

Gravett, P. B. *Over Three Hundred Years of God's Grace: A Short History of Sutcliff Baptist Church.* Olney: [n.p.], 1987.

Griggs, E. L., ed. *Collected Letters of Samuel Taylor Coleridge.* 6 vols. Oxford: Oxford University Press, 1956–1971.

Hale, J. E. *Cannon Street Baptist Church, Birmingham. Its History from 1737 to 1880.* London: [n.p.], 1880.

Hall, C. Sidney, and Harry Mowvley. *Tradition and Challenge: The Story of Broadmead Baptist Church, Bristol, from 1685 to 1991.* Bristol: Broadmead Baptist Church, 1991.

Hall, Catherine. *Civilizing Subjects, Metropole and Colony in English Imagination, 1830–1867.* Cambridge UK: Polity, 2002.

Halley, Robert. *Lancashire: Its Puritanism and Nonconformity.* Manchester: Tubbs and Brook, 1872.

Hancock, N. P. "Healing the Breach: Benjamin Godwin and the Serampore 'Schism.'" *Baptist Quarterly* 35 (1993–1994): 121-133.

Handy, Robert T. *A History of Union Theological Seminary in New York.* New York: Columbia University Press, 1987.

Hardman, James S. "Caleb Ashworth of Cloughfold and Daventry." *Baptist Quarterly* 8 (1936–1937): 200-206.

Hardy, C. M. "Former Secretaries of the Baptist Union." *Baptist Quarterly* 1 (1922–1923): 217-223.

Harrison, F. M. W. *The Story of the Collingham Baptist Church in the County of Nottinghamshire.* Newark: Collingham Baptist Church, 1970.

———. "The Nottinghamshire Baptists and Education." *Baptist Quarterly* 27 (1977–1978): 94-109.

Haslam, John. *History of the Baptist Church at Gildersome, in the County of York.* Leeds: Walker and Laycock, 1888.

Hastings, F. G. "The Passing of St. Mary's Gate, Derby." *Baptist Quarterly* 9 (1938–1939): 45-49.

Hayden, Philip. "The Baptists in Oxford 1656–1819." *Baptist Quarterly* 29 (1981–1982): 127-136.

Hayden, Roger. "Caleb Evans and the Anti-Slavery Question." *Baptist Quarterly* 39 (2001–2002): 4-14.

_____. *Continuity and Change: Evangelical Calvinism among Eighteenth-Century Baptist Ministers Trained at Bristol Academy, 1690–1791.* Chipping Norton UK: Roger Hayden and Baptist Historical Society, 2006.

_____. "Kettering 1792 and Philadelphia 1814: The Influence of English Baptists upon the Formation of American Baptist Foreign Missions 1790–1814." *Baptist Quarterly* 21 (1965–1966): 3-20; 64-72.

_____, ed. *The Records of a Church of Christ in Bristol, 1640–1687.* Bristol: Bristol Record Society, 1974.

Haykin, Michael A. G. "Benjamin Beddome (1717–1795)." In *The British Particular Baptists 1638–1910*, 3 vols, edited by Michael A. G. Haykin, 1:167-183. Springfield MO: Particular Baptist Press, 2003.

_____. "Benjamin Francis (1734–1799)." In *The British Particular Baptists 1638–1910*, 3 vols, edited by Michael A. G. Haykin, 2:17-29. Springfield MO: Particular Baptist Press, 2003.

_____, ed. *The British Particular Baptists 1638–1910.* 3 vols. Springfield MO: Particular Baptist Press, 2003.

_____. "'A Habitation of God, through the Spirit': John Sutcliff (1752–1814) and the Revitalization of the Calvinistic Baptists in the late Eighteenth Century." *Baptist Quarterly* 34 (1991–1992): 304-319.

_____. "John Sutcliff (1752–1814." In *The British Particular Baptists 1638–1910*, 3 vols, edited by Michael A. G. Haykin, 3:21-41. Springfield MO: Particular Baptist Press, 2003.

_____. *One Heart and One Soul: John Sutcliff of Olney, His Friends and his Times.* Darlington: Evangelical Press, 1994.

_____. "Robert Hall, Sr. (1728–1791)." In *The British Particular Baptists 1638–1910*, 3 vols, edited by Michael A. G. Haykin, 1:203-211. Springfield MO: Particular Baptist Press, 2003.

Hewitt, Maurice F. "Early Days at Worstead." *Baptist Quarterly* 11 (1942–1945): 165-174.

History of Bewick Street Baptist Church: A Lecture Delivered by John Bradburn, before the Bewick Street Mutual Improvement Society, on January 18th, 1883. Newcastle-on-Tyne: J. Bell, 1883.

History of the Congregational Church, at Olney. Olney: Cowper Memorial Congregational Church, 1929.

Holmes, Edward A. "George Liele: Negro Slavery's Prophet of Deliverance." *Baptist Quarterly* 20 (1963–1964): 340-351; 361.

Holyoak, Walter. *Dover Baptists. A Brief History.* Dover: Dover Express Office, 1914.

Hudson-Reed, Sydney. *By Taking Heed: The History of Baptists in Southern Africa 1820–1977*. Roodepoort, South Africa: Baptist Publishing House, 1983.

Hughes, J. *Liverpool Banks and Bankers 1760–1837*. London: H. Young & Sons, 1906.

Hulcoop, Stephen. *Extracts from the Minute Book of Potter Street Baptist Church Harlow Relating to Discipline of Members by the Church Meeting Covering the Period 1776–1827*. Harlow: S. H. Publishing, 2001.

"An Index to Notable Baptists, Whose Careers began within the British Empire before 1850." *Baptist Quarterly* 7 (1920–1921): 182-239.

Jackson, W. *One Hundred and Fifty Years of Baptist History at Waltham Abbey*. London: Elliot Stock, [1880].

James, Sharon. "John Rippon (1751–1836)." In *The British Particular Baptists 1638–1910*, 3 vols, edited by Michael A. G. Haykin, 57-75. Springfield MO: Particular Baptist Press, 2003.

_____. "Revival and Renewal in Baptist Life: The Contribution of William Steadman (1764–1837)." *Baptist Quarterly* 37 (1997–1998): 263-282.

_____. "William Steadman (1764–1837)." In *The British Particular Baptists 1638–1910*, 3 vols, edited by Michael A. G. Haykin, 2:163-181. Springfield MO: Particular Baptist Press, 2003.

Jewson, Charles Boardman. *The Baptists of Norfolk*. London: Carey Kingsgate Press, 1957.

_____. "St. Mary's, Norwich." *Baptist Quarterly* 10 (1940–1941): 340-346.

Johnson, J. H. Malins, and James Starr. *One Hundred Years: A Brief History of King Street Baptist Church, Wigan. 1826–1926*. Wigan: J. Starr and Sons, 1926.

"The Johnsonian Baptists." *Transactions of the Baptist Historical Society* 3 (1912–1913): 54-61.

Johnston, Anna. *Missionary Writing and Empire, 1800–1860*. Cambridge: Cambridge University Press, 2003.

Julian, John. *A Dictionary of Hymnology*. London: John Murray, 1908.

Kaestle, Carl F. *Joseph Lancaster and the Monitorial School Movement; A Documentary History*. New York: Teachers College Press, 1973.

Kevan, Ernest. *London's Oldest Baptist Church*. London: Kingsgate Press, 1933.

Killingray, David. "The Black Atlantic Missionary Movement and Africa, 1780s–1920s." *Journal of Religion in Africa* 33 (2003): 3-31.

_____. "Black Baptists in Britain 1640–1950." *Baptist Quarterly* 40 (2003): 69-89.

Klaiber, A. J. "Baptists at Bewdley, 1649–1949." *Baptist Quarterly* 13 (1949–1950): 116-124.

Laidlaw, Jean. *Hitchin, Hertfordshire. Monumental Inscriptions of Tilehouse Street Baptist Church, Hitchin*. Hertford: Hertfordshire Family and Population History Society, 1992.

Laird, M. A. "The Serampore Missionaries as Educationists 1794–1824." *Baptist Quarterly* 22 (1967–1968): 320-325; 312.

Langley, Arthur S. "Abraham Greenwood, 1749–1827." *Baptist Quarterly* 2 (1924–1925): 84-89.

_____. "Baptist Ministers in England about 1750 A.D." *Transactions of the Baptist Historical Society* 6 (1918–1919): 138-162.

_____. *Birmingham Baptists Past and Present.* London: Kingsgate Press, 1939.

Laquer, Thomas Walter. *Religion and Respectability: Sunday Schools and Working Class Culture, 1780–1850.* New Haven and London: Yale University Press, 1976.

Lawson, William W. "Robert and James Haldane." *Baptist Quarterly* 7 (1934–1935): 276-285.

Lee, Annie. "John Shepherd." *Lancashire and Cheshire Naturalist* 17 (1925): 157-160, 198-200.

Leifchild, John. *Memoir of the Late Rev. Joseph Hughes, A.M.* London: T. Ward, 1835.

"Letters to James Deakin." *Baptist Quarterly* 7 (1934–1935): 361-373.

Lewis, Donald M., ed. *The Blackwell Dictionary of Evangelical Biography: 1730–1860.* 2 vols. Oxford: Blackwell, 1995. Peabody MA: Hendrickson, 2004. Cited as *DEB.*

Lists of Members of the Baptist Church, Friar Lane, Nottingham, 1769–1815. Nottingham: [n.p.], 1901.

Long, Gary W. "William Knibb (1803–1845)." In *The British Particular Baptists 1638–1910*, 3 vols, edited by Michael A. G. Haykin, 3:211-231. Springfield MO: Particular Baptist Press, 2003.

Lovegrove, Deryck W. "Particular Baptist Itinerant Preachers during the late 18th and early 19th Centuries." *Baptist Quarterly* 28 (1979–1980): 127-141.

Lovett, Richard. *The History of the London Missionary Society 1795–1895.* 2 vols. London: Henry Frowde, 1899.

Lynn, Martin. "Commerce, Christianity and the Origins of the 'Creoles' of Fernando Po." *Journal of African History* 25 (1984): 257-278.

McCleery, James. *The History of Tilehouse Street (Salem) Baptist Church, Hitchin.* Hitchin UK: Carling and Hales, 1919.

McGuiness, George. "Robert (1764–1842) and James Haldane (1768–1851)." In *The British Particular Baptists 1638–1910*, 3 vols, edited by Michael A. G. Haykin, 2:219-235. Springfield MO: Particular Baptist Press, 2003.

"The McLeanist (Scotch) and Campbellite Baptists of Wales." *Transactions of the Baptist Historical Society* 7 (1920–1921): 147-181.

Manley, Ken R. *From Wolloomooloo to "Eternity": A History of Australian Baptists.* 2 vols. Studies in Baptist History and Thought, vol. 16.1-2. Milton Keynes UK: Paternoster Press, 2006.

_____. *Redeeming Love Proclaim: John Rippon and the Baptists.* Studies in Baptist History and Thought, vol. 12. Carlisle: Paternoster, 2004.

Maxted, Ian. *The London Book Trade 1775-1800: A Preliminary Checklist of Members.* Kent: [n.p.], 1977.

Mee, John. "Is there an Antinomian in the House? William Blake and the After-Life of a Heresy." In *Historicizing Blake*, edited by Steve Clark and David Warrall, 43-58. Houndsmills, Basingstoke: Macmillan, 1994.

Meek, Donald E., ed. *A Mind for Mission: Essays in Appreciation of the Rev. Christopher Anderson (1782–1852).* Edinburgh: Scottish Baptist History Project, 1992.

Miall, James. *Congregationalism in Yorkshire: A Chapter in Modern Church History.* London: J. Snow, 1868.

Michael, T. *A Brief Historical Account of the First Baptist Church, Halifax.* Halifax: S. N. Whitaker, 1890.

Moon, Norman S. "Caleb Evans, Founder of the Bristol Education Society." *Baptist Quarterly* 24 (1971–1972): 175-190.

_____. *Education for Ministry: Bristol Baptist College, 1679-1979.* Bristol: Bristol Baptist College, 1979.

Moore, G. A., and R. J. Huckle. *Salisbury Baptist Church 1655–2000.* Salisbury: [n.p.], 2000.

Morden, Peter J. *Offering Christ to the World: Andrew Fuller (1754–1815) and the Revival of Eighteenth Century Partcular Baptist Life.* Studies in Baptist History and Thought, vol. 8. Carlisle: Paternoster Press, 2003.

Murray, Derek B. "Christopher Anderson (1782–1852)." In *The British Particular Baptists 1638–1910*, 3 vols., edited by Michael A. G. Haykin, 3:171-179. Springfield MO: Particular Baptist Press, 2003.

_____. "Christopher Anderson and Scotland." In *A Mind for Mission: Essays in Appreciation of the Rev. Chrisopher Anderson (1782–1852)*, edited by Donald E. Meek, 3-7. Edinburgh: Scottish Baptist History Project, 1992.

Mursell, Arthur. *Cannon Street Baptist Church, Birmingham. Its History from 1737 to 1880.* London: [n.p.], 1880.

Naylor, Peter. "John Collett Ryland (1723–1792)." In *The British Particular Baptists 1638–1910*, 3 vols, edited by Michael A. G. Haykin, 1:185-201. Springfield MO: Particular Baptist Press, 2003.

Namier, Sir Lewis, and John Brooke. *The House of Commons 1754–1790*, 3 vols. Oxford: Oxford University Press, 1964.

Nettles, Tom J. "Andrew Fuller (1754–1815)." In *The British Particular Baptists 1638–1910*, 3 vols, edited by Michael A. G. Haykin, 2:97-141. Springfield MO: Particular Baptist Press, 2003.

Nicholson, Henry M. *A History of the Baptist Church Now Meeting in George Street Chapel, Plymouth, from 1620.* London: Baptist Union Publications, 1904.

Nightingale, Benjamin. *Lancashire Nonconformity; Or, Sketches, Historical and Descriptive, of the Congregational and Old Presbyterian Churches in* the County. Churches of Manchester, Oldham, Ashton, etc. 6 vols. Manchester: John Heywood, [1890–1893].

Noakes, Richard. "The 'Bridge Which Is between Physical and Psychical Research': William Fletcher Barrett, Sensitive Flames, and Spiritualism." *History of Science* 42 (2004): 419-464.

"Notes and News." *Bulletin of the John Rylands University Library of Manchester* 59 (1976): 5-6.

"Notes and News." *Bulletin of the John Rylands University Library of Manchester* 60 (1978): 269-274.

Nutter, Stephen Bernard. *The Story of the Cambridge Baptists and the Struggle for Religious Liberty.* Cambridge: W. Heffer and Sons, 1912.

Oddy, John. "Bicheno and Tyso on the Prophecies." *Baptist Quarterly* 35 (1993–1994): 81-89.

_____."The Dissidence of William Richards." *Baptist Quarterly* 27 (1977–1978): 118-127.

_____. *The Reverend William Richards (1749–1818) and his Friends: A Study of Ideas and Relationships.* Nottingham: [n.p.], 1973.

Olive, Dean. "Joseph Kinghorn (1766–1832)." In *The British Particular Baptists 1638–1910*, 3 vols, edited by Michael A. G. Haykin, 3:85-111. Springfield MO: Particular Baptist Press, 2003.

Oliver, Robert W. "Abraham Booth (1734–1806)." In *The British Particular Baptists 1638–1910*, 3 vols, edited by Michael A. G. Haykin, 2:31-55. Springfield MO: Particular Baptist Press, 2003.

_____. "John Gill (1697–1771)." In *The British Particular Baptists 1638–1910*, 3 vols, edited by Michael A. G. Haykin, 1:145-165. Springfield MO: Particular Baptist Press, 2003.

_____. *The Strict Baptist Chapels of England: The Chapels of Wiltshire and the West.* London: Fauconberg Press, 1968.

"The Origin of the General Baptist Missionary Society." *Baptist Quarterly* 1 (1922–1923): 270-275.

Overend, Frederick. *History of the Ebenezer Baptist Church, Bacup.* London: Kingsgate Press, 1912.

Oxbury, Harold F. *From St. Paul's to Unthank Road.* Norwich: [n.p.], 1925.

Paine, Christine. "Benjamin Evans of Scarborough 1803–1871." *Baptist Quarterly* 21 (1965–1966): 174-180.

Pattison, Samuel Rowles. *The Brothers Wiffen: Memoirs and Miscellanies.* London: Hodder and Stoughton, 1880.

Payne, Ernest A. "Abraham Booth, 1734–1806." *Baptist Quarterly* 26 (1975–1976): 28-42.

_____. "Andrew Fuller as Letter Writer." *Baptist Quarterly* 15 (1953–1954): 290-296.

_____. *The Baptist Union: A Short History.* London: Carey Kingsgate Press, 1959.

_____. "Baptist Work in Jamaica before the Arrival of the Missionaries." *Baptist Quarterly* 7 (1934–1935): 20-26.

_____. *College Street Church, Northampton, 1697–1947.* London: Kingsgate Press, 1947.

_____. "The Diaries of John Dyer." *Baptist Quarterly* 13 (1949–1950): 253-259.

_____. *The Excellent Mr. Burls.* London: Kingsgate Press, 1943.

_____. *The First Generation: Early Leaders of the Baptist Missionary Society in England and India.* London: Carey Press, [1936].

_____. "John Linnell, The World of Artists and the Baptists." *Baptist Quarterly* 40 (2003): 22-35.

_____. "The Journal of Jane Parsons." *Baptist Quarterly* 23 (1969–1970): 266-279, 311-323.

_____. "The Necrologies of John Dyer." *Baptist Quarterly* 13 (1949–1950): 303-309.

_____. *Roade Baptist Church 1688–1938.* London: Kingsgate Press, 1939.

_____. "A Yorkshire Story." *Baptist Quarterly* 19 (1961–1962): 366-369.

Payne, E. A., and A. R. Allan. *Clipston Baptist Church.* Northampton: [n.p.], 1932.

Peel, Albert. *The Congregational Two Hundred.* London: Independent Press, 1948.

_____. *A Hundred Eminent Congregationalists 1530–1924.* London: Independent Press, 1927.

_____. *These Hundred Years: A History of the Congregational Union, 1831–1931.* London: Congregational Union of England and Wales, 1931.

Pike, Godfrey Holden. *The Metropolitan Tabernacle; Or, An Historical Account of the Society.* London: Passmore & Alabaster, 1870.

Plomer, Henry Robert, et. al. *A Dictionary of the Printers and Booksellers Who Were at Work in England, Scotland, and Ireland from 1726 to 1775.* London: The Bibliographical Society, 1968.

Plumbridge, J. H. J. "The Life and Letters of John Parker." *Baptist Quarterly* 8 (1936–1937): 111-122.

Potts, E. Daniel. *British Baptist Missionaries in India, 1793–1837.* Cambridge: Cambridge University Press, 1967.

_____. "A Note on the Serampore Trio." *Baptist Quarterly* 20 (1963–1964): 115-118.

Potts, Walter D. "A Record of the Baptist Sunday School, Founded at Tuthill Stairs, Newcastle, April, 1807." In *Souvenir of the Sunday School Centenary Celebration 1807–1907.* Newcastle-upon-Tyne: Newcastle and Gateshead Baptist Council, 1907.

Powicke, Frederick James. *A History of the Cheshire County Union of Congregational Churches.* Manchester: T. Griffiths, 1907.

Price, Seymour J. "The Centenary of the Baptist Building Fund." *Baptist Quarterly* 3 (1926–1927): 81-96.

_____. "The Early Years of the Baptist Union." *Baptist Quarterly* 4 (1928–1929): 53-60; 121-131; 171-178.

_____. "Maze Pond and the Matterhorn." *Baptist Quarterly* 10 (1940–41): 202-208.

_____. *Upton: The Story of One Hundred and Fifty Years 1785–1935.* London: Carey Press, 1935.

Prosser, G. P. R. "The Formation of the General Baptist Missionary Society." *Baptist Quarterly* 22 (1967–1968): 23-29.

Ramsbottom, B. A. "Samuel Medley (1738–1799)." In *The British Particular Baptists 1638–1910*, 3 vols, edited by Michael A. G. Haykin, 1:235-249. Springfield MO: Particular Baptist Press, 2003.

_____. "The Stennetts." In *The British Particular Baptists 1638–1910*, 3 vols, edited by Michael A. G. Haykin, 1:133-143. Springfield MO: Particular Baptist Press, 2003.

Ridoutt, P. *The Early Baptist History of Portsmouth.* Landport: G. Chamberlain, 1888.

Rinaldi, Frank. *The "Tribe of Dan": A Study of the New Connexion of General Baptists 1770–1891.* Winona Lake: Paternoster, 2006.

Robb, Alexander. *The Gospel to the Africans: A Narrative of the Life and Labours of the Rev. William Jameson in Jamaica and Old Calabar.* Edinburgh: A. Eliot, 1861.

Roberts, W. Wright, "English Autograph Letters in the John Rylands Library." *Bulletin of the John Rylands Library* 25 (1941): 119-136.

Robinson, H. Wheeler. "A Baptist Student—John Collett Ryland." *Baptist Quarterly* 3 (1926–1927): 25-33.

Rooke, Patricia T. "Evangelical Missionary Rivalry in the British West Indies: A Study in Religious Altruism and Economic Reality." *Baptist Quarterly* 29 (1981–1982): 341-355.

Ross, James. *A History of Congregational Independency in Scotland.* Glasgow: J. MacLehose, 1900.

Russell, H. O. "A Question of Indigenous Mission: The Jamaican Baptist Missionary Society." *Baptist Quarterly* 25 (1973–1974): 86-93.

Salter, William Henry Gurney, ed. *Some Particulars of the Lives of William Brodie Gurney and His Immediate Ancestors. Written Chiefly by Himself.* London: Unwin, 1902.

Savannah. Savannah GA: Review Print Co., 1937.

Sellers, Ian. "The Northern Baptist College Historical Collection." *Baptist Quarterly* 32 (1987–1988): 52.

_____. "Other Times, Other Ministries: John Fawcett and Alexander McLaren." *Baptist Quarterly* 32 (1987–1988): 181-199.

_____. *Pathways to Faith: A History of Wigan Baptist Church 1796–1996.* Wigan: [n.p.], 1996.

Sennett, Richard and Henry J. Oram. *The Marine Steam Engine: A Treatise for Engineering Students, Young Engineers, and Officers of the Royal Navy, and Mercantile Marine.* London: Longmans, Green, and Co., 1898.

Shipley, C. E., ed. *The Baptists of Yorkshire: Being the Centenary Memorial Volume of the Yorkshire Baptist Association.* London and Bradford: [n.p.], 1912.

Skinner, R. F. *Nonconformity in Shropshire 1662–1816.* Shrewsbury: Wilding & Son, 1964.

Smith, A. Christopher. "Joshua (1768–1837) and Hannah Marshman (1767–1847)." In *The British Particular Baptists 1638–1910,* 3 vols, edited by Michael A. G. Haykin, 2:237-253. Springfield MO: Particular Baptist Press, 2003.

_____. "William Ward (1769–1823)." In *The British Particular Baptists 1638–1910,* 3 vols, edited by Michael A. G. Haykin, 2:255-271. Springfield MO: Particular Baptist Press, 2003.

_____. "William Ward, Radical Reform, and Missions in the 1790s." *American Baptist Quarterly* 10 (1991): 218-244.

Smith, Frank H. *The Story of Ilford (High Road) Baptist Church 1801–1951.* Ilford: C. W. Clark, [1951].

Smith, George. *Life of William Carey.* London: J. M. Dent, 1909.

Smith, G. E. "Patterns of Missionary Education: The Baptist India Mission 1794–1824." *Baptist Quarterly* 20 (1963–1964): 293-312.

Snowdon, Jacqui. *The Alcester Baptist Story 1640–1990.* Alcester: Warwick, 1990.

Spurrier, Edward. *Memorials of the Baptist Church Worshipping at Eld Lane Chapel, Colchester.* Colchester: F. Wright, 1889.

Stanfield, H. *Handbook and Guide to the Herbarium Collection in the Public Museums, Liverpool.* Liverpool: The Museum, 1935.

Stanley, Brian. *The History of the Baptist Missionary Society 1792–1992.* Edinburgh: T. and T. Clark, 1992.

Strict Baptist Chapel Southill. [n.p.], 1993.

Stuart, James. "The John Rylands Library." *Baptist Magazine* 91 (1899): 509-515.

"A Student's Programme in 1744." *Baptist Quarterly* 2 (1924–): 252–52.

Sunderland, Foster. *A Brief History of Tottlebank Baptist Church, Greenodd, Ulverston: The Oldest Baptist Church in Lancashire.* [Tottlebank]: [n.p.] 1965?

Sutcliff Centenary. Baptist Chapel, Olney, June 22nd, 1914. Northampton: [n.p.], 1914.

"Sutcliff's Academy at Olney." *Baptist Quarterly* 4 (1928–1929): 276-279.

Swaine, Stephen Albert. *Faithful Men; or, Memorials of Bristol Baptist College, and Some of Its Most Distinguished Alumni.* London: Alexander and Shepheard, 1884.

Talbot, Brian. "John Saffery (1763–1825)." In *The British Particular Baptists 1638–1910*, 3 vols, edited by Michael A. G. Haykin, 3:43-83. Springfield MO: Particular Baptist Press, 2003.

_____. *The Search for a Common Identity: The Origins of the Baptist Union of Scotland 1800–1870*. Studies in Baptist History and Thought, vol. 9. Carlisle UK: Paternoster Press, 2003.

Taylor, R. "English Baptist Periodicals 1790–1865." *Baptist Quarterly* 27 (1977–1978): 50-82.

Tibbutt, H. G. *Bunyan Meeting Bedford 1650–1950*. Bedford: Trustees of Bunyan Meeting, [1950].

_____. *Cotton End Old Meeting, 1776–1962*. Bedfordshire: Cotton End Baptist Church; Rushden: S. L. Hunt, 1963.

Thomas, Margaret F. *A History of the Tottlebank Baptist Church 1669–1999*. [n.p.], [1999].

_____. *Brassey Green & Tarporley: A Baptist History*. [n.p.], 1984.

Three Hundred Years of Free Church Life. Tercentenary 1953, Park Road Baptist Church, Peterborough. Peterborough: [n.p.], [1953.]

Todd, William B. *A Directory of Printers and Others in Allied Trade, London and Vicinity 1800–1840*. London: Printing Historical Society, 1972.

Tongue, E. J. "Dr. John Ward's Trust." *Baptist Quarterly* 13 (1949–1950): 267-275.

Tyrrell, Alex. "The 'Moral Radical Party' and the Anglo-Jamaican Campaign for the Abolition of the Negro Apprenticeship System." *English Historical Review* 99 (1984): 481-502.

Underwood, A. C. *A History of the English Baptists*. London: Baptist Union Publications Department, 1947.

Valentine, Theo. F. *Concern for the Ministry: The Story of the Particular Baptist Fund 1717–1967*. Teddington: Particular Baptist Fund, 1967.

Venn, John, ed. *Alumni Cantabrigienses*. Part II: From 1752 to 1900. 6 vols. Cambridge: Cambridge University Press, 1922–1954.

Walker, F. D. *William Carey, Missionary, Pioneer, and Statesman*. Chicago: Moody Press, 1951.

Watson, Angus. *The Angus Clan (Years 1588 to 1950)*. Gateshead: Angus Watson, 1955.

Watts, David. *A History of the Hertfordshire Baptists*. [Hertfordshire]: Hertfordshire Baptist Association, 1978.

Welch, Edwin, ed. *Bedfordshire Chapels and Meeting Places: Official Registration, 1672–1901*. Bedford: Bedfordshire Historical Record Society, 1996.

Wells, Tom. "Samuel Pearce (1766–1799)." In *The British Particular Baptists 1638–1910*, 3 vols, edited by Michael A. G. Haykin, 2:183-199. Springfield MO: Particular Baptist Press, 2003.

Wellum, Kirk. "Caleb Evans (1737–1791)." In *The British Particular Baptists 1638–1910*, 3 vols, edited by Michael A. G. Haykin, 1:213-233. Springfield MO: Particular Baptist Press, 2003.

Whelan, Timothy. "A Calendar of Baptist Autographs in the John Rylands University Library of Manchester, 1741-1907." *Baptist Quarterly* 42 (2008): 577-612.

_____. "Coleridge and Robert Hall of Cambridge." *Wordsworth Circle* 31 (2000): 38-47.

_____. "'For the Hand of a Woman, has Levell'd the Blow": Maria de Fleury's Pamphlet War with William Huntington, 1787–1791.'" *Women's Studies* 36 (2007): 431-454.

_____. "John Foster and Samuel Taylor Coleridge." *Christianity and Literature* 50 (2001): 631-656.

_____. "Joseph Angus and the Use of Autograph Letters in the Library at Holford House, Regent's Park College, London." *Baptist Quarterly* 40 (2004): 455-476.

_____. "Joseph Cottle the Baptist." *Charles Lamb Bulletin*, N.S. 111 (2000): 96-108.

_____. "'I am the Greatest of the Prophets': A New Look at Robert Hall's Mental Breakdown, November 1804." *Baptist Quarterly* 42 (2007): 114-126.

_____. "'I have *confessed myself a devil'*: Crabb Robinson's Confrontation with Robert Hall, 1798–1800." *Charles Lamb Bulletin, New Series* 121 (2003): 2-25.

_____. *Politics, Religion, and Romance: The Letters of Benjamin Flower and Eliza Gould Flower, 1794–1808.* Aberystwyth: National Library of Wales, 2009.

_____. "Robert Hall and the Bristol Slave-Trade Debate of 1787–1788." *Baptist Quarterly* 38 (1999–2000): 212-224.

_____. "Six Letters of Robert Robinson from Dr. Williams's Library, London." *Baptist Quarterly* 39 (2001–2002): 347-359.

_____. "Thomas Poole's 'Intimations of Immortality' in a Letter to John Sheppard, February 1837." *Romanticism* 11 (2005): 199-223.

White, B. R. "Samuel Whitewood, 1794–1860, at Andover." *Baptist Quarterly* 25 (1973–1974): 232-236.

Whitebrook, J. C. "The Life and Works of Mrs. Ann Dutton." *Transactions of the Baptist Historical Society* 7 (1920–1921): 129-146.

Whitley, W. T., ed. *A Baptist Bibliography.* 2 vols. London: Kingsgate Press, 1916–1922.

_____. *The Baptists of London 1612–1928.* London: Kingsgate Press, 1928.

_____. *The Baptists of North-West England.* London: Kingsgate, 1913.

_____. "J. C. Ryland as Schoolmaster." *Baptist Quarterly* 5 (1930–1931): 141-144.

_____. "The Wallis House, 1792." *Baptist Quarterly* 1 (1922–1923): 158-170.

Williams, Gwyn A. *The Search for Beulah Land: The Welsh and the Atlantic Revolution.* New York: Holmes & Meier, 1980.

Winnard, E. *The History of the Baptist Church, Barnoldswick, 1500–1916.* Burnley: [n.p.], 1916.

Witard, Doris. *Bibles in Barrels: A History of Essex Baptists.* [n.p.]: Essex Baptist Association, 1962.

Woollacott, Christopher. *A Brief History of the Baptist Church in Little Wild Street, Lincoln's-Inn Fields, from 1691 to 1858.* London: Houlston and Wright, 1859.

Wright, B. G. "Saunders, John (1806–1859)." In *Australian Dictionary of Biography*, 2 vols, edited by Douglas Pike and John Ritchie, 2:418. Melbourne: Melbourne University Press, 1967.

Wright, Philip. *Knibb "the Notorious": Slaves' Missionary 1803–1845.* London: Sidgwick and Jackson, 1973.

Wright, T. *The Life of William Huntington, SS.* London: Farncombe, 1909.

Wykes, David. "Joshua Toulmin (1740–1815) of Taunton: Baptist Minister, Historian, and Religious Radical." *Baptist Quarterly* 39 (2001–2002): 224-243.

Wylie, Robert J. V. *The Baptist Churches of Accrington and District.* Accrington: W. Shuttleworth, Wellington Press, 1923.

Young, G. H., and J. W. Barker. *A Short History of Harlow Baptist Church 1662–1962.* Harlow: Harlow Baptist Church, 1962.

Yuille, George. *History of the Baptists in Scotland from Pre-Reformation Times.* Glasgow: Baptist Union Publications Committee, 1926.

Index to the
Writers of the Letters

Index to the
Recipients of the Letters

Location Index of the Writers and Recipients of the Letters (numbers refer to the letter)

Index of Persons
named in the Letters

Ellis, Jonathan D. (d.1845), BMS missionary, India, 237, 238, 239, 259, 280, 280n, 281, 380; Mrs. Ellis, 380
Ellis, William, secretary, LMS, 457
Estlin, Anne Maria (Mrs. Prichard), 431
Estlin, John Prior, Bristol, 431
Etheridge, Samuel, 82
Etheridge, Samuel, Jr., 454
Etienne, Jean (1725-1799, 134n
Evans, Benjamin (1803-1871), Baptist minister, Scarborough, 400
Evans, Caleb (1737-1791), Baptist minister, Bristol, xxxii, xxxvi, xxxvi(n), 13n 26n, 28, 29, 29n, 32, 32n, 33, 49, 50n, 184, 380-381, 396, 398, 405, 423, 424, 456
Evans, Charles, BMS missionary, Sumatra, 187n, 192, 363, 381, 464
Evans, Hugh (1712-1781), Baptist minister, Bristol, xxxii, xxxvi, xxxvi(n), 12, 13n, 15n, 25n, 26, 32n, 380, 381, 398, 423; his wife, Sarah, 32n
Evans, James Harington (1785-1849), Baptist minister, London, 316, 381
Evans, John, Baptist minister, Foxton, 57, 382
Evans, John (1767-1827), General Baptist minister, London, 423, 424, 440
Evans, Joseph Jeffries (1768-1812), London merchant, 32n, 423, 424
Ewing, Greville (1767-1841), Baptist minister, Glasgow, 150, 151, 351; Mrs. Ewing, 151
Eyre, John (1754-1803), 66n, 76n, 90, 382, 399; Mrs. Eyre, 76

Fasbrook, Mary, 157, 159
Faulkner, Robert, Baptist minister, Thorn, 58, 77, 363
Fawcett, Benjamin, dissenting minister, 36n
Fawcett, John (1740-1817), xxix, xxxi, xxxii, xxxiii, xxxvi, xxxvi(n), 12, 13, 13n, 16n, 26-27, 61, 61n, 122, 122n, 166, 171, 173, 184, 184n, 347, 382, 387, 393, 398, 402, 405, 443, 453, 454, 458, 465; his son, John, Jr., 184, 383; Mrs. Fawcett, 184
Fawcett, Richard, Methodist layman, Great Horton, 174
Fenn (Finn), Joseph, CMS missionary, 383
Fenn, John, hosier, Cornhill, 95, 383
Fernandez, Ignatius (1757-1830), BMS associate, India, 133, 145, 146, 149, 383, 401, 404
Fido, Mrs., Bristol, 107n

Fisher, William (1789-1848), Baptist minister, Bromley, Northumberland, 286-287
Fishwick, Richard (1745-1825), Baptist layman, Newcastle, 127, 384
Fitzhugh, Charles, Northampton, 67
Fletcher, Mr., Baptist minister, Burton-on-Trent, 138-139
Fletcher, John, Dissenting minister, 36n
Fletcher, John, vicar, Madeley, 404
Fletcher, Joseph, Baptist layman, London, xxxv, 250-252, 352, 384-385
Fletcher, Joseph, tutor, Blackburn Academy, 433
Fletcher, Josiah, Baptist layman, Norwich, 296-297, 385
Fletcher, Mrs., teacher, Calcutta, 249
Fletcher, Richard (1800-1861), Independent minister, Manchester, 241, 243n, 385
Fletcher, William Roby (1833-1894), Congregational minister, Australia, 385
Fleury, Maria de, Baptist writer, 56n, 405-406
Flight, Bannister, Baptist layman, London, 330n, 386
Flight, John (1766-1791), Worcester pottery, 330n, 385, 386
Flight, Joseph (1762-1838), Worcester pottery, 330n, 385, 386
Flight, Thomas (1726-1800), Baptist layman, London, 31, 385, 386
Flower, Benjamin (1755-1829), newspaper editor, Cambridge, xxxiii, xxxiv, 83, 84n, 85, 85n, 86n, 386-387, 415, 440; his wife, Eliza Gould Flower (1770-1810), 386; his daughters, Eliza Flower (1803-1846) and Sarah Flower Adams (1805-1848), 386; his brother, George Flower, 386
Flowerdew, Mrs. Alice, Baptist poet, London, 440
Forfitt, Benjamin, founder, Book Society, London, 330n
Forsaith, Robert (1749-97), Independent minister, Northampton, 57, 387
Foskett, Bernard (1685-1758), Baptist minister, Bristol, 142n, 354, 381
Foster, Ebenezer (1777-1852), Baptist layman, Cambridge, 263n
Foster, Edward, Baptist layman, Cambridge, 263
Foster, John (1765-1847), Baptist layman, Biggleswade, 90, 199, 330n, 336, 336n, 388

Parkinson, James, Monghyr, Bengal, 236

Parkinson, Thomas, basket maker, Worksop, xxxv, 236

Parsons, George, BMS missionary, India, 234n, 428; his wife, the former Sophia Rawlings, xxxv, 234, 235, 253-255, 428

Parsons, John, BMS missionary, India, 428

Parsons, Robert, Baptist minister, Bath, 450

Pascall, James, Baptist layman, Jamaica, 454

Pasco, Mrs. Bristol, 165

Patrick, Joseph, Baptist minister, Southill, 148, 428-429

Pearce, Samuel, Baptist minister, Birmingham, xxvii, xxxiv, 50n, 57, 82, 83, 88, 88n, 89, 93, 98n, 134, 199, 334, 409, 422, 429, 438, 453, 455, 460, 465

Pearce, William Hopkins (1794-1840), 182, 185, 233n, 409, 416, 429-430, 452, 471; his first wife, Martha Pearce (later Mrs. William Yates), 233n, 409, 416, 471

Pearsan, attorney, Portsmouth, 45

Peck, Mr., Linendraper, Newbury, 167

Peel, Robert (1788-1850), 289, 319

Peggs, James (1793-1850), General Baptist missionary, India, xxxv, 235, 235n, 236, 236n, 288, 288n, 289n, 318, 319, 430

Peirce, James (1673-1726), Presbyterian minister, Exeter, 2n, 37, 430

Pell, William and Andrew, Guilsborough, 446

Pendered, William (1755-1832), Baptist minister, Newcastle, 384

Pengilly, Richard (1782-1865), Baptist minister, Newcastle, xxxv, 290, 309, 310, 311, 346, 430

Penn, William, 120, 203n

Penney, James (1792-1839), BMS missionary, Calcutta, 416, 471

Perkins, William (1558-1602), 46, 109

Pettigrew, Thomas Joseph (1791-1865), 179; his wife, Mrs. Pettigrew, 180

Petty, William, 2nd Earl of Shelbourne, 432

Phillippo, James M. (1798-1879), Baptist missionary, Jamaica, 223, 290, 311, 367, 371, 375, 413, 430-431

Phillips, Henry (1720-1789), Baptist minister, Salisbury, 442

Phillips, James, Quaker printer, London, 355

Phillips, Thomas (d.1815), Baptist layman, Shrewsbury, 9, 22, 36n, 40

Piccop, Joseph, Baptist minister, Bacup, 403

Pike, James Carey (1817-1876), secretrary, GBMS, 431

Pike, John Deodatus Gregory (1784-1854), General Baptist minister, secretary, GBMS, xxxv, 252, 430

Pike, Rev. G. T., 253

Pilkington, James, itinerant Baptist preacher, Rayleigh, 449

Pillin(g), Mary, Olney, 157, 159, 166

Plumbe, Richard, Independent minister, 446

Pomfield [Punfield], John, minister, Exeter Row, 24

Poole, Charles, Liverpool, 44

Poore, John, minister, Hope Chapel, Manchester, 243n, 385

Porter, John Paul, Baptist minister, Bath, 450

Porter, Thomas, Independent minister, Bury Street, 456

Poynder, John (1779-1849), Christian layman, London, 289, 290, 397, 431

Prescot, Charles Kenrick, Anglican minister, Stockport, 247

Price, Richard, 396

Prichard, James Cowles (1786-1848), Bristol physician, 260, 431

Priestley, Joseph (1733-1804), Unitarian minister, scientist, philosopher, 22n, 37, 85, 354, 396, 432, 437, 465

Priestley, Timothy, Independent minister, 446, 465

Prince, George K. (1800/01-1865), BMS missionary, Fernando Po, xxxv, 248n, 263-264, 284,290, 297, 308, 316, 318, 367, 422, 432, 442

Prince, Thomas (1687-1758), 147

Pritchard, George (1773-1852), Baptist minister, Keppel Street, London, 261n, 262, 432

Prowitt, Edward, Baptist minister, Newcastle, 384

Prowse, Mr. and Mrs., Exeter, 301

Prust, Edmund Thornton (1808-1886), Independent minister, Highbury, 199n

Prynne, William (1600-1669), 147

Pugsley, Nathaniel Knight (1787-1868), Independent minister, Stockport, 244, 247, 432

Purdy, Thomas, Baptist minister, Rye, 13n, 419